The Heritage

 South

This major new resource is a much-needed support to the few textbooks in the field and offers an excellent introduction and overview both to established principles and new thinking in cultural heritage management. Leading experts from Europe, North America and Australia bring together recent and innovative works in the field, with geographically and thematically diverse case studies, and examine the theoretical framework for heritage resource management.

The Heritage Reader brings together texts of the past decade with an overview of earlier literature and essays that fill the gaps in between, providing students of all stages as well as heritage professionals with a clear picture of new and older literature. A substantial introduction sets out the importance of the subject and key issues and debates, while separate thematic introductions with comprehensive reading lists provide the background to a collection of key works, many of which remained, up until now, of limited accessibility. The reader presents a series of new ideas regarding the nature and management of cultural heritage, which are set discursively within the framework of more established views of cultural heritage management.

With good coverage of major issues and solutions from around the world, *The Heritage Reader* will appeal to students internationally across the English-speaking world, and will stand as a key guide to the study and practice of heritage management.

Graham Fairclough is currently Head of the Characterisation Team at English Heritage.

Rodney Harrison is a lecturer in heritage studies at The Open University.

John H. Jameson Jnr is a senior archaeologist and Archaeology Education and Interpretation Program Manager with the U.S. National Park Service's Southeast Archaeological Center in Tallahassee, Florida.

John Schofield works for English Heritage in the Characterisation Team and is also Head of Military Programmes.

The

Heritage

Reader

Edited by
Graham Fairclough
Rodney Harrison
John H. Jameson Jnr
John Schofield

Routledge
Taylor & Francis Group

LONDON AND NEW YORK

First published 2008 by Routledge
2 Park Square, Milton Park, Abingdon, Oxon OX14 4RN

Simultaneously published in the USA and Canada
by Routledge
270 Madison Ave, New York, NY 10016

Routledge is an imprint of the Taylor & Francis Group, an informa business

© 2008 Graham Fairclough, Rodney Harrison, John H. Jameson Jnr and
John Schofield, selection and editorial matter; individual contributions,
the contributors

Typeset in Perpetua by Wearset Ltd, Boldon, Tyne and Wear
Printed and bound in Great Britain by The Cromwell Press, Trowbridge, Wiltshire

British Library Cataloguing in Publication Data
A catalogue record for this book is available from the British Library

Library of Congress Cataloging in Publication Data
A catalog record for this book has been requested

ISBN: 978-0-415-37285-5 (hbk)
ISBN: 978-0-415-37286-2 (pbk)

Contents

List of figures

List of tables

Acknowledgements

Section one: The cultural heritage: concepts, values and principles

With the exceptions of Jameson's and Clark's chapters, and Schofield's introductory chapter, the contributions to this section have been published previously. The details follow: Davison: originally published 2000, in Davison, G. (ed.), *The Use and Abuse of Australian History*, 110–30. Sydney: Allen and Unwin. Smith: originally published in the *Archaeological Review from Cambridge* 12:1 (1993), 55–75. Tilley: originally published in *Antiquity* 63 (1989), 275–80. Mason: a slightly longer version of this chapter was originally published 2002 in de la Torre, M. (ed.), *Assessing the Values of Cultural Heritage*, 5–30. Los Angeles: Getty Conservation Institute. Holtorf: originally published 2002 in Layton, B., Stone, P. and Thomas, J. (eds), *The Destruction and Conservation of Cultural Property*, 286–97. London and New York: Routledge. Dolff-Bonekaemper: originally published (no date) in *Forward Planning: The Function of Cultural Heritage in a Changing Europe*, 53–8. Council of Europe. Thomas: originally published 2004 in Merriman, N. (ed.), *Public Archaeology*, 191–201. London: Routledge. A postscript has been appended to the originally published text. Byrne: this chapter is loosely based on an earlier text from 2001, being the 'Deeper Issues' section in Byrne, D., Brayshaw, H. and Ireland, T. (eds), *Social Significance: a Discussion Paper*, 45–72. New South Wales National Parks and Wildlife Service.

Section two: Whose heritage?

With the exception of Harrison's introductory chapter, all chapters in this section have been previously published. The details follow: Lilley: originally published in 2000 in Lilley, I. (ed.), *Native Title and the Transformation of Archaeology in the Postcolonial World*, 99–120. Oceania Monograph 50. Sydney: University of Sydney. Appadurai: originally published in *Journal of Social Archaeology* 1:1 (2001), 35–49. Hall: originally published in *Third Text* 46 (1999), 3–13. Byrne:

originally published in *History and Archaeology* 5 (1991), 269–76. Tunbridge: originally published in *Canadian Geographer* 28:2 (1984), 171–80. Olwig: originally published in *International Journal of Heritage Studies* 7:4 (2001), 339–54. Layton: originally published in 1994 as the introduction to Layton, R. (ed.), *Conflict in the Archaeology of Living Traditions*, 1–21. London and New York: Routledge. Samuel: originally published in 1994 in *Theatres of Memory: Volume 1 – Past and Present in Contemporary Culture*, 288–312. London and New York: Verso.

Section three: Methods and approaches to cultural heritage management

With the exception of Fairclough's introductory chapter, all chapters in this section have been previously published. The details follow: *English Heritage*: originally published as a leaflet in 1997 by English Heritage; only an extract is reprinted here. Semple Kerr: originally published (as the opening address to the conference) in Clark, K. (ed.), 1999: *Conservation Plans in Action: Proceedings of the Oxford Conference*, London: *English Heritage*, pp. 9–19. Dick: originally published in the *APT Bulletin, the Journal of the Association of Preservation Technology*, XXXI–4–00, pp. 29–36. Stocker: originally published in 2003 as chapter 13 in Jones, M., Stocker, D. and Vince, A., *The City by the Pool, Assessing the Archaeology of the City of Lincoln*, Lincoln Archaeological Studies, 10, Oxford: Oxbow, pp. 378–82; Scott: originally published in 2002 in *Landscape Research*, vol. 27, no. 3, pp. 271–95 (only an extract is reprinted). Stoffle: originally published in 2000 in Goldman, L. R. (ed.), *Social Impact Analysis: an Applied Anthropology Manual*, Oxford and New York: Berg Publishers, pp. 191–232; a small extract is reprinted here. Lee: originally published as chapter 22 in Fairclough, G. J. and Rippon, S. (eds), *Europe's Cultural Landscape: Archaeologists and the Management of Change*, EAC Occasional Paper no. 2, Brussels and London: *Europae Archaeologiae Consilium* and *English Heritage*, pp. 193–200. English: originally published in *Parks*, vol. 10, no. 2, June 2000, pp. 13–24. Low: originally published in 2003 in Teutonico, J.-M. and Matero, F. (eds), *Managing Change: Sustainable Approaches to the Conservation of the Built Environment*, Proceedings of the 4th Annual US/ICOMOS International Symposium, Philadelphia, Pennsylvania, April 2001. Los Angeles: The Getty Conservation Institute, pp. 47–64. Council of Europe: originally published (in parallel French and English texts) in 2000 as *European Landscape Convention, European Treaty Series – No. 176*, Florence: Council of Europe, (www.coe.int/T/E/cultural-co-operation/Environment/Landscape); only an extract is reprinted here. Fairclough: originally published in 2003 in Palang, H. and Fry, G. (eds), *Landscape Interfaces: Cultural Heritage in Changing Landscapes*, Landscape Series 1, Dordrecht: Kluwer Academic Publishers, pp. 295–318.

Section four: Interpretation and communication

With the exception of Jameson's introductory chapter, all chapters in this section have been previously published. The details follow: McManamon (with comment by Holtorf and response by McManamon): McManamon's essay originally published in *Public Archaeology*, vol. 1, 2000, pp. 5–20. Holtorf's reply published in *Public Archaeology*, vol. 1, 2000, pp. 214–15, and McManamon's response in the same volume, pp. 216–19. Jeppson: originally published in Historical Archaeology, vol. 31, no. 3, 1997, pp. 65–83. Uzzell and Ballantyne: originally published in Uzzell, D. and Ballantyne, R. (eds), 1999, *Contemporary Issues in Heritage and Environmental Management*, pp. 152–71, The Stationery Office. McDavid: originally published in *World Archaeology* vol. 34, no. 2, 2002, pp. 303–14. Stone: originally published in the journal *Public Archaeology*, vol. 5, no. 2, 2006, pp. 139–49. McCarthy: originally published in Jameson, J. Jnr, Ehrenhard, J.E. and Finn, C. (eds), *Ancient Muses: Archaeology and the Arts*, 2003, pp. 15–24, Tuscaloosa, University of Alabama Press. Gibbs: originally published in Jameson, J. Jnr, Ehrenhard, J.E. and Finn, C. (eds), *Ancient Muses: Archaeology and the Arts*, 2003, pp. 25–39, Tuscaloosa, University of Alabama Press.

Afterword

Bradley *et al.*: originally published 2004 as an English Heritage booklet of the same title, with University of Bristol, University College London and Atkins Heritage, 2004.

All of the authors and publishers have given their consent for these works to be republished here, and we are grateful to all for their support and co-operation.

In addition, the editors wish to acknowledge and thank Matthew Gibbons of Routledge and Matthew Deacon of Wearset for their expertise, assistance and gratuitous patience throughout the development and preparation of this volume.

Heritage, Memory and Modernity

Rodney Harrison, Graham Fairclough,
John H. Jameson Jnr and John Schofield

Introduction

A starting point for this *Heritage Reader* is the view that how cultural heritage management is practised (and indeed, whether it is practised, and by whom) is not a 'given' but
rather the particular product of a particular historical trajectory in particular social and
cultural contexts. 'Heritage' largely exists within a historical context that has been
created by various influences that reached their zenith throughout Westernised societies
with the increasing professionalising of cultural heritage practice in the late twentieth
century. Heritage management in its various forms – 'Public' archaeology, state protection and management, museums – is the most important employer of archaeologists and
is taught routinely within archaeology departments and colleges. Most students seeking
employment within archaeology can expect to work within the cultural heritage sector
at some point in their lives, and most will work in the field for the whole of their
careers.

In the twenty-first century, it is likely that these trends will continue to shape cultural
heritage management practice. It will also engage increasingly with the new forms of diasporic and trans-national communities, with mass mobility and cyber-cohesion (the new
relationships that transcend place), which have emerged as a result of the circumstances of
late twentieth-century modernity. The papers in this collection point positively towards
the role of cultural heritage conservation in maintaining and negotiating these new forms
of community. Perhaps paradoxically, but increasingly widely accepted as a truism, heritage is no longer about the past but draws on the power of the past to produce the present
and shape the future.

This general introduction to the volume will conclude with a short summary outline of
the sections and themes that follow, but first we examine a particular and – we think –
significant context for contemporary cultural heritage management and its focus on the
materiality of the past. We think this context emerged in the twentieth century in the
'West' as a response to the changing relationship between people and objects and between
people and places as the camera (and satellites), the car (and airplane) and the computer (and
the web) have radically altered how people in Westernised, industrial and post-industrial

societies engage with their environment and with each other. If the discovery of new ways of living in the New World shattered the absolutist stance of European intellectual thought, so at an even deeper, more democratic and reciprocal level has mass global travel and migration, TV, satellites and the web, and trans-frontier migration created a new relativism which changes how people think. A democratic concept of 'World' Heritage is now almost attainable.

As 'things', however, become increasingly easily reproducible (either physically or through access), so authenticity gains a new value. Further, as Marc Antrop has said, whereas grandchildren and grand-(even great-grand-) parents would once have recognised each other's childhood landscapes, today many people experience many landscapes in a single lifetime. In addition, increasingly few people live all their lives in a small locality, so that paradoxically 'place' becomes more important to them. At the same time, like identities, people come to claim more than one place as 'theirs', an acceptance of pluralism (and of scale issues) which has major repercussions for defining 'significance', and indeed questions whether significance in its traditional sense (as opposed, for example, to context) matters all that much. Thus an attachment to the past encourages people to keep mementos, and can begin to create resistance to change at a larger scale, as well as fostering the notion of heritage as a shared and collective thing that binds society (or perhaps more accurately, parts of society) together.

Heritage and memory

> Memory's not perfect. It's not even that good. Ask the police, eyewitness testimony is unreliable. The cops don't catch a killer by sitting around remembering stuff. They collect facts, make notes, draw conclusions. Facts, not memories: that's how you investigate. I know, it's what I used to do. Memory can change the shape of a room or the color of a car. It's an interpretation, not a record. Memories can be changed or distorted and they're irrelevant if you have the facts.
>
> ('Leonard' in the film *Memento*, Newmarket/Summit Entertainment, 2000)

We can start by exploring transformations in the nature of collective memory brought about by the way that personal memory has come to be commodified and objectified throughout the course of the twentieth century. The emergence of memory as a crucial concern in Western societies is widely discussed as one of the key cultural and political phenomena of the late twentieth century (e.g. Huyssen 1995, 2000, 2003; Samuel this volume; this section after Harrison 2004). Memory discourses first emerged in the West in the 1960s in response to the rise of decolonisation, new social movements, and, in the decade after 1980, heightened debate around testimonial movements and preserving the memory of the Holocaust. Richard Terdiman (1993) goes so far as to suggest a 'memory crisis' in modern society, while Kammen (1995) situates the roots of the post-1945 heritage movement in the development of a modern sense of nostalgia and an obsession with preservation, the forcible act of *not* forgetting. This has produced a significant field of writing on the relationship between memory and anthropology (e.g. Casey 1987; Olick and Robbins 1995; Teski and Climo 1995; Climo and Cattell 2002), history and memory (e.g. Darian-Smith and Hamilton 1994; Le Goff 1996; Nora 1998), and the role of 'remembering' and 'forgetting' in the study of material culture (e.g. Forty and Küchler 1999; Kwint *et al.* 1999; Hallam and Hockey 2001; Küchler 2003). Much of the writing on memory in the late twentieth century has focused on the role of popular culture in shaping representations of the past and collective forms of memory.

In Western societies in the post-war period, cultural heritage has become one of the principal sites for the creation and contestation of memory and identity politics. Like the character Leonard in Christopher Nolan's film *Memento* (Newmarket/Summit Entertainment, 2000), who suffers anterograde amnesia and compensates through the use of a complex system of Polaroid photographs, notes and tattoos, the heritage industry might be seen as a reaction to the perceived importance of material traces as authentic triggers of memory, with the objectivity of physical things as memorials to the events of history. Of course, cultural heritage is *created* in the interpretation of material things. While archaeologists might emphasise the objective nature of heritage assessment criteria, clearly 'heritage' is not something that is self-defining; it is defined with reference to social action that selectively commodifies and emphasises particular places as important (Pearce 2000). It only exists through the reading which it is given by communities and human societies in the present. Here we begin by exploring the roots of this obsession with the authentic materiality of the past.

The age of mechanical reproduction

> The 'self-replicating rapid prototyper', or RepRap for short, is a machine that literally prints 3D objects from a digital design. Its creators hope that in the future it will be a must-have mod con for every home. Instead of queueing for this year's equivalent of Buzz Lightyear, Robosapiens or TMX Elmo, parents will simply download the sought-after design off the internet and print it out.
> (The *Guardian* newspaper, Saturday November 25, 2006 James Randerson, science correspondent)

Writing just before the Second World War, German-Jewish literary and cultural critic Walter Benjamin produced *The Work of Art in the Age of Mechanical Reproduction* (1999a). He wanted to define those aspects which set apart the art of the period before the beginning of the twentieth century, and the way in which mimetic machines such as the camera and phonograph had changed the ways in which art functioned in the modern world. Benjamin saw that the new media of his day were fundamentally altering the relations between signifying systems in society and reality, and were doing so by a process of simulation.

> The technique of reproduction detaches the reproduced object from the domain of tradition. By making many reproductions it substitutes a plurality of copies for a unique existence. And in permitting the reproduction to meet the beholder or listener in his own particular situation, it reactivates the object reproduced. These two processes lead to a tremendous shattering of tradition which is the obverse of the contemporary crisis and renewal of mankind. Both processes are intimately connected with the contemporary mass movements. Their most powerful agent is the film. Its social significance, particularly in its most positive form, is inconceivable without its destructive, cathartic aspect, that is, the liquidation of the traditional value of the cultural heritage.
> (1999a: 215)

In trying to account for the 'special' qualities of authenticity which are attributed to works of art, Benjamin used the term 'aura'. Aura describes the series of evocations and associations that surround an object or work of art, the web of inter-relations and correspondences which spiral outwards from an artefact or artwork (see also Pearson and Shanks 2001: 95). He noted that 'to perceive the aura of an object is to invest it with the ability to look at us in return' (1999b: 190).

> Above all, it [reproductive technology] enables the original to meet the beholder halfway, be it in the form of a photograph or phonograph record. The cathedral leaves its locale to be received in the studio of a lover of art; the choral production, performed in the auditorium or the open air, resounds in the drawing room.
>
> (1999a: 215)

The aura is intimately tied to the originality, or authenticity, of the artefact or art work. This aura, the basis for conceiving of an object's authenticity, became threatened during the twentieth century with the emergence of reproductive technologies such as the camera and photocopier. For Benjamin, it is the shared history of art object and the viewer or consumer that makes the artwork worthy of display and the attribution of sentimental value. As Wells notes,

> Formerly unique objects, located in a particular space, lost their singularity as they became accessible to many people in diverse places. Lost too was the 'aura' that was attached to a work of Art which was now open to many different readings and interpretations.
>
> (Wells 1997: 25)

Benjamin saw in the death of the aura the demystification of the process of creating art, making art itself much more widely available and generating radical new roles for art in mass culture. With the death of the aura, the 'distance' between the work of art and the masses grew smaller. He notes that concepts of the aura and the authentic have their roots in the associations of objects now venerated as 'art', and their creation within ritual contexts, or the 'cult' of beauty and aesthetics. When one could make a million copies of a photograph from a negative, the concept of a single 'authentic' photograph becomes untenable. And for Benjamin, 'the instant the criterion of authenticity ceases to be applicable to artistic production, the total function of art is reversed. Instead of being based on ritual, it begins to be based on another practice-politics' (1999a: 219). While on a superficial level, unlike his contemporary Theodore Adorno, Benjamin was actually reasonably positive about the death of aura and authenticity, he displayed much ambivalence towards various aspects of its demise, in particular the connection between aura and memory. He did this through drawing out the differences between the cult value of objects, and their exhibition value. He noted

> Cult value does not give way without resistance. It retires into an ultimate retrenchment: the human countenance. It is no accident that the portrait was the focal point of early photography. The cult of remembrance of loved ones, absent or dead, offers a last refuge for the cult value of the picture.
>
> (1999a: 219)

For Benjamin, the photograph (as opposed to the painting) appeared during the twentieth century as a 'means of extended discovery and control of the world' (Roberts 1982: 186).

Benjamin's 'topography of memory'

> . . . as soon as I had recognised the taste of madeleine soaked in her decoction of lime-blossom which my aunt used to give me . . . immediately the old grey house upon the street, where her room was, rose up like a stage set . . . and

with the house the town, from morning to night and in all weathers, the Square where I used to be sent before lunch, the streets along which I used to run errands, the country roads we took when it was fine.

(Marcel Proust, *À la recherche du temps perdu*)

In another essay *Unpacking my Library: An Essay about Book Collecting*, Benjamin is more explicit on the relationship between objects, authenticity and memory. He notes that 'the collector's passion borders on the chaos of memories' (1999a: 61–2). Benjamin recalls Proust's concept of *memoire involuntaire* (or, 'forced memory') to describe the process by which material objects call to mind a series of associations.

Once you have approached the mountains of cases in order to mine the books from them and bring them to the light of day . . . what memories crowd in upon you! . . . not thoughts, but images, memories. Memories of the cities in which I found so many things . . . memories of the rooms where these books have been housed . . .

(1999a: 67–8)

Indeed, it is the interaction between the object as historical and material witness, and the moment of recall in the mind of the person in the present which produces a 'spark of charged memory' (Leslie 1999: 114). As Leslie notes in an essay on Benjamin's memory-work, in his great unfinished work now known as *The Arcades Project* (2002), Benjamin draws a distinction between voluntary and involuntary memory in so far as they both operate dialectically with the object world.

The canon of involuntary memory, like that of the collector, is a kind of pro-ductive disorder . . . voluntary memory, on the other hand, is a registry, which classifies the object with a number, behind which the object disappears.

(cited in Leslie 1999: 116–17)

While institutional collecting might rely on such classificatory systems with which to notate and draw connections between objects and the material world, for Benjamin, the true collector

. . . is always anarchistic, destructive. For this is its dialectic: by loyalty to the thing, the individual thing, salvaged by him, he evokes an obstinate, subversive protest against the typical, the classifiable.

('In praise of the doll', cited in Leslie 1999: 119; see also Belk 1995 and Stewart 1993)

Thus the process of memorywork is constructed as a form of excavation, stressing the importance of the encounters of the body with material things outside of it.

Selling memories: photography and personal memory

Kodak doesn't sell film, it sells memories.

Kodak marketing slogan

As Batchen (2004, see also Tagg 1988) discusses in his exploration of the history of photo-graphy, photography and memory are now intimately connected. Throughout the course of the late nineteenth and twentieth centuries, it is possible to trace a movement from the notion of amateur photography as 'leisure' to photography as 'memory'. The increasing focus on photography as a form of forensic evidence and its role within the criminal judicial system has sealed this relationship. As Susan Sontag notes,

> Photographs furnish evidence. Something we hear about, but doubt, seems proven when we're shown a photograph of it . . . a photograph passes for incontrovertible proof that a given thing happened. The picture may distort; but there is always a presumption that something exists, or did exist, which is like what's in the picture.
>
> (Sontag 1977: 5)

While outside of the West, photography as a globally disseminated and locally appropriated medium has developed for itself alternate histories (e.g. Pinney and Peterson, eds, 2003), in the Western world, photographs have become the analogues of memory *par excellence*. While on the one hand, photography threatened the essence of what made an object 'real' by making its image easily reproducible, it also served to emphasise those things which made the real object 'authentic'; that is, its aura or 'patina' of history, the vestiges of its relations with humans in the past, all of those things we might term its 'heritage'. The growth in popularity of these individual forms of memory representation have had profound influences on the representation of collective memory in the West, both in terms of its forms, and its accelerated growth throughout the twentieth century.

Cultural heritage and the presence of the past – memory in topography

We have seen how photographs during the twentieth century became the analogues of personal memory because of their ability to capture a 'truth' in a manner that seemed objective and forensic. What we want to suggest here is that this newfound expectation of the forensic qualities of personal memory had an influence on the growth of the heritage industry as people developed new expectations of remembrance at the collective level.

If personal memories can be mediated by the materiality of photographs, then collective memories might also – and perhaps must – be buttressed by preserving authentic traces of the past as mnemonics, symbols or (an increasingly fashionable trope) 'icons'. While photographs could help mediate collective memory, however, even more important were the authentic material remains of that past. These could be 'read' by archaeologists and architectural historians and interpreted to the public at large. As the range of material remains that is absorbed into heritage broadens, however, they come closer to people's own experience and the mediation of archaeologists as experts becomes less necessary. First, for example, the remains being kept as mementos become more recent, and their origins now often still sit in living memory (Fairclough 2007a); second, they become more quotidian, and thus again people can choose their own heritage and understand it without help (opinion poll results in, e.g. HER 2000). Finally, the steady 'rise' of landscape as a unifying concept within which heritage (natural heritage as well as cultural) can be framed and made socially, individually and psychologically relevant brings us to the position where memory resides in topography as well as within memento, because landscape, perceptual and infinitely plural, is the only truly ubiquitous and wholly shared aspect of heritage.

The materiality of the past in cultural heritage conservation, at a wide range of scale and form, thus became an integral aspect of the ways in which the public could understand, and interact with, the past in the twentieth century. 'Material memories' (Kwint *et al.* 1999; Hallam and Hockey 2001; Boric 2003), that sense of 'being-affected-by-the-past'

(Ricoeur 1988: 207), became an important aspect of the significance of cultural heritage. Work on the relationship between materiality and memory has suggested that landscapes and material objects act on the body to evoke particular kinds of memories, which cannot be invoked in their absence (Connerton 1989; Küchler 1999). As Stewart (1999: 19) notes, 'the body bears a somatic memory of its encounters with what is outside of it'. Heritage places, and more latterly people's landscapes as a whole, thus came to act as authentic memorials to the events of the past and thus to an explanation of the present. As memorials, the authenticity of their 'fabric' was paramount. This produced a burgeoning industry that focused on preservation and conservation of cultural heritage places, whether they were intact, in ruins (which carried their own picturesque aesthetic and value, at least in European countries) or increasingly, even invisible (see also Davison this volume and Ireland and Lydon 2005: 5). The move towards landscape perspectives is changing this; the relevance of 'character' is slowly coming to sit alongside authenticity of fabric as a way of highlighting the past in the present (Fairclough 2007b).

If we have become obsessed with the materiality of the past in the late twentieth century, the processes of heritage conservation and preservation can be seen to be far more than neutral activities, but ones which are highly charged politically. The ownership and interpretation of the past emerges as a key issue. Heritage conservation is more than the atrophy of decay, it is selective and taphonomic in nature, and could be profitably likened to a form of collecting practice (Hall, this volume). In this way, cultural heritage management should be seen as a *discourse* that is mobilised for different social and political ends. This position is an appropriate starting point from which to approach the texts which follow.

The Heritage Reader

The Heritage Reader brings together a collection of key works that represent a combination of established principles and new thinking in cultural heritage management to emerge since the late 1980s. We use the term 'heritage management' to denote approaches to and views of cultural heritage in the broadest sense (including archaeological and cultural resource management), utilising archaeologists' perspectives of long-term change and taking as a starting point the role and significance of material culture in the modern world. We use the term 'archaeology' in its broadest sense too, as a method for interrogating and untangling both the material traces of the past and the narratives with which they are understood in the present. Like Foucault, we would suggest that pre-existing notions of continuity should be held in suspense,

> . . . we must show that they do not come about of themselves, but are always the result of a construction the rules of which must be known, and the justifications of which must be scrutinised . . .
>
> (Michel Foucault 1972, *The Archaeology of Knowledge*)

The Reader is divided into four sections, dealing in relation to the cultural heritage with issues of definition, ownership, management and interpretation. We have chosen texts that by and large propose or exemplify new approaches, sometimes quite radically new approaches that challenge longer-standing assumptions about the character and purpose of heritage practice. A newly written introduction to each section discusses and contextualises the key texts that are reproduced, identifies some of the issues that unify their new approaches, and places them in a framework of the traditional methods from which they have grown.

Section one: The cultural heritage: concepts, values and principles

What constitutes cultural heritage has formed a key focus of inquiry throughout the late twentieth century, and the introductory chapter to this section – *Heritage Management, Theory and Practice* – sets out the background to this. Governments have felt the need to form various definitions of heritage to facilitate its management by the State. The establishment of appropriate management practices and the assessment of the significance of cultural heritage places have followed definition as important areas of inquiry. As Teski and Climo note in their introduction to *The Labyrinth of Memory* (1995), memory is not simply a matter of recalling past experiences, but a complex and continuing process of negotiation and struggle over what will be remembered and what forgotten. This tension between remembering and forgetting, what to conserve and how to preserve it, clearly forms another important aspect of cultural heritage management practice.

Section two: Whose heritage? Local and global perspectives

The question of 'ownership' of heritage manifests itself differently in different cultures and nations, for example in settler and in non-settler societies, or in the context of stronger or weaker public constraints on private landownership, or of different approaches to the balance between central (or federal) and local (subsidiary) powers and controls. The co-existence of a dominant section of the population (in settler societies, for example, the usurping and non-dominant indigenous populations; elsewhere, landowning or class-based elites) produces particular kinds of friction over cultural heritage. The introductory chapter to this section, *The politics of the past: conflict in the use of heritage in the modern world*, shows that issues of the local and the global, the individual, community and nation state, and the ways in which heritage is used to build a sense of nationhood, are common to both settler and non-settler societies in the modern world. It is important to keep in mind that archaeologists are just one of many groups of people who have a role in 'creating' the past, and in locating it in many different ways in the present. The work of archaeologists, and the way they go about their business (even if supported and facilitated by a legal-scientific-intellectualised rationale), will sometimes be at odds with local stakeholders, landowners or other interest groups. There is a major interpretive divide in Australia, for example, between the views of archaeologists who see the origins of Aboriginal people in a migration out of South East Asia around 60,000 years ago, and the view of Aboriginal people themselves that they have always been here. Who has the right to interpret and control access to representations of the past is thus a critical question in all modern Western societies.

Section three: Methods and approaches to cultural heritage management

Cultural heritage management in Western Europe, Australia and North America is now the major sector of archaeological endeavour, but it is also in constant evolution. The introduction to this section – *New Heritage, an introduction – people, landscape and change* – places the papers in the context of the recent formation of a series of new approaches which together might constitute a new heritage paradigm, and indeed a new definition not simply of what heritage is but what it is for, who decides what it is, and how past heritage relates to future heritage. Archaeology as a discipline developed in tandem with legislation which established archaeological and other 'Western' knowledge systems as the expert forms of knowledge on which decisions about the preservation of the material traces of the past would rest (Smith 2004). The methods and approaches used to manage cultural heritage, then, are of critical importance to understanding the role of cultural heritage management in the modern world. Many aspects of the new ways of doing heritage which are described in this section are related to this latter concern: the present day rather than the historical value of archaeological sites, buildings and landscapes. Far more than it ever has been, heritage management – and archaeology – is coming to be focused not on the past *per se*, but on the remains of the past within the present. In particular, heritage management has come to focus on the way these traces of the past contribute to a generalised, more holistic character, and of how they contribute to issues that affect everyone such as sense of place or even quality of life (as well, obviously, as identity). In short, heritage is part of the strategy that people use to 'be' in the world. It is not coincidence that many of these new approaches operate through, or at, the scale of landscape, since it is through landscape in particular (in its conceptual sense of a perception of the environment) that people locate themselves in their surroundings and reconcile themselves to its evolution.

Section four: Interpretation and communication

'Interpretation' describes not only cultural heritage 'products', such as educational programs and museum displays, but also 'the processes by which meaning is created from archaeological materials in the public realm' (Merriman 2004: 5). Interpretation, as we have discussed above, is one of the key areas through which the public entrusts archaeologists and professional heritage managers with the role of making meaningful those traces of the past which have been obscured to the point where they are unable to 'speak for themselves'. The introduction to this section – *Presenting archaeology to the public, then and now* – challenges the notion of cultural heritage and the past as something which is finished and hence inert; instead the papers in this section of the book examine the ways in which ideas about the past can be 'constructed' and hence open themselves to multiple interpretations and representations.

Afterword: Change and creation

Change and Creation is an English Heritage programme that aims to understand and manage the archaeology of later twentieth-century landscape (1950–2000). It considers the dynamics of modern rural, urban and peri-urban landscape change and attempts to promote dialogue and collaboration in the exploration of the value of the remains of the very recent past: from football stadiums to motorways, factories to school fields, housing estates to agri-business. It explores the possibilities for archaeologies of this very recent past, and the challenges for characterising and managing the later twentieth century heritage.

In Autumn 2004, English Heritage (in partnership with Atkins Heritage, University of Bristol and University College London) published the *Change and Creation Discussion Document* (Andrea Bradley, Victor Buchli, Graham Fairclough, Dan Hicks, Janet Miller and John Schofield 2004. London: English Heritage). The discussion document brought together professionals from the public, commercial and higher education spheres of archaeology to point to the importance and challenges of engaging with the heritage of the very recent past, and to invite comment and discussion. We have included the *Change and Creation Discussion Document* as a significant paper which points to the future of heritage management in the 'West', and which brings the focus of heritage discussed in the Reader up to the present day. Recent approaches to the archaeology of the contemporary past point to the significant importance of heritage management in producing alternate histories and perspectives on the recent past. Buchli and Lucas (2001) suggest that in addressing the issue of the non-discursive realm the archaeological act comes directly into contact with the subaltern, the dispossessed and the abject. This is not simply in terms of the usual archaeological preoccupation with material remains, but the practical and social act of uncovering that which has once been hidden. The two converge here both literally and figuratively.

(Buchli and Lucas 2001: 14)

We leave the student of heritage with a snapshot of these significant new developments in both theoretical approaches to the material remains of the recent past, as well as the whole raft of complex issues about the nature of cultural heritage management as a practice itself which this document, and the process of managing the heritage of the contemporary past, raises.

Conclusion

Pearson and Shanks (2001) have drawn on the philosophy of theatre (Antonin Artaud's *Theatre and its Double* (1958)) to suggest the transformative potential of new forms of cultural heritage practice in the modern world. Artaud advocated a system of social therapy through theatre which he believed had the power to transform the audience's perception of reality and themselves. What we see emerging from many of these new approaches presented in the *Heritage Reader* is not an old fashioned equation of heritage with 'the past', but an emphasis on the performative and transformative nature of heritage as part of present day existence. This can generate new understandings of the past through the confrontations of bodies with material spaces and landscapes. It is an emphasis on the inheritance of the past as something, living only in the present; when we excavate, when we consider the historic character of landscape, when we walk over a monument, or stare into a museum case, we are experiencing those things as part of our world. They are only windows into the past if we consciously and voluntarily imagine them to be so, but to anyone who looks at them they are automatically – involuntarily – a part of the present.

We remain optimistic that new studies which provide tools to interrogate and foreground the role of political representations of the past in heritage practice, along with the rich texture of new forms of media which have arisen with the proliferation of information technologies in the last two decades, will have a very positive influence on the future directions of the practice of cultural heritage management in the twenty-first century. The texts reproduced in this Reader stand as testimony to cultural heritage management's past *and* to its future.

References

Artaud, A. (1958) *The Theatre and its Double* (trans. M.C. Richards). New York: Grove Press.

Batchen, G. (2004) *Forget Me Not: Photography and Remembrance*. Princeton Architectural Press.

Belk, R. (1995) *Collecting in a Consumer Society*. London and New York: Routledge.

Benjamin, W. (1999a) *Illuminations*. Translated and edited by H. Arendt. London: Pimlico.

Benjamin, W. (1999b) *Selected Writings Vol 2*. Translated by E. Jephcott, edited by M.W. Jennings, H. Eiland and G. Smith. Cambridge: Cambridge University Press.

Benjamin, W. (2002) *The Arcades Project*. Translated by H. Eiland and K. Mclaughlin. Cambridge: Belknap Press of Harvard University.

Boric, D. (2003) 'Deep time' metaphor: Mnemonic and apotropaic practices at Lepinski Vir. *Journal of Social Archaeology* 3(1): 46–74.

Buchli, V. and Lucas, G. (2001), The absent present: archaeologies of the contemporary past. In V. Buchli and G. Lucas (eds) *Archaeologies of the Contemporary Past*, London and New York: Routledge, pp. 3–18.

Casey, E.S. (1987) *Remembering: A Phenomenological Study*. Bloomington and Indianapolis: Indiana University Press.

Climo, J.J. and Cattell, M.G. (eds) (2002) *Social Memory and History: Anthropological Perspectives*. Walnut Creek, Lanham, New York: AltaMira Press.

Connerton, P. (1989) *How Societies Remember*. Cambridge: Cambridge University Press.

Darian-Smith, K. and Hamilton, P. (eds) (1994) *Memory and History in Twentieth-Century Australia*. Oxford, Auckland and New York: Oxford University Press.

Fairclough, G.J. (2007a) The contemporary and future landscape: change and creation in the later 20th century. In: L. McAtackney, M. Palus and A. Piccini (eds) *Contemporary and Historical Archaeology in Theory*. Oxford: Archaeopress (Studies in Contemporary and Historical Archaeology 4).

Fairclough, G.J. (2007b): From assessment to characterisation. In J. Hunter & I. Ralston (eds), *Archaeological Resource Management in the UK, Second Edition*, pp. 250–270. Stroud: Sutton.

Forty, A. and Küchler, S. (eds) (1999) *The Art of Forgetting*. Oxford and New York: Berg Publishers.

Foucault, M. (1972) *The Archaeology of Knowledge* (trans A. M. Sheridan Smith). London and New York: Routledge.

Gell, A. (1998) *Art and Agency: Towards a New Anthropological Theory*. Oxford: Clarendon Press.

Hallam, E. and Hockey, J. (2001) *Death, Memory and Material Culture*. Oxford and New York: Berg Publishers.

Hamilton, P. (1994) The knife edge: Debates about memory and history. In K. Darian-Smith and P. Hamilton (eds) *Memory and History in Twentieth-Century Australia*. Oxford, Auckland and New York: Oxford University Press, pp. 9–32.

Harrison, R. (2004) [Review of] *Archaeologies of Memory*, edited by Ruth M. Van Dyke and Susan E. Alcock. *Australian Archaeology* 58: 48–51.

Historic Environment Review (2000) Power of place, a future for the historic environment, English Heritage, London.

Huysenn, A. (1995) *Twilight Memories: Marking Time in a Culture of Amnesia*. London and New York: Routledge.

Huyssen, A. (2000) Present pasts: Media, politics, amnesia. In A. Appadurai (ed.) *Globalization*. Durham: Duke University Press, pp. 57–77.

Huyssen, A. (2003) *Present Pasts: Urban Palimpsests and the Politics of Memory* (Cultural Memory in the Present). Stanford: Stanford University Press.

Ireland, T. and Lydon, J. (2005) Introduction: Touchstones. In J. Lydon and T. Ireland (eds) *Object Lessons: Archaeology and Heritage in Australia*. Melbourne: Academic Scholarly Press, pp. 1–30.

Kammen, M.G. (1995) Some patterns and meanings of memory distortion in American history. In D.L. Schacter (ed.) *Memory Distortion: How Minds, Brains and Societies Reconstruct the Past*, pp. 329–345. Cambridge: Harvard University Press.

Küchler, S. (2003) *Malanggan: Art, Memory, Sacrifice*. Oxford and New York: Berg Publishers.

Kwint, M., Breward, C. and Aynsley, J. (eds) (1999) *Material and Memories: Design and Evocation*. Oxford and New York: Berg Publishers.

Le Goff, J. (1996) *History and Memory*. Translated by Steven Rendall and Elizabeth Claman. New York: Columbia University Press.

Leslie, E. (1999) Souvenirs and forgetting: Walter Benjamin's Memory-work. In M. Kwint, C. Breward and J. Aynsley (eds). *Material Memories: Design and Evocation*. London and New York: Berg, pp. 107–122.

Merriman, N. (2004) Introduction: Diversity and dissonance in public archaeology. In N. Merriman (ed.) *Public Archaeology*. London and New York: Routledge, pp. 1–18.

Nora, P. (1998) *Realms of Memory: The Construction of the French Past Volumes 1–3*. English language edition of *Les Lieux de Memoire*, edited by L.D. Kritzman, translation by A. Goldhammer. New York: Columbia University Press.

Olick, G. and Robbins, J. (1995) Social memory studies: From 'collective memory' to the historical sociology of mnemonic practices. *Annual Review of Sociology* 24:105–140.

Pearce, S. (2000) The making of cultural heritage. In E. Avrami, R. Mason and M. de la Torre (eds) *Values and Heritage Conservation*, Research Report, Getty Conservation Institute, Los Angeles, pp. 59–64.

Pearson, M. and Shanks M. (2001) *Theatre/Archaeology*. London: Routledge.

Pinney, C. and Peterson N. (eds) (2003) *Photography's Other Histories*. Durham, NC: Duke University Press.

Ricoeur, P. (1988) *Time and Narrative Volume 3* (trans. K. Blamey and D. Pellaeur). Chicago and London: University of Chicago Press.

Roberts, J. (1982) *Walter Benjamin*. London: Macmillan.

Smith, L. (2004) *Archaeological Theory and the Politics of Cultural Heritage*. London and New York: Routledge.

Sontag, S. (1977) *On Photography*. New York: Farrar, Straus and Giroux.

Stewart, S. (1993) *On Longing: Narratives of the Miniature, the Gigantic, the Souvenir, the Collection*. Durham and London: Duke University Press.

Stewart, S. (1999) Prologue: from the museum of touch. In M. Kwint, C. Breward and J. Aynsley (eds) *Material Memories: Design and Evocation*. Oxford: Berg, pp. 17–36.

Tagg, J. (1988) *The Burden of Representation: Essays on Photographies and Histories*. London: Macmillan.

Terdiman, R. (1993) *Present Past: Modernity and the Memory Crisis*. New York: Cornell University Press.

Teski, M.C. and Climo, J.J. (eds) (1995) *The Labyrinth of Memory: Ethnographic Journeys*. Westport, CT: Bergin and Garvey.

Wells, L. (1997) Thinking about photography: In Liz Wells (ed.) *Photography: A Critical Introduction*. London and New York: Routledge.

SECTION ONE

The cultural heritage: concepts, values and principles

Chapter 1

Heritage Management, Theory and Practice

John Schofield

Section 1 of this Heritage Reader outlines some of the guiding principles of heritage management practices as they exist in a diversity of social and political situations around the world. It addresses and contextualises some of these principles which are then further examined in the contributions that follow. By guiding principles I mean those aspects of heritage management that have determined its course, its core philosophies and the assumptions and preconceptions that have shaped practice as it exists today. However, given that some of these principles have seen significant changes of emphasis in recent years (e.g. R. Thomas, this volume), and continue to change within a rapidly evolving social, cultural and political climate, it is predominantly recent contributions that are represented in this section and discussed in this introduction. Most of the contributions, however, do contain references to significant earlier work.

* * *

This opening essay introduces the contributions that follow in Section 1, recognising that the purpose of this Reader is to outline recent approaches to cultural heritage management, rather than necessarily to present significant texts that chart its evolution, its 'heritage'. Having said that, it is necessary to understand how we arrived at the situation that exists today, and here that history and development is outlined for the United States in a previously unpublished essay by Jameson. In a wide-ranging essay, Jameson charts the emergence of heritage through an expansion of the definitions and varieties of stakeholders, the heightened importance and inclusion of traditional and indigenous cultural values, and enhanced efforts for curation, accountability, legal protection, and site stabilization. The wider relevance of Jameson's chapter is evident in the similarities that exist between this and comparable situations around the world, numerous examples of which are included in this volume.

But the emphasis here, in Section 1, is placed on the theoretical basis of heritage management, the administrative and political contexts in which management practices are conducted and decisions made, as well as the seamlessness of cultural heritage resources, both spatially (terrestrial and marine for example), chronologically (ancient and modern), as well as by type, taking in both tangible and intangible resources; the material and the immaterial. It is important to stress also that, whether we use the term explicitly or not, this is predominantly an *archaeological* resource that we are describing, in the sense of archaeology representing the study of the past through its material remains, whether buildings, monuments or artefacts, and whether of Stone Age or early twenty-first century date. Thus, as archaeology today represents 'a mode of enquiry into the relationship between people and their material pasts' (Hodder 2003: 2), heritage refers to the material world around us in its entirety, not just selected parts of it. That doesn't of course mean this area of enquiry should be an exclusive territory for archaeologists, in the conventional sense of the word; rather archaeology and heritage in their contemporary (and arguably post-modern) manifestations, I suggest are best seen as cross-disciplinary fields of enquiry, incorporating the views and expertise of, for example, architectural historians, social and cultural anthropologists, artists and geographers. This emphasis on cross-disciplinary working is clearly in evidence in the selection of works that follow.

Definitions

Far from being a new concern, the difficulties surrounding definition have a long history, compounded in recent years as the depth and breadth of what constitutes 'heritage' has increased. Of all the key concepts, how to describe the cultural heritage is a central one. Numerous authors have reviewed usage, with one of the more recent reviews (Carman 2002) recognising the three most common terms amongst archaeologists being 'the archaeological heritage' (e.g. Cleere 1984, 1989; Smith, this volume), 'the archaeological resource or resources' (Darvill 1987; McGimsey and Davis 1977) and – especially outside Europe where the heritage is often predominantly that of an indigenous population – 'cultural resources' (Lipe 1984). Another term – 'cultural property' – is used, but remains problematic, with its implication of ownership, and the diversity of particular situations this implies. Carman illustrates the problem (ibid., 29) with some possibilities. Private ownership, he says, provides exclusive access to resources with prior permission of a landowner. State ownership implies closed access, whether permission is sought or not; this might include sensitive military establishments and government buildings. Where places are under institutional or communal control and ownership, sites are preserved by the very limitations placed on access, for example in the case of hospitals. Open access (increasingly common under the various agri-environment schemes that exist, at least in the UK) could in theory introduce a lack of control, possibly and ultimately leading to a destruction of resources.

That said, a particular type of property – traditional cultural property – is increasingly of relevance to heritage management practice. Indigenous communities now routinely contribute to a dialogue concerning heritage and the historic environment, and in particular the discussions that concern value and the practical arrangements for managing specific resources and places with which they have close cultural affiliation. The principal reason for this is their status as owners of land and tradition, and their being a part of the cultural heritage per se. We should be clear what we mean by 'Traditional Cultural Properties' (TCPs). In the United States (King 2003) they are defined in *National Register Bulletin 38* thus: a TCP is:

> one that is eligible for inclusion in the National Register because of its association with cultural practices or beliefs of a living community that (a) are rooted in that community's history, and (b) are important in maintaining the continuing cultural identity of the community.

The term 'property' has obvious currency here, given the status of traditional communities as the owners of place and tradition. But this does raise a wider concern. One of the principles underlying the recognition of traditional cultural property, as well as for example characterisation programmes undertaken in England and Europe (Fairclough and Rippon 2002; Fairclough, this volume), is the point that one person's story is not necessarily any more important than another's, and everybody's treasured places deserve some recognition. Such recognition is vital as these local places help give people and community groups coherence and a degree of stability, as the world – and these places within it – necessarily change. As Archibald has said:

> The persistence of [valued] places is central to an environmental debate with future implications, but it is also reflective of a deep-seated need to find refuge from the complexities and insecurities of contemporary life in places that set humans in context, that provide constancy in the midst of profound and rapid change.
>
> (1999: 54)

This point comes out strongly in Denis Byrne's essay – that places give meaning to people's experience of the world, the traces and objects being encounter associations triggering recollections and emotions amongst those whose place, whose 'heritage' this is (see also Harrison, this volume).

So, clearly there are issues of definition here. Even 'heritage' itself is problematic, to the point where its validity, its usefulness is questionable. The UK government's use of heritage in its 'cool Britannia' initiative of the late 1990s led to a student of mine dropping the 'h' – 'eritage', reflecting this new popular (mis)appropriation (Greg Bailey pers. comm.). Raphael Samuel (1994, this volume) addresses a further difficulty. 'Lexically', he said, '"heritage" is a term capricious enough to accommodate wildly discrepant meanings' (ibid.: 205), a point also drawn out by Davison (this volume) whose essay explores usage in the context of Australian heritage management practices where heritage has additional meanings and relationships in the context of indigenous communities and landscape. His essay outlines the various ways in which the heritage has been used, reflecting on its evolution from property (appropriately defined here as meaning heirlooms, personal effects, inheritance) to that which we value about our environment, and that which we often seek to protect. He recognises also the emergence of a distinction between heritage as ideals and heritage as things, and that heritage has increasingly been linked to the workings of state and international heritage organisations. This is a point also addressed by R. Thomas (this volume) who describes a situation in which state authority is arguably being diminished, and democracy and communities are beginning to emerge as dominant forces in defining and managing 'heritage' resources.

Recently, John Humphries, presenter of the 'Today' programme on BBC Radio 4, interviewed Fiona Reynolds, the Director General of the National Trust. Their conversation began with the following exchange:

HUMPHRIES: So what's the difference between 'heritage' and 'history' then?
REYNOLDS: There isn't one: 'heritage' is the bureaucratic word, if you like.
HUMPHRIES: Ah, I thought so: well I think I prefer 'history'.

A short comment followed, from the author of an email newsletter issued by the Society of Antiquaries of London (Chris Catling pers. comm., 13 November 2006):

> It would be interesting to know whether John Humphries's views are widely shared, and whether there really is a popular antipathy to the word 'heritage'. And is it really true that 'history' and 'heritage' are synonyms? Would renaming the Heritage Lottery Fund the History Lottery Fund convey the same set

of connotations? Would English Heritage have quite so many members if it were renamed English History?

For people of antiquarian bent, heritage seems a far preferable term for our broad field of study: the term is rooted in the idea of inheritance, and the cultural legacy we inherit as a community from one generation and pass on to the next. There is a very important continuum here: heritage is about yesterday, today and tomorrow, whereas history is, by definition, primarily concerned with interpreting the past. Heritage embraces several other critically important continuities – that between culture and nature, for example, which we antiquaries have long championed through the holistic study of landscapes in their entirety – and between intangible heritage (oral history, music and the skills to make lace or cider, for example) and tangible heritage (the contents of museums, libraries and archives).

Heritage is thus a very useful term to describe the totality of the field of antiquarian study.

The defence offered here is a laudable and compelling one. But it also highlights some of the problems. If we can return this to its root, concern over 'heritage' for me originates with literal dictionary definitions which, as some of the comments above suggest, often focus on its *special* qualities, whether natural or cultural, and the fact that we *inherit* it from the past. These are sweeping and significant presumptions that deserve to be challenged, as Holtorf does in his previously published essay, reproduced here. Holtorf argues that heritage is traditionally concerned with those special places and landscapes that are worth preserving, generally unchanged, for the benefit of future generations (but cf. Byrne this volume, Chapter 16, for a non-western interpretation of heritage protection practices). Yet, it is evident in the literature, and to some extent through particular management practices, that heritage management is gradually moving away from this view that only special places matter, to a recognition that such a clear distinction between that which is valued and by implication that which is not can be unhelpful. Instead one can argue that what really matters is the diversity of features that make up the historic environment, and the particular local characteristics that contribute to this diversity (Fairclough, this volume).

Holtorf also addresses the concern that determinations of national importance, by national heritage agencies, take little account of locally held views on value and meaning, a point also drawn out by R. Thomas (this volume) who, as we have seen, recognises a growing enthusiasm for communities to develop more democratic and participatory engagements with heritage. Denis Byrne's essay on Heritage as Social Action also makes this point in relation to migrant communities and traditional owners in postcolonial Australia, who for much of the post-contact period (post 1788) were given limited visibility in the colonised landscape by white authorities. Only now, with legislation specific to Aboriginal heritage places, and studies such as those concerning the experiences of Vietnamese (M. Thomas, this volume) and Macedonian communities (Thomas 2002) of Australia's national parks, is this beginning to change.

The second fundamental concern with 'heritage' is the fact that we inherit it from the past. As both Holtorf (2005, this volume) and Graves Brown (2000) have explained, those working for heritage agencies and organisations don't (at least shouldn't) simply observe and comment upon heritage; rather, they actively engage with it, creating heritage (the archaeological resources of the future), and altering and renewing (often through particular heritage management practices) that which was inherited from the past. The heritage is constantly changing therefore; and the fact that the archaeological resource (as opposed to specific archaeological resource*s*) is non-renewable is nonsensical in these terms. We can see this most clearly in terms of later twentieth- and early twenty-first-century places and landscape now being incorporated into mainstream heritage practice (e.g. Bradley *et al.*

2004; www.changeandcreation.org). Of course, once a prehistoric burial site or medieval settlement has gone it has gone forever. But if we abandon the purist and literal assumption of archaeological resources as somehow 'ancient', it becomes evident that many more places and things are being added to the heritage resource than could ever be taken from it. As I recently wrote in the magazine *British Archaeology*:

> The Monuments at Risk Survey (Darvill and Fulton 1998) noted some 23,500 [monument] losses in 1945–95 – 470 a year; more than one per day. Yet in 1988–2004 Sites and Monuments Records grew daily by 164 records. Even if the majority of these were sites destroyed in the process of discovery, the increase in known surviving archaeological sites is significant. Additionally, modern developments generate tens of thousands of new sites a year, sites that are already starting to attract archaeological attention.
>
> (Schofield 2006: 11)

We have referred thus far only to material remains in the literal physical sense of buildings, monuments and artefacts. UNESCO now recognises a whole field of intangible heritage including the character or 'feel' of a place, its aura, as well as customs, traditions, language and dialect, musical styles, and religious or secular ritual (see http://portal. unesco.org/culture/en for the UNESCO convention on intangible heritage and chapter 31 for the European Landscape Convention). Related to this expanding view of heritage is a growing acceptance of the many ways we can experience it. As the geographer Douglass Porteous (1996: 8–9) has demonstrated, this experience is multi-sensory (Figure 1.1). It is an important point. We don't just experience place by seeing it, and processing information about it from a purely visual encounter. It is much more complicated than that. Porteous notes, for example, how the centrality of being-in-the-world depends on the four Jungian supports of thought (mind), feeling (heart), intuition (soul) and sensation (what he terms 'the gates of the body'). Sensation relates directly to aesthetics which include vision (accounting for 80 per cent of sensory input), sound, smell and tactility; we smell places and we hear them, for example. Characterisation as a means of documenting and understanding the distinctive characteristics of place is a significant new approach in contemporary heritage management practices (see Fairclough this volume), and Porteous's views have pertinence here especially. As he states:

> Environmentally, places can readily be described by the characteristic 'mix' of sense perceptions available to the average able-bodied member of the public. The identity of places is multisensory.
>
> (1996: 41)

Characterisation studies have already started to explore this complex area of enquiry, an early example being the work of Steve Mills (www.english-heritage.org.uk/characterisation), documenting the auditory characteristics of landscape character areas in west Cornwall, and extending that to a prediction of the very different auditory characteristics of a mining landscape in the past.

From this broad scope we can see the cultural heritage as including: monuments, buildings, landscape, artefacts and objects, as well as cultural traditions, music, theatre and dialect; it can be aesthetically pleasing and it can be ugly, unsafe and unprepossessing; it can be tangible – as many of these things are – or intangible. It can also be old, and it can be new. It is something valued by society, by specific groups within society, and by individuals. All these expressions and perceptions are valid, and all recognise the significance of heritage and the contribution it makes to quality of life, through its contribution to sustainable consumption and production, for example in the form of energy use and the

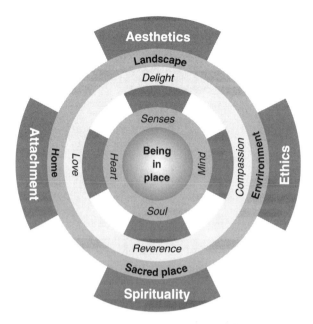

Figure 1.1   Intangible relationships with environment (after Porteous 1996: 9).

contribution of heritage to the 'green lungs' of sustainable communities (Clark, this volume). But this broad and inclusive definition does raise other questions, which provide a structure to the remainder of this introduction, and to the chapters that follow:

1   What is heritage management? Why does the heritage need to be managed, and what are the practices and infrastructure for doing so? This will include discussion of communities and the State (the subject of R. Thomas's contribution).
2   How is significance and value best judged, and what alternatives exist to heritage valuation? How does value differ from importance and significance? Does this semantic matter?
3   How can we manage change in the contemporary environment, taking account of historic features and character?

Management practices

Laurajane Smith in her 1993 essay (this volume) noted how archaeological heritage management can be usefully conceived as a process which: (a) fulfils part of a Western cultural, political and ethical concern with conservation and curation of material remains; (b) institutionalises archaeological knowledge and ideology within state institutions and discourses; and (c) is implicitly concerned with the definition of, and debates about cultural, historical, social and national identities. Management thus implies putting in place systems to oversee and control the heritage, as well as providing opportunities for it to contribute to quality of life and sustainable living. These systems exist at various levels: at an international level through conventions and protocols introduced by ICOMOS for example; nationally or state-wide through legislation; and locally through planning guidance, through local and amenity societies, and by the enthusiasm, commitment and engagement of local communities. One can view this process from the top down, with influence and the principles of good practice cascading from the state to local authorities and communities, backed up by powers of enforcement. One can also view it from the bottom up, with the wishes, values and perceptions of local communities influencing budget-holders and decision-makers (Figure 1.2). Research frameworks – perhaps driven by communities and special interest groups – are an example of how this set of relations can operate to good effect, as whatever is imposed by national government requires community support if it is to be implemented successfully. In fact in the UK at least, most subject-based research frameworks are compiled (often through dialogue and debate) by the specialist societies for a particular topic or period, while local or regional frameworks are produced by those that know those areas best. Although the initiative may be driven and part funded by the state, the frameworks themselves are locally compiled and constructed.

How the state and the local communities and authority interact is a key area of concern currently, and it is a dynamic that is changing. As Roger Thomas's chapter suggests, for the UK, as with other aspects of life, authority within heritage management practices is gradually moving away from the state and towards local authorities and the communities they serve (and who elect their members). R. Thomas's important contribution notes how the regime for protecting monuments has existed in England since the Victorian period, and is built around the authority of the state. As he explains:

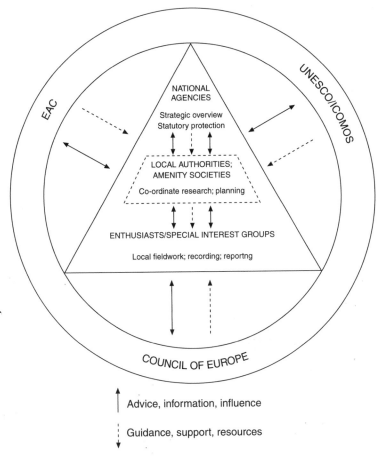

Figure 1.2 Management frameworks for cultural heritage matters in England (after Schofield 2005: 119).

Officials select monuments for protection; those selections are endorsed by board members who are appointed by the state; and the final decision is made by (or in the name of) the Secretary of State, with no real possibility of appealing against a determination as to whether a particular monument is of 'national importance' or not.

(p. 192 in original)

Such an authoritarian approach to management also exists in most other European countries and, as Carman (2005) says, it can imply closed access, physically and intellectually, to the heritage, to the decision-making process, and to the information and thought processes on which it is based. With a wide and diverse community now firmly supportive of the heritage and seeking greater access to it, property has become theft, one might argue. On this point Carman says the following:

In the case of the archaeological heritage, initial notice taken by professionals may serve to awaken interest in a local or wider community such that a range of different values and uses for the object become evident: [for example] 'cognitive ownership' can be claimed by all without any loss of the resource. Once this has happened, the conditions are met for voluntary restraints on actual use to be applied without the need for the allocation of specific property rights. Since the value of the object or the place has been increased, and new ones ascribed, it becomes an object or place of significance to all its cognitive owners: none has an interest in its depletion or destruction. No agency need appropriate use rights in order to deny them to others; and no rights of access need to be controlled by a custodian or steward. Here is the ultimate link between value and property . . .: when the value is a social value held by all, then to conserve the resource no one need be granted any right of ownership.

(2005: 116)

An ideal, maybe, but one that we are arguably and steadily moving towards. Thomas's essay explains some of the evidence for this diminution of state authority, such as the extension of market principles into areas of life previously controlled by state-run monopolies, and the notion of customer choice, impacting on what people consume and what they think. As R.Thomas says, there exists now in Britain as elsewhere a plurality of views and perceptions, many of which contradict the official and commercialised views of heritage. For that reason alone state-run heritage management and protection regimes could become harder to sustain in the long term. A current review of heritage protection in England may begin to address some of these issues, at least in part.

Examples of this more democratic and participatory approach towards the heritage abound. Carol McDavid used the example of the Jordan Plantation Project to assess democratisation in archaeology, and especially with regard to the opportunities the internet provides for giving democratic access and the opportunity for archaeologists and heritage managers to 'reach their publics' (2004: 177). Neil Faulkner provides a more radical but no less compelling model for participation, in this case challenging the conventions of officially led field archaeology projects, and of forming instead an alternative 'archaeology from below' (2000) involving fieldwork rooted in the community, open to volunteer contributions, organised in a non-exclusive, non-hierarchical way, and dedicated to a research agenda in which material, methods and interpretation are allowed to interact (ibid.: 21). Faulkner's case rests on some key principles, that

politics are about power. The politics of archaeology are about who has power over material remains from the past. The state does not allow local communities and interest groups real power over heritage. To achieve this, to take control of the archaeological record . . ., people disempowered under the present system have to fight for an alternative approach. The mass of official archaeologists, subject to the dictates of traditional workplace hierarchies, should challenge the priorities and policies of the heritage bosses they work for. The mass of actual and would-be independent archaeologists should organise their own heritage research and conservation in defiance of bureaucratic discouragement. This is not an argument for excavation improperly done without adequate record, still less for vandalising archaeological sites for profit or pleasure. Indeed, if anything, it is an argument for community mobilization against these threats.

(2000: 29)

Significance

A second area of concern, represented here in Byrne's, Dolff-Bonekaemper's and Mason's contributions is significance and value. Why, first of all, is it necessary to ascribe value to heritage sites and objects; second, how does significance differ from importance; third, how and on what basis are those values ascribed; and fourth, what are the implications of these management decisions (a point covered fully in Mason's contribution, this volume)? How do they impact upon the resource and what alternatives exist?

At the outset, it is important to emphasise the obvious merits and advantages of what has been referred to as 'informed conservation' (Clark 2002), a proactive approach to management that advocates understanding as a basis for decision-making. Without understanding, Clark says, conservation is blind and meaningless; we should strive for a system that understands buildings and monuments before we change them, not because we change them.

After Alois Riegl first determined values of historical monuments to society in 1903 (cited in Dolff-Bonekaemper, this volume), the next significant assessment of values was by William Lipe (1984), with other studies based on this seminal work following soon afterwards (e.g. Darvill 1993; Carver 1996; Darvill et al. 1987; Startin 1995; and most recently Darvill 2005). Lipe's work has particular relevance here, being the first study to state explicitly that,

> value is not inherent in any cultural items or properties received from the past, at least not in the same sense as, say, size or colour or hardness. Value is learned about or discovered by humans, and thus depends on the particular cultural, intellectual, historical, and psychological frames of reference held by the particular individuals or groups involved.
>
> (ibid.: 2)

Lipe goes on to note the characteristics of Associative/symbolic, Informational, Aesthetic and Economic values, these becoming the cornerstones of evaluative systems globally, as Mason went on to explain and analyse in some detail (this volume).

Given Mason's contribution, I'll concentrate discussion here on the wider cultural setting for these schemes and approaches, an area covered recently by Darvill (2005: 23–4) within the context of Giddens' (1990) essay, *The Consequences of Modernity*. Darvill posed the fundamental question: why do we need to create such order, and evaluate our resources in this way; what is the underlying motivation? There are two points that have particular relevance here. First, that the sources of risk and danger facing society and the world have changed. In the premodern world, according to Giddens, most threats and dangers were perceived as emanating from nature, whereas in the modern world, they are the result of increased reflexivity in society. In consequence, Darvill explains, within pre-modern society there was a series of answers provided by beliefs and received wisdom. In modern society there are only ontologically oriented questions. This change of perception can be seen in society's approach to the archaeological resource. First was the Christianizing of pagan images in the early Middle Ages; then the development of antiquarian concerns for protection and preservation coincident with the emergence of modernity; and finally current concerns about the nature of the past and the definition of what constitutes the archaeological record (Darvill 2005: 23).

The second point is the recognition that in modern society it is abstract systems that can stabilise social and economic relations across indefinite spans of space and time. Darvill explains how these systems are future-oriented and often counterfactual as a mode of connecting past and present. Thus they contrast with premodern situations in which local communities provided the setting, religious cosmologies provided a providential interpretation of human life and nature, and tradition provided a means of connecting present and future through reference to the past. These changes can also be seen in the emergence of archaeological resource management, conflated in Britain in the 100 years between the passing of the first ancient monuments protection in 1882 and the integration of archaeological issues into the town and country planning system and the emergence of Planning Policy Guidance on Archaeology and Planning in 1990 (Darvill 2005: 23–4).

Thus, for archaeology,

> The emergence of modernity provided the social context for the institutionalization, objectification, and commodification of archaeological materials. What changed was the set of relationships that allow individuals either singly or in groups to derive meaning from the physical world in which they find themselves. . . . There are no absolutes or intrinsic attributes that can be separated off from what we experience in the world. Value and importance are just as much sets of meanings and understandings derived from a body of material as is the reconstruction of Neolithic burial practices or the development of a view about medieval kingship.
>
> (Darvill 2005: 24)

It is necessary also here to understand the distinction between value and importance. They are very different, and in a further part of Darvill's (2005) essay he explains why. Value systems are conceived in a sociological sense. Values are social values, or a set of standards against which things are compared. These standards trigger feelings and emotions and provide the basis for emotional commitment. Such standards are commonly but not universally held, they are constantly being renegotiated and changed, and their formulation and acceptance is a consensual matter. Returning to Giddens, Darvill explains how changes in values are not independent of innovations in cognitive orientation created by shifting perspectives on the social world. These values are the same kind as those recognised by Lipe (1984) and others. Values currently recognised include the presumption of preservation in situ, archaeological remains providing a direct and tangible link to the past, and the recognition (expressed in numerous policy documents issued recently by English Heritage for example), that interest in the past brings social benefit in relation to the quality of life, and is a component of education and the process of socialisation (Darvill 2005: 28; Clark, this volume). A particular value is that described in Gabi Dolff-Bonekaemper's contribution, which notes how discord value contributes to the recognition of some sites whose continued survival may enable a debate that might not otherwise occur. This dissonant heritage presents particular difficulties that are addressed in this contribution, and another by David Uzzell and Roy Ballantyne in a later section.

Importance is very different (Darvill 2005: 32). Here, attention focuses not so much on the importance of archaeology as an academic and political theme, but rather on specific places or objects, comparing one site with another for instance, the importance indicators acting as parameters in the decision-making process and serving to mediate between subject and object. There are both quantitative and qualitative systems for aiding these judgements, the quantitative systems including 'scoring' of monuments, as was done for the Monuments Protection Programme in England (1986–2002), and the qualitative being driven more by research agenda, for example in the case of York (Carver 1993) and more recently Lincoln (Stocker, this volume).

There is therefore

> A distinction between 'value systems' as a set of socially defined orientations applicable to the whole resource, and 'importance systems', as an archaeological or interest-group methodology applicable to specific elements of the resource, in order to allow some kind of ranking or discrimination.
>
> (Darvill 2005: 39)

'Values' are thus generic, and culturally constituted. There seems to be consensus about the value of archaeology and heritage, for education, identity and quality of life. But how relevant are 'importance values' now, in an increasingly democratic and participatory world where state-led policies and actions are gradually diminishing? As the systems that do exist are based on higher-level decisions by state and local authority officials, and as those decisions are based on discrimination, a hard line between what we are prepared to lose, and that which we wish to retain at all costs is a clear one. In fact these two extremes are often quite easy to resolve. It is the difficult middle ground that presents most of the problems, and it is here that negotiation and dialogue with owners and a diversity of other communities is key. We should also return here to Traditional Cultural Properties, and the views of authors like Peter Read (1996) who note the significance of place to communities, including traditional indigenous communities, and individuals for whom the intangible qualities of place may hold equal significance. In other words, it isn't only the physical and extant remains that hold value, but the character of the place, local customs and memories. These factors can be the most contentious when considering the impact of development proposals.

Increasingly there are alternatives to scoring, and discrimination; to judging importance in this way. Social significance forms the basis of one approach, recognising that everyone will have their own special places, places they return to and which hold meaning for them, for a diversity of reasons. This form of valuation can also have relevance at the most intimate and personal of levels. For instance:

> Margaret Johnson had her own special places which she created by having her body there. In the homestead the old kitchen had a life of its own, cats curled up in warm corners, nappies hung on the towel rail, the iron kettle simmered on the hob, a lovely feminine brittle gum stood outside the window. Each cup of tea and brownie added to the thousands of other teas and brownies consumed in the same warmth, at the same table, on the same seats. The daily events and the physical characteristics of the country are all sort of intertwined. It's really a very special, precious, strong thing. Had the walls themselves absorbed something of this human activity? 'Oh yes, I think so. There's a patina, a richness.' There were other special places about the homestead which Margaret Johnson observed and absorbed. One

was the jasmine bush outside the bedroom window where the birds gathered.

(Read 1996: 6)

Meaning and value will often be culturally constituted, as studies by the New South Wales National Parks and Wildlife Service have established for the Macedonian and Vietnamese communities in Sydney (Thomas 2001; Thomas 2002). Mandy Thomas notes, for example, how:

[T]he array of sounds that exude from a Vietnamese landscape are frequently mentioned by both younger and older Vietnamese. The Australian landscape is seen through the lens of Vietnamese forests and mountains, in that they are often viewed as contrasting, even if the differences may not be apparent to others. For example, that the Australian bush is scentless and soundless is often commented on.

(2002: 81)

In the urban context, and in terms of strategic and spatial planning, certain narratives can take precedence over others, influencing the importance values that might ultimately determine which sites or buildings are preserved. Dolores Hayden in her seminal *The Power of Place* (1995) spoke of invisible Angelenos in their home city of Los Angeles, the second largest city in the United States with 3.5 million people, 40% of whom were Hispanic, 37% white, 13% black and 10% Asian American or Pacific Islander. While this mix of cultures projects itself onto the urban landscape quickly, and into particular and ultimately distinctive areas (and ghettoes in some cases), city biographies and official processes that recognise landmark structures favour the history of a small minority of white, male landholders, bankers and political leaders, and their architects. In 1986, 97.7% of Los Angeles's designated cultural historical landmarks were Anglo American, and 2.3% celebrated Native American, African American, Latino or Asian American history, even though these 'minority' groups comprise 60% of the population. Additionally, only 4% of landmarks were associated with women's history. As Hayden says, '[T]he major ethnic groups that have always been part of the city have been dispossessed. And the new immigrants have every reason to be confused' (1995: 86). (See also Gard'ner's (2004) study which contrasts local with official views of heritage in London's East End.)

At the higher strategic levels of management and decision-making scope exists for an alternative to quantitative valuation of specific heritage resources. Characterisation (e.g. Fairclough, this volume) represents a set of principles and methods – largely reliant upon the opportunities made available through GIS – that enable the mapping and analysis of those particular attributes that give character to specific areas, whether urban (e.g. through street patterns, building style and date, etc.) or rural (field patterns, settlement morphology). These characterisation studies provide a context within which strategic and spatial planning decisions can be made at a regional level. In England currently there are plans for large numbers of new homes in particular pre-determined growth areas. But within those areas, which places can best accommodate change, and which will be the most sensitive to it? By recognising which areas have changed in the past, and which have not, a view can be taken based on sustainable options viewed in historic context.

Also at this higher level are the guiding principles of sustainability, a broad set of guidelines, policies and parameters that originated in the 1992 Rio Earth Summit and which increasingly impact on all aspects of life. Kate Clark's essay outlines some of the key principles, and why sustainability matters so much in the context of heritage management.

Heritage in a changing world

Most countries have heritage management systems that include provision for the protection of sites, monuments, buildings and (in some cases) objects (Archaeologia Polonia 2001; Cleere 1989). As we have seen already these systems are typically state-run, and based on the principles of value and importance outlined above. More will be said on this later in the volume, but for now some of the basic principles can be briefly addressed, notably: why should we protect archaeological sites, and for whom; and how can protection best be achieved?

Fundamentally, it is accepted that archaeological sites and monuments and historic buildings are protected for the benefit of future generations, and for quality of life considerations. We are curators, stewards of the archaeological resource and have a duty of care towards it, ensuring that what we pass on to future generations reflects what we ourselves inherited from the past and what we have contributed to and shaped in the landscape, whether tangible or intangible. This remains a widely held view, and one that supports many of the heritage management systems existing around the world. But this view has been challenged. Holtorf (this volume) for example notes that:

> The significance of original archaeological sites for future generations' understanding of the past may be lower than is often assumed. Cultural appreciation of the past is not now, and never has been, to any large extent dependent on original ancient sites and objects.
>
> (p. 289 in original)

Holtorf goes on to suggest the role of ancient sites as being the product, not the origin, of cultural appreciation of the past, citing John Carman's view that 'archaeological material is not protected because it is valued, but rather it is valued because it is protected' (1996: 115).

That said, the state does and should continue to have a role. One example of state intervention at the higher level is the adoption for cultural heritage resources of a polluter pays principle, by which development costs that impact upon archaeological resources are met by the developer. This principle has been introduced comparatively recently, originating in the 1970s (OECD 1975; Graves Brown 1997), and it is one that has had significant implications for the archaeological research process, its management and the generation of data. The scale of development in the UK over the past 15 years or so, in urban, peri-urban and rural areas, and the amount of archaeological activity generated as a direct result, has led some to suggest we are now 'drowning in data' (R. Thomas 1991), and has caused some to question a system that generates data that doesn't necessarily correspond to meaningful or agreed research agenda. But there are two basic principles here that are fundamental to the way archaeological research is conducted, and accommodated in the planning process. First, that specific archaeological resources are non-renewable and should be recorded prior to their removal; and second that those responsible for their removal should cover the costs. Beyond that is an obvious need to generate intellectual frameworks within which the data generated through these numerous small interventions can be made available to researchers and given the maximum potential to be useful to others. Sites and monuments records are the obvious location for these data, supported by an effective GIS, making new data more available to academic research and syntheses. A recent review of prehistoric evidence retrieved from developer-funded archaeological work has effectively rewritten British prehistory (Bradley 2007), drawing together what had previously been considered the 'two cultures' in archaeology: the developer-funded recording of threatened ancient remains; and university-based research programmes. The vast quantities of available data have proved useful therefore. They are just not always that accessible.

The emergence of 'cultures' in archaeology and the increased availability and use of 'data' are also the subject of Tilley's contribution, noting in 1989 how archaeology needed to reconsider its priorities and the 'radical division' that all too often exists between excavation (the stage at which many wish to participate) and what happens beyond the recovery and publication of sites. Tilley presents theoretical and social justifications for limited numbers of large-scale excavation projects, to enable the discipline to continue to mature in a reflexive way, not to recover or rescue material traces necessarily, but to investigate the manner in which interpretative experience is produced, recorded and transmitted. Part of the background to this concerns power and ownership, and reflects Tilley's view that currently (or at least at the time of writing) the heritage industry 'is not supportive of archaeology', but rather challenges it as an active interpretative practice taking place today.

How we treat the archaeological resource, how we regard it and what we understand by it are fundamental in determining how it is managed. The fact that it isn't fixed, and isn't exclusively about sites 'from antiquity' represents a significant shift of emphasis from previous generations' approaches to archaeological heritage management. The first Schedule in England, established in 1882, included 24 monuments, all of which were prehistoric and monumental. Gradually, over the course of the next 100 years, the Schedule evolved, following trends and conventions to include in turn Roman, Medieval, post-Medieval and Industrial archaeology. Today, recent military sites are being included. Sites and Monuments Records, held by local authorities and the baseline for all planning decisions, even now record later twentieth-century sites, such as sections of motorway, housing developments, modern industrial sites and so on. In recent years in the UK, and reflecting a global trend (Brodie and Renfrew 2005), portable antiquities legislation has been introduced in an attempt to control illegal trade. Alongside this is a Portable Antiquities Scheme that seeks to improve relations between heritage and archaeological organisations – notably museums – and metal detector groups, the scheme providing an intellectual and curatorial context for what were previously independent groups recovering unprovenanced finds.

Things change, and the secret of good heritage management is to recognise that process, and for policy decision making and research into these new areas to keep pace with it. Ultimately this can mean enabling a debate about the world we ourselves are shaping in our everyday (including heritage) practices, and taking informed conservation and management decisions about modern buildings, landscape and sites. Of all the new dimensions and approaches covered in this collection, this is perhaps the most challenging. For that reason the text from English Heritage's (2004) Change and Creation document is included in the Reader as a final chapter.

* * *

Why do we value the cultural heritage; what do we understand by it; and how can we manage it in such a way that it can be researched without compromising it unduly, preserved without over-protective state intervention, and managed without the controlling influence that could give an impression of exclusivity? How can the heritage keep pace with the change that reshapes it with every generation? These are some of the questions this first part of the Reader will address, through key contributions from recent literature. Where gaps have been identified in the literature, or where change has overtaken the currency of key works, new or amended texts are provided. Together these contribute to a review of current thinking in some key areas, providing some of the fundamentals on which later contributions are based.

References

Archaeologia Polonia 2000. Archaeological heritage management: theory and practice. *Archaeologia Polonia* 38.

Archibald, R.A. 1999. *A place to remember: using history to build a community*. Walnut Creek: AltaMira Press.

Bradley, A., Buchli, V., Fairclough, G., Hicks, D., Miller, J. and Schofield, J. 2004. *Change and creation: historic landscape character 1950–2000*. London: English Heritage.

Bradley, R. (2007). *The Prehistory of Britain and Ireland*. Cambridge: Cambridge University Press.

Brodie, N. and Renfrew, C. 2005. Looting and the world's archaeological heritage: the inadequate response. *Annual Review of Anthropology* 34: 343–61.

Carman, J. 1996. *Valuing ancient things: archaeology and the law*. Leicester: Leicester University Press.

Carman, J. 2002. *Archaeology and heritage: an introduction*. London and New York: Continuum.

Carman, J. 2005. *Against cultural property: archaeology, heritage and ownership*. London: Duckworth.

Carver, J. 1993. *Arguments in stone. Archaeological research and the European town in the first millennium*. Oxbow Monograph 29. Oxford: Oxbow Books.

Carver, J. 1996. On archaeological value. *Antiquity* 70, 45–56.

Clark, K. 2002. *Informed conservation: understanding historic buildings and their landscapes for conservation*. London: English Heritage.

Cleere, H. (ed.) 1984. *Approaches to the archaeological heritage*. Cambridge: Cambridge University Press.

Cleere, H. (ed.) 1989. *Archaeological heritage management in the modern world*. London: Unwin Hyman.

Darvill, T. 1987. *Ancient Monuments in the Countryside: an archaeological management review*. English Heritage Archaeological Report 5. London: English Heritage.

Darvill, T. 1993. *Valuing Britain's Archaeological Resource*. Bournemouth University Inaugural Lecture. Bournemouth: Bournemouth University.

Darvill, T. 2005. 'Sorted for ease and whiz'?: approaching value and importance in archaeological resource management. In Mathers, C., Darvill, T. and Little, B.J. (eds), *Heritage of value, archaeology of renown: reshaping archaeological assessment and significance*, 21–42. Gainseville: University of Florida Press.

Darvill, T. and Fulton, A. 1998. *The Monuments at Risk Survey of England, 1995. Main Report*. Bournemouth School of Conservation Sciences and English Heritage.

Darvill, T., Saunders, A. and Startin, B. 1987. A question of national importance: approaches to the evaluation of ancient monuments and the Monuments Protection Programme in England. *Antiquity* 61, 393–408.

Fairclough, G. and Rippon, S. (eds) 2002. *Europe's Cultural Landscape: archaeologists and the management of change*. Europae Archaeologiae Consilium Occasional Paper No. 2.

Faulkner, N. 2000. Archaeology from below. *Public Archaeology* 1.1, 21–33.

Gard'ner, J. 2004. Heritage protection and social inclusion: a case study from the Bangladeshi community of East London. *International Journal of Heritage Studies* 10.1: 75–92.

Giddens, A. 1990. *The consequences of modernity*. Cambridge: Polity Press.

Graves Brown P. 1997. S/he who pays the piper ... Archaeology and the polluter pays principle. Assemblage 2. www.shef.ac.uk/assem/2/2gb2.html (accessed 30 October 2007).

Graves Brown, P. (ed.) 2000. *Matter, materiality and modern culture*. London and New York: Routledge.

Hayden, D. 1995. *The Power of Place: Urban Landscapes as Public History*. Cambridge, Mass.: MIT Press.

Hodder, I. 2003. *Archaeology beyond Dialogue*. Salt Lake City: The University of Utah Press.

Holtorf, C. 2005. *From Stonehenge to Las Vegas: archaeology as popular culture*. Walnut Creek: AltaMira Press.

King, T.F. 2003. *Places that count: traditional cultural properties in cultural resource management*. Walnut Creek: AltaMira Press.

Lipe, W. 1984. Value and meaning in cultural resources. In Cleere, H. (ed.), *Approaches to the archaeological heritage*, 1–11. Cambridge: Cambridge University Press.

McDavid, C. 2004. Towards a more democratic archaeology? The Internet and public archaeological practice. In Merriman, N. (ed.) 2004. *Public Archaeology*, 159–88. London: Routledge.

McGimsey, C.R. and Davis, H.R. (eds) 1977. *The management of archaeological resources: The Airlie House Project*. Washington, DC: The Society for American Archaeology.

OECD, 1975. The polluter pays principle: definition, analysis, implementation. Paris: OECD.

Porteous, J.D. 1996. *Environmental aesthetics: ideas, politics and planning*. London: Routledge.

Read, P. 1996. *Returning to nothing: the meaning of lost places*. Cambridge: Cambridge University Press.

Samuel, R. 1994. *Theatres of Memory Volume 1: Past and Present in Contemporary Culture*. London: Verso.

Schofield, J. 2005. *Combat archaeology: material culture and modern conflict*. London: Duckworth.

Schofield, J. 2006. Rethinking heritage management. *British Archaeology* 89: 11.

Startin, B. 1995. The Monuments Protection Programme: protecting what, how and for whom? In Cooper, M.A., Firth, A., Carman, J. and Wheatley, D. (eds), *Managing Archaeology*, 138–45. London: Routledge.

Thomas, M. 2001. *A multicultural landscape: national parks and the Macedonian experience*. New South Wales National Parks and Wildlife Service.

Thomas, R. 1991. Drowning in data? – publication and rescue archaeology in the 1990s. *Antiquity* 65: 822–28

Chapter 2

Heritage
From Patrimony to Pastiche

Graeme Davison

Few ideas are so expressive of our changing relationship with the past as the word 'heritage'. 'Heritage' is an old word, drawn from the vocabulary of traditional societies in which values were derived from ancestral relationships. But in our times it has become invested with a new cluster of meanings, characteristic of a mobile, postmodern society. Tracing its history is a valuable clue to the ways of using, and abusing, the past.

In its original sense, heritage was the property ('heirlooms') which parents handed on to their children, although the word could be used to refer to an intellectual or spiritual legacy as well. In the nineteenth and early twentieth centuries, as new nation-states fought for legitimacy, people began to speak of a 'national heritage' as that body of folkways and political ideas on which new regimes founded their identity. Australians, who modelled themselves on the new nations of Europe and America, thus created their own national myths based on the 'pioneer heritage' or 'the heritage of Anzac'. School textbooks bearing the title *Australian Heritage* showed how our love of democracy and fair play was derived from the struggles of our pioneering forebears. Charles Chauvel's film *Heritage* (1935) dramatised that message in film. (For reflections on heritage and nationalism, see Lowenthal 1988; 1996.)

In recent times, however, and especially since the 1970s, heritage has become the special name we give to those valuable features of our environment that we seek to conserve from the ravages of development and decay. When the Hope Committee of Inquiry of 1974 defined the National Estate as 'the *things* we keep' and recommended the creation of a special body, the Heritage Commission, to guard it, the new usage became official. Thus we gained 'heritage studies' to investigate old buildings, 'heritage councils' to classify them and 'heritage advisers' to tell us how to maintain them.

But, surprisingly perhaps, things don't actually have to be old or historically significant to be described as 'heritage'. The word is now freely applied to almost any commodity that purports to reproduce past *styles* of architecture, furniture, household utensils or even food. In Britain a national chain of stores called 'Past Times' is devoted to the sale of Tudor brooches, medieval tapestries and other fake heirlooms. In Australia, the Tip-Top Bread Company invites jaded consumers to sample its wholesome, old-fashioned 'Heritage' loaf. Building companies offer 'Heritage' Federation houses. In the Bristol Paint

Company's 'Australian Heritage' brochure the hallowed names of 'Phillip' and 'Macquarie', 'Ben Hall' and 'Ned Kelly' are used as labels for a range of 'authentic' Victorian and Edwardian paint colours. From the *values* of the past, to the *things* of the past, heritage has finally come to mean simply a *veneer* of pastness.

Heritage is something preserved for posterity so its framework of reference is the future – the generations yet unborn who will inherit – as much as the past. As early as the 1870s, as Tim Bonyhady (1996) has recently shown, the terms 'heritage' and 'national estate' were already part of the lexicon of those pleading for the conservation of Australian bushland and other places of natural beauty. In 1892 a plan to open a dairy farm on Tower Hill, a picturesque volcanic cone in Victoria's Western District that shortly before had been gazetted as a national park, met stern resistance from the *Warrnambool Standard*:

> The public park at Tower Hill is a priceless heritage that the generations of the future will highly prize, and it must be handed down to them with its privileges undiminished.

The nation's forests, its fauna, Sydney Harbour and Centennial Park were all described, at one time or another, as components of a 'heritage' – a gift of nature – that must be preserved for future generations.

Less commonly the word was applied to built objects (Bonyhady 1996). The architect W. Hardy Wilson, for example, called for the preservation of early colonial buildings, not just for themselves but for the conservative aesthetic and social values they represented. Similarly, in 1948, America's National Trust for Historic Preservation referred to historic sites and structures as tangible remnants of the past and monuments to the national democratic heritage. In its *Criteria for Evaluating Historic Sites and Buildings*, it saw significance residing in those places in which the broad cultural, political, economic or social history of the nation, state or community is best exemplified, and from which a visitor may grasp in three dimensional form one of the larger patterns of the American heritage (Mulloy 1976, 14).

By the 1960s the two ideas – heritage as ideals and heritage as things – were becoming more closely intertwined. In 1960 the United Nations Educational, Scientific and Cultural Organisation (UNESCO) defined cultural property as 'the product and witness of the different traditions and of the spiritual achievements of the past and . . . thus an essential element in the personality of the peoples of the world'. It was the duty of governments 'to ensure the protection and preservation of the cultural heritage of mankind, as much as to promote social and economic development'. 'Cultural heritage' was a concept well adapted to the purpose of an international agency such as UNESCO. It enlarged the concept of heritage from a familial or national setting to an international one. By employing an anthropological understanding of 'culture' as embracing both values and the objects in which they were embodied, it strengthened the moral claims of the would-be custodians of cultural property while side-stepping difficult distinctions between its 'high' and 'low', popular and elite forms. One of the important uses of 'heritage' was simply as a convenient omnibus term for all those miscellaneous items – objects and sites as well as buildings – that were in danger of being lost. In 1963 the Victorian branch of the National Trust emphasised its concern, not only for buildings but for hitching posts, Aboriginal rock paintings, fountains, graves – anything, in short, 'whose destruction would be an important loss to Victoria's heritage'.

In the 1970s the new usage was officially recognised. A UNESCO Committee for the Protection of World Cultural and Natural Heritage adopted the term 'heritage' as a shorthand for both the 'built and natural remnants of the past'. The concept soon spread among Australian preservationists, especially those who participated in UNESCO conferences, although for a time it competed for popularity with the idea of 'the National Estate' – the term which Gough Whitlam, following the example of John F. Kennedy, had adopted to emphasise the responsibility of the national government to conserve the natural and built environment. In its report on the National Estate (1974) the committee of enquiry headed by Mr Justice Hope made sparing use of the term 'heritage', preferring more precise and neutral terms such as 'built environment', 'cultural resources' and 'historic buildings'. Labor ministers for the Environment, Tom Uren and Moss Cass, and David Yencken, later to head the Australian Heritage Commission, also preferred the idea of National Estate, perhaps because it provided a more solid foundation for a radical program of state inter-vention. But the statutory body belatedly formed under the Fraser government was called the Heritage Commission (AGPS 1974).

In a period when 'quality of life' had become a leading public issue, 'heritage' was becoming a key word in the environmentalists' lexicon. When the Victorian government introduced its Historic Buildings Bill in 1973, the Leader of the Opposition, Clyde Holding, referred to the need to defend 'Melbourne's heritage in the form of historic buildings', but 'heritage' still competed in the rhetoric of debate with a host of other phrases – 'historic landmarks', 'historic legacies', 'buildings redolent of a by-gone age'. By 1977 and 1978, however, when the New South Wales and South Australian governments introduced similar legislation, they naturally described their new councils as 'Heritage Councils' and the Acts themselves as 'Heritage Acts'. (In 1996 the Victorian government belatedly followed when its Historic Buildings Council became the Heritage Council of Victoria.)

In 1981 David Yencken, Director of the Australian Heritage Commission, introduced *The Heritage of Australia*, the illustrated register of the National Estate, with some remarks on the new terminology. 'Heritage,' he wrote, 'carries connotations of buildings and monuments; conservation suggests natural environments.' But even he was not consistent, referring elsewhere to the 'natural heritage' (Australian Heritage Commission 1981).

Shades of meaning

The users of this newly popular word were often more confident of its acceptability than of its precise meaning. In his perceptive review of *The Heritage Industry* the British writer Robert Hewison quotes Lord Charteris, Chairman of Britain's National Heritage Memor-ial Fund, as saying that heritage means 'anything you want' (Hewison 1987, 32). Its value lay not in its analytical precision, but in its psychological resonance. It hinted at a treasury of deep-buried, but indefinite, values. It invoked a lofty sense of obligation to one's ances-tors and descendants. And it secured the high ground of principle for the conservationists in their perennial battle against the improvers, developers and demolishers.

Heritage – what we value in the past – is defined largely in terms of what we value or repudiate in the present or fear in the future. In its preoccupation with the material remains of the past – 'the *things* you keep' – it endorses our own materialism; yet in its reverence for what is durable, handmade or unique it also reinforces our underlying dis-taste for a culture of mass production and planned obsolescence. 'The impulse to pre-serve,' writes the geographer David Lowenthal, 'is partly a reaction to the increasing evanescence of things and the speed with which we pass them by. In the face of massive change we cling to the remaining familiar vestiges. And we compensate for what is gone with an interest in its history' (Lowenthal 1985, 399).

Ideas of psychic compensation are prominent in the theories offered by sociologists and cultural critics for the heritage boom. American sociologists, such as Fred Davis in his *Yearning for Yesterday: The Sociology of Nostalgia* (1979), invoke generalised ideas of 'future shock' and social dislocation. In a fast-moving, atomistic society, heritage, he implies, offers a sense of spiritual moorings. British neo-Marxists point to the sense of national decline and to the complementarity between a sentimentalised past and the political tenets of Thatcherism (Wright 1985). Heritage offers the consolation of a glorious, if largely fictitious, past to a nation in the midst of a painful present.

Each tradition of interpretation mirrors some of the characteristic preoccupations of the society in which it emerged. But it is hard to credit that a movement that has assumed similar forms in Britain, the United States and Australia is to be explained in purely local terms. In Australia, at least, elements of all three interpretations – the senses of disorientation, of decline and of national immaturity – may be detected in the ideology and rhetoric of the heritage movement.

In the introduction to their Report of the National Estate, the Hope Committee considered that

> It may well be that the rapidly accelerating rate of change in our society and surroundings is disorientating and bewildering to many people, and that a growing rootlessness and ugliness in their surroundings may be mirrored in aimlessness and violence.

They cited Patrick White's suggestion that Australian society was heading for 'joyless warrens from which all the peaceful and consoling aspects of village life have been banished'. 'The shock of deprivation,' they went on to argue, 'can be partly counteracted by identifying and conserving buildings and whole areas of special quality as landmarks for our cultural past, present and future . . . (AGPS 1974, 21–23).' The defence of neighbourhood integrity represented by the residents' associations of the 1970s often gave birth to an upsurge in local historical activity. The past was more than just a handy weapon against the bureaucrats and developers; the historical ambience and distinctiveness of the inner suburb was also a powerful source of community solidarity.

Australian society is not as overshadowed by an aura of national decline as British society. There, Robert Hewison has recently argued, the desire to save the past is largely inspired by a conviction that future choices are foreclosed (Bennett 1995). Heritage is something that we must 'preserve' or 'save' rather than something to be 'created' or 'built'. It expresses the unspoken conviction that there is nothing that we have made, or can hope to make, that is as valuable as what we have inherited from the past. Often, it seems, items come to be recognised as 'heritage', not for their intrinsic qualities but by being 'saved' for posterity. In 1969 the Victorian National Trust stated that not everything that was old should be preserved and that only the best of the past should be cared for – this was how culture and heritage developed.

The appreciation of heritage often grew, therefore, in proportion to the sense of peril. In stagnant and declining regions in both Britain and Australia local history museums and historic precincts abound. To the locals they provide tangible evidence of the community's better days; to the visitors they offer a pleasant respite from the visual monotony of twentieth-century architecture. As traditional industries decline, moreover, historical tourism often becomes the only economic alternative for some regions. At the Wigan Heritage Centre in the derelict British industrial town made famous by George Orwell's depression-time study of the working class, *The Road to Wigan Pier*, visitors now enter an exhibit entitled 'The Way We Were' showing a nostalgic tableau of working-class life in the halcyon days before the Great War. In Australia, too, declining regions and towns, such as the towns of Victoria's central goldfields, the ghost towns of the New South Wales slopes and the mining fields of Moonta and Burra in South Australia, dominate the heritage business.

In *The Birth of the Museum*, Tony Bennett argues that the idea of 'heritage' assumes special significance in postcolonial societies (Bennett 1995, 141). When the sense of a real past is not deeply grounded, as in Australia, the 'vacuum' is filled by 'back-projecting' onto the land itself a sense of common nationality, which is now interpreted in terms of a common patrimony of natural and built, Aboriginal and European heritage. Australia, a new nation, thus acquires a history grounded in 'deep time' rather than just the last century since Federation. Bennett associates these tendencies with the 'new nationalism' of the Whitlam years and especially with the surge of heritage activity promoted by the Hope and Pigott enquiries into the National Estate and into Museums and National Collections.

Yet the process by which Australians came to identify old objects, buildings and landscapes with a sense of national heritage long preceded the specialised use of the word 'heritage' itself. The naturalists, painters and anthropologists of the nineteenth century, like the twentieth-century promoters of national parks and pioneer monuments, were engaged in a systematic and more overtly nationalistic attempt to imbue the land with patriotic significance than the postwar heritage movement. What was new in the movement of the 1960s and 1970s was not its nationalistic focus, but its progressive redefinition from a spiritual to an essentially material concept. In this respect, as in others, Australians were following wider trends. The early 1970s was the heyday of the international environmental movement and the creation of the National Estate and the Museum of Australia might as readily be seen as an indirect creation of UNESCO as a symptom of Whitlam's new nationalism.

Heritage and history

Heritage and history are terms closely related, sometimes almost interchangeable, in the public mind (see Schofield, this volume: 17). Is history the same as heritage? Are they fellow travellers towards a common goal, or are they, as some commentators suggest, rivals for that same valuable bit of turf, the past? In his stimulating book *The Heritage Crusade*, David Lowenthal has drawn a sharp contrast between the purposes and methods of history and heritage. History aspires to be objective, precise, accurate, universal, detached, to study the past in its own terms and for its own sake. Heritage, on the other hand, is concerned not with establishing the truth about the past for its own sake but for *our* sake or our children's. It is, he says, unabashedly 'partisan', 'shallow', 'chauvinist', 'mendacious'. It bends and reshapes the past to a present purpose. It sentimentalises, fabricates, distorts.

> Heritage . . . is not a testable, or even a reasonably plausible account of the past, but a declaration of faith in that past. Critics castigate heritage as a travesty of history. But heritage is not history, even when it mimics history. It uses historical traces and tells historical tales, but these tales and traces are stitched into fables that are open neither to critical analysis nor to comparative scrutiny . . . Heritage and history rely on antithetical modes of persuasion. History seeks to convince by truth and succumbs to falsehood. Heritage exaggerates and omits, candidly invents and frankly forgets, and thrives on ignorance and error . . . Neither history nor heritage is free to depart altogether from the well-attested past. But historians ignore at professional peril the whole palimpsest of past percepts that heritage casually bypasses.
>
> (Lowenthal 1996, 121)

As illuminating as it is, Lowenthal's contrast between history and heritage oversimplifies their complex relationship. Historians are by no means as unanimously dedicated to ideals of objective truth as our academic predecessors were. Even before the discipline was exposed to the influence of postmodernism and poststructuralism, historians had largely abandoned the pretence of objectivity. Any history, they would cheerfully admit, was written from a point of view and, while they might eschew deliberate fabrication and distortion, the pasts they portrayed reflected as much of themselves as their subjects.

Nor is heritage, at least in its institutionalised forms, as 'shallow', 'chauvinist' and 'mendacious' as Lowenthal makes it out to be. A leading goal of the international heritage movement, expressed in such bodies as UNESCO, ICOMOS and the Australian Heritage Commission, has been to objectify, professionalise and systematise the process of heritage assessment and evaluation. In the hands of professionals and bureaucrats much of the heat and subjectivity – and perhaps some of the enthusiasm too – has been taken out of heritage business. In this process historians have been willing, but not uncritical, accomplices. They have been prominent as activists, working with communities to preserve heritage places, as professionals evaluating their claims to historical significance, and as critical commentators on the heritage business itself. Heritage, I once wrote, is the cuckoo in history's nest. But the relationship is really more interestingly complex than that. History is also a free-rider on the heritage bandwagon.

The politics of the past

Heritage is essentially a political idea. It asserts a public or national interest in things traditionally regarded as private. 'Heritage belongs to the people, not to the owners,' remarked Evan Walker, Victorian Shadow Minister for Planning in 1980. He did not mean that because a building or place was part of 'the heritage' its owner ceased to have legal title to it. Rather he was insisting that the public retained a right to ensure its preservation that overrode the owner's right to alter or destroy it.

Opponents of heritage legislation sometimes argue that if, indeed, heritage belongs to the people, then the people should help the owners pay for its preservation or upkeep. The government, as the people's representatives, should either pay the costs of restoration or repair, or it should pay compensation for the development opportunities that the owners of the listed building have had to forego in order to preserve it.

Even in the prosperous 1970s, when 'quality of life' issues were to the forefront, Australian governments were loath to grasp the nettle of compensation. The grants paid in assistance to owners seldom equalled the costs of preservation. The provisions contained in some state legislation to allow the remission of municipal rates or land taxes to the owners of historic buildings have seldom been used. In 1987 the Australian Council of National Trusts and the state ministers for planning jointly petitioned the Commonwealth Treasurer to adopt, as a Bicentenary gesture, the American practice of allowing owners of certain listed buildings to claim the costs of restoration as an income tax deduction. If such pleas failed in the more expansive 1970s and 1980s they seem doomed in the mean 1990s. If politicians seek to 'compensate' owners of heritage buildings, it is more likely to be by relaxing controls on use and development than by foregoing public revenue.

Some leftist critics, on the other hand, welcome heritage legislation as a minor victory over the sacred rights of private property. They look back nostalgically to the days of the Green Bans, when conservationists and trade unionists made common cause against the onslaughts of the developers. Chris McConville (1984) maintains that buildings, once presented as heritage, are no longer simply pieces of capital to be exploited for the greatest possible profit. The left wing of the conservation movement deplores the National Trust's timidity towards propertied interests and the readiness of governments – Labor and non-Labor – to compromise community values for economic development. The complaints have recently grown more vociferous as the Trust has become more preoccupied with securing the viability of its own portfolio of heritage properties.

Beyond the strict question of property rights, however, the idea of heritage also encouraged a sense of psychological or spiritual ownership over those buildings or objects brought within the National Estate. When a squatter's homestead, a miner's hut, a Catholic church or a suburban town hall is identified as part of the heritage it ceases to be in exclusive possession of a family, church or local community and becomes ours. 'Heritage conservation,' writes Jenny Walker in *South Australia's Heritage*, 'is not for governments alone; it is for us all to cherish and nurture the heritage so briefly entrusted to our care (1986, ix).' It is a concept grounded in the first-person plural.

Whose heritage?

What does it mean to 'nurture' or 'cherish' our heritage? Recent critics of the British heritage movement detect in the idealisation of a 'peaceful' rural England and of its great country houses a process whereby an aristocratic or high bourgeois culture becomes identified with the national soul or spirit. National heritage, in the words of the British critic, Patrick Wright, is 'the historicized image of an instinctively conservative establishment' (1985, 47). In Australia, too, the traditional concerns of the National Trust with squatters' homesteads and gentlemen's residences may be said to have reinforced a reverence for the conservative values of the class that inherited them. 'For the most part,' writes Chris McConville, 'the preserved building brought the ideal of the bourgeois Victorian family into the present. The balcony terrace in Gore Street and its imagined gentleman proprietor, the preserved town hall and its civic worthies, the suburban church and its lost congregation – these elements of Victorian society were represented through the preserved building' (1984, 69).

Yet, as McConville concedes, the concept of heritage in Australia has gradually been widened to take in manifestations of many decidedly non-bourgeois ways of life (e.g. Samuel 1994, 158–64). Whereas Toorak matrons once fought to save Victorian mansions, the residents of small towns and unfashionable suburbs now seek to preserve workmen's cottages and disused factories. The National Trust, once the preserve of an Anglophile upper crust, now conducts walking tours of 'Little Italy' in Carlton, Melbourne. When Ballarat Council approved a scheme to buy and restore old miners' cottages, one of its supporters emphasised that 'an important element of the city's past is the working class life of its founders and their domicile'. The Victorian National Trust, in what may be a national or even international first, recently registered a public urinal.

An analysis of the Register of the National Estate or the National Trust, or state heritage registers, would still be likely to reveal a strong bias towards grand buildings designed for wealthy clients by well-established architects. Of approximately 100 buildings or sites listed in the National Register for the Newcastle area, almost 30 per cent dated from the period before 1850, about 60 per cent were from the period between 1850 and 1900 and only about 10 per cent were drawn from the period since 1900. The area is one of the most industrialised and proletarian in Australia but, in the Register, homesteads and mansions outnumber miners' cottages and industrial sites by almost ten to one. In their pioneering study of the cultural landscapes of New South Wales, *The Open Air Museum*, Dennis Jeans and Peter Spearritt (1980) document Newcastle's rich inheritance of twentieth-century industrial buildings, but few of them have yet been included, officially, in 'the heritage'.

Though most listings of the heritage invoke the language of democracy and aspire to some kind of representativeness, the elitist values of the heritage consultants usually show through. 'We want to ensure that examples . . . of structures and remnants of each definable social group in each period, representing all important historical trends are included in the Register,' remarked David Yencken in 1981, though he conceded that 'the search for what is representative is far from complete' (Australian Heritage Commission 1981). The author of *South Australia's Heritage*, an illustrated listing of that state's Heritage

Register, claimed, with more justification, to include 'not only architectural masterpieces of the past and present, but the humble along with the great, the recent with the remote' (Walker 1986).

One way of attempting to conserve a more democratic heritage is to collect items in accordance with the main themes of Australian social history, or the social history of a specific locality. Particular attention would thus be given to the identification of sites or buildings illustrative of important phases of Australia's development or of the way of life of representative groups of people, including the humble as well as the great and famous. In such a scheme, heritage items would be selected in accordance with a general understanding of social history rather than the social history being introduced to provide a background for items collected on an *ad hoc* basis.

Thematic approaches to heritage identification have had a mixed reception among historians. While promising greater rigour and inclusiveness, they also lend themselves to remote and bureaucratic application. They rest upon a process of classification that comes more naturally to botanists and zoologists than historians. The best way of establishing the importance of a building or site, the historian will tend to argue, is by telling a rich, evocative and complex story about it; not by classifying it under a preconceived theme, however important the theme itself may be. The higher one climbs on the heritage tree, from the local to the national, and from the national to the international level, however, the more such taxonomic methods tend to prevail. World Heritage assessments are the most rarified of all. The only way in which an Australian nomination for World Heritage can be advanced is by first establishing that it represents some theme of 'outstanding universal value' (Domicelj *et al.* 1996; Dept. of Environment, Sport and Territories 1996). Historians, for whom context and narrative are the natural methods of interpretation, may welcome the inclusiveness of the thematic approach, but may resist the assumption, often made by bureaucrats, that once the historian has identified the important themes in the history of a region, the process of identification and assessment can be delegated to local planners or other heritage professionals (Davison 1990; Etherington *et al.* 1995).

Creating a more representative 'heritage' is unlikely, in any case, to satisfy other critics of the heritage movement. Indeed, it is the very tendency of the idea of 'national heritage' to subsume and obliterate cultural differences that is at the basis of their objections. Tony Bennett, for example, draws attention to the ways in which the National Estate and the National Museum, by incorporating relics of both Aboriginal and white Australia, may unwittingly 'back-project the discourse of multiculturalism into the mists of time' (1995, 151). How seriously one takes this objection may depend less on the rhetoric of those institutions than on their day-to-day practice and on how seriously one considers the alienation of those relics from their former custodians implied in the process of preservation itself (McBryde 1985).

The democratically inclined social historian, therefore, will be concerned that heritage is not only representative of the people, and conserved for the people, but that it should also be identified and conserved *by* the people. Although the public is constantly exhorted by the experts to 'cherish' and 'nurture' their heritage, the job of identifying, classifying and ensuring it belongs largely to the coterie of heritage experts, architects, historians, archaeologists and planners. The heritage business is subject to a constant tension between the demands for bureaucratic consistency and impersonal expertise, on the one hand, and for popular participation and local autonomy on the other. Since the days of the Green Bans, the balance has swung heavily towards the rule of the expert. There is now a disconcerting gap between the arcane language and specialised concerns of the professional guardians of the heritage and its lay inheritors. Sometimes, it is true, the conservation consultant simply offers a scholarly rationale for aesthetic or historical judgments which the lay person makes more intuitively. But buildings often seem to be selected in accordance with antiquarian or scholarly criteria unrelated to the concerns of the public at large. When heritage consultants come to town they always inspect the buildings, but they do not always consult the locals. There is a danger, therefore, that the buildings they identify will not necessarily reflect the community's own sense of its past.

In historic Beechworth its historian Tom Griffiths argues that the city-based experts of the National Trust and the tourists who followed them to the town were often oblivious of the town's own sense of identity and community.

> Just as the countryside became defined earlier this century as a purely visual phenomenon – to be viewed but rarely understood – so, too, had the past, Beechworth's local past, become a thing to be visited and photographed, but seen as something quite separate from the people living there. In serving the city so, the country becomes constrained to be the past. City-dwellers, who want to see 'progress' where they live, arrive in a country town and lament the careless destruction of quaint old things. Although they are ready to enter into debates about how the countryside looks, there is less concern about disappearing lifestyles or about existing relationships or feelings in that town.
>
> (1987, 98)

Griffiths may exaggerate the gulf between 'city' and 'country' attitudes and underestimate the degree to which the townsfolk, eager for tourist custom, collude with the outsiders in the transformation of their town into 'heritage'. The locals' sense of their past should surely not be regarded as sacrosanct from the more impersonal, but illuminating, interpretation of the outside heritage expert.

Sometimes, of course, the boot is on the other foot and the locals want to preserve a bit of local 'heritage' but the outside experts decree that it fails to meet the 'objective' criteria for registration. In his *Returning to Nothing*, Peter Read notes the powerful attachment, and consequent sense of loss, among residents of the old town of Yallourn, bulldozed to make way for an open-cut mine, and the residents of homes demolished in the path of a freeway in the Sydney suburb of Beecroft. These places may not 'make the grade' for heritage registration but as Read points out they are indeed someone's heritage; it is only the outsiders who fail to see it.

> Heritage and environmental impact assessors have not yet been able to appreciate the multitude of valuations among insiders who look out towards the threat. This should not be surprising, not because such assessments are so difficult, but because assessors have not yet seen the need to appreciate the valuation of the individual, the family, the neighbourhood, the suburb and the town which co-exist within the 'community'.
>
> (Read 1996, 200)

In recent years 'heritage professionals' (an oxymoron?) have responded to the disjunction between professional and community approaches to evaluation by debating the new criterion of 'social value'. In *What is Social Value? A Discussion Paper*, The Australian Heritage Commission (1994) attempts to define the nature of communities' connections to the places they recognise and value. Social value, she argues, is not about the past or about social history, but about people's attachment to places in the present (see also Byrne, this volume). Such places are important because they are 'recognised' by insiders rather than 'identified' by outsiders, and for the way they express and reinforce tradition rather than what they disclose about the past. Aboriginal meeting places, migrant hostels, main streets or pathways might have such social value. If you want to know whether a place has social value, she suggests, you can either just ask the locals, or 'threaten the place and wait to hear from the community if they care about it'. Since it was not practical (or presumably popular) to threaten every potentially valuable place, asking the community to identify valued places was the preferred methodology.

Introducting the new criterion of social value might enable the community to have a bit more say in heritage assessment; or it might encourage the entry into the heritage business of yet another tribe of experts – anthropologists, sociologists, perhaps cultural critics – to join the architects, lawyers, historians and planners who have dominated the trade until now. It might ensure that heritage assessment was not dominated by the professionals; but by insisting on a distinction between 'historical' and 'social' value it might create a distinction between professional and community concerns that many historians would reject. The fiction of heritage as a scientific enterprise in which experts assess the relative importance of heritage 'items' has been useful to governments, as well as to the experts themselves; it created a set of rules and imposed implicit limits on the number of places that belonged to the national estate. But 'social value' introduces a new degree of uncertainty into the process of heritage assessment. It remains to be seen whether federal and state governments can accommodate such open-ended criteria into existing heritage legislation or whether – as seems more likely – the local community that recognises 'social value' will also have to bear the responsibility for protecting it.

What all these disputes underline is the impossibility of reducing heritage to a simple formula. It is, by its very nature, an unstable and contested idea, as must be any idea that attempts to capture the things we count most valuable in our collective life. As soon as the net of definition is lifted over it, it takes flight.

References

AGPS 1974. *Report of the Enquiry on the National Estate (the Hope Report)*. Canberra.

Australian Heritage Commission 1981. *The Heritage of Australia. The Illustrated Register of the National Estate*. Melbourne, Macmillan.

Australian Heritage Commission 1994. *People's places: Identifying and assessing social value for communities*. Technical Workshop Series No. 6.

Bennett, T. 1995. *The Birth of the Museum: History, theory, politics*. London, Routledge.

Bonyhady, T. 1996. The stuff of heritage. In Bonyhady, T. and Griffiths, T. (eds), *Prehistory to Politics: John Mulvaney, the Humanities and the Public Intellectual*, pp. 144–62. Melbourne, Melbourne University Press.

Davis, F. 1979. *Yearning for Yesterday: The Sociology of Nostalgia*. New York, Free Press.

Davison, G. 1990. History and heritage. In Kass, T. (ed), *The role of history in conservation work*, pp. 13–15. Sydney, Professional Historians Association.

Department of Environment, Sport and Territories 1996. *World Heritage Listing: What does it really mean?* DEST.

Domicejl, J., Halliday, H. and James, P. 1996. *Australia's Cultural Estate Framework for the assessment of Australia's cultural properties against the World Heritage criteria*, volume 3.

Etherington, N., Brock, P., Dallwitz, J., Stannage, T. and Gregory, J. 1995. *Principal Australian Historic Themes Project, vol 1: Presentation and Discussion of a Thematic Framework*. Australian Heritage Commission.

Griffiths, T. 1987. *Beechworth: An Australian Country Town and its Past*. Richmond, Greenhouse.

Hewison, R. 1986. *The Heritage Industry*. London, Methuen.

Jeans, D. and Spearritt, P. 1980. *The Open Air Museum*. Sydney, Allen & Unwin.

Lowenthal, D. 1985. *The past is a foreign country*. Cambridge, Cambridge University Press.

Lowenthal, D. 1988. Identity, heritage and history. In Gillis, J.R. (ed), *Commemorations: The Politics of National Identity*, pp. 41–57. Princeton, Princeton University Press.

Lowenthal, D. 1996. *The Heritage Crusade and the Spoils of History*. London, Viking.

McBryde, I. 1985. *Who owns the past?* Melbourne, Oxford University Press.

McConville, C. 1984. 'In Trust': heritage and history. *Melbourne Historical Journal* 16: 60–74.

Mulloy, E. 1976. *History of the National Trust for Historic Preservation*. Washington, Preservation Press.

Read, P. 1996. *Returning to Nothing*. Cambridge, Cambridge University Press.

Samuel, R. 1994. *Theatres of Memory: Volume 1 The Past and Present in Contemporary Culture*. London, Verso.

Walker, J. 1986. *South Australia's Heritage*. Adelaide, State Heritage Board.

Wright, P. 1985. *On Living in an Old Country*. London, Verso.

Chapter 3

Cultural Heritage Management in the United States

Past, Present, and Future

John H. Jameson, Jr

Just as a tree without roots is dead, a people without history or culture also becomes a dead people.

Malcolm X, African-American activist

Introduction

The history of Cultural Heritage Management (CHM) in the United States can be traced to the development of what is traditionally termed 'CRM' (Cultural Resource Management) and the latter-day trends for inclusiveness and sensitivity to heritage values of multidimensional constituents or 'stakeholders.' CRM developed as a system for site and resource protection and was the result of the very rapid accumulation of archaeological and historical site information and collected artifacts following enactment of a series of federal and state historic preservation laws since the 1960s. For some, the term 'public archaeology' became interchangeable with CRM and both terms are still commonly used. The emergence of what has been called Native American or Indigenous archaeology and African-American archaeology are two recent developments. These trends saw an expansion of the definitions and varieties of stakeholders, plus heightened importance and inclusion of traditional and indigenous cultural values. Other recent trends have included enhanced efforts for curation, accountability, legal protection, and site stabilization.

CHM in the United States can be understood as encompassing the traditionally recognized legal compliance requirements with an infusion and increased emphasis on inclusiveness in education and public interpretation efforts. Public interpretation programs have focused on the methods and techniques of conveying archaeological information to the lay public in an engaging, informative, and accurate manner. These activities take place in both formal and informal settings in schools, parks, museums, public exhibits, books, brochures, interpretive artworks, and other venues. Methods and standards for public interpretation have been developed in response to increased public awareness and demand for information in national and state parks, museums, and other public arenas. These are consistent with international developments in the standards and principles of public presentation stirred by a realization that effective interpretation instills a sense of public appreciation and resource stewardship and is therefore a key component of the conservation side of emerging conservation/tourism partnerships. These approaches serve to empower the public to participate in the critical evaluations of historical and archaeological interpretations that are presented to them and to gain an understanding of how and why the past is relevant in modern societies.

Early developments

The roots of public stewardship in the U.S. can be traced to early European encounters by explorers and settlers with monumental earthen mounds that were attributed to exotic non-American cultures. The great mounds of the Lower Mississippi Valley, for example, were often attributed to wayward ancient Egyptians, Asians who pre-dated the biblical flood, or some other non-Indian and exotic sources. This is not surprising since, as far as we know, the vast pre-Columbian mound building activities had ceased by the time Europeans arrived in America. Surely, the early settlers posited, the great and intricate complexes of mounds in America could not have been constructed by the native 'savages.' This belief of non-American origins was common until the end of the nineteenth century.

Thomas Jefferson (b. 1743, d. 1826), third president of the United States, helped pique public interest in indigenous cultures when he published *Notes on the State of Virginia* in 1787, in which he describes in detail his observations from his excavation of a prehistoric Indian mound located on his property in Virginia. In perhaps the first published observation and description of what we would term 'stratified deposits,' Jefferson described the mound as containing 'different states of decay in these strata, which seem to indicate a difference in the time of inhumation.' Jefferson, a prolific writer, helped spur public interest in American Indian material culture and other exotica by putting them on public display. During his term as president, he gave instructions to the Lewis and Clark Expedition (1803 to 1806) to collect American Indian artifacts. Many of these items were displayed in the entrance hall to Jefferson's home at Monticello, Virginia, and were seen by hundreds, if not thousands, of people.

Later in the nineteenth century, the growing public interest in American Indian cultures encouraged the ethnographic work of the Smithsonian Institution. The first publicly-supported archaeology in the United States began in the 1880s through the Smithsonian's Bureau of American Ethnology (BAE) Indian mounds investigations. The International Centennial Exhibition at Philadelphia and the Chicago World's Fair in the late nineteenth century provided greater popular exposure to American Indian artifacts and culture. The growing popular appeal of things archaeological had some negative results, however, with increased commercial demands for authentic antiquities and the resultant looting of artifacts from archaeological sites, especially the prehistoric mounds in the Southeast, the greater Mississippi Valley, and pueblos of the Southwest. A growing public recognition of this unabated destruction resulted in the creation of a publicly-managed archaeological preserve at the ruins of Casa Grande, Arizona, in 1892. The late 1800s was also a period when the preservation of historic landscapes, exemplified by the concern for preserving battlefields of the American Civil War (1861–1865), captured the interest of the public.

The conservation movement of the nineteenth and early twentieth centuries contributed to public interest in protecting historic and archaeological sites. Under President Theodore Roosevelt (b. 1858, d. 1919), public policies were initiated that increased government supervision in the enforcement of antitrust laws and environmental conservation. The government authorization of thirty major irrigation projects and the mammoth Tennessee Valley Authority (TVA) projects set the precedent for large-scale federally-sponsored reservoir construction in the early- and mid-twentieth century. Creation of the

U.S. Forest Service under President Roosevelt in 1905 helped establish a precedent for public-agency management and hiring of professional staff. In the 1930s, a fledgling CHM movement received a boon when the National Park Service was authorized to employ significant numbers of professional historians, historical architects, and archaeologists.

CRM and public archaeology in the twentieth century

The development of significant public funding of archaeology in the United States arose from two major episodes tied to the economic history of the country: the Great Depression of the 1930s and the post-World War II economic boom that began in the late 1940s. Desperate to lift the spirits as well as the pocketbooks of Americans during the Great Depression, President Franklin Roosevelt initiated what he called a 'New Deal for Americans,' an ambitious program of government relief projects that continued until World War II. A massive infusion of government funds sought to put the population to work. In the name of historic preservation, multitudes of projects were launched under the auspices of the major New Deal relief programs: the Civil Works Administration (CWA), the Civilian Conservation Corps (CCC), the Tennessee Valley Authority (TVA), the Works Progress Administration (WPA), and many others. Work under these programs was also accomplished for both preservation and interpretation purposes by the National Park Service. Unemployed workers, including skilled artisans such as writers, artists, craftsmen, engineers, and architects, were widely recruited to manage or be crew members for a wide array of projects such as road construction, building large and small reservoirs, constructing and maintaining bridges, improving national park facilities, construction, and adornment of countless public buildings. Oral historians embarked on projects such as interviewing enslaved African-Americans. Archaeology, with its labor-intensive methods, was seen by the relief project administrators as ideal for putting people to work around the country. Field and laboratory personnel were often large in number and reached a scale not seen previously in American archaeology and rarely equaled since. Large-scale programs continued for almost a decade until the United States entered World War II.

During the New Deal, a whole generation of archaeologists concentrated on American Indian and historic period cultures in North America. This was the beginning of the modern Americanist specialization of many U.S. and Canadian university departments today. These archaeologists had learned to manage large-scale projects and collections. Examining extensive areas with large crews, the New Deal projects infused masses of data and collections resulting in new knowledge and making the development of new synthesis of data and artifact classification schemes possible. The birth of several major archaeology organizations occurred during this time and occupied the talents of a full generation after the 1930s. Although many of these relief projects were located in the American Southeast, the New Deal projects were truly national in scope. Many were noted for their exemplary quality. For example, in excavations in Somerset County, Pennsylvania, the methodology developed and employed was remarkably similar to modern field techniques. As in the case of many of the relief projects, the utility of this information has been nonetheless hampered by inadequacies of data collection (Anderson et al. 2000).

Besides the alarms over looting of Native American sites in the Southwest, other major events and developments, such as the opening of Colonial Williamsburg by the Rockefeller Foundation in 1933 and passage of the Historic Sites Act of 1935, furthered the cause of historic preservation and brought public, private, and professional interest in American archaeology to new heights. The resulting collection of national and state historic sites, monuments, and parks, as well as an abundance of privately administered buildings and sites, were more frequently visited by an increasingly mobile American public, a public that was becoming increasingly enamored of the physical remains of its history. By the late 1940s and 1950s, the beginnings of a new historic preservation ethic had entered the mainstream of public consciousness.

Large-scale dam and reservoir projects

A New Deal relief program, managed under the Tennessee Valley Authority (TVA), established the precedent for later reservoir salvage (rescue) programs that were to have profound influences on the development of CHM in the United States. Created in May 1933, the TVA was charged with developing a series of dams that would provide flood control and electric power, leading, it was hoped, to economic recovery. With the assistance of the Smithsonian Institution, the TVA created its own archaeological program. Much of the archaeological expertise was recruited from the anthropology departments at northern universities such as Harvard. Although the work conducted during this time failed to meet modern standards of investigation, its quality surpassed all previous archaeological research in the area. This and subsequent reservoir programs after World War II profoundly affected public and scientific community awareness of the magnitude of archaeological data loss that could occur nationwide. The decade of the 1930s provided a tremendous amount of information that has formed the basis for present-day understanding of archaeology in North America, especially the southeastern United States. These early compliance projects came to be termed 'salvage' or 'rescue' archaeology and paved the way for the broad range of historic preservation and resource protection programs that emerged in the United States in the 1960s, and that continue today. Additionally, they set precedents for new standards of archaeological management and recordation that have influenced all subsequent work (Anderson *et al.* 2000).

With the TVA projects as a backdrop and precedent, following World War II, the U.S. began an ambitious construction program for flood control, irrigation, hydroelectric installations, and navigational improvements along its many river basins. Although largely unexplored archaeologically, a few spectacular archaeological sites had been found in these areas and the scientific community faced the likelihood that considerable archaeological and paleontological information would be irretrievably lost. In response, the National Park Service and the Smithsonian Institution, in collaboration with other federal land managing agencies, developed an interagency agreement in 1946 to locate historic and prehistoric sites in threatened areas and to salvage as much information as possible prior to their inundation and destruction.

One major post-war program, the River Basin Survey, was run by the Smithsonian Institution's Bureau of American Ethnology. It attained a level of efficiency not possible during the New Deal, when work was conducted under a number of different and competing relief programs. Under this program, a core of archaeologists was hired to conduct or manage work on federally constructed projects. Contracts, grants, and cooperative agreements were also issued with public museums, universities, and colleges. Like their TVA predecessors, the River Basin Survey managers were constrained by the availability of funds and time limitations. In some instances, Native American indigenous persons were hired during these projects as field laborers, informants, and consultants. During the first five years of the program, 213 reservoir areas situated in 28 states were investigated, recording about 2,350 archaeological sites and conducting excavations at 36 sites. In 1965, the River Basin Survey was disbanded and the responsibility for reservoir 'salvage' archaeology was given to the National Park Service where it remained, under the name of the Interagency Archaeological Salvage Program, until 1974. Many of today's most senior and about-to-retire archaeologists in the United States started their careers in the salvage program (Anderson *et al.* 2000).

The work carried out in the late 1940s to early 1960s resulted in the recording of thousands of previously unknown sites. Except for the continuing TVA program, until the middle 1970s, most archaeology projects were limited in scope and budget, and were carried out by museum staff, university professors, and their students.

By the 1980s, the era of large-scale reservoir projects had come to an end. One of the last major projects was the construction by the U.S. Army Corps of Engineers of the Richard B. Russell Dam and Reservoir on the Savannah River in Georgia and South Carolina. The resultant mitigation program, carried out between 1968 and 1985, was exemplary for many reasons. First, given the sheer magnitude of the field effort, the Russell project area represented one of the most intensively studied regions in the United States. The archaeological and historical investigation reports, collectively called the *Russell Papers*, were of high quality and inspired follow-up research for more than a generation. Second, the range of investigations undertaken reflected a rare sensitivity and appreciation for the diversity of cultural resources in the area. Sites included large landmark plantations and eighteenth-century colonial fortifications as well as small farmsteads, tenant sites, and industrial occupations. Prehistoric sites included large mound complexes and village sites as well as smaller and less spectacular campsites and stone knapping stations. The program included intensive research in archaeology, history, architectural history, and oral history of the region. Complimenting the *Russell Papers* technical reports were two widely distributed award-winning popular histories that set new standards in government-sponsored popular history writing (Kane and Keeton 1993; 1994). The Russell studies collectively were one of the most successful regional investigation programs yet to be undertaken under American historic preservation mandates (Anderson *et al.* 2000).

Stronger federal protection legislation

The flow of information coming from the New Deal relief projects of the 1930s, coupled with the large-scale survey and salvage (rescue) programs of the 1940s to 1960s, raised public as well as professional awareness of the magnitude of resources and the potential for information loss to unbridled construction and development. The passage of the National Historic Preservation Act of 1966 and other key legislation and executive mandates in the 1960s and 1970s eventually exerted a transformational effect on the character of archaeological research and preservation, radically changing the way that archaeology was administratively conducted in the United States. The 1966 act formed the foundations for a system of site protection centering on a National Register of Historic Places. It also authorized the creation of the President's Advisory Council on Historic Preservation, established a National Historic Landmarks program, and provided a mechanism for the development of state-level historic preservation programs. The U.S. National Park Service took the lead in developing strong, enforceable federal regulations for the identification, evaluation, and protection of significant sites. Since the late 1970s, when regulations to enforce these mandates were finalized, hundreds of millions of dollars have been spent by federal and state governments on highway construction projects for archaeological surveys, testing and evaluation studies, laboratory analysis, and report preparation. With the resultant increased public interest and exposure to information, standards for archaeological contracting were developed that, by the late 1980s, increasingly stressed public education and outreach as recommended outcomes of compliance mitigation activities.

Two other important national laws enacted during this period were the National Environmental Policy Act of 1969 and the Archaeological and Historic Preservation Act (Moss–Bennett Act) of 1974. The 1969 act required all federal agencies to utilize a systematic interdisciplinary approach in planning and decision-making for projects that may have an impact on the environment. It also stated that a significant impact or controversy triggers an Environmental Assessment or Environmental Impact Statement which assesses impacts and unavoidable environmental effects to both natural and cultural resources and establishes alternatives, including 'no-action.' The 1974 Moss–Bennett Act had major impacts on funding levels. It required federal agencies to provide notice to the Secretary of the Interior of any constructions and other federal undertakings, and, if archaeological resources are found, for recovery or salvage of them. The law applies to any agency whenever it received information that a direct or federally assisted activity could cause irreparable harm to prehistoric, historic, and archaeological data. Most significantly, up to one percent of project funds could be used to pay for salvage (data recovery) work. Prior to the passage of the Moss–Bennett Act, federal archaeological expenditures had averaged less than a million dollars a year. By the early 1980s, estimates of annual archaeological expenditures had reached $200 million. Following the passage of the Moss–Bennett bill, the National Park Service eventually relinquished much of its role as the lead agency in conducting reservoir archaeology as other federal agencies such as the U.S. Army Corps of Engineers, Bureau of Reclamation, and TVA developed their own archaeological programs.

Protections on federal lands were further enhanced by the passage of the Archaeological Resources Protection Act (ARPA) of 1979 and the Native American Graves Protection and Repatriation Act (NAGPRA) of 1990. The 1979 law, as amended, has provided increased protection of archaeological resources located on public and Indian lands. It replaced, and significantly beefed up, the relatively weak and outdated protection provisions of the Antiquities Act of 1906. The new law also exempted information relating to location of archaeological resources from the Freedom of Information Act and established heavy civil and criminal penalties for violation of the act. An impressive litigation record since 1979 has proven the effectiveness of ARPA (Hutt 1994; Hutt 2006). The 1990 NAGPRA bill required museums and agencies that receive federal funding to inventory all human remains, funerary objects, and sacred objects in their possession. It provided a mechanism for federally-recognized Native American tribes, including Native Hawaiian organizations, to repatriate these cultural items. Part of the rationale for NAGPRA was to curb the illicit traffic in stolen and looted artifacts through a thorough inventory of artifacts. NAGPRA requires a federal agency or tribe to deal with any graves that are inadvertently discovered. They are then required to contact the affiliated Native American group. As is discussed later in this chapter, NAGPRA has had a profound influence on the archaeology and treatment of Native American sites and artifacts.

State-level and local mandates

Although budget cuts continue to hamper implementation measures, some state governments, and a number of county and municipal governments, have followed the federal lead in passing protection legislation and ordinances that protect cultural heritage sites and provide for impact mitigation. In general, however, efforts to protect and preserve sites at the state, county, and local levels have been less successful than at the federal level. State-level versions of the National Historic Preservation Act, the National Environmental Policy Act, and the Archaeological Resources Protection Act have been slow to emerge. Budget cuts and downsizings during the past decade have taken their toll on program effectiveness. Concerns about terrorist threats and security have worked to siphon off funds that otherwise would go to preservation efforts. Some faint signs of improvement have been noted in recent years as the economy in some states improves. Although partially dismantled at the turn of the twenty-first century, the preservation programs in the state of Florida, for example, seem to be on the upswing with the establishment in 2005 of the Florida Public Archaeology Network, including an underwater archaeology education coordinator (FPAN 2005) (Della Scott-Ireton, personal communication, 2006).

In many instances, states, counties, and cities make special allowances for property tax credits, historic building rehabilitation, and creation of historic districts and local protection ordinances. Archaeological and heritage preservation at these levels, however, have often been up-hill struggles, sometimes meeting with political opposition from special interest groups such as bottle and relic collectors. Notable recent exceptions have occurred in Charleston, South Carolina; Alexandria, Virginia; New York City, and Boston, Massachusetts, among others. In these cases, local communities have taken the initiative in historic preservation, educational outreach, and archaeological protection planning. The most successful local archaeological protection programs also embrace proactive preservation planning that does not rely solely on regulatory review.

A plethora of data and artifacts

As a result of effective enforcement of the later twentieth-century legislative acts, from the 1970s until the present, a virtual flood of compliance-related cultural resource investigations have been carried out throughout the United States. Work has been especially prolific in the western oil and gas states where construction projects are spurred by fuel shortages in an expanding economy. During the 1970s and 1980s, at the federal level, an army of several hundred archaeologists was hired to oversee these studies by the chief land managing agencies such as the Bureau of Land Management, the U.S. Forest Service, the National Park Service, and the U.S. Army Corps of Engineers. Studies conducted in advance of hundreds of thousands of oil and natural gas pipelines, wells, roads, dams, bridges, and other land-disturbing activities produced hundreds of thousands of reports, recording millions of archaeological and historical sites and hundreds of millions of cultural objects. Still, no more than five percent of the public lands in America have been investigated. Though some progress has been made in recent years, the thousands of reports produced and millions of artifacts collected have overwhelmed existing data management and artifact storage facilities. Despite some serious setbacks and mistakes, the continuing flow of information, as well as the evolution of field methodologies and recording standards, has sharpened our abilities to focus on the important aspects and attributes of a rich and diverse cultural heritage.

Though architectural and oral historians were sometimes members of investigation teams, most compliance-related work has been planned and carried out by archaeologists. The investigators have been stretched thin, however. Not that this will impress colleagues in large-area countries such as Australia, but the writer was once the lone cultural resources specialist for the U.S. Bureau of Land Management in an area of Wyoming that encompassed over 6 million acres (2.5 million hectares) of affected public lands. The U.S. Bureau of Land Management is responsible for 264 million acres of public land, about one-eighth of the land in the United States, and about 300 million additional acres of subsurface mineral resources.

Changes in philosophy and methodology

In addition to the much more complicated regulatory situation that was in place by the late 1970s, archaeologists both within and outside of the government had to deal with shifts in theoretical emphasis from a classificatory-historical (historical reconstruction) emphasis during the decades before and after World War II to a 'processual' paradigm beginning in the early 1960s. Before the 1960s, the goal of studies was largely the description of artifacts and chronology. The processual paradigm maintains that interpretation as well as descriptions of data is important. The new theoretical emphasis attempted to establish archaeology as a technique for recovering anthropological data. With this new approach to research, theories about cultural processes are proposed and tested through generating hypotheses and testing the hypotheses. This philosophical shift from cultural history and environmental concerns to a more scientific approach, in combination with the passage of stronger CHM laws, increased the complexity of salvage (rescue) and compliance-driven archaeology.

More recent philosophical developments have produced debates among the post processualists, who emphasize the political and public aspects of archaeology, and the more traditional logical, scientific empiricists. For example, the proponents of the post-processual 'critical theory' argue that, when the past is interpreted and becomes history, it tends to become ideology. In this line of thought, public interpreters recognize that the meanings they impose on the past are particular to their own cultural and social background. With this awareness, they can help their audiences appreciate that many, if not all, of their preconceived notions about time and space are actually part of their own, modern, historically-based ideology. Thus, audiences can appreciate that knowledge about the archaeologically-revealed past is useful in giving meaning to the present. Some American archaeologists have reacted to the critical theory approach by calling it an 'anti-science fad.' They warn against going too far in accepting the conclusions of critical theorists in that there are no facts or truths in archaeology and that the past is not knowable with any integrity. If the past has no integrity, they say, then anyone's interpretation is as good as anyone else's and the interpretation would be open to anyone's political or ideological whims (South 1997).

The 1990s saw the emergence of greater energy and funding devoted to the public interface of archaeology as the professional community became aware that intellectual introversion was no longer acceptable and that more attention should be paid to the mechanisms, programs, and standards of public presentation and outreach. In the face of an increasing public interest and demand for information, archaeologists and their cultural heritage colleagues began to more actively collaborate to devise the effective strategies for public presentation and interpretation.

Presently, for many archaeologists in the U.S., traditional definitions for the terms *historic*, *archaeological*, and *scientific* are changing to incorporate intangibles such as aesthetic, artistic, spiritual, emotional, and other values stemming from introspection. An expansion and broadening of the content of 'archaeological knowledge' to be more inclusive and less authoritative has emerged, broadening the definition and meaning of 'expert' (see Thomas, this volume). An important result has been the emergence of the interpretive narrative approach in archaeological interpretation, where archaeologists actively participate in structuring a compelling story instead of just presenting sets of derived data. The narrative is used as a vehicle for understanding and communicating, a *sharing* as well as an *imparting*, of archaeological values within the interpretation process. This trend is resulting in profound ramifications for definitions of significance in heritage management deliberations and what is ultimately classified, conserved, maintained, and interpreted (Jameson *et al.* 2003).

Crises of management

Problems of enforcement

By the early 1990s, it was evident to archaeologists and heritage site managers in the U.S. that a tremendous increase in the commercialization of the human prehistoric and historic record was contributing to looting of archaeological sites to the extent that 'if something is not done soon to curb this destruction, there will be little of our collective past left for future generations' (Smith and Ehrenhard 1991). It was also clear to many that agencies lacked adequate staff, training, and resources to enforce ARPA. At first, ARPA had proven difficult to prosecute. Americans were still generally unaware of the magnitude and destructiveness of site looting and the precise definitions contained in ARPA. As a result, until relatively recently, vandals were often prosecuted not with ARPA but with either the 1906 Antiquities Act or theft of government property statutes which were easier for the public (and many judges) to understand. Part of the problem stems from the tradition in the U.S. of right of ownership, i.e., property rights. The property owner by law owns (i.e., controls) whatever is contained on, or in, that property. This is in contrast to most other areas of the world where objects of antiquity are nationalized and owned (and controlled) by the national government. An attempt to reconcile the situation was made in late 1990 when the first President Bush signed NAGPRA into law. One of the purposes of NAGPRA was to reduce the international market by cataloguing all artifacts, beginning with museum collections. Furthermore, NAGPRA required repatriation of all sacred objects and human remains still contained within or upon archaeological sites. NAGPRA has assisted in promoting heritage values in archaeological resource management and federal land protection. It has increased ethnographic interest and awareness for Native Americans. NAGPRA also has forced agencies and museums to come to grips with curation problems and work to resolve the problems.

Crises of collections storage and information management

As has been mentioned, a virtual avalanche of reports and collected artifacts accompanied the CRM 'explosion' starting in the late 1970s. No one could have predicted the magnitude of this vast acceleration of cultural resources work. In previous years, agencies had relied upon agreements with non-federal repositories such as state and university museums to care for their collections. These agreements were often vague and usually did not provide funding or facilities support for housing, accessioning, or conservation of the materials. A government report in 1986 revealed some shocking facts. It found that a large percentage of excavation reports prior to 1975 had been lost or destroyed. There were no binding standards or criteria to guide agencies in evaluating repositories. Agencies had very poor inventory records; for example, most of the approximately 25 million artifacts stored by the National Park Service had not been cataloged, requiring $50 million to rectify, and $200 million were needed for new and upgraded storage facilities. One third of all non-federal curation facilities had already run out of storage space. Other government facilities were found to be in similar shape, with poor maintenance practices, inadequate security and fire protection, and inadequate staff.

Regulations for the curation of federally-owned collections were finally issued in 1990, only to be upstaged the same year by the newly enacted NAGPRA. NAGPRA, with its specified deadlines for compliance reporting, forced agencies and museums to focus on NAGPRA compliance to the detriment of the new curation requirements. One positive effect of NAGPRA, however, has been to force agencies to conduct artifact inventories and determine their disposition. Some agencies, such as the U.S. Army Corps of Engineers, have been able to consolidate collections. As in other aspects of historic preservation and resource protection in the United States, federal agencies are looked upon to provide leadership in acknowledging ownership of collections recovered from public lands and to provide adequate funds for curation. The lack of adequate funding, professional staff, and space to curate archeological collections over the long term remains an acute challenge and overall progress has been slow. It is certain that the curation crisis will continue well into the twentieth century (Childs 1995, 1996; Childs and Kinsey 2003).

The stampede of recorded sites and collected artifacts since the 1970s has also created a crisis of data management among responsible federal and state agencies nationwide. Since the early 1980s, site forms have become more automated as technical advances have facilitated the development of various database systems. Automation of data has facilitated the use of automated land resource distribution tools such as Geographic Information Systems (GIS) in CRM planning among government agencies at federal, state, and local levels. A major challenge among agencies has been to create systems that are mutually compatible. One of the problems has been to create dynamic systems that can evolve along with the rapidly changing technologies.

One effort to alleviate this problem was the establishment of the National Archaeological Database (NADB) by the National Park Service. NADB consists of a reports module and a NAGPRA data module. 'NADB-Reports' is an expanded bibliographic inventory of approximately 350,000 reports on archaeological planning and investigation, mostly of limited circulation. This 'gray literature' represents a large portion of the primary information available on archaeological sites in the U.S. The database can be searched by state, county, worktype, cultural affiliation, keyword, material, year of publication, title, and author, and is periodically updated. The Permits module contains records of over 3,500 federal permits, providing key information about archaeological and paleontological investigations carried out on federal and Indian lands between 1907–86. NADB-MAPS (Multiple Attribute Presentation System) is a graphical application, which contains a variety of maps (GIS) showing national distributions of cultural and environmental resources across the U.S. by state and county (NPS NADB 2006).

The NPS National NAGPRA program is a set of online databases designed to provide access to information on a variety of NAGPRA-related topics. All of the databases have search capabilities that allow the user to locate specific information. The databases are updated regularly by National NAGPRA staff. The Native American Consultation Database (NACD) is a tool for identifying consultation contacts for each Indian tribe, Alaska Native Corporation, and Native Hawaiian organization. The database is not a comprehensive source of information, but it does provide a starting point for the consultation process by identifying tribal leaders and NAGPRA contacts. The NACD is updated semiannually. More complete and updated information is regularly posted on the *National NAGPRA* Web site at http://www.cr.nps.gov/nagpra/ONLINEDB/INDEX.HTM (National NAGPRA 2006).

Challenges of managing submerged resources

The Abandoned Shipwreck Act of 1988 established protection measures for significant shipwrecks and authorized state management of them. It established United States ownership of all abandoned shipwrecks on submerged state lands that are either embedded in such lands or included in or determined eligible for the National Register of Historic Places (NPS 1991). The act transfers title of these abandoned wrecks to the states except where they are in submerged lands administered by a federal agency or Indian tribe. In cases where these wrecks are embedded in federal lands, the federal lead agency has responsibility for the abandoned shipwreck. The act only applies to formally abandoned shipwrecks. Abandonment of a wrecked military vessel requires an act of Congress. Wrecked Confederate naval vessels from the American Civil War (1861–1865), and the ships and aircraft lost to the U.S. in war, are generally the property of the U.S. government and are not subject to the terms of the act. Wrecks beyond the boundaries of U.S. waters are not subject to the terms of the act, but are subject to federal admiralty law.

States vary in how effectively they protect abandoned shipwrecks. In Florida, which has passed some of the strongest protection mandates, problems persist because of a lack of enforcement resources and conflicts with the ancient common law of treasure trove, which awards title of an artifact to the finder, whether he is a looter or an archaeologist. In recent years, however, the majority of federal and state courts have rejected treasure trove and similar common law rationales, fostering legal policies that discourage wanton trespass to real property and give protection to landowners' claims. Rejection of the rules that reward finders at the expense of landowners has also strengthened anti-looting provisions. Believing that public interpretation and outreach can serve to foster public stewardship and assist in site protection and monitoring, the state of Florida is exemplary in establishing underwater trails and preserves that seek to foster resource values as fixed points or inalienable objects in the public conscious. Since the vast majority of underwater sites that are interpreted are located *in situ* at the location where they impacted the sea floor, archaeologists and managers use interpretive strategies, rather than exhibition techniques, to illustrate and emphasize the cultural value of a shipwreck. Successful programs emphasize a combination of community involvement, effective interpretation, and active management. 'Success' in this context means that the resource is visited consistently by the public who are educated as well as entertained, and that the resource is maintained in a manner consistent with sustainable use and long-term preservation (Scott-Ireton 2007).

Philosophical trends and debates

Policies versus realities: debates on restorations and reconstructions

A controversial CHM topic since the 1930s has been the debate over the pros and cons of reconstructions vs. preservation-in-place and the role of archaeology. The focus of discussions for archaeologists has been on what is the appropriate level of archaeological investigation and knowledge that is needed prior to on-site reconstructions. Another concern is whether reconstructions of *any* nature are appropriate when *in situ* cultural materials will be damaged or destroyed. The work done at Colonial Williamsburg by the Rockefeller foundation, together with the passage of the Historic Sites Act of 1935, heightened both public and private interest in archaeology. At Colonial Williamsburg, a reconstructed historic community of the 1770s was based on detailed historical and limited archaeological research. These reconstructions proved to be immensely popular with the public.

The reconstruction technique at Colonial Williamsburg involved recreating over 450 buildings in an effort to completely restore the town. Lack of specific information on a particular building presented no problem to project designers and architects, who relied on architectural precedents and an examination of surviving colonial buildings in the region to invent building types based on general architectural practices of the period (in this case, the middle to late eighteenth century). These planners and architects saw life in eighteenth-century Virginia as more homogenous and genteel than do historians today. This popular, yet conjectural, technique became the standard applied to hundreds of reconstructions in the United States for decades to come. It pervaded and guided the work of the National Park Service and other federal agencies in scores of New Deal public works projects carried out in the years preceding World War II (Jameson and Hunt 1999). By the late 1940s and 1950s, historic preservation as the commemoration of sites and structures associated with famous people and events had entered the mainstream of public consciousness. The resulting collection of national and state historic sites, monuments, and parks, as well as an abundance of privately administered buildings and sites, became standard fare for an increasingly mobile American public.

In this backdrop of a developing preservation ethic, a small but vocal cadre of scholars (architectural historians, historians, and archaeologists) has opposed the broad use of reconstructions (or 're-creations' as some have termed it). Starting in the 1930s, there was a steadily growing outcry in the National Park Service and elsewhere, especially among cultural heritage professional staffs, to severely limit, if not abolish altogether, the use of reconstructions as an interpretive device. The debate has been between these conservative preservationists and others more concerned with effective pubic interpretation and presentation. In general, the supporters of reconstructions believe that reconstructions, if guided by extensive archival and archaeological research, can be effective if not essential to telling the story.

NPS generally defines 'reconstructions' as any measures to preserve remaining prehistoric or historic materials, features, structures, and spatial relationships. The 2006 draft of revised NPS management policies states that: 'No matter how well conceived or executed, reconstructions are contemporary interpretations of the past rather than authentic survivals from it. A structure will not be reconstructed to appear damaged or ruined. Generalized representations of typical structures will not be attempted. NPS will consider reconstruction of structure or landscapes when: 1) there is no alternative that would accomplish the park's interpretive mission; 2) sufficient data exist to enable its accurate reconstruction based on the duplication of historic features substantiated by documentary or physical evidence, rather than on conjectural designs or features from other structures; 3) reconstruction will occur in the original location; 4) the disturbance or loss of significant archaeological resources is minimized and mitigated by data recovery; and 5) reconstruction is approved by the agency director. By inference, NPS allows reconstructions to include the use of modern materials and tools only if these do not conflict with purpose of "replicating its appearance"' (NPS 2006a).

Reconstructions differ from restorations in that they involve *new* construction of various components of the cultural landscape, such as buildings, huts, towns or villages, earthworks, living areas, trails, and roads. A reconstructed cultural landscape re-creates the appearance of the non-surviving cultural landscape in design, color, textures, and, where possible, materials. Reconstructions have addressed a wide temporal range in the national park system including sites such as the prehistoric Great Kiva at Aztec Ruins National Monument in New Mexico and a ceremonial earth lodge in Georgia, to historic period buildings, trading posts, and forts of the seventeenth, eighteenth, and nineteenth centuries.

In the United States, and elsewhere, the 'value' of reconstructions often goes beyond any scientific, educational, or conservation considerations to premeditated or desired outcomes that are also influenced by a blend of other factors such as social morality, politics, local economy, and tourism. In a representative democracy such as the United States, the determining factors for creating any given national park unit revolve around these issues. Despite agency policies that have generally discouraged the use of reconstructions as public interpretation tools, a wide variance in the national park system has developed between sites that have virtually no reconstructions, such as at Jamestown, Virginia, to parks that depend almost entirely on reconstructions in their public programs, such as Fort Vancouver National Historic Site, Washington, which has a reconstructed stockade and five major buildings. At Jamestown, long a 'sacred cow' among preservationists, the preservation purist philosophy has prevailed. At Fort Vancouver and a number of other sites, *in situ* preservation has been de-emphasized in favor of a comprehensive program of reconstructions based on intensive archaeological and historical research. Archaeological research at the nineteenth-century Hudson Bay Company site has been going on intermittently for fifty years, supplying detailed information and artifacts for the public interpretation and education programs, including museum displays and living history demonstrations.

However, in light of increased pressures from the growing juggernaut of tourism, international debates on the value of reconstructions and restorations are likely to continue well into the twenty-first century. In the United States, with lessons learned from Colonial Williamsburg and other sites, and with the high cost of maintenance and the resultant reluctance to carry out reconstructions, we are likely to see less construction and more preservation-in-place.

These debates are not unique to the United States and North America (Jameson 2004; Stone 1999). In October 2005, an international colloquium on reconstructions ('restitutions') in Bezier, France, addressed the issues facing site managers in Europe on how to respond to increasing economic and political pressures to reconstruct on Roman sites such as villas and temples (MONUM 2005).

Ethnic sensitivity issues

Developments in Native American archaeology

In the 1990s, the aftermath of the passage and implementation of NAGPRA has forced many archaeologists, historians, and cultural heritage managers to rethink fundamental assumptions that traditionally guided the development of research designs and the interpretation of findings. Archaeologists found that they were no longer the sole proprietors and interpreters of pre-European history. The definition of 'cultural resources' in the archaeological sense broadened from a focus on objects, features, and architectural elements to less tangible items such as 'place,' or 'setting,' or 'traditional cultural property.' This is due primarily to the effects of new federal mandates that have made Native Americans integral players in cultural resource management, a redefinition of what constitutes 'data,' and who owns or controls the data (Edgar 2000). In this new philosophical and political environment, archaeologists and cultural resource managers can no longer rely on material culture alone to identify or describe historic and archaeological properties. This change from the traditional definition also means that cultural resources, especially archaeological resources, cannot be identified through traditional investigation procedures (Banks *et al.* 2000).

Just as the concept and context of 'cultural landscape' have been added to the evaluation criteria for National Register eligibility, so has 'traditional cultural property' (TCP). Both terms were outside the boundaries of items traditionally considered by archaeologists until the CRM developments of the late twentieth century. Many archaeologists as well as Native Americans are looking to these new definitions and concepts to help mend past animosities and provide a bridge for communication and cooperation in their common passion for Native American cultural history (Banks *et al.* 2000).

Kennewick Man: 'Native American' or European?

One of the most intriguing CHM topics from the last decade has been the ongoing investigations related to the NAGPRA-related controversy about human skeletal remains associated with the 'Kennewick Man,' or 'Ancient One.' A nearly complete skeleton was found in July 1996 below the surface of Lake Wallula, a pooled part of the Columbia River behind McNary Dam in Kennewick, Washington. Based on the preliminary 1996 study, the remains were determined to be approximately 9,000 years old, which seemed to qualify them as 'of, or relating to, a tribe, people, or culture that is indigenous to the United States, including Alaska and Hawaii' and therefore 'Native American' as defined by NAGPRA. The original scientist on the scene had retrieved a nearly complete human skeleton, with a long, narrow face suggestive, he thought, of a person of European descent. Almost immediately, a dispute developed regarding who was responsible for determining what would be done with the remains. Claims were made by Indian tribes, local officials, and some members of the scientific community. Adding fuel to the controversy were claims by another special interest group, pointing to the 1996 study, that the remains are of European rather than Native American origin. This, they said, raises the question of who came to the Americas first. It also raises a question among some researchers whether the earliest humans in North America arrived via the Bering Land Bridge, a long-held belief, or by boat or some other route. The dispute revolves around the historical connections and whether the definition of 'Native American' under NAGPRA applies to the Kennewick Man skeleton. Another aspect of the dispute is whether the involved scientists, despite NAGPRA definitions and requirements, have a legal right to study the remains.

In September 2000, the U.S. Secretary of the Interior concluded that, based on the radiocarbon dates, geographic data, and oral history accounts, the remains were affiliated with Indian tribes of the region and should be returned to the Indian Tribes as required by NAGPRA. The U.S. Department of the Interior had hoped that this work would provide conclusive evidence to determine whether or not there is a shared group identity or cultural affiliation between Kennewick Man and modern Indian groups.

Subsequent events and findings have created as many questions as answers. A 2001 report, generally confirmed by later studies, concluded that the Kennewick Man remains are of a single individual who was interred at the site instead of being left to decompose on the surface of the ground or incorporated into the deposit through some catastrophic hydrologic event. These findings are consistent with the belief by some that Kennewick Man was intentionally buried soon after death and that red ochre or some kind of staining might have been applied to his body before burial. The 2001 report confirmed previous findings suggesting that there is significant variation in the degree of intact collagen preservation in different portions of the Kennewick skeleton. From a morphological perspective, the Kennewick specimen appeared to be more similar to those of modern South Asians and Europeans than to modern Native Americans or to contemporary indigenous populations of Northeast Asia. To date, mitochondrial DNA analyses have been unable to assign the Kennewick skeleton as Asian-specific. Recent findings are reported to suggest that remnant DNA could still be found within Kennewick Man's teeth remains that were protected by hard tooth enamel (McManamon 2004; Tri City Herald 2006).

The Kennewick Man controversy has heightened the post-NAGPRA debate among archaeologists and Native Americans on who owns, controls, and interprets the artifacts and data. In the new era of Native American archaeology, many American archaeologists are questioning the appropriateness of the privileged access that professionals, such as prehistorians and physical anthropologists, have long enjoyed. The challenge will be in moving toward a greater reconciliation among divergent cultural perspectives in ways that enhance both the archaeologist's and the public's knowledge and appreciation for the past. No doubt, the controversies and litigation surrounding the Kennewick Man issue will take many years to resolve.

The emergence of African-American archaeology

Another recent focus in the 'archaeology of ethnicity' in America has been in the realm of African-American studies. An impressive collection of data has accumulated from rural plantation sites as well as urban settings. As archaeological data on African-Americans lifeways has accumulated over the last forty years, archaeologists have taken two basic methodological approaches in carrying out research.

One approach seeks to recognize the archaeological patterning of slave sites and use these as signals or markers when sites are discovered. Much of this work has been conducted on plantation sites in the southern and mid-Atlantic regions of the United States. At sites such as Mount Vernon, Monticello, and Colonial Williamsburg, new insights to the lives of enslaved African-Americans are being revealed. Most importantly, these insights are beginning to make their way into public interpretation programs and exhibits, 'to render significant what has been thought incidental; to make central the important contribution that the common person has made to America's past, not simply to add voices to mainstream history, but rather mainstream those voices into history' (Bograd and Singleton 1997). An example of this approach is the work of Leland Ferguson in the Carolinas. In *Uncommon Ground: Archaeology and Early African America, 1650–1800*, Ferguson (1992) traces the advances of African-American archaeology since the 1960s. Integrating research in artifacts, folklore, and history, Ferguson explores black lifeways along the south Atlantic coast, showing that innovative black pioneers worked within the restraints of bondage to shape their distinct identity and to lay a rich foundation for the multicultural adjustments that became colonial America. He reveals how archaeologists have compared knowledge with folklorists and historians to form a new, more complex portrait of the world the early slaves made.

The second approach, centering on the search for objects with physical or behavioral links to Africa's west coast, has moved beyond the simple transfer of objects and ideas across the Atlantic to a more refined focus which integrates behavior with material culture. The aim of the latter approach is not on direct, unaltered 'transferences,' but rather on how West African cultural traditions, as reflected in the archaeological record, were modified in the face of the new environments, different social groups, and altered power structures in which the slaves in the New World found themselves. No longer having access to the same commodities once at their disposal, West African slaves and their descendants lived in a material world populated largely with goods of English or European manufacture. The assumption is that the slave population thought about and used objects differently from what the object manufacturers had originally intended, adapting these new forms of material culture for use within African-American cultural systems (Samford 1994). This approach attempts to identify 'Africanisms' that can enable cultural heritage management practitioners to direct their efforts toward non-European historical sources and to sites where various African ethnic groups settled in America (NPS 2006b). An example of this approach is the volume *African Reflections on the American Landscape: Identifying and Interpreting Africanisms*, by Brian D. Joyner (2003). This publication highlights West and Central African cultural contributions to the nation's built environment that has been documented and recognized in the cultural resources programs of the National Park Service.

Protection and interpretation of maritime sites

Increased public attention in recent years to historic shipwrecks and other submerged cultural resources has raised concerns about protection. Protection activities in the U.S. National Park Service involve inventory, evaluation, monitoring, interpretation, and establishing partnerships to provide for the management of historic shipwrecks and other submerged cultural resources in units of the national park system. The Service does not allow treasure hunting or commercial salvage activities at or around historic shipwrecks or other submerged cultural resources located within park boundaries unless legally obligated to do so. Parks may provide recreational diving access to submerged cultural resources that are not susceptible to damage or the removal of artifacts. The Service ensures that the activities of others in park waters do not adversely affect submerged cultural resources or the surrounding natural environment. The Service consults with the owners of non-abandoned historic shipwrecks, and enters into written agreements with them to clarify how the shipwrecks will be managed by NPS. Shipwrecks owned by a state government pursuant to the Abandoned Shipwreck Act of 1988 are managed in accordance with the Abandoned Shipwreck Act Guidelines (Larry Murphy, personal communication, 2006).

The public interpretation of maritime resources can present special problems due to remoteness and accessibility. Quality public interpretation and outreach assist in managing and protecting archaeological sites in remote locations. They are also key elements in garnering public and institutional support for research and monitoring 'ownership' by local communities and frequent users who can assist in long-term preservation and public stewardship. The last decade has seen the development of effective on-site and off-site interpretative efforts such as heritage trails, virtual trails, museum exhibits, and other examples of public interpretation as a management tool. Other examples would include the successful development of maritime heritage trails, underwater parks, field schools, classroom instruction, innovative diver access programs, as well as exhibits and educational programs at maritime museums (Jameson and Scott-Ireton 2007).

Submerged sites such as shipwrecks provide special challenges. Shipwrecks are rarely entirely raised, conserved, and placed in an exhibit. The vast majority of shipwrecks that are interpreted at all are *in situ* at their resting place on the ocean floor. Thus, in order to be effective, archaeologists, resource managers, and interpreters must employ innovative and provocative interpretive strategies that go beyond traditional exhibition techniques in illustrating and emphasizing the heritage values associated with shipwrecks and other sites within the maritime landscape (Jameson and Scott-Ireton 2007).

Present and future directions: a commentary

Values-based heritage management and public stewardship

As previously mentioned, in the United States, the term 'heritage' has become synonymous with 'cultural resources' and the old acronym 'CRM' has become 'cultural heritage management' or 'CHM.' This is consistent with international forums where heritage is an emotionally charged term that connotes cultural inheritance from the past that is the evidence of human activity from Native or First Nation peoples. The term 'cultural heritage' commonly refers to both Native and non-Native places and objects, and associated values, traditions, knowledge, and cultures. 'Heritage' in the broader sense includes natural resources and the environment: it is a particular version or interpretation of the past that belongs to a person or group. Concepts of heritage play important roles in shaping group or community identities and political ideologies. Heritage attracts the attention of visitors to a location or site by providing a sense of place, a sense of purpose, and a sense of uniqueness for a community or group. Heritage also provides education about the results of research. Heritage offers distinctive experiences, fascinations, and forms of entertainment that are out of the ordinary. 'Values' in these discussions relate to tangibles and intangibles that define what is important to people, where, in all societies, a sense of well-being is associated with the need to connect with and appreciate heritage values. In heritage management, we articulate 'values' as attributes given to sites, objects, and resources, and associated intellectual and emotional connections that make them important and define their significance for a person, group, or community. An understanding of how and why the past affects both the present and the future contributes to people's sense of well-being.

Expanded emphases on community-based educational archaeology, partnerships, and public outreach

In the 1980s, having a commitment to public outreach was a major step forward beyond merely presenting and sharing the results of research among colleagues. However, these early archaeological outreach efforts often involved archaeologists working in isolation from community groups. It was the archaeologists who decided, without substantive input from community members, what type of archaeological outreach and what messages the public needed and wanted. The public lectures, tours of sites, exhibits, films, brochures, pamphlets, and articles were based on what the archaeologist wanted to say and the information that the professional archaeologist felt was most important. Questions such as who the target audience is, and what questions do they want answered, were often not on the archaeological radar screen. But, slowly, archaeologists started to move out of the isolation model and partner with non-archaeologists in order to develop more meaningful public programming. Archaeologists study communities as part of their research agenda, but now community members are moving from the category of 'research subject' into 'partner in outreach' (Jameson and Baugher 2007).

Although these efforts to increase public access to information have always been present to some degree, the picture that emerges in the early twenty-first century is one in which many archaeologists and cultural historians have come to terms with the realization that they cannot afford to be detached from mechanisms and programs that attempt to facilitate emotional and intellectual connections to archaeological information, heritage values, and resource meanings. In conjunction with efforts to instill a greater awareness and appreciation of archaeology and cultural heritage, both in and out of formal classroom settings, many archaeologists and cultural heritage specialists are devising new approaches to public interpretation in a variety of settings. The venues for these activities can include visiting an archaeological excavation, a reconstructed site, stabilized ruins, museum exhibits, or sites treated as open-air museums. Archaeologists, working with teachers and other communication partners, bring archaeology to public schools through traveling exhibits, lectures, teacher and student workshops, and hands-on activities. Communities are increasingly partnering with archaeologists and cultural historians to become active players in a variety of archaeological investigations, interpretation, and preservation of their heritage (Jameson and Baugher 2007).

The last decade has witnessed numerous applications of public interpretation and outreach models and an increased interest in establishing partnerships between professional practitioners in public interpretation and educational institutions such as museums and schools. The lessons to be derived from these modestly funded projects are that attitudes and initiatives of people make the difference. These developments have occurred in the context of a realization that community-based partnerships are often the most effective mechanism for long-term success. We have learned that successful partnerships involve years of work with partners learning from each other and that there are many diverse ways for heritage management practitioners to be involved in public outreach and community involvement (Jameson and Baugher 2007).

Heritage as inspiration

Today, many heritage management specialists are not content to rely solely on traditional methodologies and analytical techniques in their attempts to conserve resources and make human history come alive for people. They want to venture beyond utilitarian explanations and explore the interpretive potential of cognitive imagery that heritage information and objects can inspire. They realize the value and power of artistic expression in helping to convey archaeological information to the public. They are increasingly concerned with how the past is presented to, and consumed by, non-specialists. They want to examine new ways of communicating archaeological information in educational venues such as national parks, museums, popular literature, film and television, music, and various multimedia formats. Although some level of conjecture will always be present in these works, they are often no less conjectural than technical interpretations and have the benefit of providing visual and conceptual imagery that can communicate contexts and settings in compelling ways. Archaeology and archaeologically derived information and objects, many realize, have inspired a wide variety of artistic expressions ranging from straightforward computer-generated reconstructions and traditional artists' conceptions to other art forms such as poetry and opera (Jameson *et al.* 2003).

The challenges of heritage tourism

Another current and ever-growing challenge that affects the inclusiveness of heritage management and interpretation is the juggernaut of tourism. By definition, heritage tourism is collaboration between conservationists and commercial promoters. In heritage tourism, the goal is to harness people's fascination and sense of connection to the past and turn it into a commodity. It is often an uneasy association because the motives of these respective groups are not always compatible. While there is general recognition that heritage tourism can work to promote preservation of communities' historic and cultural resources, and also educate tourists and local residents about the resources, the resulting effects are not always viewed as beneficial, especially from those of us on the conservationist side of the fence. Nevertheless, because heritage tourism is a growth industry in almost every part of the world, the issues it conjures up, good and bad, must be addressed. Those of us whose primary goals and interests are conservation should be determined that our values and standards in this relationship are not compromised or diminished.

With the onset of globalization and expanded international tourism, changes and impacts to heritage management and resource conservation are likely to be profound. Heritage tourism, with its ties to the currents of rapidly evolving global economies, is causing increasing needs and demands for cross-cultural and international communication and interdisciplinary training. Emphasis is on transferable skills such as the application of interdisciplinary approaches, writing for both academic and non-academic audiences, oral presentation, and experience with multimedia packages. Heritage tourism run amok, that is, when the relationship lacks conservation-driven decision making and objectively-derived values assessments, threatens or limits inclusiveness by rendering community and other stakeholder involvement superficial.

Conclusions

This chapter has described heritage management in the United States as being shaped by the historic preservation and conservation movements of the nineteenth and twentieth centuries, the government relief programs of the 1930s, the outcomes of post-World War II CRM compliance, and recent foci on indigenous cultures, African-American cultural history, and educational archaeology. Challenges to management, such as site protection, looting, and the curation crisis, will continue to be the focus of government programs for the foreseeable future.

Lessons learned by those of us who manage, study, and present the past are that we must become aware of how the past is understood within the context of socio-economic and political agendas and how that influences what is taught, and how it is valued, protected, authenticated, and used. We know we must deal with philosophical, political, and economic forces that affect how sites and parks are managed. We are affected by political currents that threaten to weaken long-standing principles, standards, and commitments to public stewardship. Our dwindling budgets and reductions in personnel exacerbate the problem. Our interpretive messages at parks, historic sites, and museums are increasingly affected by heritage tourism pressures. Nevertheless, perhaps one measure of the status and maturity of cultural heritage management in the United States is its recent trend toward inclusiveness exemplified by a turn toward a greater recognition of multiethnic values. In this sense, a new and expanded definition of cultural resources has steered the archaeological profession toward a firmer embrace of archaeology as anthropology.

Many heritage management specialists realize that, only when they are willing to reach out to people in other professions and work with and learn from constituent communities, can successful management and interpretation partnerships be formed. Although limitations of manpower and resources continue to be sources of frustration for cultural heritage managers in the United States, we believe that our efforts in site protection, public education, and interpretation, in the Jeffersonian tradition, are producing a more informed, appreciative, and inspired public.

Acknowledgements

Portions of this chapter are derived and updated from material previously published by the author in an article entitled 'Public Archaeology in the United States' (Jameson 2004).

References

Anderson, D. G., Keel, B. C., Jameson, J. H., Jr., Cobb, J. E., and J., J. W. 2004. Reservoir Construction in the Southeastern United States: The Richard B. Russell Project as an Example of Exemplary Cultural Resources Management. In Steven A. Brandt and Fekri A. Hassan (eds), *Damming the Past: Dams and Cultural Heritage Management*, Lanham, Maryland: Lexington Books.

Banks, M. K., Giesen, M. and Pearson, N. 2000. Traditional Cultural Properties vs. Traditional Cultural Resource Management. *CRM* 23 (1): 3–17.

Bograd, M. D. and Singleton, T. A. 1997. The Interpretation of Slavery: Mount Vernon, Monticello, and Colonial Williamsburg. In John H. Jameson, Jr. (ed.), *Presenting Archaeology to the Public: Digging for Truths*, 193–204. AltaMira Press: Walnut Creek, London, and New Delhi.

Childs, T. S. 1995. The Curation Crisis. *Common Ground* 7(4). http://www.cr.nps.gov/archeology/cg/fd_vol7_num4/crisis.htm, (accessed 15 October 2006).

Childs, T. S. 1996. Collections and Curation into the 21st Century. *Common Ground* 1(2). http://www.cr.nps.gov/archeology/cg/vol1_num2/21st_century.htm, (accessed 1 October 2006).

Childs, T. S., and Kinsey, K. 2003. Costs of Curating Archaeological Collections, A Study of Repository Fees in 2002 and 1997/1998. Washington: National Park Service Archeology program. http://www.cr.nps.gov/archeology/TOOLS/feesstud.htm (accessed May 25, 2006).

Edgar, B. 2000. Whose Past is It, Anyway? Review of *Skull Wars* (2000) by David Hurst Thomas, *Scientific American*, pp. 106–107, July 2000.

Ferguson, L. 1992 *Uncommon Ground, Archaeology and Early African America, 1650–1800*. Washington: Smithsonian Institution.

FPAN (Florida Public Archaeology Network) 2005. Florida Public Archaeology Network, University of West Florida, Pensacola. http://www.flpublicarchaeology.org/ (accessed June 16, 2006).

Hutt, S. 1994. *The Civil Prosecution Process of the Archeological Resources Protection Act, Technical Brief Number 16*. Washington: National Park Service. http://www.cr.nps.gov/archeology/pubs/techbr/tch16A.htm (accessed 1 October 2006).

Hutt, S. (ed.) 2006. *Yearbook of Cultural Property Law 2006*. Walnut Creek: Left Coast Press.

Jameson, J. H., Jr. 2004. Public Archaeology in the United States. In Merriman, N. (ed.), *Public Archaeology*, pp. 21–58. New York and London: Routledge.

Jameson, J. H., Jr. (ed.) 1997. *Presenting Archaeology to the Public: Digging for Truths*. Walnut Creek: AltaMira Press.

Jameson, J. H., Jr. (ed.) 2004. *The Reconstructed Past: Reconstructions in the Public Interpretation of Archaeology and History*. AltaMira Press: Walnut Creek.

Jameson, J. H., Jr., and Baugher, S. 2007. Public Interpretation, Outreach, and Partnering: An Introduction. In J. H. Jameson, Jr. and S. Baugher (eds), *Past Meets Present: Archaeologists Partnering with Museum Curators, Teachers, and Community Groups*, pp. 3–17. New York: Springer.

Jameson, J. H., Jr., Ehrenhard, J. E., and Finn, C. A. (eds) 2003. *Ancient Muses: Archaeology and the Arts*. Tuscaloosa: University of Alabama Press.

Jameson J. H., Jr., and Scott-Ireton, D. 2007. Introduction: Imparting Values/Making Connections. In J. H. Jameson, Jr. and D. A. Scott-Ireton (eds), *Out of the Blue: Public Interpretation of Maritime Cultural Resources*, pp. 1–18. New York: Springer.

Jameson, J. H., Jr. and Hunt, W. J. 1999. Reconstruction vs. Preservation-in-place in the National Park Service. In P. G. Stone and P. G. Planel (eds), *The Constructed Past: Experimental Archaeology, Education and the Public*, pp. 35–62. London and New York: Routledge.

Joyner, B. D. 2003. *African reflections on the American Landscape: Identifying and Interpreting Africanisms*. Washington: National Park Service.

Kane, S., and Keeton, R. 1993. *Beneath These Waters: Archeological and Historical Studies of 11,500 Years Along the Savannah River*. Atlanta: Interagency Archeological Services Division, Southeast Region, U.S. National Park Service, and Savannah: U.S. Army Corps of Engineers, Savannah District.

Kane, S., and Keeton, R. 1994. *In Those Days: African American Life Near the Savannah River*. Atlanta: Interagency Archeological Services Division, Southeast Region, U.S. National Park Service, and Savannah: U.S. Army Corps of Engineers, Savannah District.

McManamon, F. D. 2004. Kennewick Man. http://www.cr.nps.gov/archeology/kennewick/ (accessed 1 April 2006).

MONUM 2005. 'Colloque International "La restitution en archéologie et la présentation au public," 12/14 octobre 2005.' MONUM (French National Monuments Agency), published conference announcement. Copy on file at the Southeast Archeological Center, U.S. National Park Service, Tallahassee, Florida.

National NAGPRA 2006. National NAGPRA. http://www.cr.nps.gov/nagpra/INDEX.HTM (accessed 1 October 2006).

NPS 1991. Abandoned Shipwreck Act Guidelines. Washington: National Park Service. http://www.cr.nps.gov/archeology/submerged/intro.htm (accessed 1 April 2006).

NPS 2006a. Draft *Management Policies*. Washington: National Park Service.

NPS 2006b. Africa in America: an Introduction. http://www.cr.nps.gov/crdi/publications/-Africanisms-Chapter1.pdf (accessed 1 April 2006).

Samford, P. 1994. Searching for West African Cultural Meanings in the Archaeological Record. http://www.diaspora.uiuc.edu/A-AAnewsltetter/Winter1994.html (accessed 1 December 2006).

Scott-Ireton, D. 2006. The Value of Public Education and Interpretation in Submerged Cultural Resource Management. In J. H. Jameson, Jr. and D. A. Scott-Ireton (eds), *Out of the Blue: Public Interpretation of Maritime Cultural Resources*, pp. 19–32. New York: Springer.

Smith, G. S. and Ehrenhard, J. E. (eds) 1991. *Protecting the Past*. Boca Raton: CRC Press.

South, S. 1997. Generalized versus Literal Interpretation. In J. H. Jameson, Jr., (ed.), *Presenting Archaeology to the Public: Digging for Truths*, pp. 54–62. Walnut Creek: AltaMira Press.

Tri City Herald 2006. Kennewick Man Virtual Interpretive Center. http://www.kennewick-man.com/index.html (accessed 1 April 2006).

Chapter 4

Towards a Theoretical Framework for Archaeological Heritage Management

Laurajane Smith

The need to theorise and 'make sense' of the competing values attributed to heritage, and the processes and strategies employed to control such values, has become increasingly important. As conflict over access to heritage objects increases, and as debates about contested pasts and cultural identity become more heated and broader in scope, it has become necessary for archaeologists to define not only their position, but their rôle in such debates. The processes and strategies employed by archaeologists and/or government organisations to regulate and control the use of heritage sites, or what are sometimes referred to as archaeological *resources*, are often identified by the term 'archaeological heritage management' (or 'cultural resource management', or simply 'heritage management').

As part of the process of theorising it is necessary to define what is meant by the term 'archaeological heritage management' (AHM). The aim of this chapter is to offer a definition and overview of AHM as it is practised in Australia. Such definitions will add to our theoretical understanding of what is a significant employment area for most archaeologists. The chapter will also briefly examine some of the recent theoretical developments in archaeology and comment upon their usefulness in theorising AHM.

Previous definitions of AHM tend to define AHM as a process or set of practices aimed at the management of cultural heritage. While such definitions are valid, AHM is much more than this and fulfills other rôles and functions. Most definitions of AHM tend to focus on the technical aspects of AHM and ignore the socio-political context of AHM practice. Even when the political aspects of AHM are acknowledged little analysis is often made of the rôle of archaeological practice and theory in political and cultural debates and conflicts.

I will argue that AHM can more usefully be conceived as:

a   a process which fulfills part of a Western cultural, political and ethical concern with the conservation and curation of material items;
b   a process which institutionalises archaeological knowledge and ideology within State institutions and discourses;
c   a process which is implicitly concerned with the definition of, and debates about cultural, historical, social and national identities.

Archaeological heritage management, especially in post-colonial societies, embodies a process of cultural domination and imperialism in which archaeological knowledge is privileged and institutionalised within the State. Through this process archaeology is used within State discourse to arbitrate on cultural, social and historical identities, and archaeology itself gains some disciplinary authority and 'identity' within this process. In Australia this process is most apparent in debates and conflict over Aboriginal cultural identity, but is no less relevant to the management of non-Aboriginal heritage. This term refers to heritage objects, sites and places relating to the European and non-European history of Australia. Although this chapter will develop a definition of AHM that has particular resonance in an Australian context, it will be argued that the conceptualisation of AHM that is advanced is of relevance also to AHM as practiced in Britain.

A history of the development of archaeological heritage management

Australian archaeological heritage management, or cultural resource management as it was then called, first developed as an organised and governmental process in the 1960s. The first government act which aimed to protect heritage objects was the New South Wales *National Parks and Wildlife Act, 1967* (since replaced by a 1974 act).

Many of the concepts and ethos of AHM were imported to Australia from the USA (Bowdler 1981, 1984; Smith 1996). The importation and development of conservation concepts, practices and policies coincided with increasing government and public concerns over environmental degradation and uncontrolled land development (Davison 1991a and this volume). It was also correlated to an increasing recognition of the importance of Australian archaeology.

In the history of Australian archaeology the 1960s is often portrayed as a period in which the discipline underwent rapid re-evaluations of the significance and value of the Australian archaeological resource (see Murray and White 1981; McBryde 1985; Mulvaney 1990). At the beginning of this decade the Aboriginal past was considered to be very recent, no more than a few thousand years old. By the middle of the decade the occupation of Australia was found to date into the Pleistocene. By the end of the decade dates in the order of 35,000 years old had been established (White and O'Connor 1983). Australian archaeology had, by the 1970s, 'come of age'. The establishment of these dates meant that Australian archaeology was finally considered to have the ability to contribute to world archaeology. This ability was reinforced by the 1960s immigration from Cambridge University of some of the first professionally trained archaeologists to work in Australia.

Archaeologists in the 1960s and early 1970s agitated and lobbied for the protection of archaeological resources and the development of government legislation to protect both Aboriginal and non-Aboriginal cultural heritage (Edwards 1975: 112–14; Mulvaney 1990; Davison 1991b). This call was reinforced and strengthened by public concerns about the environment, and by Australian building unions which placed work bans, or 'green bans', on the 'development' of historic buildings and bushland (Davison 1991b).

A further event which, I will argue later, influenced the development of AHM in Australia, was the Aboriginal Land Rights Movement. This movement obtained citizenship for Aboriginal people in 1967. Prior to this date Aborigines were not legally recognised as Australian citizens nor were they counted in government censuses. Aboriginal activism gained increasing momentum in the early 1970s, as witnessed by the establishment of the Aboriginal tent embassy on the lawns of Parliament House.

Public concern over the preservation of heritage, Aboriginal concerns over cultural sovereignty, coupled with increasing archaeological concerns to prevent the loss of what was an obviously archaeologically important resource, all worked to establish the character of AHM as practiced in the 1990s. But before I examine how these have influenced AHM, it is important to note that a further event had significant impact on the development of AHM not only in Australia, but in Britain and the USA as well.

The 1960s and 1970s also marks the development and maturation of the New Archaeology. Archaeology was firmly established in this period as a Science with rigorous and systematic methodology modeled on the physical sciences. This development had tremendous influence on the development of AHM which incorporated not only the 'scientific rigour' and methodology of the New Archaeology, but also the authority given to archaeology by its new identity as a Science. It is this development which has helped the institutionalisation of AHM and of archaeology as a whole. It is also the institutionalisation of the New Archaeology through AHM in policy discourses that had significant ramifications for the development of archaeological theory in the 1990s.

Previous definitions of archaeological heritage management

Previous definitions of AHM have often been descriptive and, with few exceptions (e.g. Carman 1991; Byrne 1991), have tended to avoid placing AHM in either a disciplinary or theoretical context. Such descriptions have relied on technical and scientist language which have tended to constrain critical analysis of AHM. Previous definitions tend to formularise its practice and underlying conservation principles and ethics (e.g. Kerr 1990; Hall and McArthur 1993a). They have also focused on describing AHM's legislative and government policy base (e.g. McGimpsey and Davis 1977; D. Fowler 1982; Ross 1986; Darvill 1987; Cleere 1984a, 1984b; Flood 1987). Other definitions or debates about AHM have been focused on particular issues, such as 'who owns the past', reburial issues, repatriation, tourism issues, or rights of access to Stonehenge, to name but a few (e.g. McKinlay and Jones 1979; Green 1984; Cleere 1989; Shanks and Tilley 1987a, 1987b; Davison and McConville 1991). While such issues are of paramount importance to AHM and archaeology as a whole, to *simply* perceive AHM as an arena where such issues are debated has two major consequences.

Firstly, such issues are seen primarily as being AHM issues, and not *necessarily* issues in which the whole of archaeology must engage. AHM is often used or conceptualised as an intellectual 'buffer' or barrier between political and cultural issues, and a pristine conceptualisation of archaeology as an intellectual and 'scientific' discipline. By identifying AHM with political issues archaeology as a discipline is one step removed from cultural and heritage politics.

Secondly, AHM as an arena for particular issues is very neatly divorced from the rest of archaeology. AHM simply becomes an area of practice which intersects with other interests in heritage. Such a conceptualisation of AHM has meant that little intellectual space has been made for conceiving of heritage as a process which is influenced by, and which in turn influences, archaeological theory and practice.

Descriptions which concentrate on AHM practice, legislation and policy or AHM issues have helped to create the opinion that AHM is separate from archaeology. Such a separation has often led to the marginalisation of AHM, and AHM is often devalued as an area that contributes little to archaeological research (Renfrew 1983; Carman 1991). As a protector and manager of archaeological data the dismissal of AHM as irrelevant to archaeological research is insupportable. How we manage archaeological sites and what we choose to conserve or destroy has obvious and irrevocable influences on archaeological research. As an embodiment of archaeological practice which is influenced by archaeological theory and ideology, the separation of AHM from archaeology in general has only confused attempts to define AHM.

Archaeological heritage management and the 'conservation ethic'

A growing body of literature exists which aims to account for why many Western countries have been concerned to save and conserve material culture. In particular debate has focused on why concerns to systematically save and preserve material culture took on more force and momentum in many countries, including Australia and Britain, in the 1960s and 1970s. These decades saw increasing urban and rural development and increasing public awareness of conservation issues. These concerns are often seen as the impetus for the escalation of conservation issues and management policy (Lowenthal 1990). However, debate continues over why Western industrial countries organise to systematically preserve material culture.

Some authors consider that as modern Western public life grows more abstract and impersonal people have turned with increasing nostalgia back to the past (Chase and Shaw 1989). Associated with this is the need to provide ourselves with material 'anchors' to a past that becomes more distant as the present becomes more complex (Lowenthal 1979; Hall and McArthur 1993b). Some warn that this phenomena is often linked with, or actively utilised by, conservative political parties, and can certainly work to retard present cultural innovations and change (Wright 1985; Hewison 1987). Others see our concern with the past as being tied to an increase in leisure, which has allowed time in which to contemplate the past (Hunter 1981). The need to conserve material from the past has also been given more urgency by the development of an economically powerful cultural tourism industry (P. Fowler 1987, 1992; Smith *et al.* 1992; Hall and McArthur 1993b).

Whatever the reason for our concern with the past, the development of a conservation ethic during the 1960s and 1970s was not simply a response to rapid development and threats to heritage. Western concerns for material culture from the past have a long history, and the development of AHM can be seen to reflect a more basic social and cultural function than the simple appeasement of a 'conservation ethic'. Western societies have, through museums, long been concerned with the acquisition and preservation of material culture from our own and other countries' pasts.

Museums play an important social and cultural rôle in helping to educate the public about history and the nature of other cultures. As a growing critical literature has argued, museums present items selected by curators as important or significant in expressing and symbolising a past that provides the basis from which we in the present construct notions of self and cultural identity (Clarke 1988; Pearce 1990; Merriman 1991; Hooper-Greenhill 1992; Moser 1996). Indeed the procurement of antiquities from colonised countries or peoples by museums occurred in association with, and as part of the processes of, imperialism, colonisation and economic domination (Gidiri 1974; Marrie 1989). The collection of such antiquities often added an element of symbolism that helped to reinforce more concrete political and economic domination.

AHM developed out of an already existing ethos or concern in Western society with the documentation and preservation of objects from the past, and simply expanded such concerns to immovable objects and places.

As part of the development of AHM in Australia there has been the continual redefining of Australian history. From the 1960s there has been an increasing number of counter and alternative histories written which criticise traditional Australian history for failing to consider the histories of the working class, women, migrants and Aborigines in accounts of the Australian past. In the build up to the Australian bicentennial and our move to become a republic, debate has increased over the definition of Australian cultural identity (e.g. Reynolds 1982; Sykes 1989; Pilger 1989; Pettman 1992; Burgmann and Lee 1988; see also the journals *Aboriginal History*; *Labour History*; *Refractory Girl*).

Such debates are often reflected in what is saved and preserved by AHM in Australia. The things that are considered important enough to conserve often reflects those things which are identified as symbolising Australian cultural identity. As the debates shift, so too do those things which are conserved.

The preservation of objects in museums or the preservation of sites and places fulfills an important social, cultural and political rôle in Western societies. The conservation of such things is important in the process of providing and/or controlling individual, cultural, social and historical identity. The conservation of material from the past is important in providing a sense of community, a sense of a shared past that helps bond community and social identity (Lowenthal 1990; P. Fowler 1992). The provision of such perceptions is political, particularly when such perceptions obscure, as they often do, inequality and divisions within communities. The political aspects of this process were intensified when heritage management was given structure and coherence by government policy and legislation.

The institutionalisation of archaeological heritage management and archaeological ideology

In fulfilling the cultural and political rôles described above AHM has become a vehicle through which archaeology has, or is at least publicly seen to have, direct cultural impact and relevance. Through this process archaeology is often given *social* authority as it is seen to impact upon and give meaning to the past and, by association, aspects of the present. In addition AHM also provides archaeology with *institutional* authority. Such authority reinforces archaeology's social authority, and ensures archaeology a rôle in the processes and strategies employed to conserve a nation's heritage. It must be noted, however, that such authority is not absolute, and although archaeology often obtains authority over non-Scientific heritage interest groups, archaeological concerns are often marginalised in relation to, for example, economic interests and concerns.

Davison (1991a: 11) notes that, despite the wide range of competing interests in, and the degree of public concern with, heritage it is inevitably professionals, such as archaeologists, historians and architects, who have come to dominate the management of material culture. In understanding why it is that professionals like archaeologists dominate heritage management it is necessary to understand the rôle and authority of intellectuals in Western societies.

Bauman (1987; 1989) offers some useful insights into the rôle of intellectuals in Western societies. Bauman (1987; 1989) identifies and defines two rôles fulfilled by intellectuals which he labels 'legislator' and 'interpreter'. Legislators speak as authoritative experts from powerful institutions, and are identified with the traditional Enlightenment view of intellectuals and knowledge. The legislator makes authoritative statements which, due to the legislator's superior knowledge, arbitrate over procedural rules which ensure the attainment of 'truth' (Bauman 1987).

Interpreters aim to facilitate communication between autonomous participants in the social order, rather than choosing 'rational' paths towards an 'improved' social order (Bauman 1987). Bauman argues that the interpreter represents intellectual practice in a post-modern sense – translating statements made in one communally based tradition so that they can be understood within a system of knowledge based on another tradition (1987). This is the intellectual practice that the post-processualists Shanks and Tilley (1987a, 1987b), Hodder (1989; 1991) and Leone *et al.* (1987; Leone and Potter 1992) aim to fulfill or imply that this is the rôle to which the discipline of archaeology should aspire. However, it is not easy for the 'interpreter' to escape the authority of the 'legislator'.

Bauman argues that these two forms of intellectual practice often operate simultaneously (1987). Individuals, disciplines and institutions *may* operate as both legislators and interpreters. Although the rôle of the interpreter may, on the face of it, be seen as more

'progressive' than the legislator, the interpreter none-the-less utilises the claims of intellectuals to meta-professional authority. The interpreter still speaks from the privileged
position of the intellectual in making binding statements on procedural rules (Bauman
1987).

Bauman's (1987; 1989) definition of the rôles of intellectuals provides a useful conceptual framework in which to illustrate the link between archaeology (via AHM) and the
State. Archaeologists within heritage management act as both legislators and interpreters.
Archaeologists act as legislators in AHM in the sense that their knowledge is often used to
arbitrate on conflicts over the use of heritage sites. At the same time archaeological knowledge is used as an interpretive bridge between different conceptualisations or understandings of the past. This is particularly the case in post-colonial societies where obviously
distinct cultural groups exist with differential political power and resources.

In any definition or discussion of heritage management the existence of *conflict* is
always emphasised. Conflict often arises over the different values attributed to heritage by
interest groups, over the use of heritage sites, over different conceptualisations and meanings attributed to heritage objects, sites and places; and over the various different expressions of cultural and historical identity. AHM is directly concerned with the management,
regulation and mitigation of conflict over the use of cultural heritage.

The interaction of the various groups who have an interest in cultural heritage is controlled and regulated by the strategies and management processes embodied in AHM.
AHM does not only manage physical objects, sites and places, but also regulates and structures the conflicts which arise between competing values and conceptualisations of the
past. Such conflicts are structured by the various pieces of heritage legislation enacted in
each country where some form of heritage management exists. The legislation establishes
a hierarchy which almost inevitably reinforces the authority of intellectuals to arbitrate on
procedure and knowledge. Heritage legislation, in effect, embodies and reinforces
Western hegemonic structures that privileges intellectual practices and knowledge. In
Australia, Britain and the USA it is archaeologists who are either explicitly recognised
under heritage legislation as arbitrators over heritage conflicts, or who are employed by
the government institutions responsible for the legislation to interpret and implement that
legislation (see D. Fowler 1982; Saunders 1983; Ross 1986; Darvill 1987; Geering and
Roberts 1992; Leone and Preucel 1992). In short, archaeological knowledge is ensured a
rôle in heritage discourse and policy, but this does not mean that this position is not itself
compromised by bureaucratic rationality and political compromises.

Historically archaeologists themselves have been concerned to ensure their primacy in
conflicts over the use of cultural heritage. In the 1960s and 1970s, when the public and
governments in Australia, Britain and the USA became increasingly concerned with the
conservation of both cultural and natural heritage, archaeologists also became increasingly
vocal in their calls for the conservation of cultural heritage. At the same time archaeologists also became increasingly concerned with delineating *who* should control conservation
processes. The discourse used in debates dating to this period, and in current debates on
heritage management, provides insight into the intellectual rôle of archaeology in heritage
management and State discourses on cultural heritage.

Since the 1960s archaeologists in the USA, Australia and the UK have argued in the
academic and popular archaeological literature and in the media about the need for archaeology to prevent the looting and destruction of sites by non-archaeologists and developers.
These concerns by archaeologists can not be assumed to be totally altruistic. Such debates
and concerns have often been expressed in terms of the rights of archaeological science as
universal knowledge to unrestricted access to the 'archaeological resource'. The debate was
often framed with references to rationality and the need for archaeology to obtain information about an objectified past. In such debates archaeologists were presented as stewards
for, and protectors of, an objective past (McGuire 1992: 817). Ideas of archaeological

stewardship abound in these debates (see for example P. Fowler 1981: 68, 1987: 411; Cleere 1988: 39; Merriman 1991: 18; Shanks 1992). So too do the concepts of *archaeological resources* or *archaeological* sites. The constant use of terminology that identified an *archaeological resource* is not simply an accident of expression. Rather the discourse is mapping out the intellectual rights of the archaeological discipline to access and control cultural heritage. The use of such language is firmly defining archaeology as an intellectual interpreter on the past. Further, the use of concepts of stewardship and arguments based on notions of rationality and archaeological 'science' is firmly denoting the legislative intellectual authority of archaeology.

It is not accidental that in Australia, at least, public expressions of archaeological concerns with conservation increased at a time when Aboriginal political movements were concerned to question the rôle of the State in controlling their cultural and political expression. During the 1960s and 1970s in both Australian and US archaeological debates on conservation there was an explicit concern to distance archaeology from concepts of 'treasure hunters' and 'grave robbers' – criticisms that indigenous people had made about archaeology. As indigenous criticism increases so too do archaeological attacks on antiquities markets, black market sales of 'archaeological' artefacts, and looting of sites by souvenir hunters and antiquities collectors (see for example Clewlow *et al.* 1971; McGimsey 1972; McGimsey and Davis 1977; Deetz 1977; P. Fowler 1977; Arnold 1978; Cockrell 1980; Gregory 1986). Such debates help, however unconsciously, to proclaim and reinforce archaeology as a legitimate intellectual discipline and practice. These debates almost inevitably employed arguments based on the rights of archaeology as a science to data, and on the concepts of science as universal knowledge. The use of such concepts again reinforces archaeological intellectual authority.

The development of the New Archaeology or processual archaeology had a significant impact on these debates. The New Archaeology firmly aligned archaeology with the physical sciences, and by doing so archaeology obtained a disciplinary identity which conformed to Western and bureaucratic notions of intellectuals based on traditional Enlightenment rationality. The emphasis which was placed on objective hypothesis testing, and the idea that through such processes general principles or 'laws' could be obtained meant that archaeology could easily be taken up and incorporated into State and bureaucratic structures. Commentators on the development of the New Archaeology have noted that one of the significant outcomes of this period was that the old order of power in the archaeological discipline was challenged. It has been noted that acceptance of the logical positivism of the New Archaeology meant that progression through the archaeological ranks was no longer based on your social status or that of your patron, but on the results of your research (Redman 1991). In short, the 'truth' of your archaeological research would ensure your success within the discipline. This of course was, and is, a simplistic view of how power is regulated within archaeology – but the important point is that such assumptions illustrate the faith that many archaeologists had in the power of intellectual authority based on rationalist philosophy. Such perceptions of the power of rationality have proved useful as such perceptions coincide with the rôle of intellectuals as structured by bureaucracies.

The use of discourse based on or influenced by the philosophical tenets of the New Archaeology in debates over cultural heritage meant that archaeology was identified as an intellectual authority. The lobbying of archaeologists for the development of heritage legislation and policy could be recognised by, and subsequently incorporated within, the sphere of State concern. Archaeology, and its conceptualisation of cultural heritage, was included within the ambit of State discourse in a way that Aboriginal and other heritage interest groups could never be. Archaeology as a 'rational' intellectual discipline could be understood by the State apparatus simply because both share common assumptions about 'rationality'. Claims to cultural heritage based on non-rationalist or non-Western knowledge were and are effectively locked out of or excluded from effective participation in the discourse.

The alignment of the discipline of archaeology with the Science of the New Archaeology came at a time when the State was increasingly concerned with cultural heritage. How much the development of each phenomena influenced the other could be speculated upon. However, one of the major consequences of these developments was the institutionalisation of archaeological science in State discourse and State apparatus as embodied by AHM.

In short AHM and the institutionalisation of archaeological philosophy and practice has provided the discipline of archaeology with institutional authority. Importantly this authority is tied to the discipline's intellectual identity. Subsequently not only does AHM provide institutional authority, it has also institutionalised the philosophy and ideology of the New Archaeology.

Contested pasts and identity: archaeological ideology and state discourse

Through AHM and the institutionalisation of archaeology, archaeologists have become intellectual arbitrators on issues surrounding contested pasts and identity. Through AHM archaeological discourse can be taken up by the State, or other participants in debates over identity, with or without the intent of the archaeological community. Archaeological pronouncements may be and often are used as legislative statements. Through AHM archaeologists and archaeological pronouncements are also used as interpretive bridges between conflicting conceptualisations of the past. For example, archaeologists and archaeological knowledge are often employed to translate Aboriginal knowledge about the past into a format that may be incorporated into the bureaucratic structures of heritage management. Further, in debates over the use of Stonehenge archaeological knowledge is often used as a 'yard stick' by management authorities to assess the validity of claims made by alternative groups.

The use of cultural heritage in defining and maintaining a sense of place, identity and/or community has been well documented in the heritage literature (e.g. Lowenthal 1990; Davison 1991a; P. Fowler 1992; Johnston 1992; Hall and McArthur 1993a). Cultural heritage and the way it is managed can play a rôle in controlling cultural expression as Hewison (1987) points out, or it may form the basis from which cultural and political challenges to normative perceptions are launched (as witnessed by Aboriginal agitation to control their heritage: Geering and Roberts 1992; Fourmile 1989a, 1989b; see also Reekie 1992; Bickford 1993).

The contestation of identity and interpretations of the past can have important political and cultural implications as I argued at the beginning of this chapter. It was argued that AHM fulfills a cultural and political rôle in Western societies, and through AHM archaeology becomes directly engaged, and often unwittingly aligned, to State arbitration and control of cultural identities.

The institutionalisation of archaeology and the use of archaeology in arbitrating on conflicts over cultural heritage and the past helps, in part, to explain why many of the issues traditionally identified with AHM are often so emotive and so intensely political. Such issues are not merely issues of conflict between competing interest groups and a politically disinterested archaeological discipline. In any conflict the use of archaeological knowledge must be seen in the context of power relations. This does not mean to say that archaeological authority is absolute; indeed archaeological interests often lose out to more powerful economic and bureaucratic interests in debates over the use of heritage. The point is that the institutionalisation of archaeological knowledge through AHM makes any debate on the use of cultural heritage intensely political. Further, the outcomes of such debates have very real consequences for all players in the debate.

The institutionalisation of archaeological knowledge also helps to explain why Aboriginal communities and other indigenous peoples have reacted with such political intensity to archaeologists and archaeology. Archaeologists are not simply perceived as disinterested intellectuals undertaking 'objective' research which may or may not support Aboriginal perceptions of their past. Rather archaeology as part of State discourses, institutions and practices impacts upon Aboriginal intellectual and cultural expression and has direct and powerful implications for Aborigines.

Discussion

I have argued that AHM may be defined as a process which has grown out of and embodies cultural and political processes in Western societies. Most importantly AHM has institutionalised archaeological knowledge, and the philosophies of the New Archaeology in particular. AHM further provides institutional authority and identity for the discipline of archaeology.

Several implications arise from such a definition of AHM. I wish to briefly pursue two in the remainder of this chapter. The first is that this definition provides an opportunity to explore the link between archaeology and State institutions, discourses and practices. Such a definition extends the conceptualisation of the political context and consequences of archaeological practice and knowledge. This is done by explicitly recognising that archaeological knowledge may be used *outside* of the discipline of archaeology and by non-archaeological interests. The second implication is that we are forced to consider the degree to which archaeology is itself controlled by external forces and interests. Archaeology is not and cannot be self-referential; what we do not only has consequences outside of the discipline, but State and institutional interests also influence the development and dissemination of archaeological knowledge.

In recent years theoretical debate in archaeology has focused on the political and subjective nature of archaeological knowledge. Post-processual and feminist archaeology have identified and discussed the theory-ladenness of archaeological research and both approaches have realigned archaeology with the social sciences. However, these theoretical developments, and post-processual theory in particular, have tended to ignore the rôle of AHM in influencing archaeological practice and theory.

Post-processual theory, for example, tends to be overly self-referential, or simply fails to identify the institutional power relations within which archaeology must operate (see Smith 1994 for further discussion). AHM which explicitly places archaeology within institutional, social and cultural hierarchies offers post-processual archaeology an arena in which to explore the power relations within which the discipline sits. Any study of AHM should provide post-processual theory with the links it so desperately lacks between the political realities of archaeological practice and the post-processual call for, what is so far, highly abstract political action.

Both feminist and post-processual archaeology, in criticising the scientist basis of mainstream archaeology, are also faced with the realisation that such a critique must challenge the institutional power base of archaeology. Such a challenge is important if feminists and post-processualists are to change the way archaeology is practiced and the way archaeological knowledge is propagated. However, any critique which challenges those aspects of archaeology which have been institutionalised within AHM runs the risk of increasingly marginalising archaeology. Critiques of the 'rationalist' bases of archaeology have no currency within bureaucratic structures that demand absolute answers in solving conflicts over the use of cultural heritage. This is not to say that we must not make such critiques, but that we need to do so in the context of a wider understanding of how archaeology is conceptualised and used outside of the discipline. We also need to provide a workable and equitable alternative to archaeology's rôle as intellectual 'legislator' and 'interpreter'.

If we do not engage with and analyse the institutionalisation of archaeology then the development of archaeological theory will remain self-referential. Further, AHM will, as many already argue, become isolated from archaeological theoretical developments. Such an isolation will not reflect the inherent lack of links between archaeological theory and AHM, but rather will result from a rejection by heritage bureaucracies of 'irrelevant and confusing' theoretical developments.

Conclusion

The definition of AHM offered in this chapter presents three levels of analysis, each increasing in complexity, through which to theorise AHM. AHM is conceived as fulfilling a cultural rôle in Western societies; this, together with the development of a Science-based New Archaeology, and the application of scientific principles within archaeology, enabled archaeology to be used as a technical/bureaucratic discourse within State institutions. The use of cultural heritage in establishing and maintaining cultural and other identities adds a further complexity to an analysis of AHM. With the institutionalisation of archaeology, archaeological knowledge plays a rôle, however limited, in State discourses to arbitrate on debates over cultural identities. Through AHM archaeology as a discipline has become directly engaged with cultural and political debate and conflict.

This definition goes well beyond dealing with AHM as a technical process, where scientific archaeology intersects with law, conservation, planning policies and so forth. My analysis allows for a fuller understanding of AHM than does post-processual theory, which tends to idealise culture, underplays the institutional rôle of archaeology, and ignores AHM as anything but a reactionary force. A definition of AHM which examines how archaeology is used, and the rôle archaeology plays, outside of the discipline offers the potential for theorising practical, policy and political aspects of archaeology. Such a theorisation can lead to a more concrete and effective political position than post-processual theory, which creates a false choice between maintaining a positivist position or adopting a post-processual position. In addition the above definition of AHM can allow nations like the United Kingdom to examine how heritage managers play a complex cultural and political rôle.

References

Arnold, J.B. 1978. Underwater cultural resources and the Antiquities Market. *Journal of Field Archaeology* 5: 232.

Bauman, Z. 1987. *Legislators and Interpreters*. Cambridge, Polity Press.

Bauman, Z. 1992. *Intimations of Postmodernity*. London, Routledge.

Bickford, A. 1993. Women's historic sites. In H. duCros and L. Smith (eds) *Women in Archaeology: a Feminist Critique*. Canberra, Department of Prehistory, RSPacS, Australian National University.

Bowdler, S. 1981. Unconsidered trifles? Cultural resource management, environmental impact statements and archaeological research in NSW. *Australian Archaeology* 12: 123–133.

Bowdler, S. 1984. Archaeological significance as a mutable quality. In S. Sullivan and S. Bowdler (eds) *Site Survey and Significance Assessments in Australian Archaeology*. Canberra, Department of Prehistory, RSPacS, Australian National University.

Burgmann, V. and J. Lee (eds) 1988. *Constructing a Culture: a People's History of Australia Since 1788*. Melbourne, Penguin Books.

Byrne, D. 1991. Western hegemony in archaeological heritage management. *History and Anthropology* 5: 269–276.

Carman, J. 1991. Beating the bounds: archaeological heritage management as archaeology, archaeology as social science. *Archaeological Review From Cambridge* 10:2: 175–184.

Chase, M. and C. Shaw 1989. The dimensions of nostalgia. In C. Shaw and M. Chase (eds) *The Imagined Past: History and Nostalgia*. Manchester, Manchester University Press.

Clarke, D. 1988. Poor museums, rich men's media: an archaeological perspective. In J. Bintliff (ed.) *Extracting Meaning From the Past*. Oxford, Oxbow Books.

Cleere, H. (ed.) 1984a *Approaches to the Archaeological Heritage*. Cambridge, University Press.

Cleere, H. 1984b. World cultural resource management: problems and perspectives. In H. Cleere (ed.) *Approaches to the Archaeological Heritage*. Cambridge, University Press.

Cleere, H. 1988. Whose archaeology is it anyway? In J. Bintliff (ed.) *Extracting Meaning From the Past*. Oxford, Oxbow Books.

Cleere, H. (ed.) 1989. *Archaeological Heritage Management in the Modern World*. London, Unwin Hyman.

Clewlow, C.W., P.S. Hallinan and R.D. Ambro 1971. A crisis in archaeology. *American Antiquity* 36:4: 472–473.

Cockrell, W.A. 1980. The trouble with treasure – a preservationist view of the controversy. *American Antiquity* 45:2: 333–344.

Darvill, T. 1987. *Ancient Monuments in the Countryside: an Archaeological Management Review*. London, English Heritage.

Davison, G. 1991a. The meanings of 'heritage'. In G. Davison and C. McConville (eds) *A Heritage Handbook*. Sydney, Allen and Unwin.

Davison, G. 1991b. A brief history of the Australian Heritage Movement. In G. Davison and C. McConville (eds) *A Heritage Handbook*. Sydney, Allen and Unwin.

Davison, G. and C. McConville (eds) 1991. *A Heritage Handbook*. Sydney, Allen and Unwin.

Deetz, J. 1977. *In Small Things Forgotten*. New York: Anchor.

Edwards, R. (ed.) 1975. *The Preservation of Australia's Aboriginal Heritage*. Canberra, Institute of Aboriginal Studies.

Flood, J. 1987. The Australian experience: rescue archaeology Down Under. In R.L. Wilson (ed.) *Rescue Archaeology: Proceedings of the Second New World Conference on Rescue Archaeology*. Southern Methodist University Press.

Fourmile, H. 1989a. Aboriginal heritage legislation and self-determination. *Australian-Canadian Studies* 7:1–2: 45–61.

Fourmile, H. 1989b. Who owns the past? – Aborigines as captives of the archives. *Aboriginal History* 13: 1–8.

Fowler, D.D. 1982. Cultural resource management. In M.B. Schiffer (ed.) *Advances in Archaeological Method and Theory* volume 5: 1–50. New York, Academic Press.

Fowler, P.J. 1977. *Approaches to Archaeology*. London, Adam and Charles Black.

Fowler, P.J. 1981. Archaeology, the Public and the Sense of the Past. In D. Lowenthal and M. Binney (eds) *Our Past Before Us: Why Do We Save It?* London, Temple Smith.

Fowler, P.J. 1987. What price the man-made heritage? *Antiquity* 61: 409–423.

Fowler, P.J. 1992. *The Past in Contemporary Society*. London, Routledge.

Geering, K. and C. Roberts 1992. Current limitations on Aboriginal involvement in Aboriginal site management in central west and northwest New South Wales. In J. Birckhead, T. DeLacy and L. Smith (eds) 1992 *Aboriginal Involvement in Parks and Protected Areas*. Canberra, Aboriginal Studies Press.

Gidiri, A. 1974. Imperialism and archaeology. *Race* 15:4: 431–459.

Green, E.L. (ed.) 1984. *Ethics and Values in Archaeology*. New York, The Free Press.

Gregory, T. 1986. Whose fault is treasure-hunting? In C. Dobinson and R. Gilchrist (eds). *Archaeology, Politics and the Public*. York, University Publications, No 5.

Hall, C.M. and S. McArthur (eds) 1993a. *Heritage Management in New Zealand and Australia.* Auckland, Oxford University Press.

Hall, C.M. and S. McArthur 1993b. Heritage management: an introductory framework. In C.M. Hall and S. McArthur (eds) *Heritage Management in New Zealand and Australia.* Auckland, Oxford University Press.

Hewison, R. 1987. *The Heritage Industry.* London, Methuen.

Hodder, I. 1989. Writing archaeology: site reports in context. *Antiquity* 63: 268–274.

Hodder, I. 1991. Interpretive archaeology and its rôle. *American Antiquity* 56: 7–18.

Hooper-Greenhill, E. 1992. *Museums and the Shaping of Knowledge.* London, Routledge.

Hunter, M. 1981. The preconditions of preservation: a historical perspective. In D. Lowenthal and M. Binney (eds) *Our Past Before Us: Why Do We Save It?* London, Temple Smith.

Johnston, C. 1992. *What is Social Value?* Canberra, Australian Government Publishing Service.

Kerr, J.S. 1990. *The Conservation Plan* (third edition). Sydney, NSW National Trust.

Leone, M.P. and P.B. Potter Jr 1992. Legitimation and the classification of archaeological sites. *American Antiquity* 57: 137–145.

Leone, M.P., P.B. Potter Jr and P.A. Shackel 1987. Toward a critical archaeology *Current Anthropology* 28:3: 283–302.

Leone, M.P. and R.W. Preucel 1992. Archaeology in a democratic society: a Critical Theory Perspective. In L. Wandsnider (ed.) *Quandaries and quests: visions of archaeology future* pp. 115–135. Carbondale, Southern Illinois University.

Lowenthal, D. 1979. Environmental perception: preserving the past. *Progress in Human Geography* 3:4: 549–559.

Lowenthal, D. 1990. *The past is a foreign country.* Cambridge, University Press.

McBryde, I. 1986. Australia's once and future archaeology. *Archaeology in Oceania* 21:1: 13–38.

McGimsey, C.R. 1972. *Public Archaeology.* New York, Seminar Press.

McGimsey, C.R. and H.A. Davis 1977. *The Management of Archaeological Resources: the Airlie House Report.* Special publication of the Society for American Archaeology.

McGuire, R.H. 1992. Archaeology and the first Americans. *American Antiquity* 94:4: 816–832.

McKinley, J.R. and K.L. Jones (eds) 1979. *Archaeological Resource Management in Australia and Oceania.* Wellington, New Zealand Historic Places Trust.

Marrie, A. 1989. Museums and Aborigines: a case study in internal colonialism. *Australian-Canadian Studies* 7:1–2: 63–77

Merriman, N. 1991. *Beyond the Glass Case.* Leicester, University Press.

Moser, S. 1996. Science and social values: presenting archaeological findings in museum displays. In L. Smith and A. Clarke (eds) *Issues in Management Archaeology* St. Lucia, Tempus, Anthropology Museum, University of Queensland, 32–42.

Mulvaney, D.J. 1990. *Prehistory and Heritage.* Canberra, Department of Prehistory, RSPacS, Australian National University.

Murray, T. and J.P. White 1981. Cambridge in the bush? Archaeology in Australia and New Guinea. *World Archaeology* 13:2: 255–263.

Pearce, S. 1990. *Archaeological Curatorship.* Leicester, University Press.

Pettman, J. 1992. *Living in the Margins. Racism, Sexism and Feminism in Australia.* Sydney, Allen and Unwin.

Pilger, J. 1989. *A Secret Country.* London, Vintage.

Redman, C. 1991. Distinguished Lecture in Archaeology: In defence of the seventies – the adolescence of the New Archaeology. *American Anthropologist* 93:2: 295–307.

Reekie, G. 1992. Women and heritage policy *Culture and Policy* 4: 91–96.

Renfrew, A.C. 1983. Divided we stand: aspects of archaeology and information. *American Antiquity* 48:1: 3–16.

Reynolds, H. 1982. *The Other Side of the Frontier: Aboriginal Resistance to European Invasion of Australia.* Ringwood, Penguin.

Ross, A. (ed.) 1986. *Planning for Aboriginal Site Management: a Handbook for Local Government Planners.* Sydney, NSW National Parks and Wildlife Service.

Saunders, A.D. 1983. A century of Ancient Monuments Legislation 1882–1982. *The Antiquaries Journal* 63:1: 11–29.

Shanks, M. 1992. *Experiencing the Past.* London, Routledge.

Shanks, M. and C. Tilley 1987a. *Social Theory and Archaeology.* Cambridge, Polity Press.

Shanks, M. and C. Tilley 1987b. *Re-Constructing Archaeology: Theory and Practice.* Cambridge, University Press.

Smith, L. 1994. Heritage management as postprocessual archaeology? *Antiquity* 68: 300–309

Smith, L. 1996. Significance concepts in Significance concepts in Australian Management archaeology. In L. Smith and A. Clarke (eds) *Issues in Management Archaeology* St. Lucia, Tempus, Anthropology Museum, University of Queensland, 67–78.

Smith, L., A. Clarke and A. Alcock 1992. Teaching cultural tourism – some comments from the classroom. *Australian Archaeology* 34: 43–47.

Sykes, R.B. 1989 *Black Majority.* Melbourne, Hudson Publishing.

White, J.P. and J. O'Connel 1983. *A Prehistory of Australia, New Guinea and Sahul.* Sydney, Academic Press.

Wright, P. 1985. *On Living in an Old Country.* London, Verso.

Chapter 5

Excavation as Theatre

Christopher Tilley

This chapter provides a theoretical and conceptual justification for large-scale rescue excavations but in a rather unusual manner. To many actively involved in rescue archaeology and so-called 'cultural resource management' there may appear to be little real need to justify the practice of excavation: are not the traces of the past diminishing and being destroyed at an alarming rate? Is it not a moral duty to rescue these traces for future generations if their preservation in the face of development proves to be impossible? This rhetoric is common among archaeologists. It is perhaps salutary to remember that such a concern is not likely to be shared by many other interest groups.

The advent of the 'new' archaeology helped to accentuate an old and unhelpful distinction, between research excavations, supposedly problem-orientated towards the solution of specific intellectual goals, and rescue excavation – which became spurned as mere data collection. The division is still upheld by many today. However, it has made very little real difference to the practice of excavation in either case and its relationship to the production of archaeological knowledge. Today, in terms of the discipline of archaeology as a whole, I believe that it may be no longer entirely self-evident on theoretical, cultural, political or economic grounds why excavation (either rescue or research) should take place, if at all, then certainly at its current rate and pace.

Nietzsche wrote in *Untimely meditations* that the historical sense is a disease of history. It might be said that digging is a pathology of archaeology. A major problem which has always dogged archaeology is the notion that it is primarily about excavation. Introductory textbooks usually place great emphasis on excavation strategies and technologies, while the literature is dominated by descriptions of sites. The effect is that the technical instrumentation of the discipline and the production of descriptive observational statements tend to become identified with its goal and purpose. It is as if the primary concern of the physicist were not to understand the physical world, but merely to perform experiments, to collect the experimental data, and then lodge them away in some archive.

By a more immediate analogy, the current state of archaeology can be compared to baking a cake. The end-product – the cake itself – rarely, if ever, gets baked. Furthermore, whether anyone will want (or be able) to eat or consume the cake is not material, so its appeal or relevancy to their own tastes and interests is hardly considered. More and more cooks obtain more and more ingredients for the cake, the flour of artefacts, the eggs of structures, the spices of bone residues. The ingredients may be lavishly described (the primary issue of publication has always been simply: how much? and in what form?) but usually little happens beyond this. There remains a striking lack of recipes as to how we should bake the cake. Those that do exist tend to produce rather dry and unappetizing products even to those responsible for their production, let alone to the public passing by the confectioner's window. Rather than placing greater emphasis on the development of conceptual structures to understand how to bake the cake – how to interpret the past – what we have today is a greater and greater emphasis on the accumulation of information, information with which very little is, or can be, done. In this sense to go on excavating as has been the case up to now is irresponsible. Much of the work appears to be a frantic attempt to accumulate more and more information 'because it is there', in the erroneous belief that some day the cake will bake itself.

What actually happens to the data accumulated has been a secondary issue. The secondary issue needs to become primary. The nature and effects of the current state of archaeology need to be spelled out clearly:

1   A discipline desperately in need of theory and the development of alternative conceptual structures appears by and large to think that it can get on quite nicely without them. If we have to decide on priorities, then it is always excavation that must take precedence. The result is that there exists a massive and disabling disparity between the amount of financial and human resources spent on excavation and post-excavation work and research going beyond the individual site.

2   Since the turn of the century, and on a European scale, the number of partially published or unpublished excavations is probably greater than those published.

3   Museums and store-rooms are already over-flowing with artefacts, often uncatalogued, sometimes lost, and in most cases remaining unanalysed.

4   The effects of many museum displays and archaeological practices appear to be the opposite to those intended. They either bore the public, turned into passive spectators of a supplied image, and/or trivialize the past and the practice of archaeology by making it desperately familiar.

5   In some cases, finds once excavated become virtually the private property of the excavator, unavailable, sometimes for decades, even to other researchers, let alone to the public for whom the past is supposedly to be rescued. It will suffice to state that none of this justifies more excavation.

Towards an integrative approach

In an ideal world all threatened sites could be excavated, all excavations could be fully published and adequate resources could also be made available for other research. Lacking such an archaeological utopia, there is a real need for rescue work to be reintegrated into the concerns of the discipline of archaeology as a whole. The gulf between rescue archaeology (not to mention museums) and university departments physically, financially and theoretically, needs to be bridged. There is a desperate need for priorities to be made both as to what to excavate and the relative cost of these excavations *vis à vis* more general research into the relationship between social structures, social strategies and material-culture production and use which may be claimed to define the most abstract goal of archaeology as an academic discipline.

In Scandinavian and British archaeology, at least, certain priorities are fairly easy to choose, and decisions are already being made. For example, the archaeology of the

Neolithic and Bronze Age has been primarily the archaeology of graves, and there are good reasons for believing that in many areas we already have a representative sample of grave sites. By contrast we know very little about settlements.

A striking characteristic of archaeological data is its patterned regularity within a region. In many respects one Bronze Age grave or Roman villa reproduces many features of another. There are very few unique sites. If all sites anyway were totally distinctive we would have little success in trying to interpret or understand the archaeological record. This very repetitiveness at a regional level means that much excavation, conceived solely in terms of data collection, may not be necessary.

Following the principle (draft 1988 International Committee of Archaeological Heritage Management charter) that the exploiter or developer should pay for the costs of excavation, it need not necessarily be the case that this money goes to the excavation of the individual threatened site; it might instead be channelled into more general archaeological research not specifically concerned with excavation or further excavation at other sites beyond the limits of the areas to be destroyed. It is pointless to rescue the traces of the past at any particular site *in isolation*, since a far more integrative approach needs to be taken at regional and national levels. A developer who wants to destroy a site must be expected to pay for this 'privilege' in *all* cases. Practically, this might be done by estimating average excavation costs on a square metre basis. It needs to be made clear, however, that such payment is a matter of *principle* – all traces of the past are important – but the principle at stake is not a myopic concern with the individual threatened site, but our understanding of the past as a whole. To repeat: rescue excavation, conceived as the collection of more and more information about the past, is not a position which can be easily supported, at least in the West (the situation is obviously very different in countries in which little archaeological research has been carried out). *The number of pieces of information we collect about the past may increase incrementally – our understanding does not.*

The rapid post-war professionalization of archaeology and the growth of rescue work has encouraged the formation of an organizational excavation structure in countries such as Sweden and Britain, based on digging units moving around from one site to another; it might be to a megalithic grave one month, a Mesolithic site the next. This approach implies that the practicalities of excavation and interpretation (on the excavation site) can be effectively divorced from wider research in the particular time period under consideration, or in more general archaeological theory.

The idea is that all possible evidence should be efficiently recorded, perhaps to await interpretation by an academic specialist (usually in a university department) at a future date. This division of labour is counter-productive, since someone actively engaging in research in a particular period, or set of problems, will almost inevitably find that the kind of evidence they are interested in has been recorded in insufficient detail, or not at all. The only way round such a problem is to integrate *all* excavations with larger-scale research projects. Perhaps a belief preventing this from becoming a *necessity* is a myth of pure objectivity, considered below.

Archaeology seriously needs to reconsider its priorities and the radical division, made all too often, between excavation and what goes beyond the 'recovery' and publication of sites. Now is a time for rethinking which might result in less excavation of any kind for the meantime; a pause will at least give us time and resources to set the larger archaeological house in order (e.g. publishing sites already excavated, analysing data in museum collections, developing explanatory frameworks, and constructing new sets of questions with which to approach the past).

A justification for large-scale excavations

Following these rather lengthy *caveats* I now want to provide a theoretical and a social justification for limited numbers of large-scale excavation projects. My remarks may only apply to those countries in which archaeological research is already well established. All archaeology is an interpretative activity. This hermeneutic dimension to archaeological research is absolutely fundamental. Yet we still know very little about the manner and conditions in which archaeological discourse is framed and produced, about why and how we produce certain interpretations and specific types of statements about the past rather than others. At present archaeological discourses are strikingly abbreviated, so much so that it is possible to claim that an unacknowledged principle of *rarity* operates. The question is: why, given that there is an almost unlimited set of possible statements to be made about the past, are only a limited number of formulations and interpretations continuously made, disseminated and repeated? We can regard archaeology itself as the largely unconscious but nevertheless rule-governed production of statements about the past. The nature of the archaeological record does not simply constrain what might be said about it, the constraints exist more importantly within the interior spaces of the discourses which purport to deal with it. To begin to analyse and understand the discourses that archaeologists produce is not mere navelgazing; it is to open out the possibility of the production of fresh discourses, new means of understanding the past and inscribing it into our present.

Continued excavations, conceived as experiments in interpretative activity rather than exercises in information collection (the division is of course only a relative one), may play a central rôle in the development of a more reflexive and mature archaeological practice. The change that I propose shifts the emphasis from archaeological excavation as a process whereby the material traces of the past are recovered and 'rescued' to being an exercise in a very different kind of production: the manner in which interpretative experience is produced, recorded and transmitted. This requires reconsidering two relationships; between the excavation and the site report; and between excavations, site reports, the archaeological community and the public at large.

The excavation and the site report

What is the relationship between an excavation and a site report? Excavation is an active *production* of material remains. As such it entails a set of producers, a series of materials, techniques and instruments for production resulting, it is hoped, in the product itself, the site report, which may then be disseminated, consumed and exchanged in various ways. Few archaeologists openly believe in the myth that archaeological excavation is a purely rigorous and technical procedure capable of standardization, the results of which are simply translated and enshrined in the site report. However, this notion does in fact seem to underlie much of the organization of excavation and the manner in which site reports are written and presented.

Third-person narrative, measured drawings (often to the level of individual cobble stones in a road or stones forming a cairn), tables, scaled photographs and detailed lists of finds are all hallmarks of the standard excavation report implying neutrality and a striving towards total objectivity untainted by human purpose: this is the empiricist dream.

Valuable or not, these procedures require deconstruction because their combined effect is to deny the importance of the fundamental basis of all excavation: that it is an autobiographic, subjective, socially determined and often fundamentally ambiguous and/or contradictory set of interpretative activities.

The excavation and its relation to the site report is an interpretative production for which the analogy of the dramatic performance and its relation to a script seems peculiarly appropriate. A play does not and cannot directly reflect, express or reproduce the dramatic text from which it is derived. The play is always a production, an interpretation which transforms or translates the text into another medium, from marks on paper to actions on a stage. Furthermore, the dramatic production is not to be judged simply in terms of its fidelity to a text as if a mirror reflecting an object. The script and the production are not commensurable entities but distinctive realms occupying different theoretical and physical spaces.

Similarly (but in reverse) the excavation performance does not transparently produce, in a relation of pure identity, the site report.

Any report which is produced remains one of any possible number of potential site reports. There exist a series of real and incommensurable transformations between the practices of digging in a trench and the drawing, recording and interpretation of a section, a disjunction between two very different material realities. Any notion of a simple homology is illusory. The relation between the processes of excavation and the text of the site report are not at all to be conceived as those existing between a shadowy essence (soil colour shades) to a concrete existence (mapped post holes in the excavation plan). The site report is not the soul or essential essence of the excavation's corpse.

An excavation report is produced as the result of interpretative labours intimately bound up with the changing conditions of the excavation process itself. There is no clear passage from the activity of excavation to that of the activity of writing. So the site report does not mime the results of the excavation. The relation between excavation and report is one of theoretical and conceptual labour founded in the theatre of excavation itself. Activities of selection, recording, organization, pattern recognition, inclusion and exclusion take place from differing perspectives of individuals and groups, and from discussions and relationships taking place on the site. These enable a determinate but non-determined product to emerge from the soil and be translated into the site report: the product of a production and inevitably a reduction of difference and a stabilization of complexity. The excavation is a complex space of different meanings, perceptions and responses to be ultimately related to individual and social circumstances. The excavation is only partly to do with the *effective* (obtaining information) but owes much more to the *affective* – socially mediated responses to the traces of the past.

The standard informational report enjoys a total hegemony today, in which with its rhetoric of neutrality, scientificity and objectivity all this is swept to one side or forgotten. In an ironic inversion that which is of vital significance becomes systematically devalued. Plurality becomes radically curtailed in a mythology founded on a dream of exact representation.

The importance of excavation as a never ending interpretative activity means it is *thought in action*. Rather than reifying the theatre of excavation into a single unchanging scene, we need site reports of a radically different nature which attempt to capture at least some of the ambiguities, disjunctions and contradictions inherent in various modes of interpretative understanding. The relationship between excavation and what gets written resembles that between an individual speech utterance and an underlying set of grammars. The excavation provides a set of grammars, often incoherent or contradictory, both constraining and enabling the production of a text. It is the nature of the production of these grammars and their relation to the act of writing that need to become a focus of attention. It is only by considering these relations that we may begin to understand how we might write differently and begin to question just why reports tend to be written in one way rather than another. The true significance of the site report must be not an attempt to redouble the supposed self-understanding of the excavation, but to reflect back on it and critically interrogate all the 'whats', 'whys', 'hows' and 'therefores'. In short what is required and can uniquely be provided by large-scale complex excavations and their reports are experiments in discovery, and more importantly, self-discovery.

Excavation: history, social relations and the politics of interpretation

Archaeology is a discipline fortunate enough to have its data base protected by law, at least in certain countries. This inevitably brings with it special responsibilities going far beyond the narrow confines of archaeology as a disciplinary practice. What is the relationship of excavation to 'real' history and contemporary society? All excavation, and indeed the very practice of excavation is value-loaded. Value-systems and ideologies do not neatly circumvent the practice of excavation and its relation to the present. Excavation has everything to do with the sociopolitical interests of the present both within the discipline of archaeology and without. These govern where excavations take place, why they take place, how they take place (excavations have their own internal micro-politics), what statements are considered acceptable to make and what are not.

In considering the relation of excavation to contemporary society we need to ask some basic questions: who is permitted to excavate and write and who is not? For exactly whom or what is this excavation and writing being done? In what social and political circumstances does it take place? The currently emerging cult of strident professionalism especially manifested in cultural resource management has by and large operated so as to effect a drastic reduction of a scope of social vision. Those who accredit themselves by their own internal rules as professionals decide on a past which the public supposedly *should* consume. Power over the past moreover, as often as not, forms part of a process of social control and constraint in the present. This control of the past turns the public into helpless spectators, to be shown selected goodies in a museum or suffered on (rather than being welcomed to) the excavation site.

Nowhere is this more evident than in the growth of the heritage industry which the culture of the New Right has actively fostered. The heritage is everywhere, all around 'us', nothing less than a kind of collective memory of an entire people or nation. Such a notion of heritage does not involve a recognition of the *difference* of the past (thus enabling it to put the present into a comparative perspective) but an assertion of sameness and identity, the creation of the fictional unity of a national collective consciousness. Instead we may ask: which people? whose heritage? whose memory? whose significance? whose values and interests? The heritage industry is not supportive of archaeology: instead it makes a direct challenge to it as an active interpretative practice taking place today. Archaeology, rather than conforming to the heritage industry, *ought to be challenging it*. In the heritage perspective archaeology tends to become increasingly abstracted as the 'historical', a diverse palimpsest of monuments frozen into a spurious unity: an imaginary nation peopled by imaginary Britons. Archaeology and history, as active interventions creating various and often incompatible pasts, the heritage industry itself as a specific production of a past, is deliberately forgotten. The specificity of the individual excavation, and the interpretative problems raised in the practice of excavation, naturally challenge, if used in the right way, any simplistic notion of heritage, that the past may provide some kind of guarantee for a conservative present.

No archaeologist interprets for him or herself. Interpretation is a social activity for an individual, a group or an audience. Such an audience for whom both excavation and site reports are produced *matter*. There is something inherently unsatisfactory and élitist about the notion that excavations should be undertaken only to satisfy the specific research goals of archaeologists. It is also equally important that archaeology reflects more deeply on precisely what it does produce on site, in museum displays and in texts so that it does not become as cultural resource management and its rhetoric seem to be directing it towards, a form of production and marketing of the past in a manner directly equivalent to any other commodity. To appreciate the past and thus value it, what archaeology must seek to create is a public consisting of cultural producers, not cultural consumers, people who discuss and interpret rather than people who are talked to and are told.

Excavation has a unique role to play as a theatre where people may be able to produce their own pasts, pasts which are meaningful to them, not as expressions of a mythical heritage. Especially in rural areas excavation provides, much more readily than museum displays or books, possibilities for enthusing an interest in and awareness of the past among non-archaeologists. Excavations need to become, much more so than they are today, nexuses of decoding and encoding processes by which people may create meaning from the past. This is to advocate a socially engaged rather than a scientifically detached practice of excavation.

Acknowledgements

An earlier version of the original paper was given as an introduction to the theoretical session of the International Committee of Archaeological Heritage Management (ICAHM) conference in Stockholm, September 1988. In revising it I have benefited from the ensuing discussions. Thanks are also due to Kristian Kristiansen for comments on the text, and to an anonymous reviewer.

Chapter 6

Only Connect – Sustainable Development and Cultural Heritage

Kate Clark

. . . these old buildings do not belong to us only; they belong to our forefathers and they will belong to our descendants unless we play them false. They are not in any sense our property to do as we like with them. We are only the trustees for those that come after us.

William Morris (1889)

Introduction

There is much confusion and plenty of cynicism about the idea of sustainable development. Yet it remains an important concept and one of great relevance to heritage, that can help us both look after our heritage, and show how heritage can contribute to wider social and economic objectives.

Sustainable development starts from the idea that we live in a world of finite resources, and that if development continues at the current rate, we will exhaust those resources. A more sustainable approach means economic development that meets the needs of current generations without compromising the ability of future generations to meet their needs. Cutting down forests, polluting the air and exhausting fish stocks, combined with growing populations and the impact of climate change, will inevitably lead to a disastrous future.

As a conservation philosophy, thinking about sustainable development represents a shift from seeing environmental conservation as a narrow branch of science, of interest only to a few ecologists, to recognising the environment as something inextricably linked to society and to the economy. The argument is that conservation cannot succeed unless it engages with economic and social issues; at the same time, the economy and society are both poorer if the environment is degraded. The three are inextricably bound together.

Over the past two decades the philosophy of sustainable development has become embedded in government policy, if not always in action. Yet heritage is rarely, if ever, mentioned. This chapter shows that caring for the heritage can contribute directly to wider sustainable development goals, through delivering economic, social and environmental benefits. It goes on to explain how sustainable development has influenced heritage practice, bringing it closer to environmental conservation. Finally, the chapter presents the emerging practices that are beginning to make heritage a powerful driver for social sustainability.

Rio and beyond – policies and strategies

In March 2005, the UK government published its new Sustainable Development Strategy (UK Government 2005). The origins of the strategy lie with the Rio summit in 1992 when 172 governments participated in the United National Conference on Environment and Development (UNCED) in Rio de Janeiro. Known as the 'Earth Summit', the event brought together governments and Non Governmental Organisations from across the world. It resulted in a document known as 'Agenda 21' and a series of other documents, including the United Nations Framework Convention on Climate Change and the United Nations Convention on Biological Diversity.

Unprecedented in both size and scope, the summit sought to help governments rethink economic development and find ways to halt the destruction of irreplaceable natural resources and pollution on the planet. The key message was that nothing less than transformation of attitudes and behaviour would bring about the necessary changes (http://un.org.geninfo/enviro.html).

The UK government (1995) was the first national government to produce its own strategy. Called 'A Better Quality of Life', it explained how economic, social and environmental outcomes could be delivered simultaneously and identified a series of indicators. A decade later, there has been some progress, but not all trends are positive. Whilst there has been strong economic growth, waste production is rising; whilst some wildlife losses are beginning to stabilise, recovery is needed. The new strategy (HM Government 2005) on sustainable development was in part a response to a critical review of progress by the Sustainable Development Commission (2004).

At the heart of the new strategy is a common purpose, which reiterates the original Brundtland definition on sustainable development:

> The goal of sustainable development is to enable all people through the world to satisfy their basic needs and enjoy a better quality of life, without compromising the quality of life of future generations.

It goes on to aim for a

> Sustainable, innovative and productive economy that delivers high levels of employment; and a just society that promotes social inclusion, sustainable communities and personal well being. This will be done in ways that protect and enhance the physical and natural environment, and use resources and energy as efficiently as possible.

Thus the economy, society and the environment are linked. The Brundtland definition recognises that unbridled economic expansion is not sustainable in the long term if it comes at a cost to the environment and resources around us, to social cohesion or to stable communities.

There are four national priorities for the UK:

• Sustainable production and consumption including reducing the inefficient use of resources

- Climate change and energy – seeking a profound change in the way we use and generate energy
- Natural resource protection and environmental enhancement
- Sustainable communities – which means giving communities more power and say in the decisions that affect them.

The strategy commits the UK to measuring progress against 20 framework indicators for sustainable development, from reducing greenhouse gas emissions and waste, to improving stocks of bird populations, to social indicators for reducing crime and childhood poverty and economic measures. It also makes clear that responsibility for sustainable development is not confined to the government departments that deal with the environment; instead it cuts across all departments, including trade and industry.

How can heritage contribute to sustainable development goals?

At first sight, there seems to be scant role for heritage in the UK strategy on sustainable development; not one of the shortlist of 20 or even the long list of 48 indicators mentions heritage. Yet a closer examination shows that there is a key role for heritage in many parts of the strategy.

The role of heritage in sustainable consumption and production

Sustainable development decouples economic progress and the destruction of the environment (WSSD 2002), and in the UK the departments which deal with trade and industry and with the environment are bringing together, for the first time, the economic and environmental case for action (DEFRA 2003). One of their key aims is reducing waste. Demolition and construction are between them the largest producer of waste in the UK, creating 24% of the estimated annual 434 million tonnes (www.defra.gov.uk/environment/statistics); the second largest producer (21%) is mining and quarrying. For every inhabitant in the UK six tonnes of building materials are used every year (English Heritage 2002: 40). Over 90% of the non-energy minerals extracted in Great Britain are used to supply the construction industry yet each year some 70 million tonnes of construction materials and soil end up as waste (quoted in English Heritage 2003: 43).

Re-using historic buildings is an important way of reducing the amount of construction waste created. English Heritage put these arguments forward during a public inquiry (part of the UK planning process) into a proposal to demolish Victorian housing as part of the Nelson West housing development plans in Lancashire. The local authority wanted to replace Victorian terraced housing with new built homes on the grounds that this represented the most cost-effective means of regenerating the area. An investigation showed that over 30 years the cost of repairing a typical Victorian terraced home in Nelson was £24,600 while a more substantial refurbishment cost around £38,500. The cost of demolishing one of the houses and replacing it with a newly built home and maintaining that home over 30 years was in the region of £64,000. The findings were instrumental in having the original plans overturned (English Heritage 2003: 45).

It is also cheaper to maintain an older property than a new one. A Victorian house is almost £1,000/100m^2 cheaper to maintain than a house from the 1980s mainly as a result of the better quality materials used in the older building (English Heritage 2003: 45) whilst a refurbished existing building performs better in environmental terms than a hypothetical new building on the same site (Carrig Conservation et al. 2004).

Whilst reusing empty older buildings may not solve all of the projected UK housing shortages there is a strong argument for making the best use of existing building stock. The re-use of former industrial buildings across the world in city centres such as New York, Liverpool, Nottingham and Sydney has shown how urban areas can be successfully regenerated without huge amounts of new construction.

The role of heritage in energy use

Long-term climate change threatens to impact on all aspects of daily life. A recent UK government report noted that,

> energy is consumed in the production of construction materials such as bricks, cement and metals and in their distribution. The energy produced from non-renewable sources consumed in building services accounts for about half of the UK's emissions of carbon dioxide.
>
> (Performance and Innovations Unit 2000, quoted in English Heritage 2003: 43)

Again, there is a role for heritage here. Re-using older historic buildings is not only cheaper than building new and creates less waste; it can reduce energy requirements. Existing building materials also represent the 'embodied' energy used to produce them. The brickwork in a typical Victorian terraced building contains energy equivalent to 15,000 litres of petrol – enough to send a car round the earth five times or half way to the moon. A similar house constructed from modern materials and modern techniques contains a higher level of embodied CO_2. If a brick building is demolished and a new one constructed, it wastes not only the embodied energy of the bricks, but uses up more energy in demolition, and even more in putting back new bricks (English Heritage 2003: 44).

The role of heritage in the economy

The economy is one of the three legs of the sustainable development 'stool' – the idea is that economic growth is good for societies but at the same time there is an interaction between the economy and the environment. It follows that if caring for the environment can benefit the economy, then economic measures that interfere with the working of the free market can be justified. Is there a similar economic case for protecting heritage?

Heritage projects can contribute to regeneration and business activities either directly through the jobs and expenditure generated by conservation or preservation work, or indirectly through the benefits of heritage-based recreation and tourism and by making places more attractive for businesses and workers.

In the UK, heritage attractions operated directly by government, by charities or by the private sector, play a critical role in the tourism industry, contributing significantly to the £26.5 billion generated by UK residents within the UK or the £11.7 billion generated by overseas visitors and the jobs that the industry supports (English Heritage 2003: 49). Similarly the National Trust (2001) found that in Wales some 40% of employment in tourism depends upon a high quality of environment.

Public funding for conservation projects can lever in new funding and contribute to job creation and a quality environment. Every £10,000 of public money invested in English regeneration projects in historic towns levers in £46,000 match funding from private sector and public sources. Together that delivers on average 41 square metres of improved commercial floor space, 103 square metres of environmental improvements, one new job, one safeguarded job and one improved home (English Heritage 2002: 3).

An investment of £6.2 million in historic building repair grants to farmers in the Lake District brought 92% of buildings (many of which were derelict and abandoned) back into productive use, improving business efficiency for farmers. Building work carried out by local firms generated between 25 and 30 jobs, and the scheme injected between £8.5m and £13.1m in the local economy (ADAS *et al.* 2005). Rykema (2004: 8) compared preservation activities with new construction and found that preservation creates more local jobs, mainly because of its greater use of local labour and materials.

Many economic studies have been criticised for over estimating economic impact and because, realistically, the economic impact of most heritage projects is quite small (Klamer and Zuidhof 1999: 33–4). For policy makers, the bigger question is whether public expenditure on heritage can be justified on the basis of the willingness of the public to pay for it. A recent review of 29 valuation studies from around the world that applied to heritage sites found that

> Positive values are attributed to the conservation or restoration of heritage assets, clearly demonstrating that the degradation of the historic environment detracts from the wellbeing of individuals and society in aggregate and showing that the public is willing to pay to mitigate this damage.
>
> (Eftec 2005)

People's willingness to pay for heritage also emerges from property prices, which can be higher near a well-kept park or waterway; older houses also tend to have higher prices.

The role of heritage in sustainable communities

The third leg of the 'stool' suggests that sustainability needs to embrace social goals as well as economic and environmental ones. Those social goals may include a society that is more cohesive or more inclusive, or a healthier population. But can heritage contribute to such goals?

There is little direct evidence for the role of the heritage (or at least the historic environment) in social goals although it is possible to draw on evidence from related sectors such as the arts and culture, the natural environment and urban parks. The arts sector has moved from assessing the impact of the arts purely in economic terms to recognising the social benefits that arise from participation (Reeves 2002). Matarasso (1997) has identified 50 potential social impacts for participation in the arts, ranging from personal benefits through to wider community benefits, including social cohesion, community empowerment and self-determination, local image and identity, imagination and vision, and health benefits.

For museums, libraries and archives activities, the best evidence for the impact of participation seems to lie in personal development, such as acquiring new skills, trying new experiences, confidence and self-esteem, changed attitudes, cultural awareness, communication and memory (Wavell *et al.* 2002). People who took part in community heritage projects say they have benefited from greater teamwork, enhanced confidence as a group and overall increased social engagement as well as learning skills (Gilmore *et al.* 2003: 6, 7).

Young people are often an under-represented audience for heritage; those who took part in projects designed to bring youth groups together with heritage reported that they had become experts in new areas of research, and through that had gained confidence and self-esteem, and were able to share their knowledge with others. Young people's attitudes towards heritage had changed as did the attitudes of youth workers who for the first time saw the value of heritage (Copeland and Hayton 2003).

Learning is another important social outcome. Learning is not simply confined to the formal educational sector; there are many different kinds of learning which can be broadly defined as,

> A process of active engagement with experience. It is what people do when they want to make sense of the world . . .
>
> (Campaign for Learning nd)

Within the formal educational curricula, heritage can contribute subjects from citizenship to science and geography (Attingham Trust 2004) and volunteering for a heritage project can help anyone of any age to learn new skills. Understanding how and why people can learn from heritage experiences not only helps make the case for supporting heritage; it can help organisations improve their own services. 'Inspiring Learning for All' is a website which helps museums, libraries and archives organisations to assess their own perform-ance, using generic learning outcomes that arise from participating in heritage projects – knowledge and understanding; new skills; new attitudes and values; enjoyment, inspiration and creativity; activity behaviour and progression (www.inspiringlearningforall.gov.uk).

The other important social agenda is health. There is some evidence that the arts and humanities can contribute to health care outcomes; a study found 385 references in medical literature to the effect of the arts and humanities in health care including reduced drug consumption, positive physiological and psychological changes, shorter time in hos-pital, better doctor–patient relationships, improved mental health care and greater empathy from practitioners (Staricoff 2004).

Similar evidence for social benefits has been found for natural heritage suggesting that biodiversity impacts on the quality of life and psychological well-being, and there is a con-nection between the opportunity to experience nature and social issues such as mental health and social development (Lees and Evans 2003; Seymour 2003).

Urban parks in particular, have many benefits; as well as acting as an environmental 'green lung', they contribute to communities and to learning and provide opportunities for play, sport and recreation (Tibbatts 2002). Obesity is one of the biggest health con-cerns in the UK; it 'costs more in public health terms and will overtake smoking as Britain's biggest killer in 10–15 years if current trends persist' (Pretty et al. nd). Urban parks provide an ideal place for exercise, sport, leisure and play; for example, the proba-bility of a group of Tokyo residents living for a further five years was linked to their ability to take a stroll in local parks and tree-lined streets (Takano et al. 2002).

These are just two examples from a review of urban parks showing how they can con-tribute to the economy, to physical and mental health, to reducing crime and fear of crime, to social objectives and to biodiversity and nature. Whilst we can't yet demonstrate a similar range of benefits for other kinds of heritage, the work does show just how broad the potential benefits of heritage can be.

Tools for sustaining heritage in its own right

Although government strategies have been slow to recognise the contribution that heritage can make to sustainable development, thinking about sustainable development is now firmly embedded in heritage management and policy.

Holistic approaches to heritage

One of the first, and most important, developments has been the use of more holistic concepts to describe and manage heritage that mirror environmental thinking.

Traditionally heritage protection has focused on isolated sites and monuments; the Venice Charter (ICOMOS 1964), a founding document of conservation practice, centres on the idea of historic monuments, and in most countries legislation relating to the heritage is based on protecting the individual bounded site or building. Yet as almost any urban or landscape-based study shows, heritage does not fit within neat red lines and there can be a potential heritage value not just in the setting of a site, but anywhere.

Within World Heritage, the idea of cultural landscapes that connect nature and culture are now well established, whilst in Australia heritage protection policies refer to the idea of heritage 'places' rather than sites (see Byrne, this volume Chapter 11). In the UK the phrase 'historic environment' is used to refer to the physical remains of the past, including historic landscapes, archaeological sites and buildings (DoE 1994) and has been central to the government's strategy for heritage (DCMS 2001: 7). Individual historic sites or monuments will always be important, but in the long term there is a greater heritage gain from managing change intelligently in the wider environment, rather as environmentalists manage ecosystems and habitats as opposed to individual species. Historic Landscape Characterisation (HLC) is a tool for capturing that wider character of whole areas, enabling heritage issues to inform planning on a bigger scale (Fairclough 2003: 25). HLC recognises that there can be something of heritage value to communities anywhere (in the same way that there can be ecological value in a back garden as well as in an internationally important site).

Once heritage is seen as part of a wider environment, the connection with sustainable development becomes more apparent. The natural environment is in itself a cultural artefact, much of it the result of thousands of years of active management by humans, and it is sensible when caring for the natural environment to also consider its cultural value. In theory, this means that any of the actions taken to care for the natural environment need to also consider cultural issues – from high-level policies to the management of a local nature reserve.

Heritage in environmental assessment

An example of how the historic and natural environment are being considered in a more integrated way is through environmental assessment. One of the basic principles of sustainability is the need to assess the impact of new development on the environment, and wherever possible to avoid or mitigate that impact. Heritage concerns have now been included in the process of environmental assessment of new developments. In the UK guidance on the treatment of archaeological remains adopts the 'polluter pays' principle, there is a presumption in favour of preservation of nationally important remains, and where remains are lost as the result of development, that loss is 'mitigated' by ensuring that excavation or recording enables knowledge about them to be made public (DoE 1990).

At a higher level, the European directive on strategic environmental assessment (2001/42/EC) requires actions that may have significant effects on the environment to be assessed. Cultural heritage is referred to in the guidance, and although much of the thinking and interpretation remains focused on natural heritage, this represents another opportunity to ensure heritage is seen as part of the wider environment.

Economic instruments

In economic terms heritage is a public good – something that many people value but which may not be provided through the operation of the market as it cannot be priced. The solution to such 'market failures' is normally some form of government intervention such as economic measures that reduce the environmental impacts of energy use or waste production; such measures can also be used to support heritage.

There are already several examples of economic measures to protect heritage in the UK; the state owns and operates some heritage assets (Stonehenge, for example, is one of over 400 sites operated by English Heritage) and there are financial incentives either in the form of tax incentives or exemptions, and of grants for conservation works available from national agencies such as Historic Scotland, Cadw and English Heritage. Perhaps the most important way of regulating heritage (in the UK at least) is through development control in the planning system. Yet an anomaly in the UK tax system ironically acts as a disincentive to care for historic buildings. Value Added Tax (VAT) is payable at the full rate on repairs and maintenance to existing buildings but only at a reduced rate on alterations to buildings or new construction, effectively giving new construction a financial incentive over maintenance.

But despite tools to protect heritage through regulation, subsidy or intervention, there is constant pressure to weaken those – whether through falling grants budgets or through debates over the weight given to new development over preservation in the planning system. Often the argument made against heritage regulation is that it acts as a brake on the economy – which is why the evidence for the economic role and impact of heritage preservation is so important.

Indicators and monitoring

If resources are finite, then it is important to measure the effect of policies on those resources. Chapter 40 of Agenda 21 calls on countries to develop indicators that will show whether progress is being made on sustainable development (UNCED 1992). In the UK, the national system of reporting against indicators for sustainable development (http://www.sustainable-development.gov.uk/performance/indicators-home.htm) is supported by more detailed work on areas such as biodiversity, waste and emissions (Environment Agency 2005), to which heritage is beginning to make a contribution.

Monitoring the loss of heritage is of course not new; from the loss of buildings in fifth-century Rome, through William Morris and John Ruskin in the Victorian period to the campaigns of the twentieth century (e.g. Harwood and Powers 2004) there has always been outrage at the loss of publicly valued sites and monuments. Until recently, however, there has been little systematic data.

In the UK data on historic attractions was compiled for many years (e.g. Hanna 1998), and there have been surveys to identify the extent of buildings and monuments at risk. In 2000 a report on the future of heritage recommended a more systematic approach (English Heritage 2000) and since 2002 annual 'State of the Historic Environment Reports' have begun to bring all this data together in one place for England. Yet as others have found, it is one thing to draw data together; it is quite another to define indicators that are robust, easily measurable and unambiguous (English Heritage 2004: 32). Although there are now indicators on buildings, monuments and landscapes at risk and levels of participation in heritage, in comparison to for example the UK Biodiversity Action Plan (UKBAP), cultural heritage is still a long way from having the kinds of robust indicators that enable other sectors to assess sustainability.

At an international level a system of periodic reporting on World Heritage sites has been introduced as a regular measure of the state of the heritage (http://whc.unesco.org);

Parks Canada operates a system for monitoring commemorative integrity of their sites, and other countries such as Australia include cultural heritage in State of the Environment Reporting (Lennon 2001).

Despite all this, monitoring heritage is not straightforward as heritage (like many other resources) is not finite – new heritage assets are protected and created every day. Over time, limits which have seemed absolute (such as the number of people the earth can feed) have proved to be more complex, and technology has enabled us to deal with problems that were once seen as insuperable (albeit at a cost). Economists such as Gilpin (2000) argue that it is no more possible for us to predict the needs of future generations than it was for prehistoric people to predict our needs. Yet this should not prevent us from either capturing robust information about what is happening to heritage, or in adopting a precautionary approach to managing change.

Social sustainability – tools for involving people in heritage

The link between heritage and the environment is a key one for making the connection to sustainable development. Yet there is another important strand to sustainable development – culture. In 1995 the World Commission on Culture and Development produced 'Our Creative Diversity', exploring the relationship between culture and development. It suggested that,

> Culture is the ultimate catalyst for development, when the latter is seen not just as a dollars and cents process, but much more broadly as a process that enhances the freedom of people everywhere to pursue whatever goals they have reason to value . . .
>
> (WCCD 1995)

A list of ten actions follows, including the need for culturally-sensitive development strategies and the recognition of cultural rights as human rights. This was acknowledged at the Johannesburg Summit in 2002 where Professor Arjun Appadurai identified an important shift in the sustainable development discourse that linked 'cultural diversity' heritage and sustainable development and noted that progress on sustainable development could not be made unless cultural values were closely embedded (quoted in Galla 2005).

Yet it can be argued that many heritage organisations are not doing enough to engage communities and reflect their values. Whilst the section above has shown how heritage has adopted some of the practices of environmental sustainability, this section explores new approaches to engaging communities.

Values-based management

Setha Low has called for a sea-change in heritage practice:

> [W]e need to shift the unit of analysis from consideration of economics and cultural landscapes to individual histories, needs and values and focus on how we can sustain the social relations and meanings that make up our complex life world.
>
> (2003: 47)

She argues that heritage has often been interpreted in terms of white male space, and that there is a need to increase the range and diversity of values that are taken into account in conservation.

The publication of the Australian Burra Charter in 1988 marked a critical moment for heritage; in contrast to the traditional European heritage documents, this put the idea of 'significance' at the heart of decision making, with the implication that significance was not something known by experts but something that needed to be discovered, and that understanding competing and conflicting values is the basis of heritage management (the updated version can be found at www.icomos.org/australia). Values-based approaches to heritage management have since been adopted elsewhere. For example, REAP (Rapid Ethnographic Assessment Procedures) involve a series of approaches drawn from anthropology to engage with communities and have been used in the US to provide a more diverse and ultimately more socially sustainable assessment of heritage sites (Low 2003); Parks Canada has adopted principles, standards and guidelines based on assessing values (Parks Canada 2005).

Across the world from Port Arthur in Tasmania to Chan Chan in Peru and Hadrian's Wall in the UK, and at heritage sites that range from historic ships to entire landscapes, management planning for heritage sites has moved from a top-down process to one that is more participatory, more consultative and takes into account a far wider range of views which in turn contributes to more sustainable conservation by creating a greater sense of ownership (and a greater voice) for those communities who live around and should benefit from heritage sites (Clark 1999; Castellanos 2003: 115).

Empowering communities

Values-based planning is just one way in which communities are becoming more involved in heritage. The specific social objective in the UK Strategy for Sustainable Development goes further – it is to give communities more power and say in decisions that affect them. Traditionally heritage decisions about heritage have been made by experts on behalf of society. However, heritage organisations are beginning to recognise the benefits of greater public participation.

To be fair the UK at least has long had a particularly strong heritage voluntary sector. The National Trust has over three million members and there are a whole range of voluntary organisations involved in caring for heritage in different ways, from amenity groups to transport enthusiasts. Yet the process of identifying and managing protected sites has generally been led by experts and there are still many barriers to accessing, enjoying or participating in heritage activities. The government wants to

> respond to the public's widening perceptions of what constitutes their heritage and consider(s) ways of involving and engaging people in decisions which affect their communities.
>
> (DCMS 2001: 25)

A more people-focused approach to heritage can be seen in, for example, the way the Heritage Lottery Fund (HLF) operates. In 1994 HLF was set up to distribute funds from the new national lottery to heritage as one of six good causes. The fund has three priorities; one is conservation, but the other two are involving more people in decisions about their heritage and increasing opportunities for access, learning and enjoyment. It has been possible to place a far greater emphasis on benefiting people than has been possible under traditional repair-based state grant schemes. The fund has given over £3bn to 18,000 projects; the majority of these are smaller awards. Many have gone to community groups or to partnerships between heritage bodies and community groups, and many have created opportunities for people to get involved in everything from archaeological excavation to biological recording projects; or from helping to manage a local park to leading an investigation of local history (Clark 2004).

The responsibility for caring for heritage is a shared one that involves sustained effort and commitment not just by experts but by wider communities. This was highlighted by the National Trust in an initiative called 'Linking People and Place' (National Trust 1995); more recently English Nature has been getting more people involved in nature conservation – for example by working more closely with fishermen who have expert knowledge of river systems (Ellis *et al.* 2005) . At the same time smaller voluntary bodies in the UK have developed a more powerful voice; over 70 bodies now belong to Heritage Link, an organisation set up in 2002 to enable voluntary bodies to speak with a more concerted voice (www.heritagelink.org.uk).

Governance

Heritage conservation involves looking after a public interest in private property, which brings with it a responsibility for experts at least to act appropriately and responsibly, and to demonstrate a level of public trust.

The collapse of a number of large corporations has recently shocked the public. Many have blamed a lack of control or effective governance and as a result, many private and public organisations are re-examining how they are governed. As part of a launch of a new Historic Places Initiative, Parks Canada set out to look at the values that should underpin it (Shipley 2005). Drawing on the work of Ottawa's Institute on Governance, on UNESCO and ICOMOS charters, and studies of heritage governance in other countries, they identified the following principles:

Legitimacy and Voice – enabling *participation* and *consensus orientation*
Direction – a *strategic vision* which includes human development and historical, cultural and social complexities
Performance – *institutions* and *processes that are responsive to stakeholders* and also *effectiveness* and *efficiency* in general
Accountability *to the public and institutional stakeholders*, and *transparency*
Fairness involving *equity* and the *rule of law*

Parks Canada is just one of a number of heritage organisations who are looking at their own institutional values – if nothing else because whatever their role (as statutory bodies, funders or curators) – the justification and legitimacy for what they do lies in the wider common public interest or value in places. As sustainable development thinking moves more towards recognising that social justice and corporate behaviour is as important as economic and environmental objectives, so this kind of work becomes more important.

Policy frameworks

In 1992 'Rescue' published a short article on archaeology and sustainable development (Clark 1992). At the time the concept was relatively new, and there was little if any recognition of the potential role that heritage might play. Over a decade later, much has changed. The protection of heritage is now included within environmental impact assessment, and is beginning to be seen as something that is relevant to wider sustainability goals. Heritage organisations have embraced thinking about sustainability in their own practices, both implicitly and through explicit policy statements (English Heritage 1997 and this volume). *Passed to the Future* – the policy statement by Historic Scotland (2002) – is one example. It sets out six basic principles which can be summarised as:

- **Recognising value** – the need to understand both the value of the historic environment in its own right, and the benefits that caring for it can deliver.
- **Good stewardship** – a commitment to caring for the heritage in the long run that takes account of both its capacity for change as well as the sustainable use of resources.
- **Assessing impact** – the need to be sure that the impact of our actions for the future historic environment is clearly understood. If this cannot be assessed with confidence, then, following the precautionary principle, potentially damaging actions should be avoided.
- **Working together** – the importance of recognising that the historic environment belongs to us all and its sustainable management should involve us all. It makes sense to work together to reduce damage, resolve conflict and maximise benefits, ensuring that the management of the historic environment is considered at the same time as other needs, both strategically and within specific projects.
- **Community involvement** – because the historic environment provides an important opportunity for community participation in making decisions about and caring for places, there is a need for greater community involvement in decision making, as well as better information that will enable communities to contribute to caring for and managing places.
- **Monitoring** – the historic environment is vulnerable to a wide range of pressures. Better monitoring is needed in order to inform policies for managing it.

This is a powerful and important document, which brings together very clearly what sustainable development means for heritage. Yet what has emerged very recently is some more thinking that can add to and complement this approach.

In February 2006 heritage practitioners from across the UK came together to look at whether or not ideas of public value were helpful in either understanding the value of heritage or in looking at how heritage organisations operate. The concept of public value was not new, but it was new to heritage. It was first put forward by Mark Moore (1997) and it is about the value created by government through services, laws, regulation and other actions. Ultimately it is defined by the public in terms of the choices they make. As Kelly *et al.* (2002) state, ultimately something is only of value if citizens – either individually or collectively – are willing to give something up. It is a useful way of thinking about the performance of public value because it is broader than traditional management approaches, addressing issues such as equity, ethos and accountability.

Hewison and Holden (2005) have shown how public value can be used to measure the performance of heritage organisations by capturing a wide range of different values, subsequently identified as:

- the **'intrinsic'** values that people put on a place (captured for example through the Burra Charter and other values-based planning techniques)
- the **'instrumental'** economic, social and environmental benefits that result from heritage expenditure and policy that are emerging from the growing corpus of impact assessment

to which they add a third kind of value drawn from Mark Moore's work – the **'institutional'** values or behaviour of heritage organisations of the kind identified by Parks Canada that generate legitimacy and trust.

This model was tested through a programme of deliberative research where members of the public were asked to assess heritage projects. It proved to be a simple way of disentangling the different types of values which can help an organisation to both make the case for future funding, but also to examine its own working practices. Given pressure from government for greater accountability and public involvement in decision taking, this kind of deliberative research which works with refined preferences is proving particularly helpful.

Sustainable development is a useful framework but it also has limits. In some ways Public Value is potentially a more helpful way of capturing the impact of heritage as it puts greater weight on two issues that are central to heritage – the significance (or 'intrinsic') values that underpin heritage practice and the ideas of governance and trust which are vital in an area that takes as its starting point what people value.

Conclusions

The Australian economist David Throsby has done much to bridge the divide between economic thinking and cultural heritage. As he says,

> Conservation cannot remain a closed and solely self-referential profession, and indeed it has not. At the same time the inexorable rise of global markets and the ascendancy of economic imperatives in policy formulation around the world does not mean that social, cultural, environmental, and other humanistic values have no role to play in shaping decisions about our future.
>
> (Throsby 2001: 3)

Throsby argues that ideas of sustainability and cultural capital can provide a way forward for integrating the ramifications of conservation decisions, in the same way that sustainability has helped with environmental decisions.

The ability to capture the impact and benefits of heritage policy and funding is one of the most important challenges facing heritage organisations today. Measuring heritage outcomes in for example crude economic terms such as number of jobs created does little to articulate the wider value of caring for the past. Sustainability appraisal techniques that take into account wider social, economic, environmental and ethical issues are essential for both helping heritage organisations to assess what they do and for communicating that to others.

This chapter began by noting that there was little explicit mention of heritage in the UK strategy for sustainable development, despite the contribution that heritage can make to sustainable development goals. This is not simply a matter of academic concern or sour grapes by heritage practitioners; lack of acknowledgement can easily put heritage at risk. For example several of the European directives designed to protect the natural environment actually have a deleterious impact on the historic environment. For example regulations on energy efficiency in buildings encourage the replacement of traditional windows with modern ones. Whilst there is no suggestion here that heritage should take priority over energy efficiency, it should be possible to use historic buildings more efficiently without losing the features that contribute to the quality and aesthetics of our historic towns (or generating additional waste).

Heritage has always acted as a bridge between culture and the environment; it is as difficult to separate the cultural dimension from a landscape as it is to isolate modern creativity from its historic cultural roots. Both the natural environment around us, and our modern culture spring from the past. This does not mean that everything should be preserved, but understanding the past and what is important about it is a good *springboard* for the future.

Although it is easy to be cynical, sustainable development now permeates much of our lives, from doorstep recycling to high-level government policy. This chapter has attempted to show how cultural heritage has the potential to contribute to much of this.

Without wanting to overstate the benefits, heritage can play a positive role in many of the wider goals sustainability seeks to achieve, from reducing waste to engaging communities. Yet, as the UK strategy suggests, there is still some way to go before cultural heritage is acknowledged as a useful contributor to sustainable development goals, and as a result, there is a risk that in achieving environmental objectives we may actually lose our heritage.

Whilst heritage can contribute to the goals of sustainable development, it is also something worth sustaining in its own right. The basic philosophy of sustainable development as set out in one of the original publications that underpinned the 1992 Earth Summit (IUCN, UNEP & WWF 1991) can – with a little bit of adjustment – be seen to provide a powerful and inspiring approach to how we can better care for our heritage. Sustainability has as much to teach heritage thinkers, as heritage has to teach the world of sustainable development.

References

ADAS UK and the Countryside and Community Research Unit 2005. *Building Value – Public benefits of historic farm building repair in the Lake District.* Retrieved 3 March 2006 from www.helm.org.uk.

Attingham Trust 2004. *Opening Doors – Learning and the Historic Environment.* Retrieved from http://www.attinghamtrust.org.

Campaign for Learning website http://www.campaign-for-learning.org.uk.

Carrig Conservation, McGrath Environmental Consultants, James P. McGrath & Associates and Murray O'Laoire Architects 2004. *Built to Last – the sustainable reuse of buildings.* Dublin: Heritage Council/Dublin City. Retrieved 3 March 2006 from http://www.dublincity.ie.

Castellanos, C. 2003. Sustainable management for archaeological sites: the case of Chan Chan in Peru. In Teutonico, J. and Matero, F. (eds), *Managing change: Sustainable approaches to the conservation of the built environment,* 107–116. Los Angeles: Getty Conservation Institute.

Clark, K. (ed.) 1999. *Conservation Plans in Action: Proceedings of the Oxford conference.* London: English Heritage.

Clark, K. 1992. Sustainable development and the Historic Environment. In H. Swain (ed.), *Rescuing the Historic Environment.* Rescue.

Clark, K. 2004. Why Fund Heritage? The Role of Research in the Heritage Lottery Fund. *Cultural Trends* 13 (4), No. 52 December 2004: 65–85.

Copeland and Hayton Associates 2003. *Young Roots – evaluation of the pilot phase.* Internal report to HLF, quoted in Clark, K. 2004.

DCMS (Department for Culture, Media and Sport) 2001. *The Historic Environment: A Force for Our Future.* London: HMSO.

DEFRA (Department for Environment, Food and Rural Affairs) 2003. *Changing Patterns. UK Government Framework for Sustainable Consumption and production.* Downloaded 3 March 2006 from www.defra,gov,uk/environment/business.

DETR (Department of the Environment, Transport and the Regions) 2000. *Building a Better Quality of Life – A strategy for more sustainable construction.* Retrieved 3 March 2006 from http://www.dti.gov.uk/construction.

DETR and DNH (Department of the Environment, Transport and the Regions, Department of National Heritage) 1994. *Planning Policy Guidance Note 15: Planning and the Historic Environment.* London: HMSO.

DoE (Department of the Environment) 1990. *Planning Policy Guidance Note 16: Archaeology and Planning.* London: HMSO.

Eftec 2005. *Valuation of the Historic Environment – The scope for using results of valuation studies in the appraisal and assessment of heritage-related projects and programmes.* Report to English

Heritage, the Heritage Lottery Fund, the Department for Culture, Media and Sport and the Department for Transport. Retrieved 6 March 2006 from www.english-heritage.org.uk.

Ellis, R., Grove-White, R., Vogel, J. and Waterton, C. 2005. *Nature: who knows?* English Nature, University of Lancaster and the Natural History Museum. Retrieved 3 March 2006 from http://www.lancs.ac.uk/fss/iepp/research.

English Heritage 1997. *Sustaining the Historic Environment.* London: English Heritage.

English Heritage 2000. *Power of Place.* London: English Heritage.

English Heritage 2002. *State of the Historic Environment.* London: English Heritage.

English Heritage 2003. *Heritage Counts 2003.* London: English Heritage.

English Heritage 2004. *Heritage Counts 2004.* London: English Heritage.

English Heritage 2005. *Heritage Counts 2005.* London: English Heritage.

Environment Agency 2005. *A better place? State of the Environment 2005.* Downloaded 19 November 2005 from www.environment-agency.gov.uk/soe.

Fairclough, G. 2003. Cultural landscape, sustainability and living with change? In Teutonico, J. and Matero, F. (eds), *Managing Change: Sustainable approaches to the conservation of the built environment*, 23–46. Los Angeles: Getty Conservation Institute.

Galla, A. 2005. *Director's Message*, Graduate Studies in Sustainable Heritage Development. Retrieved 26 December 2005 from http://rspas.anu.edu.au/heritage/message.php.

Gilmore Hankey Kirk 2003. *Evaluating aspects of the Local Heritage Initiative.* GHK for the Countryside Agency, quoted in Clark, K. 2004.

Gilpin, A. 2000. *Environmental Economics – A critical Overview.* Chichester: John Wiley & Sons.

Hanna, M. 1998. *The Heritage Monitor.* English Tourist Board.

Harwood, E. and Powers, A. 2004. *The Heroic Period of Conservation.* London: The Twentieth Century Society.

Hewison, R. and Holden, J. 2005. *Challenge and Change.* Internal report by Demos for the Heritage Lottery Fund. Retrieved February 2006 from www.hlf.org.uk.

Historic Scotland 2002. *Passed to the Future – Historic Scotland's Policy for the Sustainable Management of the Historic Environment.* Retrieved 27 December 2005 from http://www.historic-scotland.gov.uk/pasttofuture.pdf.

HM Government 2005. *Securing the future – delivering UK sustainable development strategy.* Retrieved 5 August 2005 at http://www.sustainable-development.gov.uk/publications/uk-strategy.

ICOMOS 1964. *Venice Charter. International Charter for the Conservation and Restoration of Monuments and Sites.* Retrieved 5 August 2005 from http://www.icomos.org./docs/venice_charter.html.

IUCN, UNEP and WWF (International Union on Conservation of Nature, United Nations Environmental Programme and World Wildlife Fund) 1991. *Caring for the Earth: A strategy for Sustainable Living.* Gland, Switzerland.

Kelly, G., Mulgan, G. and Muers, S. 2002. *Creating Public Value – An analytical framework for public service reform.* Strategy Unit, Cabinet Office. Retrieved 4 March from http://www.strategy.gov.uk.

Klamer, A. and Zuidhof, P.W. 1999. The Values of Cultural Heritage: Merging Economic and Cultural Appraisals. In R. Mason (ed.), *Economics and Heritage Conservation*, 33–4. Los Angeles: Getty Conservation Institute.

Lees, S. and Evans, P. 2003. *Biodiversity's contribution to the quality of life: A research report for English Nature.* English Nature Research Report No. 510.

Lennon, J. 2001 *Australia State of the Environment Report 2001 (Theme Report)* Australia: CSIRO on behalf of the Department of the Environment and Heritage.

Low, S. 2003. Social Sustainability: People, History and Values. In Teutonico, J. and Matero, F. (eds), *Managing Change: Sustainable approaches to the conservation of the built environment*, 47–64. Los Angeles: Getty Conservation Institute.

MLA (Museums, Libraries and Archives Council) 2005. Inspiring Learning for All website. http://www.inspiringlearningforall.gov.uk.

Matarasso, F. 1997. *Use or ornament? The social impact of participation in the arts.* Comedia: Bournes Green.

Moore, M. 1997. *Creating Public Value.* Harvard: Harvard University Press.

National Trust 1995. *Linking people and place – a consultation report.*

National Trust 2001. *Valuing Our Environment.* Retrieved 10 December 2005 from www.nationaltrust.org.uk.

Parks Canada 2005. *Standards and Guidelines for the Conservation of Historic Places in Canada.* Retrieved 3 March 2006 from http://www.pc.gc.ca/docs/index_e.asp.

Performance and Innovations Unit 2000. *Resource productivity: making more with less,* quoted in English Heritage 2003, p. 43.

Pretty, J., Griffin, M., Sellens, M. and Pretty, C. 2003. *Green exercise: complementary roles of nature, exercise and diet in physical and emotional well-being and implications for public health policy.* CES Occasional paper 2–3–1. University of Essex.

Reeves, M. 2002. *Measuring the economic and social impact of the arts: A review.* Retrieved 10 June 2004 from http://www.artscouncil.org.uk/information.

Rypkema, D. 2004. The economic power of conservation. *Context* 84, 18–20.

Seymour, L. 2003. *Nature and psychological well-being.* English Nature Research Report No. 533. Peterborough: English Nature.

Shipley, R. and Kovacs, J. 2005. *Principles for the Governance of the Heritage Conservation Sector in Canada: Lessons from International Experience.* Report to the Historic Places Program Branch, National Historic Sites Directorate, Parks Canada.

Staricoff, R. L. 2004. *Arts in Health: a review of the medical literature.* Retrieved 26 December 2005 from http://www.artscouncil.org.uk/publications.

Sustainable Development Commission 2004. *Shows promise, but must try harder – an assessment by the sustainable development commission of the Government's reported progress on sustainable development over the past five years.* Retrieved 6 March 2006 from http://www.sd-commission.org.uk/publications.

Takano, T., Nakamura, K. and Watanable, M. 2002. Urban residential environments and senior citizens' longevity in megacity areas: the importance of walkable green spaces. *Journal of Epedemiology and Community Health* 12, quoted in CABE Space nd. *The Value of Public Space.* http://www.cabespace.org.uk.

Throsby, D. 2003. Sustainability in the conservation of the built environment: an economist's perspective. In Teutonico, J. and Matero, F. (eds), *Managing change: sustainable approaches to the conservation of the built environment,* 3–10. Los Angeles: The Getty Conservation Institute.

Tibbats, D. 2002. *Your Parks – the benefits of parks and green space.* The Urban Parks Forum. Retrieved December 2005 from http://urbanparksforum.co.uk.

UK Government 1995. A Better quality of life – strategy for sustainable development for the UK. London: HMSO. Retrieved 6 March 2006 from http://www.sustainable-development.gov.uk/publications/index.htm.

UK Government Sustainable Development Framework Indicators updated 28 July 2005. http://www.sustainable-development.gov.uk/performance/indicators-home.htm.

UNCED (United Nations Conference on Environment and Development) 1992. *Agenda 21.* Department of Economic and Social Affairs – Division for Sustainable development. Retrieved 24 November 2005 from http://www.un.org/esa/sustdev/agenda21.htm.

UNESCO (United Nations Educational, Scientific and Cultural Organisation) 2005. Operatonal Guidelines for the Implementation of the World Heritage Convention. Paris: World Heritage Centre. Retrieved 3 March 2006 from www.unesco.org/whc/opgutoc.htm.

Wavell, C., Baxter, G., Johnson, I. and Williams, D. 2002. *Impact evaluation of museums, archives and libraries: available evidence project.* Report to Museums, Libraries and Archives (MLA) by the Robert Gordon University, Aberdeen. Retrieved 1 June 2005 from http://www.mla.gov.uk/information/evidence.

WCCD (World Commission on Culture and Development) 1995. *Our Creative Diversity.* Summary retrieved 26 December 2005 from http://www.unesco.org.culture_and_development/ocd/ocd.html.

WSSD (World Summit on Sustainable Development) 2002. *Plan of Implementation.* Retrieved 6 March 2006 from http://www.johannesburgsummit.org.

www.heritagelink.org.uk.

Chapter 7

Assessing Values in Conservation Planning
Methodological issues and choices

Randall Mason

Conservation decisions – whether they are concerned with giving a building 'heritage' status, deciding which building to invest in, planning for the future of a historic site, or applying a treatment to a monument – use an articulation of heritage values, often called 'cultural significance' (Marquis-Kyle and Walker 1992; Tainter and Lucas 1983; Tomlan 1998) as a reference point. Assessment of the values attributed to heritage is a very important activity in any conservation effort, since values strongly shape the decisions that are made. However, even though values are widely understood to be critical to understanding and planning for heritage conservation, there is little knowledge about how, pragmatically, the whole range of heritage values can be assessed in the context of planning and decision making. This chapter aims to explore value assessment as a particular aspect of conservation planning and management.

Characterizing values

As a prelude to specific discussions of value assessment, this section delves into characterizing the notion of value as a guiding idea in heritage conservation. One of the core assumptions of this chapter is the usefulness of the 'values' perspective to illuminate conservation and management planning issues and make these activities more effective.

Values in conservation

Values is most often used in one of two senses: first, as morals, principles, or other ideas that serve as guides to action (individual and collective); and second, in reference to the qualities and characteristics seen in things, in particular the positive characteristics (actual and potential). This chapter is concerned directly with the second definition. The perspective taken here is an anthropological one, and it values the attempt to understand the full range of values and valuing processes attached to heritage – as opposed to the normative, art historical view common in the conservation field, which a priori privileges artistic and historical values over others.

Value suggests usefulness and benefits. Heritage is valued not as an intellectual enterprise but because (as one aspect of material culture) it plays instrumental, symbolic, and other functions in society. This will become clearer below, as different types of heritage value are described.

In the sphere of material heritage, the simple question of 'What is the value of this thing?' provokes a whole range of answers, all meaningful and legitimate – and therein lies an important issue. In a given moment, a given heritage site, building, or object has a number of different values ascribed to it – heritage is multivalent. As an example, take a hypothetical old church: it has spiritual value as a place of worship; it has historical value because of the events that have transpired there (or simply because it is old); it has aesthetic value because it is beautiful and a fine work of architecture; it has economic value as a piece of real estate; it has political value as a symbolic representation of a certain kind of social order; and so on. What's more, the different values that can be discerned correspond to different stakeholders or expert observers. This multivalence is an essential quality of heritage and, as argued below, logically suggests a pluralistic, eclectic approach to value assessment.

A second important insight about heritage values is that they are contingent, not objectively given. The values of heritage are not simply 'found' and fixed and unchanging, as was traditionally theorized in the conservation field (i.e., the notion of heritage values being intrinsic). Values are produced out of the interaction of an artifact and its contexts; they don't emanate from the artifact itself. Values can thus only be understood with reference to social, historical, and even spatial contexts – through the lens of who is defining and articulating the value, why now, and why here? For conservation professionals, this requires some substantial rethinking of the kinds of research and knowledge that are needed to support conservation. Traditionally, values were articulated by experts' analysis of heritage as a work of art or a record of the past. Only recently has the conservation field begun to embrace such factors as economics, cultural change, public policy, and social issues – and they have yet to be fully integrated into the field.

'Where do values come from?' has been a question of considerable debate. Should material culture recognized as heritage be said to have some intrinsic value (unchanging and universal), or should heritage value be seen as radically and essentially extrinsic and constructed out of the various social contexts of the object, building, or site? The answer seems to lie somewhere in between: value is formed in the nexus between ideas and things. The viewpoint adopted in this research borrows from both ends of this spectrum: on one hand, everything anointed as heritage will, by definition, have some kind of heritage value (aside from whether the value is primarily historic, artistic, or social). In other words, anything defined as heritage is said to intrinsically and tautologically possess some kind of heritage value (though the nature of that value is not intrinsically given). On the other hand, the contingent/constructed viewpoint rightly points to value-formation factors *outside* the object itself and emphasizes the important social processes of value formation. Recognizing the fundamental contingency of heritage values does not preclude the possibility of some values that are universally held (or nearly so). These socially constructed values – think of the Great Pyramids, for instance – are seen as universal because they are so widely held, not because they are objective truths.

Value typologies

The pragmatic questions at hand are: how can a wide range of heritage values be identified and characterized in a way that (1) informs policies and planning decisions, and (2) is relevant to all the disciplines and stakeholders involved?

Values in heritage conservation have traditionally been treated in one of two ways: (1) one kind of value pre-dominates and blots out consideration of others; or (2) values are treated as a black box, with all aspects of heritage value collapsed into 'significance.' The first treatment is problematic because whole categories of value can be excluded a priori. For instance, if the economic use value of a historic site is allowed to predominate, the tourism activity that maximizes those economic values can quickly obscure or erode the site's historical values (visitor traffic destroys historic context and even the resources themselves, perhaps by careless visitors climbing on ruins or taking fragments as souvenirs). The second kind of treatment (the 'black box') is problematic because in collapsing all values to an aggregate statement of significance, the different types of heritage value are mystified or rendered secondary and are thus neglected. An example of this would be a historic church or mosque that is classified by authorities and understood by the secular public primarily as a building of historical or artistic significance; this circumstance can obscure another important value of the building as a sacred site of worship. By hanging the determination of significance too much on the artistic value of the religious building, the other ('secondary') value of religious worship or even of musical performance can be eroded, even though it would not be difficult to conserve all of these values simultaneously.

There are so many different kinds of values, and the interactions among them are so complex, that a more effective way of treating this issue has to begin with a clear, effectively neutral, agreed-upon way of characterizing different types of heritage value – as seen by the wide variety of stakeholders in conservation efforts. A *typology of heritage values* would be an effective guide to characterization and would move conservation stakeholders closer to having a lingua franca in which all parties' values can be expressed and discussed. By use of such a typology – a framework that breaks down significance into constituent kinds of heritage value – the views of experts, citizens, communities, governments, and other stakeholders can be voiced and compared more effectively.

Any effort to break down and describe the values attached to a particular heritage site immediately encounters conceptual and practical difficulties. The different articulations of heritage value (in terms of historical association, artistic merit, or dollars) are at some level different expressions of the same qualities, seen through different eyes. The units and yardsticks used by art historians, sociologists, and economists, for instance, are not readily comparable or translatable. In addition to these differences in epistemology and modes of expression, there are real differences in how a particular type of value is assessed by different stakeholders – for instance, the economic value as assessed by a corporation operating and owning a heritage site, versus a typical resident of a nearby village. A third difficulty in characterizing values lies in the fact that values are always changing in some respect, and we should expect this as part of the essential, social nature of heritage. For all these reasons, heritage values cannot be objectively measured and broken down in the same sense that a chemist, for instance, can analyze and break down a compound to determine its constituent parts.

While the subjectivity and contingency of heritage values make it difficult to establish a clear framework or even a nomenclature of values (akin to a chemist's elements and compounds), this is precisely what is needed to facilitate the assessment and integration of different heritage values in conservation planning and management. So the concept of values needs to be broken down and defined in a typology, at least provisionally. By suggesting a typology in the remainder of this section, I will to highlight its provisional nature. It is not claimed that this (or any) typology will be appropriate for all sites or situations – it is simply an attempt to create a common starting point from which a modified typology can be constructed in a variety of heritage planning situations.

The practical aspects of discussing typologies should also be emphasized. Establishing a typology of values will facilitate discussion and understanding of the different valuing processes at play in heritage conservation. This kind of knowledge ultimately can guide practitioners' choices of appropriate assessment methods for a wide range of heritage values. Typologies also constitute a first-order research tool, ordering and organizing knowledge so that research builds on itself – it keeps practitioners from having to continually reinvent the wheel. The benefit of using a common typology of values is that it lends comparability to the evaluation of different projects. This is an important goal of research on conservation planning – establishing some grounds for comparison among many types of heritage projects and deriving best-practices guidance applicable to many different situations. Finally, the typology is both an analytical tool and a way to advance wider participation in the planning process. Value categories correspond to different stakeholder positions voiced in heritage debates and projects, and devising and debating the typology are themselves means of stimulating participation.

As one would expect, given the conceptual complexities outlined so far, finding agreement on a typology or a nomenclature of heritage values has proven problematic. Nearly everyone interested in heritage – citizen, scholar, writer, professional, or organization – has a slightly different conception, advanced from a particular perspective, of how to describe these characteristics of heritage. Consider the sampling of heritage value typologies devised by different scholars and organizations and summarized in Table 7.1 (see also Kellert 1996; Rolston 1988; Satterfield 2002). In most instances, they describe the same pie, but slice it in subtly different ways.

Typologies implicitly minimize some kinds of value, elevate others, or foreground conflicts between the cultivation of certain values at the expense of others. In the Burra Charter, for instance, economic values are minimized because they are seen as derived from cultural and historical values and are therefore given secondary consideration.

It is apparent that there are several distinct, if not fully separable, categories of heritage value – economic, historical, spiritual, political, educational, aesthetic, artistic. If one were to map these value schemata, there would be a great deal of overlap even between such different frameworks as Frey's (1997 from economics) and Reigl's (1902 from art history). The typology suggested in English Heritage's recent paper on sustainability is perhaps the most comprehensive and balanced (English Heritage 1997 and this volume). This breakdown is well oriented to conservation practice because the value categories focus on how heritage is used and valued (contingently, and by people other than

Table 7.1 Summary of heritage value typologies devised by various scholars and organizations (Reigl 1982; Lipe 1984; for the Burra Charter, Australia ICOMOS 1999; Frey 1997; English Heritage 1997)

Reigl (1902)	Lipe (1984)	Burra Charter (1998)	Frey (1997)	English Heritage (1997)
Age	Economic	Aesthetic	Monetary	Cultural
Historical	Aesthetic	Historic	Option	Educational and academic
Commemorative	Associative-symbolic	Scientific	Existence	Economic
Use	Informational	Social (including spiritual, political, national, other cultural)	Bequest	Resourc
Newness			Prestige	Recreational
			Educational	Aesthetic

elites and experts), whereas many other typologies resonate more with connoisseurship and professional values and are strongly influenced by the notion of heritage's intrinsic value.

A broad distinction is often made between economic and cultural values as the two primary metacategories of heritage value. This distinction has served as a starting point for the research undertaken by the Getty Conservation Institute on values-related issues most relevant to conservation. However, defending a hard-and-fast separation of economic and cultural spheres is untenable. Economic behavior cannot be beyond, or separate from, culture, which by definition is 'ways of living together' or attitudes and behaviors passed on. Indeed, economics is one of the most dominant (sub)cultures – ways of living together – in many societies.

Nevertheless, the economic-cultural distinction is widely shared and remains a very useful analytic convenience. The economic-cultural distinction resonates because: (1) it highlights privatization and the influence of market logic into ever more spheres of social life, a most pressing contemporary social issue; (2) it connects to traditional debates around notions of economic base and cultural superstructure and their relation in modern societies; and (3) perhaps most important for our present purposes, economic and cultural spheres represent two quite distinct attitudes/perspectives toward the subject of values and valuing.

Provisional typology

The provisional typology shown in Table 7.2 – which is neither exhaustive nor exclusive – is offered as a point of departure and discussion.

This typology includes the kinds of value most often associated with heritage sites and conservation issues, but it does not assume that every heritage site has every type of value. The working assumption behind the typology presented here is that these categories encompass most of the heritage values that shape decision making and that must be considered in conservation planning and management. The danger in using such a typology is that it may suggest that one framework of values speaks equally well to all heritage sites, issues, and cultural milieus. If it were used in this normative way, and as an a priori framework, it would prefigure too much about the values of a heritage site. It is reiterated, therefore, that any value typology should serve only as a starting point and that value types will have to be adjusted and revised for each project/setting.

The two major categories – sociocultural and economic – do not actually refer to different, discrete sets of values. Economic and cultural are two alternative ways of understanding and labeling the same, wide range of heritage values. There are substantial overlaps between the values each column in Table 7.2 helps identify. The major difference between them resides in the very different conceptual frameworks and methodologies used to articulate them.

The same point must be made concerning the subcategories within the 'sociocultural values' group; they are not distinct and exclusive; in fact, they overlap quite extensively. This intermingling contrasts with the categories of the 'economic values' column, which are intended to be distinct and exclusive of one another.

Table 7.2 Provisional typology of heritage values

Sociocultural values	Economic values
Historical	Use (market) value
Cultural/symbolic	Nonuse (nonmarket) value
Social	Existence
Spiritual/religious	Option
Aesthetic	Bequest

Sociocultural values

Sociocultural values are at the traditional core of conservation – values attached to an object, building, or place because it holds meaning for people or social groups due to its age, beauty, artistry, or association with a significant person or event or (otherwise) contributes to processes of cultural affiliation.

The types of sociocultural values outlined below overlap. For instance, a quality defined as a spiritual/religious value (a congregation's ongoing use of a historic church, for example) could also be defined as a historical value (the history of generations worshipping in the church and playing a role in the development of the surrounding community) or as an artistic value (the particular design of the building and its furnishings) or as a social value (used for nonreligious gatherings – for instance, a holiday concert or soup kitchen). While these uses are closely related, it is important to understand these as different values, because they correspond to different ways of conceptualizing the value of the heritage, to different stake-holder groups, and therefore to different bases for making management or conservation decisions.

Notice that there is no separate category for political value. The reason: all values attributed to heritage are political, in that they are part of the power struggles and exertions that determine the fate of heritage. Values occupy center stage when it comes to the decisions – the politics – about the conservation of heritage.

Historical value

Historical values are at the root of the very notion of heritage. The capacity of a site to convey, embody, or stimulate a relation or reaction to the past is part of the fundamental nature and meaning of heritage objects. Historical value can accrue in several ways: from the heritage material's age, from its association with people or events, from its rarity and/or uniqueness, from its technological qualities, or from its archival/documentary potential.

There are two important subtypes of historical value that merit mention. Educational/academic value is a type of historical value. The educational value of heritage lies in the potential to gain knowledge about the past in the future through, for instance, archaeology or an artist's creative interpretation of the historical record embodied in the heritage. Artistic value – value based on an object's being unique, being the best, being a good example of, being the work of a particular individual, and so on – is also a type of historical value.

Cultural/symbolic value

History and heritage are core elements of all cultures – the ideas, materials, and habits passed through time – so cultural values are, like historical value, a part of the very notion of heritage. There is no heritage without cultural value. Cultural values are used to build cultural affiliation in the present and can be historical, political, ethnic, or related to other means of living together (for instance, work- or craft-related). As used in this typology, cultural/symbolic value refers to those shared meanings associated with heritage that are not, strictly speaking, historic (related to the chronological aspects and meanings of a site).

Political value – the use of heritage to build or sustain civil relations, governmental legitimacy, protest, or ideological causes – is a particular type of cultural/symbolic value. These values stem from the connection between civic/social life and the physical environment and from the capacity of heritage sites in particular to stimulate the kind of positive

reflection and political behavior that builds civil society. Political/civil value can be mani-
festly symbolic, or it can stem from research and understanding of how heritage sites are
created and evolve, and from learning about who has shaped the environment. Like all
heritage values, political value can be interpreted through a positive lens – as a key contributor to civil society – or, more cynically, it can be interpreted as a political tool used
to enforce national culture, imperialism, postcolonialism, and so on.

Craft- or work-related values are often very important aspects of heritage. A building
embodies the methods used to design and make it, and the values relating to the process of
making and building are often separate from (or lost among) more static historical or aesthetic values.

This category also includes heritage values used to stimulate ethnic-group identity, in
cases in which the group does not have a strong religious aspect.

Social value

The concept of social value follows closely the notion of 'social capital,' a widely used
concept in the social science and development fields. The social values of heritage enable
and facilitate social connections, networks, and other relations in a broad sense, one not
necessarily related to central historical values of the heritage. The social values of a heritage site might include the use of a site for social gatherings such as celebrations,
markets, picnics, or ball games – activities that do not necessarily capitalize directly on
the historical values of the site but, rather, on the public-space, shared-space qualities.
The kinds of social groups strengthened and enabled by these kinds of values could
include everything from families to neighborhood groups to ethnic groups to special
interest groups.

Social value also includes the 'place attachment' aspects of heritage value. *Place attachment* refers to the social cohesion, community identity, or other feelings of affiliation that
social groups (whether very small and local, or national in scale) derive from the specific
heritage and environment characteristics of their 'home' territory.

Spiritual/religious value

Heritage sites are sometimes associated or imbued with religious or other sacred meaning.
These spiritual values can emanate from the beliefs and teachings of organized religion, but
they can also encompass secular experiences of wonder, awe, and so on, which can be
provoked by visiting heritage places.

Aesthetic value

Aesthetic value is widely agreed to be a category of sociocultural value, though it refers to
a wide range of qualities. In the main, *aesthetic* refers to the visual qualities of heritage. The
many interpretations of beauty, of the sublime, of ruins, and of the quality of formal relationships considered more broadly have long been among the most important criteria for
labeling things and places as heritage. The design and evolution of a building, object, or
site can be another source of aesthetic value. It is also argued that the category of the aesthetic can be interpreted more widely to encompass all the senses: smell, sound, and
feeling, as well as sight. Thus, a heritage site could be seen as valuable for the sensory
experience it offers. Aesthetic value is a strong contributor to a sense of well-being and is
perhaps the most personal and individualistic of the sociocultural value types.

Economic values

Economic valuing is one of the most powerful ways in which society identifies, assesses, and decides on the relative value of things. Economic values overlap a great deal with the sociocultural values (historical, social, aesthetic, and so on) described above, and they are distinguished most because they are measured by economic analyses. In other words, economic values are different because they are conceptualized in a fundamentally different way (according to a fundamentally different epistemology, one not commensurable with the narrative epistemologies used for sociocultural values). According to neoclassical economic theory, economic values are the values seen primarily through the lens of individual consumer and firm choice (utility) and are most often expressed in terms of price. Not all economic values, however, are measured in terms of market prices.

Economic values stemming from the conservation of heritage are often, by definition, understood to be a public good – reflecting collective decisions rather than individual, market decisions – and are therefore not captured by market price measures. There is an important distinction between what values can legitimately be represented in terms of price (privately held values, which can be traded in a market) and what factors shape resource allocation decisions (public ones, collectively held, and provided outside of markets). Accounting for these gaps is one of the goals of the research effort. A diverse set of economic valuation methods, therefore, will be needed to span this gap between private/market values and public/nonmarket values.

The different economic values outlined here, and the relations among them, are summarized in a paper by Mourato and Mazzanti (2002) (see also Frey 1997; Throsby 2001, 2002; and Serageldin and Steer 1994). The main distinction they draw is related to use versus non-use values, corresponding to the types of economic values measured through markets and outside of markets.

Use value (market value)

Use values are market values – the ones most easily assigned a price. Use values of material heritage refer to the goods and services that flow from it that are tradable and priceable in existing markets. For instance, admission fees for a historic site, the cost of land, and the wages of workers are values. Because they are exchanged in markets, these values can be easily expressed in terms of price, and they are susceptible to economists' many analytical tools based on neoclassical theory.

Nonuse value (nonmarket value)

Nonuse values are economic values that are not traded in or captured by markets and are therefore difficult to express in terms of price. For instance, many of the qualities described as sociocultural values are also nonuse values. They can be classed as economic values because individuals would be willing to allocate resources (spend money) to acquire them and/or protect them.

The economics field describes nonuse values as emanating from the public-good qualities of heritage – those qualities that are 'nonrival' (consumption by one person does not preclude consumption by someone else) and 'nonexcludable' (once the good/service is provided to anyone, others are not excluded from consuming it). A public archaeological site would exhibit these qualities very clearly. Markets fail to provide public goods and services, and nonuse values therefore pose a difficult methodological problem for economists.

In large part, nonuse values are an alternative way of looking at the sociocultural values described and distinguished above. Sociocultural values and nonuse values are two ways of slicing the same pie, as it were.

Nonuse values are often broken down into the following, closely related categories (which are not exhaustive) in order to specify exactly which qualities of heritage motivate economic decisions:

Existence Value: Individuals value a heritage item for its mere existence, even though they themselves may not experience it or 'consume its services' directly.

Option Value: The option value of heritage refers to someone's wish to preserve the possibility (the option) that he or she might consume the heritage's services at some future time.

Bequest Value: Bequest value stems from the wish to bequeath a heritage asset to future generations.

Intrinsic values

How does the typology suggested here align with the 'intrinsic value' arguments made regarding heritage – and also made vis-à-vis nature in environmental conservation? This typology is premised on the assumption that values are fundamentally contingent – in other words, that they are socially as well as spatially constructed. But can one assume that some of the values of heritage are intrinsic (if not fixed or absolute) – i.e., that some kind of historic value is intrinsic to the whole notion of something being identified as heritage?

This intrinsic-value argument in heritage conservation would be analogous to the 'intrinsic' argument in environmental conservation, through which it is assumed that 'natural' characteristics (wildness) are intrinsically valuable. This idea parallels the notion of authenticity in the heritage field, which presumes that some kind of historic value is represented by – inherent in – some truly old and thus authentic material (authentic in that it was witness to history and carries the authority of this witness). Thus, if one can prove authenticity of material, historical value is indelibly established (but cf. Holforf 2005, Ch. 7).

Methodological issues and strategies

It was asserted above that questions of value and valuing are not, for the most part, susceptible to technical solutions. Values are embedded in culture and social relations, which are ever in flux. Political realities – the patterns of power that join and separate the various stakeholders in the heritage – are ever present: they are sometimes on the surface of conservation activities; often they lurk just beneath. The practical goal in devising value-assessment methodologies, approaches, routines, and tools is therefore not to search for the single best answer; nor is it to yield objectivity, technical precision, or a one-size-fits-all technique for effective conservation planning. Rather, the focus on methodologies (on the process of generating knowledge) will bring relevant information to bear, will lend transparency to the process, and will abet the goal of achieving wider, meaningful participation in the process.

This section of the chapter airs a number of issues regarding methodological strategies for assessing heritage values and goes on to discuss a number of tools that are, or could be, used for assessment. In a survey of these available tools, one recurring theme is the conservation field's great potential for borrowing or adapting proven value-assessment methods from disciplines such as anthropology and economics.

Before describing specific methods and tools, some strategic issues underlying the choice of methods and tools should be rehearsed.

General issues and conditions

Methodological choices for value assessment must, at some juncture in the management planning process, engage a few broad and fundamental issues (Figure 7.1).

First, the value assessment process actually consists of a few discrete but closely related parts. Value assessment is not a simple matter of simultaneous identification and measurement, like taking the temperature. Assessment can be broken down into three parts: identification, elicitation and elaboration (including exploring connections and overlaps), and ranking and prioritization.

Second, we can assume that no single value-assessment method will give perfect, total, or even adequate knowledge to inform conservation decisions on the ground. Given the varied nature of heritage values, knowledge about them is best gained by adopting a number of quite different perspectives (epistemologies) and, it follows, methodologies. To gauge sufficiently all heritage values of a project or site and to inform conservation decisions on the ground, a suite of varied methods – quantitative or qualitative, economic or anthropological – is likely to be the best course. A further challenge, addressed below, lies in matching appropriate methods to all the values identified in making a typology.

Third, context is one of the watchwords by which one can assure a varied, robust perspective on which values to assess. *Context*, as used here, refers to physical, geographical surroundings; to historical patterns and narratives; and to the social processes with discernible impact on heritage and its conservation. These include the cultural, social, economic, and other conditions contributing to significance, as well as the management setting and physical surroundings of the site. Heritage sites and objects must be understood in relation to their contexts – in other words, holistically. One cannot fully understand a site without understanding its contexts, which, perforce, extend beyond the site itself both literally and conceptually.

Conservation professionals have traditionally been very skilled in looking at certain contexts of heritage – relating to physical deterioration, environmental conditions, and other physical factors; or to art historical narratives and aesthetic canons – and have

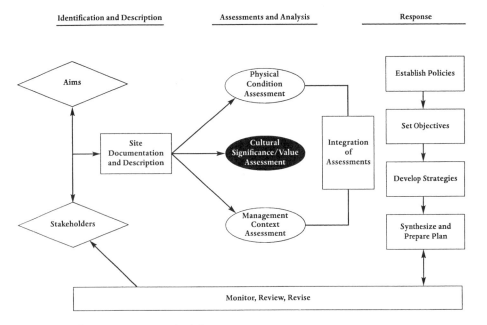

Figure 7.1   Planning process methodology.

developed methodologies and tools for analyzing these contexts. But an understanding of heritage values in the fullest sense requires that conservation professionals cast a wider net and consider more and different contexts of conservation – economic, cultural, and political. As a corollary to this, conservation professionals and planners must reach out to other fields and disciplines – which have already gained some experience in assessing such contextual issues – and bring more rigor to this engagement.

For instance, in approaching conservation planning for an archaeological site, it is often imperative to understand and deal with the pressures and opportunities presented by tourism development – not just the tourism activities that happen on the site but also the values that shape decisions well before and well after the actual visit. Such planning requires an understanding of economic forces, methods of economic analysis, public policy, cultural tensions, and trade-offs that often accompany tourism development, as well as the relationship of these factors to traditional conservation aims and principles. Moreover, the meaning of the archaeological site to the communities living around it may well be one of the driving forces behind the effort to plan and conserve. In this case, conservation professionals need to understand the values as seen by that community, which suggest a whole range of methodologies for articulating those values (ranging from ethnographic studies, to focus groups and interviews, to community involvement and 'mapping' processes).

Fourth, several complications flow from the fact that values come from people – they are opinions. Values come into play only when they are articulated and championed by stakeholders. But whom does one consult or ask? How broad is the net of informants and spokespeople and experts? Where can one draw the line to limit the number of voices so that the diversity of values is representative and manageable and not overwhelming? There is no universal solution to this dilemma, but neither does one have only intuition to follow. These questions are addressed by constituency analysis and the ethnographic methods described below. Another complication relates to how one asks the questions – or, in the terms laid out above, how does one elicit values? As Theresa Satterfield's research shows, asking for numerical responses and narrative responses to value-elicitation questions yields somewhat different sets of values (Satterfield 2002). First, one should aim for a diversity of tools and forms of knowledge (not only numerical, not only narrative); second, one can seek out the kinds of values and stakeholders that usually prove most elusive – disadvantaged communities, spiritual values, a sense of place.

Quantitative and qualitative methods

Economic and cultural modes of conceptualizing and gauging value represent two distinct and somewhat incommensurate ways of looking at value – one quantifiable and based on individual preferences, the other resistant to quantification and premised on collective meaning. In the main, economic values are best elicited and expressed by quantitative research methods. Mathematics is, after all, the fundamental language of modern economics. Conversely, cultural values submit to quantification only fitfully and inadequately. Qualitative research methods, ranging from narratives and analyses written by experts to interviews of ordinary citizens, elicit cultural values more effectively.

Grand claims have been made that economic methods based on neoclassical theory yield a comprehensive assessment of heritage values – these methods translate all types of value, it is said, into terms of dollars by simulating markets or assuming that markets exist for them. Such claims are fraught with problems, though. The best assessment of heritage values, many agree, comes from a complementary use of economic and cultural methods. Throsby (2002) reaches this conclusion, arguing from the perspective of an economist thinking about the value of culture and the arts.

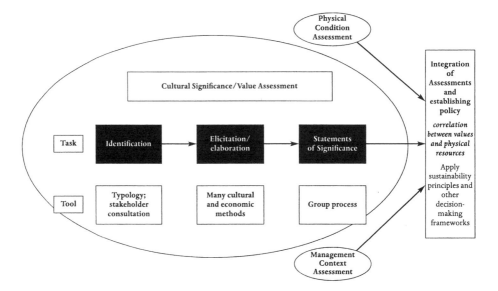

Figure 7.2   The cultural significance/value assessment process. This three-part model of value assessment is a more detailed rendering of the 'Cultural significance/value assessment' oval occupying the center of the planning process methodology (Figure 7.1). With the different parts of the value-assessment process identified, planners can apply a logical sequence of tasks to generate and collect knowledge about values and use this within the overall planning process.

Quantitative and qualitative methodologies derive from quite different epistemologies. Both provide ways of taking samples, making proxies of complex realities that cannot be described in toto. The two approaches can be seen as attempts to measure the same values, albeit from different perspectives, with different tools and discourses, and with different results. The information generated by both kinds of method is disjunct – it is difficult, if not impossible, to measure and compare them on the same scale. Though they may be seen as competing paradigms, the information they generate is often complementary.

The particular strengths and weaknesses of quantitative and qualitative approaches need to be considered carefully. By their very nature, some kinds of values resist being compared or scaled – spiritual values, for instance – and thus are more susceptible to humanist, qualitative methods. The scalable results of quantitative methods are more easily cross-compared – thus, quantitative methods remain the lingua franca for policy makers. Quantitative methods focus on causal relationships and depend on variables isolated from their contexts. However, as mentioned above, values and other forms of meaning are produced out of the interaction of artifacts and their contexts, not from the artifact itself. This arena is where qualitative research methods have a particular strength; they are sensitive to contextual relationships (as opposed to causal connections) and are therefore indispensable in studying the nature and interplay of heritage values (see Denzin and Lincoln 1994; Frankfort-Nachmias and Nachmias 1996).

A toolbox approach

Since a full assessment of heritage values will require a diverse suite of methods and a flexible approach, how does one begin to match methods to values? Can the values in the provisional typology be matched up with specific methods? Not in a hard-and-fast sense. The kinds of tools that have been brought up – expert analyses, quantitative/economic studies of use and nonuse values, ethnographic assessments – are by design quite broad in their sweep. In each instance, the specifics of the method (the survey questions, the data collected, the experts consulted) would have to be designed, on a case-by-case basis, to respond to the range of values associated with the project and to the personnel available to manage them. But it would, for instance, be sensible to imagine a planning process that used assessments with such components as economic impact analysis; surveys of tourists, including both narrative questions and quantifying methods such as a willingness-to-pay study; ethnographic studies centered on local communities (ethnic groups, indigenous people, recent migrants); interviews with local political officials and businesspeople; and thorough analyses of the historical, artistic, educational, and other values of the site from the scholarly/expert community.

The aim of the toolbox approach is to get all relevant heritage values on the table, building the fullest practicable account to inform policy and decision making. The variety of values represented in the typology requires the use of a variety of tools in their assessment. To manage this variety of available tools in the planner's toolbox, the notion of triangulation is useful. Triangulation, which requires the use of a suite of different methods in complementary ways, should be at the core of an approach to eliciting and assessing heritage values. The underlying principle is that the layering of different, complementary pieces of information will produce a more accurate answer than would the pursuit of one or two pieces of information.

Given their diversity, the elicitation of heritage values for a site requires casting this type of broad net by layering different approaches to yield the most robust results. In this vein, Denzin and Lincoln (1994) describe the contemporary social researcher as a bricoleur: one who patches together different methods to glean different sorts of knowledge, iteratively, opportunistically, to build the best composite answer to the question at hand. In the context of assessing the social impacts of environmental policies, William Freudenburg has suggested a somewhat more structured, systematic version of the triangulation-bricoleur idea. He outlines a three-part method: first, employing secondary research techniques using existing, archival data (both qualitative and quantitative); second, conducting primary research using ethnographic fieldwork techniques; and third, using 'gaps and blinders' techniques (such as structured second-guessing, consultation, and public involvement) both to fill in the blanks of knowledge and to correct for the researchers' own biases (Freudenburg 1999).

The goal of a flexible and useful methodology for value assessment has to be kept in the perspective of the larger goal of seeking more sustainable practices and policies for heritage conservation. It is a truism that the same approach will not work in all places, in all cultural contexts, for all kinds of heritage – it must be adaptable and variable. With this flexibility in mind, the frameworks developed here aim to be meaningful for a range of stakeholders, take a broad view of values as motivations behind conservation, and accept wide participation as an inherent aspect of conservation. The methodological approach to value assessment proposed here must not only be flexible – the ideas and approaches should be transferable and useful. These are among the ingredients of more sustainable conservation.

Stakeholders and participation in value assessment

Having at one's disposal the most effective methods for eliciting and assessing heritage values is important. However, the real power of a values-based approach comes through using these tools to cultivate the values as felt, conceived, and realized by actual groups concerned with the stewardship of actual heritage sites. Engaging heritage values 'on the ground' – so to speak – requires engagement with questions of influence, competition, power, and politics. One must venture questions such as: Who participates in heritage value assessment? Whose values are counted? Thus, who has power to shape conservation outcomes?

There are several different sources of heritage value: community and other culture groups, the market, the state, conservators, other experts, property owners, and ordinary citizens. In assessing values, the simplest political guideline is trying, as a matter of equity and accuracy, to work toward wide participation and account for the views of all the relevant valuers.

The question of stakeholders is an essential issue in value assessment. The importance of stakeholders to the notion of values and values assessment is clear – stakeholders do the valuing. Thus, identifying the stakeholder groups and employing methods designed to reach and hear them in light of their particular character and capacity are required of any methodology for heritage value assessment. As it is widely believed that widening of the circle of stakeholders involved in a project improves both the process and the outcome, constituency analysis and identification of stakeholders is an extremely important task.

Insiders and outsiders

As shorthand for addressing calls for wider participation and stakeholder involvement in conservation, consider the gross distinction between insiders and outsiders to the conservation planning and decision-making process. The distinction stems from the notion that some stakeholders are 'at the table' where values are identified, assessed, and ranked and where decisions are made, while other legitimate stakeholders are not present.

Insiders are those who can participate in the process by right or might – actors with power, such as public officials, bureaucrats, policy makers, those who influence them, and (to an extent) conservation professionals and other experts invited into the process. Outsiders constitute everyone else with a stake in the heritage in question but with little or no leverage on the process. In some instances, outsiders are actively excluded from the process; in other instances, they have no knowledge of the process or lack fluency in the language of conservation and policy and perhaps even lack an inclination to participate. More and more frequently, efforts are made by both sides to shift outsiders to the inside. Outsiders can be brought into the decision-making process or else they can force themselves in – which happens often enough.

Outsiders are not simply nonprofessionals; conservation professionals, in fact, are often outsiders in that they have little access to making or shaping the most important decisions affecting a site. It must be noted that the values and interests of outsiders and insiders do not necessarily conflict (despite the opposition implied in these labels). Though they have a different relation to the decision-making processes, stakeholders on both sides might very well find common ground and benefit by the same course of conservation action.

The notion of including outsiders in conservation planning is fundamentally a political issue, a matter of power and authority. In one respect, such inclusion can be addressed formally by bringing outsiders into the client/steering group of a project, acknowledging outsiders' rights to property or use of a site, and so on. The politics of participation can also be addressed in choosing methodologies and designing the planning/management process. Choosing methods is not only a matter of choosing among different expert/academic discourses; it also embodies a political gesture as to whose analysis, voices, and values are included in the decision-making mix. Participation needs to be addressed at both levels: formal membership in the process and design of the process.

The outsider/insider distinction also highlights practical problems. While the values typologies discussed here might make sense to us as conservation professionals, what would be the value categories for outsiders? Would they be different? What kind of language and phrasing and communication would most effectively abet their participation? In devising and applying a typology for a project, these questions must be considered. By what methods can those conservation professionals, officials, decision makers, and other stakeholders at the table generate knowledge about the value assessments of those outside the process?

The insider/outsider idea may be useful for identifying participants in the present. But a third set of actors (constituencies) may also be brought into the process design – potential stakeholders. These could consist of groups who may in the future exercise some interest in the heritage site in question – future generations, for instance – or who may exist at a distance from the heritage site (literally or metaphorically) but take some interest in it (for example, the 'community' of a nation's citizens). These stakeholders, too, should be accounted for in value assessment.

Addressing participation practically

Rhetorically, we all agree on the call for more participation. In principle, it is widely recognized that rigorous and meaningful participation needs to be seen as a valuable part of the planning process and integrated into many aspects of assessment and planning. But it will take real changes in professional attitudes as well as continual testing of new, context-appropriate methods. Professionals need to be open to other, nonexpert views about heritage values and decisions and embrace alternative ways of understanding value, negotiating differences, and so on.

The urban planning, environmental conservation, and development fields – and working with each, the discipline of anthropology – have wrestled with this issue a great deal, and a vast amount of practical and intellectual work has been done on participatory issues (e.g., Sanoff 2000). Such concerns have also made some inroads in heritage conservation. Progressive examples of participation in the heritage field include Australia's Burra Charter process, the Main Street process pioneered in the United States, and numerous more local efforts being pursued, for instance, in Canada (Kerr 1999).

Insiders and outsiders have to get integrated not only in how their responses to value elicitation are expressed and recorded but at the level of how they frame questions of value. Therefore, insiders and outsiders should be included in the composition of project teams and through the planning process itself (in effect, becoming insiders instead of outsiders). The alternative to this kind of effective integration of insiders and outsiders – generating separate assessments of different types of stakeholders and simply collecting them – would fall short of a full assessment of a project's heritage values.

In terms of the methods and planning process involved in this research, there are a couple of ways to address practically the issue of wider participation. First, a thorough constituency analysis is needed to identify all stakeholders: inside and outside, near and distant, present and projecting into the future. This analysis should inform composition of a project team and a consultation process representing as many different relevant stakeholder positions as possible. The constituency analysis should also be revisited periodically throughout the project, as new or different groups may come to light. A second measure for ensuring participation is the kind of ethnographic-economic suite of methodologies suggested throughout, the basic purpose of which is to engage many stakeholders in the assessment of heritage values driving conservation planning and management, engaging them with elicitation tools congruent with their 'fluencies' and the values they tend to hold dear.

Tools for eliciting heritage values

How can the views of the many parties with a stake in a heritage site be searched out, articulated, and brought to the table?

Tools suited to cultural values

The following general methodologies are offered as a spectrum of basic approaches, not specific to any one arena but, rather, applied in anthropology, archaeology, geography, sociology, city planning/urbanism, and various hybrid fields. Each one is newly used in heritage value assessment and has potential use for assessing values in conservation planning.

Expert analysis (textual/iconographic/formal/semiologic)

Detailed analysis of particular objects, things, symbols, and texts is the stock-in-trade of experts in any academic or professional field. As noted above, in the conservation field, this type of analysis has historically been exemplified by the connoisseurship judgments of art historians, curators, and collectors.

An expert interprets values and other phenomena through theoretical screens (tacitly making a great many epistemological assumptions) and interprets how they are embedded in their wider contexts. Often the outcome is some appraisal of the value of the object or phenomenon according to a scale of values internal to the profession. Such disciplinary distinctions purposely tend to isolate the judgments of these experts from other inputs (if expert knowledge is not set off from others' knowledge, it loses its value), so they work against the goal of wider participation. Who are these experts? They are the professionals trained in nearly any humanistic or professional field: historians, art historians, architects, anthropologists, geographers, and so on. Since these analyses are inherently the province of experts – analyses are de facto valuable if they are done by experts – there are few opportunities to compare or verify the judgments made.

Ethnography

Ethnography includes methods of describing and recording the characteristics of a culture. Ethnography is usually, though not necessarily, qualitative. It relies on information-gathering activities such as interviews, oral histories, observation, and recording of the characteristics of material culture. With a number of particular information-gathering tools at hand, ethnography seems well suited as an approach to eliciting heritage values.

Initially seen as a positivist methodology, ethnography has come to focus on recognizing the subjectivity of the observer as well as on recording the characteristics of the culture that is the object. Many ethnographic approaches have been developed in the field of anthropology, from participant observation studies of exotic cultures early in the twentieth century to 'thick description' (emphasizing the embeddedness of cultural practices/features in their myriad contexts, knowledge of which is built up by thick description) to today's very value-sensitive approaches to representing the many voices contributing to culture.

These types of applied social anthropology are of particular interest to heritage conservation. Indeed, some anthropologists and designers have jointly employed ethnographic methods as part of land- and community-planning projects, synthesizing information about social and physical contexts and using this information to generate design and planning solutions. Setha Low (2002) describes the specific ethnographic approach she and her colleagues have used in studying and planning heritage projects.

The tools Low and others have employed include interviews, focus groups, mapping exercises, and structured observation techniques (Low 1981; McHarg 1992). These eclectic but structured ethnographic methods have been adapted to heritage conservation as the rapid ethnographic assessment procedure (REAP), a planning method developed with the U.S. National Park Service (see Low 1991, 2002 and this volume; www.cr.nps.gov/aad).

Likewise, an applied ethnographic methodology called participatory rural assessment (PRA) is often used in the public health and development fields (particularly in agricultural development efforts in less-developed countries). PRA consists of a flexible menu of ethnographic and public-involvement techniques aimed at understanding the values and knowledge that local populations – traditional cultures and nonliterate groups in particular – wish to sustain as they encounter Western, nongovernmental organization efforts to modernize and develop their economies. PRA not only aims to glean knowledge about the values and skills of non-experts and the unempowered, it also aims directly to empower them (see www.ids.ac.uk/ids and www.unv.edu/unvpress/food 2; Bell and Morse 1999).

Surveys and interviews

As mentioned above, ethnographic methodologies often employ interviews and surveys as data collection tools. Surveys are used in myriad fields, from market research in the business world to those done to collect data for sociological studies. They can be designed and conducted in a great many ways (to elicit simple data or complex responses, gathered in person, on paper, by telephone, and so on). Interviews, too, can be designed in a variety of ways – structured or unstructured, using graphic or written or recorded responses. Interviews can be undertaken strategically, focusing on a few key informants, or extensively, with samples of hundreds. An enormous literature of applied work exists on these tools.

Other participatory methods

The field of planning/urbanism is another source of methods for engaging multiple stakeholders in planning and management efforts. Since the 1960s, many methods have been applied in many kinds of projects. Dealing with decisions on urban, social, environmental, infrastructural, and economic development issues, planners have employed varied means for understanding how ordinary citizens ascribe value and how this affects development decisions. Methods often include surveys, public meetings, focus groups, and key-informant interviews; visioning, Delphi, and other group processes; mediation and conflict resolution, in cases where a clear dispute has arisen; institutionalizing the involvement of existing community groups; and even the creation of new community groups (or capacity building among existing groups).

Mapping

Plotting data on a map or plan is one simple and distinctive way of organizing information. Mapping can be simple or very complex. It is so broad and basic a way of handling data that it is perhaps a stretch to call it a methodology; but in the broad definition being used here, it does constitute a way of generating knowledge.

Mapping is already a basic methodology in conservation, as part of the assessment of the physical conditions of the heritage being studied. Conservation professionals, architectural and landscape designers, and planners routinely use mapping and mapped information (existing conditions) as the most basic methodology for approaching any project (McHarg 1992). The analytical potential of mapping techniques has been made more powerful by the introduction and wide use of desktop geographic information systems (GIS) and the digital databases linked to them. GIS systems are not in themselves a method of value elicitation; they are a tool for organizing and analyzing data in the service of planning and management.

Another distinctive kind of mapping methodology is interactive mapping, when the choice and recording of information on a map is not managed by professionals, experts, or decision makers but, rather, by community members or other nonprofessionals. Examples of interactive mapping include 'mental mapping,' done as a kind of survey; community-generated maps (such as the 'parish map' process pioneered by the English group Common Ground, which stimulates communities to represent the identity of their place in innovative ways); and the informal rocks-and-dirt 'maps' included in some PRA models (see Greeves 1997) (see also the 1998 Getty Institute Project "Mapping Local Knowledge," available at www.getty.edu/research/programs/public/lllk/).

Primary (archival) research and writing historical narratives

The basic humanistic methodology of research, interpretation, and writing a narrative account remains one of the most effective to construct and express knowledge about values. Constructing a story, based on primary and other research, is a particular way of documenting and describing social phenomena. Narratives deal with causation in a more circumspect way than, for instance, do statistical methods. Often the contexts and settings of a phenomenon are bundled into stories alongside human actors and institutions. Understanding is gained by the unfolding of a story through characters and influences, not, by contrast, through abstracting relationships among isolated variables.

In the last few decades, the work of social historians has gained more and more influence in the heritage field. Historians' work speaks most directly to the associational (often termed historical) values that are a major motivation behind conservation.

Secondary literature research

Secondary literature research perhaps goes without saying, but it should not be overlooked as an expedient, strategic methodology for quickly generating information relevant to a project. It has become especially time effective, given the widening availability of online bibliographic and information-search resources.

Descriptive statistics

This simplest of quantitative methods is widely used by the whole range of qualitative disciplines, signaling the virtual impossibility of really separating qualitative and quantitative epistemologies. One application of the simplest kind of descriptive statistics is content analysis (of, say, media coverage or interviews: how many times was aesthetic value mentioned versus economic value?). More commonly, demographic analysis is used to characterize a population in shorthand. Tabular data are gathered and sometimes mapped or presented graphically, giving an effective, though often quite cursory, account of the current state of a population.

Tools suited to economic values

The various tools devised by economists to assess the values of cultural heritage are adapted from those devised earlier to measure the value of environmental resources as part of environmental conservation decisions. Earlier work by the Getty Conservation Institute and the growing cadre of cultural economists has summarized and evaluated these contributions to heritage valuation. Mourato and Mazzanti (2002) provide an excellent summary of this past and present work in the cultural economics of heritage, and their own work is clearly on the cutting edge of economic thinking about heritage values (see also Mason 1999; Hutter and Rizzo 1997). In light of Mourato and Mazzanti's review (ibid.) a very brief summary of economic tools for value assessment will do.

Revealed-preference methods

Revealed-preference methods draw and analyze data from existing markets for heritage-related goods and services.

Economic impact studies have become very popular because of the use of a quite simple method, and they often suggest clearly that investment in a heritage project will yield tangible economic gains. By measuring economic investments and employment gains directly related to conservation activity, and multiplying this on the theory that these direct investments yield secondary gains as they ripple throughout the economy, impact studies identify exact returns on investment (which is to say, increases in the value of the heritage). Impact studies may be useful in identifying some use values and some externalities of heritage investments, but they are often suspect because of double counting and because they fail to account for the opportunity costs of heritage investment.

Hedonic pricing methods can measure nonuse heritage values only as they are reflected in related market transactions. They measure the increments in financial value gained, for instance, from the proximity of a real estate parcel to a particular heritage resource.

Travel-cost methods measure heritage values through the proxy of travel expenditures related to the use/consumption of heritage sites or objects. By only recording values when they are translated into individual decisions to travel, these methods give highly partial accounts of heritage values.

Stated-preference methods

Stated-preference methods rely on the creation of hypothetical markets in which survey respondents are asked to make hypothetical choices, which are then analyzed as value judgments.

Contingent valuation methods measure total value ascribed to a heritage site by an individual (expressed as willingness to pay for it) but do not break down the value, leaving it undifferentiated. The method draws information from individual appraisals and decisions, in hypothetical markets, and does not see the collective picture at all, except by aggregation and inference. This method is beginning to be used more extensively for heritage projects, because it yields the sought-after conversion of qualitative values into quantified prices. (In the case of heritage, the corresponding concept of willingness to accept compensation for loss of a resource can also be relevant.) It should be noted that the insights and conclusions drawn from contingent valuation studies of heritage resources have been limited to instances where they are carried out under very stringent conditions.

Choice modeling is a potentially very interesting method for heritage in that it does break down the specific attributes of the overall value expressed by study participants.

Therefore, it could be used to measure the values (the utility to individuals) associated with the different characteristics of a heritage site, according, for instance, to the typology outlined above. Though people do respond well to these types of scenarios and comparisons, the method presumes very well-informed participants, and it will not capture well the intangible, difficult-to-price values (such as spiritual values).

Economic methods in general have gained a great deal of credibility by (1) presenting data in a seemingly objective form (prices), and (2) appealing quite directly to the business-thinking mentality of global decision makers and, increasingly, of society at large. Economic methods are used more widely and for new purposes, and they are gaining credibility. But there remains a great danger in relying on quantitative economic methods alone – this is a view strongly endorsed by some economists. The neoclassical economic model is so well refined, so tightly theorized to block out uncertainties, that it sets a tone in which other values seem a priori excluded (or devalued). This situation is problematic in several respects, among them that people cannot talk about certain kinds of value in monetary terms; cognitively, quantitative language doesn't work very well, for instance, to express spiritual values. In other situations, the ability to express a commonly held qualitative value in quantitative terms has been critical to getting proconservation decisions made, so the urge to quantify remains very strong.

All the methods described in this section need professional economists to direct them; there are many technical problems to be dealt with, and the methods can easily be abused if applied in an uninformed manner. But the stated-preference methods, which include extensive survey processes, open up a lot of common ground (and potential collaboration) with the approaches used by anthropologists and other social researchers. The ways that economists create and adjust survey instruments are basically identical to the ways that anthropologists do it (an iterative process of piloting, refining, rolling out).

Integrating assessments and frameworks for decision making

Once the broad array of values linked to a site are assessed, how does one go forward? How does one connect these assessments with the difficult, politicized work of prioritization and decision making? As with most issues regarding planning processes, there is no prescription, but this section outlines a series of steps – necessarily conceptual, until they are developed in relation to particular projects – for building on the value assessments to tackle decision-making tasks. These steps must realistically involve some integration and even prioritization of the values assessed. Suggesting how this can be done – without prescribing it – is the goal of this section.

The second part of this section describes (in broad terms) how sustainability principles could be adapted to provide some frameworks for making and evaluating management planning decisions both within projects and across multiple sites.

The steps are described conceptually, not as a rote set of tasks and not to the level of detail that would perforce arise from actually adapting and executing them. While specifying the steps in great detail would need to be done in the case of a specific site, project and team, that process is beyond the scope of this chapter.

Integrating value assessments

Four steps are suggested for integrating value assessments and implementing them as part of the planning process: creating statements of significance, matching values to physical resources and site characteristics, analyzing threats and opportunities, and making policies and taking actions. The steps, which are discussed below, are not to be undertaken in a linear fashion – indeed, some of them can and should be done in parallel (Figures 7.1 and 7.2).

Creating statements of significance

Statements of significance flow directly out of the value assessments. Their function is synthesizing the reasons behind all the actions one might propose for the site – conservation, development, interpretation, and so on – and providing clear positions that would form the basis of later decisions and evaluation. Generating a statement of significance is standard practice in conservation planning in, for instance, the United States. The professional team looks at all the varied values and assessments, culls and winnows from these the dimensions of significance and meaning, and articulates significance in terms that will be understandable to all stakeholders (and indeed, they should be understandable to the general public, to decision makers, investors, and so on).

The statements proposed here depart from the convention by emphasizing the plural, and perhaps even contradictory, nature of a site's significance. The statements do not necessarily have to be boiled down to one or two points, nor do they need to reflect a single consensus or universal view about the site. In fact, one would expect conflicting statements of significance to be articulated for a site (for instance, one set of stakeholders may see significance overwhelmingly in terms of profit, while other stakeholders' significance would exclude the possibility of profit-making activity). Thus, the plural *statements* is emphasized, and it signals the intent of this step to identify the main themes of significance arising from the value assessments, as interpreted from the perspectives of the various stakeholder groups involved.

The creation of statements involves two distinct parts. First is the cataloguing and articulating of all aspects of site significance. In this sense the statements are unabashedly plural. These would be framed by the overall set of values and stakeholders identified earlier in the process. It is important to stay away from statements that privilege some values over others – that is, if one decides early on that value A is less important than values B and C, the tendency in case of conflict would be to sacrifice A for the sake of B and C; if the values are not ranked, more efforts are likely to be made to find policies that respect them all. Second, one can begin to introduce some sense of priorities by assessing and stating the uniqueness or importance of the site's values vis-à-vis other sites in the nation/region/world (whatever the decision-making domain is).

This recognition and articulation of the relative importance to the values – without ranking categorically their importance for the site – is borrowed from Pearson and Sullivan (1995) and from Kerr (2000). They suggest at this point an assessment of the degree or level of significance of each value, as seen against the universe of site and values in the decision-making domain. This is not where one would say that the historical value of the site is more important than its recreational value. Rather, what is suggested is an evaluation of the degree of importance of a particular value (unique, important, typical, etc.) of a site when compared with that value in related sites.

Matching values to physical resources and site characteristics

Management, plans, and decisions must integrate articulations of value and the physical properties and resources of the site. The integration has traditionally been part of the analysis contributed tacitly by conservation professionals, but the correspondences between values and the physical attributes of heritage need to be made explicit. Without consciously evaluating the connections between specific physical aspects of heritage and specific values, as well as the appropriateness of the tools chosen to the values present, it will be difficult to predict or monitor how values are affected by material interventions or management decisions.

Therefore, some sort of mapping of the values invested in specific site elements and characteristics is an important reference both for informing decisions and for evaluating their results. In the Getty Conservation Institute's model planning process (Figure 7.1), this matching occurs at the end of the assessment phase, in which assessment of physical conditions is linked with the assessment of significance. How this is achieved practically and in detail can be worked out in any number of ways, in light of a specific planning project. At the least, all types of value identified in the values assessments should be 'mapped' onto the site; all the main physical elements of the site could be linked with specific types of value.

The benefits of this step would be twofold: first, simply, a clear delineation of how each of the values identified for the site is expressed, embodied, or otherwise represented in the materials of the site (ranging in scale from artifacts to buildings to landscapes); second, key 'complexes' of (material) resources and (immaterial) values could be identified. By identifying these complexes, the planning/management team is deliberately associating the values held with regard to the site to the actual physical resources making up the site. For instance, the key historical value complex for a historic building might associate the site's most important historical events, narratives, and concepts with the arrangements of buildings on the site or with the decoration of particular rooms or with landscape elements such as walls or hedgerows. The most important complexes will likely be the focus of conservation and management interventions.

Analyzing threats and opportunities

Against the background of the statements of significance and their association with particular material aspects of the site, the analysis should turn to the potential threats to the identified complexes of material and significance. Threats can be quite varied and could be categorized, for instance, according to the following categories: physical threats stemming from environmental factors, from vandalism or violence, from neglect or poor management, or from economically driven redevelopment; and social, cultural, or political forces that produce changes in meaning and valuing. Conservation planners should not be looking only for threats, however. The opportunities encountered at sites should also be brought into this analysis, as decisions to take advantage of opportunities (whether economic, political, interpretive, logistical) are very likely to have an impact on the value-material complexes – sometimes positive, sometimes negative.

The professional team, by this juncture, should be able to identify the threats. The threats, of course, can only be defined against the context of the conservation/management goals of the stakeholder groups governing/influencing the site. One stakeholder's threat may be another's opportunity.

Making policies and taking actions

At this point, the planning process has moved on to 'response' (Figure 7.1). Here the actions needed involve not so much integrating values but, rather, acting upon them. The specific steps by which these actions are worked out and implemented will vary widely from site to site, depending more than anything on institutional setup, organizational cultures, and other issues raised in the management context assessment.

In light of the plural, varied, often conflicting nature of heritage values and in light of the political processes inescapably shaping and usually governing decisions about conservation, are there any generalizations that can be made about conservation decision making? It is argued here that there are some robust principles useful for framing decision making in any number of circumstances. These suggestions take up the next and final section.

Assessing management context

Well before the integration steps outlined in this section, an assessment of the management context needs to be undertaken. This is best undertaken at least as early as the physical conditions and values assessments are begun, and perhaps earlier (Figure 7.1).

Management context refers to a number of factors that affect the capacity of people and organizations to decide, direct, and implement any plans that are formulated. This includes pragmatic concerns such as financing, institutional architectures, legal and regulatory frameworks, and available personnel, as well as political factors such as the patterns of power and influence known to shape the interactions and capacities of the various stakeholders in the site. The issues arising in the management context – especially those of power relationships – are crucial to the ultimate success of management planning and must be dealt with as systematically and as openly as possible.

The management context assessment through which these factors are documented and analyzed has not been studied in detail, though some version of it is part of most management planning processes. The review – and possibly the adaptation – of some of the methods for management assessment used in the fields of urban planning and business management can provide a starting point for the conservation field.

Frameworks for decision making

A number of decision-making processes and protocols are available and widely used in other fields, but none of them are a priori appropriate to heritage conservation or robust across all situations. Therefore, no specific decision-making tools are advocated here. However, this chapter does suggest frameworks for decision making, establishing a series of guides useful for assembling information to fuel decision making and frameworks for evaluating decisions afterwards.

While there are no prescriptions or recipes for heritage conservation decision making, guidance for planning/management decisions (ranking, prioritizing) can be drawn from other fields – in particular, environmental conservation. Research, application, and evaluation of decision making have been the subject of considerable work in the environmental sphere, and much of this is quite relevant to heritage conservation decisions. The concept of sustainability, in particular, has been an effective and influential organizing principle in environmental decision making. Although full sustainability remains an ideal, sustainability principles have, in practice, been merged with extensive experiences in cultivating public participation. The result is a growing body of practical lessons drawn from the use of sustainability principles.

The use of sustainability principles for guiding such complex decisions is the state of the art in the environmental conservation field. There are many parallels between heritage planning/management decisions and environmental decisions: comparable complexities in the systems and processes being managed, diversity and incommensurability of values attributed to the resources being conserved, and political difficulties and power differences among stakeholders, to name a few.

A recent publication by several scholars and practitioners in the environmental field provides a good source of intelligence for addressing the decision-making challenges set forth in this chapter (Sexton *et al.* 1999). Having identified critical issues and cases in environmental decision making, Sexton and colleagues evaluated state-of-the-art decision-making tools. The conclusion reached was that there are no hard-and-fast rules or procedures for making effective decisions. The goal of fostering integrated decision making requires a lot of experimentation and improvisation. The authors offered the following guidelines, derived from twenty or so years of experience with decision-making strategies in the environmental conservation field (Sexton *et al.* 1999: 447–58):

- build mutual trust and understanding;
- adopt sustainability as a unifying principle;
- take shared responsibility;
- institutionalize public participation;
- continually refine and use decision-making tools;
- collect and analyze important information (gather data for evaluation);
- use incentives to encourage innovation.

For the most part, the advice represented in these points is not specific to environmental issues and resources and is readily applicable to any other field. In order to retool and reorient this research for the heritage conservation field, though, the notion of sustainability needs to be rethought in terms applicable to heritage. The following section considers the second of these guidelines and discusses how sustainability principles for heritage conservation might be approached. (See also Clark, this volume.)

Sustainability principles for heritage conservation

Principles of sustainable development have proved quite useful, influential, and robust, not only in environmental conservation and the fostering of ecological sensitivity in the development field but also, increasingly, in the urban development field. Sustainability has already been proposed as an ideal and as a guide to policy in the heritage field (English Heritage 1997; US/ICOMOS 2000). David Throsby has proposed a set of sustainability principles that could form the basis of a useful set of guidelines and norms for decision making in the conservation-planning model (Throsby 2001; 2002). The principles are built on the notion of sustainability developed in the fields of ecological conservation and economic development and adapted in light of Throsby's notion of cultural capital (heritage resources) as analogous to natural capital.

The notion of sustainability accords with the principles underlying values-based conservation planning in that it adopts a holistic view of resources (in this case, cultural resources) and their contexts and aligns with the goal of taking account of the widest range of heritage values. It deals directly with the problem of making decisions in the present but for the very long term – essential for acknowledging the role of heritage as an inheritance to be stewarded and passed on to future generations. Sustainability has also proven to be politically resonant (even after twenty or so years) and practically useful because the principles are a flexible frame of reference rather than a fixed benchmark or rigid method (and, not surprisingly, sustainability has been criticized for the same reason by those who wish for inflexible environmental standards).

Ideally, the sustainability principles will influence the planning model in several ways, at several stages. First, they constitute an ideal, which could shape the setting of project goals, the composition of the stakeholder group, the analysis of significance and management contexts, and the evaluation of project outcomes. The principles will have most direct impact, however, at the policy-setting stage: the principles would be designed to serve as tests, or criteria, against which the policies (and thus the actions that follow from them) can be judged. Individually and as a group it can be asked, do not Do these policies meet the tests of sustainability? Each decision can be evaluated (informally, or with formal indicators) against each of the principles. The same tests can be applied to the actions as they are being formulated. In this way, the sustainability principles play the role of guidelines.

The fact that sustainability principles are a flexible, negotiable set of standards could be seen as a weakness. In the environmental field, a distinction is made between 'strong' versus 'weak' sustainability in the environmental sphere. Strong sustainability insists on immediate and total conformance to sustainability principles and is not negotiable – so it is generally seen as infeasible (and therefore unsustainable!). Weak sustainability allows change, is flexible, and doesn't attempt to freeze things in place. These two versions of sustainability parallel the notion of distinguishing 'sacred' versus 'tradable' heritage and the a priori privileging of cultural values over economic values by preservationists (or vice versa by investors or policy makers). Whereas it is easy to insist on the total protection of things deemed sacred, in light of practical considerations, this is not possible and becomes mere rhetoric. A more pragmatic strategy recognizes the need for trade-offs and recognizes that some heritage is in fact tradable or convertible to other forms of capital.

Sustainability principles also recognize the moral aspect of sustainability, through principles regarding intergenerational and intragenerational equity, which overarch and strengthen the scientific, economic, and pragmatic arguments for sustainability. The notion of equity, which requires moral vision and ethical reflection, should be closely allied with our collective sense of professional ethics and purpose. These ideas could, indeed, provide the conservation field with something of an ethical–moral compass as it navigates through a period of great change.

So as we see, sustainability holds great potential as a framing concept for the task of integrating heritage values, yet the concept needs to be developed further and applied to specific projects. As in the environmental and development applications of sustainability, sustainability indicators could be created to bring rigor and clarity to the application of sustainability principles (Hart 1999; Bell and Morse 1999).

Additional work is needed to make the argument for using these sustainability principles and to describe how they can be used in real situations. For instance, how are the various sustainability criteria/tests weighted? Are they all equally important in a particular project? Also, what exactly is being sustained – cultural resources themselves (buildings, artifacts, sites) or cultural memory and meaning? Answers to these questions can help connect the sustainability principles with the issues of heritage values and valuing.

Finally, decisions need to be continually evaluated and checked against the original aims set out at the beginning of the process. This continuous revisiting of the effectiveness of decisions is a key ingredient to the successful implementation of planning measures and to the realization of effective management for heritage conservation.

References

Bell, S., and S. Morse. 1999. *Sustainability Indicators: Measuring the Immeasurable*. London: Earthscan Publications.

Denzin, N., and Y. Lincoln, eds. 1994. *Handbook of Qualitative Research*. Thousand Oaks, Calif., and London: Sage Publications.

English Heritage. 1997. *Sustaining the Historic Environment: New Perspectives on the Future*. English Heritage Discussion Document. London: English Heritage.

Frankfort-Nachmias, C., and D. Nachmias. 1996. *Research Methods in the Social Sciences*. Fifth ed. New York: St. Martin's.

Freudenburg, W. 1999. Tools for understanding the socioeconomic and political settings for environmental decision making. In Dale, V. and English, M. (eds), *Tools to Aid Environmental Decision Making*. New York: Springer.

Frey, B. 1997. The evaluation of cultural heritage: Some critical issues. In Hutter, M. and Rizzo, I. (eds), *Economic Perspectives on Cultural Heritage*, London: Macmillan.

Greeves, T. 1987. *Parish Maps: Celebrating and Looking after Your Place*. London: Common Ground.

Hart, M. 1999. *Guide to Sustainable Community Indicators*. North Andover, Mass.: Sustainable Measures.

Holtorf C. 2005. *From Stonehenge to Las Vegas: Archaeology as Popular Culture*. Walnut Creek: AltaMira Press.

Hutter, M., and I. Rizzo, eds. 1997. *Economic Perspectives on Cultural Heritage*. London: Macmillan.

Kellert, S. 1996. *The Value of Life: Biological Diversity and Human Society*. Washington, D.C.: Island Press.

Kerr, A. 1999. Public participation in cultural resource management: A Canadian perspective. Draft manuscript, March 31.

Kerr, J. 2000. *Conservation Plan: A Guide to the Preparation of Conservation Plans for Places of European Cultural Significance*. Fifth ed. Sydney: National Trust of Australia (NSW).

Lipe, W. 1984. Value and meaning in cultural resources. In Cleere, H. (ed), *Approaches to the Archaeological Heritage*, 1–11. New York: Cambridge University Press.

Low, S. 1981. Social science methods in landscape architecture design. *Landscape Planning* 8:137–48.

Low, S. 2002. Assessment of Cultural Values in Heritage Conservation. In de la Torre, M. (ed), *Assessing the Values of Cultural Heritage*, 31–49. Research Report. Los Angeles: The Getty Conservation Institute.

McHarg, I. [1967] 1992. *Design with Nature*. Reprint, New York: John Wiley & Sons.

Marquis-Kyle, P., and M. Walker. 1992. *The Illustrated Burra Charter*. Sydney: Australia ICOMOS/Australian Heritage Commission.

Mason, R., ed. 1999. *Economics and Heritage Conservation*. Los Angeles: Getty Conservation Institute.

Mourato, S. and Mazzanti, M. 2002. Economic valuation of cultural heritage: evidence and prospects. In de la Torre, M. (ed), *Assessing the Values of Cultural Heritage*, 51–76. Research Report. Los Angeles: The Getty Conservation Institute.

Pearson, M., and S. Sullivan. 1995. *Looking after Heritage Places: The Basics of Heritage Planning for Managers, Landowners, and Administrators*. Carlton, Victoria: Melbourne University Press.

Reigl, A. [1902] 1982. The modern cult of monuments: Its character and its origins. Reprint, trans. D. Ghirardo and K. Forster. *Oppositions* 25:21–51.

Rolston, H., III. 1988. *Environmental Ethics: Duties to and Values in the Natural World*. Philadelphia: Temple University Press.

Sanoff, H. 2000. *Community Participation Methods in Design and Planning*. New York: John Wiley & Sons.

Satterfield, T. 2002. Numbness and sensitivity in the elicitation of environmental values. In de la Torre, M. (ed), *Assessing the Values of Cultural Heritage*, 77–99. Research Report. Los Angeles: The Getty Conservation Institute.

Serageldin, I., and A. D. Steer. 1994. *Valuing the Environment: Proceedings of the First Annual International Conference on Environmentally Sustainable Development Held at the World Bank*. Washington, D.C.: World Bank.

Sexton, K., et al., eds. 1999. *Better Environmental Decisions: Strategies for Governments, Businesses, and Communities*. Washington, D.C.: Island Press.

Tainter, J., and J. Lucas. 1983. Epistemology of the significance concept. *American Antiquity* 48(4):707–19.

Throsby, D. 2001. *Economics and Culture*. Cambridge: Cambridge University Press.

Throsby, D. 2002. Cultural capital and sustainability concepts in the economics of cultural heritage. In de la Torre, M. (ed), *Assessing the Values of Cultural Heritage*, 77–99. Research Report. Los Angeles: The Getty Conservation Institute.

Tomlan, M., ed. 1998. *Preservation of What, for Whom?: A Critical Look at Historical Significance*. Ithaca, N.Y.: National Council for Preservation Education.

Chapter 8

Is the Past a Non-renewable Resource?

Cornelius J. Holtorf

Archaeological heritage management of our times is normally based on four key tenets:

1   Archaeological sites and objects are authentic, in other words, of true antiquity, and
    have a distinctive aura which fakes and copies do not have. Safeguarding this authen-
    ticity and the aura of the original is the rationale of many museum collections and
    justification for preserving ancient sites in the landscape. In a famous article 'The
    work of art in the age of mechanical reproduction', Walter Benjamin (1992) has
    given the notion of aura some philosophical grounding.
2   Archaeological sites and objects are irreplaceable and non-renewable, because we cannot
    go back into the past and remake them. Timothy Darvill argued accordingly that:

> the archaeological resource is finite in the sense that only so many examples of
> any defined class of monument were ever created.... The archaeological
> resource is non-renewable in that . . . once a monument or site is lost it cannot
> be recreated . . . Reconstructed archaeological remains lack authenticity.
>
> (Darvill 1993: 6)

3   In the modern Western world, archaeological sites and objects are in danger of
    being destroyed by forces such as changes in ground-water levels, deep ploughing,
    wars, industrial and housing development and the antiquities trade. It has become a
    cliché to lament the loss of ancient sites and objects in the modern Western world in
    much the same way as we do the continuous reduction of the tropical rain forests
    and the gradual decline of remaining oil reserves (cf. Lomborg 2001). David Lowen-
    thal reckoned (1985: 396) that 'this generation has . . . destroyed more of prehistory
    than was previously known to exist.' As a consequence, rescue archaeology and the
    preservation of ancient sites have become the order of the day.
4   Professional archaeologists save archaeological sites and objects from further
    destruction on behalf of future generations who are expected to be grateful that they
    too can appreciate these sites and objects, and thus the past. The UNESCO World
    Heritage Centre, for example, writes about its task:

With 754 cultural and natural sites already protected worldwide, the World Heritage Centre is working to make sure that future generations can inherit the treasures of the past. And yet, most sites face a variety of threats, particularly in today's environment. The preservation of this common heritage concerns us all.
(http://www.unesco.org/whc/nwhc/pages/sites/s_worldx.htm
4 October 2004)

Philosophies and ethics of resource conservation and preservationism name economic, academic, aesthetic and spiritual reasons for conserving archaeological resources. Other reasons to preserve the past for the future are based on ideological, political, educational and psychological considerations. All these reasonings have been often rehearsed in the theoretical literature on archaeological heritage management (Lipe 1984; Cleere 1989; Greeves 1989; Darvill 1993; Carman 1996; Carlie and Kretz 1998) and heritage management in general (Lowenthal 1985; Siegel 1985; Samuel 1994).

These four tenets derived from specific contexts in Western European cultural history (Jokilehto 1995), but have now been adopted by global organizations such as UNESCO and ICOMOS as well as by states around the world as a general basis for archaeological heritage management (such as Charter 1990). In this chapter I will challenge the paradigm outlined above, and suggest that archaeological heritage management needs a different approach. This is done very much in a spirit of intellectual debate, and I hope others will take up and further discuss some of the issues raised. Let me discuss the four tenets one by one.

Archaeological sites and objects are authentic, that is, of true antiquity, and have a distinctive aura which fakes and copies do not have

The actual physical age of an archaeological site or object can in many cases only be determined by specialists; even they will often still need the help of complicated apparatus to get a reliable date. Yet it can empirically be shown that visitors to archaeological sites or museums experience authenticity and aura in front of ancient originals to exactly the same extent as they do in front of fakes or copies – as long as they do not *believe them to be* fakes or copies. In virtually all circumstances, age, authenticity and aura are not essences of sites or objects but human constructs in particular contexts, dependent on specific meanings and particular experiences of archaeological sites and objects (see Larsen 1995; Holtorf and Schadla-Hall 1999; Holtorf 2005a, ch. 7). There is nothing special about an original ancient artefact: it is the assumption of antiquity that matters, not its veracity (Lowenthal 1985: 242; Tunbridge and Ashworth 1996: 8–9).

> To be credible historical witnesses, antiquities must to some extent conform with modern stereotypes. . . . Moreover, the very process of conforming to current expectations tempts renovaters to feel that the past they reconstruct is not only faithful, but *more* faithful than what once existed, just as they themselves are more knowledgeable about times past than those who lived in it.
> Nashville's reinforced-concrete Parthenon of the 1920s is a case in point. Like many replicas, it is more complete than the original . . . So 'authentic' is their replica, Tennesseeans brag, that the Greeks would have to study the correct details in Nashville in order to rebuild the original.
> (Lowenthal 1985: 291, 354)

Rather than reflecting its 'material' value and worth, the experienced aura of an object we possess, or at least view, in fact authenticates our taste and thus *our own* worth (Lowenthal 1989: 846). Perhaps this can explain why public interest in copies or reconstructions is not necessarily reduced when they are acknowledged or revealed as such (Lowenthal 1985:

290–91; 355–56). The rapidly expanding British High Street chain of shops *Past Times* advertises in its catalogue what it calls 'authentic replicas', while Greek tourist shops praise their 'original copies' (Holtorf 2005a, 126). A German producer of archaeological replicas, who specializes in metal jewellery, has created a catalogue which resembles in both content and layout a museum catalogue. The products advertised are praised as 'authentic' in two seemingly contradictory ways: they are not only strictly based on 'archaeological finds of particular quality' but at the same time contain irregularities and mistakes originating from the handicraft replicating process in which the new originals are being manufactured (Neidhardt 1998).

I will now discuss the third tenet, and return to my second point later on.

In the modern Western world, archaeological sites and objects are in danger of being destroyed by forces such as changes in ground-water levels, deep ploughing, wars, industrial and housing development and the antiquities trade

This statement is highly misleading. As a matter of fact, no society has surrounded itself with as many archaeological sites and objects as modern society in the Western world. Sinking ground-water levels, deep ploughing, the effects of wars, industrial and housing developments, and the activities of antiquity dealers, among other factors, tend to produce and reveal ever more 'new' ancient sites and objects which are then being preserved. If it were not for such admittedly brutal forces many sites and artefacts would forever remain in the ground and we would never know about them – in effect, they would not exist for us: discovery is invention (Shanks and Hodder 1995: 11). Typical for our Western world is thus not the loss of archaeological sites and objects but their accumulation, for example in museums, shops and the landscape. In 1995, England alone had more than 657 000 registered archaeological sites – this number having increased by 117 per cent since 1983 – and its archaeological sites and monuments records were expected to contain over 1 million entries by the end of the millennium. Between 1983 and 1995 on average 'nearly 100 entries' were daily added to the records, while only one recorded site per day has been lost since 1945 (Darvill and Fulton 1998: 4–7).

The trend is therefore not that we will one day have no archaeological sites and finds left, but that in the future more and more of our lifeworld will be recorded as some sort of historical object worthy of preservation. But what do we need all these sites for (Borst 1993; Wienberg 1999)? Some observers already question why anyone should value ancient sites and objects at all (Treanor 1997). Even archaeologists will agree that the rapidly growing numbers of archaeological sites and objects create considerable challenges for responsible heritage management and finds administration, making it difficult to keep up with the overall task of 'writing history' (Tilley 1989 and this volume). As Roger Thomas put it in relation to the huge accumulation of data from extensive rescue work, 'we are, in a sense, the victims of our own success' (Thomas 1991: 828; cf. Merriman and Swain 1999; Robbins 2001). If there is any problem concerning the preservation of archaeological sites and objects in the modern Western world, it could therefore be that we are overwhelmed by the sheer number of them. Other regions of the world should learn from this and reject Western rationales that might lead nowhere (Byrne 1991).

Professional archaeologists save archaeological sites and objects from further destruction on behalf of future generations who are expected to be grateful that they too can appreciate these sites and objects and thus the past

If this is indeed one of the aims of professional archaeology it is fundamentally flawed. The significance of original archaeological sites for future generations' understanding of the

past may be lower than is often assumed. Cultural appreciation of the past is not now, and
never has been, to any large extent dependent on original ancient sites and objects:

> The resource endowment sets, at most, a determining limit, on which final
> heritage products may be developed, and frequently not even that, as conser-
> vation moves along the spectrum . . . from preservation of what remains, to
> maintenance, replacement, enhancement and fascimile construction of what
> might, could or should have been.
>
> (Tunbridge and Ashworth 1996: 7–8)

If anything, the reverse is true: ancient sites and objects are not the origin but the product of
cultural appreciation of the past. The past can be seen as a cultural construct which is experienced at certain places and on certain occasions. This construct does not necessarily rely on
archaeological sites and objects. Their significance for our understanding of the past depends
largely on wider socio-cultural contexts within which they are given value and meaning
(Leone and Potter 1992; Shanks and Hodder 1995). John Carman (1996: 115) even argued
that 'archaeological material is not protected because it is valued, but rather it is valued
because it is protected'. This view appears to imply that if archaeological material had not
been protected and preserved, the past could have been created using other means. Among
the most powerful 'alternative' sites and objects evoking the past in our present are:

- Artificial ruins and Greek temples in landscape parks from the eighteenth and nine-
  teenth centuries
- Rebred, formerly extinct animal species such as Przewalski's horse
- Buildings and town districts reconstructed in their entirety, such as Warsaw's town
  centre which was rebuilt after the Second World War
- Carefully restored or reconstructed heritage attractions
- Historical walks, plays and re-enactments (in life or on film) in the spirit of 'living
  history'
- Facsimile reprints of ancient texts and replicas of artefacts such as the crafts offered
  in Mediterranean tourist shops (Figure 8.1)
- Souvenirs, retrochic and other items of popular culture which are appreciated for

Figure 8.1   Original replicas in a craft shop on Crete, Greece.

Figure 8.2   Tal der Könige (Valley of the Kings) at Hamburg's biannual funfair Dom, Germany.

their connection with the past: for example, the ride 'Valley of the Kings' at a funfair in Hamburg (Figure 8.2)

- Models and dioramas as part of exhibitions, either in miniature or to a scale of 1:1 suggesting actual time-travel
- Neo-Gothic, neoclassical and certain elements of contemporary architecture
- Places where traditions are enacted, such as the annual initiation ceremony of the Welsh *Gorsedd of Bards* taking place in a modern stone circle.

In none of these cases is an explicit claim about true antiquity made, but they are all fully satisfactory in supplying people with 'authentic' experiences of the past and in satisfying most of our educational, economic, aesthetic and spiritual needs (Lowenthal 1985; Samuel 1994; Tunbridge and Ashworth 1996). As David Lowenthal noted (1985: 240), the felt past is, more than anything else, 'a function of atmosphere as well as locale'. Current fashions in retrochic, revivalism, resurrectionism, and re-enactments give substance to Jean Baudrillard's supposition (1988) that simulacra – copies for which there are no originals – can take the place of originals with no loss. It is probably fair to predict that when future generations remember the past, they too will not have to be terribly worried about the number of original archaeological sites and objects at their disposal; the past is made elsewhere. At any rate, it is quite impossible to know, and perhaps a peculiar kind of arrogance to assume that future generations will be grateful to us for what we preserve for their benefit (Moore 1997: 31).

As far as future archaeologists are concerned it can be argued that, given the expected methodological advances, it will matter less and less if actual sites and objects from the past have been preserved or not, and it may even stimulate research and interpretation if the amount of data available are limited rather than overwhelming. Moreover, large quantities of preserved archaeological sites are perhaps not as essential for scientific research as is often stated. This is *not* because I trust that we can record them 'in full' at the time of their destruction, or because a small sample of sites would in any case be representative. Rather, I am inclined to think that the success of archaeology is determined by how satisfactory the norms of its craft, or discourse, are exercised in practice and not by some objective measure of how close we have come to an understanding of the 'real' past (Shanks and McGuire 1996). In other words, archaeologists will be happy to do their field-work and analyse site and monument records with ever-new questions and methods to write smart academic books and papers, and to teach their students, no matter how many archaeological sites are left at their disposal.

Having said all this, I now turn to the second tenet in my list.

Archaeological sites and objects are irreplaceable and non-renewable, because we cannot go back into the past and remake them

I have already argued that a meaningful understanding of the past and an appreciation of archaeological sites and objects as authentic has never required a very close link with sites and objects that are actually very old. Virtually every generation has constructed its own range of ancient sites and objects, which were fully sufficient to evoke the past for them. I use the words of George Herbert Mead (1929: 240) to remind you of the truism that 'every generation rewrites its history – and its history is the only history it has of the world'. Over the centuries, many novel pasts have replaced others which had become redundant. With every new past, new archaeological and historical sites and objects are created or become significant in relation to this past (Samuel 1994). A similar argument can be made about the various pasts, and sites and objects associated with them, created in different contexts and for different social groups, within any one time period. Tunbridge and Ashworth argued in respect to modern society that

> There is an almost infinite variety of possible heritages, each shaped for the requirements of specific consumer groups. . . . An obvious implication . . . is that the nature of the heritage product is determined . . . by the requirements of the consumer not the existence of the resources.
>
> (Tunbridge and Ashworth 1996: 8, 9)

Conservationists, druids, New Age followers, archaeo, astronomers, ley hunters, political parties and others each reinvent the past in terms and at sites which can be very different from those of academic archaeology. The past as well as specific ancient sites and objects have been replaced and are renewed all the time.

It is ironic that modernism with its fetishization of the new and its desire to shape ever new futures (Samuel 1994: 110) was also characterized by a particular obsession with maintaining a supposedly unchanging and 'objective' past: all was to be modernized, apart from the remains of the past which needed to be preserved as they were. Such modern views of the past and of archaeological sites and objects were the construct of a relatively small group of intellectuals and their supporters, living mostly within very specific contexts of the Western world during the nineteenth and twentieth centuries. But even within the framework of modern and contemporary archaeology, which puts so much emphasis on original sites and artefacts, it has virtually always been accepted that ancient sites could be legitimately destroyed, even where they were not threatened, as long as they could later be renewed from information recorded during the excavation and later published in reports. Ironically, in many cases it seems preferable for archaeologists to replace actual sites with records kept in archives and published catalogues (Lucas 2001: 159; Merriman and Swain 1999: 250). In effect, therefore, creating new parts is a part of modern archaeology too.

In conclusion, I argue that archaeological heritage management should be concerned with actively and responsibly renewing the past in our time. There is little sense in preserving too much of the material past that might not be needed in the future, and in spending not enough thought and resources on providing experiences of a past that is beneficial to our own present (Leone and Potter 1992; Moore 1997: 30–31). Archaeologists have the skills, experience and responsibility to assist our society in constructing one or more pasts that are appropriate for all of us. If this is what we aim for, archaeologists must focus first and foremost on the character of experiences of the past in a given society, and not concern themselves excessively with the side-issue of how some archaeological sites and objects will decay and disappear as time goes on. As Tunbridge and Ashworth argued, the production of heritage becomes a matter for deliberate goal-directed choice about what uses are made of the past for what contemporary purposes.

> The recycling, renewal and recuperation of resources, increasingly important in the management of natural resources, can be paralleled in historic resources where objects including buildings can be moved, restored and even replicated. . . . the deliberate manipulation of created heritage can be a valuable instrument [in an efficient management of historic resources].
> (Tunbridge and Ashworth 1996: 9, 13)

I envisage that the future work of archaeologists will continue to involve the preservation, conservation, restoration, reconstruction and replication of established ancient sites and objects. But it will also require creating open spaces for the needs of the present, including the construction of new pasts. A certain amount of destruction of archaeological resources is therefore not only unavoidable but indeed desirable (Holtorf 2005b). This rationale may well accommodate the interests of archaeologists on the one side and those of politicians, developers, farmers, and antiquities dealers on the other side better than it often seems possible at present. We should welcome an opportunity of making some of the established battles between archaeological preservationists and modern land- and artefact-users redundant.

I end with a very brief anecdote, told by Steven Kemper (1991: 136), which also answers the question in the title of my chapter. When visiting a relic mound with a friend, Kemper asked him whether the place was ancient. The friend replied: 'Yes, it was restored just last year.'

Acknowledgements

I would like to thank the World Archaeological Congress and the Department of Archaeology, University of Wales, Lampeter, where I was based at the time, for enabling me to attend the conference on Braè. I am extremely grateful to Kathryn Denning and Kristian Kristiansen for the elaborate and very critical comments they sent me after reading earlier versions of this chapter. Thanks are also due to Henry Cleere for drawing my attention to and sending me a copy of the proceedings of the Nara conference.

References

Baudrillard, J. 1988. Simulacra and simulations. In J. Baudrillard, *Selected Writings*, pp. 166–84. Cambridge: Polity.

Benjamin, W. 1992. The work of art in the age of mechanical reproduction. In W. Benjamin, *Illuminations*, pp. 211–44. London: Fontana.

Borst, O. 1993. Vom Nutzen und Nachteil der Denkmalpflege für das Leben. In W. Lipp (ed.) *Denkmal—Werte—Gesellschaft. Zur Pluralität des Denkmalbegriffs*, pp. 85–119. Frankfurt: Campus.

Byrne, D. 1991. Western hegemony in archaeological heritage management. *History and Anthropology* 5: 269–76.

Carlie, A. and Kretz, E. 1998. *Sätt att se på fornlämningar. En teoretisk och metodisk grund för värdebedömning inom kulturmiljövården*. University of Lund, Institute of Archaeology, Report Series no. 60.

Carman, J. 1996. *Valuing Ancient Things. Archaeology and Law*. London: Leicester University Press.

Charter 1990. The charter for the protection and management of the archaeological heritage. *Antiquity* 67: 402–5.

Cleere, H. 1989. Introduction: the rationale of archaeological heritage management. In H. Cleere (ed.) *Archaeological Heritage Management in the Modern World*, pp. 1–19. London: Unwin.

Darvill, T. 1993. 'Can nothing compare 2 U?' Resources and philosophies in archaeological resource management and beyond. In H. Swain (ed.) *Rescuing the Historic Environment. Archaeology, the Green Movement and Conservation Strategies for the British Landscape*, pp. 5–8. Hertford: RESCUE, The British Archaeological Trust.

Darvill, T. and Fulton, A. K. 1998. *The Monuments at Risk Survey of England 1995. Summary Report*. London: English Heritage.

Greeves, T. 1989. Archaeology and the Green movement: a case for perestroika. *Antiquity* 63: 659–66.

Holtorf, C. 2005a. *From Stonehenge to Las Vegas. Archaeology as Popular culture*. Walnut Creek: Altamira.

Holtorf, C. 2005b. Iconoclasm. The destruction to loss of heritage reconsidered. In G. Coulter-Smith (ed.) *Art in the Age of Terrorism*, 228–40. London: Holberton.

Holtorf, C. and Schadla-Hall, T. 1999. Age as artefact. On archaeological authenticity. *European Journal of Archaeology* 2: 229–47.

Jokilehto, J. 1995. Authenticity: a general framework for the concept. In K.E. Larsen (ed.) *Nara Conference on Authenticity*, pp. 17–34. Proceedings of the Conference in Nara, Japan, 1–6 November 1994. Trondheim: Tapir.

Kemper, S. 1991. *The Presence of the Past. Chronicles, Politics, and Culture in Sinhala Life*. Ithaca and London: Cornell University Press.

Larsen, K.E. 1995. *Nara Conference on Authenticity*. Proceedings of the Conference in Nara, Japan, 1–6 November 1994. Trondheim: Tapir.

Leone, M.P. and Potter Jr, P.B. 1992. Legitimation and the classification of archaeological sites. *American Antiquity* 57: 137–45.

Lipe, W.D. 1984. Value and meaning in cultural resources. In H. Cleere (ed.) *Approaches to the Archaeological Heritage. A Comparative Study of World Cultural Resource Management Systems*, pp. 1–11. Cambridge: Cambridge University Press.

Lomborg, B. 2001. *The Environmentalist Measuring the Real State of the World*. Cambridge: Cambridge University Press.

Lowenthal, D. 1985. *The Past is a Foreign Country*. Cambridge: Cambridge University Press.

Lowenthal, D. 1989. Art and authenticity. In I. Lavin (ed.) *World of Art: Themes of Unity in Diversity*, pp. 843–7. University Park, Pennsylvania: Pennsylvania University Press.

Lucas, G. 2001. *Critical Approaches to Fieldwork*. London: Routledge.

Mead, G.H. 1929. The nature of the past. In J. Coss (ed.) *Essays in Honor of John Dewey*, pp. 235–42. New York: Henry Holt.

Merriman, N. and Swain, H. 1999. Archaeological archives: serving the public interest? *European Journal of Archaeology* 2: 249–67.

Moore, K. 1997. *Museums and Popular Culture*. London: Cassell.

Neidhardt, M. 1998. Das Geschmeyde unserer Ahnen. Katalog Juli 1998. Nidderau: Replikate & Schmuckdesign Markus Neidhardt.

Robbins, C. 2001. No room for riches of the Indian Past. *The New York Times*, Nov. 24.

Samuel, R. 1994. *Theatres of Memory. Past and Present in Contemporary Culture*. London: Verso.

Shanks, M. and Hodder, I. 1995. Processual, postprocessual and interpretive archaeologies. In

I. Hodder, M. Shanks, A. Alexandri, V. Buchli, J. Carman, J. Last and G. Lucas (eds) *Interpreting Archaeology. Finding Meaning in the Past*, pp. 3–29. London: Routledge.

Shanks, M. and McGuire, R. 1996. The craft of archaeology. *American Antiquity* 61: 75–88.

Siegel, M. 1985. *Denkmalpflege als öffentliche Aufgabe: Eine Ökonomische, institutionelle und historische Untersuchung*. Göttingen: Vandenhoeck & Ruprecht.

Thomas, R. 1991. Drowning in data? – publication and rescue archaeology in the 1990s. *Antiquity* 65: 822–8.

Tilley, C. 1989. Excavation as theatre. *Antiquity* 63: 275–80.

Treanor, P. 1997. Archaeo-spatial Europe. URL: http://web.inter.nl.net/users/Paul.Treanor/archaeo-spatial.europe.html (visited 13 December 2000).

Tunbridge, J.E. and Ashworth, G.J. 1996. *Dissonant Heritage: the Management of the Past as a Resource in Conflict*. Chicester: Wiley.

Wienberg, J. 1999. The perishable past. On the advantage and disadvantage of archaeology for life. *Current Swedish Archaeology* 7: 183–202.

Chapter 9

Sites of Memory and Sites of Discord

Historic monuments as a medium for discussing conflict in Europe

Gabi Dolff-Bonekämper

The educational power of beauty

The congruence between beauty, goodness and truth is an old myth, which, in spite of all experiences to the contrary, has remained ingrained to this day. How we would love beautiful things to be good, good things to be true and true things to be beautiful! The union of these three values has been widely seen as the criterion of the perfect work of art, preferably by a master of supposed perfection, such as Raphael, Rembrandt or Poussin. This has led art theorists to posit that works of art – beauty – have an educational impact on people's minds and not just on their senses. Early twentieth-century art educationalists made this the basis for their cultural and social strategy of educating the people by improving their access to art. Workers' movements and trade unions adopted the same approach in their cultural policies; the educational impact of experiencing beauty thus became linked to the strategy of social advancement through knowledge of art.

The educational power of monuments/the heritage

Where heritage education is concerned, for 'beauty' read 'heritage'. However, identifying heritage items is a more complex process than identifying works of art in a museum, involving a dialectic between scientific discovery and social appreciation. Usually, moreover, heritage discourse remains anchored to an actual site, on terra firma as it were. It is concerned with a tangible contribution to identity, rather than seeking a more general, civilising effect. The objective of social advancement is replaced by social bonding of a group, of whatever size, around a common identity. However, as soon as heritage discourse is made to pursue more general aims – such as a European cultural policy – it becomes dominated by idealistic metaphors, as in the following example:

> Heritage education should underline the historical, artistic and ethical values that the cultural heritage embodies for the community, teaching respect for multiple identities, development of tolerance, and opposition to inequality

and exclusion. The quality and objectivity of the educational message depend on the values of those who are interpreting the cultural heritage.

(Final Declaration of the European Conference of Ministers responsible for the Cultural Heritage, Helsinki, 30–31 May 1996)

This amalgam of heritage-related, political and moral objectives appears plausible and persuasive, and I would not wish to dismiss the declaration as unrealistic. But at the very least, it leaves me wondering whether this rhetorical embellishment of our task misses the point somewhat. How can anyone claim that the cultural heritage only embodies positive historical, artistic and ethical values (truth, beauty and goodness), when heritage often comes down to us from periods of deep social and political conflict? Does historical conflict disappear when its physical legacy becomes heritage? Put another way, is the educational message of those who interpret the heritage always to be the same? Surely the message depends on the social and local, or national, environment? A monument may feature in different, even contradictory narratives on different sides of a border or a class divide for example.

Of course, it could always be argued that rhetorical embellishment is merely a stylistic trait of declarations issued by international organisations and that they should not be taken too literally. Well, they should be taken very literally indeed!

Letters on the Aesthetic Education of Man, by Friedrich Schiller

The very concept of education through art – or, indeed, the heritage – is of course idealistic. For a better understanding of its merits and possible shortcomings, I would suggest taking a look back at the author who invented the concept, or at least built a theory around it. In 1795, the German poet and philosopher Friedrich Schiller published his 'Letters on the Aesthetic Education of Man' (Schiller 1994), which he had been working on since 1792. Shaken by the events of the French Revolution and scarred by his personal experience of the draconian regime at his sovereign's Karlsschule in Stuttgart, he formulated a philosophy describing the transformation of the subject (*Untertan*) into a free citizen, without explicitly discussing the political and economic conditions underpinning the miniature states found in Germany at the time. Schiller proposed that human beings should be raised from a sensuous (*sinnlich*), material, submissive state to a moral (*sittlich*), rational, active, responsible state by experiencing beauty. In his view, the experience of beauty brought together sensuality and reason (*Sinnlichkeit und Vernunft*) in a complementary relationship: beauty was impossible to perceive without the senses, and impossible to understand without reason. Sensuality and reason – concepts which Kant placed in hierarchical order, arguing that reason/the mind should dominate the senses/the material (*der Geist macht sich die Materie untertan*) – still appear to be opposites, but may be reconciled in aesthetic experience:

> Haben wir uns hingegen dem Genuß echter Schönheit dahingegeben, so sind wir in einem solchen Augenblick unsrer leidenden und tätigen Kräfte in gleichem Grad Meister, und mit gleicher Leichtigkeit werden wir uns zum Ernst und zum Spiele, zur Ruhe und zur Bewegung, zur Nachgiebigkeit und zum Widerstand, zum abstrakten Denken und zur Anschauung wenden.

> But on the other hand, if we have resigned ourselves to the enjoyment of genuine beauty, we are at such a moment of our passive and active powers in the same degree master, and we shall turn with ease from grave to gay, from rest to movement, from submission to resistance, to abstract thinking and intuition.

(22nd letter, German version from Schiller's Werke in der Büchergildenausgabe, p. 786)

Aesthetic experience allows people to choose one direction or another, granting them freedom of choice. It is therefore a constructive part of their education as citizens. Experiencing beauty becomes a prerequisite for knowledge (*Erkenntnis*) and formation of convictions (*Gesinnung*).

Beauty itself cannot, however, give any practical guidance. It is defined as an autonomous value, entirely separate from the content of the work of art, whether a poem, a sonata or a painting. In this way, Schiller circumvents an argument that he himself raises; he is well aware that, in the hands of evil forces, beauty can become a dangerous tool. He readily admits that in the real world, art can be used for the ends of power and ideology. Yet he is reluctant to accept it in his philosophical thinking. He treats beauty as an isolate, an abstract quality, unsullied by any iconographic or semantic significance or political relevance. Clearly, then, the idealistic nature of the concept and the idealisation of the means have gone hand in hand from the outset. I must stress that I am not opposed to the concept itself; I merely wish to reconsider the means.

Historicisation and representation, re-semanticisation and the potential for dispute/discord (Streitpotential)

All researchers involved in listing monuments must look at history to ascertain the physical, political and social circumstances in which they were created. Often, the historical background was one of conflict, not harmony. Evidence or traces of conflict may be found both in the artistic concept behind the particular monument and in its physical substance. They are there to be discovered and deciphered. There is nothing unusual about this; all art historians use exactly the same method in their research. The difference between art history and a heritage conservation is that the report must include enhancement of the monument and of features of it, which are thought to be of significance to the heritage, in their present condition. The need to convince a committee, and the conservation specialist's desire to present the monument in a favourable light, mean that an affirmative slant is likely. Emphasis is usually placed on the monument's positive aspects. Historical conflict is as if resolved, peacefully reflected in the monument, to be experienced from a distance like a folly in an English garden. The monument's value of present-day relevance, the one that enables it to reach the olympic realms of patrimony through protection, will of course be once more its beauty.

Where, then, is the problem?

When Chancellor Kohl decided in 1993 to use Friedrich Schinkel's Neue Wache, built between 1816 and 1818 on the Unter den Linden boulevard in Berlin, as the site for a memorial to the victims of war and tyranny, the tiny building suddenly found itself at the centre of a fierce political controversy. The fact that the guardhouse had been built to commemorate the victory of the Prussian troops over Napoleon's army in 1814–15, as could easily be ascertained from the type of building and the iconography of the sculpted décor, had been of little interest to anyone for a long time. The new use of the building by the federal state, the victor in the German unification process, resurrected its semantics: the iconography of victory assumed importance once again, becoming a bone of contention. Was it still permissible to return monuments commemorating victorious generals to their historical location next to the building, thereby restoring the original effect of Schinkel's work? Or did the new function of the building's interior as a national memorial to the victims of war and of Nazism and Stalinism rule out any return to a triumphalistic narrative?

The Neue Wache dispute turned into a debate on the state of Germany four years after the fall of the Berlin Wall, on similarities and differences in the collective cultural memory of West and East Germans, and finally on Prussian history, in particular the era of reforms prior to the 1814–15 victories, when the idea of a German nation-state was still on the horizon. The Neue Wache became a *site of discord*, triggering a debate which had hitherto not taken place precisely because there was no venue for it.

I would like to demonstrate that a monument's capacity to cause dispute/discord is not a failing but an inherent quality which can be measured in terms of both the fierceness of dispute and the intensity of the ensuing debate. To classify this quality, I would suggest the term '*discord value*', or the neater German expression '*Streitwert*'.

Streitwert/discord value – a new category

Since the publication of Alois Riegl's famous essay 'Der moderne Denkmalskultus' ('The Modern Cult of Monuments') in 1903 (Riegl 1982), we have had recourse to an impressive range of value categories to express observations and ideas of the utmost complexity:

'Erinnerungswerte'/values of recollection

- '*Alterswert*' (age value) – highlights the traces left by time on a monument's surface and in its substance, even where this involves deterioration or ruin;
- '*historischer Wert*' (historical value) – refers to the monument's value as a reflection of history or art history;
- '*gewollter Erinnerungswert*' (intentional commemorative value) – concerns monuments and buildings which were intended from the outset to stand as an eternal testimony to the event or person represented.

'Gegenwartswerte'/present-day values

- '*Gebrauchswert*' (use value) – concerns safety and practical function;
- '*Kunstwert*' (artistic value) – see 'relative artistic value';
- '*Neuheitswert*' (newness value) – requires a monument to have no traces of deterioration and be complete in form and colour;
- '*relativer Kunstwert*' (relative artistic value) – since there is no objective standard for all eras, artistic value can only be defined in relation to the *Kunstwollen* (artistic will) of the curator's time.

These categories make it possible to highlight all the qualities of a monument, some of which may be conflicting. Age value will naturally require different conservation measures from those relating to newness or use value. In this way, Riegl encourages consideration of a variety of intervention strategies, including that of non-intervention.

I would suggest the inclusion of '*Streitwert*' (discord value) in his system as one of the 'present-day values'. This new category would enable conservators to give recognition to something that is part of their constant experience: their work is carried out amidst a multiplicity of conflicts. Of course, they cause some of these conflicts themselves – in applying the legislation on conservation, they are going against owners' financial interests. Other types of conflict – the ones with which we are concerned here – derive from the nature of certain monuments, which, like the Neue Wache in Berlin, may provoke strong opinions and discord, encouraging debates which had not taken place before for want of a suitable venue.

Suppose people wanted – at last – to preserve what is left of the Cité de la Muette in Drancy, a northern suburb of Paris – a large social housing project designed by Lodz,

Beaudouin and Prové in the early 1930s as one of the first examples of prefabrication and serialisation. Standing on its own and structured in a way that made surveillance easy, it was later converted into a detention camp and used as a deportation centre during the German occupation. The building's (positive) historical and architectural value is considerable, but its (painful) historical value as a deportation camp is even greater. The two cannot be separated. Moves to award the site listed status would cause huge controversy. The monument's discord value would perhaps even surpass its historical value – but hopefully only for a limited period, because at the end of any dispute, one would hope to achieve a consensus, or at the very least compromise. Its discord value would then fade immediately. Later it would re-emerge as an aspect of historical interest.

However, it is quite possible that the opposing sides would be unable to agree and that differences of opinion would persist: the monument would keep its discord value. The aim would then be to come to an understanding that the monument would remain a site of discord and that this state of affairs (*Sachverhalt*) was to be accepted. As a result, an object on which it had been impossible to reach a consensus would become part of the heritage by consensus.

Aiming at the evaluation of a contemporary impact rather than posterity, the '*Streitwert*' category provides an opportunity to consider places of recent historical significance and, possibly, to take action to conserve them from an early stage. It would encourage the conservation of pointers to recent history such as the Berlin Wall, traces of the Iron Curtain or other remnants of dictatorships or civil conflict. Such objects are often a source of fierce argument and in danger of disappearing before the controversy for which they may well provide a venue dies down. At a later stage, the '*Streitwert*' will probably turn into historical value, serving as justification for lasting conservation. Otherwise, the conservation may remain short-term.

References

Riegl, A. 1982. *The Modern Cult of Monuments: Its Character and its Origin/Translation*. Harvard University: Institute for Architectural and Urban Studies.

Schiller, F. 1994. On the aesthetic education of man, in a series of letters (trans. Reginald Snell). Bristol: Thoemmes.

Chapter 10

Archaeology and Authority in the Twenty-first Century[1]

Roger M. Thomas

From the late nineteenth century onwards, the authority of the state has played a signific-ant role in shaping the view of Britain's archaeological past, through the process of identi-fying selected monuments as being of 'national importance', and thus meriting protection under the ancient monuments legislation. Today, people are less ready to accept the 'authorised' view of the archaeological past, preferring to choose for themselves what kind of past they wish to believe in. This has implications for the role of the state archaeological official, who may have to change from being a figure of unquestioned authority to playing a role of facilitator in other people's exploration of the past. Recent developments in the 'heritage' field in England seem to pre-figure a re-orientation of this kind.

Introduction – the state and archaeological value

In 1882, after a prolonged struggle against property interests, the first Ancient Monu-ments Protection Act was passed in Britain (Chippindale 1983; Murray 1989; Saunders 1983). This Act enabled the British state to place selected monuments on a list, or 'sched-ule', thereby giving them legal recognition and protection. This approach has formed the basis of ancient monuments legislation in Britain ever since (Carman 1996, ch. 5). Under the present statute (the Ancient Monuments and Archaeological Areas Act 1979, s. 1): '. . . the Secretary of State may include [in the Schedule] any monument which appears to him to be of national importance'. Note especially the use of the term 'national' – the modern nation state provides the framework for valuing the archaeological past. The selection of monuments to be 'scheduled' has, since 1882, been made by archaeological officials of the state – Inspectors of Ancient Monuments, to give them their formal title.[2] In recent years, archaeological officials in local authorities have also been involved in the selection process (J. Schofield, pers. comm.). The selections of monuments made by offi-cials have been guided or endorsed by advisory committees or boards (the Ancient Monu-ments Boards or their equivalents). These boards are made up of eminent scholars in the field of archaeology. Their members are appointed by the Secretary of State (or, in England, by the Commissioners of English Heritage).[3] These appointments are made on the advice of officials – broadly, the same officials as the ones who are responsible for selecting monuments to include on the Schedule.

The archaeological officials and board members are drawn from very much the same circle. They are members of the same profession, they tend to come from fairly similar backgrounds and they have often attended the same universities. In earlier decades this was especially so, with graduates of the universities of Oxford and Cambridge especially well-represented both on the boards and among the cadre of officials. In this, of course, the complexion of these groups was simply reflecting that of the political and administrative class as a whole in Britain (Ponting 1985: 75).[4]

There is no system of appeal against the Secretary of State's decision to designate (or not to designate) a monument as being of 'national importance'. There is a convention by which the owners and occupiers of monuments are consulted in advance if it is intended to schedule a monument on their land. This pre-notification is taken seriously, but it is a matter of courtesy and good administrative practice rather than being a legal requirement. The Secretary of State's decision – and especially the decision as to whether the monument appears to him to be of 'national importance' – is to all intents and purposes final.

Thus, the regime for protecting ancient monuments which has existed in Britain since the Victorian age is built around the authority of the state. Officials select monuments for protection; those selections are endorsed by board members who are appointed by the state; and the final decision is made by (or in the name of) the Secretary of State, with no real possibility of appealing against a determination as to whether a particular monument is of 'national importance' or not.

In this way, the authority of the state has played a significant role in establishing the view of Britain's archaeological past, through the choices that have been made about which things were, and which were not, considered to be of national importance. The same point holds broadly true for many European countries, with antiquities legislation generally being administered by archaeological officials of the state (see papers in Cleere 1984, 1989).

The changing patterns in the selection of monuments of different types for protection form an interesting subject for study in their own right (J. Schofield, pers. comm.; Robertson 2000). One example serves to illustrate this very clearly. In Scotland, abandoned rural settlements of the medieval or later periods – many of them resulting from the notorious 'clearances' of the eighteenth and nineteenth centuries, when people were evicted from their homes and land by large landowners – were until recently seriously under-represented in the schedule of protected monuments. This fact, and the recent growth of interest in these sites, can be seen as reflecting the changing political relationship between the British state and the Scottish nation (and the changing consciousness of Scottish history, as pressure for the devolution of power to Scotland has grown) (see Mackay 1993; Hingley 1993, 2000).

The extension of choice

It is perhaps ironic that the present Ancient Monuments Act was passed in 1979, because that year marked something of a watershed in Britain: 1979 was, of course, the year in which Margaret Thatcher was elected Prime Minister, ushering in a very new set of political philosophies. Since 1979, the role of the state in British life has changed and, arguably, diminished, substantially. Certainly, there is a widely held view that the authority of the state is not held in the same respect now as it was previously (e.g. Hutton 1995: 28).

A significant factor in this claimed diminution of the authority of the state in Britain has been the extension of market principles into many areas of life which were previously controlled by state-run monopolies (Hutton 1995). Central to those principles has been the notion of 'choice' for consumers. A few examples may be offered. In 1979, the public utilities (electricity, water, gas), telecommunications and public transport were almost entirely provided by state monopolies. Now, they are run by private companies, and the virtues of 'consumer choice' between competing suppliers are heavily promoted. Very importantly (given the influence wielded by the media) there has been deregulation of broadcasting – first by the introduction of new commercial radio and television channels, and latterly through the introduction of satellite and digital broadcasting, with its promise of a multitude of different channels to choose between. There have also been attempts to extend the notion of choice into school education and public health. All of these things have, to some extent or another, diminished or altered the role of the state within society as as whole.

'Globalisation' of the economy has also helped to erode the position of the state as a key source of authority (Harvey 1989; Giddens 1999). Capital flows do not respect national boundaries or the wishes of governments; multinational corporations wield considerable power and influence across frontiers; and the Internet is a global information and communication tool which dissolves geography and opens up an extraordinary potential for individuals to choose what information they would like to receive – *and* to distribute – anywhere in the world.

It comes as no surprise, then, that the widespread extension of the notion of choice has affected not just what people consume. It has also affected what they think. There is now a much greater plurality of ideas, interests and belief systems than before – people wish to be able to choose what they believe in, as well as what they buy. At the broadest level, this is seen in relation to religion – far fewer people now follow the established Church of England, while at the same time there is growing interest in a wide range of alternative beliefs, from Buddhism to paganism and a wide spectrum of so-called 'New Age' philosophies. Also (and linked to the preceding point) there has been a substantial rejection of science as the only valid belief system. There has been a proliferation of alternative medicines and therapies, and these are now very popular. Such things as astrology and other forms of divination have many adherents. In essence, what a lot of this amounts to is a rejection of the official or 'authorised' view of the world, in favour of choice from a multiplicity of different ideas.

As one might expect, this trend is also apparent in relation to interest in the past. In Britain, as in many other places, interest in the past has never been greater (Lowenthal 1998). Again, however, many people – rather than simply accepting the 'official' version of what is interesting – have developed their own ideas about the past, about which aspects of it matter to them and why. The spectrum of this interest is extremely wide. At one end of it, there are such subjects as industrial archaeology, or recent military history, which have actually evolved from being 'popular' or 'amateur' interests, not regarded as matters for professionals, to areas of serious academic study (Dobinson *et al.* 1997; Samuel 1994). Such topics as local history, family history and battle re-enactments have considerable followings. There is a great interest in all things 'Celtic', some of it linked to the revived interest in paganism mentioned above.[5]

At the other end of the spectrum from such things as local or military history, many 'New Age' beliefs draw heavily on the past. Stone circles and other prehistoric monuments are often revered by 'New Age' believers as foci of earth forces, or as evidence of the 'lost wisdom' of largely mythical 'ancient Britons'. An interesting example of this general kind of approach is to be found in Cope's *The Modern Antiquarian: a Pre-Millennial Odyssey through Megalithic Britain* (Cope 1998). This is an illustrated guide to many of Britain's best known prehistoric monuments, but one in which the text places as much emphasis on the sacred and spiritual aspects of the monuments as it does on the narrowly archaeological ones. The enormous controversy which arose in 1999 over the treatment of the 'Seahenge' prehistoric timber circle on the Norfolk coast (Champion 2000) illustrates particularly vividly the sharp divergence between 'establishment' and 'alternative' views of the value of ancient monuments. The long-running debate over access to Stonehenge highlights exactly the same point (Bender 1998; see below).

Some of these 'alternative' ways of thinking offer an interesting contrast to establishment and 'commercial' presentations of 'heritage'. The latter often dislocate the past from the present and emphasise the notion of historical progress towards an increasingly rosy future (Walsh 1992), while the former weave motifs and ideas about the past into a present-day belief system, and regard the spiritual awareness and beliefs of 'the ancients' as greatly superior to the debased mainstream values of today. Cope, for instance, regards the pre-Roman past of Britain as 'a magical story, yet one which has been covered up, denied or ignored' from Roman times onwards (Cope 1998: ix).

Other current philosophies reflect related trends towards plurality and the empowerment of the individual. This is particularly so in the area of protecting the environment. This is one of the great popular causes of our time, and one of which historic conservation is an important, albeit often rather neglected, part (MacInnes and Wickham-Jones 1992). The injunction to individuals to 'think global, act local' in environmental matters is well-known, and is essentially concerned with empowering people. In the same vein, the doctrines of sustainability emphasise the need to involve local people actively in decision-making about their environment, and to recognise that different groups of people may value the same resource for very different reasons (English Heritage 1997 and this volume). In essence, sustainability recognises that there can be more than one version of 'truth', and tries to harness and to reconcile differing perceptions, recognising in particular that the authority of the state should not automatically take precedence over local perceptions of local environments.

A recognition of the possibility of acknowledging multiple perspectives on the past has also arisen from the claims of indigenous people over their cultural heritage (Simpson 1996; Potter and Chabot 1997) and from the post-modern shattering of consensus about 'truth' (Walsh 1992). The sustainability agenda of community involvement is therefore linked to a wide renegotiation of the traditional lines of authority and power in relation to the representation of the past. In an English archaeological context, Bender has sought to involve multiple voices in discussion about the meaning of Stonehenge, and about access to the monument (Bender 1998). She treats the issue as a matter of 'appropriation and contestation' of both the monument and the interpretation of it, and discusses an 'alternative' exhibition, entitled 'Stonehenge belongs to You and Me', about the monument. In a very similar vein, Cope's *The Modern Antiquarian* is addressed to 'the culturally dispossessed' of Britain (Cope 1998: ix).

Looking to the future

If this analysis is accepted, then the present regime for ancient monuments protection in Britain (which is essentially Victorian in origin) may be quite hard to sustain unchanged in the long run. In the present system, a small group of officials and academics (drawn largely from the same social and educational backgrounds) decides which monuments are important and then declares – without possibility of appeal – that these are what is 'nationally important'. This approach sits uneasily with notions of choice, plurality, empowerment and the claimed diminution in the authority of the nation state.

In England, in the past years, the state has recognised and begun to respond to the implications of these new imperatives for the 'heritage' field. In November 1999, at a conference in Manchester entitled 'Whose Heritage?', Chris Smith MP, the then Secretary of State for Culture, Media and Sport (which covers heritage), gave a speech on 'Cultural Diversity'. He said, among other things: 'Our heritage and culture need to be reflected from the perspectives of different communities' and 'If organisations wish to speak for all society . . . they must find out how communities want to have their history reflected and told'.

In February 2000, the United Kingdom Government asked English Heritage to co-ordinate a 'Review of Policies Relating to the Historic Environment in England' (the exercise was also widely referred as the 'heritage review') (Morris 2000). Following widespread consultation, a set of five discussion papers was published in June 2000. The papers were titled, respectively, 'Understanding', 'Belonging', 'Experiencing', 'Caring' and 'Enriching' (English Heritage 2000a). Again (and clearly taking a lead from the Secretary of State) these papers explicitly recognised the need to acknowledge other perspectives. A small selection of quotations suffices to make the point:

> At present [the language currently used to explain the significance of the historic environment] is often elitist and academic. We need a vocabulary which . . . encourages the exploration of alternative narratives.
>
> (*Belonging*, para. 38)

> Whose values? . . . in practice value is usually defined within national and academic criteria. The 'expert' holds a central role. Value, however, needs to be considered more broadly than this.... It involves assessing non-expert personal and spiritual viewpoints, as well as the more familiar scientific and academic ones.
>
> (*Caring*, paras. 11 and 12)

> National institutions, organisations and funding bodies must become, first and foremost, facilitators.
>
> (*Belonging*, para. 30)

The final report of the review, entitled *Power of Place: The Future of the Historic Environment* (English Heritage 2000b), was submitted to Government by English Heritage in December 2000. The Government's response, *The Historic Environment: A Force for Our Future*, was published in December 2001 (DCMS 2001). Sentiments similar to those in the discussion documents feature prominently in both reports. Again, a couple of examples make the point:

> In a multi-cultural society, everybody's heritage needs to be recognised' . . . 'Good history . . . accommodates multiple narratives and takes account of the values people place on their surroundings.
>
> (English Heritage 2000b)

> These decisions [about legal designation] are taken by central government on the advice of professionals within a framework of national criteria but do not always take account of other factors which might be of importance to the local community.
>
> (DCMS 2001: 30)

These quotations – and, indeed, the tenor of the exercise as a whole – can perhaps be taken as an indication of how great the tension had become between the 'authority' role of the British state in archaeological protection (with its roots in the late nineteenth century) and the demands of people in an increasingly diverse and plural society in Britain to create their own engagement with the past.

As part of the review process, the market research organisation MORI was commissioned to carry out a major survey of people's attitudes to the historic environment. This showed widespread support for the subject. It also revealed that heritage is a very personal matter, that the relevance of heritage to individuals is a key issue and that heritage has a major contribution to make to meaning in people's lives today (MORI 2000).

Two things, then, are clear. First, different groups of people and individuals wish to create their own histories and heritage, rather than simply to accept an 'official' one. Second, the state itself has recognised this and has begun to think through the implications. Against that background, then, what should the proper role of the state archaeological official in the twenty-first century be? Clearly, the role can no longer be one of unquestioned, and unquestionable, authority. More importantly, I would argue that it *should* no longer be that. Despite – or more probably because of – the fluid, multi-vocal and uncertain times in which we live, there is a tremendous interest in the past, and in its material remains, in many parts of the world today. The past has much to offer in the search for identity and meaning, and to the desire to retain some sense of distinctiveness in the face of an increasingly homogenous global material culture.

I would therefore argue that the role of the state archaeological official in the twenty-first century should become one of guide and facilitator, rather than of authority figure. But what, in practice, might such a change in role involve? In essence, it may be about engaging more closely with other groups in society who wish to explore their own pasts, or the pasts of others. It may involve developing dialogues with such groups, rather than being somewhat aloof from them. And it may involve helping to empower those groups, giving them tools and guidance to pursue their own explorations of the past.

Merriman (2000) has explored this argument in relation to museums, but how might it apply in the archaeological field? One can envisage various possibilities. As archaeologists (and as state archaeological officials) we have many advantages. We have ready access to enormous quantities of existing archaeological information, and we know our way around the plethora of potential sources – what material exists, what its qualities are, what the problems and pitfalls of using it are. We are familiar with a body of specialised archaeological techniques and procedures – one might mention the principles of stratigraphy, or such techniques as aerial photography, geophysical survey, pollen analysis and radiocarbon dating. And – perhaps this is the really significant point – we work within a long and well-established tradition of *interpretation* of the past. To say that is certainly not to claim that this tradition of ours has a monopoly of 'truth', or of understanding (far from it). But we have subjected the theoretical foundations of our subject to searching examination in recent years, we draw on a body of established procedures and our models of the past incorporate a wide range of empirical observations, many of which have been replicated many times. So, I would argue, we do have things to offer.

Of course, not all of what we can offer will appeal to everybody – creationists, for instance, are unlikely to warm to our enthusiasm for absolute dating methods. The professional's rejection of cherished popular myths, such as cavemen or ancient Britons, is not always welcomed by the lay person. But there *is* a demand to know about the past, and also to engage directly with it. The Archaeological Resource Centre in York, where people can handle archaeological material for themselves and learn about archaeological techniques, is extremely popular (Jones 1995); interest in the techniques of archaeology themselves seems to be considerable. 'Community archaeology' programmes in some parts of England have been very successful (Liddle 1989; Start 1999).

Two current developments in this area are worth mentioning. The first is the 'Local Heritage Initiative'. This is a programme, funded from the National Lottery, to provide grants to help local people and groups to explore and present their local heritage (including, but not limited to, the archaeological heritage). It is notable that this programme is administered, not by English Heritage (the state agency for archaeological matters in England), but by the Countryside Agency (a state body with responsibility for rural matters) (DCMS 2001: 30). The second development, also funded from the Lottery, is the 'Portable Antiquities Scheme' (Bland 2004). The aim of this programme is to work with metal detectorists (a very large constituency which is making its own engagement with the archaeological past) to ensure that their finds are properly identified and recorded. The emphasis is, in essence, on collaboration and facilitation.

We must, then, recognise that many people wish to make their own explorations of the past, in their own way. In Merriman's survey of public attitudes, for instance, people were asked how they would prefer to find out about local historical places. Some 20 per cent said they would like to visit them on their own (while 19 per cent would prefer a guided tour) (Merriman 1991). Whether for the unaccompanied visitor or for the tour party, we have much to offer – by using our own, very privileged position, we can help people to see for themselves, to understand and to question. This must be preferable to presenting people with an apparently factual and scientific 'authoritative' account of our own invention, allowing little opportunity for the validity of that account to be questioned.

By adopting a more 'open' approach, we may be able to help people to discover for themselves (among other things) a sense of place and locality, and of history and historical process. In what seems to be an increasingly ephemeral and rootless world, this may be a valuable thing indeed.

Conclusion

I have argued that the authority of the state has helped to create a particular view of the archaeological past in Britain. This has been done through the system of selecting monuments of 'national importance' (decisions against which there is no appeal). Now, I would argue, the significance of the nation state has diminished, and there has been a substantial rejection of 'authorised' views of all kinds, including those about the past. This obviously calls into question the role of the state archaeological official. However, interest in all aspects of the past, including the archaeological past, has never been greater. This interest takes many different forms, some of them involving fairly wholesale rejection of conventional views of the past and, indeed, of the nature of the world. The task for state archaeological officials (and, indeed, for all archaeologists) is to respond constructively and positively to this new situation, in which many people are extremely interested (potentially or actually) in 'our' subject, but will not necessarily accept our views of it unquestioningly. The best response to this situation will be to use our own, privileged positions to help others to engage with the past for themselves. This will undoubtedly present new challenges. It is likely to involve accepting that the former role of unquestioned (and unquestionable) authority figure of the state may well have had its day. But this need be no bad thing. I suspect that, if we concentrate on trying to enrich the experience of others, we are likely to find that we have enriched ourselves in the process.

Acknowledgements

My colleagues Martin Cherry and John Schofield kindly read this chapter in draft. John Schofield provided helpful comments on current practice in the scheduling of monuments. Mairi Robertson provided me with details of her Master of Studies dissertation. Nick Merriman provided helpful guidance on the original paper, and showed remarkable patience in waiting for my text. I am most grateful to all of these people.

Quotations from *Power of Place* and associated discussion papers, and from *The Historic Environment: A Force for Our Future* are reproduced with grateful thanks to English Heritage and the Department for Culture, Media and Sport respectively.

Responsibility for the views expressed in this chapter is mine alone. Those views are personal ones, and the chapter does not necessarily reflect the policies or views of English Heritage.

Notes

1   In the contents page of Merriman (ed.) 2000, the title of this chapter is incorrectly given as 'Archaeology and authority in England'. The correct title is that given in the chapter itself: 'Archaeology and authority in the 21st century'.
2   The first such Inspector was General Pitt Rivers, the well-known soldier, anthropologist and archaeologist: see Bowden (1991).
3   English Heritage is the government agency responsible for ancient monuments and archaeology in England.
4   Lists of board members and senior officials can be found in the *Annual Reports* of the Ancient Monument Boards, or for England from 1984 onwards, in the *Annual Reports* of English Heritage.
5   This is attested by the large number of recently published books with the word 'Celtic' in their title, or with paganism as one of their themes.

Bibliography

Bender, B. 1998. *Stonehenge. Making Space*. Oxford: Berg.
Bland, R. 2004. The Treasure Act and the Portable Antiquities Scheme: a case study in developing public archaeology. In Merriman, N. (ed.), *Public Archaeology*, 272–91. London: Routledge.
Bowden, M. 1991. *Pitt Rivers. The life and archaeological work of Lieutenant-General Augustus Henry Lane Fox Pitt Rivers, DCL, FRS, FSA*. Cambridge: Cambridge University Press.
Carman, J. 1996. *Valuing Ancient Things: Archaeology and Law*. Leicester: Leicester University Press.
Champion, M. 2000. *Seahenge: A Contemporary Chronicle*. Barnwell: Timescape Publishing.
Chippindale, C. 1983. The making of the first Ancient Monuments Act 1882 and its administration under General Pitt Rivers. *Journal of the British Archaeological Association* 136: 1–55.
Cleere, H. (ed.) 1984. *Approaches to Archaeological Heritage Management*. Cambridge: Cambridge University Press.
Cleere, H. (ed.). 1989. *Archaeological Heritage Management in the Modern World*. London: Unwin Hyman.
Cope, J. 1998. *The Modern Antiquarian – A Pre-Millennial Odyssey through Megalithic Britain*. London: Thorsons.
DCMS (Department for Culture, Media and Sport). 2001. *The Historic Environment: A Force for Our Future*. London: DCMS.
Dobinson, C., Lake, J. and Schofield, A.J. 1997. Monuments of War: defining England's twentieth century defence heritage. *Antiquity* 71: 288–99.
English Heritage 1997. *Sustaining the Historic Environment: New Perspectives on the Future*. An English Heritage Discussion Document. London: English Heritage.
English Heritage 2000a. *Review of Policies Relating to the Historic Environment*. Discussion papers circulated in June 2000. London: English Heritage.
English Heritage 2000b. *Power of Place. The Future of the Historic Environment*. London: English Heritage.
Giddens, A. 1999. *Runaway World: How Globalisation is Reshaping our Lives*. London: Profile.

Harvey, D. 1989. *The Condition of Postmodernity*. Oxford: Basil Blackwell.

Hingley, R. 1993. Past, current and future preservation and management options. In R. Hingley (ed.) *Medieval or Later Rural Settlement in Scotland. Management and Preservation*. Historic Scotland Ancient Monuments Division Occasional Paper Number 1. Edinburgh: Historic Scotland: 52–61.

Hingley, R. 2000. Medieval or later rural settlement in Scotland – the value of the resource. In J.A. Atkinson, I. Banks and G. MacGregor (eds) *Townships to Farmsteads. Rural Settlement Studies in Scotland, England and Wales*. BAR British Series 293. Oxford: BAR: 11–19.

Hutton, W. 1995. *The State We're In*. London: Jonathan Cape.

Jones, A. 1995. Integrating school visits, tourists and the community at the Archaeological Resource Centre, York, UK. In E. Hooper-Greenhill (ed.) *Museum, Media, Message*. Leicester: Leicester University Press: 156–64.

Liddle, P. 1989. Community archaeology in Leicestershire museums. In E. Southworth (ed.) *Public Service or Private Indulgence?* The Museum Archaeologist 13. Liverpool: Society of Museum of Archaeologists: 44–6.

Lowenthal, D. 1998. *The Heritage Crusade and the Spoils of History*. London: Viking.

MacInnes, L. and Wickham-Jones, C.R. (eds) 1992. *All Natural Things: Archaeology and the Green Debate*. Oxbow Monograph 21. Oxford: Oxbow Books.

Mackay, D. 1993. Scottish rural Highland settlement: preserving a people's past. In R. Hingley (ed.) *Medieval or Later Rural Settlement in Scotland. Management and Preservation*. Historic Scotland Ancient Monuments Division Occasional Paper Number 1. Edinburgh: Historic Scotland: 43–51.

Merriman, N. 1991. *Beyond the Glass Case. The Past, the Heritage and the Public in Britain*. Leicester: Leicester University Press.

Merriman, N. 2000. The crisis of representation in museums. In F. P. MacManamon and A. Hatton (eds) *Cultural Resource Management in Contemporary Society. Perspectives on Managing and Presenting the Past*. London: Routledge: 300–309

MORI. 2000. Research conducted for English Heritage. URL: www.english-heritage.org.uk.

Morris, R. 2000. On the Heritage Strategy Review. *Conservation Bulletin* 37: 2–5.

Murray, T. 1989. The history, philosophy and sociology of archaeology: the case of the Ancient Monuments Protection Act 1882. In V. Pinsky and A. Wylie (eds) *Critical Traditions in Contemporary Archaeology*. Cambridge: Cambridge University Press: 55–62.

Ponting, C. 1986. *Whitehall: Tragedy and Farce*. London: Sphere Books.

Potter, P.B. and Chabor, N.-J. 1997. Locating truths on archaeological sites. In J. Jameson (ed.) *Presenting Archaeology to the Public. Digging for Truths*. London: Altamira Press: 45–53.

Robertson, M. 2000. *Conservation Practice and Policy in England, 1882–1945*. Master of Studies dissertation, Department of Continuing Education, University of Oxford.

Samuel, R. 1994. *Theatres of Memory Volume 1: Past and Present in Contemporary Culture*. London: Verso.

Saunders, A.D. 1983. A century of ancient monuments legislation. *The Antiquaries Journal* 63: 11–33.

Simpson, M.G. 1996. *Making Representations: Museums in the Post-Colonial Era*. London: Routledge.

Start, D. 1999. Community archaeology: bringing it back to local communities. In G. Chitty and D. Baker (eds) *Managing Historic Sites and Buildings: Reconciling Presentation and Preservation*. London: Routledge: 49–59.

Walsh, K. 1992. *The Representation of the Past. Museums and Heritage in the Post-Modern World*. London: Routledge.

Postscript

This chapter is based on a paper which was given at the World Archaeological Congress in Cape Town, South Africa, in January 1999. The chapter as published tried to take account of developments up to about the start of 2002 (although it did not appear in print until the end of 2004).

Since 2002, a number of further developments in England have underlined the move away from an 'authority-based' approach to heritage and its protection.

In 2003, for example, the Department for Culture, Media and Sport (DCMS) published a consultation paper on changing the system for heritage protection (scheduling of ancient monuments, listing of historic buildings and so on). In the Foreword, Tessa Jowell, Secretary of State at DCMS, said that the aim of the proposals is to ensure 'a means of deciding what needs protecting which reflects not only the knowledge of experts but also the values of our diverse communities'. Public consultation on listing decisions is now very much the order of the day.

Particularly notable are remarks made in 2005 by David Lammy MP, Minister at DCMS. In a speech at a major conference on 'The Public Value of Heritage' he said:

> Perhaps most importantly, we are looking at how we give ownership [of the heritage] back to the local communities themselves.
> We have some way to go. The heritage sector is perceived as experts talking to themselves. There is a lack of trust. The experts are seen as only willing to engage with communities on their own terms . . .

The Minister then went on to talk about a project in Castleford, where local people had been encouraged (with funding from English Heritage and the Heritage Lottery Fund) to explore their own heritage – apparently in the face of various obstacles placed in their way by the heritage 'establishment'.

He also quotes an unnamed 'heritage expert' (the Minister's phrase) as saying:

> The Castleford project has given me an opportunity to explore what these words ['facilitation', 'advocacy' and 'enabling'] might mean . . . Heritage management is about the technical aspect of conservation, but it is equally about encouraging and drawing out local skills, knowledge and experience of place rather than dictating what is of cultural significance.

It is argued in the chapter above that the age of deference to authority and to experts has passed, and that people today wish to be able to choose what they know and what they believe in, just as they choose what to consume in material terms. Politicians in England in the early years of the twenty-first century have both responded to and encouraged these trends, with strong emphases on social inclusion and public participation in decision-making and policy-forming. Heritage professionals in turn have responded by embracing these new agendas. What remains to be seen, however, is whether this represents a real change of outlook on the part of 'heritage experts' (including, or perhaps especially, officials of the state) or whether this is an expedient response to the political orientation and discourse of a particular administration. The next few years may make clearer whether some of the changes in attitude which 'heritage officials' are now professing are simply skin deep, or really come from the heart.

Chapter 11

Heritage as Social Action

Denis Byrne

Introduction

An earlier version of the present chapter first appeared in a discussion paper (Byrne, Brayshaw and Ireland 2001) on the social significance of cultural heritage places prepared by the New South Wales National Parks and Wildlife Service. This organisation had responsibility for the management of Aboriginal heritage places across the whole of NSW (a total of *c*.60,000 places) and also for those non-indigenous heritage places that lay within the State's national park system (*c*.9,000 places). The discussion paper was written against a background of concern that inadequate attention was being given by heritage practitioners to the social significance of these heritage places. As far as Aboriginal heritage was concerned, practitioners inside and outside government had stressed the archaeological significance of places that included rock art sites, shell middens, rock shelter deposits, stone artefact scatters, ceremonial rock arrangements and initiation sites, carved trees, and human burial sites. In the case of the on-park non-indigenous places, belonging to the period after the British settlement of Australia in 1788, the emphasis was on architectural significance. These places included old homesteads and the infrastructure of sheep and cattle stations, old mines, lighthouses, the remains of convict-built roads, and nineteenth- and twentieth-century defence installations around Sydney Harbour.

It was appreciated that the ordinary citizens of NSW might also value these places for their archaeology and architecture. But it was clear that these two 'values' by no means exhausted the meaning that heritage places had for people in their everyday lives. The term 'attachment' would seem to go a long way towards encompassing this everyday-life significance of heritage places. The subject of 'place attachment' has received considerable attention in the field of environmental psychology (e.g., Altman and Low 1992; Williams *et al.* 1992), however, the focus of this work has tended to be on attachment to the natural rather than the cultural environment. In the cultural heritage field in Australia, while there has been a general assumption that people do form attachments to what we refer to as heritage places, there appears to be little understanding of the nature of such attachments, how they are formed and how they change over time. For this reason, over the last few years our agency's cultural heritage research team has taken the issue of attachment as a primary focus of its work (Byrne and Nugent 2003; Harrison 2004; Schilling 2003; Veale 2001).

The present chapter, in revised form, was part of my own contribution to the social significance discussion paper (Byrne, Brayshaw and Ireland 2001). My intention in the chapter was to stimulate thinking and debate about the social significance of heritage places by reviewing some of the relevant literature in the fields of history and anthropology. It was hoped this review would prove useful to heritage practitioners working in private practice (as consultants) or in government agencies where background reading tends not to be considered 'core business' in the way it would be if they were working in universities. It is characteristic of publications and reports produced in the field of social significance assessment that the literature they reference consists almost entirely of other heritage publications and reports. This relatively closed circle has contributed to the undertheorised nature of the cultural heritage field. Also relevant here is a tendency for heritage practice in particular regions of the world to develop in a way that is tailored to the heritage laws and heritage bureaucracies that exist there and to the particular conservation paradigm that is locally accepted. There is often little incentive to be inventive outside of these local models.

Finally, by way of introduction, it should be mentioned that the issue of social significance is nested inside that larger sphere of cultural heritage work known as significance assessment or values assessment (e.g., Avrami, Mason and De la Torre 2000; De la Torre 2002; Lipe 1984; Walker and Marquis-Kyle 2004). This assessment activity is based on a 'values approach' to cultural heritage which posits that any given heritage property will have multiple values and that these should be understood and assessed prior to any action carried out for the purposes of management or conservation. The various value or significance typologies in use include the following among other categories: aesthetic, archaeological or scientific, economic, educational, historic, spiritual/religious, and recreational. Mason (2002 and this volume) provides a useful overview of value typologies. In the present chapter, and in keeping with normal convention in Australia, a definition of social value/significance is employed that encompasses the spiritual/religious.

Culture and landscape

What is culture?

Raymond Williams (1963: 13, 16) tells us that the English word 'culture' only took on its meaning as 'a whole way of life, material, intellectual, and spiritual' in the course of the nineteenth century. It is no coincidence that the movement for the conservation of historic monuments emerges at around the same time. These developments reflect, on the one hand, the idea that the nation state was a 'cultural' as well as a political entity and, on the other, the idea that a national culture was a form of patrimony that needed to be cared for. Until very recently, cultural heritage sites were considered to be a form of national property to be managed and conserved by the state, by state-authorised bodies such as National Trusts, and by authorised professions of archaeology, architecture and art history. Only in the last few decades has it been acknowledged by heritage practitioners and agencies that heritage places might also 'belong' to ordinary people and to local communities who might have particular associations, feelings, attachments, and so on, to these places. And this idea that heritage places may have a 'social significance' that should be taken account of in the conservation process is still weakly developed.

In anthropology the term culture denotes the coherent totality of everything that is learned group behaviour. So it includes the kinship system of a society as well as its political system, high culture as well as popular culture, religious beliefs as well as attitudes to nature, the agricultural system as well as the manner of organising domestic space, table manners, how close you stand to a stranger at a bus stop, and so on. In other words 'culture' is taken to mean the whole package, everything that makes one society distinct from another.

During the course of the last century the culture concept replaced racial classification as a means of accounting for human differences. In the first half of the twentieth century, though, we tended to see non-Western cultures as consisting of a kind of unchanging *essence*, a quality that was deeply embedded in individuals. Our conceptualisation of this essence was not that different from the way we had thought about 'blood' (Cowlishaw 1987). Not until the 1960s was it generally accepted that all cultures were constantly changing, constantly remaking or re-inventing themselves. The earlier view came to be described as 'essentialist'. There is a residue of essentialism present in the heritage field where the urge to conserve old places sometimes goes hand-in-hand with an urge to conserve old ways. In other words, an urge to freeze culture at some ideal stage of its past. The importance of the new anthropological understanding of culture for cultural heritage practice cannot be overestimated. Among other things, it implies that the social significance of heritage places is subject to change, innovation, improvisation.

It might be said that we in the West have found it difficult to get away from the idea of culture as consisting of structures. We often refer, for instance, to social, economic, and political structures. Frequently we think and speak about such structures as if they have physical substance. This view of culture is associated with the functionalist and structuralist schools of anthropology which were dominant in the early and middle decades of the twentieth century. It is a view that the anthropologist Johannes Fabian sees as embodying a 'law-and-order' view of culture, a phrase which captures the sense of a somewhat rigid set of rules, customs and practices which you inherit at birth and which determine your social existence thereafter (Fabian 1998: 4). Another anthropologist, Arjun Appadurai, notes that 'This substantialization seems to bring culture back into the discursive space of race, the very idea it was originally designed to combat'. What Appadurai is referring to here is the way that, though we have rejected race in favour of culture as a way of classifying people, we are still somehow pulled back into a way of thinking about behaviour – about culture – that makes an object out of it. Heritage practitioners might be said to be particularly prone to this 'substantialization' of culture. Our focus on physical fabric/substance, whether in the form of artefacts or built structures, often resembles a kind of fetishism. It is easy for us to forget they are products of culture rather than constituting culture itself.

The structuralist view of culture was thoroughly critiqued and dismantled in anthropology in the latter decades of the twentieth century. It was replaced with a view of culture which emphasised practice over structure. Cultures came to be seen as fluid, inventive, and responsive to changing circumstances. The boundaries around cultures came to be seen as porous zones rather than hard shells or impervious skins. In the old way of thinking, the idea of culture contact evoked the idea of cultures as billiard balls, a vision in which 'European culture bumped into non-European culture without merging' (Leach 1989). By contrast, we now speak of cultures becoming 'entangled' when they come into contact with each other. They readily borrow from each other and what they borrow they often 'rework' for their own purposes (Thomas 1991).

The discussion in the pages that follow does not attempt to comprehensively answer the very large question, 'what is culture?' This is a question central to the projects of anthropology, sociology, history and cultural studies and there is a huge body of research and literature pertaining to it. Instead, a few facets of the 'culture question' have been chosen for discussion because they bear particularly upon the subject of the social significance of heritage places.

Local knowledge and the lived world

One of the most notable trends in the social sciences in the last few decades has been the call to the local and specific, a call that represents a turning away from or loss of confidence in sweeping general theories of how society works (Marcus and Fischer 1986: 8; Moore 1996: 2). The best known pioneer in the investigation of the 'view from the inside' has been Clifford Geertz, famous for his concept of 'local knowledge' which he describes as 'significant worlds and the indigenous outlooks that give them life' (Geertz 1983). Geertz emphasises the particular; his focus is the local community and the small-scale worlds of ordinary people. It is these worlds we turn to when considering the social significance of heritage places.

One immediately has to caution, though, as Geertz does, that you can never put yourself inside the local world of other people. You can only ever interpret, and interpretation lacks closure or finality. Critics of Geertz, who include Marshal Sahlins (1985) and Eric Woolf 1982), though they admire his work, are concerned at what they see as his treatment of cultures as islands unto themselves, 'spaces' which are not subject to external or even global influence and power. They are also concerned at the limited scope in his model for local 'actors' to be self aware and to be agents of change. Some of the implications of this are taken up below.

In the field of history, the trend to particularity in the course of the 1980s produced a great volume of research concerned with the question of how ordinary people experience the world and make sense of it (Biersack 1989: 76). Perhaps the best known example of this type of history, from the 1980s, is Natalie Zemon Davis's (1983) book (later a film), *The Return of Martin Guerre*. Davis 'uses a series of incidents from the peasant life of sixteenth century France to probe local sentiments, motivations, values, feelings, and *the lived world*' (emphasis added) (Biersack 1989: 76). At a certain level, this list of headings could almost represent the agenda for social significance assessment. In the assessment of social significance we are concerned not with the meaning of heritage places in the fields of archaeology or architecture, but their meaning in 'the lived world' of ordinary people. One would hope that part of our motivation for understanding the latter is to enable us to devise conservation strategies that are protective of old places and things in the context of their own 'local world' rather than according to some global template.

Anthropology tells us that we are symbolic beings. In the course of our lives we assign symbolic meanings to places and things which differ from the 'obvious' or practical meanings they have for us. In a scenario described later, a shell midden comes to signify for local Aboriginal people the fate of the 'old people' who originally produced the site and occupied it. Every local landscape is populated with places to which local people have given symbolic meaning (Field and Basso 1996; Stewart 1994; Tilley 1994). These meanings are 'inscribed' invisibly onto places and although these meanings can be easily 'read' by local people, they will normally be invisible to outsiders.

Places function as signs in the sense that they are signified with meaning (hence the concept of *significance*). When we assess the social significance of heritage places we seek to gain access to this local knowledge in order to conserve places not just for their 'obvious' meaning (e.g., a shell midden as a shell midden) but for the meanings assigned to them by local people.

For much of the post-contact period (post-1788) in Australia the white authorities strove to limit the visibility of Aboriginal people in the colonised landscape as well as to suppress any aspect of Aboriginal culture not considered to be in line with the white 'civilising' mission. Even under such circumstances, though much of the old knowledge was lost, elements of the meaning of the 'traditional' landscape were still able to survive. No amount of official surveillance or suppression can control meanings people give to places in the privacy of their own minds or which they communicate in private conversation. The keeping alive of this 'landscape of signs' can become almost an act of defiance in its own right, an element of what Gillian Cowlishaw (1988: 132–137) has called 'oppositional culture'.

Up until very recently, the Aboriginal side of Australia's post-1788 history received little public attention and was largely 'written out' of school history books, white local histories, and heritage registers. Aboriginal people themselves, however, recorded their own local histories, partly in the form of the invisible meanings they inscribed places with – i.e., meanings invisible to 'outsiders'. The old massacre site, the old fringe camp which is now a vacant paddock, the land they cleared for a white farmer, the 'sites of segrega-tion' such as the town hospital, picture theatre and public swimming pool – the meanings of these places were 'mapped' and recorded in people's minds (Byrne 1996–1997, 2003a; Byrne and Nugent 2004). One of the reasons for documenting the meaning places have for local communities is, then, that there are histories there which would otherwise be invisi-ble. The scenario described here lends itself to the notion of 'encrypted' (Mueggler 1998) significance, both in the sense of a secret or semi-secret knowledge (unknown to official-dom) and in the sense of a buried, underground knowledge. We thus come to an under-standing of how any given landscape can have several different layers of signs, some of them more publicly accessible than others.

Since the 1950s, many historians, particularly those influenced by the French *Annales* school, have focused on the narrative aspect of historical production. Hayden White, drawing upon the work of Paul Ricoeur, describes historical productions as allegorical. He has it that the historian is engaged not in fiction, because the events dealt with are and were real, but in imagination.

> How else can any past, which by definition comprises events, processes, struc-tures, and so forth, considered to be no longer perceivable, be represented in either consciousness or discourse except in an 'imaginary' way? Is it not pos-sible that the question of narrative in any discussion of historical theory is always finally about the function of imagination in the production of a specifi-cally human truth?
>
> (White 1987: 57)

While there is a fair degree of acceptance for the view that there can be no final, definitive version of an historical event, this obviously does not stop professional historians combing the archives to ensure their 'narratives' have maximum possible accuracy in representing what happened in the past. On the other hand, it seems clear that the acceptance of the proposition that there will always be different versions of history has given impetus to the public history movement and to the recording of oral histories.

In the field of environmental impact assessment (EIA), which is the context for so much of the work in cultural heritage carried out these days, there is understandably a concern to establish objective truths. The primary responsibility of the cultural heritage practitioner always remains, however, that of representing the 'specifically human truth', to borrow Hayden White's (1987: 57) phrase. The specifically human truth of the meaning of places to individuals and communities is rarely the quantifiable, provable truth familiar to us from the fields of physics, biology or geology. The cultural meaning of a place may be contested locally and different local people may 'narrate' a place differently. It is not the role of the heritage practitioner to resolve such contestation. In relation to this it is worth noting the ICOMOS 'Draft Code on the Ethics of Co-Existence in Conserving Significant Places', 1997, Article 14, which advises practitioners: 'where appropriate, [to] seek co-existence of differing perceptions of cultural significance rather than resolution'. Too often, one suspects, heritage practitioners are placed under pressure by their clients or by government agencies to come up with simplified accounts of place-meaning or to establish the validity of one individual or community group's view of significance over that of others.

While historians were becoming interested in culture, anthropologists from the 1970s were becoming increasingly interested in history (Kuper 1996: 182). Eric Woolf's (1982) work on historical change in non-Western cultures is an example of this. Not only were anthropologists becoming more interested in the history of the peoples they studied, they were becoming increasingly interested in their own history as anthropologists. The seminal work of Talad Asad (1973), for instance, situated anthropology firmly within the project of colonialism, arguing that it had provided colonial powers with the means to understand and manipulate or govern their colonial subjects. Historians and anthropologists could thus both be said to have turned to consider themselves not just as interpreters of history and society but also as subjects of history and society.

The cultural heritage field is something of an oddity in the humanities and social sciences in the extent to which it has been relatively disinterested in its own historical development. Most of the writing over the last few decades that has situated heritage practice in a historical and political perspective has come from academic historians (e.g., Anderson 1991), archaeologists (e.g., Silberman 1989) or geographers (e.g., Lowenthal 1985, 1996) most of whom are not professionally engaged in heritage conservation. There has been a strong tendency for we heritage practitioners to 'naturalise' our area of work, seeing what we do as a natural or obvious response to an obvious need (e.g., a nice old building is collapsing, we go out and conserve it). We do not see our own work as 'producing' heritage, in the sense of constructing it discursively, or as producing a particular view of heritage.

What is a cultural landscape?

The discourse and practice of heritage conservation is comparatively recent. We have not always regarded old places as 'heritage', and yet nobody these days can disregard their heritage without running the risk of being left out of history. In describing what cultural landscapes are, it might thus be wise to begin by saying they are contested. In Australia, the Aboriginal post-contact experience exemplifies this.

In settler colonies such as Australia, Canada and the United States, it was not enough for colonists simply to occupy the country of Indigenous peoples; they needed to reinscribe it culturally. To cease being foreigners and start being citizens, to start being *of* a place instead of merely being *in* a place, the landscape needs to begin to tell your story. In rural Australia the history of white settlement is commemorated in local history books, local museums and local government heritage studies. Especially in the southeast of the continent, where white settlement was earlier and more concentrated, there is a marked tendency for these cultural productions to be interested in Aboriginal occupation prior to, but not after, white settlement. Aboriginal fringe camps and missions from the nineteenth and twentieth centuries rarely get a mention; Aboriginal participation in local industries such as sheep shearing, crop picking, fishing, logging, or mining, is rarely mentioned either. The touchy subject of race relations is routinely left out altogether. Effectively, the history and heritage of Aboriginal presence and experience in the local landscape after the time of white settlement is hidden from public view. In its place we find a landscape 'filled in' with the heritage of white settlement, one in which there is no space for the heritage of the Aboriginal experience.

This is hardly surprising. Heritage is a field that is highly contested and social groups which have most power have most chance of having their story or experience commemorated as history. Dolores Hayden (1995) has shown, for instance, how heritage landscapes in the USA have not only routinely excluded African-Americans and their historical experience, they have also excluded the white working class and its historical experience, just as they have tended to exclude women and their historical experience. If you are a minority group, heritage visibility is often a matter of struggle. Not to struggle for visibility is to remain invisible in the heritage landscape. The proper role of heritage managers and professionals is not to participate in this struggle over visibility in the cultural-historical landscape. Our role is to facilitate the visibility of all.

Having noted that cultural landscapes are contested, my second point is that they are socially constructed. Much of the space-related work in the social sciences and humanities since at least the 1960s is founded on this understanding. To say that they are socially constructed is to say that they derive their meaning, and often even their physical form, from the actions and imaginations of people in society. We are familiar with the idea of landscape formation as a geomorphic process involving erosion and sedimentation, a process whereby mountains are gradually broken down and river deltas gradually built up. Cultural landscapes are created through time by a form of cultural sedimentation in which past human action leaves traces – the traces, for instance, of houses, campsites, shrines, battles, fences and pathways – that accumulate. Julian Thomas (2004: 214) cautions us against regarding this accumulation as a 'Cartesian world of inert substance'. Rather the cultural landscape we inherit should be thought of as meaningfully constituted (Thomas 2004). The actions represented by the traces had meaning and these meanings are embodied in the traces. We in the present landscape are thus always in a form of contact with those who occupied it before us. Their presence interacts with our presence. This does not mean that a heritage site means to us in the present exactly what it meant to its creators in the past. In the course of the interaction referred to above we interpret the meaningful traces in the context of our own lives, our own imaginations, desires and ambitions. It is this interpretation that constitutes the social significance of heritage places and landscapes.

We should also consider the role of memory. People who move through a landscape where they have lived or spent time in the past inevitably encounter traces of themselves there. These are not just physical traces, like old bicycles and discarded toys, left behind by their younger selves. They also 'encounter' associations. Recollections and emotions are triggered by the sight of traces in the form of objects; they are also triggered by the sight, smell and feel of familiar places even where there is no tangible/physical trace of their former presence. Gradually, though it has been a painfully slow process; heritage practice has come to acknowledge the importance of 'intangible heritage' and hence to recognise the importance of memory.

The anthropologist, Susanne Küchler (1993: 100), describes how for natives of the Melanesian island of New Ireland the experience of walking through the landscape is an experience of collecting or 're-collecting' memories:

> The secondary forest and the garden land surrounding each settlement offers an extended journey into the burial places of memory. The pathways which connect gardens, settlements and villages connect also past settlements, so that each journey done by foot is a journey in which a buried, forgotten landscape is quite literally re-collected as nut and fruit trees are harvested by the passers by.

One of the ways we 'memorise' cultural landscapes is in the form of mental maps. Many of us have had the experience of trying to locate a feature on a topographic survey map with the help of a farmer or a member of a local Aboriginal community. Often, on first examining the map, they will say that 'they' (the map makers) 'have got it wrong' because the mental map they have of their local landscape is so different from the one shown on the published map. These mental maps have often been built up though a lifetime's sedimentation of experiences and are far more complex than any map on paper could ever be.

In the heritage field, the process of social significance assessment partly aims to give validity to the maps that people hold in their minds (e.g., Byrne and Nugent 2004). One of the obstacles to effective social significance assessment is the habit which heritage professionals sometimes have of forcing the local, mental map into the straitjacket of the official printed map. A fascinating example of local people reinserting their own maps into an official map occurred in Cape Town in the 1990s. After the forced removal of the 'coloured' population from District Six, near the city centre, beginning in 1966, and the razing of the terraced houses there, the only obvious trace of this former cosmopolitan residential precinct (apart from a few public buildings standing in isolation) was the remaining grid of streets and lanes. The street grid later became a 'memory aid' when it was reproduced as a map on the floor of the District Six Museum that was opened in 1994 in a vacant church building. During visits to the museum, many former residents have inscribed their names, the locations of their former homes, and other information on the map using marker pens. Former victims of apartheid were in this way able to symbolically recover a lost space and reinscribe themselves in it. District Six has become a key site for a post-apartheid heritage of segregation (Malan and van Heyningen 2001).

Societies tend not to be homogeneous entities. Rather, they consist of coexisting fractions, such as ethnic minorities, sub-cultures, genders, socio-economic classes, and religious congregations. These fractions each 'construct' different landscapes. We might assume that a resident of the up-market Sydney suburb, Vaucluse, will 'map' Sydney in a different way to a resident of the less affluent Blacktown. The former may map it as a landscape populated with private schools, corporate office towers, Italian designer boutiques, yacht anchorages and cocktail circuits. The latter's map may populate it with state schools, suburban shopping malls, George Street cinemas, and football clubs. This is not to say there are not areas of overlap – the Sydney Cricket Ground, for instance, might be a key site on both maps. Yet it seems fair to say that each of these people experience Sydney as a somewhat different place – in cultural landscape terms, they *are* two different places.

To convey the idea of how two landscapes can occupy the same place at the same time I offer the following description of an imaginary country town somewhere in NSW in the 1950s. This snapshot draws upon the work of Byrne (2003a) and Byrne and Nugent (2004).

> The town, with its paved streets, cinema, pubs, streets of houses, the surrounding landscape of fenced paddocks, the highways and other infrastructure, is a product of Anglo-Celtic settlement. But half a kilometre away from the edge of town is an Aboriginal reserve whose occupants carry around in their minds a map of the local landscape which, though it accurately represents the reality of daily life for these people, would likely be unrecognisable to the town's white citizens.
>
> The Aboriginal landscape consists of the reserve and its immediate environment, spaces that are intimately known and signified by Aboriginal people but are either a no-go area for whites or a place they prefer not to see. The landscape includes fishing and hunting places in the swamps, creeks and forests as well as the Christmas camp down on the coast where the reserve community spends several weeks a year camping. It also consists of a web of routes and pathways, many of which follow trajectories dictated by the spatial disposition of 'friendly' as opposed to 'unfriendly' landowners who might or might not allow Aboriginal people to come onto their land or cross it in order to fish, hunt, or camp. This web and the vast amount of information supporting it is critical to the 'underground' occupation or utilisation of a topography they no longer own. This duality of landscapes has been maintained by the policies and practices of segregation and oppression. The town's picture theatre is used by both populations but the people of the reserve are forced to sit in a

roped off section up the front. The police station is also a site where the two landscapes ostensibly coincide but for a disproportionately large number of Aboriginal people it is the inside of the lockup which they know most intimately. None of them has ever worked behind the front desk.

Connectivity

One of the obstacles to greater recognition of the social significance of heritage places has been the tendency for heritage managers to deal with these places as discrete points in a landscape rather than as elements of a connected pattern of places associated with the lives of people. In Australia this site-based approach is deeply embedded in heritage practice and heritage bureaucracies. It may be more convenient to list and manage places as discreet entities but this easily leads to a misrepresentation of cultural significance. People are mobile and mostly they live their lives across some portion of a landscape rather than at a single point in it. Aboriginal people in Australia have often found it particularly difficult to reconcile their holistic experience of 'country' with the piecemeal approach that heritage practitioners favour.

We know that many of the places we call heritage 'sites' are often really just points on pathways (or 'trajectories'). They are 'moments' in a journey or trip across a landscape. When using a site-based approach to heritage, the points on the pathway have tended to dominate our thinking and the pathway is lost sight of. The following scenario draws upon the author's reflections on his role as an archaeologist and 'site' recorder.

> In the course of an oral history recording project on the NSW North Coast an archaeologist asks two Aboriginal women if they would show him some fishing sites along the big river which lies between the mission community, where they live, and the nearby town. As the three of them are driving down the narrow road from the mission to the river the women remember how, when they were children in the 1960s, they would always walk along this road to go fishing at the river, often in the company of their parents or relatives. They remember one time when they took a short cut across a paddock belonging to a farmer known to be unfriendly towards local Aboriginals and were chased into a pond by the farmer's dog. They recall how scared they were and they laugh about this and it triggers other memories of things that happened on the walk to the river. Having reached the river they walk down through the long grass to the riverbank where they talk about the variety of fish that had been caught there over the years by themselves and others. There is some friendly disputation about the size of some of these fish. The remembering of these fishing events sparks off talk about some of the other people involved: where they are now or when they passed away, details about their lives and personalities.
>
> The archaeologist, who has been plotting the fishing site on his map then gets down to business and asks them to describe the significance of this fishing place, the spot they are standing on. What does this place mean to them? After a pause, one of the women says, 'Well, this is a place we used to come and fish. We still do come here, with our kids.' There is another pause while they look around again at the spot. The other woman says, 'Well, there's not a lot you can say about it really.' It is as if she is lost for words. But on the way back in the car they chat away again about the days when they were kids walking down to the river from the mission.
>
> What the archaeologist has recorded, what he goes away with, is a dot on the map: a fishing site/place. But what the women were talking about – what

apparently they had 'in mind' – was the act of going fishing. The memory of 'going fishing' was in no way contained by the fishing site. For them, the path there and back was just as rich in memories as 'the site'. The act of going fishing involved the whole tract of landscape that you passed through and experienced in the course of 'going fishing'. And even when people were at the fishing site they spent a lot of time looking up and down and across the river, enjoying the view, thinking about the weather, wondering where the fish were, noticing other places along the banks and remembering times they'd fished from those places, who they were with at the time and what they caught. Their field of vision was continuous with the spot they were standing on and this field of vision pushed out the boundaries of the 'site'.

The archaeologist's act of recording the fishing site as a 'site' effectively disconnected or dis-located it from almost everything that made 'going fishing' meaningful to the women. The accuracy with which the archaeologist plots the 'site' on the map disguises the gross *inaccuracy* of the whole recording exercise. It is a misrepresentation of social reality. The 'site' in this case didn't exist for them as an independent place. To think of it in that way was like taking a bead off a necklace, holding it up between your fingers and saying, 'this is a necklace'. What the archaeologist was doing, essentially, was asking them to try to translate the full meaning and richness of 'going fishing' into his exotic and alien 'site' concept.

It is not difficult to see that what is happening here is that the social meaning of a place is taking second place to its archaeological meaning. It is a case of privileging the physical over the social.

The old model: heritage as material

The relatively low priority currently given to the social value of heritage places is a product of a heritage conservation paradigm that objectifies or materialises these places. In what follows, some of the characteristics of this paradigm are discussed.

For the staff of many government heritage agencies it is often a struggle to keep in mind, and to remind others, that cultural heritage is about people, communities and the values they give to heritage places. In their role of 'operationalising' heritage legislation, the staff interact with land owners and developers who seek timely decisions on the management of the physical aspect of heritage places and are reluctant to acknowledge that these places may have social significance. At another level, cultural heritage staff often struggle to convince staff in the environmental protection area that natural landscapes are also cultural landscapes, that they have a human landuse history and they often are valued by communities for cultural reasons. Often it seems as if people have forgotten that cultural heritage, in the last resort, is about culture.

It may appear that the relative neglect of the social significance is a result of archaeologists and architects having monopolised the field of cultural heritage management. We should bear in mind, though, the role that developers, planners and land managers have had in maintaining the primacy of archaeology and architecture. The latter often prefer to deal with archaeologists and architects than with local communities. They find archaeological and architectural priorities easier to deal with than community priorities. This is understandable. But it is also increasingly untenable in a world where conservation is an arena of community action.

Culture commodified

It would be naïve to suppose that the materialist approach to cultural heritage practice (the focus on physical fabric) is not related to deeper social and historical forces. One of these is the tendency of capitalist societies to commodify things.

In Karl Marx's critique of capitalism, ordinary people (workers) are alienated from the things they produce because their employers, the controllers of capital, are only interested in the monetary value of their output. The industrial revolution, in this view, ushered in a world in which the production of objects and wealth was privileged over the well-being of ordinary people. This new value system quickly naturalised or normalised itself so that soon whole populations – both the owners of capital and the slaves of capital – internalised its values. The accumulation of capital and goods and the endless labour involved in acquiring them came to be seen as morally good.

It was in those northern European societies which in the nineteenth century were leading the world in capitalist development that our present concept of cultural heritage first appeared. Many commentators have attributed its appearance to a linkage between the economic capital and cultural capital. In particular, it is linked to a tendency for nation states to begin to think of themselves as possessing a 'heritage' or patrimony in the form of cultural capital (Anderson 1991). Cultural capital (national wealth) included those old places and objects which now were regarded as a form of *property* belonging to the nation (Handler 1985, 1988).

A refinement of the understanding of commodification has come through the notion of reification. In a famous essay of 1922, Georg Lukacs attacked the distinction held to exist between 'objectivity' and 'subjectivity', arguing that this distinction was itself a product of the capitalist value system. The concept of reification has been absorbed into the social sciences where it is used, for instance, to describe how we have come to think of culture as a thing rather than as a set of ideas, actions, and beliefs residing in people's minds.

The notion that we could or should preserve culture is a good example of reification. The assumption here is that culture is a thing, an object that can be acted upon from the outside, an entity that is *available* to conservation. The implication is that culture is something that can be lost, as if it were a set of car keys. In actuality, however, culture is just a word we give to the whole pattern of a particular people's thoughts and actions. As pointed out earlier, culture is a process rather than an object.

Many in the social sciences see the heritage field as contributing to the increasing reification or 'thingification' (Taussig 1992: 84) of culture. There has been considerable discussion of the role of the discourse of heritage in objectifying Australian Aboriginal culture and of the extent to which Aboriginal people themselves have had little choice but to also engage in this power-laden discourse in which artefacts and 'traditions' are privileged over social action (Keefe 1988; Lattas 1990; Merlan 1989). As an example of reification at work, one might imagine a scenario in which a heritage practitioner, in the course of recording an Aboriginal person's oral history, records a story told about a post-contact Aboriginal mission site or a Dreaming (mythological) site. The practical outcome of this work is likely to be the recording of these places on a heritage inventory such that the places take priority over the stories – i.e., what is inventoried are places with associated stories rather than stories with associated places.

Inventories and commodification

Heritage inventories, while they are indispensable to the task of heritage conservation, also lend themselves to the commodification of heritage. This is partly through their tendency to describe places in terms of their physical fabric rather than their values (e.g., their social significance). Once a recording of a place is entered on an inventory the danger arises that the recording will be treated as the equivalent of the place. In the case of Aboriginal archaeological sites, normally what is recorded by archaeologists is only that part of a site visible to them on the ground (e.g., the stone artefacts visible along road margins or on eroding surfaces) rather than the real extent of the site. Clearly, in this case, the recording is an incomplete representation of the place.

The inventory record may even take on a greater reality than the place represented. It is frequently the case that once an Aboriginal archaeological site is on an inventory it is the inventory recording that will be referenced in subsequent environmental impact assessment reports rather than information gained from revisitation of the site in the field. It is likely that a majority of the approximately 50,000 sites recorded on the NSW Aboriginal heritage inventory (AHIMS) have never been revisited in the field subsequent to their initial recording. These sites become familiar to us mainly through the inventory data. In a sense, the real place, the place in the ground, fades away as continuing references are made to the always more readily accessible inventory data.

Heritage inventories, if not carefully managed, can thus bring about the commodification of hertitage. They contain locational details (cartographic and cadastral) of the places as well as quantifiable data on them. As a matter of principle there may be agreement among heritage professionals that social values have priority over, or at least equity with, scientific or architectural values. Yet once they are included on an inventory, the places can easily break free of their community context. The locational and archaeological data can come to be regarded as having stand-alone meaning that is separable from other aspects of a place's significance.

Intrinsic significance and immanence

Built into most cultural heritage legislation in Australia is the principle that the significance of a heritage place resides in the physical fabric or form of the place. The assumption is that significance or meaning is intrinsic to or inherent *in* a place rather than being given *to* a place by people. This principle is based on flawed logic. A critique of the principle of inherency is necessary as part of any serious consideration of the role of social significance in heritage management.

In perhaps the most important contribution to the debate on significance in the USA, Tainter and Lucas (1983) noted that cultural heritage charters and laws in the USA, from the 1930s to the 1950s, all embodied the idea that heritage properties possessed 'intrinsic qualities' which made them unique and inherently valuable or significant. They traced this to the influence of the Western philosophical tradition known variously as empiricism or positivism. This tradition privileged direct experience or observation of phenomena in determining empirical reality. In the empiricist–positivist view, significance was to be thought of as present in a cultural property rather than in the mind of the observer, the observer's role being to objectively report the property's observable–verifiable nature.

Post-structuralist thinkers, on the other hand, have debunked the idea of observation and language as objective and theory-neutral. During the great paradigm shifts in the history of science (as Kuhn has shown) not only is theory altered, 'But more fundamentally, the basic perception of the object of study changes, so that it is often seen to have a different nature' (Tainter and Lucas 1983: 713). Citing other post-structuralists, Tainter and Lucas (1993: 713) note that 'the theories to which we subscribe, as well as our education and training, fundamentally influence our sense experiences'. They point out that the assertion

> . . . that meaning is inherently fixed in the object of perception . . . contradicts basic anthropological theory and experience. To anyone familiar with cross-cultural variation in symbol systems, it should be clear that meaning is assigned by the human mind.
>
> (1983: 713)

Before looking at the wider implications of this critique we might consider its implications for archaeology. The archaeological profession has rejected virtually unanimously the notion of inherent significance – the 'inherency thesis' as Leone and Potter (1992) call it. In a review of 83 peer-review publications on significance assessment in archaeology, covering the period 1972–1994, Briuer and Mathers (1996: 11) found a high level of consensus among authors on the principle that significance is a dynamic and relative concept, that it is ascribed rather than inherent, and that is it changeable rather than static.

Since the 1970s, archaeologists in both the USA and Australia have, in practice, replaced the principle of inherent significance with the principle of *representativeness*. Beginning from the premise that all sites are unique and significant – but acknowledging the reality that all sites cannot be preserved – they have focused their energy on determining which sites are representative of the range of variation present at various geographic scales (e.g., the local scale, the regional scale).

While archaeologists reject the principle of inherent significance, they tend to do so only in relation to their own archaeological assessments. While adhering to the position that significance is ascribed rather than inherent, they have nevertheless been reluctant to acknowledge that values ascribed to places by non-archaeologists are as valid as their own. Yet if the critique of inherency is taken to its logical conclusion we must concede that non-archaeologists are highly unlikely to signify places the same way we do. If significance is to be acknowledged as ascribed rather than inherent then one person's inscription, presumably, is as valid as another's. This is not to say that significance, as a subjective and variable quality, is impossible to delineate. In most cases there are degrees of consensus within given groups about the meaning of places. Most archaeologists might agree, for instance, that a certain site is valuable for its particularly long sequence of stratified occupation deposits. Most members of an Aboriginal community might agree that the same site is significant for its association with a Rainbow Serpent Dreaming story.

The attention I have given here to the concept of intrinsic/inherent significance reflects the influence I believe it has had in the heritage profession in regard to the neglect of social significance assessment. By regarding heritage objects and places as having meaning-in-themselves they are cut loose, in a sense, from their social context. We should take heed, though, that the critique of inherency, while it debunks one Western intellectual tradition is in danger of installing another. The proposition that significance is inscribed and socially constructed is democratic insofar as it recognises the diversity of meanings a place can have but it could also gloss over the fact that a very large proportion of the world's population believes that many heritage places are inherently sacred and empowered. It may be true that a majority of those in the Western world in the time since the Protestant Reformation have rejected the idea of 'real presence', meaning that the presence of God (or deities, saints etc) can be manifest in objects and places such that they have divine agency. But millions of others do believe this. For them, the power possessed by such objects and places is not installed (inscribed) in them via their own belief but is present there on a prior basis. Their belief is often reinforced by witnessing the miraculous efficacy of objects and places such as cases in which illness is cured by touching a sacred object or place. That such belief systems are sometimes described as religions of immanence (Eire 1986) attests to the central role played in them by the belief in inherent power.

Our tendency, of course, is simply to say that immanence also, ultimately, rests on belief. But this amounts to an imposition of our rationality upon their reality. For a Thai villager making propitiatory offerings to the animist spirit (*phi*) that inhabits the site of an old Buddhist temple, the spirit that embodies the place exists quite independently of themselves. In the everyday world that such people inhabit, its power is manifest in numerous ways (for instance, in the bad luck visited upon those who infringe its tutelary rights over the place). In such an order of things, places have agency. They have quite as much ability to act upon people as people have to act upon them.

In countries like China, Taiwan, Thailand and Vietnam, religious beliefs and practices of this type, which are often described as belonging to the magical–supernatural dimension of popular religion, appear to be flourishing rather than declining under the conditions of modernity and rapid economic development (Jackson 1999; Keys, Hardacre and Kendall 1994). Our failure to engage with the lived reality of such beliefs and practices risks the realm of heritage conservation remaining remote from the everyday lives of the majority of the population in these countries.

A new model: heritage as social action

Reference was earlier made to Appadurai's (1996: 12–13) concern that the idea of culture as 'substance' takes us back to an earlier idea of culture as race, an idea one would have hoped had been left behind. Appadurai suggests we think of culture mainly as being to do with the 'mobilizing of group identities'. In the pages that follow I explore the idea that cultural heritage is a field of social/cultural action.

Cultural change and social significance

In a book that had a major impact on the way anthropologists think about culture, Eric Wolf (1982) pointed to the amount of time members of a culture spend adapting to new circumstances, interpreting their history and inventing new practices. Wolf wrote that, '[a] culture is thus better seen as a series of processes that construct, reconstruct, and dismantle cultural materials . . .' (1982: 378). Cultures are these days seen as more fluid and changeable than they were before. People are seen not as inheritors or passive recipients of culture but as active owners and modifiers of culture.

It may be useful at this point to reflect on the way that culture and cultural space is communicated intergenerationally. The cultural landscape at any one time can be thought of as being populated by several generations who, in a sense, form different strata. The landscape that is culturally configured by one generation is 'inherited' by the succeeding generation but is reinterpreted in the eyes of their own experience rather than being taken on as a given. In this way they are agents in the history-making process, not passive receivers of historical knowledge. Different generations, or age-cohorts, have different experiences of history (Colson 1984: 1–13; Rosaldo 1980) and the significance or meaning of heritage places is simultaneously inherited and reinvented by the living. The living can be thought of as constantly re-producing significance.

The historical landscape is inherited by any one generation as a configuration of places whose significance was established by the previous generation. This significance is communicated by members of the previous generation who are now more or less old. In Australian Aboriginal society, as in other societies which privilege oral over textual transmission, such communication is obviously only possible because generations overlap. If a generation spans twenty years, for argument's sake, then members of at least four generations are likely to be alive and sharing the landscape at any one time. Also, those in the middle generations, the 40–60 age bracket, are layered between both older and younger generations of the living. Those in the newest generation 'inherit' the historical landscape of their parents' generation as well as that of their grandparents' generation, as reinterpreted or mediated by their parents' generation. But they are also able to receive it directly from the grandparental generation. The complexity of the situation can be appreciated if we acknowledge that each individual's reworking of the landscape is not something accomplished and then concretised but is a process of 'becoming' which continues until death.

But nor is it merely the process of reinterpreting physical traces which renders the historical landscape dynamic. Succeeding generations add their own traces in the form of the things they build, the places they frequent, the cars they drive and abandon, and the events they witness and participate in. The landscape is thus authenticated or personalised by each generation in a transactional manner, transactional in the sense that present and past lives act on each other.

It is critical for any assessment of the social significance of heritage places and landscapes that inter-generational transmission and change be treated seriously. Allowance has to be made for the fact that this significance can and does change through time: an assessment of social significance carried out twenty years ago is an historical document, not a basis for determining the significance of a place in the present.

In Australia, one of the most important 'projects' of the field of Aboriginal studies over the last couple of decades has been to show how the old perception of Aboriginal culture as traditional, timeless and static has served to oppress contemporary Aboriginal people, especially in areas like New South Wales. Western society has a history of viewing other cultures as custom-bound and as less 'alive' and dynamic than its own cultures (Thomas 1989: 39). Other cultures are seen as less able to change and innovate. We would not think of referring to the eighteenth- or nineteenth-century British as 'traditional' because history tells us that this, the period of the industrial revolution, was a time of great change in British society. By the same token, these changes are not believed to have made Europeans culturally less European. The West, in other words, has seen change as natural and proper to its own culture. But when non-Western 'traditional' cultures – Aboriginal cultures, for instance – are observed to be undergoing change in the colonial context this is perceived to be a symptom of cultural breakdown or collapse. It is seen to represent a loss of integrity and authenticity. The changes are also almost always seen as being forced on these cultures, almost never seen as innovative responses by people who, while they did not choose to be colonised, may nevertheless be determined to take advantage of whatever opportunities the new situation has to offer.

The anthropologist, James Clifford (1988: 5), has described the way the West has typically seen the situation of the colonised:

> Entering the 'modern world', their distinct histories quickly vanish. Swept up in a destiny dominated by the capitalist West and by various technologically advanced socialisms, these suddenly 'backward' peoples no longer invent local futures. What is different about them remains tied to traditional pasts, inherited structures that either resist or yield to the new but cannot produce it.

Like Native Americans in the USA, contemporary Aboriginal people in Australia were always seen as 'survivors', a category redolent with connotations of passivity. As survivors they 'could not by definition be dynamic, inventive, or expansive' (Clifford 1988: 284).

Places with local futures

The dramatic under-recording of Aboriginal historic period (post-contact) heritage places in Australia suggests that much of the old thinking, outlined above, still holds sway in the field of Australian heritage practice (Byrne 2003b). As noted earlier, there appears to be a perception that Aboriginal pre-contact (pre-1788) heritage is more authentically Aboriginal than that of the later period. It need hardly be said that such thinking is likely to produce a climate in which the social significance that heritage places have for Aboriginal people in present-day NSW will not be taken seriously.

Faced with this situation, Aboriginal people have felt compelled on occasion to use the language of the 'sacred' to describe the value of heritage places which ostensibly are secular. A shell midden, for instance, may in the present day take on symbolic meanings and emotional associations which have no precedent in 'traditional' culture. Some Aboriginal people, when they are present at such places are overcome by a sense of the presence of the 'old people' and a sadness for what happened to them – a sadness about the violence of the frontier period and the oppression suffered by their forebears under the government's Protection policies. In a situation where the heritage system only has one category for these sites (shell midden – archaeological) and has only been responsive to two categories of value or significance (archaeological and sacred/Dreaming) it sometimes happens that Aboriginal people describe such sites as 'sacred'. In a similar vein, Jane Jacobs (1988) points to the way legal frameworks relating to Aboriginal land rights in South Australia have placed an over-emphasis on the sacred site, leading it to be seen as *the* authentic Aboriginal site. When Aboriginal people resort to the category of the 'sacred' in these contexts they do so not so much for want of a better word as for want of a legal system and heritage system capable of acknowledging that there are authentic ways of valuing places in present-day Aboriginal society which are uniquely to do with the present day.

Clifford writes that 'It is easier to register the loss of traditional orders of difference than to perceive the emergence of new ones' (Clifford 1988: 15). Lamentably few heritage professionals have been sensitive to the uniquely modern/contemporary discourses of heritage that we see among Indigenous people today. In the scenario involving the shell midden, referred to above, there is a failure on the part of the heritage system to concede that an old place can be recycled back into Aboriginal culture with a new meaning. There is a failure, in other words, to acknowledge that a place's significance can be up-dated, a failure, to use Clifford's terms again, to acknowledge that an old place could be given a 'local future'.

Part of this process of 'local futuring' involves the 'new' self-consciousness or reflexivity that local people now have about the way they live. This indeed is one of the symptoms of modernity. There is a general acknowledgement that one of the features of modernity has been an acceleration in the rate at which social practices are altered by the arrival of new information and by the habit of reflecting on those practices (Giddens 1990: 38). This particular self-consciousness was enabled by the advent of print media and later, of course, by the electronic media. There can, for example, be few local communities in the world that are unaware of that sphere of the activity that involves the identification and conservation of cultural heritage places. One of the consequences of this is that a heritage professional cannot these days go into a local community to assess the social significance of an old place without finding that the community's expression of that significance is not in some way influenced or structured by received concepts of heritage. The discourse of heritage has arrived in the community in advance of the heritage professional and local expressions of a place's significance will be filtered through this discourse.

This does not, of course, mean that these local expressions of significance are inauthentic. It simply means that local people are engaged, as we heritage professionals are, in the self-conscious, reflexive business of producing their heritage. Taking this further, we might also note the development in the post-colonial world, from the time of the 1950s, of the practice of 'talking back' or 'writing back'. These catch-phrases of the field of post-colonial studies describe the way previous colonial subjects in places like India, Africa, and the Caribbean have turned the West's own system of knowledge back on it. Scholars in the developing world have used their Western training in fields like history, anthropology, and cultural studies to mount an attack on the West and its behaviour towards them. It is not difficult to find instances of Aboriginal people engaging with heritage discourse in this way. When John Ah Kit (1995: 34–36), for instance, uses his understanding of existing heritage processes in the Northern Territory to launch a critique of the way these processes have excluded Aboriginal experience from the Territory's historic heritage he is no longer, if he ever was, a passive subject/recipient of heritage practice but, rather, is an active interlocutor.

While it is clear that a desire to 'reform' public perception is not a good premise for a program to assess social significance there is an argument that intervention is justifiable when it takes the form of 'enabling'. Chris Johnston (1990: 35) has been a proponent of this in Australia. Rather than formal education in heritage, she argues, the community needs to be given 'opportunities for discovery and participation' in the heritage process. Johnson is recognising, here, that from a local community's point of view, the fact that they have attachment to a place and knowledge of it is not enough to ensure they will have a real role or stake in the heritage arena. If a local community is to become an effective, rather than notional, stakeholder in local heritage outcomes then it will need to develop certain skills.

The heritage conservation process has its own established concepts and language. Heritage is a discourse which non-professionals need to learn if they want their views to register with officialdom. In Johnson's (1990: 36) terms, they need to become 'connoisseurs'. Presumably she has in mind a scenario where it may not be enough for a community simply to value an old building or a landscape feature; they will also need, for instance, to be able to describe the history of the place and perhaps record oral histories relating to it.

All of this reflects the heightened consciousness in the present-day social sciences of the equation between language and power. This consciousness to a great degree stems from the work of the French philosopher Michel Foucault (1972, 1980). After Foucault, it is possible and useful to think of a field like archaeology not so much as a discipline (the old term) but as a discourse. The discourse of archaeology is a formation of concepts and language that can be deployed in order to make a certain sense of the physical traces of the human past. Over the last 100 years or so archaeologists have been successful in gaining recognition, by governments and institutions, as possessing the legitimate expertise on the physical traces of the human past. For better or worse, archaeology is now recognised as constituting the 'proper knowledge' of these traces. Under these circumstances there is considerable advantage to other people (i.e., non-archaeologists) in borrowing bits of the discourse of archaeology to describe old places. Aboriginal people in Australia increasingly deploy the discourse of archaeology to describe certain of their old places, presumably because this language carries more weight in getting protection for places than other forms of language. Presumably for the same reasons, they increasingly deploy the discourse of heritage. They might even be said to have appropriated or 'hijacked' the heritage discourse, a discourse whose origins were in white society.

The issue of agency

The French sociologist, Pierre Bourdieu, has had a significant influence on current understandings of how society is experienced by the individual (the individual social 'actor'). He coined the term 'habitus' to refer to the accumulated knowledge which individuals use in order to be acceptable and successful in society (Bourdieu 1977). An individual's habitus might include his or her ability to take part in a group conversation, their ability to be humorous, their ability to use forms of speech appropriate in different situations, their command of table etiquette, their taste in art, or their knowledge of the conventions of sportsmanship. This might seem simply to describe the process of an individual's 'sociali-sation', except that Bourdieu is interested in describing the individual's own initiative in acquiring these skills and deploying them. Such initiative might best be called *agency*.

It is clear that in each culture or society there are commonly accepted ways of think-ing about old places and expressing attachment to them, knowledge of them, or interest in them. These ways would be part of an individual's habitus. A key element of the concept of habitus, though, is the idea that we continue to work at acquiring knowledge and skills all through our lives. We do this in the interests of social advancement. It is well known that certain forms of what might be called 'heritage appreciation' are associated with 'high class' or élite culture. Examples of this might include the collecting of 'fine art' and antiques, the acquiring and display of knowledge about the ancient monuments of Egypt or about Victorian or Edwardian domestic architecture.

Another of Bourdieu's concepts, that of 'cultural capital', is useful here. The skills and knowledge people accumulate in their lives are a form of cultural capital not unlike eco-nomic capital (or money). Cultural capital is more than just a form of status in itself. It can be deployed to a variety of ends such as gaining public office or gaining entry to influential social circles where there are more opportunities to accumulate more cultural capital. It is well known that in some countries the extent to which antiquities have become a form of cultural capital is causing a boom in the trade in antiquities often illegally obtained by 'looting' heritage sites (e.g., Byrne 1999; Hamilakis and Yalouri 1996).

But even for those who are not collectors, simply being able to speak about old places and objects can also be an important factor in the sort of 'upward mobility' that comes under Bourdieu's term 'personal trajectories' (Postone, LiPuma and Calhoun 1993). There can be no doubt that this accumulation of cultural capital is a fact of life in communities the world over, that it is a driving force in local historical societies, National Trusts, museum volunteer groups and other less structured forms of heritage participation. Nor can there be any doubt that it is a dynamic that is present on the ground in many assessments of social significance. It would be wrong, however, to try to separate this form of knowledge and appreciation from supposedly more 'authentic' forms. Bourdieu, after all, is not describing how 'social climbers' operate but how people in general operate. Appreciation of heritage places is not something people are born with, it is something acquired.

An in-depth understanding of the social significance of heritage places calls for an awareness of such processes. It also requires an awareness of when and how certain places become a focus of, or come under the heading of, cultural capital. In most parts of Aus-tralia, for instance, a knowledge of the site of an old Aboriginal fringe camp will not be useful for social advancement in white society. There is more cultural capital to be gener-ated from an interest in pre-contact Aboriginal heritage places (e.g., rock art sites) than post-contact heritage places. This is because the former are generally perceived by white society to be a more authentic expression of Aboriginality than the latter which are seen as representing a period when 'real' Aboriginal culture had been lost. The local historical societies that are to be found in most Australian country towns and whose members tend to be exclusively Anglo-Celtic are nodes of activity in the accruing of cultural capital through the celebration of settler history and heritage. In many cases their members, who have often grown up and gone to school with Aboriginal people, display an aversion to the idea that the continuing Aboriginal presence in the local colonised landscape could be a subject of heritage recording and conservation. In a similar vein, Dolores Hayden (1995) describes how an appreciation of the heritage of Afro-Americans, women, the working classes and immigrants has not traditionally been socially sanctioned in white establishment culture in the United States.

The social science debate on cultural change is closely related to the concept of agency. Social scientists are increasingly aware that individuals and groups are not passive subjects of social systems but, rather, are actively engaged in shaping their society just as their society shapes them. Congruent with the dynamic nature of societies, the social significance of a heritage place should not be thought of as a social *fact*. Rather, it is part of a social *process*. When heritage practitioners go into communities they are not in a position to simply download those communities of information (social facts) about the way they value old places. More realistically, they are engaging the community in a dialogue, the outcome of which will have as much to do with the heritage practitioner as with the community itself.

Promoting heritage values

The idea of cultural heritage as a form of social action is likely to meet resistance from those heritage practitioners who might argue that this condones the 'invention' of significance. Their view would be that the social significance of a place is embedded in that community in a relatively unselfconscious manner. This sits uncomfortably, it is argued below, with the fact that heritage practitioners and heritage agencies have themselves always been energetic 'educators', even manipulators, of public opinion and community values. There is no question that many of the expressions of public value that social significance assessors collect from community groups were 'seeded' by other heritage professionals. While there is an undeniable circularity in this, there is nothing necessarily wrong with it. It simply underlines the point that heritage is a field of social action.

What is questionable, however, is the failure of heritage professionals to acknowledge reality in this area. At worst, this obfuscation (the right hand pretending not to notice what the left hand is doing) has produced the lack of transparency so characteristic of the way that social significance is currently discussed by most heritage professionals.

'Heritage' is a relatively recent concept in Western society. Pierre Nora (1989), in a well-known article, observes that prior to the nineteenth century 'the milieu of memory' was a pervasive part of everyday life and not something subject to commemoration in the way that it became later. In John Gillis's (1994: 6) words, '[o]rdinary people felt the past to be so much a part of their present that they perceived no urgent need to record, objectify, and preserve it'. The industrial revolution and the European political revolutions of the late eighteenth and early nineteenth centuries changed all that:

> The demand for commemoration was then taken up by the urban middle and working classes, gradually expanding until, today, everyone is obsessed with recording, preserving, and remembering. According to Nora, 'we speak so much of memory because there is so little of it left,' referring to the kind of living memory, communicated face to face, that still exists in rural Ireland, but which now has to compete with a multitude of other memories, some official, others commercialized.
>
> (Gillis 1994: 7)

Most heritage commentators note the linkage between the concept of national heritage and the enterprise of national identity building (e.g., Anderson 1991; Lowenthal 1985, 1996). There is by now a well-entrenched belief by governments across the globe that the identification of the national population with certain sites and monuments helps to foster a sense of cohesion and consensus. Nobody would suggest that such cohesion or social bonding is a bad thing if it results in an avoidance of communal violence and blood-letting. The benefits, it would have to be said, are less obvious where national heritage has been used to prop up military dictatorships (examples of which range from Hitler's Germany to Myanmar under its present military regime).

This critique of 'national heritage' sites does not imply that these places had no value or significance to communities prior to the appearance of the modern nation state (i.e., prior to the eighteenth century in Europe). What it does imply is that the identification of these places with the nation is recent and 'invented' (Hobsbawm and Ranger 1989). It could certainly be argued that a large part of the Australian Heritage Commission's mission in the last quarter of the twentieth century was to make Australians conscious of a shared national heritage, a heritage embodied in the list of the National Estate. Many of the places in the National Estate were unknown to the average Australian prior to the publicising of them by the Commission and related bodies.

From the beginning of the preservation movement – in Europe in the nineteenth century, later in Australia – architects, archaeologists and historians have energetically promoted an appreciation of heritage values in the population as a whole. It is not insignificant that in England in the second half of the nineteenth century both John Ruskin and William Morris, the two most significant public voices on the protection of built heritage, both saw themselves as educators of public opinion and were deeply committed to the education of the lower classes. In 1931 the influential Charter of Venice (and later international conventions) took as one of its principles the promulgation of the conservation ethic among the general public. Later, National Trusts and then government heritage agencies joined this project of public education.

There can be little doubt that many of the heritage places we now value and even love have only survived because of a groundswell of public support for their preservation, support which has been at least partly a product of this educational enterprise. The point here is that the promulgation of a particular way of valuing old places has, from the beginning, been an integral feature of the heritage discourse.

A typical expression of the proselytising mission of heritage practitioners and agencies is the following statement in the NSW Heritage Office's *Heritage Assessments* publication under the heading, 'What is meant by integrity':

> an item '. . . must be capable of being successfully interpreted now or in the future so that the general public can appreciate its significance'.

There is no separation, here, between the process of instilling heritage values and that of assessing them. Almost every publication on cultural heritage contains exhortations to enhance the community's appreciation of heritage. One might conclude that heritage practitioners themselves are implicitly committed to the concept of heritage as a form of social action.

Much heritage legislation and policy cites the interests of future generations as a reason for protecting heritage in the present. The job of deciding what future generations will appreciate, and how they will appreciate it, falls to present-day heritage professionals who make their determinations largely on the basis of scientific, historical and aesthetic significance (which largely translate as the sectoral values of the archaeological, historical and architectural professions). The most problematic dimension of this 'appeal to the unborn' is where the assumed value system of future generations is used to over-ride the expressed values of present-day communities. This was what was at stake in the campaign by a faction of Australian archaeologists in the 1980s to prevent Aboriginal communities reburying Aboriginal skeletal remains that had been repatriated from museum collections. In the face of a clearly stated and virtually unanimous desire by these communities to rebury or otherwise dispose of the remains, the archaeologists argued against reburial on the grounds that it would be against the interests of future generations of Aboriginal people.

In calling for more reflexivity on the part of heritage practitioners, in other words, a greater consciousness of the origin and historic-political context of our ideas, a comparison might be made with the discipline of anthropology. Up until about 1960 the extended periods of intensive ethnographic field observation engaged in by anthropologists were seen as producing a true picture of the social reality of non-Western cultures. After 1960 it began to be seen that these 'true pictures' were still very much interpretations. Non-Western peoples were still being portrayed the way the West wanted to see them (e.g., as passive, unchanging, gullible, superstitious). Rather than trying to get rid of the filter of interpretation, anthropology embraced it. It was acknowledged that the anthropologist could not leave his or her own culture behind when he or she travelled into the field. They took it with them and it inevitably acted as the lens through which they observed other cultures. This did not mean that no understanding of the Other was possible. It simply meant that any understanding has limits. Anthropologists came to appreciate how important it was to include themselves as a subject of their study, how essential it was to understand the preconceptions and biases they took with them into the field and how these might affect their interpretations. Heritage professionals might do well to strive for a similar self-awareness when assessing the social significance of heritage places and landscapes. This might entail an understanding of the extent to which we are advocates as well as practitioners of conservation.

This is an opportune point at which to return to the notion of heritage as social action. The attachment that a person feels for a heritage place may be based on stories that have been passed down to them about the place or on experiences they have had at the place in their own lifetimes. Equally, though, their attachment may have been formed or enhanced in the course of the struggle to preserve the place from development. Or it might have been formed in the context of the sort of 'cultural revival' activities in which many Aboriginal communities in Australia are involved. These activities often entail organising 'culture camps' where elders explain the significance of places and landscapes to young people. Or, again, an interest in and attachment for a place may be acquired in the course of improving one's social position (developing one's social 'trajectory', in the words of Bourdieu). Most often, though, attachment will involve combinations of these, combinations which may well defy any heritage practitioner's efforts to untease them.

James Clifford (1988: 14) writes that:

> Twentieth-century identities no longer presuppose continuous cultures or traditions. Everywhere individuals and groups improvise local performances from (re)collected pasts, drawing on foreign media, symbols and languages.

Everywhere, in other words, cultures (societies) are inventive. Cultural identity is improvised partly by drawing on the past. The term '(re)collected' conveys the sense of remembering and 'gathering together'. We are inclined, when we think of cultural heritage, to think of it as something we just protect, keep an eye on, and perhaps restore. What Clifford is referring to, though, is the way we use heritage as a resource in the on-going project of creating our identity. One could say that heritage is *deployed* in this aspect of social life.

Another way of putting this is that landscapes, with all the heritage places and traces they contain, and also our minds, with all their memories, are an archive of our culture's past and an archive of ourselves as individuals. We *mobilise* elements from this archive in the process of forming and expressing our identity. There is nothing sinister about this deployment of heritage. It would be difficult to find an example of heritage work in which heritage is not being deployed in identity formation. Heritage is the very stuff of social identity and to this extent can be regarded as a form of social action. The implication is that we all – people in communities as well as heritage practitioners – are 'heritage workers'. We are all engaged in the work of signifying places, deciding what should be done with them, deploying them as identity markers.

Heritage and identity

Local communities are not natural phenomena. They are cultural constructions in the sense that they come into being and maintain their integrity only through the ceaseless work of local identity building. Crucial here is the work entailed in identifying a particular community with a particular place, that limited piece of terrain that the community comes to regard as its neighbourhood.

The relationship between a community and its neighbourhood is essentially two-way (i.e., dialectical). Arjun Appadurai (1996: 182), who describes locality as 'a structure of feeling', observes that the association of a community with a locality can never be taken for granted; locality should never be considered a 'given'. Anthropologists working all over the globe have noticed that local communities themselves never seem to take locality as a given. 'Rather they seem to assume that locality is ephemeral unless hard and regular work is undertaken to produce and maintain its materiality' (Appadurai 1996: 181). An example of such work would be the relationship of a local Aboriginal community in Australia with its cemetery (Byrne 2004). The 'work' that goes into maintaining the association between the space of the cemetery and the community includes not just the activity of decorating and maintaining the graves, or maintaining the fence around the cemetery that keeps stock from trampling the graves. It also includes the attendance by often large numbers of community members at funerals. The cemetery becomes a local place partly because the community has 'stamped' its identity upon the place (the names of its members are quite literally 'stamped' on the wooden crosses and the headstones). But the place, in a sense, has also stamped itself on the identity of the community in the way that the community is known, and knows itself, partly as being that group of people who periodically gather at this particular place. Such place-based activity, while it would rarely be thought of as 'work', is nevertheless precisely the work of identity building.

The fact that a local community, Indigenous or non-indigenous, may live in a landscape that is scattered with places where physical traces of past occupation are present, does not in itself create an identity association between those traces and the community. The association comes about through certain activities. These may include the work carried out to protect the traces from erosion or vandalism or the taking of visitors out to see the traces as part of a local cultural tourism venture. It may consist of a community member talking to a class at the local school about the traces, or it may consist simply of the reminiscences about the place which appear in an autobiography written by a community member. Rodney Harrison (2004: 208–212) goes so far as to propose that the space of a heritage site, such as the former Aboriginal pastoral camp at Dennawan in western NSW (c.1890s–1950s), is only brought into being in the present by performative actions in the present. He describes the way that Aboriginal people continue to maintain Dennawan as their place by semi-ritual visits to the site which entail walking a particular unmarked route around it and encountering objects (remains of huts and old cars, old buttons, brooches, clay pipe stems) that trigger memories, emotions and stories.

Indigenous people in many countries are struggling for recognition of their rights to traditional land. They have become aware that something that may previously have been taken for granted (their attachment to locality, their sense of belonging) now has to be made public and demonstrable. It is no longer enough for people to have their own sense of 'who they are', they have to be able demonstrate a tangible linkage between their community and the local landscape. The need for this linkage, it might be suggested, has brought about a merging of 'heritage work' and the work of identity building.

The position argued here is that the way that local places 'become' heritage places is not merely a normal aspect of community identity building; it is probably critical to the viability or survival of a community. It is something all communities engage in. All communities are emplaced and the work of place-making, whether conceptualised as heritage or not, is fundamental. The whole field of activity we now think of as heritage work might be seen as driven by what one commentator has described as the 'tenacious and fragile desire' of people to belong to a place and a community (Probyn 1996: 8).

References

Ah Kit, J. (1995) 'Aboriginal aspirations for heritage conservation', *Historic Environment* 11: 34–36.

Altman, I. and Low, S. (1992) *Place Attachment*. New York: Plenum Press.

Anderson, B. (1991) *Imagined Communities*. London: Verso.

Appadurai, A. (1996) *Modernity at Large*. Minneapolis: University of Minneapolis Press.

Asad, T. (1973) *Anthropology and the Colonial Encounter*. London: Ithaca Press.

Avrami, E., Mason, R. and de la Torre, M. (2000) *Values and Heritage Conservation*. Los Angeles: Getty Conservation Institute.

Biersack, A. (1989) 'Local knowledge, local history: Geertz and beyond'. In Hunt, L. (ed.) *The New Cultural History* pp. 72–76 Berkeley: University of California Press.

Bourdieu, P. (1977) *Outline of a Theory of Practice*, translated from the French by R. Nice. Cambridge: Cambridge University Press.

Briuer, F.L. and Mathers, C. (1996) *Trends and Patterns in Cultural Resource Significance: An Historical Perspective and Annotated Bibliography*. Vicksburg, Mississippi: US Army Corps of Engineers, Center for Cultural Site Preservation Technology.

Byrne, D. (1996–97) 'The archaeology of disaster', *Public History Review* 5/6: 17–29.

—— (1999) 'The nation, the elite and the Southeast Asian antiquities trade', *Conservation and Management of Archaeological Sites* 3: 145–153.

—— (2003a) 'Nervous landscapes: race and space in Australia', *Journal of Social Archaeology* 3(2): 169–193.

—— (2003b) 'The ethos of return: erasure and reinstatement of Aboriginal visibility in the Australian historical landscape', *Historical Archaeology* 37(1): 73–86.

—— (2004) 'Archaeology in reverse'. In Merriman N. (ed.), *Public Archaeology*, 240–254. London: Routledge.

Byrne, D. and Nugent, M. (2004) *Mapping Attachment*. Sydney: Department of Environment and Conservation (NSW).

Byrne, D., Brayshaw, H. and Ireland, T. (2001) *Social Significance: A Discussion Paper*. Sydney: NSW National Parks & Wildlife Service.

Clifford, J. (1988) *The Predicament of Culture*. Cambridge (Mass): University of Harvard Press.

Colson, E. (1984) 'The reordering of experience: anthropological involvement with time', *Journal of Anthropological Research* 40: 1–13.

Cowlishaw, G. (1987) 'Colour, culture and the Aboriginalists', *Man* (N.S.) 22: 221–237.

—— (1988) *Black, White or Brindle*, Cambridge: Cambridge University Press.

Davis, N.Z. (1983) *The Return of Martin Guerre*. Cambridge, MA: Harvard University Press.

De la Torre, M. (ed.) (2002) *Assessing The Values of Cultural Heritage*. Los Angeles: Getty Conservation Institute.

Eire, C.M. (1986) *War Against the Idols*. Cambridge: Cambridge University Press.

Fabian, J. (1998) *Moments of Freedom: Anthropology and Popular Culture*, Charlottesville: University of Virginia Press.

Field, S. and Basso, K.H. (eds) (1996) *Senses of Place*. Santa Fe: School of American Research.

Foucault, M. (1972) *The Archaeology of Knowledge and the Discourse on Language*, translated from the French by A.M.S. Smith. New York: Pantheon.

—— (1980) 'Two lectures'. In Gordon, C. (ed.), *Power/knowledge: Selective Interviews and Other Writings 1972–1977 by Michel Foucault*, pp. 78–101. New York: Pantheon.

Geertz, C. (1983) *Local Knowledge: Further Essays in Interpretive Anthropology*. New York: Basic Books.

Giddens, A. (1990) *The Consequences of Modernity*. Stanford: Stanford University Press.

Gillis, J.R. (1994) 'Memory and identity: the history of a relationship'. In Gillis, J.R. (ed.) *Commemorations: The Politics of National Identity*, pp. 3–24. Princeton: Princeton University Press.

Hamilakis, Y. and Yalouri, E. (1996) 'Antiquities as symbolic capital in modern Greek society', *Antiquity* 70: 117–129.

Handler, R. (1985) 'On having a culture: nationalism and the preservation of Quebec's *Patrimoine*'. In Stocking, G. (ed.) *Objects and Others*, pp. 192–215. Madison: University of Wisconsin Press.

—— (1988) *Nationalism and the Politics of Culture in Quebec*. Madison: University of Wisconsin Press.

Harrison, R. (2004) *Shared Landscapes: Archaeology of Attachment and the Pastoral Industry in New South Wales*. Sydney: NSW University Press and the Department of Environment (NSW).

Hayden, D. (1995) *The Power of Place*. Cambridge, MA: MIT Press.

Hobsbawm, E. and Ranger, T. (eds) (1989) *The Invention of Tradition*. Cambridge: Cambridge University Press.

Jackson, P. (1999) 'Royal spirits, Chinese gods, and magic monks: Thailand's boom-time religions of prosperity', *South East Asian Research* 7: 245–320.

Jacobs, J. (1988) 'The construction of identity'. In Beckett, J. (ed.) *Past and Present*, pp. 31–43. Canberra: Aboriginal Studies Press.

Johnson, C. (1990) 'Whose views count?: achieving community support for landscape conservation', *Historic Environment* 7: 33–37.

Keefe, K. (1988) 'Aboriginality: resistance and persistence', *Australian Aboriginal Studies* 1: 67–81.

Keyes, C.F., Hardacre, H. and Kendall, L. (1994) 'Introduction: contested visions of community in East and Southeast Asia'. In Keyes, C.F. Kendall, L. and Hardacre, H. (eds) *Asians Visions of Authority*, pp. 1–16. Honolulu: University of Hawaii Press.

Küchler, S. (1993) 'Landscape as memory: the mapping of process and its representation in a Melanesian society'. In Bender, B. (ed.) *Landscape: Politics and Perspectives*, pp. 85–106. Oxford: Berg.

Kuper, A. (1982) *Anthropology and Anthropologists*. London: Routledge. Revised edition 1996.

Lattas, A. (1990) 'Aborigines and contemporary Australian nationalism: primordiality and the cultural politics of otherness', *Social Analysis* 27: 50–69

Leach, E. (1989) 'Tribal ethnography: past, present, future'. In Tonkin, E. McDonald, M. and Chapman, M. (eds) *History and Ethnicity*, pp. 34–47. London: Routledge.

Leone, M.P. and Potter, P.B. (1992) 'Legitimation and the classification of archaeological sites,' *American Antiquity* 57: 137–145.

Lipe, W. (1984) 'Value and meaning in cultural resources'. In Cleere, H. (ed.) *Approaches to the Archaeological Heritage* pp. 1–11. New York: Cambridge University Press.

Lowenthal, D. (1985) *The Past is a Foreign Country*. Cambridge: Cambridge University Press.

—— (1996) *The Heritage Crusade and the Spoils of History*. London: Viking.

Malan, A. and van Heyningen, E. (2001) 'Twice removed: Horsley Street in Cape Town's District Six, 1865–1982'. In Mayne, A. and Murray, T. (eds) *The Archaeology of Urban Landscapes*, 39–56. Cambridge: Cambridge University Press.

Marcus, G.E. and Fischer, M.J. (1986) *Anthropology as Cultural Critique*. Chicago: University of Chicago Press.

Mason, R. (2002) 'Assessing values in conservation planning: methodological issues and choices'. In de la Torre, M. (ed.) *Assessing The Values of Cultural Heritage*, 5–30. Los Angeles: Getty Conservation Institute.

Merlan, F. (1989) 'The objectification of "culture": an aspect of current political process in Aboriginal affairs', *Anthropological Forum* 6: 105–116.

Moore, H.L. (1996) 'The changing nature of anthropological knowledge.' In Moore, H.L. (ed.) *The Future of Anthropological Knowledge*, pp. 1–15. London: Routledge.

Mueggler, E. (1998) 'A carceral regime, violence and social memory in Southwest China', *Cultural Anthropology*, 13: 167–192.

Nora, P. (1989) 'Between memory and history: *les lieux de memoire*', *Representations* 26.

Postone, M., LiPuma, E. and Calhoun, C. (1993), 'Introduction: Bourdieu and social theory'. In Calhoun, C. LiPuma, E. and Postone, M. (eds) *Bourdieu: Critical Perspectives*, pp. 1–13. Chicago: University of Chicago Press.

Probyn, E. (1996) *Outside Belongings*. New York: Routledge.

Rosaldo, R. (1980) *Ilongot Headhunting 1883–1974*. Stanford: Stanford University Press.

Sahlins, M. (1985) *Islands in History*. Chicago: Chicago University Press.

Schilling, K. (2003) *Aboriginal Women's Heritage: Nambucca*. Sydney: NSW National Parks and Wildlife Service.

Silberman, N.A. (1989) *Between Past and Present: Archaeology, Ideology, and Nationalism in the Middle East*. New York: Holt.

Stewart, K. (1996) *A Space on the Side of the Road*, Princeton: Princeton University Press.

Tainter, J.A. and Lucas, G.J. (1983) 'Epistemology of the significance concept', *American Antiquity* 48: 707–719.

Taussig, M. (1992) *The Nervous System*. New York: Routledge.

Thomas, J. (2004) *Archaeology and Modernity*. London: Routledge.

Thomas, N. (1989) *Out of Time: History and Evolution in Anthropological Discourse*. Cambridge: Cambridge University Press.

—— (1991) *Entangled Objects*. Cambridge, MA: Harvard University Press.

Tilley, C. (1994) *A Phenomenology of Landscape*. Oxford: Berg.

Veale, S. (2001) *Remembering Country*. Sydney: NSW National Parks and Wildlife Service.

Walker, M. and Marquis-Kyle, P. (2004) *The Illustrated Burra Charter*. Melbourne: Australia ICOMOS.

White, H. (1987) *The Content of the Form*. Baltimore: Johns Hopkins University Press.

Williams, D.R., Patterson, M.E., Roggenbuck, J.W. and Watson, A.E. (1992) 'Beyond the commodity metaphor: examining emotional and symbolic attachment to place', *Leisure Studies* 14: 29–46.

Williams, R. (1963) *Culture and Society 1780–1950*. Harmondsworth: Penguin.

Wolf, E. (1982) *Europe and the People Without History*. Berkeley: University of California Press.

Whose heritage? local and global perspectives

Chapter 12

The Politics of the Past
Conflict in the use of heritage in the modern world

Rodney Harrison

Introduction

During the early 1990s, it was common to see a large, colourful poster distributed by the Australian Heritage Commission designed to raise awareness of the Register of the National Estate hanging on the walls of the waiting rooms of a number of Australian State Heritage Management Agencies. A series of these posters were produced showing glossy shots of picturesque Australian heritage places and the words *'Places we want to keep'*. The success of this campaign rested on the simplicity of the language and the directness of the message. But who is the 'we' in this phrase, and why do we want to keep particular places and not others? These are the questions which are central to this section of the Reader, and an area of debate which I will try to summarise in this introduction to the section.

The role of heritage in settler societies and non-settler societies compared

Before moving on to the issues pre-empted above, it is important to suggest a distinction between the way in which heritage management and conservation can be seen to operate in settler societies, as opposed to non-settler societies, and to outline an argument which I hope to develop in parallel with a consideration of the issues of the 'for whom?' and 'why?' of heritage management. In doing so, I draw generally on Laurajane Smith's (2004) application of the later works of Foucault to explain the governmentalisation of archaeology as a tool by which the state, which holds an intermediary position between Indigenous people and archaeologists in settler societies, exercises power and control of heritage and the past (see also Palus, Leone and Cochran 2006). Lilley's paper (this volume) defines settler societies and introduces the idea of the peculiarities of indigenous heritage management in colonial and post-colonial contexts of settler societies. He notes that settler societies are an invention of postcolonialism, and can be defined as the overseas extensions of the states of Western Europe, places that were established as colonies or outposts of European empires in which existing indigenous populations were dislocated by settler-colonists. While Lilley follows Eddy and Schreuder (1988) in suggesting a difference between the United States and the other major Commonwealth Anglophone settler societies of Australia, New Zealand and Canada, in this chapter I would like to explore some broader differences between the ways in which heritage is managed in the United Kingdom as opposed to *both* the US and the other major settler societies. Clearly the co-existence of an original indigenous population and a population which derives from later usurpers, whether numerically dominant (as in the cases of Australia, the US, New Zealand and Canada) or not (as in the case of South Africa), has important implications for the ways in which settler nations deal with heritage as a way of representing the history and cultural identity of the nation (see also Lilley 2006; Smith 2004).

'Predatory' heritage

In his interview with Ian Hodder, Ashish Chadha, Trinity Jackman and Chris Witmore, Arjun Appadurai (this volume, see further discussion below) develops the idea of 'predatory' forms of heritage, suggesting that some forms of recollection which are manifest in the selection and management of particular cultural heritage places require the elimination or removal of other memories or forms of recollection. An idea that I will return to at several points in the course of this introductory chapter is that because of their peculiar colonial histories, heritage management in settler societies is necessarily predatory in nature, requiring the metaphorical and/or physical erasure of traces of prior Indigenous occupation and emphasising the roots of nationhood in colonial settlement. In Australia, as a number of authors have recently observed (Byrne 1996; 2002; 2003a; 2003b; Godwin and L'Oste-Brown 2002; Harrison 2000; 2004), the material traces of Aboriginal life from after the European invasion of Australia have largely been neglected in Australian cultural heritage management. Concurrent with this has been a general academic neglect of post-invasion Aboriginal archaeology or 'contact archaeology' (Murray 1993; Torrence and Clarke 2000; Williamson and Harrison 2002; see Lightfoot 1995 for similar observations about the US). The division of management and legislation used to protect Indigenous and historic heritage in Australia has further compounded this problem. By studying and managing Indigenous (read 'prehistoric', or 'black') and historic (read 'European', or 'white') heritage places separately, Indigenous heritage management in Australia has emphasised what Byrne (2002) calls the 'lavish, almost obsessional recording of pre-contact (or pre-colonisation) places' to the neglect of post-colonisation places. This has led to the illusion of a break between the pre-colonial past – when 'authentic' Aboriginal people lived as hunter-gatherers – and the present – when contemporary Aboriginal Australians generally live a radically different lifestyle (Griffiths 1996; Russell 2001). This has been supported by the settler colonial myth of *Terra nullius* (Reynolds 1982; 1987), the idea that lands were not legally occupied at the time of European invasion and sovereignty, and hence European occupation was not an act of war or invasion, but one of the settlement of vacant land. In settler societies, 'foundational' mythologies regard the arrival of European settlers as the starting point of history (Thomas 1994; 1999). This has resulted in a radical disassociation of Indigenous people from the heritage of the recent colonial past – a metaphorical usurpation of history (and hence, heritage) by the colonising group.

While I have drawn predominately on an Australian literature here, that heritage management in settler societies must necessarily be predatory in nature, emphasising particular heroic aspects of the colonial experience at the expense of those which speak of the ongoing presence and continuity of Indigenous people, seems almost a given. This observation can be coupled with Gosden's (2005) comments regarding the various forms of colonialism that can be seen to have existed throughout the past 5000 years in the world. Gosden suggests colonial 'middle grounds' are exemplified by the peripheries of the Greek colonies and the Roman Empire, and early modern contacts with indigenous peoples in North America, Africa, India and the Pacific. These forms of colonialism were characterised by experimentation and creativity, and consist of accommodation on the part of both indigenes and colonists and the development of regularised social relations. He contrasts these with '*Terra nullius*' forms of colonialism, as evidenced by the major settler societies of Australia, New Zealand, North America and Russia from the mid-eighteenth century, but also by the Mongols and Spanish in Peru and Mexico, which were characterised by extreme violence, mass appropriation of land, and the spread of disease which enabled the destruction of existing forms of social relations. Active resistance to colonial forms which allowed indigenous cultural continuity often existed in such circumstances. *Terra nullius* colonialism is differentiated from the other forms by the existence of relatively fixed categories of difference, whereas in middle-ground colonialism new categories of difference are often created by cross-cultural encounters. It is this requirement of *Terra nullius* forms of colonialism in settler societies to construct fixed notions of difference, in addition to any need to establish a legal basis for colonial occupation, that underlies the need for heritage in such contexts to develop predatory forms which (at least metaphorically) undermine or erase traces and memories of prior indigenous occupation.

'Places we want to keep': heritage conservation as a form of collecting

As Schofield outlined in the introduction to Section One, many literal 'dictionary' definitions of heritage focus on special places and landscapes which are considered worthy of preservation for future generations, generally in some way unchanged from (or at the very least reflecting) their original state. Hall's paper (this volume), a keynote address given at a conference: 'Whose Heritage: The Impact of Cultural Diversity on Britain's Living Heritage' in 1999, takes this notion to its logical conclusion, suggesting that heritage conservation needs to be seen as a form of collecting practice, and hence one which is both selective and political in nature. As he notes:

> Since the eighteenth century, collections of cultural artefacts and works of art have also been closely associated with informal public education. They have become part, not simply of 'governing', but of the broader practices of 'governmentality' – how the state indirectly and at a distance induces and solicits appropriate attitudes and forms of conduct from its citizens. The state is always, as Gramsci argued, 'educative'. Through its power to preserve and represent culture, the state has assumed some responsibility for educating the citizenry . . . this was the true test of their 'belongingness': culture as social incorporation.

He goes on to add:

> We should think of the Heritage as a discursive practice. It is one of the ways in which the nation slowly constructs for itself a sort of collective social memory. Just as individuals and families construct their identities in part by 'storying' the various random incidents and contingent turning points of their lives into a single, coherent, narrative, so nations construct identities by selectively binding their chosen high points and memorable achievements into an unfolding 'national story'. This story is what is called 'Tradition'.

Hall is concerned most specifically with Britain, and the ways in which the notion of what constitutes cultural heritage has been/could be transformed by 'Black British' and the explosion of cultural diversity and difference (see further discussion below). But the history of the development of collecting and the museum itself is instructive on the ways in which predatory forms of heritage management are employed in settler societies. The impetus for developing such collections derived from the historical specificities of Euro-American colonial expansion, and the relationship between natural history collections and newly emerging research in the biological sciences in the early to mid 1800s in Europe (Herle 1998: 80). Museums were to assemble complete sets of material culture with which to reconstruct the very cultures that they were 'modernising' in the process of collecting them. Fabian (1983) and Clifford (1988: 202) draw our attention to the ways in which the narratives of ethnography rest on an allegory of modernity in which the non-Western world is always in decline and ruin, emphasising the project of collecting cultures as one of salvaging the authentic in the wake of the modernisation of the tribal world. These collections were the very essence of a colonial narrative that fossilised Indigenous culture, by emphasising it as 'pure', essential and un-creolised (papers in Thomas and Losche 1999), but most importantly, *vanished*, an extinct strata covered over by European invasion and modernity (see Thomas 1999: 109). Understanding heritage conservation as a selective process by which places which represent the nation are collected and displayed for the education and integration of citizens into a particular notion of society and national identity immediately raises a number of issues about the 'for whom?' and 'why?' of heritage conservation.

'The nervous force and density of a lived cultural poetics': theorising community

Recent work on the production of community by anthropologists and sociologists draws attention to the way in which community is defined in contrast with an 'Other'. Gupta and Ferguson (1997: 13) note that:

> Community is never simply the recognition of cultural similarity or social contiguity but a categorical identity that is premised on various forms of exclusion and construction of otherness.

If one of the main areas of research through which modern anthropology has tackled issues of radical alterity has been through the study of colonialism and ethnicity (Keesing 1994: 301), it has also been the domain within which anthropology has most critically theorised the notion of 'community' (Amit and Rapport 2002: 44). There are a broad range of 'forms' of community, which may be developed primarily with reference to that which is held in common by its members, or in contrast, in terms of oppositional categories between insiders and outsiders. Shared participation can be used to constitute a sense of community in the same way that discourses of alterity can be mobilised to construct a collective sense of otherness. Such ascribed categorical identities as ethnicity or religion often derive symbolic power through the experiences of social relations or activities that are associated with them (Amit and Rapport 2002: 60). In using the word 'community' in this chapter, I am describing both those symbolic categories that may be employed to establish a sense of radical alterity as well as that sense of community which local people 'work' to produce through a series of social relations. These social relations often focus on particular important places in the landscape, and it is here that conflicts between local community understandings of heritage may come into conflict with the state (see further discussion below).

Heritage and the 'imagined community'

Both Hall and Appadurai (this volume) share a very particular idea of the connection between heritage and the nation state which is informed by a close reading of Benedict Anderson on 'imagined communities'. Benedict Anderson (1983) developed the concept of the 'imagined community' to attempt to account for the power and spread of nationalism in the West at the same time that the links between community and locality were becoming increasingly broken. Following Anderson, Cohen (1985) and Appadurai (1996) have argued that the dissolution of the spatial boundaries of a localised community has lead to the increased importance of the symbolic and imagined forms of community. Recent work on community has sought to explore the alternate forms of community which have arisen in response to the uncoupling of community and locality (e.g. papers in Amit ed. 2002). While some of these forms of community are best thought of as 'imagined', other forms which manifest themselves through both long-distance and face-to-face social relationships which may or may not be centred on place are increasingly becoming apparent. Such dual forms of 'imagined' and 'social' community may actually develop as part of a process of social mobility, or even physical movement and diaspora (Clifford 1997). Drawing on shared experience, interest, histories and common experiences, these new articulations of community 'arise . . . out of an interaction between the imagination of solidarity and its realization through social relations' (Amit 2002: 18).

'Congealed scenes for remembered events': theorising locality

Byrne's chapter (this volume) makes a series of crucial connections between heritage and local identity. Following Appadurai (1996 and this volume), he notes that communities use heritage as a part of the 'work' which maintains their effective links with particular localities (see also Byrne 2003a; 2003b; Byrne and Nugent 2004; Harrison 2004).

Appadurai's work on the production of locality emerges from his writings on globalisation and cultural flows, and the place of the local in the context of a world in which the traditional nation-state has become destabilised by processes of transnationalism. For Appadurai, locality is primarily a relational concept, rather than a spatial or scalar one, 'a complex phenomenological quality, constituted by a series of links between the sense of immediacy, the technologies of interactivity, and the relativity of contexts' (1996: 178). He uses the term *neighbourhood* to describe the formal social structures in which locality is realised. Neighbourhoods are thus 'life-worlds constituted by relatively stable associations, by relatively known and shared histories, and by collectively traversed and legible spaces and places' (1996: 191). There is a dialogic relationship between the neighbourhood and local subjects in which each is related to, and creates, the other. The production of the neighbourhood is intimately related to its context; it is both historically and environmentally grounded. However, all locality building activities also produce extra-local contexts for themselves, so the production of locality is intimately related to the production of itself in contrast with a non-locality (which Appadurai describes using the term *ethnoscape*). Locality is thus context-generative (as ethnoscape) as well as context-providing (as neighbourhood).

Appadurai's concern with locality here is primarily political and economic, but there are other articulations of the concept of locality to which he refers only tangentially, but which are equally relevant to this paper. Phenomenologist Edward Casey (2000: 189) notes on the connection between locality and memory:

> Places are *congealed scenes* for remembered contents; and as such they serve to situate what we remember . . . Place is a *mise en scène* for remembered events

precisely to the extent that it guards and keeps these events within its self delimited parameters. Instead of filtering out . . . place *holds in* by giving to memories an authentically local habitation.

[original emphases]

The potential for locality to embody, symbolise and evoke both individual and collective memory is an important aspect of the role of heritage in community building. On the flip side, commemoration and memorialisation are tools with which communities can produce locality and through collective participation, community. Casey (2000: 253) goes on to note that 'commemoration brings together such seemingly disconnected things as past and present, self and other, body and mind . . . it draws on powers of participation that are at play in every act of remembering'. The recursive nature of community, locality and commemorative acts/objects is central to understanding the role of heritage in building a sense of place.

National heritage vs local heritage

Locality is not a given, and Appadurai notes that the fragile condition of locality gives rise to a series of techniques, or *technologies*, for the production of locality, the sorts of activities which anthropologists often refer to as 'rites of passage'. The production of neighbourhood requires a foundational moment in which a *space* is transformed into a *place*. This foundational moment may be associated with events of extreme violence, ritual or warfare (1996: 183), but may later be remembered as relatively routine. In a later interview which specifically addressed the relationship between *Modernity at Large* and heritage (this volume), Appadurai emphasises the politics of remembering and forgetting and the role of the nation-state in controlling 'the apparati through which the economy of remembering and forgetting is configured'. He notes that archaeology plays a role in the development of 'specific mechanisms for remembering and forgetting' which should be set against popular and diasporic memory practices, the media, and the state's articulation of national heritage. Through the relationship between archaeology and state heritage institutions, Appadurai sees the profession of archaeology as a 'key site through which the apparatus of nations can reflect on the politics of remembering'. He suggests the focus of archaeology on the politics of recovery and remembering might mask the need to equally examine the politics of erasure and forgetting. Instead he advocates an examination of the narratives of political 'layering' which is sensitive both to the politics of remembering and forgetting, as well as the struggle between the local and the nation-state.

Byrne's chapter (this volume) suggests, following Bowdler (1988), that appealing to the universal or transcendent category of heritage is a means by which people with a particular interest in heritage places are excluded by the State from having a role in managing them. He draws on two case studies to suggest that notions of 'Universal' heritage value have been employed to argue for the application of Western notions of heritage management in the non-Western world. In his first example, Aboriginal people were criticised for maintaining a centuries-old cultural tradition of re-painting rock art images in the Kimberley region of Australia due to the insistence of a local land owner that this practice was damaging ancient paintings that were the 'universal heritage of all mankind'. In his second example, Byrne discusses continuous repair and enlargement of the Confucius Temple complex at Qufu, Jiangsu Province in China as a violation of the 1964 Venice Charter, but a project which is true to the Chinese approach to authenticity, which holds that the spirit of a place can only be maintained and enhanced through such activities in the present. This contrasts markedly with the kind of Western approach to heritage discussed by Holtorf (this volume) which sees the role of heritage as one of conserving or preserving the past in a relatively unmodified form, and draws a clear connection between the original fabric and form of a place or object, and its authenticity, and hence value, as a piece of cultural heritage. A more radical reading of Byrne's chapter may lead one to suggest that notions of Universal heritage value are another way in which the West is continuing a colonial project even in what could be considered to be a post-colonial world.

A challenge to the nation-state? Heritage and multiculturalism

Another major theme in Hall's chapter is the challenge of multiculturalism for heritage management. Observing that the very idea of 'Englishness' has been challenged by the presence of a growing diasporic community, he writes:

> These communities are, as C.L.R. James once put it, 'in but not of Europe'
> . . . Nevertheless, they have known 'Europe' for three or four centuries as
> what Ashis Nandy, in his unforgettable phrase, calls 'intimate memories'.
> They are what David Scott has called 'conscripts of modernity'. They have
> dwelled for many years, and long before migration, in the double or triple
> time of colonisation, and now occupy multiple frames, the in-between or
> 'third' spaces – the homes-away-from-homes – of the postcolonial metropolis.

The theme of the challenge of multiculturalism for cultural heritage management discussed in Hall's chapter pre-empts Thomas' case study in Vietnamese perceptions of National Parks in Sydney, Australia (2002). Thomas presents a series of interviews with Vietnamese Australians about their experiences and perceptions of 'nature' and national parks. The chapter illustrates key themes about how heritage places, and the way in which they are managed, are conceptualised in different ways by different groups in multicultural societies.

These issues are also raised in Tunbridge's chapter (this volume), which looks at the relationship between political power and urban heritage conservation, with particular reference to settler (which he terms 'plural') societies. Comparative insights are drawn from the Canadian and southern African experience. Tunbridge contends that:

> In any urban society the answer to 'whose heritage?' should be 'everyone's', if
> values and goals are shared sufficiently to promote a stable future. If conserva-
> tion does not accord recognition to the landmarks of politically powerless
> groups as part of this common heritage, it is likely to become an instrument of
> social stress. This is true in principle with respect to Chinese in Vancouver as
> to Coloureds in Cape Town, notwithstanding differences that may exist in the
> degree of stress involved.

Tunbridge (see also Tunbridge and Ashworth 1996) highlights the dominance of urban over rural heritage conservation and suggests ways in which this might influence what is being conserved (and for whom), and produce biases in heritage conservation practices. He sees this dominance as evidence of political elites using heritage conservation practices in urban contexts in the exercise of political power, noting the ways in which non-dominant groups are marginalised through heritage conservation.

Despite this, both Tunbridge and Hall are positive about the potential for the interpretation and management of multicultural heritage to produce positive values that lead to greater social inclusion and harmony, at least in the urban environments to which they refer. Hall's vision of the role of multicultural heritage in questioning English society as one which is imagined as culturally unified and homogenous in favour of ways of representing the 'palimpsest of the post-colonial world' provides a positive challenge to 're-write the margins into the centre, the outside into the inside', and alternative to the ways in which Appadurai represents the use of heritage by the nation-state.

> The agenda will itself have to be open and diverse, representing a situation which is already cross-cut by new and old lateral connections and reciprocal global influences and which refuses to stand still or stabilise. We ourselves should recognise that there will be many complementary but different ways of being represented, just as there are many different ways of 'being black'.

This agenda evokes Michel de Certeau's vision of stratigraphic layering in *The Practice of Everyday Life* (1984: 201):

> Beneath the fabricating and universal writing of technology, opaque and stubborn places remain . . . This place, on its surface, appears to be a collage. In reality, in its depth it is ubiquitous. A piling up of heterogeneous places. Each one, like a deteriorating page of a book, refers to a different mode of territorial unity, of socioeconomic distribution, of political conflicts and identifying symbolism.

Nature vs culture in cultural heritage management

Thomas (2002) also suggests that 'natural' heritage, as much as 'cultural' heritage, is a key site through which citizens are educated about what constitutes 'national' culture. Indeed, the term 'national park' clearly suggests this is so.

> The wilderness in Australia historically came to represent national distinctiveness as well as the separation from Europe. This separation was manifest through the enduring images of the wildness and untameability of Australia's bushland. The Australian colonisers to a large degree rejected the landscapes of Europe and increasingly valued the native flora and fauna . . . national parks came to symbolise emerging nationhood and played an important role in establishing a national culture.
>
> (2002: 129)

Olwig's contribution to this collection raises another area of conflict in cultural heritage management – a conflict between what are often perceived to be the dualities of 'natural' and 'cultural' values in cultural landscape management. An opposition between 'natural' and 'cultural' landscapes is explicit in beliefs that derive from movements such as 'deep ecology' that maintain an essential disjuncture between nature and culture. 'Deep ecology' (or biocentric egalitarianism), a term coined by Norwegian philosopher Arne Naess (1973; see also Seed *et al.* 1988 and Naess 1994), utilises a spiritual or 'self-actualising' approach to the issue of the relationship between human beings and the natural world, challenging the 'human centredness' of the dominant Western worldview (Devall and Sessions 1995). In emphasising the duality of 'humans' and 'nature', and expressing this duality as a quasi-mystical or moral duality (Bookshin 1994: 21), deep ecology requires the existence of non-cultural landscapes as a fundamental part of its doctrine. The deep ecology movement has been a powerful force in the environmental movement throughout the world and has influenced approaches to natural and cultural heritage management. Ideas deriving from deep ecology and its variants (e.g. 'Gaian consciousness' and 'eco-theology') have influenced the way in which many heritage management agencies undertake nature conservation and land rehabilitation through an assumption of the moral right of nature conservation and rehabilitation and a perceived opposition between nature and culture. Critics of the deep ecology note that the concepts developed by the movement 'do not help move us forward as a global society faced by critical choices made between varying and often conflicting . . . values' (Hurwich 1986: 770).

This notion of a strong opposition between a 'natural' and 'cultural' landscape emerges most strongly in the national parks movements in settler societies such as Australia, New Zealand and the US. The emphasis on the management of 'pristine' or 'wild' landscapes in the national parks movements in these settler societies can be linked once again to the predatory nature of heritage management, which seeks to establish *Terra nullius* landscapes in an attempt to uncouple Indigenous people from their colonial environment. This idea has been explored by Spence (1999) in relation to the establishment of the earliest national parks in the US, where there is an explicit connection between the removal of Indigenous Americans from areas that were established as national parks during the late nineteenth century. While the idea of 'wilderness' as an unpopulated area which has not been modified by humans is now widely accepted within the settler societies discussed, the notion of a natural landscape that is not in some way cultural is difficult to comprehend for many Indigenous people in settler societies. Australian Aboriginal people, for example, would understand all of the 'natural' environment as textured and layered with social meaning and value. As Rose explains,

> A definition of wilderness which excludes the active presence of humanity . . . miss[es] the whole point of the nourishing Australian terrains. Here on this continent, there is no place where the feet of Aboriginal humanity have not preceded those of the settler. Nor is there any place where the country was not once fashioned and kept productive by Aboriginal people's land management practices. There is no place without history, no place that has not been imaginatively grasped by song, dance and design, no place where traditional owners cannot see the imprint of the sacred nation.
>
> (Rose 1996: 18)

The perception of 'wilderness' itself clearly needs to be seen as a cultural construction with a complex history, derived in part from the Enlightenment and the Romantic pastoral landscapes of late-nineteenth-century Europe (Nash 1973; Valenti 1996). However, it remains important to note that the UK as well as in many other Western European countries, such a clear distinction between the 'natural' and 'cultural' environment is not a feature of national heritage management principles as in the settler societies represented in this collection (this issue is also touched on by Samuel's chapter in this volume).

Olwig suggests that the 'paradise/progress' dialectic is one which is pervasive in Western societies, but is a kind of 'trap' which forces researchers to see the world in terms of either unchanging tradition or progress. By deconstructing this dialectic, he suggests that we can begin to understand how principles of custom work to preserve both a sense of historical continuity and community as well as to conserve environments in an economically and socially sustainable way. Like other contributors to this volume, Olwig emphasises a vision of heritage as something that is constantly being created, not fossilised in the past.

Conflict in the archaeology of living traditions and the politics of the past

An issue pre-empted by both Lilley's and Byrne's contributions to this volume re-emerges in Layton's chapter on conflict in the archaeology of living traditions (this volume), originally written as an introduction to one of two books which arose from sessions held during the World Archaeological Congress in Southampton. The chapter has been reproduced in its original form here, including its extensive discussion of the papers which constituted the edited volume, both as a historical record of the debate which accompanied the conference on the issues surrounding archaeologists and Indigenous cultural heritage, as well as an extensive summary of the points of view put forward by a range of archaeologists and Indigenous people from throughout the world on the topic. The issues surrounding the study of Indigenous skeletal remains and other forms of cultural materials by archaeologists, and Indigenous calls for such materials to be treated according to Aboriginal custom, have famously caused significant recent legal and academic controversy in the case of the repatriation of the Kennewick/'Ancient One' skeleton in the US (e.g. see Anderson 2004; Harris 2005; Owsley and Jantsz 2001; Smith 2004; Thomas 2000). However, since the late 1970s, archaeologists in settler societies have been forced to engage with increasingly emotive and vocal calls to recognise indigenous rights and interests in the pasts which they study and conserve as archaeological heritage (e.g. Kelly 1975; Langford 1983; McBryde 1985; Tasmanian Aboriginal Land Corporation 1996; Watkins 2000; 2003; and reviews in McGuire 2004 and Lilley 2006). Layton notes that a corner stone of this debate has been the ways in which archaeologists have understood their position as one of the 'expert', whose role it is to assess and analyse archaeological material objectively. Authors such as Trigger (1990) have charted the development of the archaeologist as 'expert', and others have noted that archaeological values, as much as indigenous ones, are clearly governed by subjective understandings about cultural processes and the past (e.g. Shanks and Tilley 1987; Shanks 1991).

Layton takes up the issue of objectivity at great length in his chapter, suggesting that archaeologists must modify their goals and ways of thinking about the past if they are to avoid conflicts with the descent communities of the people who they wish to study, suggesting that 'all explanatory models rest on certain assumptions and are capable of political application'. He goes on:

> Much of the evidence archaeologists use to reconstruct the past is the product of cultures whose values differ from those of the West, but it is through these values that the significance of much archaeological evidence is constituted.

Indeed, that all representations of the past managed as heritage are political is the theme of the final chapter in this section, written by Raphael Samuel. Originally published as part of his *Theatres of Memory*, this chapter considers the ways in which heritage and preservationism have been used by various political interests in Britain to establish political ideals to which they appeal. His detailed history of the political roots of various heritage campaigns in Britain demonstrates that notions of heritage preservationism have been employed by both right- and left-wing interests throughout the course of the nineteenth and twentieth centuries. By historicising the heritage movement in this way, Raphael reveals fundamentally the subjective nature of heritage conservation, despite the notions of 'universal value' to which heritage conservationists in the West might appeal (Byrne, this volume). Indeed, Samuel is clear in documenting conservation and preservation as an *active* process:

> Conservation is not an event but a process, the start of a cycle of development rather than (or as well as) an attempt to arrest the march of time. The mere fact of preservation, even if it is intended to do no more than stabilize, necessarily involves a whole series of innovations, if only to arrest the 'pleasing decay'. What may begin as a rescue operation, designed to preserve the relics of the past, passes by degree into a work of restoration in which a new environment has to be fabricated in order to turn fragments into a meaningful whole.

He continues:

> Politically heritage, like conservation, draws on a nexus of different interests. It is intimately bound up with competition for land use, and the struggle for urban space. Whether by attraction or repulsion it is shaped by changes in technology. It takes on quite different meaning in different national cultures, depending on the relationship of the state and the civil society, the openness or otherwise of the public arena to initiatives which come from below or from the periphery.

Like Tunbridge and Hall, Samuel is positive about the potential role for heritage in 'the construction of post-colonial identities'. '. . . heritage helps to support both a multi-ethnic vision of the future, and a more pluralistic one of the past'. Similarly, Layton suggests that when archaeologists 'take account of the values, aspirations, and knowledge of indigenous peoples . . . the result will in the long run benefit both archaeological theory and practice'.

> If people from other cultural traditions question the archaeologist's models of stability, change, and discontinuity, or the associations of cultures and genetic populations, their criticisms should not too hastily be dismissed as unscientific. Instead, the evidence should be looked at afresh . . . archaeology can benefit from such a reappraisal.

Conclusion

The chapter in this section suggest that by understanding heritage as part of the 'educative' apparatus of the nation-state, practitioners can begin to challenge the homogenous perceptions of national identity from the inside. This is particularly the case for those chapter that consider the positive role that heritage might take in multicultural or plural societies. While heritage and archaeology might be understood on the one hand as tools for nation building employed by the middle classes, developing programs of heritage interpretation and management that are mindful of, and indeed, celebrate difference, promises to lead to a more dynamic understanding of both our collective pasts, and our futures. While there is potential for conflict between local and national heritage values, by acknowledging and interpreting such differences, we pave the way for a radical decolonisation of heritage practice. And by celebrating the continuous, local and heterogenous uses of heritage in locality and community building in preference for the fossilised, national and homogenous uses of heritage in the employ of the nation-state, heritage practitioners might find themselves engaged in re-writing 'the margins into the centre, the outside into the inside', as suggested by Hall.

The chapters in this section also need to be read as emphasising a difference between the ways in which heritage is used in settler and non-settler societies. In settler societies, I have suggested, following Appadurai, that predatory forms of heritage management operate, in which colonisers seek to erase or override memories of prior Indigenous land occupation. Such predatory forms of heritage management can be seen to operate both in the field of 'nature' conservation, as well as in cultural and archaeological heritage management. Appadurai notes that the focus of archaeology on the recovery has the potential to obscure the need to study the politics of forgetting. Instead, archaeologists in settler societies should concern themselves with the narratives of political 'layering' in a way that is mindful both to the politics of remembering and forgetting, as well as the struggle between the local and the nation-state.

References

Amit, V. (ed.) (2002) *Realizing community: Concepts, social relationships and sentiments*, Routledge, London and New York

Amit, V. (2002) Reconceptualizing community, in V. Amit (ed.) *Realizing community: Concepts, social relationships and sentiments*, Routledge, London and New York; pp. 1–20

Amit, V. and N. Rapport (2000) *The Trouble with Community: Anthropological reflections on Movement, Identity and Collectivity*, Pluto Press, London and Sterling

Anderson, B. (1983) *Imagined communities: reflections on the origin and spread of nationalism*, Verso, London and New York

Anderson, D.G. (2004) Kennewick man: a Paleoamerican skeleton from the northwestern U.S., in B.T. Lepper and R. Bonnichsen (eds) *New perspectives on the first Americans.* Center for the Study of the First Americans, College Station, TX, distributed by Texas A & M University Press

Appadurai, A. (1996) *Modernity at Large*, University of Minneapolis Press, Minneapolis and New York

Bird, Rose D. (1996) *Nourishing Terrains: Australian Aboriginal Views of Landscape and Wilderness*, Australian Heritage Commission, Canberra

Bookshin, M. (1994) Will Ecology become the dismal science?, in Murray Bookshin (ed.) *Which way for the Ecology movement? Essays by Murray Bookshin*; pp. 21–29. AK Press, California

Byrne, D. (1996) Deep nation: Australia's acquisition of an indigenous past, *Aboriginal History* 20: 82–107

—— (2002) An archaeology of attachment: Cultural heritage and the post-contact, in R. Harrison and C. Williamson (eds) *After Captain Cook: The Archaeology of the Recent Indigenous Past in Australia*, Sydney University Archaeological Methods Series, no. 8, pp. 135–146

—— (2003a) Nervous landscapes: Race and space in Australia, *Journal of Social Archaeology* 3(2): 169–193

—— (2003b) The Ethos of Return: Erasure and reinstatement of Aboriginal Visibility in the Australian Historical Landscape. *Historical Archaeology* 37(1): 73–86

Byrne, D. and M. Nugent (2004) *Mapping Attachment*, Department of Environment and Conservation (NSW), Sydney

Casey, E.S. (2000) *Remembering: A Phenomenological Study*, Second Edition, Indiana University Press, Bloomington and Indianapolis

Clifford, J. (1988) *The Predicament of Culture: Twentieth-Century Ethnography, Literature and Art*, Harvard University Press, Cambridge, Mass. and London

Clifford, J. (1997) *Routes: Travel and translation in the late twentieth century*, Harvard University Press, London and Cambridge, Mass

Cohen, A.P (1985) *The symbolic construction of community*, Routledge, London

Connerton, P. (1989) *How Societies Remember*, Cambridge University Press, Cambridge

De Certeau, M. (1984) *The Practice of Everyday Life* (trans S. Randall), University of California Press, Berkeley.

Devall, B. and G. Sessions (1985) *Deep Ecology: Living as if Nature mattered*, Peregrine Smith Books, Salt Lake City

Eddy, J. and D. Schreuder (eds) (1988) *The rise of colonial nationalism: Australia, New Zealand, Canada and South Africa first assert their nationalities, 1800–1914*, Allen and Unwin, Sydney

Godwin, L. and S. L'Oste-Brown (2002) A past remembered: Aboriginal 'historic' places in central Queensland, in R. Harrison and C. Williamson (eds) *After Captain Cook: The Archaeology of the Recent Indigenous Past in Australia*, Sydney University Archaeological Methods Series, no. 8, Archaeological Computing Laboratory, University of Sydney, pp. 191–212

Gosden, C. (2005) *Archaeology and Colonialism: Cultural Contact from 5000BC to the Present*. Cambridge University Press, Cambridge

Griffiths, T. (1996) *Hunters and Collectors: The Antiquarian Imagination in Australia*, Cambridge University Press, Cambridge and Melbourne

Gupta, A. and J. Ferguson (1997) Culture, Power, Place: Ethnography at the end of an era, in A. Gupta and J. Ferguson (eds) *Culture, Power, Place: Explorations in Critical Anthropology*, Duke University Press, Durham, NC and London; pp. 1–21

Harris, H. (2005) The politics of American archaeology: cultural resources, cultural affiliation and Kennewick, in C. Smith and H.M. Wobst (eds) *Indigenous archaeologies: decolonizing theory and practice*. Routledge, London and New York

Harrison, R. (2000) Challenging the authenticity of antiquity: Contact archaeology and native title in Australia, in I. Lilley (ed.) *Native Title and the Transformation of Archaeology in the Postcolonial World*, Oceania Monograph 50, University of Sydney, Sydney

—— (2004) *Shared Landscapes: Archaeologies of attachment and the pastoral industry in New South Wales*, UNSW Press, Sydney

Hurwich, E.M. (1986) Review of *Deep Ecology: Living as if Nature mattered*, edited by Bill Devall and George Sessions, *Ecology Law Quarterly* 13: 770–771

Keesing, R. 1994 Theories of culture revisited, in R. Borofsky (ed.) *Assessing Cultural Anthropology*, McGraw-Hill, New York; pp. 298–316

Kelly, R. 1975. From the 'Keeparra' to the cultural bind, *Australian Archaeological Association Newsletter* 2: 13–16

Langford, R. 1983. Our heritage – your playground. *Australian Archaeology* 16: 1–6

Lightfoot, K. (1995) Culture contact studies: redefining the relationship between prehistoric and historical archaeology, *American Antiquity* 60(2): 199–217

Lilley, I. (2006) Archaeology, diaspora and decolonisation, *Journal of Social Archaeology* 6(1): 28–47

McBryde, I. (1985) *Who owns the past?* Oxford University Press, Melbourne

McGuire, R. (2004) Contested pasts: Archaeology and Native Americans, in L. Meskell and R. Pruecel (eds) *A Companion to Social Archaeology*, pp. 374–395, Blackwell, Oxford

Murray, T. (1993) The childhood of William Lanne: Contact archaeology and Aboriginality in northwest Tasmania, *Antiquity* 67: 504–519

—— (1996) Contact archaeology: Shared histories? Shared identities?, in S. Hunt and J. Lydon (eds) *SITES Nailing the Debate: Interpretation in Museums*, Historic Houses Trust of NSW, Sydney, pp. 199–213

Naess, A. (1973) The shallow and the deep, long range ecology movements: A summary, *Inquiry* 16: 95–100

Naess, A. (1994) Self-realization: An ecological approach to being in the world, in Donald VanDeVeer and Christine Pierce (eds) *The Environmental Ethics and Policy Book*; pp. 226–230. Wadsworth Publishing Company

Nash, R. (1973) *Wilderness and the American mind*, Yale University Press, New Haven

Owsley, D.W. and R.L. Jantz (2001) Archaeological Politics and Public Interest in Paleoamerican Studies: Lessons from Gordon Creek Woman and Kennewick Man, *American Antiquity* 66(4): 565–575.

Palus, M.M, M.P. Leone and M.D. Cochran (2006) Critical Archaeology: Politics Past and Present, in M. Hall and S.W. Silliman (eds) *Historical Archaeology*; pp. 84–104. Blackwell Publishing

Reynolds, H. (1982) *The Other Side of the Frontier: Aboriginal Resistance to the European Invasion of Australia*, Penguin, Melbourne

—— (1987) *The Law of the Land*, Penguin, Melbourne

Russell, L. (2001) *Savage Imaginings: Historical and Contemporary Constructions of Australian Aboriginalities*, Australian Scholarly Publishing, Melbourne

Seed, J., J. Macy, P. Flemming and A. Naess (1988) *Thinking like a mountain: Towards a council of All beings*, New Society Publishers, Philadelphia

Shanks, M. (1991) *Experiencing the Past: On the character of archaeology*, Routledge, London

Shanks, M. and C. Tilley (1987) *Social Theory and Archaeology*, Polity Press, Cambridge

Smith, L. 2004 *Archaeological theory and the politics of cultural heritage*, Routledge: London and New York

Spence, M.D. (1999) *Dispossessing the Wilderness: Indian removal and the Making of the National Parks*, Oxford University Press, New York

Tasmanian Aboriginal Land Council (1996) Will you take the next step? in *Australian Archaeology '95 Proceedings of the 1995 Australian Archaeological Association Annual conference Tempus, vol. 6* (eds S. Ulm, I. Lilley and A. Ross), St Lucia: University of Queensland; pp. 293–299

Thomas, D.H. (2002) *Skull Wars: Kennewick Man, Archaeology, and the Battle for Native American Identity*, HarperCollins Publishers

Thomas, M. (2002) *Moving Landscapes: National Parks and the Vietnamese Experience*. NSW National Parks and Wildlife Service, Sydney

Thomas, N. (1991) *Entangled Objects: Exchange, material culture and Colonialism in the Pacific* Harvard University Press, Cambridge, Massachusetts and London

—— (1994) *Colonialism's Culture: Anthropology, Travel and Government*, Polity Press, Cambridge

—— (1999) *Possessions: Indigenous Art, Colonial Culture*, Thames and Hudson, New York

Torrence, R. and A. Clarke (2000) Negotiating difference: Practise makes theory for contemporary archaeology in Oceania, in R. Torrence and A. Clarke (eds) *The Archaeology of Difference: Negotiating Cross-Cultural Engagements in Oceania*, Routledge, London and New York, pp. 1–31

Trigger, B. (1990) *A history of archaeological thought*, Cambridge University Press, Cambridge

Tunbridge, J.E. and G.J. Ashworth (1996) *Dissonant Heritage: The Management of the past as a Resource in Conflict*, New York: Wiley

Valenti, P. (1996) *Reading the landscape: writing a world*, Harcourt Brace College Publishers, New York

Watkins, J.E. (2000) *Indigenous Archaeology: American Indian values and scientific practice*. Walnut Creek, CA: AltaMira Press

Watkins, J.E. (2003) Beyond the Margin: American Indians, First Nations, and Archaeology in North America, *American Antiquity* 68(2): 273–285

Williamson, C. and R. Harrison (2002) Too many Captain Cooks?: An archaeology of Aboriginal Australia after 1788, in R. Harrison and C. Williamson (eds) *After Captain Cook: The archaeology of the recent indigenous past in Australia*, Sydney University Archaeological Methods Series, no. 8, University of Sydney, pp. 1–14

Chapter 13

Professional Attitudes to Indigenous Interests in the Native Title Era
Settler societies compared

Ian Lilley

In this chapter, I consider how the principal archaeological associations in the world's main English-speaking settler societies approach the questions surrounding indigenous cultural heritage which are emerging or evolving with recent developments in the recognition of indigenous land title on the basis of prior occupation.

The essay has four main parts. In the first I define what I mean by "settler societies", then show how despite many obvious similarities shared by all Anglophone settler societies, the Commonwealth constitutional monarchies of Australia, Canada and New Zealand can be distinguished on sociohistorical grounds from South Africa and, more particularly, the United States, and other principal Anglophone settler nations. The U.S. forms the principal case in point because relations in that country between archaeologists and indigenous people mirror those in the three Commonwealth countries to a much greater degree than they do in South Africa, though there are commonalities there too. I refer to South Africa at various points through this first part of the work, however, because thinking about politics and the practice of our discipline in that nation should help us understand what is going on in the other nations under discussion as much as it does about what may be unfolding there.

In the second part of the chapter, I argue that the sociohistorical features which distinguish the three Commonwealth nations from the U.S. on a general level help explain why the approaches to indigenous cultural heritage of the national archaeological associations of the Commonwealth countries differ from that of the Society for American Archaeology. With particular emphasis on the Australian scene, the third main section of the chapter discusses some theoretical reasons why archaeologists in the U.S. and the three Commonwealth settler societies might behave as they do with regard to indigenous cultural heritage issues.

The final part of the essay is a postscript which reflects on the implications for South African archaeology and cultural heritage management of the differences between the U.S. and the three Commonwealth countries considered in the earlier parts of the work. I conclude that South African archaeologists and cultural heritage managers may be better off following the approaches of the Commonwealth nations, rather than that of the U.S., even though there is significant sociohistorical pressure to do the reverse.

I should note I am not specifically concerned with technical or procedural issues arising from the involvement of archaeologists in land rights or native title cases. Rather, I use the term "native title era" in the title of the chapter to signify the milieu in which archaeology is now pursued in postcolonial settler societies, a milieu in which rights to land have effectively come to subsume rights to archaeological material and other aspects of cultural heritage. The recognition of such rights is the most potent symbol of the march of postcolonialism in societies where physical decolonization is impossible.

Settler societies

Settler societies thus described are an invention of postcolonialism. With roots buried deep in colonial history, postcolonialism at its most fundamental is best thought of as an attitude which had its initial articulation in relatively recent British Commonwealth and Francophone colonial literatures. It is not simply about what came after colonialism in historical terms, which is sometimes distinguished as "post-colonialism" (e.g. Boehmer 1995:3; the hyphen is the issue). Rather, it concerns "writing about empire, and about writing in opposition to empire" (Boehmer 1995:1). Described by Okri (cited in Boehmer 1995:4) as "literature of the newly ascendant spirit", postcolonialism critically examines the colonial relationship and resists colonial perspectives on issues such as race in an effort to shift power relations between colonized and colonizer. Building on this, it can be said that "postcoloniality" is the condition which sees (de)colonized peoples everywhere assert their place in the world as historical agents (Boehmer 1995: 3). In short, one might say that postcolonialism is how "the Empire strikes back" (*pace* Luke Skywalker).

And struck back the Empire certainly has, across an array of scholarly fields including anthropology, archaeology and geography as well as in literature. In geography, for example, postcolonial scrutiny of settler societies began to emerge soon after World War Two, through the work of the Australian scholar A. Grenfell Price in particular (see Griffiths and Robin 1997). Anthropology saw its earliest explicit articulation in the work of Asad (1973). The gist of the criticism of anthropology and archaeology, as well as of fields such as cartography, is that the disciplines have been and by some accounts remain complicit in the (neo)colonial subjugation of indigenous peoples. Though a global phenomenon, the postcolonial critique has a particular grip on the West, as might be expected, and informs many aspects of left-liberal (and oppositional conservative) discourse. The critique has caused a great deal of soul-searching amongst Western anthropologists and archaeologists. The developments discussed below and in other chapters in this volume have emerged in this milieu. They form part of a Western professional response to the critique which seeks to maintain archaeology's relevance by advancing the discipline's emancipatory potential (see Wolfe 1999 for a cogent and detailed account of the impact of postcolonialism on anthropology which in large part applies also to archaeology; see also Sahlins 1999).

So what *are* settler societies? They are those which, in his global discussion of nation-building, Smith (1983:122) described as overseas offshoots of the "old continuous nations" (Eddy and Schreuder 1988:4) which became the states of Western Europe. He distinguished both from "ethnic" nations such as those he thought characteristic of Eastern Europe and the Middle East, as well as from newer, usually decolonized nations of the sort that abound in Africa and the Indo-Pacific. Smith's definition could conceivably apply to a great many Anglo-, Franco- and Hispanophone societies in addition to the countries in focus in this essay. It could even encompass the Caribbean, for instance (Prof. Helen Tiffen, Department of English, The University of Queensland, pers. comm. 1998). There, the physical extinction of the indigenous peoples resulted from the political and economic dominance of very small numbers of European settlers and the numerical dominance of relatively large numbers of their African slaves (see Sued-Badillo 1992). Conventionally, however, it is the United States which many scholars including Smith (see also, for example, Spillman 1997) would be most likely to include as the only Anglophone settler society of note in addition to the three Commonwealth countries emphasized in most of the other chapters in this volume. This is because like them, and unlike other possible contenders such as India, South Africa or the complex case of the Caribbean, in the United States the European colonizers of an extensive territory came to overwhelm colonized Native American populations numerically as well as politically and economically.

In contrast to the view just described, scholars who research "colonial nations" (e.g. Eddy and Schreuder 1988) would undoubtedly add South Africa to the list of major Anglophone settler societies instead of the U.S. They would do so on the grounds that like Australia, Canada and New Zealand, South Africa was a self-governing Dominion of the British Empire (India was refused Dominion status in 1919 (Boehmer 1995:108), but with the separation of Pakistan in 1947, both countries became Dominions just prior to their complete independence (Morris-Jones 1971:17)). The strength and time depth of South Africa's Afrikaner heritage notwithstanding, in a world dominated by Britain the nation was treated as one of "the great colonial branches of the firm ['John Bull and Co.']" (O'Rell 1894), at least after Britain won the second South African War. Despite the similarities of the sort distilled by Smith and discussed again below, scholars such as Eddy and Schreuder exclude the U.S. from their considerations of colonial nations on the grounds that the ideology of colonial nationalism in the Dominions differed dramatically from that which has underpinned U.S. politics and nation-building since the Revolutionary War. This difference is critical to the thesis I develop below.

Colonial nationalism was the ideology of the American Loyalists who after the American Revolution fled to what later became Canada. Unlike the American Revolutionaries and their ideological descendants – and despite a lingering Anglophilia amongst east-coast elites in the U.S. (Spillman 1997:67–68) as well as what appear to be Britain's best efforts to cut the apron strings on several occasions (e.g. Lipset 1990:46) – colonial nationalists sought to remain part of the metropolitan power through the mechanism of home rule (Eddy and Schreuder 1988:5–6). The Americans Revolutionaries, on the other hand, separated violently from Britain at roughly the same time Britain was first colonizing Australia and New Zealand and wresting control of what became Canada from the French.

Many postcolonial scholars would probably agree with the foregoing position regarding South Africa vis-à-vis the U.S. They would most likely add that the relatively small numbers of European settlers in South Africa were/are not the issue so much as their relative power (Prof. Helen Tiffen and Assoc. Prof. Alan Lawson, Department of English, The University of Queensland, pers. comm. 1998). As should be apparent later in the piece, however, my position on this differs from both of those I have just sketched. To tackle the issue of South Africa first, it is, as we all know, South Africa's White population rather than its indigenous population which is significantly in the minority numerically, despite the former's long-term sociopolitical and economic control of the nation. To anticipate discussion at the end of the work, it is clear from the archaeological literature alone that this fact has had a profound bearing on how settlers and indigenes saw and see themselves, each other, and their nation-state. On this basis, it is inconceivable to me that the dynamics of the relationship(s) between the two groups and of each to the South African state should not differ radically from the relationships which obtain in nations where indigenous people comprise only a few percent of the population, as they do in the U.S. and the three Commonwealth nations in focus here. Moreover, South Africa has had its own Head of State since it left the Commonwealth in 1961. This fact would compound the differences to which I refer, for reasons that should become apparent in the following discussion of the United States. My views on these issues seem to be supported by writers on South Africa as a colonial nation, such as Schreuder (1988:222, also 193), who argues that "the deeper origins of the anguished modern history of apartheid South Africa – 'Union', then 'Republic' (1961) outside Commonwealth – . . . [are] to be located in the rise of [tribal] white colonial nationalism in South Africa before [union in] 1910". As mentioned, I will return to discuss such matters explicitly in the third main part of the discussion.

At first glance, the U.S. is less readily separated than South Africa from the three Commonwealth nations I have identified, if only because the minority status of its indigenous inhabitants. There are significant differences, however, which arise from the fact that the U.S. has been an independent nation for as long as the three Commonwealth societies have been British colonies. Canadian scholars see the distinction resting on their compatriots' "confidence in the social order", which is bred of a conviction that "freedom wears a crown" (McNaught, cited in Lipset 1990:14–15; see also Spillman 1997:146). Such sentiments are closely tied to a "greater sense of [political] restraint in Canada and other elitist democracies [such as Australia and New Zealand]" (Lipset 1990:15), and a greater tolerance, indeed, an expectation, of considerable government intervention in people's lives. The tenor of these comments is echoed from an Australian perspective in a paper contrasting Australian and U.S. legal traditions by then-Supreme Court judge F.C. Hutley (1981:64). He said:

> Since I have been in America, I have been surprised on a number of occasions when I have been asked what was an Australian's view of the justification for the law. This is a kind of question which has no meaning for those who do not have to rely on a revolutionary situation or conquest . . . [thus, while Aborigines often see things differently,] for the European population in Australia, the authority is based in powers which have been legitimate for nearly a thousand years, and therefore it is not necessary in Australia to appeal to God or the people or to any other source. The law is there and has always been there, and its origins are historically based in the powers of the British Parliament, going back to ancient times.

The settler society position contrasts irreconcilably with the classical liberalism of the American view that freedom "means laissez faire and also implies rejection of aristocracy and social class hierarchy" (Lipset 1990:35). According to the U.S. scholar Lipset (1990:14), Canadian historians argue that U.S. anti-elitism and individualism in fact result in "greater political intolerance in the United States . . . [because] repression of minority opinion must occur in a society with unlimited popular rule". Needless to say, if people in the U.S. ever pause to compare themselves with Canadians, which apparently is a rare event (Lipset 1990:xvi–xvii, 5) they do not see things that way, and the Left in the U.S. as much as the Right finds an exuberance and virtue in the 'American way' that contrasts with a dour conformity in Canadian ways that even many Canadians acknowledge (Lipset 1990:27–30, 45).

These propositions are borne out by Spillman's (1997) examination of nation-building in Australia and the U.S. through a comparison of their centenary and bicentenary celebrations. To quote her (1997:3–4) at length:

> many people from other places would see the United States and Australia [or New Zealand or Canada] as more similar than different. Visitors to both countries will now find functioning democracies, predominantly English-speaking peoples, extensive and varied lands, big cities, and developed economies. The two countries also share important historical experiences: European conquest, British settlement, long-established liberal political culture, extensive exploration, immigration and settlement, the joining of smaller parties to form the

nation-state, and economic growth ... In such circumstances, one might expect that American and Australian national identities would be very similar. On the other hand, uniqueness can be an important claim in a national identity. So do Americans and Australians [Canadians, New Zealanders] think of themselves in the same ways? Or have their national identities developed very differently?

In their centenary celebrations, Spillman (1997:13) finds that:

> while both Americans and Australians talked about international recognition in their centennials, they did so in somewhat different ways – Australians stressing more their identification with powerful others, Americans stressing more national display to powerful others.

After also considering the respective bicentenaries, she (1997:13) concludes that:

> overall, producers of Australian national identity have been more deeply and persistently influenced by concerns about the position of their forming nation in the world, and producers of American national identity by problems associated with the internal integration of their populations.

As Spillman implies, it would not do to overemphasize the differences between the U.S. and the three Commonwealth settler societies in focus here, for they are so very closely allied in so many ways. Nor should undoubted sociohistorical differences amongst the three Commonwealth societies be disregarded. In the present context, however, it remains the case that significant differences arise between the United States of America on the one hand and Australia, Canada and New Zealand on the other because unlike the latter, the U.S. has historically devolved much more power from the central government to state/provincial and, more particularly, local administrations. This is because it "achieved its sovereignty at a time when ideas and institution forms for nations were shaky innovations" (Spillman 1997:148; also 22–24 and Lipset 1990:1–18). Indeed, the United States is sometimes referred to as "the first new nation" (e.g. Lipset 1979). That this feature has long distinguished the U.S. from Canada is demonstrated by the fact that the problems of national integration it produced from the time the American Revolutionaries declared independence were explicitly recognized by those who framed Canada's strongly centrist original constitution in the 1870s (Lipset 1990:42–56; provincial authorities now have considerably more power than was then the case, Wylie pers. comm. 1999).

The tension between centre and periphery in the U.S. led to the American Civil War over states' rights a decade or so before the nation's centenary. The war left profound divisions which remain still. On the basis of Lipset's (1990:8–9, 13, 231) comments on the matter, I do not think such fissures can be directly compared with the tension between the Quebecois and English-speaking Canada, deep-seated and of long-standing though that may be. Nor can it be compared except in jest with the periodic calls for secession from Far North Queensland or Western Australia. In addition, the U.S. has long had a significant non-indigenous population of non-Anglophone origin, most notably African slaves and their descendants on the one hand and migrants from neighbouring Hispanophone regions on the other. The reaction of African Americans in particular to their oppression, especially during the mobilization for civil rights in the 1960s, as well as its flow-on effects to Native Americans, Hispanics, women and, most recently, homosexuals, have taxed the integrity of the "imagined community" (Anderson 1991) of the U.S. even further (Spillman 1997:149; also Lipset 1990:38–39). In short, nation-building elites in the U.S. have had their work cut out for them from the start, owing to complexities of non-indigenous population movements over the last 500 years and the centripetal forces inherent in the U.S. form of liberal democracy as it has developed over the last 220 years or so.

Canada and Australia have become very multicultural nations, primarily since World War Two, but neither of the foregoing factors applies to the same degree in either country, much less New Zealand, owing to the different colonial histories and constitutional arrangements of these nations vis-à-vis the United States. Thus, as the likes of Lipset and Spillman imply, their "nation-building elites" can be argued to feel much less vulnerable to threats to national integrity posed by social division.

It could be objected that the foregoing ignores the fact that Native Americans have long been treated differently from other sectors of U.S. society, including other important minorities, despite any threat to national integrity that such treatment might have encouraged. A recent instance of this can be found in Spillman's (1997:128) observation that "much more effort seems to have been devoted by U.S. bicentennial organizers to assuaging Native American critics than to programs and talk integrating African Americans". She sees this as "curious", presumably because issues of unequal treatment are usually argued to focus on African Americans first and other groups later (e.g. Lipset 1990:38).

Historically, the most notable instance of ostensibly distinctive treatment of Native Americans in the U.S. is the arrangement built on treaties which see Federally-recognized Indian tribes treated as "dependent sovereign nations" with some quite wide-ranging rights. In Lipset's (1990:176) view, this meant that "until recently, the U.S. courts generally accepted the legitimacy of Indian property rights, as defined in treaties, more easily than the courts . . . [in Canada]". He (1997:176) casts doubt on the degree to which this arrangement did in fact amount to special treatment through an acknowledgement that it "presumably reflected the greater commitment to due process and constitutionally protected property rights [for all citizens] in the United States". In fact, Lipset greatly overestimates the "commitment to . . . [the] constitutionally protected property rights" of Native Americans. There are actually two forms of Native American title acknowledged in the U.S., "Indian (or aboriginal) title" and "recognized title". The latter is property title to specified areas of land recognized through treaties and agreements, and covers about half of the two billion acres of Native American land acquired by the U.S. government between the end of the Revolutionary War in 1783 and 1900. Indian title, on the other hand, has to be claimed over parcels of the remaining billion acres on a case-by-case basis. It is not conceived of as *property* title, but rather as "impaired" *possessory* title, meaning that outside the treaty lands, Native American title is not seen as commensurate with settlers' land rights (Rigsby 1997:28–30, 37 endnote 28).

While Lipset may be overly-generous in his assessment of the judicial protection afforded Native American property rights, Rigsby's position is in line with Lipset's (1990:39) qualification that the U.S. judiciary has "gradually been modifying, though not eliminating" policies recognizing the rights of special interest groups, on the grounds that "they violate the equal protection sections of the Bill of Rights, which emphasize individual, not group, rights". Politicians such as the State of Washington's Senator Slade Gorton also play their part, seeking to initiate Federal bills to roll back treaty rights in regions such as the Pacific Northwest (Shapiro 1998). So, too, with the citizenry, which, through means such as citizen-initiated referenda, has halted affirmative action programs in education and the like, as has recently occurred in California and Texas (Cohen 1998). In other words, any tendency in the U.S. to recognize and protect the rights of special interest groups such as Native Americans is counter-balanced by an effort to diminish if not eliminate such rights as contrary to the individualistic tenets of U.S. liberal democracy.

To take the argument regarding treaties in particular along a slightly different tack before concluding this section, I draw attention to the fact that New Zealand's foundation as a nation rests on the 1840 Treaty of Waitangi between Britain and the Maori, while historically Canada concluded treaties with various First Nation groups (see Klimko and Wright, this volume). Winks (cited in Lipset 1990:175; cf. Kidd 1997) has shown Australian race relations to have been the worst of the four countries in question, and New Zealand's "the least harsh", with the U.S. tending to the Australian end of the spectrum and Canada to the New Zealand end. This finding suggests I can extend Franks's observations (cited in Lipset 1990:177) regarding North America and argue that both New Zealand and Canada have been "more consistently supportive than . . . [the U.S.] of 'communal land and tribal identity'". That the U.S., with its treaties and judicial support for native title to land, can be argued to rate in this regard like Australia, which has never concluded a treaty with any Indigenous Australians and explicitly rejected judicial and legislative recognition of Native Title until the closing decade of the twentieth century, while New Zealand and Canada rate so highly, even without the judicial protection of private property of the sort offered by the U.S. constitution, to my mind conclusively negates the issue of long-standing treaties as a critical factor in the present context, whether or not they represent special treatment of Native Americans' land tenure. This position is in keeping with the demonstration in the next part of the chapter that Australia, New Zealand and Canada are more similar to each other than any of the three is to the U.S. in terms of relations between indigenous peoples and archaeologists acting in groups.

Archaeology

I contend that the broad historical and sociopolitical distinctions just described allow us to separate the relationships between archaeologists and indigenous people in Australia, Canada and New Zealand as a group from the relationships of this sort that obtain in the U.S. This is the case even though, as Trigger (1984) brought to our attention, all can be lumped as exemplars of "colonialist" archaeology (with qualifications regarding "imperialist" tendencies in the U.S.), even though all four nations share a great many features of professional practice, such as a longstanding emphasis on scientific approaches to the past, and even though all have had very similar recent experiences as far as indigenous reactions to archaeological research are concerned (e.g. Deloria 1992, 1973; Langford 1983; Nicholas and Andrews 1997; O'Regan 1990). The critical difference, in my view, lies in the reaction to indigenous concerns of the archaeological communities *as groups* in these various countries. This proposition began in my mind as little more than an impression based on unsystematic reading about the issue and my experiences at the 1998 Society for American Archaeology conference in Seattle. It was bolstered by the discovery of a paper by Rosenswig (1997) in the *Canadian Journal of Archaeology* and borne out by subsequent more detailed study of the relevant archaeological literatures of the countries in question.

   Rosenswig undertook content analyses of six documents: the codes of ethics of the national archaeological associations of the U.S. (SAA), Australia (AAA), Canada (CAA) and New Zealand (NZAA), of the World Archaeological Congress (WAC) and of the (U.S.) Society of Professional Archaeologists (SOPA). The last two were controls (note that SOPA has recently been replaced by the Register of Professional Archaeologists, known as "the Register" (Aldenderfer 1999:2)). The WAC code was seen as an example of a code explicitly formulated to acknowledge the primacy of indigenous interests in the archaeological record. The SOPA code was included as an example of standards regulating accreditation as a professional archaeologist, and thus focused on archaeological rather than indigenous interests. The idea was to determine which of the two more closely matched the codes of ethics of the four national archaeological bodies, to see if the latter emphasized the primacy of archaeological or indigenous interests. Rosenswig concludes that the SAA Principles of Ethics most closely resemble the SOPA guidelines, and do not acknowledge "the *distinctive* role of Native peoples . . . whose cultural heritage is the focus of investigation" (Rosenswig 1997:108, his emphasis). The AAA, CAA and NZAA codes, on the other hand, mirror the WAC statement. Indeed, the AAA and NZAA have for all intents and purposes just borrowed the WAC code, while the CAA independently arrived at a very similar document following wide consultation with First Nations groups.

Rosenswig (1997:108) notes that "the lack of direct focus on indigenous peoples in the SAA principles of ethics does not reflect a lack of attention paid them by the SAA more generally", as indicated by the column-inches devoted to the matter in *American Antiquity* and the *SAA Bulletin*. I wholeheartedly second this important proviso, and add that a visit to the SAA web site (www.saa.org), and particularly the Government Affairs area, under-lines the point, as there is a significant amount of material on-line dealing with repatriation of Native American skeletal remains and cultural property and the like. In search of other answers, Rosenswig (1997:108) puts the difference between the SAA Principle of Ethics and the codes of the other national groups partly down to "the hyperlegalized context in which it was formulated". "[P]otential legal interests in the material record of the human past" were certainly an explicit consideration of the SAA in its 1986 *Statement Concerning the Treatment of Human Remains* (cited in Hubert 1989:125), and people from other coun-tries are certainly often struck by that nation's litigiousness, a characteristic Lipset (1990:21–22, citing Nettl 1968) argues arises from the ideology that "only law is sover-eign" that has prevailed since the country was founded. However, Rosenswig (1997:108) goes on to propose that:

> [p]erhaps a more fundamental factor ... [is that] the archaeological communities in Canada, Australia and New Zealand have identified improved relations with their respective indigenous populations as the single most important ethical issue facing the discipline of archaeology.

He emphasizes this point by noting that despite the very positive attitudes and efforts reflected by the aforementioned material in *American Antiquity* and the *SAA Bulletin* (and, I might add, many other publications), McManamon (1991:127) was still able to allude to the considerable irony that

> the segment of the public most directly connected to the past societies that most American archaeologists study has not been a primary audience for archaeological public education.

On this basis, Rosenswig (1997:110) distils the conclusion that:

> [t]he fundamental distinction between the four national organizations is not *if* sharing control of archaeological resources is necessary but *with whom* such sharing of authority should occur.

Wylie (1997) responded to Rosenswig's paper as a respected senior scholar centrally involved in the development of the SAA Principles of Ethics. Her position is that Rosenswig is not comparing like with like, on two principal grounds. First, she (1997:115–116) notes that the SAA Principles are an extension of the SAA By-laws, whereas the Australian, Canadian and New Zealand codes were specifically formulated to govern relations between archaeologists and indigenous peoples. She thus sees the SAA Principles closely parallel the "general statements of disciplinary or society purpose" found in the Constitution of the CAA. The constitutions of the AAA and NZAA contain similar general statements (for N.Z., Janet Davidson pers. comm. 1998). Wylie points out that the Goals in the CAA Constitution make no mention of Native Americans, nor "indeed, to any special responsibilities archaeologists may have to those who regard archaeological material as part of their cultural heritage". The same can be said of the constitutions of the AAA and NZAA.

Wylie's (1997:116) second line of argument regarding Rosenswig's comparison is that the SAA is not a "national organization" in "quite the sense described by Rosenswig", in that it focuses on all the Americas rather than just one country, and unlike the CAA, at least, "its articles on membership and executive structure impose no citizenship or residency restrictions". This is seemingly borne out by Wylie's Canadian citizenship and work history. Moreover, while she (pers. comm. 1999) acknowledges that only about 20% of the SAA membership is "non-U.S./non-North American", she has also pointed out to me that "40% of member responses [to a survey of the SAA] identify non-North American field areas as a primary research interest (half of this 40% are 'Old World' and the other 60% includes Canada . . .)".

That may be true, and there can be little doubt that doing all one's field work in, say, the Dordogne would colour one's perspective of indigenous relations differently from spending one's field time with the Navaho Nation. Nonetheless, I think there are two reasons why her position on this matter can be seen as something of a red herring. First, in the present context it is not so much where people focus their field research that concerns me. Rather, it is where they are from and where they usually live and work from day to day that interests me, and how the sociohistorical complexion of their usual milieu might influence what they think and do in relation to indigenous people.

On that basis, Wylie's 20% figure becomes more significant than the others. She made her calculation in the late 1980s, but examination of addresses listed in the SAA *1998 Administrative and Member Directory* strongly suggests the vast majority of members, and certainly virtually all members of the Society's Executive (including committee chairs), are still U.S. archaeologists. I would also draw attention to Aldenderfer's editorial in the *SAA Bulletin* of March 1999. He says (1999:2, my emphasis) that the early SAA

> was focused mostly upon research in North America, but through time, it became more inclusive, *reaching out to colleagues in Latin America*, Europe and other parts of the world. Intellectually, however, and despite the changes that have swept through how we conceptualize archaeology, *we remain a strongly Americanist organization.*

The explicit reference to Latin America as "another part of the world" implies to me that the last few words of the quote actually mean "a strongly *North* Americanist organization". Coupled with the aforementioned evidence of the SAA *Directory*, the fact that the Canadians have their own CAA suggests that "[North] Americanist" means "U.S." for all practical purposes in the present context. What this boils down to is that even if Wylie has a different personal perspective as a Canadian, in her response to Rosenswig she is representing the collective opinion of a group of archaeologists who for the most part normally live and work in (and in all probability were born and bred in) the U.S. and who are thus influenced to a greater or lesser degree by the broad sociohistorical patterns sketched in the first part of the paper.

The second and more important reason why Wylie's point about national associations can be considered a distraction is that the survey results she quotes (pers. comm.) indicate clearly that it is the archaeology of Native Americans which forms the focus of inquiry of most SAA members who work in any part of the Americas, North, Central or South.

Be these observations as they may, it is the question of the nature of the SAA Principles that I, like Wylie, want to pursue further. As she (1997:117) remarks,

> [t]he real question is not whether, or why, the SAA Principles show a different word count on cognates for terms that are central to the purpose-specific

codes, but why the SAA has not adopted, in addition to the new Principles and the Objectives set out in its by-laws, something like the WAC code or the CAA Principles which specify the particular responsibilities archaeologists have to aboriginal and indigenous peoples.

Despite the evidence quoted earlier that the SAA has taken legal considerations into account in closely-related situations in the past, Wylie (1997:117–118) dismisses Rosenswig's suggestion regarding legal concerns because "defensive caution about legal implications" did not play a significant part in the process leading to the promulgation of the SAA Principles. Rather, she says (1997:118, my emphasis), the over-riding concern

> was that archaeologists must explicitly acknowledge the *growing number* of descendant communities and other constituencies who are affected by their practice . . .

Wylie points out that Native American positions were "most strongly represented", but contributors to the process emphasized the existence of many non-indigenous constituencies

> who insist their interests must be respected . . . [i]ncluding the descendants of African American, Asian, Hispanic, and mixed heritage populations in North America; mestizo and indigenous peoples of meso- and South America; and the poor and dispossessed of all backgrounds throughout the Americas[,]

as well as people not historically connected with archaeological material in their vicinity but who are impacted by its investigation. She (1997:118) notes that a principle reason for a strong commitment to outreach to these groups is that it is vital to bolstering respect for, and to combat "exploitative or destructive appropriations" of, archaeological heritage.

As I have mentioned, it is common knowledge that, with the U.S., Australia and Canada are among the most multicultural societies in the world. It is true that Australian archaeologists were and in some cases remain profoundly disturbed by the prospect of their access to the archaeological record being restricted or precluded by Aboriginal interests (see Hubert 1989:149–156; Layton 1994; also the "Repatriation Issues in Australian Archaeology" papers in Ulm *et al.* 1986:291–322). However, in neither Australia nor, from what I understand from Rosenswig's paper, Canada, do archaeologists exhibit the profound concern of the SAA to treat equitably all of what McManamon (1991) called "the many publics for archaeology" as it is expressed in Wylie's paper. Rather, they have acknowledged the priority of indigenous claims over those of all other interested parties. On this basis, it can be proposed that the SAA's position as described by Wylie reflects precisely the concerns with social integrity and fair dealing across multiple constituencies that would be anticipated from discussion in the first part of the paper regarding the broad sociohistorical differences between the U.S. and the three Commonwealth nations in question here.

The deep-rootedness of this concern in the U.S. archaeological community is abundantly clear not only in Wylie's response to Rosenswig, but also in her paper and those of others in the special 1992 edition of *American Antiquity* which considered the archaeological implications of the quincentenary of Columbus's voyage. While Reid's (1992:583) brief editorial focuses almost exclusively on Native Americans, Wylie's paper also takes in African American and Hispanic concerns by way of introducing following papers by a Native American (Deloria 1992), a Puerto Rican (Sued-Badillo 1992), and an African American (Williams 1992). Similarly, material on SAAweb concerning renewal of the "National Archaeological Program" (Lipe and Redman 1998:5) discusses "the multiplicity of legitimate interests in archaeology and archaeological resources" without explicitly mentioning Native Americans, except to note that along with "Federal agencies . . . and SHPOs", "tribes" should ensure "recognition of multiple interests". SAAweb documents (e.g. Steponaitis 1998) also demonstrate that just as the Native American positions in other areas are being diminished, so too with NAGPRA, in the form of the recently defeated H.R. 2893, *A Bill to Amend the Native American Graves Protection and Repatriation Act*. According to the SAAweb material, the Bill was supported by the SAA for two main reasons. The first was that it acknowledged scientific concerns to a greater extent than is the case with NAGPRA at present. The second was that it sought to recognize multiple interests in the archaeological record by repealing NAGPRA's provisions affording blanket Native American ownership of pre-European cultural heritage regardless of whether it is found on Federally-recognized tribal land. The intention of the SAA's support was "to bring NAGPRA closer to SAA's policy without undoing the important and positive effects of NAGPRA" (SAA 1997:1).

I do understand that NAGPRA technically applies not to all U.S. archaeologists but only to Federal agencies and museums which accept Federal funds. I also recognize that matters such as those just outlined are never black-and-white, and that, for example, there are Native American archaeologists with mixed views on the issues, and that some Native American groups (especially those lacking Federal recognition) supported H.R. 2893 (Donald Craib, pers. comm. 1998). Nonetheless, as one with a long involvement in Australian Aboriginal archaeology, as well as in the AAA Executive during some turbulent times, I must say I find SAA's approach very different in conception and execution from that of the Australian Archaeological Association (see Hubert 1989 for further description of the differences), as well as from what I understand to be those of the professional bodies in Canada and New Zealand. That the SAA is attempting to move NAGPRA towards its policy rather than the reverse really does make it seem to me as if the organization misses NAGPRA's central implication for relations between archaeologists and indigenous people in the U.S. A lawyer might well see NAGPRA *de jure* as a straightforward property statute which strictly speaking has no intentional moral dimension and applies only to a particular, narrowly-defined segment of the archaeological community. However, I do not think anyone would deny NAGPRA has galvanized the U.S. archaeological community like few if any issues before or since. On that basis, it seems to me that *de facto*, NAGPRA's most profound implication applies to *all* U.S. archaeologists, and is very much an issue of social justice rather than property law. To wit, the U.S. government had to *legislate* to make most Native Americans feel more confident that U.S. archaeologists *as a group* will take Native American claims to their cultural heritage seriously, regardless of how much progress U.S. archaeologists have made in this connection (see, for example, Russell's (1997) comments concerning what he calls the "Indian-Archaeologist Wars").

At the end of her reply to Rosenswig, Wylie (1997:119) asks whether "the next step for the SAA should be to develop guidelines that set out members' obligations specifically to Native peoples". It has to be asked whether the passage of NAGPRA in 1990 and defeat of H.R. 2893 in 1998 have not seen events already well-and-truly overtake the SAA in this regard. Would NAGPRA have been necessary at all had the SAA moved to formulate guidelines concerning indigenous heritage *before* expanding and updating the general ethical principles in the association's by-laws? In effect, this is what the CAA, AAA and NZAA did (for N.Z., Janet Davidson pers. comm. 1998). In Australia, for example, government heritage agencies have moved more-or-less in tandem with the AAA on ethical matters, and archaeologists throughout the country are now legally obliged to acknowledge and accommodate the primacy of indigenous concerns regarding native heritage. However, this is usually done in ways the professional archaeological community negotiates with indigenous people on an on-going basis rather than in ways which have been imposed and to a much greater degree set in legislative stone by non-archaeological interests.

To my mind, a negotiated settlement ought to be the preferred arrangement in any liberal- or social-democratic polity. In view of the particularly strong and long-standing U.S. focus on small government and individual rather than group rights, it is especially ironic that the opportunity to achieve such a result in the U.S. appears to have been missed, whereas it was seized upon in the three Commonwealth settler societies, where government intervention has historically been the rule, not the exception. I can only surmise that the overwhelming priority to meet Native American concerns that is embodied in NAGPRA was simply not apparent to the SAA. Wylie's reply to Rosenswig and the 1992 quincentenary edition of *American Antiquity* make it clear that the organization was preoccupied by an intense (and entirely honourable) countervailing concern to treat all interests equitably. Such a concern is perfectly understandable as the product of long-standing and deeply-rooted tensions in the U.S. polity, but may in fact result in a reduced capacity on the SAA's part for flexible responses in a rapidly changing postcolonial world.

I am emphatically *not* saying by any of this that U.S. archaeologists collectively do not in fact consider Native Americans' claims about their heritage seriously. *Nor* am I saying that in the great majority of individual cases they do not go to considerable lengths to accommodate such concerns sincerely and sensitively, even if at least some Native Americans do not see either matter that way and thus vehemently resist attempts to alter NAGPRA (see earlier citation of Russell). Such assertions may well have been true at the time of the first WAC congress (e.g. Hubert 1989:137–149; Zimmerman 1989a, b; though see, for example, Lipe 1974 for an early acknowledgement of the need for consultation with Native Americans). However, the timbre and content of most of the vast literature about such matters that has accumulated in the decade or so since the first WAC indicates they would be untrue today (though see Clark 1998 and Watkins 1998, whose exchange indicates beyond any doubt that the argument is far from over). What I *am* saying, however, is that despite this fact and despite the outward similarities between the U.S. and the three Commonwealth settler societies, it is clear that when *acting in concert* through the SAA, U.S. archaeologists have approached relations with Native Americans very differently from the ways in which Australian, Canadian and New Zealand archaeologists *acting in concert* through their respective national archaeological associations have approached relations with indigenous peoples.

I have intimated that this difference has had a less than favourable outcome for archaeologists in the U.S., in the form of imposed Federal legislative solutions to questions which need not have been resolved in this manner. I argue that the reasons for this phenomenon go well beyond those sketched in Wylie's response to Rosenswig's analysis, and are to be found in the fundamentally different approaches to nation-building that attend the sociohistorical differences between the U.S. and the Commonwealth settler societies which I outlined earlier. There are of course differences among the three settler societies too, but in the terms I have set here, they are much more similar to each other than any of the three is to the U.S. In addition to any more general value this conclusion has for our understanding of important but not immediately obvious variations in politics and the practice of our discipline in these closely allied countries, it suggests that the lessons learned and solutions found regarding relations between archaeologists and indigenous peoples in the U.S. may not be as relevant to the Commonwealth settler societies as they might seem, or vice versa.

Discussion and conclusion

Trigger (1981:139) quite reasonably thinks most Anglo-American prehistoric archaeologists are members of the middle class and thus that "the various problems . . . addressed [in Anglo-American prehistoric archaeology] reflect the reactions of . . . [the] middle class to its changing fortunes". His propositions and their elaborations by others (for a more recent overview see McGuire and Walker 1999; see also Patterson 1999) help place my commentary in a larger theoretical framework. In this view, the fortunes of the middle class are perhaps tied more closely to national political integration of the nation than to any other sociopolitical goal, or for any other class, for it is the middle class which usually has the most to lose from significant variations in the political and economic status quo. The very rich can just rearrange the transnational disposition of their capital if the status quo changes to their disadvantage, or if they see a better offer elsewhere, while the very poor are at the best of times only marginally involved in the core political or economic processes of the nation-state and have little influence over them one way or the other.

If my analysis bears any scrutiny, a relative lack of concern about national integration amongst the middle classes of the three Commonwealth settler societies discussed here results from their membership of numerically as well as politically and economically dominant colonists *as well as* a conviction about the stability of the social order rooted in the supposed stability of Britain's ancient monarchy and the constitutional arrangements it has bequeathed to them. These factors freed middle-class archaeologists to confront the emergent problems of doing colonialist archaeology head-on and, much more than has been the case in the U.S., on their own terms and schedule. That they wanted to deal with such matters as a matter of urgency, as Rosenswig proposes, rather than pursue other goals in the way the SAA has done, can I think be put down to a lack of confidence amongst middle-class settlers in the standing of their societies in the eyes of other nations rather than any concern for social integration, as Spillman discusses in relation to Australia and Lipset to Canada. I think this lack of confidence has been heightened by the postcolonialist tenor of much commentary from opinion leaders in predominantly left-liberal institutions such as the media and universities. Just as this problem surfaced in Australia's centenary and bicentenary celebrations, so we now see it very clearly in the reactions of prominent figures in that country's press to inconsistencies in the conservative government's approach to a referendum on an Australian republic held in 1999. Addressing the Prime Minister, then-senior Commonwealth parliamentary press-gallery journalist Michelle Gratton (1998:26, my emphasis) states:

> You've been assuring us . . . that whatever happens with the referendum, there's no danger to the community fabric.
> *Well, the fabric might remain intact but the image will be somewhat battered* if the referendum is lost. Most of the world, or at least those parts that bother to watch, will see the result as, at best, an exercise in national absurdity, and, at worst, a manifestation of a confused identity. In any case, it's a pretty limp way to start the new millennium . . . [the referendum *was* lost]

In this connection, I contend that in Australia, if not Canada or New Zealand, most archaeologists share a pervasive, middle-class, postcolonialist view that our country cannot be considered a "whole" nation in the eyes of important others unless we achieve reconciliation with the continent's indigenous populations (cf. Bird Rose 1996; Rothwell 1999). This notion can certainly be detected behind the nervousness expressed in the nation's quality press (e.g. Manne 1997; Wood 1997) about international reaction to the racist policies of a political party which recently emerged (and may now be disappearing) on the Far Right. It is probably seen most clearly in the effectiveness of the common cry of Aboriginal protestors that "the whole world is watching". I am sure this last perception was behind what Spillman (1997:129) calls "a startlingly cooptive move" that saw Aboriginal demonstrations against the nation's bicentenary "numbered among the myriad activities . . . [marking] the year".

In contrast to the situation in Australia, the analyses discussed earlier suggest that to ensure its own well-being over the long term, the middle class in the United States has

focused for a considerable period on keeping an ethnically diverse and highly individualistic nation together. It has done so by trying to treat everyone equally and by promoting
social harmony above all else. This has meant that as a collectivity, its archaeological
members seem not to have recognized an emergent pressing need to single out Native
Americans for attention before such a course of action was imposed upon them by interests which are not naturally sympathetic to archaeological concerns and perhaps even
middle-class concerns more generally. This does not mean NAGPRA spells the end of
Native American archaeology, of course. The same underlying emphasis in the U.S. polity
on individual rights for everybody that diverted the SAA's attention from the special case
of group rights for Native Americans will ensure that archaeologists' interests will be preserved, if not through H.R. 2893 then perhaps by judicial *fiat*. It just seems to me to be a
pity that relations between archaeologists and Native Americans have come to this, but
perhaps I simply do not understand the "American way".

Postscript: whither South Africa?

It would not be right for a settler Australian (and particularly a Queenslander like me) to
even think about lecturing South African archaeologists about relations with colonized
indigenous groups, owing to our appalling history of race relations (e.g. Evans *et al.* 1993;
Kidd 1997). In closing this chapter I will nonetheless ask what pointers, if any, my conclusions regarding such matters in the U.S. and the three Commonwealth settler societies
provide the profession in South Africa. Something obviously has to be done in answer to
Hall's (1997:vi) lament that he and his colleagues "are finding it difficult to attract black
students to the discipline, or even a representative cross-section of South Africans to our
public lectures and open courses", and that to "any outsider, archaeology in the 'New
South Africa' must seem very white". While I empathize with his concerns, particularly in
the light of the deep funding cuts he and others (e.g. Schoeman *et al.* 1997:vii) describe, I
would nonetheless respond optimistically that it is early days yet.

  There are, however, clear signs that the South African archaeological community
needs to keep the lines of communication with the wider community not only open but
busy as it moves to encourage and accommodate indigenous interests in the archaeological
record. Despite the country's history as a British Dominion, and the apparent rejection by
"many South Africans . . . [of] American multiculturalism . . . [as something] uncomfortably similar to the rhetoric used by the Apartheid state" (Engela 1997:iv), it may be that
South Africa is more like the U.S. than the three settler societies discussed above, owing
to the centripetal forces a very long colonial history has built into the South African state.
There is perhaps also a lack of "confidence in social order" that emerged with the end of
authoritarian government in the absence of a stable institution such as the Crown or a
republican structure closely resembling the present arrangements in the three Commonwealth nations' constitutional monarchies, such as that proposed by the "minimalist" position on the proposed Australian republic.

  These factors may explain why several of the short notes in a special southern African
section in a recent *WAC News* (Ouzman 1997) raise the issue, somewhat obliquely it must
be said, of multiple interests in the archaeological record in terms very reminiscent of
H.R. 2893 in the U.S. rather than of any policies and principles pursued in the Commonwealth settler societies. It can be seen in Engela's "Why archaeology, now, in South
Africa?" (1997:iv) as well as in Schoeman *et al.*'s "Challenging perspectives from our past:
a student view". Most importantly, Deacon's (1997:iii) summary of the nation's new heritage legislation expresses concern for multiple interests in archaeological heritage in its
discussion of "communities" with "*bona fide* interests" in graves and objects. I might note,
however, that while unlike the articles of NAGPRA or in the policies or laws of the three

Commonwealth settler societies, the proposed new South African legislation makes no provisions for blanket ownership by indigenous people, such ownership may be understood to be there in a remote sense, insofar as all cultural material will be deemed the property of the State, which is now politically as well as numerically dominated by black South Africans.

While it may be true, such a reflection is really only grasping at straws. Apart from anything else, it ignores the intensifying tensions between the Khoisan, "South Africa's first people", and other black South Africans (Agence France Presse 1999; also Jordan 1999). Moreover, many South African archaeologists have long promoted socially and politically unpopular views regarding the formation and meaning of the South African archaeological record (Shaw 1989:16), but, as Blundell (1997:ii) despairs, this appears to have had very little impact on the wider South African community.

On the basis of that observation and my foregoing comments, I think that if archaeologists in the "New South Africa" want their discipline to seem less White, while at the same time they try to avoid whatever problems they may perceive in "American multiculturalism", they should try to ensure the heritage legislation that controls access to archaeological resources, as well as the teaching, research and outreach programs which describe and explain those resources to people both within South Africa and beyond, explicitly recognize that the vast bulk of those resources were created by indigenous Africans and belong to their descendants, Khoisan and others more recently arrived. This is *not* the same as saying that indigenous people constitute merely one amongst many groups with an interest in the archaeological record, or even that they have a "special interest" in archaeological material which really belongs to "all humanity". If the SAA had seen that, U.S. archaeologists generally, and *not* just those in the agencies and institutions to which its application is technically restricted, might not have found themselves devoting so much time, energy and money to coping with the moral and practical implications of NAGPRA. Would that South African archaeologists recognize this, and map their way ahead accordingly.

Acknowledgements

This essay has benefited from comments by Donald Craib (U.S.), Janet Davidson (N.Z.), Bruce Rigsby (Australia), Bruce Trigger (Canada), Alison Wylie (Canada/U.S.) and two anonymous referees. Of course, all faults of omission or commission remain my responsibility. I thank the ATSIS Unit, University of Queensland, for making my participation in WAC-4 and the production of this volume possible.

References

Agence France Presse. 1999. Bushmen win back Kalahari. *The Australian* March 23:12.

Aldenderfer, M. 1999. Editor's Corner. *SAA Bulletin* 17(2):2.

Anderson, B. 1991. *Imagined Communities: Reflections on the origins and spread of nationalism.* London: Verso.

Asad, T. (ed.) 1973. *Anthropology and the Colonial Encounter.* New York: Ithaca Press.

Bird Rose, D. 1996. Rupture and the Ethics of Care in Colonized Space. In Bonyhady, T. and T. Griffiths (eds) *Prehistory to Politics. John Mulvaney, the Humanities and the Public Intellectual*, pp. 190–215. Melbourne: Melbourne University Press.

Blundell, G. 1997. Archaeology in a dangerous time. *The World Archaeological Congress Newsletter* 5:ii.

Boehmer, E. 1995. *Colonial and Postcolonial Literature. Migrant Metaphors.* Oxford: Oxford University Press.

Clark, G. 1998. NAGPRA, the conflict between science and religion and the political consequences. *SAA Bulletin* 16(5)22, 24–25.

Cohen, A. 1998. Back to square one. *Time* April 20:22–23.

Deacon, J. 1997. South Africa's new heritage legislation. *The World Archaeological Congress Newsletter* 5:iii.

Deloria, V. Jr. 1973. *God is Red*. New York: Delta Books.

Deloria, V. Jr. 1992. Indians, archaeologists and the future. *American Antiquity* 57:595–598.

Eddy, J. and D. Schreuder (eds). 1988. *The Rise of Colonial Nationalism. Australia, New Zealand, Canada and South Africa first assert their nationalities, 1800–1914*. Sydney: Allen and Unwin.

Engela, R. 1997 Why archaeology, now, in South Africa? *The World Archaeological Congress Newsletter* 5:iv.

Evans, R., Saunders, K. and K. Cronin 1993. *Race Relations in Colonial Queensland: A history of exclusion, exploitation and extermination*. Brisbane: University of Queensland Press.

Gratton, M. 1998. PM makes world of differents. *The Australian Financial Review* October 17–18:26.

Griffiths, T. and L. Robin (eds). 1997. *Ecology and Empire. Environmental History of Settler Societies*. Melbourne: Melbourne University Press.

Hall, M. 1997. The transformations and future of South African archaeology. *The World Archaeological Congress Newsletter* 5:v–vi.

Hirst, K. 1997. The roots of NAGPRA: Steve Russell. http://archaeology.tqn.com/library/weekly/aa083197.htm

Hubert, J. 1989. A proper place for the dead. In Layton, R. (ed.) *Conflict in the Archaeology of Living Traditions*, pp. 131–166. London: Unwin Hyman.

Hutley, F. 1981. The legal traditions of Australia as contrasted with those of the United States. *Australian Law Journal* 55:63–70.

Jordan, B. 1999. Row erupts as Khoisan call for return of old bones. *Sunday Times* [Cape Town] January 17. http://www.suntimes.co.za/suntimesarchive/1999/01/17/news/news16.htm#top

Kidd, R. 1997. *The Way We Civilise. Aboriginal Affairs – The Untold Story*. Brisbane: University of Queensland Press.

Langford, M. 1983. Our heritage – your playground. *Australian Archaeology* 16:1–6.

Layton, R. 1994. Preface and recent developments. In Layton, R. (ed.) *Conflict in the Archaeology of Living Traditions* (2nd ed.), pp. xxv–xxix. London: Routledge.

Lipe, W. 1974. A conservation model for American Archaeology. *The Kiva* 39(3–4):213–245.

Lipe, W. and C. Redman 1998. National Archaeological Program. www.saa.org/About-SAA/Ethics/renew.html

Lipset, S. 1979. *The First New Nation: The United States in Comparative and Historical Perspective*. New York: W. W. Norton and Co.

Lipset, S. 1990. *Continental Divide: The Values and Institutions of the United States and Canada*. New York: Routledge.

McGuire, R. and M. Walker 1999. Class confrontations in archaeology. *Historical Archaeology* 33(1):159–183.

McManamon, F. 1991. The many publics for archaeology. *American Antiquity* 56:121–130.

Manne, R. 1997. Our delayed reactionaries. *The Australian* May 12:13.

Morris-Jones, W. 1971. *The Government and Politics of India*. London: Hutchinson University Library.

Nicholas, G. and T. Andrews (eds) 1997. *At a Crossroads: Archaeology and First Peoples in Canada*. Burnaby: Archaeology Press, Department of Archaeology, Simon Fraser University.

O'Regan, S. 1990. Maori control of Maori heritage. In Gathercole, P. and D. Lowenthal (eds) *The Politics of the Past*, pp. 95–106. London: Unwin Hyman.

O'Rell, M. 1894. *John Bull & Co: The great colonial branches of the firm, Canada, Australia, New Zealand and South Africa*. London: Warne.

Ouzman, S. (ed.). 1997. Southern Africa Focus. *The World Archaeological Congress Newsletter* 5:i–xvi.

Patterson, T. 1999. The political economy of archaeology in the United States. *Annual Review of Anthropology* 28:155–174.

Reid, J. 1992. Quincentennial truths and consequences. *American Antiquity* 57:583.

Rigsby, B. 1997. Anthropologists, Indian Title and the Indian Claims Commission: The California and Great Basin Cases. In Smith, D. and J. Finlayson (eds) *Fighting over Country*, pp. 15–45. Centre for Aboriginal Economic Policy Research Monograph 12. Canberra: Centre for Aboriginal Economic Policy Research, Australian National University.

Rosenswig, R. 1997. Ethics in archaeology: An international, comparative analysis. *Canadian Journal of Archaeology* 21:99–114.

Rothwell, N. 1999. Everyday heroes [comments on Miriam Dixson's *The Imaginary Australian*]. *The Weekend Australian* June 5–6:29.

Sahlins, M. 1999. What is anthropological enlightenment? Some lessons of the Twentieth Century. *Annual Review of Anthropology* 28:I–xxiii.

Schoeman, A., Sales, K. and J. Behrens. 1997. Challenging perspectives from our past: A student view. *The World Archaeological Congress Newsletter* 5:vii–viii.

Schreuder, D. 1988. Colonial nationalism and 'tribal nationalism': making the white South African state, 1899–1910. In Eddy, J. and D. Schreuder (eds) 1988 *The Rise of Colonial Nationalism. Australia, New Zealand, Canada and South Africa first assert their nationalities, 1800–1914*, pp. 192–226. Sydney: Allen and Unwin.

Shapiro, N. 1998. Gorton Rides Again. http://www.seattleweekly.com/archives/07_16_98/shapiro0716.html

Shaw, T. 1989. African archaeology: Looking back and looking forward. *The African Archaeological Review* 7:3–31.

Smith, A. 1983. *State and Nation in the Third World*. Brighton: Wheatsheaf Books.

Society for American Archaeology 1998. *1998 Administrative and Member Directory*. Washington DC: Society for American Archaeology.

Society for American Archaeology 1997. Questions and answers regarding HR 2893. Prepared by the Committee on Repatriation December 8, 1997. www.saa.org/Government/Lobby/hr2893q&a.html

Spillman, L. 1997. *Nation and commemoration. Creating national identity in the United States and Australia*. Cambridge: Cambridge University Press.

Steponaitis, V. 1998. Testimony of Society for American Archaeology and Society for Historical Archaeology. U.S. House of Representatives Committee on Resources Hearing on H.R. 2893 A Bill to Amend the Native American Graves Protection and Repatriation Act. www.saa.org/Government/Lobby/hr2893-testimony.html

Sued-Badillo, J. 1992. Facing up to Caribbean history. *American Antiquity* 57:599–607.

Trigger, B. 1981. Anglo-American archaeology. *World Archaeology* 13:138–155.

Trigger, B. 1984. Alternative archaeologies: Nationalist, colonialist, imperialist. *Man* 19:355–370.

Ulm, S., I. Lilley and A. Ross (eds) 1996. *Australian Archaeology '95. Proceedings of the 1995 Australian Archaeological Association Annual Conference*. Tempus Vol. 6. Brisbane: Anthropology Museum, University of Queensland.

Watkins, J. 1998. Native Americans, Western science, and NAGPRA. *Society for American Archaeology Bulletin* 16(5):23, 25.

Williams, B. 1992. Of straightening combs, sodium hydroxide, and potassium hydroxide in archaeological and cultural-anthropological analysis of ethnogenesis. *American Antiquity* 57:608–612.

Wolfe, P. 1999. *Settler Colonialism and the Transformation of Anthropology. The Politics and Poetics of an Ethnographic Event*. London: Cassells.

Wood, A. 1997. You can't split the Hansonite agenda. *The Australian* May 20:15.

Wylie, A. 1992. Rethinking the quincentennial: Consequences for past and present. *American Antiquity* 57:591–594.

Wylie, A. 1997. Contextualizing ethics: Comments on ethics in Canadian archaeology by Robert Rosenswig. *Canadian Journal of Archaeology* 21:115–120.

Zimmerman, L. 1989a. Made radical by my own: An archaeologist learns to accept reburial. In Layton, R. (ed.) *Conflict in the Archaeology of Living Traditions*, pp. 60–67. London: Unwin Hyman.

Zimmerman, L. 1989b. Human bones as symbols of power: Aboriginal American belief systems towards bones and 'grave-robbing' archaeologists. In Layton, R. (ed.) *Conflict in the Archaeology of Living Traditions*, pp. 211–216. London: Unwin Hyman.

Chapter 14

The Globalization of Archaeology and Heritage

A discussion with Arjun Appadurai

Arjun Appadurai (with Ashish Chadha,
Ian Hodder, Trinity Jachman and Chris Witmore)

One aspect of social archaeology is the historical and contemporary use of archaeology within nationalist movements. And yet, many would argue today that there are increasingly global processes that undermine the nation-state and its sovereign ownership of the national past. In his book *Modernity at Large* (1996), Arjun Appadurai dwells on issues of globalization and the relationship between modernity and tradition. For these reasons it was felt that a discussion with him might help to explore the contemporary role of a social archaeology in the context of a new journal devoted to that topic. Appadurai is also known to archaeologists for his work on material culture in *The Social Life of Things* (1986). So in sitting down to this interview we were interested in examining the broad question of the role of archaeology and material culture studies in a changing world, and in exploring links between social archaeology and wider interdisciplinary debates. The following discussion took place at Stanford University on 14 April 2000 between Arjun Appadurai, Ashish Chadha, Ian Hodder, Trinity Jackman and Chris Witmore.

TJ: It has been argued that the development of the discipline of archaeology was directly linked to the rise of nationalism and the spread of colonialism. In *Modernity at Large*, you write that the nation-state is entering a period of 'terminal crisis' and that culture is increasingly becoming an arena for conscious choice, justification and representation, the latter often to multiple and spatially dislocated audiences. If this process is coming about, do you see the 'politics of the past' becoming more intense as claims to the past increasingly proliferate? Or, do you think this fluidity and spatial dislocation will neutralize and de-politicize the past? Finally, what role do you imagine archaeology playing in these changes?

AA: My views have not changed but have become slightly more nuanced on the matter of the crisis of the nation-state. I think in *Modernity at Large* I might have overstated the terminality of the nation-state because I wanted to point to certain issues, but clearly the empirical evidence is mixed as to what exactly is going on. I still believe that there is a crisis. The question is what is the nature of that crisis. Now, I would say it's not a matter of a yes/no, terminus/non-terminus, ending/non-ending, kind of apocalyptic debate, yet I am not convinced by the explanation that the nation-state is simply changing: this explanation is too banal, for it's always changing. I certainly think that there is a widening of the field of sovereignty. I would still argue that as corporations, grass-roots interest groups and the like have become more powerful, the nation-state is no longer the only player with large-scale claims to sovereignty. It must contend with being only one player among many. That seems to me certain. Whether it means the nation-state literally ends is another matter but I'm certainly ready to consider this possibility. I often say to people that the nation-state did not receive an eternal contract but developed historically, as archaeologists know, and can come and go. The question of what would constitute signs of a terminal crisis is an open question, but I would love to ask this question to those individuals who say the nation-state is alive and well.

So I think there is a crisis, and a complication of sovereignty, and that there is a question of multiple sovereignties, etc., but I would not simply assert that the end of the nation-state is here, in a way I at least occasionally imply in the book. There is a normative impulse there too, and that impulse remains, as I'm not sure that the nation-state is the most desirable form for the management of large-scale human affairs. Its downside is, on the whole, more striking than its up-side. That is the background to the question of whether the reorganization of the experience and the structures of space and time will have a diffusing effect on the politics of the past or whether they will intensify it. At the moment, in so far as we can read the evidence, we see very little sign that the politics of the past are disappearing. I think they are stretching and deepening in lots of ways as more people become bi-national, multi-national or diasporic. The coherence of location and recollection cannot be taken for granted. A question that particularly interests me now apropos the nation-state is the shifting relationship between the politics of remembering and the politics of forgetting. Some people stress the business of remembering and that's quite justified for a lot of these groups, but not enough attention has been paid to the economy of forgetting and remembering in any given place or situation or in any given national space. In that economy, the nation-state plays a significant role in so far that it significantly controls the apparati through which the economy of remembering and forgetting is configured. The nation-state is in this respect a powerful player; media obviously plays a powerful independent role through documentaries, fiction, history channels, and popular memory and diasporic memory practices all join to complicate this field. Specific mechanisms for remembering and forgetting are still crucial to the national inflection of this economy. Here archaeology plays a vital role as it always has.

Professional archaeology is intimately tied to state institutions, national institutions and the ruling political party; as we saw during the recent World Archaeology Conference in Delhi[1] even the question of how archaeology could enter the space of conversation reminded us that archaeology is a key site through which the apparatus of nations can reflect the politics of remembering. It still remains very salient. In short, in so far as archaeology professionally remains very closely tied in many countries to what Etienne Balibar would call 'producing the people' it remains a critical player in the economy of remembering and forgetting. At some risk of exaggeration we could say that we must invert our weighting of the crude politics of erasure, of forgetting as opposed to that of recovery and remembering. The spatial diffusion of identities surely complicates the field within which the work of archaeology as a national discipline by and large exists.

AC: I ask this question in the context of recent reports about the targeting by right-wing archaeologists, government officials and academicians, of secular sites of Mughal India such as the Fatehpur Sikri which are claimed to be built upon destroyed Hindu temples. You mention in your book *Modernity at Large* that the diasporic community has played an important role along with electronic media in the withering of the nation-state, and has been responsible for the weakening of the hyphen between the nation and the state. How would you then explain the recent increase in NRI (Non-Resident Indian) funding to the Sangh Parivar organizations, whose politics are directly contributing to the strengthening of the nation, and of the state, especially when they are actively reinterpreting the past and denying any multivocality, thus contributing to the opposite of the effect that you talk about?

AA: Again, I would probably reformulate that in a less total form than the metaphor 'withering' would suggest. I do think that it is possible to go too far in one direction with the information on the NRIs. Though the NRI factor is important, no one has shown how important it is, i.e. does the Sangh Parivar fundamentally rely on it? Is it just an addon? Who needs whom more? Do the NRIs need them more or does the Sangh Parivar need the NRIs more?

Obviously, there are many worrisome developments in the history of India in the 150 years, arguably in the last 400 to 500 years, in the relations between 'Hindus' and 'Muslims'. These developments continued through the colonial period, etc., through the Partition and finally have been woven into the party politics of the present. So there is what in *Modernity at Large* I would have called a history as well as a genealogy to this relationship. The genealogy may look out to the NRI phenomena, but the history does not. My cautionary statement would be to not over-emphasize the salience of what the NRIs are doing or what the BJP (Bharatiya Janata Party) and its allies are doing. These activities may be very important for the NRIs, but I think that it is essential to ask exactly who within this vague category they are important to and in what precise NRI project such interests come to be important.

Once you ask that question, it connects to the earlier part of your query, which concerns the issue of space. Some of these activities are profoundly bifocal and seem clearly to be about what Benedict Anderson calls 'long-distance nationalism'. He has parenthetically suggested that such interventions are somewhat illegitimate and have often got to do with a reproduction of cultural practices driven by anxieties about identity here in the United States, or wherever the non-resident Indian may be, in England, Hong Kong, etc. My conception of a diasporic public sphere does not generate such draconian criticisms of long-distance nationalism.

It is not clear to me how one can read these processes in terms of contemporary Indian politics, in particular the question of the nation and the state in India. How can we be sure what is being fortified? How can we be sure what is being advanced? In fact, is it the project of the Indian nation that is being advanced, or is the effort to delete other histories, other groups (Muslims notably) actually producing new crises of hegemony in India? It is not self-evident that these inputs are simply fortifying, consolidating and drowning everything else. They might, in fact, be complicating the task of producing a hegemonic consensus in India.

As far as the state is concerned, on the other side of the hyphen, so to speak, it is even less clear what NRI support, whether fiscal or otherwise, means to the Sangh Parivar. What is the value of their support to the project of the state, broadly speaking, to development, to the theory of justice, to state economics? I am inclined to think that the issue is less the question of NRIs (though they are surely a part of it), than the contradiction, which is now very widespread but takes a particular form in India and elsewhere, between the opening of the market and the closing of national cultural space. The BJP-led coalition that rules India is certainly involved in this contradiction. Just the other day, we saw that the Indian Minister of Commerce and Industry, Murasoli Maran, has announced that there will be a flood of new opportunities for the middle classes to buy consumer goods, without licenses and restrictions. So, the market is opening wide, while the space for cultural plurality is shrinking. This perspective is related to the kind of argument about globalization that people like Samuel Huntington and Benjamin Barber and others have made. But I think we need a more complex picture of how the opening of markets relates to cultural closure, and here we should focus on the market ideology of the ruling coalition, in which the NRI story is a part, but certainly not the entire story.

Going back to the beginning of your question, I think it is clear that there is a continuing, but not very apparent, pressure on a party like the BJP, as they open the market, to find new ways of establishing their credentials as the trustees of cultural sovereignty, of cultural purity, cultural authenticity. This guardianship acts in their favor because they are caught between the pressure of their commercial supporters to favor liberalization, but also to account to their hardline ideological supporters, notably the RSS (Rashtriya Swayamsevak Sangh) for their pro-Hindu credentials. And one option is certainly to move towards some kind of mono-ethnic nationalism, which can then become xenophobic and even turn genocidal.

I think that there is a story to be told about the actual politics of the monuments and the politics of the 'layering', so to speak, and the narrative of the layer. Underneath the material presence of Islamic ruins is a whole living material world of human monuments, and the earlier narrative of submergence is now being complemented with a narrative of destruction, the narrative of a project of architectural submergence that the Muslims had allegedly undertaken, which has to be unpeeled from the top to reveal a kind of landscape. This politics of layers brings together contemporary spatial politics, such as the demolitions of slums, with the deep politics of monuments and archaeology.

This relationship is part of what I am struggling with now in Bombay. In some sense, urban spaces, increasingly, are being re-inscribed as national spaces or national soil, and a lot of the practices of ethnic rioting and violence in Bombay can be seen as violent practices of spatial re-inscription, so that, to take one example from the rumors that spread during the ethnic riots of 1992–93, the coastline of Bombay needs protection against the Pakistanis – a kind of implosion of two landscapes. So where does the story of the temples and the mosques, the double layer, with the Hindu layer underneath, fit into this global project, particularly that of reconstructing urban spaces? Which people are ritually and politically mobilized to be associated with the kind of ethnic violence which occurred in Bombay? This kind of re-writing of cities as national spaces, requiring protection, requiring fortification, requiring defense and so on, is constantly occurring. Something is moving between the centers and the borders. From this point of view, you can view the Babri Masjid as the center in the national imagination and military borders, territorial borders and the recent war with Pakistan as borders. And somewhere in between, there are these cities, which are not the centers, but where you can replay the Babri Masjid story, by attacking a mosque in Bombay. In this, there is not just the simple replication of the events but also a complicated rewriting of these spaces as markedly national, not just as routine components of the national.

So, to return to the question of NRIs. We need to distinguish between the question of the NRIs, which is important in its own right, the question of whether or not the BJP is deepening its own crisis in regard to economic opening and cultural closure, and the question of the politics of trying to find an undisturbed Hindu layer through archaeological practices. I would pull these questions slightly apart and not bring them together very tightly yet.

CW: We recently had a member of a local Native American tribe, Otis Parish (Kashaya Pomo), as a visitor to Stanford who, along with his community, is overseeing a set of unique excavations upon tribal land along a stretch of the Californian coastline just north of San Francisco. This community has taken traditional scientific methods of archaeological excavation, which are seen as universalizing, and made them 'safe' in a hybridized form through the incorporation of ritual. Here we have an example, in the context of archaeology, of a blending of local tradition and science as a facet of modernity. Concomitantly, the story that is being brought to light is one of continuity with the past. Is it possible to address the question of how notions of the theory of rupture, transition and fracture between modernity and tradition, explicit in your work *Modernity at Large*, can be understood and articulated in such a situation where that distinction is purposely blurred? In this particular case the global/local dynamic can also be highlighted since this is a local issue, which is broadcast globally through the Internet.

AA: That is a very interesting and challenging question in two or three different ways. On the one hand, it speaks to a kind of basic dilemma in anthropology and in the humanities and social sciences more generally. We keep deconstructing the idea of the primordial and the primordialist thesis. Yet all sorts of groups act on the assumption that their peoplehood is primordially real. We can say that there is something wrong with the latter view, that it is a form of false consciousness that ethnic or religious groups such as the Serbs or the Hindus may have. People seem to operate without questioning how they transfer 'things' from the historical to the non-historical and thus, somehow, to the physical, hardwired, biological, racial, etc. So people faced with peculiarly modern dilemmas tell a story about who 'we' are which is time-deep, unambiguous and primordial. My response to this point of view is that both the question and the answer are very modern.

There are certain questions that never arise except under these conditions of modernity. A specific example is the question of long-term materially certified authenticity. Some kind of tribal or other identity itself only arises under the conditions of modern debate about who you are, what your claims are and where you would stake them; and again the nation-state affects the terms of this debate in a specific way. This is due to the fact that it has, in the US for example, put into place the idea that genuine claims to certain forms of community have to be anchored in some kind of spatial sovereignty. Once you have that argument in place then claims to some type of special standing or autonomy, as in the case of most Native American groups, have to be somehow connected up to a story of spaces that are 'ours' over the long run, stories of originality. It is not just that the answer and the ways of answering rely on modernity, but that the question too comes out of debates about who we are and what our claims are, which in turn could not have happened except under the conditions of modernity.

I sense something else in your question of why this orientation to deep-time exists. It is the question of continuity vs. rupture. One could say that certain tropes of continuity and certain ways of materializing continuity, which would bring archaeology into the picture, become particularly salient under conditions of rupture. Here it is only *when* the question of peopleness comes into play, that the national and the archaeological, as mediated by the social sciences more generally, seem to acquire special relations. It is not so much the case that the question is modern and the answer is traditional: I think both are from the same sort of conditions. This is not the kind of debate about deep continuity that you might find, I think, if you had access to inscriptional records from the thirteenth century. You would get other statements about who we are, why we are special and so on, but you would not get this notion of deep-time, unbroken continuity and so on. Such discourses may be themselves historical, and modern.

CW: In the historical situation I was referring to before, approximately 150 years ago a Russian trading post was founded upon this stretch of coast, which opened up these

indigenous populations to the outside world through the fur trade. Processes of
globalization present at that time had a profound impact upon their conception of
identity and understandings of tradition. Believing these contacts to be dangerous,
they eventually closed themselves off from the outside world and only in the 1950s
did they again make contact. Extreme caution toward the outside world has been a
practice for over a century with this tribe. And so when I mentioned how this
community dealt with the universalizing process of the scientific method, something
that can be associated with modernity and the global, I wished to play upon that
dynamic where the global is brought into, utilized and made necessarily safe in a
local context through ritual and then is projected back globally through the Internet.
This invention of a 'local tradition' is not only heavily influenced by the global but is
meant to have influence globally.

AA: The invention of tradition argument does not invite one adequately to ask whether
people invent tradition as they please, just like history. And the answer is *no*. They
invent it under conditions that are themselves historical. In this case you are pointing
to one set of conditions where there is an expanding world and then a shrinking
world so that depending on the group in question they are not in a linear progression, but work in ebbs and flows.

    Amitav Ghosh, in his book *In an Antique Land* (1992), suggests that we are less
cosmopolitan now than we were in the pre-modern epoch in the region of the
Indian Ocean. It is an interesting argument and for someone like me it is very challenging. This is not because I have a linear evolutionary view, but I have not known
very well how to engage with earlier cosmopolitanisms, earlier global contacts and
divisions. I am now trying to reconnect *The Social Life of Things* argument to the
Modernity at Large essays. I see there is something important to do in reconnecting
the idea of commodities and the realities of their movement explicitly to the arguments found in *Modernity at Large*. For a long time, I had not quite seen that *Modernity at Large* is very much animated by the same sorts of impulses as in *The Social Life
of Things*.

IH: One of the themes that was very interesting in the Otis Parrish example was that he
was taking the scientific archaeological methods and embedding them in rituals, so
that the excavation would take place in the context of, for example, prayer or
dance. That raises the wider issue of how we deal with different forms of knowledge, including non-academic forms of knowledge, and how we provide institutional arrangements for better dialogue. The Parrish example is about science and
ritual knowledge coming together. I wonder whether you could say something more
general about the problems of dealing with different forms of knowledge, perhaps
specifically in relation to the past, museums and heritage and how we can provide
structures to deal with these sorts of relationships.

AA: I am glad that you highlighted that interesting dimension. I can enter into the debate
about multiple knowledges through the idea in the last chapter of *Modernity at Large*
about the production of locality. The question is 'what are the kinds of conditions
under which locality is produced?' Sometimes it is produced with explicitly
hybridizing techniques like the ones that have been mentioned. In such cases the aim
is to produce the local, but it is found expedient or compelling to do so by bringing
in the discourse of science. Science is introduced into a space which was otherwise
separate from it in order to more fully, more plausibly, more attractively and more
credibly, perhaps to a wider public sphere, produce the local.

    So for me one part of the scaffolding for considering multiple knowledges
would be the conditions under which locality is produced. There is a set of historical
conditions, at different points in time and space, in which the production of the local
involves a quite complicated traffic in knowledges. Sometimes that traffic seems

thinner or less stressed, less hybrid, less negotiated. But in the particular case you mention there is a more conscious negotiation in order at the end of the day to somehow both produce a local that is more durable and is also produced in a way that is more credible. The claims are made through a certified apparatus of truth, which is what archaeology in this case is taken to be. It is taken to somehow ratify or sustain the production of a pattern that might otherwise seem more vulnerable.

Important issues surround efforts to conserve, materialize, record and represent heritages for broad publics. One angle on that might be the distinction that my friend and colleague Valentine Daniel (1996) makes in his recent book on Sri Lankan ethnic violence between history and heritage. He tries to speak of these as two modalities associated with Sri Lankans and Tamils as they apprehend the past of that island, and he makes a very sharp normative, or idealtypic, break between the two, while recognizing that leakages between them do occur. Such distinctions are salient to the question of museum building practices at the end of this century and concern, among other things, whether museums should properly be speaking about history or about heritage? In Val Daniel's terms, heritage becomes a more fixed, a more worrisome and more essentialist notion, and history becomes more open and more mobile. If museums are going to be about history, how can this be achieved when their very materiality as well as the disciplines which produce them conduce to the other type of typological fixity?

There is another angle on these issues that I would like to bring out. I am thinking here of issues such as the contestation of the past, archaeology as a discipline, museums as institutions. I am also thinking of the retrieval of the material, and of the fact that nation-states or, in the broadest sense, national imaginations require (as Fredric Jameson might put it) signatures of the visible, and that museums and archaeology as a practice are about signatures of the visible. I think we have choices both in what archaeology does in its practices as a discipline and in what museums that are driven by excavation can do.

I want to make just one point about this that I think deserves development. In the general business of retrieving the past, remembering, materializing that memory and further commemorating it, leads directly to the business of the nation, and does so through certain regimes or techniques of truth provided mainly by archaeology. This process, and I think this is not just true of history but of all social practices of recollection, ties into my interest in ethnic violence and returns to the question of what large-scale violence is about, whether in Eastern Europe or India or Rwanda or anywhere else. In such contexts, there are forms of recollection that do not seem to require the elimination of other memories, and there are other forms of recollection which seem more, to use a term I am trying to develop, predatory. That is, they seem to be premised on that idea that for them to subsist something else must go. So one of my big concerns now is why certain identities, which are parts of pairs or sets which have been in some form of workable juxtaposition at a certain point in time, become predatory. Why does one of them, or sometimes both, become animated by the idea that there is only room for one of them? When and under what circumstances does this happen?

This is a broad and challenging comparative question. But with regard to archaeology and museums, it seems to me one could ask whether a particular exercise in excavation or in documentation or in museumization is going by its form and nature to tend towards predation, which is to say the exclusion of others. How can one organize things so that there is an opening of memory in which there is room for others, for contesting perspectives and so on? I have no clear idea about how one might put items into an exhibit hall in such a way as to discourage predation. That is a complex question for museum curators, but in principle it seems to me to be one consideration to be taken up. One can look at opening exhibits to debate. One can look at using modern information technologies in a non-superficial manner in so-called interactive exhibits. There are many such possibilities, but unless you have good answers to the central question, even excellent answers to exhibit presentation issues will not make museums benign places.

IH: We could go on and talk about 'origins' because very often issues concerning the display of the past get linked to the question of origins. There I think we would have to think through whether it is possible to claim an origin without excluding, and whether the search for origins is not always predatory.

But can I move on to our final topic which is to do with the authentic. I would like to bring up the idea of the commodification of the past and the role that is playing in globalization. You talk in *Modernity at Large* about the past being placed into museums, and the past becoming less a *habitus* and more a choice. One can go from there to wider questions of choice in the marketing of nostalgia, and to ideas of pastiche and depthlessness. But archaeologists often observe that many people today remain absolutely absorbed in the past as real and authentic. The search for the authentic, however much commodification goes on, is very strong. So tourists will ask 'is this produced by indigenous people?', and 'who exactly produced it; how authentic is it?' and so on. There is a fascination with the authentic which is not necessarily reducible to nationalism. The public point of view is not always 'this is my . . .'. Rather visitors or tourists say 'I want to have the real thing' and they presume that 'real' things have higher market value. I wondered if you could make sense of this fascination for the authentic in a very highly commodified world where the past too has become commodified.

AA: The whole field of the authentic in whatever domain, in tourism or whatever else, is very important to continue to study. I have different kinds of responses. One is that just as particular kinds of authentication through tradition are parts of particularly modern debates about identity that may not have occurred before, likewise the pursuit of the signature – 'who really made this' – arises under the empire of the commodity. The endless effort to singularize, as my colleague Igor Kopytoff would say, occurs because of the constant expansion of the empire of the commodity so that the two (the singular and the commodity) are like scorpions in a bottle constantly feeding off each other. I have begun to write a little essay on the gift in the age of the commodity, playing with the idea of what gifting in this context might mean. In a fully commodified culture, what gift is there that has any singularity to it? Who could possibly make a singular gift other than by cutting off their hands or something like that? Even then it is not clear what you would have to do to be absolutely singular. So the force that you refer to is perfectly understandable in such a context.

I think there are two choices here and I am not sure how one might referee or arbitrate between them. One is to say that the urge you describe is strictly accounted for by the energy of its other, and tourism is the perfect case in that people want precisely to be only there themselves, wanting the unspoilt place. The eternal trope of the travel journals is 'this place is unspoilt, so go find it'. The place then will thus no longer be unspoilt but still you got there first. So the two things are literally two sides of the one coin. But I think there is another way to think about these tensions which is both more benign and more worrisome. This is when one says that there is a metaphysics of presence and recollection and rootedness which is independent of the question of the commodity. That is, people are always seeking to anchor themselves in a relatively unmediated material world that sustains their sense of themselves, their cultural worlds, their modes of signification. It is in that world that the world of the commodity intervenes. So there is an endless search for the margins, for the place where the commodity is not yet king, where one is slightly free of it. In such places one may feel, not entirely without justification, that one has found the signature, found the maker, nailed the case so to speak. Such a space would not be produced by the working of the commodity but would be seen as residual but free of the relentless expansion of commodification.

I don't know how one would arbitrate between these views and I have a feeling one cannot do so deductively. One would have to look at the practice. One would have to look at the actor or the institution and analyze the claims that are being made, the practices, the justifications and the debates and then assign them to one or the other situation. I could accept that some groups, especially some groups that have to struggle for the means of cultural survival, attach themselves to this or that object, space, monument, etc., in a manner that is precisely not predatory, which is only about survival and dignity, which does not require someone else to disappear. I am perfectly prepared to see that exercise and that effort as not driven by the dynamics of the commodity. It is driven by something else that may have its own dangers from a Foucauldian perspective – that is it may be humanistic in a limited way. But it would not have the problem of being just the other of the commodity. So, briefly, I am less inclined than I and others would have been five or ten years ago to see authenticity always invariably as the sign of something else negative. Now I am prepared to see that there may be legitimate strivings for connections to the material world and to the past.

In the whole business of identity and ethnicity and so on which preoccupies me now and which is not at all unconnected to the materialities of mosques and destructions of collections, heritage and so on, I have come to see that there are processes and projects of identity building which are fundamentally future-driven. They are 'projects', you might say. And there are the others that are fundamentally driven by the past, at least in their self-understanding. My sense is that those that are projected usually are likely not to be predatory. But those that are excessively driven by the past tend to crowd others out. Why this should be so is not clear to me.

IH: I am digging in Turkey at the moment. When tourists visit this 9000-year-old site, quite a number of them stay quite a long time. Some have worked hard reading about the site, or it may have a religious value to them. It's a site where the Goddess is supposed to originate. They get a feeling of authentic association with that place even though they have only been there a short period of time. Such diasporic tourists have a sense of locality which is global. They move around as part of their holidays or their searching lives, creating a sense of an authentic relationship with the past in a number of different localities. They put together a story of themselves which is a product of that tour through the past or through time and space. One begins to get this notion of people constructing multiple authentic identities on a global scale. This observation then problematizes the opposition between the global and the local in relation to the past in a very clear way. And then of course there are many imagined communities, like groups in Europe who think they are Native Americans. There are people constructing real authentic relationships with the past that are very separate from them, which are very multiple, and they can move through them. They construct their sense of identity by putting all that together in complex ways.

AA: I have not reflected very much about that kind of experience, that kind of authentication, but the mediating term there would be 'life-style'. That is, you acquire a lifestyle, a way of being, assuming the time and money and leisure, in which the delinkage of a single location from a single authentic history is now made possible. But the worry about it is that there is something fundamentally unstable, frivolous or over-privileged about it. That is always the worry about these kinds of complex Bohemian habits of self-authentication. They are dubious because they are so restricted.

IH: Of course the ability to travel and tourism are restricted, but there are nowadays huge numbers involved in a variety of income groups

AA: I am very sympathetic to that fact, but I think that the more complex experiential aggregation of memories in relation to places and so on requires more than travel; it requires a whole series of other things. Not that the growing practices of travel are always elitist or exclusive (in the age of mass tourism) but I think they are necessarily partial and occasional experiences. I do not think their specialness disqualifies them in any way. It just opens the question of what kind of requirements are there for having this experience. But you are quite right, in that whatever these experiences are, if one takes them seriously they open other ways to connect space, history, materiality.

IH: It is perhaps important to consider travel as a mechanism and metaphor for relating to the past in order to try and get away from the idea that someone owns the past.

AA: Yes, the property dimension is a little bit connected to something I tried to develop up to a point a long time ago in a completely different context. This is the idea of the past as a scarce resource. In 1981 I published an essay based on my research on a temple and its history, in the British journal *Man*. That debate about the past happens within certain normative parameters. It was a sort of anti-Malinowski argument. One could, of course, think about the past as a boundless resource, endlessly open to variety, elaboration, re-invention and social empowerment. But if indeed the past is a scarce resource, because its construction is subject to cultural as well as material constraints, this means that the economy which governs the production of the past has to be examined even more critically. Specifically, since the most violent social dramas of recent times have involved those contexts in which the material past has been converted into national or ethnic property, it may be helpful to encourage more plural appropriations of the past, such as those encouraged by tourism and travel. So we find ourselves on the horns of our largest contemporary dilemma: whether to be slaves in the empire of the commodity or puppets in the shadow of the state. Recognizing that the past does have an economy, and debating the forms and functions of that economy, may yet point to a way out of this impasse. And archaeology, always and legitimately concerned about the material past, may hold a large part of the answers for an ethics and a politics appropriate to this ambiguous future.

Note

1   The third World Archaeological Conference was hosted in New Delhi by the Archaeological Society of India in December 1994.

References

Appadurai, A., ed. (1986) *The Social Life of Things: Commodities in Cultural Perspective*. Cambridge: Cambridge University Press.

Appadurai, A. (1996) *Modernity at Large: Cultural Dimensions of Globalization*. Minneapolis: University of Minnesota Press.

Daniel, E.V. (1996) *Charred Lullabies: Chapters in an Anthropology of Violence*. Princeton: Princeton University Press.

Ghosh, A. (1992) *In an Antique Land*. London: Granta Publishers.

Chapter 15

Whose Heritage?

Un-settling 'The Heritage', re-imagining the post-nation

Stuart Hall

This conference on 'Whose Heritage?' provides an opportunity to look critically at the whole concept of 'British Heritage' from the perspective of the multicultural Britain which has been emerging since the end of World War II. How is it being – and how should it be – transformed by the 'Black British' presence and the explosion of cultural diversity and difference which is everywhere our lived daily reality?

In preparing to say something useful on this topic, I was struck again – as many of you may have been – by the quaintness of the very term, 'Heritage'. It has slipped so innocently into everyday speech! I take it to refer to the whole complex of organisations, institutions and practices devoted to the preservation and presentation of culture and the arts – art galleries, specialist collections, public and private, museums of all kinds (general, survey or themed, historical or scientific, national or local) and sites of special historical interest.

What is curious in the British usage is the emphasis given to preservation and conservation: to keeping what already exists – as opposed to the production and circulations of new work in different media, which takes a very definite second place. The British have always seen 'culture' as a vaguely disquieting idea as if to name it is to make self-conscious what well-bred folk absorb unconsciously with their mother's milk! Ministries of Culture are what those old, now discredited, eastern European regimes used to have, which is altogether the wrong associations! Culture has therefore entered the nomenclature of modern British government only when sandwiched alongside the more acceptably populist terms, 'Media' and 'Sport'.

This gives the British idea of 'Heritage' a peculiar inflection. The works and artefacts so conserved appear to be 'of value' primarily in relation to the past. To be validated, they must take their place alongside what has been authorised as 'valuable' on already established grounds in relation to the unfolding of a 'national story' whose terms we already know. The Heritage thus becomes the material embodiment of the spirit of the nation, a collective representation of the British version of *tradition*, a concept pivotal to the lexicon of English virtues.

This retrospective, nation-alised and tradition-alised conception of culture will return to haunt our subsequent thoughts at different points. However, it may also serve as a warning that *my* emphasis does include the active production of culture and the arts as a living activity, alongside the conservation of the past.

We spend an increasing proportion of the national wealth – especially since The Lottery – on 'The Heritage'. But what is it *for*? Obviously, to preserve for posterity things of value, whether on aesthetic or historical criteria. But that is only a start. From its earliest history in western societies – in the heterogeneous assemblages of the 'cabinets of curiosity and wonder' – collections have adorned the position of people of power and influence – kings, princes, popes, landowners and merchants – whose wealth and status they amplified. They have always been related to the exercise of 'power' in another sense – the symbolic power to order knowledge, to rank, classify and arrange, and thus to give meaning to objects and things through the imposition of interpretative schemas, scholarship and the authority of connoisseurship. As Foucault observed, 'there is no power relation without the relative constitution of a field of knowledge nor any knowledge that does not presuppose and constitute . . . power relations'.[1]

Since the eighteenth century, collections of cultural artefacts and works of art have also been closely associated with informal public education. They have become part, not simply of 'governing', but of the broader practices of 'governmentality' – how the state indirectly and at a distance induces and solicits appropriate attitudes and forms of conduct from its citizens. The state is always, as Gramsci argued, 'educative'. Through its power to preserve and represent culture, the state has assumed some responsibility for educating the citizenry in those forms of 'really useful knowledge', as the Victorians put it, which would refine the sensibilities of the vulgar and enhance the capacities of the masses. This was the true test of their 'belongingness': culture as social incorporation.

It is important to remember that the nation-state is both a political and territorial entity, *and* what Benedict Anderson has called 'an imagined community'.[2] Though we are often strangers to one another, we form an 'imagined community' because we share an *idea* of the nation and what it stands for, which we can 'imagine' in our mind's eye. A shared national identity thus depends on the cultural meanings which bind each member individually into the larger national story. Even so-called 'civic' states, like Britain, are deeply embedded in specific 'ethnic' or cultural meanings which give the abstract idea of the nation its lived 'content'.

The National Heritage is a powerful source of such meanings. It follows that those who cannot see themselves reflected in its mirror cannot properly 'belong'. Even the museums and collections apparently devoted to surveying the universal, rather than the national, achievements of culture – like the British Museum, the Louvre, or the Metropolitan Museum in New York – are harnessed into the national story. Carol Duncan and Alan Wallach have argued that these institutions 'claim the heritage of the classical tradition for contemporary society and equate that tradition with the very notion of civilization itself'.[3] Much the same could be said about the museums of Modern or Contemporary Art in terms of the way they have colonised the very idea of 'the modern', 'modernity' and 'modernism' as exclusively 'western' inventions.

Heritage is bound into the meaning of the nation through a double inscription. What the nation means is essentialised: 'the English seem unaware that anything fundamental has changed since 1066'.[4] Its essential meaning appears to have emerged at the very moment of its origin – a moment always lost in the myths, as well as the mists, of time – and then successively embodied as a distilled essence in the various arts and artefacts of the nation for which the Heritage provides the archive. In fact, what the nation 'means' is an ongoing project, under constant reconstruction. We come to know its meaning partly *through* the objects and artefacts which have been made to stand for and symbolise its essential values. Its meaning is constructed *within*, not above or outside representation. It is through identifying with these representations that come to be its 'subjects' – by 'subjecting' ourselves to its dominant meanings. What would 'England' *mean* without its cathedrals, churches, castles and country houses, its gardens, thatched cottages and hedgerowed landscapes, its Trafalgars, Dunkirks and Mafekings, its Nelsons and its Churchills, its Elgars and its Benjamin Brittens?

We should think of The Heritage as a discursive practice. It is one of the ways in which the nation slowly constructs for itself a sort of collective social memory. Just as individuals and families construct their identities in part by 'storying' the various random incidents and contingent turning points of their lives into a single, coherent, narrative, so nations construct identities by selectively binding their chosen high points and memorable achievements into an unfolding 'national story'. This story is what is called 'Tradition'. As the Jamaican anthropologist, David Scott, recently observed, 'A tradition . . . seeks to connect authoritatively, within the structure of its narrative, a relation among past, community, an identity.' He goes on to argue that,

> A tradition therefore is never neutral with respect to the values it embodies. Rather a tradition operates in and through the stakes it constructs – what is to count and what is not to count among its satisfactions, what the goods and excellences and virtues are that ought to be valued . . . On this view . . . if tradition presupposes 'a common possession' it does not presuppose uniformity or plain consensus. Rather it depends upon a play of conflict and contention. It is a space of dispute as much as of consensus, of discord as much as of accord.[5]

The Heritage is also a classic example of the operation of what Raymond Williams called the 'selective tradition':

> Theoretically a period is recorded; in practice, this record is absorbed into a selective tradition; and both are different from the culture as lived . . . To some extent the selection begins within the period itself . . . though that does not mean that the values and emphases will later be confirmed.[6]

Like personal memory, social memory is also highly selective, it highlights and foregrounds, imposes beginnings, middles and ends on the random and contingent. Equally, it foreshortens, silences, disavows, forgets and elides many episodes which – from another perspective – could be the start of a different narrative. This process of selective 'canonisation' confers authority and a material and institutional facticity on the selective tradition, making it extremely difficult to shift or revise. The institutions responsible for making the 'selective tradition' work develop a deep investment in their own 'truth'.

The Heritage inevitably reflects the governing assumptions of its time and context. It is always inflected by the power and authority of those who have colonised the past, whose versions of history matter. These assumptions and co-ordinates of power are inhabited as natural – given, timeless, true and inevitable. But it takes only the passage of time, the shift of circumstances, or the reversals of history, to reveal those assumptions as time- and context-bound, historically specific, and thus open to contestation, re-negotiation, and revision.

This is therefore an appropriate moment to ask, then, who is the Heritage *for*? In the British case the answer is clear. It is intended for those who 'belong' – a society which is imagined as, in broad terms, culturally homogeneous and unified.

It is long past time to radically question this foundational assumption.

It is, of course, undeniable that Britain has been in recent times a relatively settled society and 'culture'. But as something approaching a nation-state, the United Kingdom of Great Britain and Ireland (subsequently 'and Northern Ireland') is in fact a relatively recent historical construct, a product of the eighteenth, nineteenth and twentieth centuries. Britain itself was formed out of a series of earlier invasions, conquests and settlements – Celts, Romans, Saxons, Vikings, Normans, Angevins – whose 'traces' are evident in the palimpsest of the national language. The Act of Union linked Scotland, England and Wales into a united kingdom, but never on terms of cultural equality – a fact constantly obscured by the covert oscillations and surreptitious substitutions between the terms 'Britishness' and 'Englishness'.[7]

The Act of Settlement (1701) secured a Protestant ascendancy, drawing the critical symbolic boundary between the Celtic/Catholic and the Anglo-Saxon/Protestant traditions. Between 1801 (the date of the Act of Union which brokered Ireland into the Union) and Partition in 1922, the national story proved incapable of incorporating 'Irishness' into 'Britishness' or of integrating Irish Catholic migrants into an imagined 'Englishness'. Their culture and presence remains marginalised today.

Though relatively stable, English society has always contained within it profound differences. There were always different ways of being 'English'. It was always fissured along class, gender and regional lines. What came to be known, misleadingly, as '*the* British way of life' is really another name for a particular settlement of structured social inequalities. Many of the great achievements which have been retrospectively written into the national lexicon as primordial English virtues – the rule of law, free speech, a fully-representative franchise, the rights of combination, the National Health Service, the welfare state itself – were struggled for by some of the English and bitterly resisted by others. Where, one asks, is this deeply ruptured and fractured history, with its interweaving of stability and conflict, in the Heritage's version of the dominant national narrative?

The British Empire was the largest *imperium* of the modern world. The very notion of 'greatness' in Great Britain is inextricably bound up with its imperial destiny. For centuries, its wealth was underpinned, its urban development driven, its agriculture and industry revolutionised, its fortunes as a nation settled, its maritime and commercial hegemony secured, its thirst quenched, its teeth sweetened, its cloth spun, its food spiced, its carriages rubber-wheeled, its bodies adorned, through the imperial connection. Anyone who has been watching the Channel 4 series on *The Slave Trade* or the 'hidden history' of the West India Regiment or the BBC's *The Boer War* will not need reminding how deeply intertwined were the facts of colonisation, slavery and empire with the everyday daily life of all classes and conditions of English men and women. The emblems of Empire do, of course, fitfully appear in the Heritage. However, in general, 'Empire' is increasingly subject to a widespread selective amnesia and disavowal. And when it does appear, it is largely narrated from the viewpoint of the colonisers. Its master narrative is sustained in the scenes, images and the artefacts which testify to Britain's success in imposing its will, culture and institutions, and inscribing its civilising mission across the world. This formative strand in the national culture is now re-presented as an external appendage, extrinsic and inorganic to the domestic history and culture of the English social formation.

Despite all this, the idea of Heritage *has* had to respond to at least two major challenges. The first we may call the democratisation process. Increasingly, the lives, artefacts, houses, work-places, tools, customs and oral memories of ordinary everyday British folk have slowly taken their subordinate place alongside the hegemonic presence of the great and the good. The inclusion of domestic vernacular architecture and the agrarian and industrial revolutions, together with the explosion of interest in 'history from below', the spread of local and family history, of personal memorabilia and the collection of oral histories – activities witnessed to in, for example, Raphael Samuel's memorable celebration of the 'popular heritage', *Theatres of Memory*[8] – have shifted and democratised our conception of value, of what is and is not worth preserving. A few courageous if controversial steps have been taken in our direction – the Liverpool Museum on the Slave Trade, the Maritime Museum's re-hang. However, by and large, this process has so far stopped short at the frontier defined by that great unspoken British value – 'whiteness'.

The second 'revolution' arises from the critique of the Enlightenment ideal of dispassionate universal knowledge, which drove and inspired so much of Heritage activity in the past. This has to be coupled with a rising cultural relativism which is part of the growing de-centring of the West and western-oriented or Eurocentric grand-narratives. From the 'Magiciens de la Terre' exhibition at the Pompidou Centre in Paris in the 1980s, on through the 'Te Maori' exhibition from New Zealand at the Metropolitan Museum of New York, the 'Paradise' exhibition from New Guinea at the Museum of Mankind, 'The Spirit Sings' exhibition of Canada's 'first peoples' at Calgary, the 'Perspectives: Angles on African Art' at the Centre for African Art in New York, and on and on, the exhibiting of 'other cultures' – often performed with the best of liberal intentions has proved controversial. The questions – 'Who should control the power to represent?' 'Who has the authority to re-present the culture of others?' – have resounded through the museum corridors of the world, provoking a crisis of authority.

These two developments mark a major transformation in our relation to the activity of constructing a 'Heritage'. They in turn reflect a number of conceptual shifts in what we might loosely call the intellectual culture. A list of these shifts would have to include – a radical awareness by the marginalised of the symbolic power involved in the activity of representation; a growing sense of the centrality of culture and its relation to *identity*; the rise amongst the excluded of a 'politics of recognition' alongside the older politics of equality; a growing reflexivity about the constructed and thus contestable nature of the authority which some people acquire to 'write the culture' of others; a decline in the acceptance of the traditional authorities in authenticating the interpretative and analytic frameworks which classify, place, compare and evaluate culture; and the concomitant rise in the demand to re-appropriate control over the 'writing of one's own story' as part of a wider process of cultural liberation, or – as Frantz Fanon and Amilcar Cabral once put it – 'the decolonization of the mind'. In short, a general relativisation of 'truth', 'reason' and other abstract Enlightenment values, and an increasingly perspectival and context-related conception of truth-as-interpretation – of 'truth' as an aspect of what Michel Foucault calls the 'will to power' . . .

Each of these developments would take a whole lecture on their own to elaborate. But I take them here as together marking an unsettling and subversion of the foundational ground on which the process of Heritage-construction has until very recently proceeded. We see it reflected in different ways: in how the texts supporting art works and framing exhibits are written by museums; in the attempts to make explicit the 'perspective' which has governed the selection and the interpretative contextualisation, so as to make it more open to challenge and re-interpretation; in the exposing of underlying assumptions of value, meaning and connection as part of a more dialogic relationship between the cultural institutions and their audiences; and in the tentative efforts to involve the 'subjects' themselves in the exhibiting process which objectifies them. These are only some of the manifest signs of a deep slow-motion revolution in progress in the practices of cultural representation.

They have taken hold, but are certainly not yet extensively or ubiquitously deployed in the institutional complex of the British Heritage 'industry' as a whole. Their appearance is at best patchy, more honoured in the breach – in profession of good intentions – than actual practice. Nevertheless, the question 'Whose Heritage?', posed in the context of the current 'drift' towards a more multicultural Britain, has to be mounted on the back of this emerging 'turn'. I take the appearance of 'cultural diversity' as a key policy priority of the newly restructured Arts Council, its greater visibility in statements of intent by the government and the Ministry of Culture, Media and Sport, the recent efforts by the British Council to project a more 'diverse' image of British culture abroad, and even the much-delayed declaration of a 'Year of cultural diversity' – two years after Amsterdam, but much to be welcomed nevertheless – as potential but uncertain harbingers of change.

Suppose this *were* to turn out to be a propitious moment. What would those new constituencies who feel themselves woefully inadequately represented in the mirror of culture which the Heritage holds up to British society want out of it?

It goes without saying that we would need more money specifically targeted at this objective. The corners of the government's mouth tend to droop significantly when the money and material resources required to meet objectives are mentioned, and the weary muttering about 'not simply throwing money at the problem' rises to a quiet crescendo. However, the idea that a major culture-change – nothing short of a cultural revolution – could take place in the way the nation represents the diversity of itself and its 'subject-citizens' without a major redirection of resources is to reveal oneself as vacantly trivial about the whole question.

In fact, however, money really *is* not enough. For if my arguments are correct, then an equally powerful obstacle to change is the deep institutional investment which the key organisations have in going on doing things in the ways in which they have always been done; and the operational inertia militating against key professionals re-examining their criteria of judgement and their gate-keeping practices from scratch and trying to shift the habits of a professional lifetime. It will require a substantially enhanced programme of training and recruitment for curators, professionals and artists from the 'minority' communities, so that they can bring their knowledge and expertise to bear on transforming dominant curatorial and exhibitory habits. It also will take the massive leverage of a state and government committed to producing, *in reality rather than in name*, a more culturally diverse, socially just, equal and inclusive society and culture, and *holding its cultural institutions to account*. There are some straws in the wind and a lot of wordage, but so far no consistent sign of this.

Nevertheless, it seems to me that *we* have here an opportunity to clarify our own minds and to refine our agendas so that we can seize every opportunity to challenge institutions, shift resources, change priorities, move practices strategically in the right direction. The rest of my talk is devoted to this task of clarification.

First we need a better idea of who the 'we' are in whose name these changes are being articulated. Principally, we have in mind the so-called 'ethnic minority communities' from the Caribbean and Indian sub-continent, whose presence in large numbers since the 1950s have transformed Britain into a multicultural society, together with the smaller groups of non-European minorities from Africa, the Middle East, China and the Far East and Latin America. Their impact on diversifying British society and culture has been immediate and significant. It may therefore surprise you to hear me say that it is really very complex to understand how appropriately these communities should now be culturally represented in mainstream British cultural and artistic institutions. Our picture of them is defined primarily by their 'otherness' – their *minority* relationship to something vaguely identified as 'the majority', their cultural difference from European norms, their nonwhiteness, their 'marking' by ethnicity, religion and 'race'. This is a negative figuration, reductive and simplistic.

These are people who have formed communities in Britain which are both distinctively marked, culturally, and yet have never been separatist or exclusive. Some traditional cultural practices are maintained – in varied ways – and carry respect. At the same time, the degrees and forms of attachment are fluid and changing – constantly negotiated, especially between men and women, within and across groups, and above all, across the generations. Traditions coexist with the emergence of new, hybrid and crossover cultural forms of tremendous vitality and innovation. These communities are in touch with their differences, without being saturated by tradition. They are actively involved with every aspect of life around them, without the illusion of assimilation and identity. This is a new kind of difference – the difference which is not binary (either-or) but whose '*differances*' (as Jacques Derrida has put it) will not be erased, or traded.[9]

Their lives and experiences have been shaped by traditions of thought, religious and moral values, very different from the Judeo-Christian and classical traditions whose 'traces' still shape 'western' culture; and by the historical experience of oppression and marginalisation. Many are in touch with cultures and languages which pre-date those of 'The West'. Nevertheless, colonisation long ago convened these cultural differences under the 'canopy' of a sort of imperial empty 'global' time, without ever effectively erasing the disjunctures and dislocations of time, place and culture by its ruptural intrusion into their 'worlds'. This is the palimpsest of the postcolonial world.

These communities are, as C.L.R. James once put it, 'in but not of Europe'[10] . . . Nevertheless, they have known 'Europe' for three or four centuries as what Ashis Nandy, in his unforgettable phrase, calls 'intimate enemies'.[11] They are what David Scott has called 'conscripts of modernity'. They have dwelled for many years, and long before migration, in the double or triple time of colonisation, and now occupy the multiple frames, the in-between or 'third' spaces – the homes-away-from-homes – of the postcolonial metropolis.

No single programme or agenda could adequately represent this cultural complexity – especially their 'impossible' desire to be treated and represented with justice (that is, as 'the same') simultaneously with the demand for the recognition of 'difference'. The agenda will itself have to be open and diverse, representing a situation which is already cross-cut by new and old lateral connections and reciprocal global influences and which refuses to stand still or stabilise. We ourselves should recognise that there will be many complementary but different ways of being represented, just as there are many different ways of 'being black'.

Without becoming too specific, what would be the basic elements or building blocks of such an agenda?

First, there is the demand that the majority, mainstream versions of the Heritage should revise their own self-conceptions and rewrite the margins into the centre, the outside into the inside. This is not so much a matter of representing 'us' as of representing more adequately the degree to which 'their' history entails and has always implicated 'us', across the centuries, and vice versa. The African presence in Britain since the sixteenth century, the Asian since the seventeenth and the Chinese, Jewish and Irish in the nineteenth have long required to be made the subjects of their own dedicated heritage spaces as well as integrated into a much more 'global' version of 'our island story'. Across the great cities and ports, in the making of fortunes, in the construction of great houses and estates, across the lineages of families, across the plunder and display of the wealth of the world as an adjunct to the imperial enterprise, across the hidden histories of statued heroes, in the secrecy of private diaries, even at the centre of the great master-narratives of 'Englishness' like the Two World Wars, falls the unscripted shadow of the forgotten 'Other'. The first task, then, is re-defining the nation, re-imagining 'Britishness' or 'Englishness' itself in a more profoundly inclusive manner. The Brits owe this, not to only us, but to themselves: for to prepare their own people for success in a global and decentred world by continuing to misrepresent Britain as a closed, embattled, self-sufficient, defensive, 'tight little island' would be fatally to disable them.

This is not only a matter of history. London and other major cities have been, throughout this century, 'world cities', drawing to themselves the creative talents of nations far and wide, and standing at the centre of tremendously varied cross-cultural flows and lateral artistic influences. Many distinguished practitioners who chose to live and work in Britain – Ronald Moody, Aubrey Williams, Francis Souza, Avinash Chandra, Anwar Jalal Shemza, David Medalla, Li Yuan Chia, Frank Bowling, and many others – have been quietly written out of the record. Not British enough for the Tate, not International enough for Bankside, I guess. The ways in which the 'modernist' impulse in western art drew inspiration from what it defined as 'primitive' is now an art-historical cliché. But the numbers of non-European artists who played a central part in European, and especially British, modernism, is far less widely acknowledged. – what Rasheed Araeen called, in his historic retrospective, 'The (Largely Untold) Other Story' (1989). The existence of major 'other modernisms', with their own indigenous roots elsewhere, passes without serious attention. The incontestable truth of the observation that 'The search for a new identity expressed in modern forms has been the common denominator of most contemporary art movements in Africa' is, for western curators and art-historians, still a well-kept secret.[12]

Then, second, there is the enormous, unprecedented, creative explosion by contemporary practitioners from the so-called 'minority' communities in all the arts (painting, visual arts, photography, film, theatre, literature, dance, music, multi-media) which has marked the last three decades. Unless this work is funded and exhibited, young talent and promise will simply dribble away. And it needs to be said loud and clear that this is not work which is likely immediately to appeal to the new culture-heroes of the art world – the corporate sponsors – who are already in search of their next Monet outing at some prestigious venue. For a time the work of contemporary artists from the minority communities was patronisingly secured within an 'ethnic' enclave, as if only non-European work reflected the cultural idioms in which they were composed – as if only 'we' had 'ethnicities'. However, the movement has long ago breached its boundaries and flooded – but only when permitted by the cultural gate-keepers – into the mainstream. Its visibility has depended largely on a few pioneering figures and the efforts of a whole fleet of small, local and community based galleries.

Like the rainbow, this work comes and goes. Major practitioners surface and pass quietly from view into an early and undeserved obscurity. Their work occasionally surfaces in mainstream venues – and has an innovative vitality which much 'indigenous' work lacks. But they cannot be properly 'heritaged'. The critical records, catalogues and memorabilia of this great tide of creative work in the visual arts since the 1980s, for example – from which, one day the histories and critical studies of black diaspora visual culture will be written – existed for many years in boxes in a filing cabinet in Eddie Chambers' bedroom in Bristol before they found a resting place – in AAVAA, the Asian and African Visual Arts Archive, courtesy of The University of East London. No proper archive, no regular exhibitions, no critical apparatus (apart from a few key journals like *Third Text* and the now-defunct *Ten 8*), no definitive histories, no reference books, no comparative materials, no developing scholarship, no passing-on of a tradition of work to younger practitioners and curators, no recognition of achievement amongst the relevant communities . . . Heritage-less.

Third, there is the record of the migrant experience itself. This is a precious record of the historical formation of a black diaspora in the heart of Europe – probably a once-in-a-life-time event – still *just* within living memory of its participants. Anyone who watched the *Windrush* programmes and listened to their moving and articulate interviews, or saw the images which Autograph (The Association of Black Photographers) helped to research and mount at the Pitshanger Gallery in Ealing or read the first-hand evidence of the political struggles of the period 1940–90 being put together by the unfunded George Padmore series edited by a veteran figure – John LaRose – whose autobiography we await, will know the rich evidence in visual imagery and oral testimonies which is waiting to be consolidated into a major archive.

It needs, of course, to be supplemented by extensive oral histories, personal accounts, documents and artefacts, from which, alone, 'the black experience' in Britain since the 1950s could be recreated. We know, from a few bold efforts to build the everyday concerns of migrant people into 'daily life' local exhibitions (for example by the adventurous Walsall Museum and Art Gallery) of the rich and complex details – customs, cuisine, daily habits, family photographs and records, household and religious objects – which remain to be documented in these domestic settings, poised as they are on the edge of and constantly negotiating between different 'worlds'. There is no such systematic work in progress though the Black Cultural Archives with its recent Lottery grant *may* at last be able to make a small start on oral histories. Some selective attempts have been made to do this for some Afro-Caribbean communities. So far as I know, there is very little comparable work as yet on the Asian experience(s). Heritage? *Which Heritage?*

Fourth, there is the question of those 'traditions of origin', so often deployed to represent minority communities as immured in their 'ethnicity' or differentiated into another species altogether by their 'racialised difference'. These 'traditions' are occasionally on view in performances by visiting companies, framed as an exotic entertainment. But in general terms, the public is deeply uninformed about them. The complexities of practice, interpretation and belief of Hinduism or Islam as world systems of religious belief are virtually a closed book, even to the intelligentsia. The long, highly complex and refined traditions of Indian music or dance, the key texts, poets and novelists, of these great civilisations, the extraordinarily varied cultural history of the Indian sub-continent itself, are beyond the reach of even the well-educated. Equally obscure are the complexities of tribe, language and ethnicity in sub-Saharan Africa.

These basic building blocks of the new global universe we inhabit confront a blank and uncomprehending provincial 'Englishness' as if fitfully glimpsed from outer space. Beyond sea, sun, sand, reggae and ganja, the fantastic intricacies of the 'transculturation' of European, African and Indian elements over centuries, which have produced the variety and vibrancy of Caribbean 'creole' cultures, is another Great Unknown. Latin America with its highly evolved Hispanic and Amerindian cultures may well be less familiar than the surface of Mars. The 'peculiarity' of Afro-Caribbeans – that they are simultaneously deeply familiar because they have lived with the British for so long, and ineradicably different because they are black – is regarded by most of the British (who have never been asked by their 'Heritage' to spare it a thought) as culturally inexplicable. Here, the National Curriculum and the truncated remnant of History as a discipline which remains, with only its most simplistic relationship to notions of 'Heritage' intact, has done irreparable damage.

And yet many of the creative talents of these communities are still 'framed' within a familiarity with the practices of these richly-traditional arts, so deeply are they interwoven with the textures of a lived culture itself; and even new and experimental work draws on their repertoires, idioms and languages of representation. Unless the younger generation has access to these cultural repertoires and can understand and practice them, to some extent at least, from the inside, they will lack the resources – the cultural capital – of their own 'heritage', as a base from which to engage other traditions. They will in effect be culturally 'monolingual' if not silenced – literally, deprived of the capacity to speak – in a world which requires us all to be or become culturally bi- if not multi-lingual.

There is no intrinsic contradiction between the preservation and presentation of 'other cultures' and my fifth point – the engagement with the production of new diasporic forms. The popular culture of our society especially has been transformed by the rich profusion of contemporary hybrid or 'cross-over' cultural forms – in music, dance, street-style, fashion, film, multi-media – which mark the production of 'the new' and the transgressive alongside the traditional and the 'preservation of the past'. Here, 'modernity' (or postmodernity) is not waiting on some authority to 'permit' or sanction this exploration of creativity in contemporary media and form. This is the leading-edge cultural phenomenon of our time – the 'multi' in multicultural, the 'Cool' in 'Cool Britannia'. For a time, black Afro-Caribbeans were in the vanguard of these avant-garde cultural practices, like cultural navigators crossing without passports between ragga, jungle, scratch, rap and electro-funk. In recent years, they have been decisively joined by the 'disorienting rhythms' of Asian youth. Perhaps this aspect of cultural production needs no 'archive' or 'heritage'. But it is proceeding unrecorded and unanalysed, consigned to the ephemera of its day – expendable. Yet it represents one of the most important cultural developments of our time: the stakes which 'the margins' have in modernity, the local-in-the-global, the pioneering of a new cosmopolitan, vernacular, post-national, global sensibility.

What I have offered is a wholly inadequate sketch – leaving out whole tracts of activity and countless examples aside. The account is inevitably skewed by my own interests and preoccupations. The detail does not matter. What matters is some greater clarity about 'the big picture'. I have tried to suggest not only *what* but *why* the question of 'The Heritage' is of such timely and critical importance for our folks at this time. 'British' most of us were, at one time, but that was long ago and, besides, as Shakespeare said, 'the wench is dead'. 'English' we cannot be. But tied in our fates and fortunes with 'the others' – while steadfastly refusing to have to *become* 'other' to belong – we do, after all, have a stake, an investment, in this phase of globalisation, in what I might call 'the post-nation'. But only if it can be re-imagined – re-invented to include us. That is the bet, the wager, the gamble we are here to discuss.

This is the text of the keynote speech given on November 1st, 1999, at the national conference 'Whose Heritage? The Impact of Cultural Diversity on Britain's Living Heritage' that took place at G-Mex, Manchester, England.

Notes

1   Michel Foucault, *Discipline and Punish*, Tavistock, London, 1977.
2   Benedict Anderson, *Imagined Communities*, Verso, London, 1983
3   Carol Duncan and Alan Wallach, 'The Universal Survey Museum', *Art History*, no 4, December, 1980, p. 451.
4   Norman Davies, 'But We Never Stand Quite Alone', *The Guardian*, 13 November, 1999.
5   David Scott, *Re-fashioning Futures: Criticism After Post-Coloniality*, Princeton, New Jersey, 1999.
6   Raymond Williams, *The Long Revolution*, Pelican, Harmondsworth, 1963.
7   On this whole question, see Norman Davies, *The Isles: A History*, Macmillan, Basingstoke, 1999.
8   Raphael Samuel, *Theatres of Memory*, Routledge, London, 1997.
9   Jacques Derrida, *Margins of Philosophy*, Harvester, Brighton, 1982.
10 C.L.R. James, 'Popular Art and The Cultural Tradition', in *Third Text*, no 10, Spring 1990, pp. 3–10.
11 Ashis Nandy, *The Intimate Enemy*, Oxford, New Delhi, 1983.
12 Salah Hassan, in *Reading The Contemporary: African Art From Theory to Market-Place*, (eds) Olu Oguibe and Okwui Enwezor, Institute of International Visual Arts (inIV A), London, 1999.

Chapter 16

Western Hegemony in Archaeological Heritage Management

Denis Byrne

In 1981 and 1982 two consecutive numbers of the journal *World Archaeology* were devoted to the development in various parts of the world of regionally distinctive traditions of archaeological research. The editors (Trigger and Glover 1981) were sceptical of the prospects of a single theoretically and methodologically 'correct' approach, such as that advocated by the American processual school, taking hold globally. They and others of the authors showed how the modern study of archaeology had developed in Europe and been exported as part of the baggage of colonialism throughout the world in the nineteenth century. It had then been moulded by the unique social conditions of the recipient countries, had been used in the service of a great many regimes and political ideologies, and had taken on the particular national and regional styles which we now see in places like India, Australasia, South America, Japan and Vietnam.

But this vision of a global mosaic could also be misleading. It accounted for the use of archaeology to justify and maintain relations of power at a local level but was perhaps too inclined to portray the discipline as one which was open to manipulation rather than as being itself essentially constituted in global politics and reconstituted according to major switches in political ideology and the balance between global powers. One of the editors (Trigger 1984, 1989) has since taken up the issue of 'world-orientated' or imperialist archaeology, detailing the manner in which three imperial powers, Britain, the Soviet Union, and America, had sought to impose particular brands of archaeology over areas of the world comprising their cultural spheres of influence.

Trigger's imperialist archaeology follows logically from the equation of knowledge and power. Where there are world powers there will be world archaeologies extending outwards the concepts the powers had of themselves and their place in history. In the case of nineteenth-century Britain, for instance, the fact of European technological pre-eminence was explained in terms of a continuing process of unilinear cultural evolution, historians and archaeologists ordered the past of countries where they found themselves in terms of a hierarchy of 'progress' with themselves at the pinnacle. This arrangement of world history was one which provided a powerful justification for Europe's dominating presence in almost every corner of the globe. Trigger is not, of course, suggesting that imperial governments had actually directed the activities of archaeologists but rather that archaeologists were are imbued with the ideological colour of their own societies. Their influence stemmed from the opportunities they had to work in other countries – archaeology following the flag either directly or through the favourable climate created by economic aid and military alliance – and from sponsoring the education of archaeologists from non-Western countries at 'home' universities, their ability to publish and disseminate research over large areas, and from the intellectual thrall in which leading exponents at great universities could hold their less advantaged colleagues over large parts of the world.

So much for the global spread of archaeology as a discipline. One might go on to wonder about the archaeological record itself, the archaeological deposits, ruins, monuments, and artefacts which are archaeology's subject matter, and question whether the West's attitude or approach to the conservation of these has also been disseminated abroad.

At the time archaeology began in the West industrialization was radically changing the face of the landscape. Well aware that their data would not survive without active protection, the early archaeologists lobbied for legislation and policies to conserve what is now referred to as the archaeological heritage (apart from royal decrees relating to treasure the first laws protecting ancient monuments were enacted in Europe during the nineteenth century and in America in 1906). Thus began archaeological heritage management which went on to develop as a profession in its own right – now employing far more people and attracting much more funding than research archaeology. The liaison between research and management archaeology has always been close, the latter being considered the 'public' side of the discipline. But if archaeologists are often thought of as practical people with a fairly cavalier attitude to theory and epistemology this is much more true of their colleagues in heritage management. Perhaps this is because of the urgency of their mission – in a world where ancient places are disappearing almost as fast as they can be recorded there is little time to dwell on theory. But the result is that a remarkably coherent style of archaeological heritage management has come to be practised throughout the world with almost no discussion of how this came about.

The publication in 1989 of the 23 volumes emanating from the 1986 World Archaeology Congress in Southampton provides an interesting opportunity to look at what heritage management is and where it came from. The Congress drew attendance from 70 countries and featured a number of symposia on issues relating to heritage management – contributions to these have been collected in five volumes.

There does seem to have been a general understanding among archaeologists and heritage managers at Southampton as to what heritage management is. It is based on what has been termed the 'conservation ethic' by which archaeologists are enjoined to minimize the impact of their own research on the non-renewable 'archaeological resource' while at the same time championing its conservation in government and public spheres. In *Archaeological Heritage Management in the Modern World* (Cleere 1989a), several articles addressing general management issues – mostly by Europeans and Americans – are followed by papers dealing with the problems faced in particular countries or at particular sites. Despite the diversity of local circumstances it is clear that a fundamentally similar approach to heritage management has been taken in most countries and it seems equally clear, to my mind at least, that this approach is essentially the one which was developed in Europe and America. By this approach the conservation ethic has been put into action through the establishment of heritage agencies attached to state museums or the government departments responsible for cultural or environmental affairs. The agencies compile inventories of sites deemed worthy of legal protection, they carry out surveys ahead of development projects and may salvage excavation sites in the projects' impact zones, they conduct or supervise restoration of ruins, attempt to stop the looting of sites and illegal traffic in antiquities, and they generally run or sponsor programmes to educate the public in the value and conservation of their national archaeological heritage.

Though accounts are given of these activities in places as diverse as Ecuador, Nigeria, Madagascar, Togo, the Philippines, China and Arizona there is little clarification of why they are necessary and appropriate in these places or how they relate to local cultural values. Heritage management seems simply to appear with the passing of the first protective legislation which itself occurs because an obvious 'need' is recognized. What is obvious is that the archaeological record is rapidly being destroyed, but why is this necessarily a problem for non-Western countries with urgent development priorities, unless, of course, the conservation ethic is truly universal rather than specific only to the heritage of the West?

In Henry Cleere's paper he traces desire for the preservation of cultural relics to the European Enlightenment and the idea of 'cultural continuity' which he contrasts to the idea of 'spiritual continuity' in less-developed societies (1989b: 7). The European interest in cultural continuity led to an appreciation of the material culture of times past – the old buildings, monuments, factories, gardens and even landscapes which are now listed on European heritage inventories and the moveable items which now fill the museums. In the less-developed societies, by contrast, interest and group identity focuses on places of spiritual or religious significance such as the Dreamtime sites of Australian Aboriginal mythology; material culture and secular sites in such societies tend not to be given significance lasting beyond their utilitarian lifespan. If the heritage management we now see in the West derived from an Enlightenment shift in Western thinking then how is one to account for the presence of this same heritage in countries of the non-Western world which did not experience the Enlightenment? Is it a straightforward case of Western imperialism, of heritage management following the flag, in which case it would be an imposition? Cleere notes that departing colonial powers often left a legacy of heritage legislation in the newly independent states. The legacy was not rejected; in fact there has been a widespread tendency for the new states to use and conserve precolonial and even colonial archaeological heritage in the name of national identity (1989b: 7–8).

Evidently Western notions of heritage do have a place in the non-Western world. But this does not mean they have not been imposed. Dozens of contributors representing indigenous minorities and underclasses spoke out at Southampton against archaeologists and the practices of archaeological heritage managers (these have been collected in two volumes edited by Robert Layton (1989): *Conflict in the Archaeology of Living Traditions* and *Who Needs the Past?*). It was about the time of the Southampton Congress that the demands of the indigenous minorities, particularly in North America and Australia, for return of human skeletal remains began to attract the widespread media attention. *Conflict in the Archaeology of Living Traditions* (Layton 1989) contains papers in which indigenous people demand that these remains be treated not as archaeological evidence but as remains of their dead relatives and ancestors. These people seem quite unconvinced by the valid research interest of archaeologists whose attitude they see – often in relation to 'archaeological' sites generally – as alien and macabre. The indigenous challenge is exemplified by Carlos Condori, speaking of the situation in Bolivia where the colonial/mestizo regime controls and manages pre-Spanish Indian sites:

> The message of both archaeology and history in Bolivia is clear: the evidence of our past, the age-old historical development of our societies and the Indians are for them only prehistory, a dead and silent past.
>
> Prehistory is a Western concept according to which those societies which have not developed writing – or an equivalent system of graphic representation – *have no history*. This fits perfectly into the framework of thought typical of Western culture.
>
> (Condori 1989: 51)

For such people the relentlessness of invasion has gone beyond loss of land and liveli-hood; often the bones of their ancestors are on museum shelves, their religious sites are being grazed by cattle behind fences on private land, and they must pay an entry fee to visit former settlements turned into historical parks; the grabbing hands have appropriated their past.

But over most of the non-Western world heritage management, like modern environmental management, has spread by a process of ideology transfer rather than imposition. This applies not only to the post-colonial states but also countries like Thai-land which also have heritage agencies modelled on those of Europe and America. Several of the papers in *Archaeological Heritage Management in the Modern World* are by employees of such agencies and their tone reflects an ideal shared with their Western colleagues: the problems they speak of are the same but simply bigger. To what extent, though, is the conservation ethic in their countries a thin veneer? None of these contrib-utors explain how or if heritage conservation is rooted in national culture. Certainly there seems to be little popular demand for it. Lack of public appreciation or awareness is a major problem in Ecuador (Norton 1989: 143), the Philippines (Henson 1989: 115), Nigeria (Myles 1989: 122), Madagascar (Rasamuel 1989: 128). Most spectacularly it is evident in the widespread looting of sites to feed the local and foreign antiquities markets. One is impressed by the enormity of the task facing Third World heritage managers and their frustration with governments who will not provide the funds or per-sonnel necessary to implement their own legislation. It is tempting to conclude that these countries essentially have no interest in their heritage but the problem is more likely to lie in a lack of fit between the Western approach to heritage management and indigenous social systems and values, a case of what the development experts call 'inap-propriate ideology transfer'. Non-Western countries do have an appreciation of their past but they are finding it difficult to develop appropriate mechanisms to implement it beset, as they are, by outside insistence on the Western model.

This, I would suggest, is what is missing in *Archaeological Heritage Management in the Modern World* and what is missing in the consciousness of heritage management practitioners generally: an understanding of the values underlying the Western management ethos and an openness to alternatives. If, in the postmodern world there can be alternative histories why can't there be alternative heritages and alternative models of heritage management?

The idea of a universal significance for archaeological heritage is one which is prima-rily associated with international heritage bodies such as UNESCO and ICOMOS but is cropping up increasingly in archaeological literature. There are two aspects to this. There is the idea that all peoples of the world share an interest in and concern for their archaeo-logical heritage, an idea which implies that it is characteristic of the human species to hold these values. This may, of course, be true but it is certainly not proven. And then there is the related notion that this inherent bond exists not only between people and the archaeo-logical heritage at a local or even a national level, but that the people of any one country have a concern for the heritage of other countries, a concern which takes on global dimen-sions – this appears to be the rationale for the World Heritage List. Peter Ucko, in his foreword to *Archaeological Heritage Management in the Modern World* (1989: xii–xiii) is alert to the imperialist underpinnings of the world heritage concept but it is not a concern echoed by any of the contributors to the volume.

The first aspect of the universal ethos perhaps explains why archaeologists and her-itage managers spend so much time invoking the conservation ethic and so little time explaining its origin. Heritage management 'appears' in non-Western countries not because of Western intervention, although Western experts may have assisted to develop and refine it, but because it is a response to an inherent, universal value. This is taken to be obvious. There is even a sense that good old nineteenth-century unilinear evolution is at play: left to their own devices all societies would eventually embrace heritage conservation so the question of timing, or whether in particular cases it is introduced by colonial powers, the World Bank, or UNESCO is not that important.

What is more serious, though, is the tendency to blur the distinction between the idea of heritage management and the practice of it. Two cases come to mind where a concern for conservation in non-Western societies has been expressed in a manner radically different to that advocated by 'international' (read: Western) heritage conventions. In the Kimberley area of Western Australia numerous rockshelters and overhangs contain paintings of Wandjina figures which are ancestral beings of the local Aboriginal tribes. Aborigines periodically repaint the figures, often superimposing new figures on old, in a practice which is traditionally sanctioned and is an integral part of their relationship with the powerful Wandjina. However, in 1987 their right to continue this practice was threatened after an outcry initiated by a local white landowner that ancient paintings which were 'part of the heritage of all mankind' were being desecrated by Aborigines engaged in a repainting project (Bowdler 1988: 520). The dispute was eventually resolved in favour of the Aborigines after it was shown that the 'damage' to the 'original' paintings (mostly repaintings themselves) were exaggerated and that in the terms of their own culture the Aborigines were actually engaging in the conservation of the living significance of the sites. But as Bowdler observes in retrospect: 'The phrase which seems to have acted like a bell on the Pavlovian dogs of the heritocracy is "cultural heritage of all mankind . . ." and ". . . defining something as belonging to that transcendent category is a means of excluding anyone who might have a particular interest in it"' (Bowdler 1988: 521).

The second case concerns the Confucius Temple Complex at Qufu, Jiangsu Province, China. The original components were constructed by the Prince of Lu in 478BC; by AD 959 it had been restored and enlarged 15 times and covered 11,000 square metres; by 1949, 54 restorations and enlargements later (an average of once every 16 years between 1368 and 1949), it extended over 96,000 square metres; restoration is continuing at the present time (Wei and Aass 1989). The point which the architects Chen Wei and Andreas Aass make is that whereas in the West the emphasis in conservation is on authenticity to the original and historical legibility, in China it is on the spirit of the place, the 'genius loci'.

> Consequently, in the field of conservation of monuments such as Qufu, the Forbidden City or Cheng De, the allowing of continuous repairs or even rebuilding all respect this concentration on the spirit of the original monument. Although the physical form may change, the spirit and purpose of the original is not only preserved as a continuity, *but can be enhanced through the contributions of succeeding generations* (my emphasis).
>
> (Wei and Aass 1989: 8)

It may come as no surprise that this Chinese approach violates the 1964 Venice Charter, supposedly the universal benchmark for architectural conservation and a document which Wei and Aass see as 'having been written to address the Western experience only' (1989: 8).

There is no denying that a great deal has been achieved by the Western approach to heritage management but, as the two examples above indicate, there are alternatives. Moreover, the alternatives may point to a more socially integrated management style which seems to promise relief from the relentless commodification of a Western style grounded in the rational tradition.

A theme in many of the Southampton papers is the role archaeological heritage plays in affirming cultural identity – indeed, this is held to be one of the major justifications for heritage conservation. Herrmann maintains that archaeological heritage has a particular role to play in multi-cultural societies in 'helping to develop the population's awareness of a shared historical identity' (Herrmann 1989: 35). Rare, though, is the country where ethnic groups balance each other in terms of numbers, wealth or political influence and, consequently, it is not uncommon for the dominant group to use its power to push its own heritage to the fore, minimizing or denying the significance of subordinate groups as it crafts a national identity in its own image. In Bolivia the Indians find themselves losers in the nation-forming project of the 1952 revolution as the white colonizers sought to integrate pre-Spanish archaeology into a Bolivian national heritage at the same time as integrating the Indian population into the 'stream of civilization' (Condori 1989: 47). It seems equally likely that at a global level an emergent universal heritage will be weighted in favour of the West – not so much in terms of Western heritage but of the categories of sites intelligible to the Occidental mind and of the Western way of experiencing the past. Writers such as Edward Said (1978) and Janet Abu-Lughod (1989) have shown that powers such as Europe and America situated at the hub of world systems are quite capable of generating and sustaining constructions of the 'outside' world which are quite at odds with historical reality and with the experience of the inhabitants of those colonized regions. The reluctance of heritage managers to look closely at their own values makes such bias inevitable.

References

Abu-Lughod, J. (1989) "On the remaking of history: how to reinvent the past", in Kruger, B. and P. Mariani (eds), *Remaking History*, Seattle: Bay Press.

Bowdler, S. (1988) "Repainting Australian rock art" *Antiquity* **62**: 517–523.

Cleere, H. (ed.) (1989a) *Archaeological Heritage Management in the Modern World*, London: Unwin Hyman.

Cleere, H. (1989b) "Introduction: the rationale of archaeological heritage management", in Cleere, H. (ed.), *Archaeological Heritage Management in the Modern World*, London: Unwin Hyman.

Condori, C. M. (1989) "History and prehistory in Bolivia: what about the Indians?", in Layton, R. (ed.), *Conflict in the Archaeology of Living Traditions*, London: Unwin Hyman.

Henson, T. (1989) "Historical development and attendant problems of cultural resource management in the Philippines", in Cleere, H. (ed.), *Archaeological Heritage Management in the Modern World*, London: Unwin Hyman.

Herrmann, J. (1989) "World archaeology – the world's cultural heritage", in Cleere, H. (ed.), *Archaeological Heritage Management in the Modern World*, London: Unwin Hyman.

Layton, R. (ed.) (1989a) *Conflict in the Archaeology of Living Traditions*, London: Unwin Hyman.

Layton, R. (ed.) (1989b) *Who Needs the Past?*, London: Unwin Hyman.

Norton, P. "Archaeological rescue and conservation in the North Andean area", in Cleere, H. (ed.), *Archaeological Heritage Management in the Modern World*, London: Unwin Hyman.

Said, E. (1978) *Orientalism*, New York: Pantheon Books.

Trigger, B. (1984) "Alternative archaeologies: nationalist, colonialist, imperialist" *Man* **19**: 355–370.

Trigger, B. (1989) *A History of Archaeological Thought*, Cambridge: Cambridge University Press.

Trigger, B. & I. Glover (1981) "Editorial" *World Archaeology* **13**(2): 133–137.

Ucko, P. (1989) "Foreword" in Cleere, H. (ed.), *Archaeological Heritage Management in the Modern World*, London: Unwin Hyman.

Wei, C. and A. Aass (1989) "Heritage conservation: East and West" *Icomos Information* 1989/3.

Chapter 17

Whose Heritage to Conserve?

Cross-cultural reflections on political dominance and urban heritage conservation

John E. Tunbridge

Urban heritage conservation as a geographic phenomenon is a subject of increasing comment in the academic literature.[1] Its significance for different aspects of urban development has been discussed, more or less explicitly, with reference to both Western and socialist cities. Even for the developed world, however, contributions to date have been piecemeal; a balanced perspective on conservation and urban geography awaits development. For the Third World city, the subject remains largely terra incognita; more tangible concerns dominate both development programmes and academic investigations, and there is little documentation of the geographic impact of, for example, the restoration of sixteenth-century Santo Domingo or redevelopment–conservation conflicts in Singapore.

From a global perspective, there is a considerable void in our understanding of urban conservation. This chapter is concerned with a significant element of that void: the relationship between political power and urban heritage conservation, with particular reference to plural societies. Comparative insights are drawn from North American and southern African experience, but the underlying contention is that this theme has a wider relevance to the equity and harmony of urban life, given the human diversity of most of the world's major cities.

What constitutes heritage from the perspective of the urban environment? Heritage structures reflect a society's cultural and historical background, in both general terms and through associations with specific events and people. Urban landmarks are commonly perceived as heritage structures; and heritage elements in an urban environment are conducive to the development of a sense of place, which in turn may exert a positive influence on the perception of what is heritage. Even the urban plan has heritage significance, for it may imprint historic values of space and scale on structures and movement paths long after all original buildings have disappeared. St John's, Newfoundland, is a prime Canadian example.

In the Western world, there has been a radical change in social attitudes toward the conservation of the built environment in recent years. The manifestations are all around us and are now widely documented. It has been shown that this development has significant implications for the evolving geography of the city; urban geographers cannot ignore it, whether their concerns be primarily morphological, social, or economic.[2] It is also well known that conservation issues are contentious. There are invariably those who, through predilection or vested interest, would conserve either less or more in general, and specific merits of individual heritage buildings are frequently debatable. Less well known, however, are the background tensions as to which of a townscape's diverse components matter most for posterity. In short, whose heritage should we be conserving?

The significance of the city's physical character to the sense of place, security, and stability of its inhabitants is now well established and has become a prime rationale for conservation.[3] The landmarks, nodes, and other structural components to which Lynch first drew attention have thus acquired a focal significance in urban conservation activity.[4] But one person's landmark may be an object of indifference or hostility to another.

The protagonists of conservation have so far tended to deal with urban heritage as a monolithic issue. To geographers, however, it is a central fact that an urban population is not homogeneous. Urban residents are divided by political outlook, by socio-economic class, and by deep-seated cultural and ethnic values, and their heritage perceptions will vary accordingly. Notwithstanding this diversity, it is contended in this essay that the way the character and image of a city develop is a reflection primarily of the values of whichever social group is ascendant at the time. The dominant group is by no means necessarily a majority, yet will typically mould the city in its own image by deliberate or unconscious bias in its approach to conservation and alternative redevelopment.

The prominent conservationist Harold Kalman has noted a conservation bias in Canadian cities resulting from the values of the political party currently in power.[5] He observes that Liberal landmarks (such as birthplaces of the party's notables) have a better chance of survival in contemporary Canada than those important to opposition parties. This, however, is just the tip of an iceberg that geographers are well placed to chart more comprehensively. With respect to political values, the mild distortions identified by Kalman could be considered a pale reflection of totalitarian states such as Nazi Germany and the Soviet Union, where authorities have commonly manipulated urban heritage by enhancing their own monuments and playing down or destroying those of opposing values.[6]

The class dimension appears to be intrinsic in conservation issues. In the Western world, promotion of conservation has come predominantly from élite groups, which has caused a double bias against the poorer classes. A generation ago, ruling élites in most Western countries held a narrow view of what merited conservation. They readily consigned poorer districts to the bulldozer in the name of slum clearance or freeway construction. When the prevailing view subsequently deemed vernacular architecture and values worthy of conservation, the poor suffered dispossession by gentrification from those run-down areas that became fashionable. Too often an embarrassing discord exists between heritage (élite-defined) conservation and community conservation, a problem to which solutions have only recently begun to appear.[7] Even if this issue fades for residential structures, how often are we likely to see the conservation of urban landmarks justified on the grounds that they matter to the sense of place and security of the poor in their vicinity?

The question of whose heritage we are conserving acquires a sharper significance when we consider culturally diverse societies. In other contexts, geographers are quick to note that most large urban societies are culturally diverse, and nowhere more so than in North America. Yet we appear to be backward in recognizing what this means for the conservation of our townscapes. In the United States, it would be interesting to compare the proportion of recognized urban heritage landmarks with 'WASP' (White Anglo Saxon Protestant) associations with the proportion of WASPS in the population, for it might be argued that the 'melting pot' has been greased disproportionately with the physical symbols of the original mainstream. The symbolism conveyed by the landmarks of Boston (to take an example that is prominent in conservation terms) has little to do with the Irish, Italians, and other 'minorities' that collectively dominate the city, but it has been used to good political effect in asserting pre-established values in the national consciousness. This is not to deny the local highlighting of particular ethnic heritages (e.g. San Francisco's Chinatown, New Orleans's *vieux carré*, or Albuquerque's old Hispanic quarter), but for the most part these are latter-day revitalizations with decidedly commercial overtones. There are, however, currently signs of a greater willingness to acknowledge minority heritage values in localities that lack attraction to the mainstream population and thus lack commercial appeal. One example is the recent establishment of a Chicano heritage district in San Diego, covering a small park beneath a freeway intersection.[8]

In Canada's case, the recognition of ethnic minority (non-English or -French) contributions to the urban heritage is generally more recent still. In the late 1960s the homes and landmarks of the Chinese communities in Toronto and Vancouver were disappearing in favour of 'mainstream' redevelopment, and those in Montreal were still at risk a decade later.[9] Toronto's city hall is perhaps the classic example of mainstream landmark creation at the expense of a minority's sense of place, having displaced part of Chinatown. The levelling of Africville in Halifax, whatever its intrinsic merits, might be seen in a similar light.[10] It is no coincidence that ethnic minorities have also tended to be poor and politically weak, a combination that appears to have retarded ethnic heritage recognition in Canadian cities, as elsewhere. The problem would appear to be twofold: lack of concern for minority welfare (or even outright hostility, as toward Asiatics in British Columbia before 1945),[11] and failure to recognize those elements of the townscape that might constitute the minority heritage. (The question of definition remains problematic here and will be considered further below.)

Cultural exclusiveness has by no means operated only against non-whites. Winnipeg provides an outstanding illustration of cultural dominance by the WASP 'charter group' at the expense of eastern European immigrants, who were systematically disadvantaged in all aspects of the city's life throughout the first half of this century.[12] The cultural monuments inherited by a more egalitarian age are heavily biased in favour of the original social élite. The provincial legislature, remnants of Fort Garry, and prominent commercial structures are located close to élite South Winnipeg, whereas the socially 'outcast' northern area (now partly native Indian) was separated, prior to the Old Market Square restoration, by a barrier of decrepit warehouses as well as by the proverbial 'tracks.'[13]

The 'outcast' group has not always been a minority. The case of Montreal is uncomfortably close to the African situations considered below, in that its heritage as Canada's former leading city is primarily that of a minority WASP élite. The city's image cannot be speedily adapted to be more reflective of its francophone majority. This is illustrated in the rue St-Denis area of east-central Montreal, where a francophone heritage localized around a variety of institutions, such as convents, schools, hospices, and clubs, is gradually being reinforced.[14]

It should be noted that all the disadvantaged groups mentioned have experienced significant spatial segregation. This has undoubtedly insulated the dominant group from an appreciation of the subordinate groups' needs in the urban environment and of their contributions to that environment. It might also be hypothesized that segregation has prevented, or inhibited, subordinate groups from identifying with the dominant landmarks of the élite and created an accordingly greater need for sensitive conservation of their own.

In the past decade of greater social and environmental awareness, Canadian attitudes to the urban contributions of minorities have undergone a substantial change. Culturally distinctive streetscape improvement by groups such as the Italians and Portuguese has been noted and appreciated.[15] Some minorities have formed their own organizations to promote conservation of their ethnic heritage, sometimes receiving government support.[16] Further, the proliferation of specialty restaurants and the like has helped to provide a powerful commercial incentive for conserving both ethnic and general heritage environments. As a consequence, there is hope that the future management of Canadian cities will result in a better balance between the heritage contributions of different ethnic groups, surely the most tangible expression of multiculturalism.[17] Whether this will in time include contributions by the native peoples is a sensitive point worth contemplating, particularly in light of the African cases discussed below. The projected growth of native populations in the prairie cities would create a parallel to rapid black urbanization in southern Africa.[18] In both cases the question arises of how the newcomers will relate to existing white heritage and what they may create or adapt to supplement or supplant it.

Returning to the question of what constitutes heritage, there are difficulties of interpretation with minority and disadvantaged groups. In line with their economic status, their material heritage may be quite humble and so not be perceived, let alone respected, by politically dominant groups. In addition, minorities are commonly sequent occupiers of pre-existing structures to which they have experienced a relatively short period of attachment. In confronting these difficulties, it is necessary to remember that structures of heritage significance are continuously being created. Many that already express the culture and identity of minorities have yet to acquire distinction in the eyes of others, being relatively recent adaptations of pre-existing buildings with or without prior heritage significance.

This is not to assert that every structure built or adaptively reused by minority or disadvantaged group members (who may have few options of personal space available to them) will become part of the heritage of the group, and by extension of the wider urban society. Belated recognition of minority heritage values leaves us with a lag in our thinking on the subject; but the starting point should be the views of the minority itself, without prejudgement of their wisdom. We may expect that the landmarks around which minority life revolves will be perceived as heritage. In particular, places of worship are usually consciously distinctive in their design and associations. But we should not be surprised if dwellings, stores, and workshops of modest character (to others) turn out to be vital to the sense of place, security, and identity of the people concerned. The case of the Chicano park in San Diego is a striking example of unpromising institutional space having sense of place for that group. This was reflected by residences before their demolition and subsequently by an effusion of Latin and pre-Columbian mural art.[19]

Further scholarly research is appropriate to determine what constitutes distinctive heritage from a wider, comparative perspective. How far we stretch the interpretation of heritage may, however, become an academic point when the key issue is the conservation of the valued environment in which a social group can exist, happily and peaceably. The lesson of Third World shanty developments may be instructive here. It is now widely accepted that their inhabitants may prefer to upgrade apparent slums with which they can identify rather than accept alternative shelter. There are century-old *barriadas* in some Latin American cities that could fairly claim to have upgraded themselves to a very real heritage of sustained community effort.[20] In comprehending the urban heritage of minority and disadvantaged groups, therefore, it would be well to start with a certain breadth of vision and openness of mind, before applying our critical faculties to argue (perhaps) for a more selective approach. This perspective would appear to be equally desirable in Canada, southern Africa, and elsewhere.

It is in the truly plural societies that our question of 'whose heritage' comes to a head. Where divergent identities and goals exist among competing social groups, urban heritage conservation becomes a political exercise, frequently with sinister overtones for those groups out of power. The case of Belfast, where rival factions have been busily destroying each other's sense of place for years, is a healthy reminder that the point is not remote from our Western values. Divergent plurality is most in evidence in recently colonial countries, however, and the rest of this chapter will be focused on southern African cities, with specific reference to pertinent cases that I have had the opportunity to examine in some depth. Urban heritage conservation in this environment, though a relatively recent concern, has acquired profound significance to social and, hence, to political attitudes during the painful process of liberation from minority rule. For white minorities, urban heritage is implicitly seen in terms of cultural survival.

The case of Harare (Salisbury), the capital of Zimbabwe, is of particular interest, having experienced three years of black majority rule after ninety of white control. Salisbury was cast in the mould of an ideal tropical city as seen through the eyes of British settlers. Its wide streets and spacious, floral quality reflect this, though a more general kinship with western Canadian streetscapes of the same vintage is readily apparent. Its landmarks and symbolism were those of a pioneer settler society, to the complete exclusion of black African values. Most notably, Cecil Square, the central focus, is coextensive with the original Fort Salisbury of 1890. The city's heritage was, in fact, disproportionately strongly linked with the pioneer leaders of 1890, above all Cecil Rhodes; the fact that its white administrations tended to pursue 'progress' with little regard for general conservation served to accentuate the importance of monuments commemorating the pioneers. No majority government responsive to black African sensitivities could allow the near-deification of Rhodes to continue, and so his statues have been removed and several pioneer street names changed in favour of 'front-line' state leaders, such as Kenneth Kaunda and Samora Machel.

But no other detectable changes have occurred in the city's morphological quality. This reflects at least three factors.[21] The priority of present national and urban governments is to provide for the mushrooming urban black population, which naturally focuses attention on peripheral township development (to which most black residence was formerly restricted) rather than the established city. It is particularly worthy of note that Heroes' Acre, the national war memorial and principal monument of the present government, overlooks townships on the outskirts of Harare. Second, inner-city commercial development has remained slow (as in the war years) because of corporate uncertainty over the government's economic and political policies. Third, the present city government has so far shown somewhat greater sensitivity to heritage conservation than the pro-development white governments that preceded it.[22]

Thus the image of Harare – reflecting core rather than periphery – continues to project the heritage of a settler society. The persistence of most familiar landmarks cannot but reinforce the central government's policy of reconciliation between blacks and whites, notwithstanding some better-publicized negative influences. The historical legacy, treated with such restraint, certainly places the white minority in a remarkably favourable heritage position by comparison with urban minorities on other continents. The question of 'whose heritage' does arise, but it affects the subtle details of emphasis among what are still the monuments of a settler society. Rhodes's statues have gone; St Mary's Cathedral remains a non-racial landmark, conserving the memorabilia of Rhodesia along with a continuing vital role in the city's life; but several buildings of the 1890s that may have housed the black trials after the Matabele War (1896) are seen as shrines by the present city government which, tribal rivalries notwithstanding, is more likely to ensure their conservation than its predecessors.[23]

Bulawayo, Zimbabwe's second city, likewise continues to project its settler image, in its plan as well as its buildings. Rhodes's wide streets, designed to permit an ox-wagon to turn, remain even though his statue no longer overlooks them. There has also been little structural change, and city hall still physically projects a settlers' perspective on municipal affairs. Its square is coextensive with the settlers' fortifications during the Matabele War.

Zimbabwe is of particular contemporary interest and, along with the Republic of South Africa, is the best example in southern Africa of urban heritage dominated by the symbols of a white minority. Angola and Mozambique also possess a distinct colonial heritage, but aside from the question of how culturally exclusive the Portuguese settlers may have been, their virtual disappearance after 1975 implies that urban heritage is unlikely to be a contentious issue. Botswana contains little urban development, having been governed from Mafeking in South Africa during the British colonial period. Its new capital, Gaberone, contains no divisive heritage, even though it has an obvious physical kinship with British 'new towns.' Namibia, however, could experience heritage-related tensions when it achieves majority rule, to judge from the increasing references in the South African press to conservation of the German colonial heritage, as at Lüderitz, for example.

In Lesotho and Swaziland, the issue is generally minimized by the small size of the cities and their few white residents. However, Mbabane, capital of Swaziland, is a further example of a multiracial urban centre that has experienced stable continuity since independence. Under the late King Sobhuza II it retained the fine details of its settler heritage, including street names. The city was founded by British expatriates as a trading centre nearly a century ago, and many whites of Commonwealth or South African origin continue to live and work there. Its lasting congeniality to white residents appears to owe much to the comfortable persistence of an urban heritage that is entirely British colonial or Afrikaner rather than that of a tribal kingdom.[24] The conservative political order following Sobhuza's death seems likely to perpetuate the status quo.

Urban heritage in South Africa is a particularly noteworthy case in that its political ramifications may have a very significant bearing on the country's future. In essence, South African cities are the principal repositories of white civilization in the country, even though largely constructed by non-white hands. They have been strenuously denied to black residence by successive governments, albeit with diminishing success as the forces of black urbanization have grown. The present government's alternative policy of creating quasi-independent black homelands is gaining momentum, notwithstanding global opposition, as successive homelands acquire sufficient independence to form a vested interest in this concept of the country's future. However, the homelands' greatest deficiency is their lack of adequate urban nodes, and their leaders have pressed the white government for the transfer of smaller urban centres that might act as strategic foci for economic growth. One has already been transferred: Mafeking was ceded to Bophutatswana in 1980 and is currently being integrated with the homeland's capital, for which it serves as the chief commercial centre. Notwithstanding a pivotal historical role in southern Africa, Mafeking is a small town, relatively lacking in distinction. Most of its buildings post-date the siege of 1900.

The Mafeking precedent has not yet been followed elsewhere. When Ciskei requested King William's Town in 1981, the South African government refused to cede it, despite its obvious focal value to that homeland.[25] The reasons for this refusal appear to be partly electoral,[26] but my own examination of the town indicated an undocumented and perhaps subconscious reason. King William's Town was a key focus of white settlement in the eastern Cape, and its architectural heritage makes it a living monument to that settlement. To cede such a bastion of 'white' South Africa would be galling; but so too would the cession of other long-established 'white' communities. A particular case might be cessions from Natal to Kwazulu, a homeland that is severely fragmented by 'white' settlement areas and has refused co-operation with the government's homeland-independence policy, partly on this account.[27] Thus urban heritage could have the far-reaching political consequence of obstructing one possibly viable route out of South Africa's present impasse between the aspirations of both blacks and whites for self-determination.

More generally in South Africa, white attitudes to racial confrontation cannot but be conditioned by their urban heritage. The overwhelmingly white orientation of that heritage perpetuates the belief of the (mainly urban) white population that theirs is a settler society comparable to North America or Australasia, and that they are entitled to retain it as such. Western has observed that the central monumental area of Cape Town constitutes white 'sacred space,'[28] and the same could be said of Pretoria. But nowhere is this more evident than in Pietermaritzburg, capital of Natal, a charming Victorian city grafted onto Boer Voortrekker roots and now largely surrounded by sections of the fragmented

Kwazulu homeland. In the city centre the familiar built environment, replete with an impressive heritage of British colonial associations and past military victories, beguiles the white perception with its sense of permanence and security, notwithstanding the human mix in the streets. Black symbolic space has been confined to two bus stations, the vicinity of which has a Third World atmosphere as in most southern African cities. Such an urban environment fosters traditional values, not least through the flourishing system of private schools. It also dulls awareness of the exploding homeland populations only a mile or two away and, undoubtedly, of the need to reach a political accommodation with them. Wills notes that the white sacred (or 'defensive') space is being gradually eroded as black, informal-sector trading (street-hawking) spreads out from the bus stations, and he criticizes white resistance to this black survival mechanism. He also notes that when several historic buildings (including the Natal Supreme Court) were damaged by terrorist bomb blasts, the outrage of the white population was exactly compatible with the idea of ethno-centric sacred space.[29] Pietermaritzburg is a classic, and disturbing, illustration of the maxim that we shape our buildings and they then shape us.[30]

While the blacks have been excluded as far as possible from urban residence and any claim on urban heritage, the Coloureds and Indians have been allowed only a subordinate identification with it. The Coloureds in Cape Town, though culturally sharing in the general urban heritage, have largely been dispersed in suburban locations in an implicit denial of their identification with a city they have always dominated numerically. The levelling of the inner-city District Six, in which the Coloureds had a deeply rooted sense of place, was a most explicit denial, in the guise of urban renewal; but no white developers will intrude on this spiritually Coloured space, and the cleared area stands in mute testimony to partisan manipulation of urban heritage.[31] Most of the large Indian population in Durban and Pietermaritzburg has likewise been physically relocated away from an inner-city heritage on which, despite cultural differences, it traditionally had some claim; residual inner-city dwellers are generally restricted to poorer areas designated Indian without any necessary reference to Indian sense of place.[32] As in North America, the established perception of what constitutes urban heritage derives from the ruling white groups. Cape Dutch architecture is revered and widely copied, and British colonial styles not much less so. Only in the present decade have 'minority' structures started to appear in the lists of national monuments, the principal South African means of conserving heritage structures.[33] The Natal authorities have remained reluctant to include Indian temples, shops, and so on in their current efforts to list the province's urban heritage buildings.[34] This may result in part from a perception problem by no means confined to South Africa: 'minority' structures were usually built in off-centre locations, even before apartheid, and seldom form part of the image-making central urban focus.

Exclusive claim on urban heritage leads too naturally to a reluctance to share control of a community and the wider society of which it is a focal point. While this is a dimension of the South African dilemma that the outside world should note, it is also a dimension that Western urban society might take greater care to avoid. In any urban society the answer to 'whose heritage?' should be 'everyone's,' if values and goals are shared sufficiently to promote a stable future. If conservation does not accord recognition to the landmarks of politically powerless groups as part of this common heritage, it is likely to become an instrument of social stress. This is as true in principle with respect to Chinese in Vancouver as to Coloureds in Cape Town, notwithstanding differences that may exist in the degree of stress involved.

One of the more positive signs for the future is the growing dependence internationally on the tourist trade. Cities must increasingly sell themselves on their claims to distinctiveness, which means not only the conservation of their mainstream heritage but also the accentuation of their various ethnic spaces. This has become readily apparent throughout North America; it is a significant moderating force on majority governments in cash-starved former colonies such as Zimbabwe; and even 'white' South Africa now finds it profitable to compete for the tourist dollar under the rubric 'a world in one country.' Growing recognition of the advantages of a tangibly multicultural environment could make life distinctly more secure for urban minorities, a point that might possibly not be lost on those still clinging fearfully to power – notably white South Africans. Recreational geographers might find it profitable to explore such wider overtones of the urban tourist industry.

Whether bias or balance exists in conserving urban heritage, it implies a specific direction in which the character of the city is evolving, in its socio-economic as well as morphological dimensions. Either way, it is of geographic concern. But geographers have a long-standing involvement with cultural landscape and the patterns of sequent occupance that this commonly entails. They are, therefore, excellently placed to draw attention to the cultural diversity of urban heritage, to examine how it is perceived by the groups involved, and to evaluate its comparative significance beyond one particular city. In the contemporary spirit of social relevance, they may thereby contribute to its defence and thus to the greater goal of social harmony.

Acknowledgements

I am most grateful to T. Wills, R. Haswell, and the Department of Geography, University of Natal, Pietermaritzburg, for numerous insights into the subtleties of the South African situation, both during my stay in Pietermaritzburg and in subsequent correspondence. A GR-6 travel grant from the Faculty of Graduate Studies, Carleton University, made my visit to Zimbabwe possible and is gratefully acknowledged.

Notes and references

1   Related articles are increasingly prominent in a variety of historical, social, and environmental journals, such as the *Journal of Historical Geography* and *Landscape*, in addition to specifically urban periodicals.
2   See, for example, L.R. Ford, 'Urban preservation and the geography of the city in the U.S.A.,' *Progress in Human Geography*, 3 (1979), pp. 211–38; D. Lowenthal, 'Environmental perception: preserving the past,' *Progress in Human Geography*, 3 (1979), pp. 549–59; J.E. Tunbridge, 'Heritage Canada: the emergence of a geographic agent,' *Canadian Geographer*, 25 (1981), pp. 271–7.
3   This field was pioneered by J. Jacobs, *The Death and Life of Great American Cities* (New York: Random House, 1961).
4   K. Lynch, *The Image of the City* (Cambridge, Mass.: MIT Press, 1960). See also J.D. Porteous, *Environment and Behavior* (Reading, Mass.: Addison-Wesley, 1977), pp. 101–8.
5   H. Kalman, 'Politics, patriotism and preservation,' *Canadian Heritage* (August 1982), p. 5.
6   A case in point is the negative Soviet treatment of churches, which have been de-emphasized or closed while monumental socialist architecture and planning have come to dominate most Soviet cities. See S.D. Brunn and J.F. Williams, *Cities of the World* (New York: Harper and Row, 1983), pp. 147–9. Somewhat similarly, Nazi Germany had planned to rebuild Berlin around monumentalia glorifying the regime, having earlier let the democratic Reichstag burn. In contrast, Polish cities have been rebuilt with greater regard to traditional cultural and religious monuments (notably Old Warsaw), and it is interesting that the Polish government appears less able to control the minds of its people than do other totalitarian regimes.

7   See Heritage Canada, 'Rich in, poor out: how do we solve the displacement dilemma?,' *Canadian Heritage* (August–September 1981), pp. 8–11.

8   L.R. Ford and E. Griffin, 'Chicano Park: personalizing an institutional landscape,' *Landscape*, 23, No. 2 (1981), pp. 42–8.

9   See A. Frampton, 'Down in old Chinatowns: the Chinese in Toronto,' *Canadian Heritage* (February 1982), pp. 28–30; and H. Kalman, 'Our institutions let us down,' *Canadian Heritage* (May 1981), p. 9.

10 See Porteous, op. cit., pp. 290–1; a quotation from a former resident of Africville asserts its heritage value.

11 See, for example, Heritage Canada, 'The Japanese in Canada,' *Canadian Heritage* (October 1980), pp. 10–12; and 'Chinatowns,' *Heritage Canada* (May 1979), pp. 23–4.

12 See A.F.J. Artibise, *Winnipeg: An Illustrated History* (Toronto: James Lorimer and Co./National Museum of Man, 1977).

13 See C. Brook, 'Winnipeg's market,' *Canadian Heritage* (October 1980), pp. 44–6.

14 Research on this process is being conducted by P. Kestelman, a graduate student at Carleton University.

15 Morphological adaptation by a cultural minority is discussed in detail in J. Intscher, 'Little Italy,' *Canadian Heritage* (October 1981), pp. 22–4. See also Heritage Canada, 'The Portuguese in Canada,' *Canadian Heritage* (February 1981), pp. 11–12. Examples of these groups' structural additions are, respectively, porches for wine-cooling and ornamental ironwork.

16 For example, the Chinese of Victoria, from 1970. See Heritage Canada, *Canadian Heritage* (October–November 1982), p. 22, and 'Tong Ji Men,' *Canadian Heritage* (May 1982), pp. 8–9. There are now also various types of government involvement, such as Canada Mortgage and Housing Corporation's recent development of culturally distinctive infill housing in Strathcona (Chinatown), Vancouver; personal communication from B. McGrath, CMHC, Vancouver, October 1983.

17 This is an important element in comprehensive management of the built environment, currently advocated by Jacques Dalibard, executive director of Heritage Canada. See Heritage Canada, 'The major trend,' *Canadian Heritage* (December 1982), supplement pp. v–vi; and 'Conserving the cultural landscape,' *Canadian Heritage* (August–September 1981), pp. 30–3.

18 L. Krotz, *Urban Indians: The Strangers in Canada's Cities* (Edmonton: Hurtig, 1980).

19 Ford and Griffin, op. cit.

20 C. Stadel, 'The structure of squatter settlements in Medellin, Colombia,' *Area*, 7 (1975), pp. 249–54. I have observed a similar outcome in Lima.

21 These points were drawn from discussion with public servants, academics, and conservationists in Harare, September 1982; in particular G. Goodwin and D. Lewis of the Buildings Directorate, City of Harare, and M. Spencer-Cooke of the History Society of Zimbabwe.

22 The conservation ethic appeared late in white private circles also, as evidenced by the uncontested demolition of significant landmarks in the 1970s, notably the old Meikles Hotel (1974).

23 A.M. Spencer-Cook, 'F.S.A.D. Building: and the trial of Mbuga Nehanda,' *Heritage 2* (History Society of Zimbabwe, 1982), pp. 7–14. It should be noted, however, that the street atmosphere in central Harare is changing subtly as black street-hawking spreads.

24 From general discussion with white residents it was learned that heritage, the 'highveld' climate, and conservative politics all contribute to the city's congeniality.

25 Ciskei's government buildings are about 3 km from King William's Town. Note also that Venda has subsequently been refused urban nodes in the strategic northern Transvaal, apparently for fear of right-wing backlash. See *South African Digest*, 16 July 1982, p. 17.

26   Loss of Nationalist votes and fear of white backlash against the Nationalist government are considered likely reasons: personal communication, R.F. Haswell, Department of Geography, University of Natal, Pietermaritzburg, October 1982.

27   Practical objection to the fragmentation of Kwazulu has now become inextricably linked with political opposition to apartheid in general. In 1982 Kwazulu's chief minister, Gatsha Buthelezi, sponsored a commission report proposing a means of reintegrating Natal and Kwazulu (*South African Digest*, 12 March 1982, pp. 11–21). Since he is widely regarded as the principal leader of non-violent black opposition, this was seen as a pilot scheme for the general ending of apartheid as well as an attempted resolution of the geographic problem of Kwazulu vis-à-vis Natal.

28   J. Western, *Outcast Cape Town* (Minneapolis: University of Minnesota Press, 1981), pp. 139–42.

29   T. Wills, Department of Geography, University of Natal, Pietermaritzburg, quoted in *Echo* (black supplement to the *Natal Witness*), 16 June 1983; and personal communication.

30   Attributed to Sir Winston Churchill (with respect to houses) by J. Vance, *This Scene of Man: The Role and Structure of the City in the Geography of Western Civilization* (New York: Harper and Row, 1977), p. 2.

31   Western, op. cit., pp. 142–59. However, other formerly Coloured areas that have been legislated white under the Group Areas Act have experienced profitable white gentrification.

32   T. Wills, *Pietermaritzburg: An Introduction for Geography Students* (Pietermaritzburg: University of Natal, 1981), p. 4.

33   See *South African Digest*, 17 September 1982, p. 5, and 19 November 1982, p. 24.

34   Personal communication from R.F. Haswell, Department of Geography, University of Natal, Pietermaritzburg, currently heritage consultant to the province of Natal. His report, 'An Historic Townscapes Conservation Scheme for Natal' (1982 – presently unpublished) attempts to correct this ethnic bias.

Chapter 18

'Time Out of Mind' – 'Mind Out of Time'

Custom versus tradition in environmental heritage research and interpretation

Kenneth Robert Olwig

Introduction

Our environmental heritage is often interpreted as reflecting a fall from grace in which modern society is seen to destroy tradition through an increasingly unnatural relationship to its environment. At the same time, modern science promotes itself as providing a means to restore that natural environment. There is an apparent contradiction between a modernity that is seen as being capable of destroying society's natural environmental heritage and, at the same time, is seen as also providing the curative to save it. This apparent contradiction, it is argued here, represents two sides of the same narrative coin, going back to the Bible and the Greek and Roman classics. This article proposes that by an examination of the distinction between unchanging tradition and custom, as the source of ever-changing practices, rooted in a vital sense of the past, it is possible to re-conceive heritage interpretation, presentation and preservation in more dynamic terms.

The environmental heritage research and interpretation complex

The idea of the 'Military Industrial Complex' is probably known to most, even if they do not know the origin of the expression.[1] It refers to a symbiotic relation between the military and industry. Another such complex might be the relation between environmental research and heritage interpretation. This complex can be illustrated by the personal experience of making a joint interdisciplinary research grant proposal for a project to study the management and ecology of mountain-meadow grazing lands. Several colleagues, from the natural sciences, kept slipping phrases into the application that referred to how, until very recent times, these meadowlands had for centuries, if not millennia, represented a stable biodiverse environment, managed by an equally stable traditional society. Now, however, modern industrial agriculture was suddenly bringing a heritage of ancient, ecologically balanced farming practices to a bitter end. This abrupt change of affairs was, fortunately, recent enough that with the application of our scientific wisdom, and a large amount of research funding, something might be done to salvage the situation.

The application was to a state funding body heavily involved in the preservation and interpretation of landscape heritage. This exemplifies how a particular narrative, expressing a particular interpretation of the historical and ecological heritage of a particular environment can influence both the formulation of a research project and its chances of funding. This classical 'declensionist' narrative, which interprets environmental history in terms of a modern fall from landscape grace, resounds with much that is received wisdom amongst scientific researchers and heritage interpreters, but in what sense is it 'true'?[2]

Out of time, out of mind

The way in which differing narratives result in differing interpretations of the same environmental heritage can be illustrated by a recent exchange between landscape researchers at a conference. The first narrative was produced by a group of cultural ecologists, the second by a biogeographer with strong historical interests. The first paper contained the following lines:

> In earlier times the agrarian landscape in this place was characterised by its small-scale pattern of variation, a mosaic of small tilled fields and hay meadows, pastures, wooded hay meadows, pollarded and coppiced woodlands and summer farms, resulting in a great diversity of plant communities and ecological processes. Agriculture influenced competition and favoured biological diversity since many species found niches in the agricultural landscapes that resulted from the farmer's efforts to produce sufficient food and fodder. In other cases, domestic animals favoured certain wild plants by eliminating their competitors. As long as agriculture was mainly conducted on the basis of local conditions and without major inputs of outside resources, its impact on the environment was moderate, the effect was stable and the semi-natural vegetation types were maintained through generations.[3]

This received wisdom sounded both agreeable and unproblematic until the biogeographer got up and spoiled things by pointing out that the local peasants, driven by borderline starvation conditions, historically had been forced to employ bone crushingly laborious methods that extracted every possible nutrient from the soil, even to the point of wasting the soil down to the bedrock. Bare bedrock was not, he pointed out, notable for its biodiversity (whatever biodiversity, a notoriously difficult concept to define, might be). The regeneration of these soils, furthermore, would take millennia. Finally, he noted that the environment had probably never been as biodiverse as it was now as a consequence of its abandonment and its subsequent regrowth. This physical geographer's line of argument might have been pursued further, as cultural geographers are wont to do, by pointing out that the rural economy of even remote areas has almost never, in historical times, simply been a product of local conditions. The difficulties of generating a subsistence from the soil have nearly always been compounded by the need to extract a surplus, whether simply to acquire needed goods through exchange or, for example, to pay taxes or the interest on a loan. This need to extract a surplus has added to the human burden upon the environment that has created the highly unstable ecosystems that scientists are now labouring to preserve as a form of 'semi-natural' heritage.

These conflicting narratives lead to larger questions concerning why it is that we tend to interpret our heritage in terms of an opposition between a natural, stable, harmonious and unchanging traditional society and a modern society which brings flux and disharmony, also to nature. Why do we think this way? The English literary critic and writer on culture Raymond Williams has sought to answer this question. Williams once observed that a recent book on rural England had proclaimed that 'a whole culture that had preserved its continuity from earliest times had now received its quietus'. But then, looking back further in time, he saw that this culture should actually already have died in 1932, judging from a book from that year on the disappearance of 'the organic community' of 'old England': 'its destruction is very recent indeed'. But this prediction, it turned out, was based on books which appeared between 1907 and 1923 proclaiming that *now* the rural England 'is dying out'. . . . Williams goes on to write that 'if we mount a kind of historical escalator and begin to move back in time, we see that this "now" is everywhere'. Williams's escalator takes him from Thomas Hardy, to Richard Jefferies, to George Eliot, to Thomas Bewick, John Clare, Goldsmith, Thomas More, Langland, and so on, each of whom saw the disappearance of the last remnants of a contiguous stable, tradition-bound, rural age. In mock desperation Williams asks:

> Or shall we find the timeless rhythm in Domesday, when four out of five were villeins, bordars [sic], cotters or slaves? Or in a free Saxon world before the Norman rape and Yoke? In a Celtic world before the Saxons came up the rivers? In an Iberian world before the Celts came with their gilded barbarism? Where indeed shall we reach before the escalator stops?
>   One answer, of course, is Eden.[4]

Williams satirises here the exaggeration of historical continuity – counterpoised to commensurably abrupt contemporary changes – which characterises not only the perception of the pastoral upland grazing lands of north-western Europe, but much discourse on environmental heritage interpretation and preservation more generally. This pattern of thought can also be found, I would add, in Wordsworth's mourning the entry of the railway to the Lake District because it would bring both change and tourists. The tourists, on the other hand, were attracted to the area by their reading of Wordsworth's *A guide to the district of the Lakes*, with its presentation of the district's heritage as a once 'perfect republic of shepherds'.[5] In the end, Williams argues, this line of reasoning goes back to the biblical Garden of Eden and the classical myth of the pastoral golden age.

Most of those who write about the paradise myth see it as an expression of desire for a lost rural idyll, which is identifiable with childhood. The universality of the experience of childhood can thus explain the universality of this myth. In childhood time seems to stand still and the world is ordered by an external authority, but in adulthood we must labour by the sweat of our brow to maintain the stability necessary to survival – not least the survival of our own children. The historical process of society's increasing urbanisation also means that childhood is often identified with a rural background (or at least visits to rural family or summer homes), whereas adulthood is identified with the urban. This personal experience of a lost childhood, as strengthened by pervasive myths, is reinforced by the apparent tendency of 'traditional rural society' to appeal to the 'time out of mind' values of custom. This sort of explanation means that our tendency to dichotomise our heritage into a timeless, natural, traditional rural society, and a modern urban society of flux and disharmony, basically represents a nostalgia for a lost personal and historical past. This approach to the paradise myth, however, characteristically overlooks the opposite side of the coin, which is just as central to this myth as the idea of loss. This is the idea of development and progress through the transcendence of a necessary loss of innocence.

Paradise and progress

The biblical Garden of Eden and the classical myth of a pastoral golden age both tend to be cast as timeless natural utopias that are run according to the equally timeless natural laws of a godhead who oversees the world of humankind. In the ancient classics – as in the

versions presented by the Greek philosopher Plato or those of the Roman poet Virgil –
when the godhead of the golden age ceases to regulate the world according to godly laws,
humankind, of necessity, must gradually rediscover these laws, and learn to use them to
re-create a world organised like it once was under the godhead. Paradise is thus both a lost
age and a natural utopian model which society seeks to regain by developing its own
human resources in imitation of the gods. The loss of the godhead's natural golden age is
thus the dialectical prerequisite for Promethean human progress towards a utopian future
of its own creation, and by its own hard labour.

Virgil (70–19 BC) is often seen to be the source of many of our ideas regarding the sad
loss of an idyllic pastoral golden age. This significance is due to the enormous influence of
his collection of pastoral lyrics, the *Eclogues*, which synthesises both Greek and Roman
myth and literature. The pastoral idyll, however, represents only one aspect of Virgil. The
Eclogues are, in fact, brought to an end when one of the pan-piping shepherds, lazing under
a shady tree, gets tired of his *ennui* and admonishes the shepherds 'let us rise, it is late, and
shade is harmful to crops'.[6] He seems hereby to be arguing that society needs to get on
with human progress by moving from the laziness of golden age pastoralism to the hard
work of cultivation, the subject of Virgil's next book, *the Georgics*. After the end of the pastoral golden age, according to Virgil, the godhead 'suffered not his realm to "slumber
neath inveterate sloth"', as had been the case previously. Now the godhead 'spurred the
wits of men by cares' in order 'to make men prove and hammer out by practice divers
arts'. He then describes humankind 'now slowly learning how to plough and sow, now
striking from flint vein the lurking fire'. Gradually, in this way, humankind learns the
science of metallurgy, shipbuilding and navigation and eventually, as described in Virgil's
epic *Aeneid*, creates the vast city and empire of Rome. Each step in human progress leads,
however, to new setbacks and cares, as when, for example, cultivation is countered by
invasions of weeds, pests and disease, spurring mankind on to ever greater effort.[7] As in
the Judeo-Christian story of Adam and Eve, the founders of humankind, the loss of paradise is related to the gain of human knowledge, symbolised by the eating of the apple of
the tree of knowledge. It is this ingestion of knowledge which forces humanity to leave its
childhood paradise garden and live, henceforth, by the sweat of its adult brows.

My diversion into the ancient classics, and the Bible, may seem to have taken us very
far from the grant application mentioned at the outset, but, actually, it brings us back to it.
For if one re-examines what we were doing, one will see that the application contained
both sides of the paradise myth. On the one hand, we were bemoaning the loss of a form
of human community in which people lived in stable harmony with their environment,
guided by Nature's laws. But since this loss, given the exigencies of progressive modern
society, is final, we therefore promise the research grant gods that we will henceforth
work by the sweat of our brow and develop new scientific ways to restore the natural har-
monies which contemporary society has destroyed. Our science, of course, is no longer at
the stage of 'striking from flint vein the lurking fire'. Now we're striking lurking information from cyber space. And we no longer tell 'the number of the stars', in the manner of
ancient mariners, now we read satellite images in order to learn the *sat* of the *land*. In our
project, furthermore, we have promised not just to disseminate our results to scientific
specialists, but to interpret and present our study of this vital heritage to the general
public. Though our methods are as modern and effective as can be, there is a real risk that
our interpretive framework belongs to the realm of 'mind out of time' myth. But this is
clearly a myth with a solid track record.

The myth of a lost, natural, golden childhood of humankind, which must be replaced
by reflective adults, working to achieve god-like knowledge and reason, provides the background for Plato's influential *Republic*, in which a board of philosophers is set to run the
ideal post pre-lapsarian utopia of the future. Plato, of course, was a philosopher himself,
and his interpretation of the heritage of humanity certainly did not hurt his profession's

employment opportunities. Francis Bacon modernised this idea in his *Atlantis* in which a board of scientists gets the job of advising the leadership of the ideal future utopia, thus creating the ideational foundation for modern applied scientific research centres. Bacon, the chancellor and legal adviser to a would-be benevolent despot, was, of course, himself a person with scientific pretensions. His utopia would have been an ideal setting for the ambitious Bacon, who would have naturally become an adviser on both natural and human law. Karl Marx, one of the founders of the modern idea of modernity, for whom Bacon's idea of science was an inspiration, gave the idea of learning from the lost idyllic childhood of humanity, while simultaneously transcending it, a particularly poignant form:

> A man cannot become a child again, or he becomes childish. But does he not find joy in the child's naiveté, and must he himself not strive to reproduce its truths at a higher stage? . . . Why should not the historic childhood of humanity, at its most beautiful unfolding, as a stage never to return, exercise an eternal charm?[8]

These observations raise the question of whether this myth is so rooted in our experience of a lost childhood, and in our conception of science and social development, that it has become second nature. I think there is good reason to question this mode of thought as creating a mental trap from which, once one accepts its premises, it is almost impossible to escape.

The paradise/progress trap

The paradise myth has two enticing, but ultimately questionable, dimensions. It is built, first, on the surprisingly pervasive assumption that there is a natural parallel between the childhood and youth of society and the childhood and youth of the individual. And, second, it is built on the related assumption that in the natural state of childhood, or of primitive existence, we behave spontaneously according to natural principles. In the state of adulthood, and social maturity, we must consciously learn the natural laws that once governed our behaviour without reflection. Thus, though the childhood idyll might continue to inspire us, we must leave this Eden and, as adults, shoulder the responsibility of reasoning out the eternal laws once taken for granted in a more natural, but juvenile, past.

This chapter began by relating a personal experience of writing a grant application in which we depicted a timeless traditional society in stable harmony with its environment which is suddenly overwhelmed by a progressively changing modern society. In examining the genesis of this idea, I have suggested that tradition and modernity define each other, that they are two sides of the same dialectical coin, with deep roots in our culture. By defining traditional society both as idyllic, unchanging and harmonious, and as the sadly outmoded and passive prisoner of a lost time, the way is paved for the purveyors of change to promote new and modern rationalities and sciences by which to organise the world and achieve power. The minds of traditional people are essentially defined as being out of time, and this is why traditional society is always seen to be running out of time, and on the verge of extinction. This idea, however, contains something of a self-fulfilling prophecy because it means that by destroying traditional society one proves that it is not viable and that it, therefore, necessarily must be replaced by a modern society, which is defined as being the opposite of traditional society.[9] The point is made even stronger if one is able to preserve remnants of this traditional society as musealised heritage, in order to illustrate the nostalgic contrast to the modern in all its inevitability. The 'paradise/ progress' dialectic is thus a kind of trap, the premises of which it is difficult to escape. But a possible way out will be explored in the following section.

Escaping the heritage paradise/progress dialectic

One reason why the idea of the existence of timeless traditional societies seems plausible is that tradition is confused with custom, and custom plays a concrete role in the legal workings of many societies deemed to be traditional. Custom, however, is not timeless and unchanging, and it belongs by no means to a fossilised past. Custom is, in fact, the foundation for much, though not all, law in contemporary Western society. This is particularly the case in most of the countries, including the United States, which have inherited the traditions of English Common Law. There is nothing backward about custom as a legal tradition, quite the opposite.[10] Custom-based principles of law, as the distinguished Huguenot jurist Francois Hotman already recognised in the 16th century, were in fact more up to date than the kind of eternal 'natural' principles which are characteristic of, for example, Roman law, as well as such natural sciences as physics or astronomy.[11] These principles, because they do not change, are in the long run inappropriate for human societies, which are always changing. Laws based upon timeless principles of the sort which were seen to govern both the stars and the earth, and which thereby also seemed appropriate to the governance of the eternal city, are sadly out of date a few centuries later, as Hotman noted. Customary law, on the other hand, is always updating itself, though it appears to be rooted in the heritage of the past.

The historian Eric Hobsbawn has explained the logic of custom by comparing it with a motor:

> 'Custom' in traditional societies has the double function of motor and fly-wheel. It does not preclude innovation and change up to a point, though evidently the requirement that it must appear compatible or even identical with precedent imposes substantial limitations on it. What it does is to give any desired change (or resistance to innovation) the sanction of precedent, social continuity and natural law as expressed in history.[12]

The remembrance of custom is fundamentally flexible. 'The human memory', according to the historian Marc Bloch, 'is a marvellous instrument of elimination and transformation – especially what we call collective memory.'[13] Custom gives a community possession of its past because it is based upon the idea of 'time out of mind' which, in practice, means that aspects of the past can be conveniently forgotten and reinterpreted according to the contemporary situation. Tradition, by contrast, creates a situation in which people become, as it were, possessed by a given past.[14] Eric Hobsbawn argues that tradition 'must be distinguished clearly from "custom" which dominates so-called "traditional" societies':

> The object and characteristic of 'traditions,' including invented ones, is invariance. . . . 'Custom' cannot afford to be invariant, because even in 'traditional' societies life is not so. Customary or common law still shows this combination of flexibility in substance and formal adherence to precedent. The difference between 'tradition' and 'custom' in our sense is indeed well illustrated here. 'Custom' is what judges do; 'tradition' (in this instance invented tradition) is the wig, robe and other formal paraphernalia and ritualised practices surrounding their substantial action. . . . Inventing traditions, it is assumed here, is essentially a process of formalisation and ritualisation, characterised by reference to the past, if only by imposing repetition.[15]

Custom, thus, is reinvented as tradition when it is reified as *costume*.

A recent newspaper article exemplifies how the principle of custom works in a modern contemporary society. A number of the thirteen English colonies that eventually formed the nucleus of the USA have traditionally based the rights of owners of beach-front property upon special colonial laws dating back to 1647. These ordinances gave the owners control of the beach beyond the high water mark, out to a maximum distance of 1,650 feet into the sea. Based on these statutes present-day property owners have been increasingly exercising what they see as their right to exclude bathers from the beach. Fowlers (hunters), fishermen and navigators, however, did have rights of access to this area under colonial legal practice. The New Jersey Supreme Court used this precedence when it recently ended the monopolisation of the beaches by private landowners. Today's beach bathing, in the court's opinion, is the modern recreational equivalent of such popular colonial pursuits as fowling. As one source is quoted as saying: 'The Supreme Court decided what they [the promulgators of colonial law] really meant was to incorporate change, and that to include recreation and sunbathing was in keeping with that intent.'[16] So what we see here is the application of a time-out-of-mind principle to a thoroughly modern activity. These same issues, this paper argues, are also highly applicable to the way we think about heritage interpretation.

Petrified golden age heritage and the Midas touch

If we see upland pastoralists as managing their land according to unchanging traditions, then any change in the pattern of land use will appear to signal the abrupt end of a hallowed way of life and its corresponding environment. This is the sort of thinking which was leading us, in our grant application, to fall into what I have called the paradise/progress trap. Using this mode of thought we would inevitably wind up painting an idyllic picture of past land-use practices, which could never be compatible with the exigencies of modern society. Actually, of course, we were dealing with forms of customary land use that had always undergone a constant process of modification and adaptation, in relation to changing economic and environmental exigencies. This land use was not always in harmony with the environment. Sometimes, as the biogeographer pointed out above, it wore the land down to the bare bedrock. But the people using the land by and large survived because they were able to learn from, and adapt to, changing circumstances.

The interpretation of upland land use is tied to the larger agrarian heritage. Several of my students recently made a brief study in an area noted for its heritage of preserved traditional Norwegian farms.[17] Preservation, here, did not focus on the changing relationship between the farm buildings and the complex pattern of upland and lowland farming, but rather upon the physical appearance of the architecture in the lowland farm base. Selected farms, which were known to be many centuries old, had been placed under strict preservation orders by the state. This preservation severely limited the owners' right to make any changes in the buildings, even within the living quarters of the family. Special permission was thus required even to change the type or the colour of the paint in the living room. Preservation, by and large, sought to preserve these buildings according to a standard imagined to be characteristic of a stable traditional culture such as was known largely from 19th-century sources. These buildings thus became petrified as timeless tradition in a form that never, historically, would have looked like this, because they would always have been undergoing a process of change. This kind of preservation naturally also leads to a form of heritage interpretation and presentation that eulogises an equally timeless traditional society, which is seen to inhabit such houses.

The transformation of living and changing farmsteads into a petrified, idealised golden age tradition can have the Midas effect of creating valuable properties for people who can afford to, and desire to, possess such cultural capital.[18] These are the sorts of financially endowed people, with independent incomes, for whom, for example, old farm tools are valuable antiques, and the ownership of an authentic old traditional farm gives social status. This form of preservation can lead to the meticulous care of particular properties, while forcing other potential owners (generally those who must make their living strictly from agriculture) out of the market.

The burden placed by heritage preservation upon the farmer can have an effect on the overall use of the farm. Resources that might have been devoted to the tending of a marginal upland meadow, for example, might instead be devoted to the laborious maintenance of de-modernised buildings. The fact that the agricultural economy is inherently weak in areas with physically difficult farming conditions, such as mountain Norway, means that the disposition of scarce resources is important to economic survival. Ideally, the state should be supplying these farmers with the necessary funds to offset the exorbitant cost of maintaining these buildings, but in practice no government can afford such an expense and most of the farmers complained that these funds were not forthcoming. The end result of this kind of heritage preservation, and its attendant form of interpretation, is an untenable situation in which a few farms are preserved in mint condition, while the remaining either fall into disrepair or, by default, are not maintained according to regulations. But is there an alternative to a situation in which buildings seem to be either preserved according to strict regulations, or despoiled with modern additions that seem to show no continuity with the original structure? A greater sensitivity to the actual workings of custom might offer a solution that, though it will not appeal to purist preservationists, might have a chance of working. This can be exemplified by recent experience from the Faeroe Islands.

Faeroe 'pastoral'

During a recent visit to the Faeroe Islands a young shepherd and his sheep dog took me, as part of a group of landscape researchers, on a walk that ended at a cliff with a drop so precipitous that I was afraid even to look over the edge. The day before, we learned, this shepherd had crawled over the edge, with a sheep on his back, and shimmied down a rope in order to put the animal out to summer pasture on the rich, sea bird fertilised, grass on a ledge below. He had done this six times. Those of my colleagues who were not afraid to look over the edge informed me that there were indeed six sheep down there. The sight of these pastures, tended according to centuries-old principles, and the presence of the shepherd, who shared the land with eight others from the village, made me feel as if I had walked into the pages of the *National Geographic*, or perhaps even stumbled upon a scene from Virgil's pastorals. Then I made the mistake of asking the young shepherd if he was able to make a living from farming. Oh no! he exclaimed, almost nobody can make a living from farming on the Faeroes. On asking what he did to earn his keep, he explained that he was the manager of the village bank. He added that he would probably be skippering his father's factory trawler if it were not for the fact that the ocean made him seasick.

This fellow's story destroyed my illusion of the young shepherd as the son of nature, and the Faeroes as an idyllic, timeless, traditional society, surviving far away from modern society in the North Atlantic. Yet this knowledge helped explain other things, such as the line of fencing, and the rather nondescript concrete block barn, which seemed out of place. This was clearly still a working landscape and not a museum piece. The young man may have earned his income from a bank, but he was still participating in productive farming practices, organised according to customary principles, which, by and large, maintained the historical continuity and biological values of the cultural landscape. The market value of the lamb and mutton produced could not recompense for the time expended producing it, but home-grown and cured meat remained a priceless delicacy in Faeroese culture, the sort of thing which makes the ideal gift. Even the process of working together to care for the sheep and tend the pastures played an important role in cementing social relationships in the village – thus reminding one that the word *fellowship* originally appears to have derived from a word meaning a club or association (the *low* in fel*low* deriving from *lag* meaning association) for managing sheep (*fe*).[19] The term *Faeroe* Islands, in fact, would be a misnomer without the sheep, since *Faeroe* means 'sheep' (*fae*) 'island' (*oe*). Though this particular contemporary sheep-raising association still collectively managed an undivided section of pasture affiliated with their farm lots, they had decided to fence their parcel from that of adjacent farmer collectivities in order to save labour. Custom was hereby being transformed to suit changing circumstances, but the cultural landscape was still productive, and the Faeroes were still very much sheep islands.

In travelling around the Faeroes, despite the occasional presence of rather ugly modern structures, many buildings looked as if they had been built according to ageless tradition. Some, indeed, were ancient structures that had been preserved according to official regulations. Often, however, when one came closer to one of these 'traditional' buildings, they proved to be of recent origin, and had been built of decidedly untraditional materials, such as reinforced concrete or corrugated iron. The shape and form was 'right', but the material was 'wrong', though it was practical and inexpensive. What we were seeing here was an architectural example of structures constructed according to customary principles. The origin of the forms was time out of mind, but the materials had been brought up to date.

The Faeroese case exemplifies how environmental heritage can be maintained within a living modern society, without subjecting that environment to 'the Midas touch'. Once one becomes familiar with the Faeroese landscape one even learns to appreciate the somewhat indiscreet charms of even the brightly painted corrugated iron siding, which can also be found elsewhere on the islands of the North Atlantic.

Conclusion

The example of places like the Faeroe Islands, where the force of custom is strong, and the promoters of tradition have yet to gain the upper hand, can provide inspiration for different ways of researching, interpreting and presenting heritage. If we are able to think about heritage as something that is constantly being created, through a process based on principles of custom, which are both time-out-of-mind and up to date, perhaps then we can escape the trap of the paradise/progress dialectic. This trap leads to the dichotomy between timeless traditional societies and modern, rootless, changing societies. To escape this trap is not easy, however, owing to the unexamined epistemological foundations that underlie much of our work as researchers and interpreters. The very separation between research and interpretation, and between the different disciplines of the natural, cultural and social sciences, blinds us to the ways in which scientific research, itself, is driven by interpretive narratives.

Part of what makes the concept of nature and the natural so complex is that the term simultaneously refers both to certain material phenomena and to the laws which, behind the scenes, generate and shape those phenomena. Science tends to seek unchanging laws, in the spirit of Bacon, and governmental agencies, again in the spirit of Bacon, are attracted to those who can provide them with what appear to be scientific certainties. The divide in modern education between the sciences and the humanities also means that few are capable of comprehending the ways in which age-old narratives, and age-old conceptions of law, continue to infuse the way we think about our environmental heritage. The more ignorant we are of our cultural heritage, the more likely we are to be blind to the way such narratives, and such notions of law, influence our interpretation of our environmental heritage. Our environment, as students of the humanities and the social sciences have become increasingly aware, has been shaped by human beings whose environmental perceptions have, in turn, been shaped by centuries of custom. Unless one understands the workings of custom one will never be able effectively to interpret the human environment, or effectively influence its future development.

The trap of the paradise/progress dialectic forces researchers and interpreters to dichotomise the world in terms of either unchanging custom, or the juggernaut of the rampant change governed by progress. Escaping this trap should help us to develop approaches to heritage that can increase the understanding of how the principles of custom might work to create environments that both preserve a sense of historical continuity and remain economically and socially viable. Unfortunately, however, this trap is not simply the figment of the individual researcher or interpreters' imagination, it is built into the way our society structures education, research and interpretation. Unless we work to deconstruct the 'research and heritage interpretation complex' itself, our disciplinary development will continue to be governed by the 'paradise/progress' dialectic.

Acknowledgements

I would like to thank Anders Lundberg, University of Bergen, Norway, for useful commentary. I would also like to thank the students who produced the field report *Kulturminner i Hegra – verdier og visjoner ved vern* (see note 17), for their inspiration (and for the use of some of their photographs). They are: Jorunn Elin Olden, Elin Gjevre, Marte Sletten, Heidi Grethe Betten, Astrid Tveteraas, Susan Helena Ørjansen, Torgeir Haavik, Marit Skanche Langen, Ine Cecilie Mork Olsen, Lene Marie Grennes, Helene Kvarberg Tolstad and Heidi Grethe.

Notes

1   The term is from a speech written by Malcolm Moos (now a former president of the University of Minnesota) for a presidential speech by Dwight D. Eisenhower.
2   On 'declensionist' narratives see C. Merchant, 'Reinventing Eden: Western culture as a recovery narrative', in W. Cronon (ed.) *Uncommon ground: towards reinventing nature*, New York: W.W. Norton, 1995, pp. 132–159.
3   The account of our grant application, and the critique of the paper referred to here, has been slightly fictionalised. There is no reason to pillory particular colleagues for exemplifying a mode of thought which is endemic, in my experience, amongst heritage researchers and interpreters.
4   R. Williams, 'Literature and rural society', *The Listener*, November 16, 1967, pp. 630–632.
5   W. Wordsworth, *A guide to the district of the Lakes in the North of England*, New York: Greenwood Press, 1968 (orig. 1810).
6   Virgil, *Eclogues* X 74–77: quoted and interpreted in M.C.J. Putnam, *Virgil's pastoral art*, Princeton: Princeton University Press, 1970, pp. 386–394.
7   K.R. Olwig, *Nature's ideological landscape: a literary and geographic perspective on its development and preservation on Denmark's Jutland Heath*, London: Allen & Unwin, 1984, pp. 1–10; Virgil, *Eclogues and Georgics*, London: Dent, 1946, pp. 69–71.
8   K. Marx, *Grundrisse*, Harmondsworth: Penguin, 1973, pp. 110–111.
9   K.R. Olwig, 'Landscape, place and the state of progress', in R.D. Sack (ed.) *Progress: geographical essays*, Baltimore: Johns Hopkins University Press, 2002.
10 Francis Bacon, as Chancellor and legal adviser to a royal court with absolute despotic ambitions, hated customary and common law, and hence parliament, but he lost out, in fact, to parliament, and I personally doubt that England would have become more modern and progressive under Bacon's council of ruling scientists, than it did under parliament.

11   J.G.A. Pocock, *The ancient constitution and the feudal law*, Cambridge: Cambridge University Press, 1957; F. Hotman, *Francogallia*, Cambridge: Cambridge University Press, 1972 (orig. 1573).

12   E. Hobsbawn, 'Introduction', in T. Ranger & E. Hobsbawn (eds) *The invention of tradition*, Cambridge: Cambridge University Press, 1983, pp. 1–14 (pp. 2–4).

13   M. Bloch, *Feudal Society*, Chicago: University of Chicago Press, 1961 (orig. 1940), p. 114; see also D. Lowenthal, *The past is a foreign country*, Cambridge: Cambridge University Press, 1985, pp. 206–210.

14   D. Lowenthal, *Possessed by the past. The heritage crusade and the spoils of history*, New York: The Free Press, 1996.

15   Hobsbawm, pp. 2–4.

16   D. Fraser, 'Day at the beach: access still a thorny issue', *Sunday Cape Cod Times*, July 4, 1999, pp. 1, 6, 7.

17   Betten *et al.*, *Kulturminner i Hegra-verdier og visjoner ved vern. Feltkurs i Stjørdal kommune*, Geo 200, Trondheim, Norway: NTNU, 1999.

18   In the myth of King Midas the king achieves his wish of having everything he touches turned to gold, only to discover that this means that everything he touches becomes useless and inedible. The term cultural capital is generally associated with the French sociologist Pierre Bourdieu, who argues that culture can also be used as a form of capital within given social groups. P. Bourdieu, *Distinction: a social critique of the judgment of taste*, London: Routledge & Kegan Paul, 1984.

19   *Oxford English Dictionary*, Oxford: Oxford University Press, 1971, *fellowship*.

Conflict in the Archaeology of Living Traditions

Robert Layton

Recent controversy surrounding the exhumation and reburial of indigenous human skeletons in the United States and Australia has called into question the relationship between archaeologists and contemporary native peoples. This is turn has led some archaeologists to deny the existence of a continuous native cultural tradition linking living people with the remains of the past, upon which indigenous claims for control of those remains frequently rest. The debate has raised a number of issues concerning the connections between archaeological theory, research methods and politics.

The US archaeologist B. D. Smith, for instance, challenges contemporary Native American demands for the reburial of indigenous skeletons held in museums and other collections, on the grounds that Native American beliefs varied over time and place, and that no cultural or genetic continuity is demonstrable between modern Indian groups and many pre-colonial skeletons. He characterizes the linked contentions that there exists a cultural unity among all Native Americans, which permits living people to demand the reburial of skeletons, as ' "articles of faith" which are not open to logical debate . . . the defense of their initial assumptions rests on the inherent rejection of the western concept of logical reasoning' (Smith n.d., p. 15).

In a recent public lecture the Australian archaeologist John Mulvaney takes a more cautious line with regard to Australian Aboriginal participation in archaeology. He accepts that Aboriginal people are the guardians and custodians of Aboriginal history and culture (Mulvaney 1986, p. 56), but argues that custodianship should not be equated with an exclusive right to interpret that material. In particular, Mulvaney challenges the view of some Aboriginal Australians that their race originated in Australia, a contention which 'could produce unforeseen political consequences. Obviously', he continues, 'if scientific evolutionary theory is rejected by Aboriginal creationists, who also ignore the archaeological evidence for human antiquity in South-East Asia, the claim is lodged for a separate human origin within Australia' (Mulvaney 1986). Like Smith, Mulvaney also takes exception to the claim that there exists a unitary Aboriginal culture which privileges contemporary Aboriginal interpretation of the remains of past indigenous culture (Mulvaney 1986, p. 54).

Both archaeologists quoted appeal to scientific method, and its ability to examine data objectively, to validate their stance. Smith dismisses the native position as one which lies wholly beyond the limits of scientific method. Although Mulvaney sees scope for dialogue over the proper interpretation of data derived from the past's remains (Mulvaney 1986, p. 55), not surprisingly he dismisses the theory of a separate origin for Australian Aborigines as unscientific. Smith considers that the value of skeletal evidence justifies control of indigenous skeletons by archaeologists, but Mulvaney distinguishes between ownership and study. Neither archaeologist addresses a set of issues which, to indigenous peoples, appear crucial: to what extent does archaeological theory itself embody subjective assumptions about cultural process? Have archaeologists' presuppositions prevented them from correctly interpreting the response of indigenous peoples to colonial domination? Have they similarly neglected the dynamics of non-Western society prior to colonial contact? Can indigenous peoples contribute to a reassessment of their own past, or does Western culture have a monopoly on scientific method?

The reburial issue has confronted American and Australian archaeologists with the kind of moral dilemma that faced British anthropology at the end of the colonial era (Asad 1973), and American anthropology during the Vietnam War (Berreman 1968, Hymes 1974). Research supposed by its practitioners to be disinterested was found to have contributed to the furtherance of partisan political goals at odds with the aspirations of indigenous peoples. Some academics respond to such challenges by retreating from the real world. It is my view that the popularity of structuralism in British anthropology during the late 1960s had something to do with the manifest irrelevance of structural imagery in myth, or dietary restrictions, to contemporary political issues, and was motivated in part by the fear that politics compromised scholarly activity. The rise of structuralism coincided with claims that anthropology had up until then furthered the aims of colonialism (e.g. Asad 1973). Opponents of reburial such as Smith and ACPAC (1986), on the other hand, respond to the challenge in a different way, by evoking the image of science as a kind of intellectual Gatling Gun: whatever happens, we have got science and they have not. A more measured response to either of these is to ask whether archaeological theories or methods themselves need to be revised if they are clearly at variance with other peoples' perceptions of the data.

Can we be objective about objectivity?

Objectivity is often something one seems to posses in greater measure than one's opponents. It is necessary to establish some common grounds for assessing competing theoretical stances. Otherwise the debate is vulnerable to the accusation that it is merely a matter of competing subjectivities.

What, then, is objectivity? The word objective refers to an object of perception or thought, as distinct from the perceiving or thinking subject; it is, in other words, something that is, or is held to be, external to the mind. Sometimes it is used in a medical sense, to refer to symptoms observed by the practitioner, in distinction to those which are only felt by the patient (*Shorter Oxford English Dictionary*). In the social sciences, the view that the objective consequences of a person's behaviour do not correspond to their subjective intentions is comparable to the SOED's medical sense of the word. The view, often adopted in the history of science, that the presuppositions of earlier generations of scientists prevented them from objectively noticing some aspect of variability in the data under study, corresponds to the SOED's more general sense.

The former usage is exemplified by the Functionalist theory of religion, proposed by Durkheim (1938) and relied upon in many ethnographies from the 1920s to the 1950s. According to this interpretation the objective consequence of practising religious rituals, apparent to the detached observer, is to promote social harmony. The participants (subjectively) believe they are worshipping spirits, the observer finds the (objective) consequence to be increased solidarity in the congregation.

The second usage is illustrated by Ardener's discussion of Newton's belief in 1669 (Westfall 1980) that the spectrum should display seven discrete colour bands, even though cross-cultural comparison shows that other cultures classify colour variation in other ways. Newton reversed the received view that white is a pure colour, and showed it rather to be a composite of other colours. Unable to identify discrete bands in the spectrum by his own observation, Newton attributed this to his poor eyesight, and requested a friend to trace the boundaries between the colours for him. Newton felt there should be seven bands of colour in the spectrum, a presupposition apparently based on the existence of a seven-note scale in music. The name indigo was adopted for a seventh, supposedly discrete band (Ardener 1971, pp. xx, lxxxiv). His subjective expectations prevented Newton from objectively recognizing that the spectrum exhibited continuous variation.[1] The Linnean classification of species is a similar case. The 18th-century naturalist Linnaeus did not (except in limited instances) believe in evolutionary change. His classificatory system treated natural species as discrete and immutable (Davis and Heywood 1963). For that reason, he regarded variation within a species as nothing more than the effect of soil and climate. Our understanding of genetics allows us, with hindsight, to recognize such an approach as subjective, and a consequence of his presuppositions about natural order.[2]

How do these two definitions of objectivity relate to the issues addressed in this debate?

In the context of the reburial debate, the first usage identified above resembles Smith's indictment of the Native American position on reburial. Contemporary Native Americans conceive of burial as a means of caring for the spirit of the deceased, but really the objective consequence of burial was to store archaeological data for the future scientist. The second usage is adopted by a number of authors in their critical assessment of archaeological theories. Static models of culture areas, the equation of material culture complexes with genetically distinct populations, concentration on certain eras of history, all betray an insensitivity to the full character of variability in archaeological data, and result from prior suppositions on the part of the analyst which do a disservice to the people whose history is under investigation.

What is not contended here is that political expediency justifies selection of a particular theoretical orientation. This is the position taken by Binford in a recent paper. Although strict empiricism, that is, observation of data without the guidance of a theory is impossible (Binford 1987, p. 394), nonetheless we cannot adhere to a theory merely because it seems politically expedient or morally right (Binford 1987, pp. 401–2). We must test our theories against observation. Trigger reaches a similar conclusion, namely that, although a 'value-free' archaeology is probably impossible to achieve, 'the findings of archaeology can only have lasting social value if they approximate as closely as possible to an objective understanding of social behaviour' (Trigger 1984, p. 368). On the other hand, any theory that has a bearing on the real world may have political implications, if it is used to formulate or justify policy, even though this consequence may be unintended by the analyst.

There are cases when it is hard to believe that a particular interpretation of archaeological data is not advanced for political reasons, since it seems palpably contrary to the empirical evidence. For some years an institution in Canberra publicly displayed a case containing the skulls of a gorilla, an Aboriginal and a White Australian, arranged in ascending order. The caption asserted that the three skulls displayed the principal trends in human evolution. In other cases, the political implications of a scientific interpretation may be less apparent. The view that Tasmanian Aborigines were extinct disregarded the descendants of Tasmanian women and White Whalers (Ryan 1981). From their point of view, the assertion could underpin the denial of land rights or the right to dispose of indigenous skeletons in a culturally appropriate manner (Bickford 1979, Ucko 1983). In such cases of conflict, the use of theory to underpin policies imposed on indigenous minorities by power inevitably politicizes archaeology. Mere protestations of objectivity cannot free the archaeologist from the political implications of research. Ucko has documented the way in which Australian archaeology was transformed by Aboriginal participation, bringing to archaeologists a new awareness of the implications inherent in their theoretical positions (Ucko 1983). I have elsewhere reviewed the use of alternative anthropological theories in interpreting the evidence for Australian Aboriginal land claims, and the practical consequences which ensued in the success or failure of the claim (Layton 1985). Mulvaney points out that although the Australian Institute of Aboriginal Studies was never expected to formulate policy for the government, its research findings on such matters as education and health were bound to have policy implications (Mulvaney 1986, p. 51).

Where Binford's (1987) argument is misleading is its apparent rejection of Hodder's insight that much archaeological material is the product of conventional cultural codes that had meaning for the participants (e.g. Hodder 1982). The discovery that cultural codes are relatively arbitrary or conventional does indeed deny the archaeologist access, in the absence of informants, to specific meanings (Binford 1987, pp. 396–9). Objectivity here consists rather of attempting to construe the intersubjective meaning of material for members of the culture that produced it. An archaeologist examining the jaw of an ancient skeleton, for instance, might discover toothware patterns that allowed him to deduce aspects of diet by comparison with toothware on unrelated living populations. But if certain teeth had been artificially removed before death, only ethnographic information about that cultural tradition would allow the archaeologist to deduce the significance of the missing teeth (Mulvaney 1986, p. 54, cf. Geertz 1973). Another good example is provided by Rubertone (1994) where she argues that historical ethnographic sources throw a different light upon 17th-century New England culture to that previously inferred by archaeologists from inspection of the material. Rubertone finds evidence of resistance to domination rather that passive assimilation.

Objectivity and intersubjectivity in the study of culture

In the physical and natural sciences it is assumed that the data under investigation exist independently of any theory about them. In the social sciences there is a limit on the extent to which an observer, inspecting the material elements of a cultural tradition, can 'objectively' determine their significance. This is because the meaning of artefacts, their place in a system of signification, is largely determined by cultural convention. Even representational art is less open to naive interpretation by members of other cultures than is sometimes supposed, since different artistic traditions select different aspects of the perceived world to represent, and organize their representations according to different styles (Layton 1977). The meaning of artefacts is culturally constituted, and to discover what it is the analyst must go to the negotiated, intersubjective and sometimes changing elements of cultural interaction. This imposes a limit on the use of ethnographic analogy, as Binford recognizes (1987, p. 399). But Binford has himself employed such analogies (e.g. Binford 1980), and inferences having some degree of probability are not precluded. The sciences of information theory and linguistics have demonstrated that the patterning of messages into 'bits' of information can be objectively studied both in human and animal communication. Although we will probably never know what the mental construct 'bison' symbolized in Palaeolithic European culture(s) we can document the relative frequency with which bison, horse, etc. were depicted, and the non-random selection of caves to decorate (Layton 1987). We do not need to attempt to intuit the precise symbolism of prehistoric burials to appreciate that deliberate burial signified, beyond reasonable doubt, something different to the casual abandonment of the body (cf. Binford 1971, but see Ucko 1969). The failure to attend to cultural patterning in the archaeological record would be to disregard important aspects of variability in the data, even if the uninformed outsider cannot fully explain it.

It was a weakness of the Functionalist theory mentioned above that it paid relatively little attention to the intellectual content of religion. The same accusation can be directed at the opponents of reburial, who oppose the 'objective' explanations of science to the 'subjective' explanations of religion. The Functionalist stance seemed permissible as long as Durkheim's explanation was accepted. Durkheim, as is well known, believed that religious experience was generated by the congregation's coming together, creating a social current such as may grip people in a crowd. Once this interpretation was rejected (see Needham 1963), the question which Durkheim had hoped to answer, why do beliefs persist which appear to the outsider to be contradicted by experience, is posed once again. The answers which anthropologists have offered throw light on the general issue of the limits of objectivity. Horton, in a series of papers (e.g. 1960, 1964), argued that religion offers a type of explanatory model which conceives of non-human forces as socialized entities. He argued that such models appeal to communities who experience social life as ordered and predictable, but do not seem useful to members of cultures undergoing rapid social change.

Much anthropological and philosophical attention has been devoted to the case of the Azande, described by Evans-Pritchard (1976 [1937]). Although not a naive Functionalist, Evans-Pritchard explained the persistence of Azande witchcraft beliefs and practices in terms of their functional consequences rather than their intellectual content. Fear of being thought a witch discouraged anti-social behaviour, and the procedures for identifying witches gave Azande the confidence to act, in the belief they could limit misfortune. When an accused witch promised to desist, this helped to resolve quarrels. But how could the beliefs persist if experience refuted them? Evans-Pritchard had less success in explaining the intellectual content of the beliefs. He was particularly puzzled by the technique for identifying a witch that involved feeding 'poison' to chickens and posing the questions to the 'poison': 'if x is the witch kill (or spare) the chicken' (Evans-Pritchard 1976, pp. 131–40). Evans-Pritchard admitted that he found conformity with Azande practice as reasonable a way as any of conducting his affairs during fieldwork with them (1976, p. 126). He even admitted once seeing a witch (1976, p. 11). Yet he believed there were inconsistencies in Azande thought which they were unable to address because they were trapped inside their (more limiting) system of logic (1976, pp. 155–9). Consequently, he held, they could not recognize empirical disproof of their belief even though they recognized empirical evidence within the system of thought (1976, p. 25).

Philosophers and later anthropologists have attempted to better Evans-Pritchard's analysis. Three of their proposals are particularly relevant to the kinds of problem concerning objectivity posed in this book. Gellner (1970, p. 241) points out that it is in the political interests of Azande princes to maintain the system even if they recognize its logical shortcomings (cf. Evans-Pritchard 1976, p. 7). Both parties in the reburial debate might interpret their opponents' position in these terms. Winch (1970, p. 82) alternatively argued that Azande wanted to explain events which we dismiss as accidental. Their valuation of human life demands that unexpected death be attributed a cause (cf. Evans-Pritchard 1976, pp. 18, 23). The explanations offered by witchcraft and science are therefore directed to different ends. Ahern (1982) argues a more fundamental point, that every explanatory theory rests on certain constitutive rules, which are not open to question within the theory. The exercise of objectivity is directed by these rules. Ahern draws an analogy with the rules of a game. Tennis is constituted by certain rules; it would be silly or meaningless to ask a player why he didn't knock two balls over the net to be sure of beating his opponent with one – it wouldn't be tennis. In a parallel fashion, Azande oracles are constituted on the principle that the 'poison' is not a chemical but a sentient force. When Evans-Pritchard asked what would happen if you went on feeding more and more poison to a chicken (Evans-Pritchard 1976, p. 147), he intended the Azande to realize the chicken would inevitably die. But Evans-Pritchard's frame of reference was constituted on the supposition that the poison acted chemically. The Azande, on the other hand, replied that they supposed the chicken would eventually burst! They found such questions silly, and told Evans-Pritchard 'you do not understand such matters'. Contrary to his expectation, they did not seem distressed, nor did they feel their position to be insecure; the fault lay with Evans-Pritchard's failure to understand (Ahern 1982, pp. 308–9). Ahern's concept of constitutive rules is derived from linguistic theory (Ahern 1982, p. 305), but it may be compared with Kuhn's concept of the unquestioned rules that constitute a scientific paradigm (Kuhn 1970, pp. 4–5, 44–8) and Geertz's contention that cultures must be understood in their own terms (Geertz 1973). Trigger's paper 'Alternative archaeologies' (1984) examines some of the assumptions underlying three basic types of archaeology (Nationalist, Colonialist and Imperialist), and his conclusions match closely those of some contributors to this book. No theoretical orientation is exempt from constitutive propositions.

Does functionalism itself have constitutive rules?

Suppose Functionalist explanation is subjected to this type of critique. Functionalists modelled their approach on the natural sciences, and prided themselves on having devised an objective approach to studying other cultures.

The School of Functionalism arose in reaction to the earlier theories of Evolutionism and Diffusionism, the former tending to explain customs as survivals from earlier 'stages in social evolution', the latter explaining customs as elements that had spread more or less randomly from 'centres of civilization'. The rise of Functionalism was closely connected with the development of lengthy field research in a single community as a method of investigation. It offered a much more detailed explanation of human social behaviour, viewed at first hand from a synchronic perspective. Nonetheless Functionalism rested on certain constitutive propositions: that the history of a custom was irrelevant to its current function, or contribution to social solidarity (Radcliffe-Brown 1952, p. 185), that societies tend naturally to remain in equilibrium (1952, p. 183), that communities are governed by consensus (1952, p. 180, but see p. 181 note 1). Although Radcliffe-Brown emphasized that the notion of functional unity among the customs of a community was an hypothesis (1952, pp. 181, 184), these propositions were not normally tested in functional analysis, partly because the relevant historical data often seemed unobtainable, partly because the analysis often sought implicitly to reconstruct the society as it was imagined it would be in the absence of colonial domination.

Yet the Functionalists' research also depended, to a significant extent, upon the colonial order for prolonged access to the field. This, in Asad's view, played an important part in determining how research findings were presented: 'anthropology does not merely apprehend the world in which it is located, but the world also determines how anthropology will apprehend it' (Asad 1973, p. 12). 'It is because the powerful who support research expect the kind of understanding which will ultimately confirm them in their world that anthropology has not very easily turned to the production of radically subversive forms of understanding' (Asad 1973, p. 17).

The realization that a theory does not wholly explain variability in the data under investigation does not necessarily negate its usefulness in circumscribed areas. Functionalism provided a useful guide to the fieldworker which helped him or her to examine the structure of social life in the community under study. The same is true of archaeological theories (cf. Trigger's appraisal of Soviet archaeology, 1984, pp. 365–6), and more generally. Although the theory that the stars revolve around a sphere with the Earth at its centre has long since been discredited, charts which predict the location of stars in the sky through successive nights are still constructed on this principle. Although Linnaeus' creationist theory is no longer accepted in the biological sciences, his principles of classification are adequate to describe natural species, even though contemporary theory regards genetic variation within more or less transient breeding populations as of equal importance to barriers inhibiting cross-fertilization between populations. It is when such theories are applied inappropriately that they become dangerous. No space programme could be predicted on the pre-Copernican theory of the universe. The view of species as fixed and 'pure' has led by extension to the obscenities of Nazi policy toward 'Jews' and 'Slavs', and recent South African policy on so-called mixed marriages.

Whether Functionalists intended their research to provide an ideological justification for colonialism is a moot point. It is true that some argued, without much success, for the practical value of social anthropology to colonial regimes (Kuper 1983, Ch. 4, Grillo 1985, pp. 9–16). Others contend that their intention was to improve the lot of colonized peoples (e.g. Gulliver 1985). One could, however, turn the Functionalist approach to religion (see above) upon the Functionalists themselves and argue that the objective consequences of their practice were quite different to their stated goals. Wherever archaeological theories become used to justify policy, it is equally essential to look again at the assumptions that underpin them and ask whether they are used to promote injustice.

Theories of stability, change and adaptation

Static models

The chapters in *Conflict in the archaeology of living traditions* examine two related topics. The first is the ability of archaeological theories to account for change in non-Western societies, both those wrought by colonialism and those which took place earlier. The second topic concerns the disjunction that sometimes arises between the research aims of non-Western people, whether archaeologists or not, and the archaeologists of Western society. The two issues are related, for we must understand how Third and Fourth World communities responded to the colonial impact to appreciate why, today, they may hold different analytical objectives and evaluate the use of information about the past in different ways. Chapters 1–9 discuss the first topic and chapters 10–16 deal with the issues related to the disposition of the dead. Chapters 17 and 18 pick up some of the threads of the previous chapters, and concentrate on the ways forward for co-operation between archaeologists and indigenous communities.

The relationship of Functionalism to colonial policy is raised in Gilliam (1994), where anthropology is held particularly responsible for the view of Third World cultures as discrete and inherently static. The critique of Olderogge, whom Gilliam cites, resembles that of Eric Wolf in his survey of interaction between *Europe and the people without history* (Wolf 1982), which emphasizes the dynamism of human cultures and their continual interaction.

Beauregard (1994) and Rubertone (1994) similarly contend that the 'culture area' principle does little justice to the dynamics of interaction between native Americans and early colonial settlers, endowing the principle with misleading political implications. Beauregard demonstrates the diversity of economic strategies adopted in response to new modes of production imposed on the area during the colonial period. Both contributors conclude that Indians were not passively becoming assimilated to colonial society, an argument which puts the modern Indian struggle in a different light.

Evolutionary models

For many contributors, the application of evolutionary theories has been responsible for even greater misrepresentation of the evidence of social process. Any theory that ranks human societies in successive stages rests on the constitutive principle that evolution has a single goal. It is extraordinary how little acknowledgement exists in the social sciences that the concept of unilinear progress has no part in the neo-Darwinian theory of evolution. Since genetically determined traits can only be defined as 'useful' (i.e. contributing to the individual's reproductive success) by reference to a given environment, the concept of natural selection provides no objective basis for speaking in general terms of 'higher' or 'lower' forms of life. This applies just as much to the evolution of social behaviour as it does to physiological evolution (Trivers 1985, pp. 31–2).

In Darwinian terms the evolutionary value of agriculture over hunting and gathering, for instance, is to be measured in the contribution of the new behavioural strategies to reproductive success. In some environments a hundred-fold increase in population resulted, but in environments to which agriculture is maladapted, hunting and gathering continued to provide the most effective set of behavioural strategies (Irons 1983, pp. 172–3, 198).

To the extent that Native American and Aboriginal Australian peoples have succeeded in surviving the colonial onslaught this is due in part to their ability to adapt indigenous cultural strategies. Once the persistence of distinctive cultures is acknowledged (Castile 1974) it becomes of immediate interest to investigate how it was achieved. Rubertone and Beauregard examine this issue. The origin of such flexible strategies in pre-colonial tradition further challenges the assumption that non-Western societies are characteristically static, as Rakotoarisoa shows (1994 and cf. Trigger 1984, pp. 361–2).

Twagiramutara (1994) interprets the origin of agriculture in sub-Saharan Africa as an adaptation to climatic change. He argues that historically related communities adopted different modes of production, according to the diversity of ecological niches they occupied. This, as he shows, is not incompatible with the view that innovations in technology, crops, and methods of production could enhance specific adaptations, and the latter may legitimately be described as 'progress', in a specified context. Such judgement, however, would not deny the adaptive quality of a hunting and gathering way of life in other settings, due either to the drought-prone character of the natural environment or to displacement by more powerful social groups.

Kishani (1994) argues that linguistic diversity in Africa is not the sign of barbarism (conceived as a stage in social evolution) that some Europeans have contended, but has specific historical causes: partly the failure of any single indigenous empire to establish lasting dominance, but also the continual disruption and fragmentation brought about by centuries of slave raiding. The Aikios (1994) document the response of Sámi (Lapp) reindeer herders to the encroachment of farmers upon their land, and to the closing of national borders across which Sámi had previously moved without constraint. Attention is drawn to the irony that outsiders asserted the Sámi to be politically weak and immature, even though their life-style was well adapted to the subarctic environment. In order to sustain their way of life, moreover, the Sámi had to master many languages and become expert at the interpretation of legal agreements; the idea of nomads living outside civilization is, the Aikios conclude, a politically convenient myth created by outsiders.

Rubertone (1994) argues that US colonial archaeology's view of the past confirms popular beliefs about the past without calling them into question. It disregards evidence that indigenous peoples contributed actively to the construction of colonial society, and remains constituted upon the ideology that colonization represents the successful challenge of civilization to savagery. Rubertone shows how an alternative model can account more fully for the ethnographic and archaeological data.

Condori (1994) cites the predilection among descendants of Spanish settlers in Bolivia to describe the pre-colonial past as 'prehistoric'; a contention that fits Western evolutionist thought, but is refuted by ethnohistorical research which shows that techniques existed in the pre-colonial state for keeping records pictorially. He further contrasts the Western tendency to regard the future as lying 'before us' – something we strive to attain – with the Aymara concept that it is the past which lies, visible, before our eyes, and the future, unknown, behind our backs.

Gilliam (1994) points out that it is the politically dominant who assign 'backwardness' to others, thereby not only denying the validity of alternative contemporary cultures and alternative directions for economic development, but justifying the continued expropriation of other people's land, labour and resources in the name of progress. Assertions that Western technology offers the only means to bettering a community's condition denies the value of localized traditional knowledge for self-reliant development.

Race and culture

Historically, the assumption that evolution constituted progress has been rather closely linked in Western thought with the view that the 'level' of cultural attainment of non-Western populations (so-called 'races') is linked to their biological constitution. Although this provided archaeologists in the past with a convenient shorthand – 'the Beaker People', 'the Battle-Axe people' – the premise has no part in neo-Darwinian theory. On the contrary, socioecologists generally accept that humans as a species have evolved a substantial capacity for learned behaviour, the content of culture. The capacity is genetically determined, but not the content (Alexander 1979, pp. 65–7, Irons 1983, p. 199). Culturally acquired traits may in turn influence our genetic constitution, as is shown by the evolution of sickling and the maintenance of lactose in adulthood in response to agriculture (Irons 1983, pp. 172–3). Genetic variation in humans, however, occurs predominantly within rather than between populations (Lewontin 1972). There are a number of ethnographic studies which demonstrate that individuals may rapidly shift from one cultural configuration to another if it appears a profitable strategy: from hunter-gatherer to pastoralist or vice versa (Schrire 1980, Hodder 1982, p. 98); from farmer to pastoralist (Barth 1967); from shifting cultivator to member of a centralized state (Leach 1954, Condori 1994).

Twagiramutara (1994) argues that the Rwanda categories *Twa, Hutu*, and *Tutsi* are cultural constructs, the names aiding recognition between heterogeneous social units, so that anyone integrated into a neighbourhood practising a predominantly agricultural mode of production was considered a Hutu, and so forth. He regards the concept of them as genetically distinct populations on different levels of cultural evolution as a colonial imposition. Twagiramutara further questions the likelihood that people attributed the widespread clan name Abasinga (and its variants) constitute a biologically discrete unit. Rakotoarisoa (1994) criticizes Malagasy researchers for their willingness to identify with their Arab or Austronesian antecedents, but not with their Africanness. He plausibly argues that this attitude derives from the supposition that certain ethnic groups are intrinsically superior to others, and points out that the absurdity of such a contention in the light of evidence that later Austronesian settlers possessed a different mode of production to earlier groups from the same region, which allowed them to impose their political and economic system upon the earlier arrivals. Mangi (1994) questions the need to explain the diversity of contemporary cultures in Papua New Guinea in terms of waves of immigration from Asia, arguing that local diversification offers a more likely explanation.

Richardson (1994) describes how Tasmanian Aborigines were formerly thought to be related to the Neanderthals, and gives instances of the barbaric treatment of Aborigines brought about by the consequent rush to acquire specimens. Similar evidence regarding the treatment of Native Americans is cited by McGuire (1994). Just as Australian Aborigines were at first regarded as a dying race, incapable of adjusting to the colonial onslaught, so the excavation of Indian graves was misled by the assumption that either as a race or cultural group the Indians would inevitably disappear, either because they were already 'the veriest ruins of mankind' or because contact with civilization had reduced them to 'savagery'. Indians were said to be incapable of progress along the supposed unilineal evolutionary ladder, and doubt was cast on their ability to have constructed complex monuments (cf. Trigger's assessment of 'Colonialist archaeology', 1984, pp. 360–3). Westerners frequently have difficulty accepting the scale of non-Western cultural achievements. Mangi (1994) draws attention to the achievements of New Guinea peoples, having developed the technology to cross to offshore islands by 10,000 years ago, and constructing irrigation channels in the Highlands 9,000 years ago (cf. Trigger's 'Nationalist archaeology', 1984). Gilliam's opening quotation is apposite (1994).

Appropriation of the past's remains

Perhaps the most pervasive theme of this book is the extent to which outsiders' research interests fail to match the concerns of indigenous communities. A number of contributors conclude that this problem cannot be rectified unless indigenous peoples take control over access to their own past. Rakotoarisoa (1994) graphically documents the obsession of archaeologists working in Madagascar with the colonial period. The Aikios (1994) note a similar imbalance between the paucity of archaeological research into the nomadic Sámi's past as against research into the incursion of peoples practising agriculture. Beauregard (1994) finds a tendency among New England archaeologists to assume that changes in indigenous culture arose from continuous European contact, and that 'events prior to the establishment of the colonies there were relatively unimportant'. Kishani (1994) looks at the way in which Africans have been encouraged to believe that only European languages provide an adequate vehicle for the analysis of African culture. The Inuit, according to Bielawski (1994), class archaeologists with other whites, as people who will never stay for long, will barely begin to understand Inuit culture, and will at worst take something away with them for profit: income, minerals or artefacts.

More contentious even than these instances are those in which indigenous material remains are appropriated as symbols of national identity, and human skeletons exhumed for purposes of biological research. The former is documented by McGuire (1994) and Condori (1994). The latter problem constitutes another major theme in this book. Hubert (1994) has provided an overview of this issue, bringing together for the first time the evidence of variability in Judeo-Christian practices, as well as the current demands and problems of indigenous peoples. Her information derives both from interviews of participants at the World Archaeological Congress and from first-hand experience in American Indian and Australian Aboriginal communities.

McGuire notes that the notion of the Indian as the first 'American' was part of the effort to construct a distinctive national identity in 19th-century United States, in much the same way that Australians and New Zealanders have appropriated indigenous art styles as emblems of their country's uniqueness on tea towels, tourist advertisements, and commercial logos. But McGuire argues that Native American cultures were more specifically appropriated by archaeologists and natural historians as the base on which to establish themselves as academic disciplines. When efforts to conserve the natural wonders of the United States landscape were initiated, the surviving features of indigenous culture were regarded as national monuments and archaeological resources, not as elements of a continuing and distinct Indian way of life.

It is not surprising that American Indians construe such activities as an attack on their religious practices, customs and traditions, as Hammil and Cruz (1994) make plain. The same is true in Australia where, Richardson (1994) argues, indigenous groups are entitled to be involved in handling material that is both spiritually and morally theirs. Condori (1994) describes a similar situation in Bolivia.

Who owns indigenous burials?

A careful examination of the arguments against indigenous control of Native American skeletons shows that there is more to them than empirically orientated propositions. No doubt, as Reeder has put the anti-reburial position, 'human skeletal remains are particularly useful in studying prehistoric social structure and status systems, health and diet, and demography' (Reeder 1985, p. 8). The validity of such a position is not called into question by pointing out that its proponents also voice constitutive propositions that are not open to empirical test. The assertion that 'ancient skeletons are the remnants of unduplicable evolutionary events . . .' is empirically testable. To continue '. . . which all living and future peoples have the right to know about and understand. In other words ancient human skeletons belong to everyone' (ACPAC 1986, p. 2) is to move to another level. There is no obvious way in which the value of an object determines who owns it. It will determine how anxious people are to keep or acquire ownership. The analogous claim 'all peoples value good art, therefore no valuable paintings should remain in private collections' may make its political implications clearer.

Smith puts a similar view, contending that although it is not ethical to accede to requests for reburial unless they come from living members of the dead person's tribe (Smith n.d., pp. 12, 14), it is ethical for archaeologists to 'protect the data base of their discipline' by opposing reburial (p. 13); in other words, the value of the exhumed skeletons for archaeology is deemed sufficient to determine who owns them. A second constitutive proposition which emerges from the ACPAC Newsletter cited is that living Native Americans are 'Indians', not Indians. By some unspecified criterion, the continuous transformation of Indian culture in response to colonial domination has been represented, rather in the manner adopted by Newton and Linnaeus, as an absolute dichotomy. Smith adopts a similar, but not identical, position by choosing the 'tribe' as an arbitrary cut-off point. If the dead person did not demonstrably belong to the tribe of those who demand reburial, 'the biological/genetic or cultural tie to the skeletal remains is so weak, so tenuous, that any reburial request should be denied' (Smith n.d., p. 12). Statistics are notoriously open to several interpretations but Smith cites a survey which showed not only that 39 per cent of Indian tribal leaders felt non-Indian burials should be avoided in construction work, but that 54 per cent felt 'non-tribal prehistoric' burials should be avoided, in support of his position (Smith n.d., p. 11).

The opponents of reburial have no difficulty in detecting beliefs in the fate of the soul as constitutive propositions. They are less ready to accept that the pro-reburial lobby also has empirical evidence to support its position. Buried skeletons are not purely biological material. The act of burial demonstrably renders them artefacts of culture, and their value is therefore in part constituted on cultural premises. American Indians Against Desecration contend that native burials contain the remains of their ancestors, and physical anthropologists are generally prepared on empirical evidence, to identify a skeleton as indigenous or European. Christy Turner's assumption 'that the present state of knowledge about worldwide genetic prehistory is so inadequate that very few if any living populations can scientifically validate claims for exclusive *genetic* ancestry with prehistoric skeletal populations' glosses over this general congruence of Indian and White opinion (cited ACPAC 1986, p. 2).

The link between the advocacy of archaeological theory and the enactment of policy emerges clearly from the differential treatment accorded White and Indian bones in the United States. The handling of White people's bones is premised on the contention that they are meaningfully located in a continuing cultural tradition, albeit one in which, as McGuire (1994) shows, burial practices have changed markedly over time. Indian bones, however, are consigned to a lapsed cultural tradition or, worse, are considered not to constitute cultural artefacts at all but mere biological data. McGuire deals frankly with the different constraints that guided his research into colonial and native burials. He concludes that relations of power govern such differences, and that the political dimension is obscured, both to the public and to the archaeological community, by historically constructed ideologies. Zimmerman (1994b) describes his similar experience, and the poignant effect upon him of discovering personal goods in an Indian burial. He argues that archaeologists make political use of their theories in defence of access to Indian skeletal material. Moore (1994) documents the way in which US federal law continues, with the support of archaeologists, to define Indian grave sites as 'archaeological resources', sanctioning the storage of Indian skeletal material and grave goods in museums. Why, he asks, should the bodies of Custer's soldiers who died at Little Big Horn be reburied, but not those of the Sioux? Moore shows that from the outset, Indian burials were deemed in federal legislation to be 'scientific resources'. It is fair to ask whether 'science' should rest content with thus becoming an agent of government policy. In other words, does such policy do justice to the nature of the data constituted in burials? The premise that indigenous human bones constitute biological, not cultural artefacts is discussed by a number of contributors. Richardson describes how Australian Aboriginal skeletons were studied to answer questions supposedly raised by Darwin's theory of evolution. McGuire argues that Native Americans were similarly regarded, in the 19th century, 'as objects of natural history, their remains to be collected like fossils and botanical specimens'. Zimmerman contends that such an approach continues among some modern archaeologists.

It is noteworthy that the Louisiana Court of Appeals, cited by Moore, recognized in 1986 that the burying of goods in a grave did not constitute their abandonment. Chief Seattle, whose speech is quoted by Turner (1994), expressly stated that in ceding land to the Whites, his people did not relinquish an interest in the graves of their ancestors. Hammil and Cruz (1994) present ample evidence that other Indian communities continue to hold such concerns.

Respect for Indian graves does not demand a denial of empirical evidence, but rather an acceptance that within the data lies part of the evidence that indigenous burials belong to an alternative cultural tradition. The issue, as Hammil and Cruz (1994), Moore and Zimmerman (1994b) argue, is one of the right to cultural self-determination, to religious freedom, not the suppression of objectivity.

The situational relevance of cultural unity

Although some archaelogists are willing to accept that changes in indigenous material culture over time refute Indians' contention that the sanctity of burials has a basis in cultural tradition, much of the material of value to colonial archaeology was once household refuse or abandoned house sites. Does this prove the argument a developer might advance, that the value archaeologists attribute to broken or discarded artefacts had no basis in colonial cultural tradition? Of course it does not. The contemporary value of surviving artefacts for archaeologists lies precisely in the transformation of White American culture through time. The concern of living Indians for indigenous burials regardless of arguments about tribal affiliation derives in part from the opposition *brought about by the colonial impact*, between indigenous and European cultures. Smith, I consider, misrepresents

King's arguments on this score (Smith n.d., pp. 13, 14, 16). Mulvaney, similarly, neglects to note that although Australian Aboriginal cultures vary in time and space, when contrasted to other hunter-gatherer traditions, let alone European Australian culture, they do have a distinctive unity (cf. Layton 1986).

The narrowness with which a continuing interest in the remains of the dead is defined in US law is arguably a consequence of the fact that disputes over exhumation will normally arise within the community. The parties are situationally defined as those uniquely connected to the deceased versus the proponents of other interests within the community, such as road widening or building construction. Where the opposed parties belong to different cultural traditions, the situational relevance broadens.

As McGuire notes (1994), the ability to demonstrate genealogical connectedness is conditioned by cultural factors. Evans-Pritchard argued that among the Nuer of East Africa, socially recognized common descent was situationally relevant. He exemplified his point through an analogy with British culture: if asked where he belonged his answer would depend on who posed the question. To another resident of Oxford he would give the name of his street; elsewhere in Britain he would reply 'Oxford'; if abroad, and asked by a foreigner, the appropriate reply would be Britain. In the same way Nuer identify themselves as members of a hamlet, lineage or tribe according to context (Evans-Pritchard 1940). The Louisiana Court of Appeal finding cited by Moore captures this phenomenon without abandoning the notion of genealogical connectedness, reasoning that at least some members of the Tunica-Biloxi tribe are descendants of the buried Indians, and therefore the tribe is the owner of their remains. In some cases the situationally defined opposition is even wider. It may seem an irony that a sense of national identity among Native Americans or Australians has been brought about by external domination, but it is this which explains why, for instance, a modern Sioux is concerned about the exhumation of the skeleton of an Indian from another group (Zimmerman, 1994b), and why pan-Indian groups such as American Indians Against Desecration (Hammil and Cruz, 1994) form collectively to oppose the actions of European Americans.

It is not only in the definition of legally valid objections to reburial that the law may favour certain sectors of society. The Aikios refer to the recurrent legal convention that nomadic peoples possess no ownership rights over the land they exploit. This doctrine contributed to the failure of the first attempt to gain legal recognition of Aboriginal land ownership in the Northern Territory of Australia. Nancy Williams has published a detailed study of the origin of the concept that nomadic people lack land ownership in the period of the colonial expansion (Williams 1985). She demonstrates that it was not based on empirical evidence of land tenure among nomads, but on speculative theoretical constructs which presented the opposition between European and exotic societies in terms favourable to European expansion.

The way forward

It is not the intention of contributors to argue that the interests of archaeologists must always be opposed to those of indigenous communities.

Mangi (1994), putting the view of an indigenous researcher from Papua New Guinea, looks at ways in which the findings of archaeology might be communicated to ordinary citizens. Bielawski (1994) reports on the success with which young Inuit have been involved in an archaeological field school. Richardson (1994) urges that research results be communicated more freely to Aboriginal communities in Australia (a view also promoted by the Australian Institute of Aboriginal Studies), and notes that information about past diet, medical, and cultural practices may be of benefit to such communities. For this reason, she argues, indigenous control over archaeological material will not necessarily prevent further research. Research funded by the AIAS must have the approval of the Aboriginal community involved. Hammil and Cruz (1994) report the benefits gained from collaboration between American Indians and archaeologists, as do Zimmerman (1994b) and Reeder (1985). Bielawski (1994) notes that indigenous Inuit organizations are hiring their own archaeologists. The Avataq Cultural Institute of Northern Quebec encourages outside agencies to consult with Inuit prior to undertaking research which directly involves Inuit cultural and environmental concerns. Kishani (1994) laments the failure of Western linguists to involve Africans as equal partners in their research, with the consequence that informants may not benefit from the research to which they have contributed. The Avataq Institute has sought to establish an Inuit language commission.

Several contributors question the academic assumption that indigenous communities lack an interest in their own past, a fallacy which is examined in detail in the related volume in this Series, *Who needs the past* (Layton 1994).

While contributors to the present book urge their fellow archaeologists in various ways to take account of the values, aspirations, and knowledge of indigenous peoples, they consider that the result will in the long run benefit both archaeological theory and practice. Zimmerman (1994b) takes archaeologists to task for their arrogant assumption that they alone are interested in Native American peoples' past. He links the inference with the propensity to regard Indian culture as extinct. In his second chapter (1994a), however, Zimmerman notes that Native Americans do not regard their history as a series of discrete episodes; there is, rather, continuity between past and present. Bielawski similarly observes that traditional Inuit views of the past were structured in a very different way to the archaeologist's chronology. Gilliam (1994) and Kishani (1994) see such different modes of interpretation in a positive light, although Rakotoarisoa (1994) and Twagiramutara (1994) anticipate that archaeology may undermine indigenous cultural constructs. Rakotoarisoa (1994) concludes that it would be politically imprudent to propagate archaeological evidence which undermines political ideology. Mangi (1994) and the Aikios (1994), however, demonstrate that the results of archaeological research may have an effect on policy of benefit to indigenous communities, in the first instance by providing evidence of a common origin for the diverse groups of Papua New Guinea, in the second by substantiating long-term occupation by Sámi.

Co-operation with archaeologists from the Third World and minority groups will frequently mean that Western archaeologists must modify their goals, or rethink their ideas. It is no longer possible to make the comfortable assumption that non-Western peoples live in a timeless present, that their cultures are inherently unchanging or that such people have willingly assimilated to Western ideas and practices. Appropriating the material remains of other peoples' past can no longer be justified by the arrogant assumption that 'we know best', that the advance of knowledge is a Western prerogative. All explanatory models rest on certain assumptions and are capable of political application. When archaeological theories are used to justify policy decisions it is not enough to disclaim an interest in politics and retreat into an ideal world of pure 'science'. Rather, the archaeologist must ask whether the theoretical premises on which he or she relied remain justifiable, or demand revision. The intimate connection between the politics of colonial domination and the collection of exotic material must be acknowledged (Gidri 1974). Much of the evidence archaeologists use to reconstruct the past is the product of cultures whose values differ from those of the West, but it is through these values that the significance of much archaeological evidence is constituted. If people from other cultural traditions question the archaeologist's models of stability, change, and discontinuity, or the association of cultures and genetic populations, their criticisms should not too hastily be dismissed as unscientific. Instead, the evidence should be looked at afresh. This book sets out to show how archaeology can benefit from such a reappraisal.

Acknowledgements

I am grateful to David Knight and Malcolm Smith for their help in examining the two case studies in the notes. A special note of thanks is owed to Rob Foley. Our discussions about the problems of recognizing objectivity formed the germ of this introduction. Peter Ucko made helpful comments on a draft version.

Notes

1   The quotation which Ardener provides from Newton's published correspondence for the year 1675 (Ardener 1971, p. lxxxiv) seems unequivocal; Newton sought a friend's help 'to draw with a pencil lines cross the image . . . where every one of the seven afore-named colours was most full and brisk, and also where he judged the fullest confines of them to be'. However, the story is more complex. Westfall points out that Newton's theory of colour reversed the basic assumption of 2 000 years of optical research in positing that white was not the pure and simple colour it seemed, but a heterogeneous mixture of individual, pure and simple colours (Westfall 1980, p. 170). Newton at first thought in terms of a two-colour system comprising blue and red (Westfall 1980, p. 161); by 1666 he had identified five – red, yellow, green, blue, purple; from 1669 he frequently spoke of seven colours (Westfall 1980, pp. 171, 213). In Westfall's assess-ment, however, although Newton compared the positions of the seven colours 'in the spectrum to the divisions of the musical octave, he understood that such divisions were wholly arbitrary' (Westfall 1980, p. 213).

2   In later life, Linnaeus modified his position and contended that God had created a smaller number of species than exist at present, many extant species and genera having arisen through hybridization between members of the original set. Linnaeus had experi-mental evidence for hybridization (Davis and Heywood 1963, pp. 19–20).

References

ACPAC 1986 *ACPAC Newsletter*, November 1986. Garden Grove, Calif.: The American com-mittee for the preservation of archaeological collections.

Ahern, E. M. 1982. Rules in oracles and games. *Man* (n.s.), **17**, 302–12.

Aikio, M. and P. Aikio 1994. A chapter in the history of the colonization of Sami lands: the forced migration of Norwegian reindeer Sami to Finland in the 1800s. In R. Layton (ed.) *Conflict in the Archaeology of Living Traditions*, 116–130. London and New York: Routledge.

Alexander, R. 1979. Evolution and culture. In *Evolutionary biology and human social behaviour*, N. Chagnon & W. Irons (eds), 59–78. North Scituate, Mass: Duxbury.

Ardener, E. 1971. Introductory essay: social anthropology and language. In *Social Anthropology and Language*, E. Ardener (ed.), ix–cii. London: Tavistock.

Asad, T. (ed.) 1973. *Anthropology and the colonial encounter*. London: Ithica Press.

Barth, F. 1967. On the study of social change. *American Anthropologist* **69**, 661–9.

Beauregard, A. D. 1994. Relations of production and exchange in 17th-century New England: interpretive contexts for the archaeology of culture contact. In R. Layton (ed.) *Conflict in the Archaeology of Living Traditions*, 22–31. London and New York: Routledge.

Berreman, G. 1968. Is anthropology alive? Social responsibility in anthropology. *Current Anthropology*, **9**, 391–6.

Bickford, A. 1979. The last Tasmanian: superb documentary or racist fantasy? *Filmnews* (Sydney), January, 11–14.

Bielawski, E. 1994. Dual perceptions of the past: archaeology and Inuit culture. In R. Layton (ed.) *Conflict in the Archaeology of Living Traditions*; pp. 228–236. London and New York: Routledge.

Binford, L. R. 1971. Mortuary practices: their study and their potential. In *Social dimensions of mortuary practices*, Memoir No. 25, Society for American Archaeology. *American Antiquity*, **36**, 6–29.

Binford, L. R. 1980. Willow smoke and dogs' tails. *American Antiquity*, **45**, 4–20.

Binford, L. R. 1987. Data, relativism and archaeological science. *Man* (n.s.), **22**, 391–404.

Castile, G. 1974. Federal Indian policy and the sustained enclave: an anthropological perspective. *Human Organization*, **33**, 219–28.

Condori, C. M. 1994. History and prehistory in Bolivia: what about the Indians? In R. Layton (ed.) *Conflict in the Archaeology of Living Traditions*, 46–59. London and New York: Routledge.

Davis, P. H. & V. H. Heywood 1963. *Principles of angiosperm taxonomy*. Edinburgh: Oliver & Boyd.

Durkheim, E. 1938. *The rules of sociological method*. (Trans. S. A. Solovay & J. H. Mueller.) New York: Free Press.

Evans-Pritchard, E. E. 1940. *The Nuer*. Oxford: Oxford University Press.

Evans-Pritchard, E. E. 1976. *Witchcraft, oracles and magic among the Azande*. Oxford: Oxford University Press. First edition 1937.

Geertz, C. 1973. Thick description: toward an interpretive theory of culture. In *The interpretation of cultures*, C. Geertz, 3–30. London: Hutchinson.

Gellner, E. 1970. Concepts and society. In *Rationality*, B. Wilson (ed.), 18–49. Oxford: Blackwell.

Gidri, A. 1974. Imperialism and archaeology. *Race*, **15**, 431–59.

Gilliam, A. 1994. On the problem of historicist categories in theories of human development. In R. Layton (ed.) *Conflict in the Archaeology of Living Traditions*, 68–81. London and New York: Routledge.

Grillo, R. 1985. Applied anthropology in the 1980s: retrospect and prospect. In *Social anthropology and development policy*, R. Grillo & A. Rew (eds), 1–36. London: Tavistock.

Gulliver, P. H. 1985. An applied anthropologist in East Africa during the colonial period. In *Social anthropology and development policy*, R. Grillo & A. Rew (eds), 37–57. London: Tavistock.

Hammil, J. and R. Cruz 1994. Statement of American Indians Against Desecration before the World Archaeological Congress. In R. Layton (ed.) *Conflict in the Archaeology of Living Traditions*, 195–200. London and New York: Routledge.

Hodder, I. 1982. *Symbols in action*. Cambridge: Cambridge University Press.

Horton, R. 1960. A definition of religion and its uses. *Journal of the Royal Anthropological Institute* **90**, 201–26.

Horton, R. 1964. Ritual man in Africa. *Africa* **34**, 85–104.

Hubert, J. 1994. A proper place for the dead: a critical review of the 'reburial' issue. In R. Layton (ed.) *Conflict in the Archaeology of Living Traditions*, 131–166. London and New York: Routledge.

Hymes, D. (ed.) 1974. *Reinventing anthropology*. New York: Random House.

Irons, W. 1983. Human female reproductive strategies. In *Social behaviour of female vertebrates*, S. K. Wasser (ed.), 169–213. New York: Academic Press.

Kishani, B. T. 1994. The role of language in African perceptions of the past: an appraisal of African language policies and practices. In R. Layton (ed.) *Conflict in the Archaeology of Living Traditions*, 97–115. London and New York: Routledge.

Kuhn, T. S. 1970. *The structure of scientific revolutions*. Chicago: University of Chicago Press.

Kuper, A. 1983. *Anthropology and anthropologists: the modern British school*. London: Routledge.

Layton, R. 1977. Naturalism and cultural relativity in art. In *Form in indigenous art*, P. J. Ucko (ed.), 33–43. Canberra: Australian Institute of Aboriginal Studies.

Layton, R. 1985. Anthropology and the Aboriginal land rights act in northern Australia. In *Social anthropology and development policy*, R. Grillo and A. Rew (eds), 148–67. London: Tavistock.

Layton, R. 1986. Political and territorial structures among hunter-gatherers. *Man* (n.s.) **21**, 18–33.

Layton, R. 1987. The use of ethnographic parallels in interpreting Upper Palaeolithic rock art. In *Comparative anthropology*, L. Holy (ed.), 210–39. Oxford: Blackwell.

Layton, R. (ed.) 1994. *Who needs the past? Indigenous values in archaeology*. London and New York: Routledge.

Leach, E. R. 1954. *Political systems of highland Burma*. London: Bell.

Lewontin, R. C. 1972. The apportionment of human diversity. *Evolutionary Biology*, **6** 381–98.

Mangi, J. 1994. The role of archaeology in nation building. In R. Layton (ed.) *Conflict in the Archaeology of Living Traditions*, 217–227. London and New York: Routledge.

McGuire, R. 1994. The sanctity of the grave: White concepts and American Indian burials. In R. Layton (ed.) *Conflict in the Archaeology of Living Traditions*, 167–184. London and New York: Routledge.

Moore, S. 1994. Federal Indian burial policy: historical anachronism or contemporary reality? In R. Layton (ed.) *Conflict in the Archaeology of Living Traditions*, 201–210. London and New York: Routledge.

Mulvaney, J. 1986. 'A sense of making history': Australian Aboriginal Studies 1961–1986. *Australian Aboriginal Studies* **2**, 48–56.

Needham, R. 1963. Introduction. In *Primitive classification*, E. Durkheim & M. Mauss, xii–xviii. London: Cohen and West.

Radcliffe-Brown, A. R. 1952. On the concept of function in social science. In *Structure and function in primitive society*, A. R. Radcliffe-Brown, 178–87. London: Cohen and West.

Rakotoarisoa, J. 1994. The burden of an encumbered inheritance upon the study of the past of Madagascar. In R. Layton (ed.) *Conflict in the Archaeology of Living Traditions*, 82–87. London and New York: Routledge.

Reeder, R. L. 1985. Reburial: science versus religion? *Missouri Archaeological Society Quarterly* **2**(4), 7–16.

Richardson, L. 1994. The acquisition, storage and handling of Aboriginal skeletal remains in museums; an indigenous perspective. In R. Layton (ed.) *Conflict in the Archaeology of Living Traditions*, 185–188. London and New York: Routledge.

Rubertone, P. 1994. Archaeology, colonialism and 17th-century Native America: towards an alternative interpretation. In R. Layton (ed.) *Conflict in the Archaeology of Living Traditions*, 32–45. London and New York: Routledge.

Ryan, L. 1981. *The Aboriginal Tasmanians*. Brisbane: University of Queensland Press.

Schrire, C., 1980. An enquiry into the evolutionary status of San hunter-gatherers. *Human Ecology* **8**, 9–32.

Smith, B. D., n.d. URPIE logic: an analysis of the structure of the supporting arguments of universal reburial proponents. Washington, DC: Department of Anthropology, National Museum of Natural History, Smithsonian Institution.

Trigger, Bruce G. 1984. Alternative archaeologies: nationalist, colonialist, imperialist. *Man* **19**, 355–70.

Trivers, R. 1985. *Social evolution*. Menlo Park, California: Cummins.

Turner, E. 1994. The souls of my dead brothers. In R. Layton (ed.) *Conflict in the Archaeology of Living Traditions*, 189–194. London and New York: Routledge.

Twagiramutara, P. 1994. Archaeological and anthropological hypotheses concerning the origin of ethnic divisions in sub-Saharan Africa. In R. Layton (ed.) *Conflict in the Archaeology of Living Traditions*, 88–96. London and New York: Routledge.

Ucko, P. J. 1969. Ethnography and archaeological interpretation of funerary remains. *World Archaeology* **1**, 262–80.

Ucko, P. J. 1983. Australian academic archaeology: Aboriginal transformation of its aims and practices. *Australian Archaeology* **16**, 11–26.

Westfall, R. S. 1980. *Never at rest: a biography of Isaac Newton*. Cambridge: Cambridge University Press.

Williams, N. 1985. *The Yolngu and their land*. Canberra: Australian Institute of Aboriginal Studies.

Winch, P. 1970. Understanding a primitive society. In *Rationality*, B. Wilson (ed.), 78–111. Oxford: Blackwell.

Wolf, E. 1982. *Europe and the people without history*. Berkeley: University of California Press.

Zimmerman, L. J. 1994a. Human bones as symbols of power: aboriginal American belief systems toward bones and 'grave-robbing' archaeologists. In R. Layton (ed.) *Conflict in the Archaeology of Living Traditions*, 211–216. London and New York: Routledge.

Zimmerman, L. J. 1994b. Made radical by my own: an archaeologist learns to accept reburial. In R. Layton (ed.) *Conflict in the Archaeology of Living Traditions*, 60–67. London and New York: Routledge.

Chapter 20

Politics

Raphael Samuel

I

Historically, preservationism is a cause which owes at least as much to the Left as to the Right. The founders of the Society for the Protection of Ancient Buildings – William Morris and Philip Webb – were socialists. 'Green belts' – the exclusion zones around the city where property developers were forbidden to build – were a creation of the 1930s Labour-led London County Council. National Parks were legislated into being by the Attlee Labour government, which also laid the legislative groundwork for Nature Conservancy and wildlife reserves. From the point of view of the National Trust, as John Gaze, one of its land agents at the time recalls, the landslide Labour victory of 1945 was an unquestioned good.

> The advent of a Labour Government with a large majority in 1945 brought new influences to bear on the Trust. Governments had never been hostile to the Trust, some had been positively helpful and we have seen how Baldwin felt about it. Nevertheless, now for the first time there was a Government not only prepared but anxious to advance the Trust's interests. In part this was due simply to the feeling that the Trust was a Good Thing; its work had been very much in line with the attitude of middle-class Fabians whose influence was strong in the Labour Party. There was also a feeling that the old order really was at an end, that there were some pieces which needed to be picked up. It was thought that the organisation would be a useful instrument to do that and might later be taken over by Government when convenient.[1]

In Australia, though heritage came under attack, at the time of the bi-centenary celebrations of 1988, as giving a licence to racism, it seems on the contrary to have been serviceable to the coming out of hitherto stigmatized and inferior minorities. Indeed, the recovery and advancement of Aboriginal culture seems to have been the fulcrum for the emancipatory movement which, on the issue of land rights in the Northern Territories, has just registered so signal a victory.[2] The conservation movement in Australia has at least one of its origins in the 'green' initiatives of the left-wing, semi-syndicalist building workers' union. The establishment of a Committee of Inquiry into the National Estate in 1973, leading in 1976 to the enactment of the Australian Heritage Bill and the subsequent compilation of a register of protected properties; and the establishment of a Committee of Inquiry on Museums and National Collections, leading to the Museum of Australia Act of 1980, were all measures of Labour administrations, while the environmental direct action groups – such as the one which involved itself in tremendous struggle over wilderness sites in Tasmania – were ultra-radical in character. A recent commentator ascribes the success of these campaigns to a fund of radical patriotism:

> . . . the willingness of Labour administrations, state and federal, to preserve historic sites from threatened destruction by developers served as a key emblem of this 'new nationalism' and its commitment to representing the interests of 'all Australians' against what were seen as the socially destructive activities of both international corporations and domestic élites.[3]

In the United States 'heritage' is notoriously the name given to one of the New Right's best-funded foundations, dedicated, in the 1980s, to the global fight against Communism. But the term has been adopted, no less affirmatively, for black-power cultural initiatives in the field of museology while 'Afro-American', the term adopted since the 1960s by black consciousness movements of all kinds, highlights the tremendous preoccupation with historical roots.[4] In the sphere of conventional politics, conservation-led redevelopment, on the lines of Lowell, Mass., has been the grand Democratic Party panacea for disindustrialization in the rust-belt states. Preservationism in the United States may take one of its inspirations from such exercises in historical make-believe as the Rockefeller-funded Williamsburg (the old colonial 'living history' town established in 1928) or Henry Ford's Greenfield Village, but it also owes a good deal to the cultural initiatives of the liberal New Deal era, which legislated the first protection for historic buildings and set in train a remarkable project of federal-funded ethnography – notably in the recording of slave narratives, and in the collection of negro spirituals and blues.[5]

In France, the historical association of 'heritage' with the Left comes from the French Revolution itself. The term *patrimoine* was a Jacobin coinage, an inspiration of the egalitarian priest, l'Abbé Grégoire, who used it both to combat iconoclasts and wreckers (he invented the term 'vandal' to describe them) and to establish the nation's claim to the treasures of the châteaux, the monasteries and the palaces.[6] For a century and more the idea of *patrimoine* ran in tandem with that of republican education and the creation of republican consciousness, and this embraced *all* aspects of heritage, not only 'arts et traditions populaires' (in which a notable museum was set up in the period of the Popular Front),[7] but also the châteaux: when they were opened up to *son et lumière* historical displays in the 1960s, some at least of the promoters hailed it as a further triumph of the republican idea.

In Germany, where *Volkskunde* was appropriated wholesale by the Nazis,[8] and used to give historic credence to the idea of a racial soul, the 'new-wave' social historians of the 1960s, like Enlightenment-oriented radicals generally, steered clear of anything with a *Volkisch* taint. By the same token, because of Nazi instrumentalization of former movements, any idea of back-to-the-land was deeply suspect. Yet in practice, the Federal Republic of the 1970s and 1980s was second only to Britain in its enthusiasm for industrial archaeology; it was the Social Democratic *Länder* who took the lead in promoting working museums, just as it was Social-Democratic municipalities who were most generous in initiating and resourcing town heritage centres, oral history projects and 'people's exhibitions'.[9] Historical suspicions of Nature mysticism did not prevent the green movement from capturing the imagination of a whole generation of the student Left, and indeed of presenting itself, as it did to the dissident Rudolph Barho, as the alternative to a histori-cally exhausted and ethically bankrupt Communism.[10]

II

In Britain, when 'heritage' first came under attack, in 1987, it seemed quite plausible to think of it as reactionary, and to argue that it fitted into, and could be seen as an expres-sion of, the dominant ideology, and ruling politics, of the time. The Conservatives were riding high after three general election victories, and the Falklands War – politically popular as well as being a military success – seemed to mark the comeback of a know-nothing 'Little Englandism' in which dreams of vanished supremacies served as consola-tions for the collapse of British power. By the same token the museums explosion – and in particular the rise of the open-air industrial museum – was seen as consolation for decline of the British economy and the departure of manufacture and production from these shores. Likewise in the property boom of the 1980s, 'gentrification' – the name given to the middle-class led rehabilitation of the inner city – was thought to be creating a new *rentier* class. Heritage, in short, was Thatcherism in period dress. It represented a posthu-mous victory of the aristocratic spirit over the levelling tendency, and egalitarian poten-tial, of the post-war settlement.

In the light of subsequent development, as well as perhaps a belated recognition of heritage's popular roots, these confident equations and (from a radical point of view) pejo-rative associations may seem over-done. For one thing the Conservatives' attachment to the notion of heritage seems quite shallow. Nicholas Ridley, at the Department of the Environment, was quite as ruthless in ignoring or overriding conservationist opinion as any modernizer of the 1960s, though doing so on grounds of the sanctity of private prop-erty rather than the imperatives of comprehensive redevelopment. The increasingly restrictive character of environmental legislation makes it obnoxious to the free-market right, while the Tory Party's 'Little Englanders' are offended by the European (or Ameri-can) provenance of ecology.

There is no doubt that from a capitalist point of view, whatever the discomfort to the motorway lobby or the property developers, 'heritage' has been a success, or at any rate a project which it can accommodate. The rent-map of London shows far higher premiums for office accommodation in Mayfair – where Westminster Council has listed more than half the buildings, and where the Grosvenor Estate jealously protects the eighteenth-century street grid – than the City of London, where the Corporation, ever since the great rebuilding got under way in the 1950s, has been even more destructive than Hitler's bombers.[11] Then again, one could point to the way in which the property developers have learnt to incorporate an element of conservation in their clearances; indeed it sometimes seems that for a comprehensive work of destruction to begin (I am thinking of the business village which has been built on the corpse of the old East India Company offices in Houndsditch) it needs the accolade of English Heritage, or the Fine Arts Commission, to say that a really imaginative redevelopment is envisaged.

Nevertheless, among property owners, to judge by a stream of attacks on 'retrophilia' in the quality press, there is a rising tide of complaint about heritage officers – a bunch of crazed aesthetes, as they sometimes appear, attempting to regulate the shape of the last corbel; and when the motorway lobby resumes its onward march, as it is threatening to do, the chorus of recrimination seems likely to grow. The reversal of the conservation order on Mappin and Webb – the last block of Victorian building in the Golden Mile – and the refusal of one for the Bankside power station (the government has sold the site to British Nuclear Fuels) perhaps marks the turning of the tide (government-instigated cuts in the archaeological services point in a similar direction). Mrs Thatcher, a ruthless modernizer, though espousing 'Victorian values' was not averse to using the word 'Victorian' as a pejorative, and treating it as synonymous with the out-of-date.[12] Her successors follow suit. 'We are not in the heritage business', the Minister of Health declared, when, to the outrage of both medical and metropolitan opinion, she announced her determination to press ahead with the closure of London's most ancient and prestigious teaching hospital.

On the other side of the party-political divide, 'heritage' in the 1980s proved very serviceable to hard-pressed Labour authorities. Deprived of their building programmes (from 1918 onwards the lodestar of municipal idealism) they turned instead to consortium-led redevelopment, using 'historic' buildings as a bargaining counter to negotiate with would-be developers – as Glasgow City Council has done with its recreated 'Merchants' City'; or, like Southwark Council with its newly opened Thames Path – trading off planning permissions in exchange for schemes of environmental enhancement. Labour councils also turned to 'heritage', or heritage-related projects, as a new source of service-sector jobs. In a climate of spending cuts and Exchequer-imposed economies, it was one of the very few fields of municipal enterprise in which they could still attract outside support – if not from government itself, then from the county council, or from one of the Department of the Environment's burgeoning quangos. Faced, as many of them were in the recession of 1977–83, with the run-down of local industries and the near collapse of the local economy, they turned to conservation as the grand remedy for urban blight.

In ways such as the foregoing, heritage and its allies have arguably given a new lease of life – and a new visual form – to what used to be called, in the 1890s and 1900s, when it found expression in municipal libraries, swimming baths and bandstands, the Civic Gospel. It is one of the very few areas in which local government can still take a lead, and almost the only one where public-sector employment has increased.

Notionally backward-looking and apparently reactionary, conservation has been for some twenty years or more a magnet for cultural dissidents. It makes utopianism feasible. The cry of 'heritage in danger' has proved by far the most potent of mobilizing forces – and of networking – in environmental campaigns. It is a popular cause even if the activists get much of their energy from the self-conscious righteousness of minorities. 'Heritage' is in fact one of the few areas of national life in which it is possible to invoke an idea of the common good without provoking suspicion of party interest, and it is also one of the few where notions of ancestry and posterity can be invoked without embarrassment or bad faith. It has notched up real achievement – reclaiming streets from the motorist and creating traffic-free zones, greening the inner city, restoring, or creating wildlife habitats.

What distinguishes conservation from other kinds of public issue – and perhaps accounts for the radicalism of many of those who take up its causes – is its predilection for direct action. It does not wait for the tedious processes of representation or the often unalterable processes of the law, but, in the manner of the Oxleas Wood campaigners, pins its faith on interventions in the here-and-now. At a time when mass membership parties are in precipitous and secular decline, and party politics very largely the preoccupation of self-regarding élites, the politics of the environment are one of the few places where individual action, and collective participation, counts, and it is no doubt indicative of this that Greenpeace – or for that matter the Royal Society for the Protection of Birds – have much longer membership lists than the Labour Party, and a much more vivid life. Conservation also allows for some measure of the politics of the personal, giving space for the unilateral action of the individual, asking us to practise its precepts in our lives, and giving us some say on who our neighbours might be – a dangerous power, and one which can be turned to ethnocentric or class-exclusive ends, but at the same time one of the inescapable components of any folk radicalism.

Heritage could also be described as a residuary legatee of the planning idea.[13] It is by its nature interventionist – one reason perhaps why it is currently attracting such obloquy.

Like planning in the 1940s – though on the strength of popular initiative rather than central authority – it is an attempt to make a new landscape, both indirectly, through the take-up of improvement grants, and directly, through schemes of environmental enhancement. Like 1940s town and country planning, too, it wants to control land use, restrict market forces, and to integrate old and new. Its conservation areas, though less strict in segregating occupational and residential use, could be seen as late offspring of that favourite child of the 1940s town planners, 'zoning', while its urban regeneration schemes could be seen as a lineal descendant of 1960s comprehensive redevelopment, albeit in the name of a traditionalizing rather than a modernizing aesthetic.

Though ostensibly concerned to protect a particular environment, preservation usually involves a more or less systematic attempt to improve it, and quite often to effect a total transformation, as in such brilliant inventions as Covent Garden's Floral Hall. It also has an affinity to the comprehensive redevelopment schemes of the 1960s. It subordinates private interest to what it conceives of as the public good. In its own way it is quite collectivist in spirit, believing that new buildings should 'blend' with their surroundings and be 'in keeping' with their neighbours,[14] and it is indeed this predilection for theming and integration which is the solid basis for the historical and aesthetic arguments which can be advanced against it.

Whatever the criticisms of conservation areas – widely attacked for being Disneyfied, historical toy-towns – they at least involve a recognition that the ideal home does not begin on the doorstep but involves a total environment; and that – as Ian Nairn and the authors of the Architectural Review's *Outrage* (1955–6) knew – street furniture, kiosks, benches, even tree-irons are involved in it.[15] In its own way 'heritage' thus raises questions about whether or not an environment is to be planned, and it seems possible that some of the hatred aroused by it, though voiced in the name of the Left, bears the impress of that recoil from planning which has not yet run its course.[16] Those who want to do dirt on heritage might pause on the fact that after a decade and a half in which privatization and monetarization have seemed to carry all before them, and when the very idea of public service has been poisoned at its source, the politics of the environment is one of the few spheres in which the idea of the public has been given radical new extensions. We are not so rich in counter-examples as to be able to jettison one in which there is a popular support for an extension of the public sphere.

So far from standing for entropy or stasis, heritage and conservation could be seen as growing points in the national culture. Economically, at a time when micro-electronics are making almost every form of human skill redundant, it is one of the very few forms of labour-intensive employment which is actually growing. Politically it rests on a broad base of do-it-yourself retrieval projects in which local initiatives serve, in some sort, as a surrogate for municipal enterprise or state intervention. It puts a premium on cultural innovation and experiment.

It is customary to counterpose futurism and resurrectionism, the one forward-looking, the other a throw-back to the past. Yet historically speaking – as in England's first modernizer, the Arts and Crafts Movement of the 1880s – they might be seen as symbiotic, complementary and antagonistic at the same time, or even as two sides of the same coin, each testifying to a felt absence in the present. Each, typically, arises as an expression of cultural dissidence, and involves a radical rejection of the present in favour of an idealized (or fantasized) other. Under an optic like this the rise of heritage might be seen as a vehicle for the pursuit of the visionary, an idiom for the expression of otherwise forbidden, or forgotten, desire. It allows utopia to occupy the enchanted space which memory gives to childhood, promising a new age which will be simpler and purer than the present. It joins the practical and the visionary, the future and the past. When, for instance, in the winter of 1993–4, the *Independent* offered a £30,000 award, inviting readers to submit a statement on how they would use the money to change their lives – 'by fulfilling a dream, perhaps, or liberating themselves to take on a new job, or complete a long-nurtured project' – the winning entry was that of a 28-year-old marketing manager who wanted to return with his brother to the small village of Grampound, in Cornwall, to run the business that has been in his family for 300 years – 'one of only two in Britain still using natural oak bark tanning methods, selling high quality leather to top-of-the-range shoe-makers'.[17]

III

Heritage criticism in Britain has been particularly severe on notions of rusticity which it treats by turn as risible and sinister. A powerful influence was Raymond Williams's *The Country and the City* (1973), which argued that pastoralism was always an exercise in bad faith. In Ben Jonson's time ('To Penshurst' is his text) it was a cloak for the spoliation of the peasantry; in Raymond Williams's own day it had been a licence for 'unconscious reaction'. In either case it involved historical illusion, nostalgia for a past that never was.[18] Martin Wiener's brilliant squib, *The Decline of the Industrial Spirit*, amplified this for the nineteenth and early twentieth centuries, making ruralism the villain of the piece in a narrative of English decadence.[19] Then, in 1987, Patrick Wright and Robert Hewison accused the National Trust of aggrandizing country house owners while reducing the rest of us to a forelock-pulling deference.

In the light of the foregoing, it seems worth pointing out that rural preservation has often been associated with both social protest and cultural dissidence, as it was for Sir Thomas More and the sixteenth-century 'Commonwealth' opponents of enclosure, or, later, for Cobbett and Clare at the time of Captain Swing. From the 1860s, when it began to emerge as a continuous cause, down to very recent times, rural preservation and revival – or rural 'reconstruction' as it was called in the 1920s – was a 'progressive' cause, one which found many of its most ardent supporters and exponents at the radical end of the political spectrum. The Commons, Open Spaces and Footpaths Society, founded in 1865 – the remote ancestor of the National Trust – was a kind of Liberal front, championing the claims of villagers and commoners against the encroachments of landlords and property developers.[20] Robert Hunter, the lawyer, one of the three founders of the National Trust, had been fighting common rights cases for some thirty years, winning such famous battles as those for Hampstead Heath and Epping Forest. As a young man he had come under the influence of Christian Socialism, while his political affiliations, whether working on commons preservation with John Stuart Mill, or in the service of government with Henry Fawcett, placed him on the radical side of mid-Victorian liberalism.[21] Octavia Hill, the second of the Trust's founders, was proclaimedly a disciple of John Ruskin, her mentor, and by the nature of her fresh air and open space enthusiasms, a critic, even at times an enemy, of the idea of private property. Canon Rawnsley, the third of the Trust's founders, had also come under the influence of Christian Socialism as a young man and he was a life-long follower of John Ruskin, though in his belligerent defence of the Lake District, where he spent his life, he owed as much perhaps to the Tory-radicalism of Wordsworth.[22] William Morris's 'anti-scrape' agitation seems to have been one of the influences on the founding of the National Trust, and a letter from him to Canon Rawnsley in the Trust archives datelined 10 February (1887?) and written from Kelmscott House, Hammersmith, conveys something of the combative spirit of organized preservationism's early years:

> As to the Commission on the rights of way; my firm opinion is that we shall be quite helpless against the landowners as long as there is any private ownership of land. If I lived in the Country I should rage against these pickers and stealers

with the best: but if you will not think it too cruel a paradox I must say I am not sorry that well-to-do people should feel the tyranny of the system, as it will thereby be more likely to come to an end.
From Dear Sir
Yours faithfully
William Morris[23]

The Arts and Crafts Movement, according to their own lights, and their admirers and imitators abroad (among them the great American architect Frank Lloyd Wright) were modernists and experimentalists, avatars of light, space and freedom.[24] They were pioneers of both 'rational' dress and the labour-saving home, exalting the Simple Life against the suffocating claims of convention, the freedom of the open air against the claustrophobia of the Victorian interior. Baillie Scott and Raymond Unwin – the latter a revolutionary socialist by formation – were housing reformers as well as propagators of cottage architecture, the virtual inventors, for the middle class, of the two-storey, servantless home, and for working-class housing of the garden city ideal.[25]

Cecil Sharp, the discoverer of Morris dancing, and collector of traditional song, was a Fabian, and in his folkloric work at Headington Quarry contrived to combine musical notation with canvassing support for the Liberal Party during the stormy period of the People's Budget and the House of Lords crisis.[26] Percy Grainger, the musicologist who was largely responsible for the popularization of folk-song in the schools, was a socialist, albeit of a racist Nordic kind;[27] so too was Mary Neal, who performed a similar function for Morris dancing. Ruralism between the wars was also quite largely in the hands of progressives, notably in the attempt to revive village crafts (Leonard Elmhirst of Dartington, a disciple of Tagore, was a representative and influential figure);[28] and in the opposition to 'ribbon' or bungaloid development, of which Clough Williams-Ellis was the energetic co-ordinator,[29] gathering about him a formidable array of writers and artists. And it was very much of a piece with this that Labour in its propaganda should have treated ribbon developments as a capitalist atrocity, the very epitome of the evils of unrestricted competition.

The early promoters of the country house cult – very much a lost cause, it seemed, between the wars – were also, curiously enough, in their politics if not in their preservationism, 'progressives'; and indeed as late as 1936, when George Lansbury was Vice-Chairman of the National Trust,[30] the rescue of doomed country houses was thought to be more of a Labour than a Conservative cause. In the 1930s a quite remarkable amount of socialist business seems to have been transacted at country houses, either because they had been converted into conference centres – like those in which the ILP, the Fabians and the Liberals held their summer schools; or because, like Dartington Hall, or Garsington, or Hinton Manor (host, in the 1930s, to a large part of Labour's future cabinet),[31] they were a weekend home for the radical intelligentsia. Or because in the manner of the Countess of Warwick's Easton Lodge in the 1890s,[32] or of Lord Faringdon's Oxfordshire estate (watering-hole of Bevanism in the 1950s) there was a radical aristocrat in place.

Vita Sackville-West, who championed the 'organic' country house against the more grandiose, Palladian alternative, was no progressive, but via marriage her connections were as liable to be Labour as Tory, and even before her affair with Virginia Woolf, at least one of her existences seems to have been on the outer fringes of Bloomsbury. In any event her notion of the 'informal' country house seems to be closer in spirit to the cottagey look, affectionately caricatured in Osbert Lancaster's 'Home, Sweet Home' than to the Roman fantasies of Sir John Vanbrugh.[33] Sybil Colefax, whose celebrated shop in Mayfair was one of the nurseries of what today is known as 'the country-house look', was in her other persona (that of a literary hostess) the friend and patron of left-wing writers and artists: along with Nancy Cunard and the Duchess of Atholl she was one of those dissident aristocrats who subscribed to Spanish Aid, and championed the Republican cause in the Civil War.

In a more popular vein, National Parks were Labour policy;[34] hiking was a major, if unofficial component of the socialist lifestyle;[35] and 'freedom to roam' was a left-wing campaigning issue.[36] It had been given a mass basis, in Edwardian times, by the Clarion League, the 40,000 strong organization of the young who combined Sunday cycle meets with preaching the socialist message on the village green. In the inter-war years it was forwarded by the Woodcraft Folk – a kind of anti-militarist, co-educational version of the Boy Scouts and Girl Guides who combined pacifist advocacy and nature mysticism;[37] by the Youth Hostels Association, formed in 1930; and by that great army of hikers who on high days and holidays went rambling on the mountains and moors. Hiking had a particular appeal to working-class Bohemians, as a mainly intellectual alternative to the dance hall, and one that cost no money. They seem to have figured largely among those who poured out of Manchester, Sheffield and Leeds for the mass occupation of Kinderscout in 1934, one of the actions which heralded the long-drawn-out campaign for the opening of the Pennine Way.[38]

None of these left-wing enthusiasms survived the post-war years, though (as a correspondent to the *History Workshop Journal* remarked) septuagenarian cyclists, 'with their bums up and their pedals working like pistons', could still be seen on country roads, while hikers with knapsacks on their backs turned out *en masse* for the Aldermaston Marches of 1958–62. The 1960s editors of the *New Statesman* no longer felt obliged to write on country matters, as Kingsley Martin had done, or to write an occasional column under the pseudonym of Mr Park; while Labour, when it began to take notice of conservationist matters, showed itself more interested in civic amenity than in rural integrity. The counter-culture of the 1960s was much more metropolitan in its enthusiasms than its inter-war predecessors ('Make London a 24-hour city' was one of the watchwords of *International Times*), and though it staged huge open-air pop concerts, rambling was hardly its scene. But the counter-culture did have its Arts and Crafts side. 'Ethnic' clothes stalls were the original kernel of today's mega-market at Camden Lock; the macrobiotic restaurants and 'whole-food' shops promoted the idea of 'organic' farming. 'Cranks', the health-food restaurant which opened at Carnaby Street in 1961 – using only '100% whole meal flour, raw Barbados sugar, free-range eggs, fresh fruit and dairy produce' – could be said to be the pioneer of some of the vernacular lines to be found on the supermarket shelves today, while the now familiar but then revolutionary surroundings – 'handthrown stoneware pottery, solid natural-coloured oak tables, heather-brown quarry tiles, woven basket lampshades and hand-woven seat covers' – prefigured the stripped-pine look. More generally, it was in the nature mysticism, transcendental meditation, wistful songs and droopy clothes of 1960s hippiedom, and in the communes, squats and settlements of the early drop-outs, that the idea of 'back-to-the-land' resurfaced, not only as an environmental panacea but also as a private utopia (A. Rigby, *Communes in Britain*, 1974, shows the movement in its earlier phase).

In this context it seems pertinent to point out that Edith Holden, the so-called 'Edwardian Country Lady' of *The Country Diary of an Edwardian Lady* – an international best-seller when it was published in 1977, and one which, by judicious franchising, gave rise to a vast profusion of 'Edwardian Country Lady' products – was not in fact a country lady at all, but a Birmingham socialist, and an artist, somewhat akin, in origins, occupation and outlook, to the Miriam of D.H. Lawrence's *Sons and Lovers*.[39] On weekdays, at the time she was compiling her 'country diary', she was a mistress at a Birmingham elementary school; on Sundays, following in the wake of her socialist father, she was a teacher at the Birmingham Labour Church, Hurst Street. Along with her family she was also in the habit of attending Sunday evening services there at which (as the researcher who went in track of her life put it) 'a socialist spoke every week'. Like her older sister Effie, Edith was an ardent follower of Arts and Crafts, and the Birmingham Art College where she received an 'excellent' for her drawing had apparently been started by disciples of William Morris.[40]

The publishers' blurb of *The Country Diary of an Edwardian Lady*, concerned, perhaps, to defend his opportunistic choice of title, cunningly notes that the diary was found 'in a country house' but there is no evidence that Edith Holden herself actually stayed in a country house, still less that she wrote her diary in one, indeed the diary has no reference to any domestic interior at all: it is made up entirely of flower sketches juxtaposed against verse. Her 'diary' is in fact very much akin to those of the nineteenth-century working-men botanists who (as Sabbatarians occasionally complained) spent their Sundays collecting specimens or taking sketches from nature. There is not a word in her diary about, nor a visual hint at, any of those commodities which have been manufactured in her name, neither the 'Edwardian Country Lady' set of bedroom co-ordinates which Marks and Spencer were still featuring in 1987–8 (in the following year it was replaced by the 'Versailles look'); nor the 'Edwardian Lady's Country Kitchen' which competed for favour with the 'Balmoral' and the 'Elizabeth Ann' in the monthly glossies, still less the 'Edwardian Country Lady' notelets on sale in the stationery department of W.H. Smith's and John Menzies.

IV

In the 1930s the modern movement in architecture and design went hand-in-hand with the organization of preservationist lobby and pressure groups. The Council for the Preservation of Rural England, founded in 1926, was definitely an advocate of the planning idea – seeing rural reconstruction and the prevention of ribbon development as the only way of preventing a new expropriation of the countryside.[41] It was also an early friend of the idea of National Parks, and a supporter of the 'freedom to roam' of hikers. Inevitably, too, it was an early advocate of those ideas of land-use control which were collectivism's grand panacea for rural ills. Sir Patrick Abercrombie, Secretary of the Council for the Preservation of Rural England, was the most famous planner of his day, a disciple of Geddes, and author in 1943 of that most remarkable of the utopian blueprints for post-war reconstruction, *The County of London Plan*.

Aesthetically, too, in the inter-war years, modernism and revivalism were partners. 'Regency Style', an invention of the interior decorators which became fashionable in the early 1930s, was offered as a parallel to the Modern Movement (symptomatically it was popularized by the ultramodern Chelsea department store, Peter Jones).[42] So was Georgian architecture, with its supposedly simple lines and predilection for a light airiness. No less influential – a ruling philosophy with the Design and Industries Association established in 1915 – was the combination of the Arts and Crafts tradition with a belief in machine aesthetics. It was anticipated in the mystic socialism of W.R. Lethaby,[43] at the Central School of Arts and Crafts; taken up in the 1930s by Nikolaus Pevsner in *Pioneers of Modern Design* (1935) and by Herbert Read in *Art and Industry* (1934); and found its apotheosis in the war-time 'Utility' schemes and the founding of the Council of Industrial Design.

J.M. Richards, a founder of the Georgian Group in 1937, and in later years the long-running editor of the *Architectural Review* and an influential popularizer of modernism, combined a belief in social planning with a whole series of very strong attachments to the old. His *Functional Tradition* (1958) is given over to the analysis and celebration of such early industrial buildings and plant as Albert Dock, Liverpool (then falling into ruin, today a Grade I listed building); Snape Maltings (later adopted by Benjamin Britten and Peter Pears for the Aldeburgh Festivals) and the fishermen's sheds at Hastings, recently secured for the fishermen after a sixty-year campaign.[44] 'Structures of this kind', he writes of nineteenth-century storage sheds, 'may seem too modest to deserve the name of architecture, but they demonstrate better than any others the unselfconscious rightness of taste – based on robustness and simplicity – displayed by nineteenth-century engineers and builders.'[45]

Another figure who seems worth pausing on, partly because he was the writer of preservationism's finest contribution to the history of the built environment, partly because he helped to marry love of the Georgian with the planning idea, is John Summerson, author of *Georgian London*, and in his later years curator of that remarkable memorial to late eighteenth-century antiquarianism, Sir John Soane's Museum. As Mandler shows in his new study, Summerson was an enemy of what he once called 'architectural Toryism'; he was a supporter of the refugee scholars and architects coming to England from continental Europe, and the neo-Marxism of his history has been ascribed to the influence of the Warburg. As well as being an exemplary marriage of economic history and aesthetics, *Georgian London* is also a tremendous vindication of the planning idea and in its own way as much a tract for the times as Clough Williams-Ellis's *Britain and the Beast* and *Britain and the Octopus*.[46]

Educationally, as well as architecturally, heritage arrived on the scene as a progressive force. Thus country dancing was introduced to the Edwardian school, by teachers like Mary Neal, as an early experiment in eurhythmics, a way of freeing the limbs from Victorian tight-lacing.[47] Likewise handcrafts, in the form of pottery and woodwork, were promoted as an example of education through art.[48] Scouts and Guides, or in the Labour and Co-operative movement the Woodcraft Folk, represented the principles of the New Hygiene as well as a return to Simple Lifeism (forest camps seem to have something of the same function for ecologically-minded children and parents today). Later, in the 1950s, industrial folk-song was taken up by the promoters of the New English as a way of introducing 'working-class experience' into the school curriculum, and bringing the language of the classroom closer to that of everyday life.[49]

The open-air museums, derided today by cultural critics as the quintessence of sentimentality and Little England conservatism, were at the outset, in the 1960s, in the hands of the museum profession's Young Turks – curators who wanted to untether the exhibits from their mooring and position them instead in free-floating open space. Barrie Trinder, one of the founders of Ironbridge Gorge, writes that they took their aesthetic models from best-practice Scandinavian design:

> The projects of the 1960s shared many aspirations, and used many of the same expressions in justifying their existence. All were concerned with the monuments of the Industrial Revolution, with providing opportunities for voluntary labour, with potential visits from educational groups and with encouragement of crafts. The expression 'Open-Air Museum' was used in much the same way as a term which was thought to command instant approval, although few people understood its implications. The enthusiasm for Open-Air Museums is best explained by the fashion for all things Scandinavian which was in vogue in Britain in the late 1950s and early 60s. Girl students adorned their rooms with smoky glass and gonks. Stainless steel dishes were universal wedding presents, and the Saab 96 was widely admired. A generation of student filmgoers regarded Wild Strawberries and Smiles of a Summer Night as peaks of cinematic achievement. Almost every primary school of the 1960s contained echoes of Munkegard School in Copenhagen, and its architect was invited to design what proved to be the finest twentieth century building in the University of Oxford. Scandinavia meant good design, in buildings, furnishing and fabrics, a serious concern for the arts, and a life-style which, in England, seemed blissfully hedonistic. Open-Air Museums were part of this general impression.[50]

Post-war preservationism, in its early phases, was a movement in which the Establishment had little or no part. The Body Shop emerged from Brighton counter-culture;[51] the Campaign for Real Ale from beer-swilling radicals.[52] Covent Garden, in its present form, sprang from a 'community' agitation in which the newly radicalized students of the Architectural Association played a big part. Impossibilists were no less prominent in the early agitation against the motorway box, as they have been, in recent times, in the mass trespasses which have blocked the way of the road-builders. The idea of 'heritage centres' was introduced into this country by an ex-journalist of the *Daily Worker* who, in his passage from 'red' to 'green', had become the press officer of the Royal Institute of British Architects. As he wrote in a letter:

> Heritage centres were, in fact, my brainchild. I got the idea of 'interpreting' the natural environment to an urban population that had lost its contact with nature from the US national parks, and developed the idea in 1973–4 when working on a Leverhulme Fellowship study of the crisis in architecture that people should understand both the history and the actual working (including the allocation of social space) of environments in which they live. As a member of the committee for European Architectural Heritage Year 1975 I persuaded the Arts Council to fund three experimental 'architectural interpretation centres', and I was personally involved in the development of the York centre. I still think it was a good idea, although I never liked the name 'heritage centre', which was given to it by Lady Dartmouth (now the Countess Spencer and, God help him, the Prince of Wales' step-mother-in-law). I always argued that the concept of a centre where people could learn about their environment should not be restricted to the special 'conservation areas' and in that sense I'm delighted that Wigan has one![53]

At the other end of the political spectrum, preservation owes a great deal to right-wing cultural dissidents. Here James Lees-Milne, the long-standing secretary of the National Trust, with his hatred of the levelling tendencies in post-war Britain, and his determination to bring the rescue of imperilled country houses within the ambit of the Trust's work, was clearly an influential figure (there is an illuminating discussion of him in Patrick Wright's *Journey Through Ruins*); so was the anarcho-Tory architectural correspondent of the *Daily Telegraph*, Ian Nairn, one of the very first to extend the notion of 'conservation' from the protection of wild nature to that of the built environment. Railway preservation, the first of the post-war resurrectionist crazes, and arguably the one with the largest mass following, owes little to either right-wing aesthetes or left-wing intellectuals, but seems to have prospered on its own.

V

One reason why heritage cannot be assigned to either Left or Right is that it is subject to quite startling reversals over very limited periods of time. Conservation is not an event but a process, the start of a cycle of development rather than (or as well as) an attempt to arrest the march of time. The mere fact of preservation, even if it is intended to do no more than stabilize, necessarily involves a whole series of innovations, if only to arrest the 'pleasing decay'.[54] What may begin as a rescue operation, designed to preserve the relics of the past, passes by degree into a work of restoration in which a new environment has to be fabricated in order to turn fragments into a meaningful whole. Nature reserves are by definition pretty fragile places, which only the most vigilant and interventionist management (using electronic fences to keep out potential predators and engaging in complex hydrographical exercises to maintain optimum mud conditions) can keep in a wilderness state.[55] Reconstituted ruins are if anything even more vulnerable, being exposed both to the press of the visiting public, and to the aestheticizing hand of heritage management. Heritage, in short, so far from being a stationary state, is continually shedding its old character and metamorphosing into something else.

Industrial archaeology, when the term was first coined, presented itself as no more than a natural extension of the traditional dig, mapping and identifying the visible remains of the past. It was concerned with relics rather than the environment. The advent of the 'working' museum, and the attempt to re-create a realistic and total 'period' setting — shops as well as factories, mill-streams as well as mules, hearths as well as tools — had the collateral effect of aestheticizing the labour process and animating what had been inert. At the 'living history' museums, the demonstrators, drawn from retired or redundant workers, are prize exhibits. The blacksmiths at their forge are monuments of manly strength; the shoemaker stitching away at his awl is the old-time craftsman incarnate. The little piecers, darting in and out of the machines, are miracles of survival. What had begun as a rescue operation, concerned with material remains, was thus elevated, by degree, into a celebration of manual labour. 'Hurrah for the Factory' was the expressive title chosen by Manchester Studies when, in 1979, they put on a photographic display of old-time mill interiors.

Museum display introduces a further set of displacements since, as with any exhibition, it must choose objects for their expressive quality, turning them into a public spectacle and investing them with a public, and very often a historical narrative. The Museum of Rural Life in Emilia is an example. It began life, some thirty years ago, in 1964, when Ivano Trigari, a former peasant employed in an agricultural co-operative near Bologna, found an old farming tool, half-covered by earth, and locally known as a *stadura*. Putting it on show, he set off a fever of emulation, with *festa della stadura* — demonstrations of old hand tools — spreading through the province. The humours it seems were carnivalesque. Institutionalized in a museum, and with captions provided by the economic history department of the University of Bologna, the objects looked quite different — not wonders or marvels or curiosities but documentary illustrations of a quite predictable narrative.[56]

The mere fact of preservation aesthetizes, turning warehouse walls into townscape, derricks and cranes into obelisks, alleys into picturesque lanes. It makes backwardness visually appealing and turns subjects of study into objects of desire. The 'dark satanic mills' no longer seem horrors when they are exhibited as historical monuments or reassembled in picturesque settings. No one who visits the Greg mill at Styal, Cheshire, a National Trust property, can fail to be impressed by the giant water wheel, a veritable cyclops of Vulcan's arts. But no cotton waste sticks to the factory walls; the ground has been lovingly landscaped; and the restored looms, though 200 years old, are producing modern designer-ware — in 1986 'beautiful cotton cloth, incorporated by top designer Pat Albeck into the Styal Calico Collection'. The same cognitive dissonance awaits visitors to Robert Owen's old mill at New Lanark; it has been turned into a conservation village and given over to modern craftspeople. A factory can no longer be associated with the machine age — still less with 'sweating' — when its manufactures appear as art products.

Then, the historical object, however scrupulously preserved, or, as critics sometimes complain, mummified, is as much subject to time's whirligig as any living organism. Canal restoration began as an attempt to resuscitate a dying culture. In 1946, when the Inland Waterways Association was formed, it was still plausible — just — to think of reactivating the canals for inland transport, and also (Tom Rolt's peculiar and intense vision when he was writing *Narrow Boat*) of preserving the 'indigenous working life' of the boatmen. Even the much more practical Robert Aickman, a joint founder of the IWA and its full-time president, dedicating himself to 'an all-consuming campaign to breathe life into a corpse', believed that they might be opening the way to a second front in inland trade.[57] Today, when the canal basins have become showcases of urban pastoral, sprouting conference centres, leisure complexes, luxury apartments and brand new cobbled walkways, and when the Inland Waterways Board declares itself to be the only nationalized leisure industry, the canals, though boasting more than a thousand listed buildings, seem more a pointer to the future than to the past.

Even when the objects have remained the same, we can be sure that they are seen with different eyes, partly because of changes in the environment, but even more, it may be, because of the lens through which they are perceived. Thus at a time when, under the impact of agribusiness, field names are becoming a thing of the past, the subject matter of 'history on the ground' threatens to become as remote as the 'lost villages of medieval England' were when Professor Hoskins and Professor Beresford set out on their muddy walks. Likewise the farm labourer – still neighbours when George Ewart Evans[58] took his tape recorder to them – is an endangered species. Canal boats, too, 'splendidly restored . . . in traditional livery' and painted in the harlequin colours of the Victorian fairground rather than rotting on their hulls, are inconceivably more 'historic' than they were when Tom Rolt began campaigning for them.

The meaning of industrial archaeology has been transformed out of all recognition by the disappearance, or near disappearance, of heavy manual labour and the unexampled haemorrhage of industrial jobs. In its early years, despite the name, industrial archaeology was largely concerned with the forerunners of the industrial revolution, windmills and canals in particular. Later, the decline of smokestack industry put the Lancashire and West Riding textile mills on the conservationist agenda, while more recently the robotization and computerization of the labour process has turned even assembly-line work into a potential museum-piece. The saving of the Oxo tower on the South Bank, and the floodlighting of the Hoover factory – the first of the sights of London which greets travellers from the West – testifies to the remarkable updating in the archaeological agenda (the youngest listed buildings now date from the 1970s).[59]

The metamorphoses that have overtaken the folk revival, though less publicly visible, are hardly less striking in character. It was highly political in origin, the work initially, of two Communist singer-scholars, A.L. Lloyd and Ewan MacColl, who more or less single-handedly uncovered a forgotten corpus of industrial song and at the same time established a particular style of performance art. Musically, it was quite closely allied to the New Orleans of 'revival' jazz, promoting concerts as 'Ballads and Blues' and using a jazz banjo or even clarinettist as a kind of modernist counterpoint to traditional song. Ethnically, it was quite *anti*-English, drawing much of its repertoire, and some of its most notable singers, from the Scottish ballad tradition and from Irish rebel song. The proletarian idiom, borrowed partly from American work-songs, partly from coalfield ballads, was pronounced: 'rough songs . . . made by rough men . . . as coarse and awkward as the day they were first sung'. It offered a heroic view of manual labour rather than an elegiac one, and indeed, like the Northern voice in 'new wave' British cinema, it was widely acclaimed as announcing the arrival of a working-class presence in the national culture.

The folk club movement of the 1960s, though drawing on many of the same singers, was quite different. It was still highly political, being closely associated with what were then known as 'protest' politics (in Scotland the revival ran in tandem with the campaign against nuclear submarines in Holy Loch), but the politics were those of middle-class radicalism rather than a socialism of the working class. The transatlantic influences were those of Joan Baez and Bob Dylan rather than the little red song book of the Wobblies. Jazz idiom was left to rock, the banjo to country-and-western, while in the clubs it was the unaccompanied purist who set the pace. The Critics Group, with Ewan MacColl as teacher, resuscitated eighteenth-century and pre-industrial song, while recordings from Sam Larner, a Yarmouth fisherman, and Harry Cox, a Norfolk farm labourer, helped to inspire the discovery of an alternative heritage of *English* country song. With the harmony singing of the Copper family – recorded in print as well as on disc and much imitated in the clubs – the revival put down its roots in deepest Sussex. The clubs themselves seem to have served as some kind of refuge for the sociologically orphaned – the ex-working class from whose ranks the new generation of singers were largely recruited.

VI

Politically heritage, like conservation, draws on a nexus of different interests. It is intimately bound up with competition for land use, and the struggle for urban space. Whether by attraction or repulsion it is shaped by changes in technology. It takes on quite different meanings in different national cultures, depending on the relationship of the state and civil society, the openness or otherwise of the public arena to initiatives which come from below or from the periphery. In one aspect it is a residual legatee of the environmental campaigns of the 1960s, the aesthetic revolt against 'gigantism', and the rediscovery of simple lifeism. In another aspect it could be seen as the epicentre of a whole new cycle of capitalist development; the spearhead, or cutting edge, of the business recolonization of the inner city, a style-setter for post-Fordist small-batch production. In Eastern Europe on the other hand, where the mobilization and use of tradition was at least as much a feature of the politics of the 1980s as it was in the West, cultural nationalism and the revival of religion seem more pertinent than the restructuring of the economy.

Ideologically, too, heritage is chameleon, being subject to startling reversals over comparatively short periods of time. Like conservation, with whose causes it is umbilically linked, it is incapable of remaining in a stationary state, but is constantly metamorphosing into something else. That is why the focus on the 'manufacture' or 'invention' of tradition – the only way in which the heritage-baiters and the deconstructionists seem able to engage with the commemorative arts – seems often wide of the mark. Focusing on the 'strategies' of supposedly all-powerful and far-seeing elites, it cannot begin to address the great mass of pre-existing sentiment which underpins sea-changes in public attitudes and revolutions in public taste.

The notion that nostalgia is a peculiarly British disease, and that the rise of 'heritage' in the late 1970s and 1980s represented a recrudescence of 'Little Englandism' is not one which could survive comparative analysis intact. Conservationism is a global phenomenon, and the notion of heritage as an environment under threat, and as a cultural asset to exploit, has been a feature, for some thirty years, of the advanced capitalist economies of the world. Landmarks Conservancy in New York has been systematically 'listing' historic buildings for some twenty-five years, while the Environmental Protection Act of 1969 laid the groundwork for US industrial archaeology. The Garden Festival idea was German in origin. The historicist preservation and adaptive re-use of old commercial and industrial premises has been for some thirty years the cutting edge of the business recolonization of the inner city, as familiar in Lakeside Zurich as it is in Southwark Bankside.[60]

Nature conservancy is even more strikingly transnational, and it was indeed in recognition of this that, when Peter Scott in 1961 launched the initiative to which, more than any other, we owe the preservation of our ancient woods and surviving wetlands, it took as its name the World Wildlife Trust. As the ecological disasters in Russia and Eastern Europe painfully demonstrate, a preoccupation with wildlife habitat and ecosystem balance, is – like the preservation of industrial monuments – prosperity-led, a privilege of the advanced, or relatively advanced, economies. It was at the very height of the post-war boom, when in the EEC countries talk of 'economic miracles' was giving way to fears of 'over-heating', and when in Britain the government was struggling with the problems of 'brimful' employment, that, in 1970, European Conservation Year was celebrated, 'the closest that the nature conservation movement has yet come to embracing all aspects of conservation'. Friends of the Earth was founded in the USA in 1969, the World Heritage Convention – under which European Architectural Heritage Year of 1975 was promoted – was held in 1971, the year that TB was first identified in British badgers, and that the Otter Trust was formed. The International Convention on Wild Flora and Fauna, which Britain ratified in the Endangered Species Act of 1976, was held in the following year.

Heritage is also proving quite crucial in the construction of post-colonial identities, and indeed the demand for the restitution of national art treasures – for some two or three centuries plundered by the metropolitan powers – is not the least of the effects of the coming-of-age of newly independent states. Through the medium of cultural tourism it is allowing, and indeed encouraging, a whole new class of historic nations to emerge, e.g. Sicily, which now appears as an outer limb of Hellas, or a detached province of Byzantium, rather than as the place which Christ forgot. Building on cultural difference – as in the celebration of Native American art, or the nations within a nation which have been the high point of the exhibition year at the Smithsonian Institute, Washington, since 1976 – heritage helps to support both a multi-ethnic vision of the future and a more pluralist one of the past.

Australia, currently re-making itself for the second or third time this century, and on the eve of becoming a republic and throwing off the imperial British legacy, is a particularly striking, indeed exciting, case in point. Here the creation of a post-colonial society, in which both historians and heritage have been quite decisive as consciousness raisers, has gone hand in hand with a wholesale revaluation and indeed discovery of the pre-colonial past. Instead of *terra nullius* – before the Mabo judgement of 1993, the formal status of the pre-European Antipodes – there is now a 20,000-year history of 'dreamways' for which archaeologists, geologists, ecologists and Aboriginal campaigners are creating a whole new narrative.

Notes

1   John Gaze, *Figures in a Landscape, A History of the National Trust*, London 1988. In 1946 Hugh Dalton, as Chancellor of the Exchequer, introduced the National Land Fund to resource National Parks, one of his great enthusiasms – legislated into being in the Town and Country Act of 1948 – and the National Trust. This was the Fund which SAVE called on in its late 1970s battle to rescue Mentmore. In *Practical Socialism for Britain* (1935) Dalton had described the National Trust as 'Practical Socialism in Action'. Like many Socialists of his generation he was an enthusiastic walker, and had been in the habit of walking the Pennine Way for some years before, as Minister of Town and Country Planning in July 1951, giving it state protection. Ben Pimlott, *Hugh Dalton*, London 1985, pp. 218, 455–6, 553–4, 578–81.

2   The recent exhibition of Aborigine art, ancient and modern, at the Hayward Gallery gave the clearest indications of the role of art, history and heritage in consciousness-raising movements among native Australians. Peter Sutton, ed., *Dreamings, the Art of Aboriginal Australia*, New York 1988 is a fine catalogue.

3   Tony Bennett, 'Museums and "the People"' in Robert Lumley, ed., *The Museum Time Machine*, pp. 76–82.

4   Geoffrey C. Stewart and Faith Davis Ruffins, 'A Faithful Witness: Afro-American Public History in Historic Perspective, 1828–1984' in Susan Porter Benson *et al.*, eds, *Presenting the Past, Essays on History and the Public*, Philadelphia 1986. For Malcolm X's advocacy of the lost Afro-American identity, *The Autobiography of Malcolm X*, Harmondsworth 1968, pp. 41, 85, 276–7; ed. S. Epps, *The Speeches of Malcolm X*, London 1969, pp. 61–2, 77, 168–9. Alex Haley, *Roots*, London 1979 for an ambitious and very successful attempt to make the Afro-American the basis for a family history. Alice Walker's novel *The Color Purple* is a brilliantly successful fiction in this vein.

5   Michael Wallace, 'Professionalizing the Past, Reflections on the History of Historic Preservation in Benson et al.; Charles E. Peterson, 'The Historic American Buildings Survey: Its Beginnings', in *Historic America, Buildings, Structures and Sites*, Washington 1983, pp. 7–21.

6   For a splendid account of the role of this in the cultural politics of the 1790s, B. Deloche and J.-M. Leniaud, *La Culture des sans culottes, le premier dossier du patrimoine 1789–1798*, Paris 1989. Daniel Hermant, 'Destructions et vandalisme pendant la révolution française', *Annales*, July–August 1978.

7   Marcel Maget, 'A Propos du Musée des arts, 1935–44', *Genèses*, IV, 1992.

8   A sinister reminder of what this meant – and of its potential appeal – comes in the chapter on 'Lessons from other Countries' which Lord Howard of Penrith contributed to Clough Williams-Ellis's 1938 rural preservationist volume *Britain and the Beast*. It quotes with approval the law for protecting the natural beauties of the Reich passed by the National Socialist Government on 26 June 1935, 'signed by the Führer and Chancellor of the Realm Adolph Hitler', and countersigned by General Goering and other ministers.

> Today as formerly Nature in Wood and Field is the object of the desire, the joy, and the recreation of the German people. The landscape of the countryside has however been completely changed in these latter years, its garb of trees and flowers owing to intensive agriculture and afforestation, to narrow minded cleaning up of meadows and to the cultivation of conifers has been in many places completely altered. Many species of animals which inhabited wood and field have disappeared with the disappearance of their natural haunts. . . . The protection of objects of natural interest (*Naturdenkmalpflege*) which has been growing for centuries could be carried out with but partial success, because the necessary political and cultural conditions were lacking. It was only the transformation of the German man which created the preliminary conditions necessary for an effective system of protection of Natural Beauty.

Lord Howard of Penrith comments:

> Whatever we may think or feel about Nazi political philosophy all must I think acknowledge that in this introduction to a Law, which I hope will in many things become a model for the rest of the world, its draughtsmen have expressed a deeply felt sense of the beauties of their country and of the necessity of preserving these for the 'desire, the joy, and recreation' of future generations. We who share their views in this matter can at least applaud the effectiveness of the measures they are taking to attain their laudable object.

9   Michael Wildt, 'History Workshops in Germany', in R. Samuel, ed., *History Workshop, A Collectanea, 1967–1991*, Oxford 1991.

10   R. Bahro, *The Alternative in Eastern Europe*, London 1979. *Building the Green Movement*, London 1986.

11   Hillier Parker research. *Market Briefing*, June 1992. I am grateful to Robert Thorne for a copy of this document.

12   I have argued this in 'Mrs Thatcher's Return to Victorian Values' in T.C. Smout, ed., *Victorian Values*, Oxford 1992.

13   Bailly, *The Architectural Heritage of European Cities*, Cambridge, Mass. 1979, pp. 97–8. English Heritage, says a former member of the GLC Historical Buildings Department, 'is now the only strategically effective body for London . . . The only form of public interest property men will listen to'. Robert Thorne in discussion, January 1994.

14   *British Architectural Design Awards*, Macclesfield 1984.
15   *Architectural Review*, 'Outrage', June 1955; 'Counter-Attack', December 1956.
16   Peter Hall, *Great Planning Disasters*, London 1980; Alice Coleman, *Utopia on Trial. Vision and Reality in Planned Housing*, London 1985.
17   'Free to Save a Traditional Cornish Craft', *Independent*, 10 January 1994.
18   Raymond Williams, *The Country and the City*, London 1975.
19   Martin J. Wiener, *English Culture and the Decline of the Industrial Spirit 1850–1980*, Cambridge 1981.
20   Lord Eversley (G.J. Shaw-Lefevre), *English Common and Forest, the Story of the Battle during the last Thirty Years for Public Rights over the Commons and Forests of England and Wales*, London 1894; *Commons, Forests and Footpaths*, London 1910; W.H. Williams, *The Commons, Open Spaces and Footpaths Preservation Society, 1865–1965, A Short History of the Society and its Work*, London 1965; J. Rawlett, 'Checking Nature's Desecration; Late Victorian Environmental Organisation', in *Victorian Studies* 22, 1983, pp. 197–222. On C.R. Ashbee's role as Council member of the National Trust, National Trust Archives Acc. 42/25–6 lectures to be delivered in the USA by Canon Rawnsley and C.R. Ashbee 1899–1900. 'Sydney Olivier is on the Executive Committee of the Commons Preservation Society', runs a notice in *Fabian News*, May 1893, '... Members are specially requested to inform him of any cases of enclosure of Commons, roadside strips, or footpaths which may come under their notice.'
21   Robert Hunter, *Preservation of Commons*, London 1880 for some of his battles with railway companies and property owners. Christopher Helm, *Founders of the National Trust*, London 1987 for a not very illuminating collective profile.
22   Eleanor F. Rawnsley, *Canon Rawnsley, An Account of His Life*, Glasgow 1923.
23   National Trust Archives, Acc. 6/4, letter of William Morris to Canon Rawnsley, 10 February (1887?). Morris did not take part in the foundation of the National Trust, but C.R. Ashbee, in some sort his successor on the anarchist and community-building aesthetic wing of English Socialism, did. Cf. National Trust Archives, Acc. 42/25–26 for the prospectus of the lectures he delivered for the Trust in the USA in 1900; and Acc. 1/30 for a letter to Ashbee in 1897.
24   G. Naylor, *The Arts and Crafts Movement, A Study of its Sources, Ideals and Influence on Design Theory*, London 1990. Fiona MacCarthy, *The Simple Life; C.R. Ashbee in the Cotswolds*, London 1981. Elizabeth Cumming and Wendy Kaplan, *The Arts and Crafts Movement*, London 1991. For the community-building side of Arts and Crafts, cf. Jan Marsh's excellent *Back to the Land, the Pastoral Influence in Victorian England from 1880 to 1914*, London 1982; Dennis Hardy, *Alternative Communities in Nineteenth Century England*, London 1979; W.H.G. Armytage, *Heavens Below, Utopian Experiments in England, 1560–1960*, London 1961.
25   M.H. Baillie Scott, *Houses and Gardens*, London 1900; Raymond Unwin and M.H. Baillie Scott, *Town Planning and Modern Architecture at the Hampstead Garden Suburb*, London 1909; James D. Kornwolf, *M.H. Baillie Scott and the Arts and Crafts Movement*, London 1972.
26   Cecil Sharp House, Sharp Correspondence, Box 2, Correspondence with William Kimber.
27   John Bird, *Percy Grainger*, London 1982.
28   On Dartington there is Michael Young's excellent and loving *The Elmhirsts of Dartington*, London 1982; cf. also Maurice Punch, *Progressive Retreat, A Sociological Study of Dartington Hall School, 1926–1957*, Cambridge 1977; Victor Bonham-Carter and W.B. Curry, *Dartington Hall, the History of an Experiment*, London 1958; Anthony Emery, *Dartington Hall*, Oxford 1973.
29   Clough Williams-Ellis, *England and the Octopus*, London 1928; (ed.), *Britain and the Beast*, London 1938; *Architect-errant*, London, 1971, for his autobiography.

30 Lansbury's support of the National Trust was of a piece with his lifelong attention to environmental issues, his promotion of farm colonies and – as Minister of Works in the 1929–31 Labour government – his championship of open-air lidos. Raymond Postgate, *The Life of George Lansbury*, London 1951.

31 Nicholas Davenport, *Memoirs of a City Radical*, London 1974 for the place of Hinton Manor in the XYZ Club where the young Hugh Gaitskell cut his political teeth.

32 Modern Record Office, Warwick University, Mss. 74/6/2/105, Letter of Countess of Warwick to Ben Tillett, 21 December 1936 is a poignant reminder of what Easton Lodge had once meant.

33 Vita Sackville-West, *English Country Houses*, London 1941; Jane Brown, *Vita's Other World, a Gardening Biography of V. Sackville-West*, London 1985; Suzanne Raitt, *Vita and Virginia, the Work and Friendship of V. Sackville-West and Virginia Woolf*, Oxford 1993 for a hostile though interesting account.

34 John Sheail, 'The Concept of National Parks in Great Britain, 1900–1950', *Trans. Inst. of British Geographers*, 66, 1975; *Rural Conservation in Inter-War Britain*, Oxford 1981.

35 Ruth Adler, *A Family of Shopkeepers*, London 1985, Ch XVIII for the rambling craze among young Stepney Jews.

36 C.E.M. Joad, *A Charter for Ramblers*, London 1934; Joad, who became a national figure during the Second World War when he emerged as one of the stars of the BBC 'Brains Trust', was chosen to compile the BBC's 50th anniversary tribute to the National Trust – see National Trust Archives, Acc. 45 'The National Trust. Past Achievements and Present Activities', script to BBC Third Programme 10 August 1947.

37 For a splendid new account of the Woodcraft Folk in relation to the nature mysticisms of the 1920s, Derek Edgell, *The Order of Woodcraft Chivalry 1916–1949 as a New Age Alternative to the Boy Scouts*, 2 vols, Lampeter 1992. Also D. Prynn, 'The Woodcraft Folk and the Labour Movement, 1925–1970', *Journal of Contemporary History*, 1983, vol. 8, pp. 79–95.

38 Howard Hill, *Freedom to Roam*, Ashbourne 1980. Ewan MacColl, *Journeyman, An Autobiography*, London 1990 for the young motor mechanic whose 'I'm a Rambler' written for the mass trespass became, thirty years later, one of the unofficial anthems of the folk club movement. John Lowerson, 'Battles for the Countryside' in Frank Gloversmith, ed., *Class, Culture and Social Change*, Brighton 1980.

39 Josephine Poole, *The Country Diary Companion*, London 1984, p. 12.

40 Arthur Holden, Edith's father, a paint and varnish manufacturer, was 'in financial difficulties', and about the time she may have been compiling the diary, the family had been forced to move to a suburban house in a fast-growing commuter village, though 'Edith was still within cycling distance of her beloved childhood scenes', ibid., p. 20.

41 The CPRE, as the monthly *Reports* show, worked in tandem with such organizations as the National Housing and Town Planning Council, and took a full part in parliamentary pressure for land use legislation, planning powers and access to the countryside. For an interesting memoir on the founding of the CPRE and its early campaign for the Derbyshire Peak, North West Sound Archive, interview with Garard Haythorn Thwaite, 17 December 1991. 'Skeffington-lodge's spiritual home was the Fabian Society, in which he was exceedingly active until his late eighties', runs an obituary on the former MP for Bedford. 'He was chairman and president for many years of the Brighton and Sussex branch, which is among the most active in the country. He was very friendly with John Parker, Arthur Blenkinsop, and Arthur Skeffington (no relation), all Fabians deeply concerned about the countryside. This led him to give vigorous support to the Council for the Protection of Rural England, of which he was chairman of the Brighton district committee, the Royal Society for the Protection of Birds and the Friends of the Lake District. He was an ecologist long before it became fashionable.' Tam Dalyell, 'Tom Skeffington-lodge', *Independent*, 26 February 1994.

42 John Cornforth, *The Inspiration of the Past, County House Taste in the Twentieth Century*, Harmondsworth 1985, pp. 146–7.

43 W.R. Lethaby, *Home and Country Arts*, London 1924; *Form in Civilisation*, London 1938; R.W.S. Weir, *William Richard Lethaby*, London 1938; Godfrey Rubens, *Richard Lethaby, His Life and Work*, London 1986.

44 For an account of this campaign by the leader of its latest and most successful phase, Steve Peak, 'The Battle on the Beaches Since 1945', in his *Fishermen of Hastings; 200 Years of the Hastings Fishing Community*, Hastings 1985.

45 J.M. Richards, *The Functional Tradition in Early Industrial Buildings*, London 1958, p. 165.

46 Peter Mandler 'John Summerson, the Architectural Critic and the Quest for the Modern', in S. Pendersen and P. Mandler, eds, *After the Victorians; Private Conscience and Public Duty in Modern Britain*, London 1994, pp. 229–46.

47 Georgina Boyes, *The Imagined Village*, Manchester 1993, pp. 72–86, 94–5, 155–6 for Mary Neal and the Espérance Club – the most determined, if controversial, attempt to translate the principles of the Revival into elementary school practice. Roy Judge, 'Mary Neal and the Espérance Morris', *Folk Music Journal*, V:5, 1989, pp. 545–91. Cecil Sharp, *Folk Singing in Schools*, London 1912.

48 For progressive ideas in English education between the wars, R.J.W. Selleck, *English Education and the Progressives, 1914–1939*, London 1972; Trevor E. Blewitt, ed., *The Modern Schools Handbook*, London 1934; W. Boyd and W.T. Rawson, *The Story of the New Education*, London 1965.

49 S. Clements, J. Dixon and L. Stratta, *Reflections*, Oxford 1963; and *Things Being Various*, Oxford 1967; John Dixon, *A Schooling in English; Critical Episodes in the Struggle to Shape Literary and Cultural Studies*, Milton Keynes 1991, pp. 150–54 for a retrospective account. In *Things Being Various* black-and-white photographs were introduced in the same spirit as folk-songs had been in *Reflections*.

50 Barrie Trinder, 'A Philosophy for the Industrial Open-Air Museum', in Claus Ahrens, ed., *Report of the Conference of the European Association of Open-Air Museums*, Hargen-Detmold 1985, pp. 87–95.

51 Anita Roddick, *Body and Soul*, London 1991; Gilly McKay and Alison Corke, *The Body Shop, Franchising a Philosophy*, London 1986.

52 Richard Boston, *Beer and Skittles*, London 1977. I am grateful to Mr Boston for letting me read the file of his weekly articles. Apart from their interest for the progress of CAMRA, they are a fascinating commentary on changing mores.

53 Letter to the writer from Malcolm MacEwan, 10 October 1987. For some of MacEwan's other activity in this field, see his autobiography, *The Greening of a Red*, London 1991.

54 'Pleasing Decay', the subject of a justly famous chapter in John Piper's *Buildings and Prospects*, London 1949.

55 For the RSPB reserve at Minsmere, see Simon Barnes, *Flying in the Face of Nature; A Year in Minsmere Bird Reserve*, London 1992.

56 Alessandro Triulzi, 'A Museum of Peasant Life in Emilia', *History Workshop Journal*, 1, Spring 1976, pp. 117–20 for an acount of the origins of the museum. I am drawing on memories and notes of a visit there, with one of the museum's founders, in 1983. Interestingly the one room really crowded with visitors was the kitchen, where there had been no attempt to caption the objects or even, in any museological way, to display them. My guide seemed irritated that the local Italian people were more interested in domestic and culinary bric-à-brac than the story of agricultural change carried in the main panels.

57 Robert Aickman, *The River Runs Uphill, A Story of Success and Failure*, Burton-on-Trent 1986, for a personal account. Robert W. Squires, *Canals Revived, the Story of the Waterways Restoration Movement*, Bradford-on-Avon 1979, for a history.

58   George Ewart Evans, *The Strength of the Hills, An Autobiography*, London 1983; *Ask the Fellows Who Cut the Hay*, London 1956, for the first of his ethnographies.

59   Kenneth Hudson, *The Archaeology of the Consumer Society; the Second Industrial Revolution in Britain*, London 1983, for the Thirties turn in industrial archaeology.

60   Dan Cruikshank points to the interesting parallel to the early development of the English seaside, when, in Regency times, ramshackle fishing ports, such as Brightensholme, were turned into fashionable resorts, cultivating 'views' and 'prospects' that looked out to sea, rather than turning its back on them.

Methods and approaches to cultural heritage management

Chapter 21

New Heritage, an Introductory Essay – People, Landscape and Change

Graham Fairclough

1 Attitudes and aspirations

Introduction

Of the developments in 'western' style heritage management (and archaeological or cultural resource management) of the past two or three decades, those in methods and approaches have been as great as any. 'Traditional' methods derived from later 19th century attitudes (such as that experts and connoisseurs objectively identify on everyone's behalf the qualitative 'best' of heritage, which is then 'kept') are no longer the only option. New approaches are emerging which move away from traditional methods, while building on the lessons and experiences to be learnt from past practice.

These new approaches use broader holistic and comprehensive definitions of the historic environment. They try to create greater democratic involvement in the heritage process, recognising this can lead experts to revise their views on what (and why) society values something. More fundamentally, the new approaches increasingly recognise that their goal is the management of future change rather than simply the protection of the fabric of the past.

This opening essay offers a discursive introduction to the eleven chapters in section three (22 to 32) which present a little of the great diversity of methods and approaches that are beginning to put these new ideas into practice. Each chapter describes a different method, but these have all been designed or adapted to deal with specific identified problems that traditional Heritage paradigms do not resolve. They all have in common an interest in practicality; most have been written mainly for practitioner or even non-specialist audiences rather than for academia.

Changing definitions

The current more comprehensive scope of heritage has been reached over the past century or so by incremental expansion. In the UK, for example, the first state-endorsed definition of the archaeological heritage (the original 1882 Schedule of legally protected monuments) was concerned almost only with major mainly prehistoric monuments. This was broadened in later legislation during the 20th century to include Roman and medieval ruins and 'standing buildings', buried deposits and remains, later medieval and post-medieval earthworks and finally (so far) industrial archaeology and late 20th century military remains. It has also stretched to some 'non-monumental' heritage, though not all, e.g., palaeo-environmental deposits, are protected in law. The spatial dimension of heritage has grown from 'monument' to the slightly larger concept of 'site', thence to 'setting', areas and 'landscapes' (chapters 24, Dick and 28, Lee) and cities (chapter 25, Stocker) and, finally, to the landscape (chapter 32, Fairclough). The chronological spread of heritage has been expanded until there are no significant temporal boundaries at all. Growing interest in 'contemporary archaeology', and the concepts of future heritage, suggests that heritage dos not even need to be of the past.

This widening of view has of course been followed in other disciplines too. In building conservation circles, vernacular buildings, industrial buildings and so on were quite rapidly added in the later 20th century to an initial concern with 'polite' architecture (the buildings of the rich, the landed and the powerful). Townscape and 'the local scene' were embedded in the 1960s in the UK's historic urban areas legislation (known as 'conservation areas') as an early pre-view of current interest in landscape and character. Similarly, 'nature conservation' evolved via 'ecology' into 'biodiversity', expanding its concerns from individual animals or plants to species, to habitats and to the whole of the environment.

The various successive enlargements of 'heritage' have created an all-inclusive concept of the 'historic environment'. From originally being a qualitative measure or a badge of significance, the word 'historic' has become an adjective applied to the whole environment, irrespective initially of significance. The term 'historic environment' carries a dual implication: the environment is not purely natural but has a strong (and culturally predominant) humanly-created aspect, and, conversely and in consequence, the historic environment is not free-standing but part of a wider interconnected environmental whole.

All this can be characterised as a landscape-based way of looking at heritage, or indeed of spatial planning in general (for instance, Antrop 2005, Fairclough 2002, Sarlov-Herlin 2004, Selman 2006, or Stoumann 2002). It is necessary to emphasise that 'landscape' here is taken to be a complex, multiple concept not simply (as some archaeologists treat it) just as heritage covering large areas. Many of these ideas are included in the European Landscape Convention (ELC), which in its principles is of universal as well as European relevance (chapter 31, Council of Europe 2000), and they are stimulating vigorous debates across Europe (e.g. Fairclough & Rippon (eds) 2002, Doukellis & Mendoni (eds), 2004, Ruiz del Árbol & Orejas, 2005, Meier (ed.) 2006).

The landscape viewpoint brings different levels of scale into play but it also carries with it other important presumptions. One is about the need for trans-disciplinary integration. Landscape is perhaps the most inter-disciplinary forum of all (chapter 32, Palang & Fry 2003, Antrop 2005), and liaison with those working with other aspects of the environment within other academic disciplines is essential, a theme which runs through many of the next twelve chapters. Inter-disciplinarity is not enough, however. Landscape as a concept is also heavily democratic because landscape is everyone's neighbourhood, and a greater inclusion of public and lay voices as well as expert and professional opinion is necessary. There is thus a need for new heritage approaches to adopt *trans*-disciplinary approaches that go beyond all of the disciplines into 'real' life (Tress *et al.* 2005).

A second presumption stems from the view of landscape as perception. Because landscape is a way of seeing and a way of *being*; it only really exist in people's perception; "an area of land as perceived by people . . ." is the beginning of the ELC's definition (Chapter 30). 'Real' people ('normal' people) automatically have a holistic view which specialists and experts sometimes have to struggle to re-discover. People do not readily divide the world, or heritage or landscape, into natural or cultural features, instead they think in terms of place or landscape; additionally, people talking during public participation projects about landscape as 'beautiful' or 'natural' often subsume the cultural within this, and it is not always easy for experts to unpack (chapter 26, Scott). There is still also an important debate to be had on what constitutes a 'good' landscape in cultural or archaeological, as opposed to aesthetic or 'green', senses (Fairclough 2006b).

An even more important consideration, also reflected in the ELC, is that the enlarged definitions are not restricted to the actual 'stuff' of heritage but extend to definitions of who defines heritage, and of how it is perceived by 'audiences' and stakeholders. An increase in public access to heritage, both real and virtual, has brought with it a recognition of the validity and usefulness of a multiplicity of values and of ways of valuing (such as chapters 28, 29, 30, van de Stoep & van den Brink 2005, or the newly-emerging politically-aligned and economically-based concept of 'public value' in the UK: Clark (ed.) 2006, National Trust & accenture, 2006). This complements but nevertheless extends far beyond the essentially evidential, scientific or pedagogic values that have traditionally been attached to heritage. This has been covered in previous parts of this book, specifically with reference to Lipe's work, but its influential appearance in the public action domain derives from the debate about sustainable development and in particular how this affected the historic, as opposed to the 'green' environment that properly started in the 1990s (chapter 22).

This line of thought has promoted awareness that people as well as experts determine what is especially valued in the heritage, a concept central to the new 'Faro Convention' – the Council of Europe Framework Convention on the Value of Cultural Heritage for Society CETS No.: 199 (Council of Europe 2005). This very new Convention, not yet in force, reflects, as the official résumé says, a shift from the question "How and by what procedure can we preserve the heritage?" to the question "*Why* should we enhance its value, and for whom?". What 'ordinary' people value might be different to what experts value, or they might value the same things but for quite different reasons, such as for reasons of association, memory, or locality.

Changing attitudes

Whilst definitions of scope have been revised, definitions of objectives and purpose have not changed to the same degree, although if heritage itself is constantly renewed so too should be the ways in which we choose to manage it. Heritage has conventionally been about protecting things – fabric – against loss. Like conservation, its origins during the 20th century lie in a reactive, confrontational and last-minute opposition to proposals for change in the twin context of a society largely wedded to the notion of progress and growth and of an under-resourced heritage sector reduced to slogans such as 'Rescue' or 'Save'. Heritage conservation and archaeological resource management, however, have become better-resourced, their procedures stronger, their data sets ever-larger (e.g. HLC, chapter 32). They have also gained a broader degree of public support. The *principle* and value of conservation (at least of keeping old buildings) is now rarely challenged. Heritage is one of the 'usual suspects' of local grass-roots opposition to change. In the light of this increased confidence and capacity, chapters 22–32 show heritage practitioners beginning to revisit their aims to see if they are as suited to a climate of agreement as they were to the climate of opposition in which they were first framed.

A great deal has changed. Westernised societies now include an inherently and quite often influential conservationist constituency. This is demonstrated by the existence of extensive networks designed to conserve the land (e.g. the National Trust movement), nature or the 'countryside' (a word whose very meaning was (re)constructed to carry a preservationist message; a 'google' of 'countryside' on US web pages shows it to be as used as 'heritage' as a marketing term, Fairclough & Sarlov Herlin 2005). The economics of mass heritage-tourism also creates a preservationist stance (and a re-creationist one, as the removal of later 'inappropriate' development in the vicinity of WH sites). It can also be said that there is a widespread fear of change, fuelled perhaps by factors such as Cold War anxieties, the traumas of de-industrialisation, and new anxieties surrounding climate change, that together have led to a loss of belief in progress that manifests itself in a rejection of modernity. The idea of conservation has become a deeply embedded social phenomenon, and future generations may well look back to the later 20th and perhaps the 21st century in the 'west' as an era characterised by the self-conscious conservation of its past.

It could be thought that heritage practice can cling to its traditional protectionist ways simply because of this strong predisposition towards preservation. The growing social resistance to change has indeed proved helpful to the heritage 'cause', but it should be asked whether it always remains the best horse to pull the heritage carriage. The desire to keep all things old and 'traditional', especially when it operates within ever-expanding heritage definitions, is problematic. How can heritage remain dynamic and contested (one of its characteristics) if it does not change? How is 'future heritage' to be constructed without change? More important, is it sustainable, economically, socially or politically, to apply to the whole historic environment methods that were originally designed to protect only a few examples or a small sample of 'the heritage'. Traditional heritage methods worked well as a pragmatic last-resort defence, but at best they poorly reflected local or personal concerns such as context or sense of place. This approach still haunts UNESCO and the World Heritage List. Not all heritage, as Kerr for example points out (chapter 23), is for keeping, we must decide what to let go and what to change. These are questions which underline new heritage approaches. Some of the papers that follow begin to lift the curtain on such a new view.

Sometimes the evolution of methods has preceded theoretical development. The development of archaeological records that aspired to, or could claim, completeness was inevitably going to produce different philosophy and methods. In the UK, Sites and Monuments Records (today termed Historic Environment Records) gradually became a more important indicator of the whole heritage than the lists of protected monuments (which only 'flagged up' a small proportion even of the known sites). SMRs had an involvement with almost all proposed development whether or not it affected an already known or a designated site. They provided a register of locations where archaeological remains were known to exist or where they might be predicted or suspected, and this allowed a much larger proportion of the resource (or more accurately of new impacts upon it) to be managed. The concept of testing a proposal site before any permissions are granted – a version of the precautionary principle – has been instrumental in both massively increasing archaeological knowledge and in changing perceptions of the character and value of that resource, and thus of the discipline's objectives.

Techniques such as selective designation or ways of identifying special value on national scales are thus coming to monopolise heritage policy to a lesser extent. It becomes more realistic for archaeologists and heritage managers to work actively and in a forward-looking way to inform future change (e.g. Bloemers 2002, 2005) as well as to protect things. More importantly, they can start to think about engaging with the contribution of the past to the present day everywhere, in all places, not just at the most special sites; to do so for or with anyone who wishes to be included; and to see heritage in terms of people-centred issues such as landscape, place, identity and quality of life. These are issues at the heart of the most recent heritage Conventions in Europe, notably the Landscape Convention (Council of Europe 2000, chapters 31, 32, Fairclough 2002, 2006a).

When this new landscape perspective is linked to the stronger social support for heritage, the use of mainstream policies provides a better context for new heritage approaches than heritage-specific policies, procedures and controls. Mainstream policies are those such as the spatial planning system and similar over-arching ways of managing the environment (agricultural policy for example) that are applied more or less to all land, whether public or private, and which are concerned with all aspects of its value. Management of change throughout the historic environment as a whole, is coming to be the main goal of heritage, aiming not to retain all historic fabric, or to protect highlights whilst all else changes around them, but to create a future in which the past in one form or another plays an appropriate part everywhere. Overall historic character, present and future, is the focus, with heritage conservation (as a process not merely a product) embedded in local as well as national communities.

Changing aspirations

Some of the reasons for adopting new heritage approaches are mundane, such as access to new IT systems, particularly Geographical Information Systems, which both change how the heritage resource is defined and offer new opportunities for dealing with it. Other reasons follow from the developments of philosophy already described in chapters 1 and 12). Others are more fundamental still, such as the effect of introducing the concept of sustainability development into heritage management or the implications of the landscape concept as a unifying theme; these required re-examination of many givens, including attitudes towards future change, and are part of foundations of what is coming to be known under the shorthand term of 'characterisation' (EH 2005, Clark *et al.* 2004, Fairclough 2003, 2006d). This is an approach which looks at a bigger picture through a process of holistic generalisation. It creates a series of contextualisations: of individual components of the heritage in their setting, of the past in the present and of contextualised people in their habitat, their landscape, and their lives. It helps people to see the overall historic character of an area or region and to use this new perspective as the frame for both strategic and more detailed decisions that affect all heritages.

Another factor in the appearance of new approaches has been increased sharing of experience between national and continental cultures. Heritage management, with many nationally or regionally distinctive approaches, is still very diverse. It will always be so, because heritage practice (as any cultural and socially based systems) is deeply rooted historically and culturally. The idea that 'better' or superior methods can be imported simply and un-problematically into one country from another is delusional. This introductory chapter, for example, has a European perspective but it largely reflects practice in the UK, and indeed mainly within England; the detail of English practice could not easily be transferred even to the other parts of the UK because of their different cultural attitudes, legal history and mentalities, let alone to the rest of Europe. On the other hand, valuable lessons can be learnt from comparing approaches.

There has been a great growth over the past 20 to 30 years in opportunities to share experience and expertise, whether at trans-national conferences or through the web, and this has added a more sophisticated layer of conscious relativity. Diversity offers opportunities for learning and self-reflection. In Europe alone, for example (particularly since the changes of 1989–91), many European network projects, the annual conferences of the European Association of Archaeologists, or the many workshops, publications and conferences of the Council of Europe have started to create pan-European communities of practice in many different heritage and archaeological fields. Such examples exist in most continents, and books such as this draw on this diversity in global practice to inform its further development.

In many countries the most important factor in the development of new methods may well be the success of various forms of heritage management during the 1970s and 1980s that provided the encouragement and the solid platform for pursuing more ambitious approaches. Markers of this success are many, and building on them is a more positive and obstructive way forward than continually noting threats and losses as if the gains of the past few decades had not been made. In Europe, for example, the introduction of EIA, and in the UK the introduction of robust principles and procedures ('PPG16') for embedding archaeological resource management into the development control system with their adoption across Europe as the Valetta Convention, meant that it was commonplace in the early 1990s to hear the phrase 'coming to maturity' used in relation to archaeological management. Ten years later in England, as building conservation 'caught up', the publication of *Power of Place* in the UK was similarly hailed as a 'coming of age'. Steps forward such as these allowed and encouraged new thinking

In short, stable and widely-accepted mechanisms (and methods and approaches) for protecting monuments and sites seen as the most important were largely fully in place by the late 1980s. By and large they worked well, so that, for example, the total loss of really significant buildings or sites became rare, at least without full, indeed often prolonged, public and occasionally highly politicised debate (e.g. the Rose Theatre or Seahenge) and almost never without mitigation of some sort such as excavation which simultaneously added to the strengthening confidence of the heritage profession. This stronger position allowed heritage disciplines to start to look outwards (for example, to start to use main-stream policy and laws), and to pursue grander ambitions. Recently emerged methods can be seen as a manifestation of new aspirations.

Greater expectations – people in their (local) landscapes

The growing-up of heritage management – which seems to be what the new heritage represents – cannot be separated from its social context, whether public attitudes towards change (a now-inherent conservatism) or the economics of mass tourism (which has given 'heritage' the economic value which even a few decades ago it mainly lacked). These have pushed heritage and conservation higher up political agendas; it is less common now to hear arguments against preservation of a building or even an archaeological site on the grounds that they are value-less in monetary terms; most areas of rural Western Europe market themselves on their landscape heritage in one way or another. All this has given greater expectations of what heritage practice can aspire to and achieve

The larger goals of new heritage approaches are generally based on three grounds, of *scale, scope* and *ambition*, which can be discerned in most of the chapters in this Section:

–   an expansion in *scale*, notably involving an emphasis on landscape (or context), not only to protect 'landscape' in itself, but more importantly to use the concept of landscape to manage the whole heritage resource, a more mature acceptance of the complexity and ubiquity of heritage;
–   an extension of *scope*, through which more recent heritage, and in some countries heritage that is less monumental and non-'built' (such as semi-natural features like hedges, woodland, moorland, peat-lands and heath) have been drawn into the 'canon' of heritage, while intangible heritage now receives a little more attention;
–   an enlargement of *ambition*, stemming from an increase in the perceived size of the resource and in the proportion that is being successfully managed (expanding constantly 'adds' to heritage), and routine developer-funded evaluation and excavation established by Valetta (e.g. INRAP 2006) demonstrate that what has so far been 'discovered' from the past is a small proportion of what still exists.

Other environmental disciplines have also re-focused themselves. The IUCN Protected Areas movement, for example, is re-branding itself as an approach with universal applicability well beyond its traditional reserves (Brown *et al.*). Originally emerging from the US wilderness movement, its aim was to protect from future human activities areas seen as being unspoilt nature. From the 1940s, however, it began to operate in more populated areas such as IUCN Category V areas ('lived-in, peopled' landscapes, classically the English and Welsh 'National Parks') and more recently Category VI areas ('Managed Resource' areas, where the need for sustainable human exploitation is recognised even in biosphere reserves). The experience of working in these areas is now being promoted as a new paradigm for managing all areas where a human influence contributed to, and is necessary to maintain, inherited character – in other words, as the biodiversity establishment is coming to recognise, almost everywhere.

Additionally, re-introducing a democratic note, it is not politically sustainable to expect members of a community (whether one of interest or place) to agree to the public protection and maintenance of someone else's idea of what is important whilst not attempting to look after what they themselves value (or even to find out what they value most). Many people would willingly support the protection of major monuments (e.g. Stonehenge, Taj Mahal) which they themselves may never see, but by the same token they expect some measure of interest from heritage 'authorities' in the monuments of their quotidian landscape, no matter how unimportant on a national or global scale these may appear (Low, chapter 30). Context is all, it might be said, and most people's context is their local areas. Heritage, especially when distilled as landscape (with its temporal unities, its focus on place and the commonplace, its link to *being*) is a material and intangible bequest from the past that exists everywhere and not just in special places but whose recognition is contingent on people and their viewpoint. What matters to someone is quite usually what is around them in their daily life, and this is the arena within which new heritage tries to work, hence the emphasis of chapters 22–32.

In contrast, national criteria were normally used in traditional systems of heritage designation protection. In immature systems, the role of experts' training and taste to reveal 'intrinsic' value was strong. More mature systems (e.g. Startin 1993) were more systematised and rigorous (intra-thematic comparison for instance) but still followed the principle of selecting the 'nationally important' or the 'special interest'. The tension between selecting and preserving the 'best' (at a national or even global level) on the one hand and paying attention on the other to how important a building (say, but equally a tree, chapter 29) is to its locality irrespective of the values that might be attributed to it nationally or by specialist experts, is at the heart of recent and continuing methodological development. Put simply, the key heritage dimension in many individuals' historic landscape is very often going to be made by humble, more commonplace features that will rarely if at all figure on national or even regional lists.

'Whose heritage?' is therefore a question not just about ownership and conflict, but about definition. The answer to the question is not only 'everyone's' but – most particularly in terms of landscape and place – also 'whatever someone wishes it to be', thus giving rise to multiple values which co-exist even if conflicting (chapters 26, Scott, 27 Stoffle, and 30, Low). There is a caveat, however, that no one can be forced to accept heritage, and heritage can legitimately be disowned, as for example the earliest post-industrial generations in England of the 1960s and 1970s often wished to see the destruction of the architectural legacy of their recently-lost industries, such as textile mills and coal spoil heaps, symbols of a past they were partly glad to lose. The next generation thought rather differently. Values are attributed rather than intrinsic.

Landscape (or place) and 'character' are central to many of the new heritage approaches. Landscape is quintessentially multiple in its meanings, significance, 'ownership', social and individual relevance and its possible futures. The conservation or protection of an individual building is heavily concerned with fabric (Kerr, chapter 23), whereas the management of areas and landscape is linked to character (Dick, chapter 24). Character is a less tangible but more powerful and pervasive concept that includes fabric but also transcends it (and does not always require it, chapters 28, Lee and 29, English). Trying to manage landscape is a very different task to managing or protecting a site or monument. Landscape is inherently dynamic. It is always open to significant change on a variety of time-scales even without physical human intervention; its perceptual aspects are just as dynamic as its physical ones. People change their view of the world and thus their landscapes for many reasons, for example as fashions in landscape appreciation change what they sense, as knowledge and understanding change what they notice, or as they themselves change through age or circumstance (Fairclough 2007). Landscape in other words cannot be preserved unchanged, and perhaps this is its main lesson for heritage practice.

Conclusions

Many of the ideas touched on in this essay, reflecting chapters 22–32, arise ultimately from the concept of sustainability, brought into the heritage debate in the 1990s in the years after the 1991 Rio summit by documents such as *Sustaining the Historic Environment* (1997) (chapter 22) and its equivalents (e.g. Historic Scotland 2002). From being an attempt to harness this new politically-influential concept to support traditional heritage management, the encounter with sustainability in fact proved to be a mirror that reflected existing practice, not always flatteringly and usually showing alternative avenues. The debate very rapidly brought into common usage the notion that value is attributed and relativist and perhaps most importantly multiple but inclusive; at a stroke this made us look closely at the role of experts – what is a good balance between being 'priests' to hand down wisdom or facilitators to help people 'find' their heritage?

The centrality of people to heritage was underlined by sustainability, and with it connections were made to local distinctiveness. That was the spatial dimension of bringing Sustainable Development into heritage – a shift to include local heritage, a shift to include the whole. The equivalent temporal shift was to start focusing on the present day not on the past for its own sake, and to remind ourselves that heritage and the archaeological resource as a whole are 'contemporary', whatever role they may also have had in the past. Heritage practitioners study, protect and manage the remains of the past not only (or even mainly, apart from their evidential value) because they are from (or of) the past but principally because they exist in the present and contribute to the present, whether as part of the environment or as part of peoples' landscape.

2 The papers

The first paper (chapter 22) is an extract from English Heritage's 1997 statement, *Sustaining the Historic Environment*. This grew out of collaborative research between EH and its sister government agencies the Countryside Commission and English Nature; indeed unusually – but productively – the sectoral statement followed rather than preceded the inter-disciplinary work, which is surely the correct approach. The leaflet proved very influential, and presaged similar work elsewhere; it coloured the sector-wide publication *Power of Place* (EH 2000) which started the recent rapid political acceptance in Britain (and elsewhere in Europe) of heritage ideas such as characterisation, multiple values, inclusion and participation and the Public Value debate.

The next paper, James Semple Kerr's description and analysis of the Australian practice of Conservation Plans (chapter 23) reminds us that many of these newer heritage principles were developed quite independently in different parts of the world. Kerr's introduction to the concept of Conservation Plans discusses the question of place and its significance, but also the practicalities of bringing together multiple viewpoints and the perils of un-integrated multi-disciplinary approaches. Different disciplines do not just contribute different areas of knowledge or different sets of facts, but often also different philosophies of knowledge and perspectives on the world; it is these that need some type of integration.

One aim of Conservation Plans is to codify existing but disparate knowledge; knowledge held by experts is most useful once it as been mediated and explained in ways that non-specialists and other people wish to see it (see also Stocker, chapter 25). They also offer a chance to resolve conflict between disparate viewpoints (although one might ask whether different viewpoints might not be able to co-exist quite legitimately, even perhaps offer a constructive tension to heritage management). Finally, this paper discusses the timing of decision making, and the value of separating assessments of significance (or character) from statements of policy, one of the tenets of characterisation that separates it from designation (where the act of selection, designation, is so often implicitly but naively tied up with future management).

Conservation Plans are about managing change – they seek to reconcile future use to inherited significance, and to ensure that what happens to a place is compatible with both its character and the demands of its continued or future use – in Kerr's words, 'to evolve policies to guide work that are *feasible* and *compatible* with . . . significance' (p. 322) (my emphasis). They thus place a foot on both sides of the traditional/new heritage divide: for example, they are traditional in being concerned (just like a listing description) with identifying value but they do so in a context of recognising multiple viewpoints, interdisciplinary approaches and the contested and provisional nature of any assessment.

Kerr's paper also starts to question whether Heritage is necessarily for keeping – 'inherit(ed.) . . . things we do, *and do not*, wish to keep as well as things we want to modify or develop further' (p. 323, my emphasis). Heritage can sometimes be commemorated in ways other than by being retained. It can be modified and re-used, kept as abstracted traces or markers rather than as a whole, it can even be taken away, its absence showing the past to the future (absence, negative evidence, missing layers, discontinuities are all important parts of the archaeological record); all these are legitimate 'heritage' responses to the past.

The third selected paper (chapter 24, abbreviated), offers an example of another similar approach from Canada. Lyle Dick uses different language to Kerr, and is also concerned with slightly different outputs, but there are bigger similarities of approach. Commemorative integrity is a concept that encourages values to be defined by relevant heritage managers and stakeholders; its value, and its similarities to the Australian model of Conservation Plans, is that the exploration of value is tied to future action. The act of considering why a place is significant, and what stakeholders consider constitutes that significance is not an end in itself but a step towards future management and where necessary change (Clark (ed.) 1999, or Van de Stoep and van den Brink 2005/6 for a non-UK European example). Management objectives are as much a product of this method as are statements of value.

This method has been in common use by the governmental agency Parks Canada but also by non-state owners were in receipt of state support, since the 1990s. It reflects the focus on landscape that new heritage approaches often show: the complexity and size of 'cultural resources distributed over a larger . . . area than . . . individual buildings or monuments' throw up different challenges; different approaches are needed. Despite this, it remains relatively faithful, like Conservation Plans, to monumental approaches, particularly in its assumptions about goals and purposes – to maintain a monument's fabric, to isolate it to some extent from its surroundings (or at least to demarcate it clearly), to define its value largely in terms of national thresholds of importance and thus in effect to proclaim that the defined thing is special, and pertains to the national state as well as (even instead of?) to the neighbourhood. Other, alternative innovative approaches to defining value and deciding on management have been developed by Parks Canada for their non-western indigenous intangible landscape (see Lee, chapter 28).

In the next paper, chapter 25, David Stocker offers another parallel approach. LARA (the Lincoln Archaeological Research Assessment) takes a whole city as its subject, across the whole 2,000 years of its existence. The project that it describes is a form of characterisation designed to inform decisions about the future of the archaeological resource. It was focused on research questions for using the archaeological resource in Lincoln, but continuing work (the Lincoln Township Assessment) is adapting the approach to future management issues to do with the character and appearance of contemporary townscape, and with the experience of living in the city. The relationship to change and redevelopment that LARA assumes is not the same as the traditional one of conservationists because it is not necessarily concerned with stopping change – it sees heritage as a resource not just an asset.

As part of English Heritage's national programme of urban and rural characterisation (EH 2005), LARA offers a method that can be used in other circumstances. It takes evidential value (and associative values that might arise from that) and asks what more can we learn area-by-area about a place's long human history that will enlarge our understanding on a wide variety of fronts, from the most distant past to modern-day sense of place (associative as well as physical) and to the character of modern and future Lincoln. LARA is therefore a tool of heritage construction, both in terms of helping to (re)construct the city's heritage in people's minds (again, codifying existing knowledge) and by helping to shape decisions about 'what happens next' in Lincoln: how the future townscape (the future heritage) is to be made, and what of the past, it will include, in what form and to what degree.

LARA is also interesting for setting itself explicitly within a theoretical model of expert mediation. It envisages a pyramid of understanding: at the base, 'raw' data (which in turn of course sits upon the 'stuff' that archaeologists study, whether this might be buildings, the layout of towns, buried structures or deposits, artefacts, or the remains and records of older excavations); in the middle of the pyramid sits interpretation, synthesis and explanation ('ideas', the product of expert mediation), and the pinnacle, people. These people (and their 'politicians' and planners) will be involved in taking decisions about the future, but they might or might not choose to accept the expert synthesis, or they might add to or modify it with their own knowledge, experience, ideas or preferences.

Chapter 26 moves debate on this question into a landscape context, or perhaps a landscape-scale context, because "LANDMAP", the context for the work, is an environmental database rather than a landscape assessment tool (although public perception studies like the ones described here go far towards correcting this). Alister Scott raises issues about intangibles (seemingly always one of the main arenas within which public values need to be placed, Gwyn 2002), about the nature/culture interface, interdisciplinary-ness, and the relation between environment and landscape which are all central to the emerging new heritage approach. It offers a rare worked-through analysis of how landscape becomes a way to share disciplinary experience and how it can draw in public perception (or the difficulties of doing so). The research reported asked (more or less) whether people 'liked' particular areas of landscape as shown on photographs; it is a moot point to ask how the results might have differed if they were asked whether they found the areas 'historically interesting', whether they could read stories in them, and if not what impact would their be on perceptions if stories in the landscape were shown to them (cf. Clark *et al.* 2003).

The paper raises other questions, such as whether people in the experiments reacted to landscape or merely to the photographic images (see Olwig's thoughts on the relationship between perception and depiction, Olwig 2004). More significantly, what do people mean when they use the word 'beauty' to describe an area of landscape? If we only protect landscapes that people 'like', where would that leave history that has left uncomfortable remains; more, what would that say about our lives – can no longer live with pain, do we wish to deny the hardships of the past, do we wish always to be happy? Landscape without disliked areas (if only to provide contrast and shadow) is like climate without seasons.

The next paper (chapter 27) introduces ways of reconciling the view of disinherited indigenous populations with those of the state. Richard Stoffle offers in detail (the original 41-page manual is here very heavily abbreviated) a methodology established in the USA to give some 'ownership' (or at least influence) to the indigenous groups that lay claim to land in state ownership, for instance while formulating proposals for change or management. The 'consultation' that sits at the centre of this method adds 'new ways of seeing' to more conventional (and conventionally western) methods such as issues of affiliation, and understanding, for example a perspective based on the less tangible aspects of cultural landscape that also uses landscape as a frame for broader and more detailed definition and management of cultural heritage resources. Perhaps most interesting is Stoffle's observation that 'native peoples approach CRM from what as been called "holistic conservation"', which is also one of the distinguishing marks of new heritage approaches (e.g. characterisation) that have been developed elsewhere in non-indigenous contexts.

In Chapter 28, Ellen Lee offers an alternative but related view to Stoffle's paper as well as a pendant to Dick's earlier Canadian paper (chapter 24). Like the methods described by Stoffle (as in the next paper too), this second Parks Canada approach brings into a heritage framework indigenous views of the intangible and semi-natural. It does this, however, in the context of landscape – of perception and construct – rather than solely in terms of environmental assessment, recognising that landscape is multiple. The result is a quite different view of heritage, one that reflects a different relationship to the land and to society.

As with the next chapter by English, Lee is describing a way of finding out how people relate to their environment physically and psychologically, mentally and emotionally, in other words, landscape as a way of being in the world, and as the construction of perception. Low describes the same thing in chapter 30: 'defining who we are – as individuals and as groups', what she terms 'place attachment'.

Similar concerns inform the next paper, chapter 29, about Social Impact Assessment, a method used in Australia to broaden ways in which indigenous communities can engage – either more effectively and perhaps for the first time – with state-led planning procedures (notably EIA) that affect their lives. Beneath his description of dialogues with two local communities about their relationship to the land, Anthony English has unearthed fundamental issues. These have been teased out in the context of aboriginal relationship with modern society (where they are most acute, significant and most overlooked or misunderstood), but they apply much more widely. The paper enlarges the definition of cultural heritage – not merely the 'sites' or artefacts that are easy for traditional heritage methods to deal with but also ways of using the land and the resource that are needed, and not just within protected parks but also 'off-Park', that is everywhere. It considers questions of nature and culture, of the tangible and the intangible, and ultimately two issues at the heart of many papers in this Reader – multiple values and landscape.

The paper's example of 'the last quandong accessible on foot by the Muruwiri people' is particularly relevant. That this tree was destroyed by a road scheme whilst archaeological sites were 'saved' demonstrates as the paper says that a whole area of aboriginal culture and heritage was not officially recognised; but it also serves to exemplify the ways that values of a very wide range of type are not inherent but are attributed – had the tree been

of a scientifically rare species, it might have been avoided, because EIA is largely predic-
ated on scientific or evidential values; the types of cultural values inherent in a thing
(whether a tree, or pathway, a view) have traditionally been more difficult to capture in
e.g. EIA or spatial planning or heritage protection. This is not an issue necessarily unique
to aboriginal heritage, and in countries such as the UK, for instance, topics such as
'amenity' or 'local distinctiveness' address similar issues of empowering ordinary people
to engage with otherwise specialist debates.

English's paper is also about 'landscape' in the broad perceptual sense of the ELC,
although he scarcely uses the word, perhaps considering it too linked to western ideas. But
his dichotomy between 'sites such as middens and rock art' and 'biodiversity and environmental health' or 'contact with the land' is very familiar in a European context as a
description of the efforts of more than ten years to expand archaeological resource management from sites to landscape. 'I know sites are very important, but sites are only part
of the land. . . . The land is the base of your culture, your tradition' (Corindi Beach Elder)
recalls to us the preamble of the ELC (chapter 31).

Setha Low's paper, chapter 30, comes from a collection that as a whole is a good
reflection of the new heritage (Teutonico & Matero (eds) 2003). She looks at ways of
engaging all parts of a community living in an area in the decisions about the future of
places, to make design meet local needs, and to strengthen identity and 'place attachment'. Her work has been with communities that are urban, so they are non-indigenous in
one sense but at the same time equally marginal from traditional definitions of heritage.
They are rooted in places and landscape that are being created through use and activity.

Like the method described by Stoffle, Rapid Ethnographic Assessment Procedures
(REAP) looks, through interview- and observation-based techniques, at how people relate
with each other through the medium of place and landscape. REAP originated in US
federal procedures for Parks, but it has been taken up much more widely. Echoing
English's insistence on the need for methods of recognising and protecting cultural values
in off-park contexts, Low's paper introduces an absolutely real world, one that is
dynamic, political and messy. This is another important dimension of the 'new'
approaches to heritage that this book seeks to explore. Heritage is everywhere, everyday,
everyone's; heritage is where people live, not something museum-ified or Reserved but
something being used by people all the time. Archaeological remains, and heritage in
general, are as a resource not an asset, landscape is where we live not just as a piece of
pretty scenery. Low's paper also leads again into the discussion of multiple and diverse
values, and into the recognition that heritage, identity and landscape are continually being
redefined.

Chapter 31 offers an extract (the full text is available on the web (Council of Europe
2000) or reprinted in Fairclough & Rippon 2002, 227–32) from the Florence Convention:
the European Landscape Convention, published by the Council of Europe in 2000 and
already in force in 26 countries. This important milestone in the development of new
heritage approaches is included here because it sums up much of the preceding discussion.
First, it approaches heritage through the medium of landscape, and draws together seam-
lessly both cultural and natural heritage. Second, it is concerned with all landscape, and
therefore the whole environment, not just with special areas, as the definition and scope of
'landscape' set out in Article 1(a) and 2 demonstrates so elegantly. Third, it is a modern-
style 'enabling' convention – it suggests and facilitates ways forward that depend on
democratic consensus and inter-disciplinary co-operation; it is not a top-down prescriptive
directive in the tradition of earlier 20th-century heritage paradigms. Fourth, as its Preamble makes very clear, the ELC regards heritage as a contemporary issue – a resource for
social and economic development, for the enhancement of cultural diversity and the
promotion of inter-cultural dialogues and as part of an economic development model
based on the principles of sustainable resource use. Fifth, it looks forward to how to

enhance or create new landscape that contains heritage more than it looks to protect existing heritage against all change; in its embrace of change it adopts an optimistic view of heritage as a process not a reaction.

The final paper in this section on methods, chapter 32, also summarises several of the main themes of the whole section by means of presenting a method of understanding heritage through landscape ('Historic Landscape Characterisation', HLC), with all that this entails in terms of scale, inclusiveness and comprehensiveness. It also starts to look at the question of new objectives. There are more up-to-date summaries of the Historic Landscape Characterisation (HLC) programme (e.g. Fairclough 2005, Fairclough & Wigley 2005, Turner 2006, Fairclough 2006(c), 2007),Turner & Fairclough 2007, Lake & Edwards 2006a, b), and other papers have begun to unpick some of its wider and more far-reaching ramifications (cf. Fairclough 2006 (a) and (b)), but the paper from the book 'Landscape Interfaces' has been chosen for this Reader because it focuses on the importance of inter-disciplinary partnership, and of heritage as a part of a larger whole.

The paper also underlines the idea of landscape as a 'new' and growing subject with heritage, and more importantly as a vehicle for even bigger changes and concerns such as Sustainable Development and interdisciplinary work. Working through landscape is a clear demonstration that values are attributed not inherent, because for landscape it is abundantly clear that values reside in the intellect, the eye and the emotion of the 'beholder' as part, but only part, of the mental construction of landscape. HLC type approaches (and characterisation more generally as a new and increasingly-used technique of engaging with the future) are successfully changing approaches to resource management heritage protection in the UK (Fairclough 2006d), EH 2005).

HLC also encourages a reconsideration of attitudes to change, leading us to embrace the idea of managing change everywhere rather than over-protecting individual heritage assets (Fairclough 2006 (a), (b)). A presumption against change might be a defensible starting point when dealing with the fabric of discrete monuments or buildings but needs to be justified more specifically before being applied to the whole of landscape (being dynamic, subject to multiple and contested values, living). Two complementary avenues are opening up.

If it is accepted that the evidence for and results of change are actually part of the character of landscape, then future change of some sort becomes desirable as well as being an impact, sometimes, negative, to be mitigated or minimised. Add to this an interest in very recent, even contemporary, heritage at landscape scale, and the case presented in 'Change and Creation' (included in this Reader as its final chapter) becomes a central part of the new heritage approach. Second, if the whole landscape is considered as heritage of one sort or another (national or local, high quality or needing enhancement) it is the management of change, not just the protection of 'stuff', that offers a way to mediate (or not) proposed changes, and to assist in the process and enabling our successors to construct their own future landscape in which the past remains legible and relevant to them. This is the basis of the new approaches to heritage management explored in the eleven papers reprinted as Section 3 of this Reader.

References

Antrop, M. 2005: From holistic landscape synthesis to trans-diciplinary landscape management, in Tress *et al.* (eds), 27–50.

Bloemers, J.H.F. 2002. 'Past- and Future-oriented archaeology: protecting and developing the archaeological-historical landscape of the Netherlands', in Fairclough and Rippon (eds), 89–96.

Bloemers, J.H.F. 2003. *Op weg naar een duurzaam archeologisch-historisch landschap in 2015?*, Inaugural lecture, University of Amsterdam; Amsterdam: Vosiupers UvA.

Bradley, A., Buchli, V., Fairclough, G.J., Hicks, D., Miller, J. and Schofield, J. 2004. *Change and Creation, Historic landscape Character 1950–2000*, English Heritage/Atkins. www/changeandcreation.org.uk

Brown, J., Mitchell, N. and Beresford, M. (eds) 2005. *The Protected Landscape Approach – Linking Nature, Culture and Community*, IUCN: Gland (CH) and Cambridge (UK).

Clark, J., Darlington, J. and Fairclough, G.J. (eds), 2003. *Pathways to Europe's Landscape.* Heide: European Pathways to the Cultural Landscape/EU, www.epcl-eu.int.

Clark, J., Darlington, J. and Fairclough, G.J. 2004. *Using Historic Landscape Characterisation.* London: English Heritage/Lancashire County Council.

Clark, K. (ed.) 1999. *Conservation Plans in Action: proceedings of the Oxford Conference*, London: English Heritage

Clark, K. (ed.) 2006. *Capturing the Public Value of Heritage, The Proceedings of the London conference, January 2006.* English Heritage, with Department of Culture, Media and Sport, Heritage Lottery Fund, National Trust, London.

Council of Europe 2000. European Landscape Convention, European Treaty Series – CETS no. 176, Florence: Council of Europe (www.coe.int/T/E/cultural-co-operation/Environment/ Landscape).

Council of Europe 2002: The European Landscape Convention, *Naturopa* Issue 98/2002 European Landscape Convention, Strasbourg. (www.coe.int/T/E/cultural-co-operation/Environment/Landscape) (accessed 14 November 2006).

Council of Europe 2005. Framework Convention on the value of Cultural Heritage to Society, European Treaty Series – CETS no. 199, Faro: Council of Europe (www.coe.int/T/E/cultural-co-operation/Environment/) (accessed 14 November 2006).

Doukellis, P and Mendoni, L.G. (eds) 2004. *Perception and Evaluation of Cultural Landscapes.* Athens: National Hellenic Research Foundation.

English Heritage, 2000. *Power of Place, A future for the historic environment*, EH on behalf of the Historic Environment Review, London.

English Heritage, 2005: *Characterisation*. Themed issue, *Conservation Bulletin* 47 (Winter 2004/05). www/english-heritage.org.uk/characterisation (accessed 10 Nov 2006).

Fairclough, G.J. 2002. Cultural landscape and spatial planning: England's Historic Landscape Characterisation Programme. In L.M. Green and P.T. Bidwell (eds) 2002. *Heritage of the North Sea Region: Conservation and Interpretation: Papers Presented at the Historic Environment of the North Sea InterReg IIC Conference 29–31 March 2001, South Shields*, 123–149. Shaftesbury: Donhead.

Fairclough, G.J. 2003. Cultural Landscape, Sustainability and Living with Change?, in Teutonico, J.M. and Matero, F., (eds), pp. 23–46

Fairclough, G.J. 2005. Wider Horizons, Wider Aims: Historic Landscape Characterisation in England, in Kelm, R (ed.) 2005: Frühe Kulturlandschaften in Europa: Forschung, Erhalting und Nutzung, papers from the 3rd and 4th Albersdorfer Kolloquium Albersdorfer Forschungen zur Archäologie und Umweltgeschichte, Band 3, Heide, ÄOZA and Boyens, 176–194

Fairclough, G.J. 2006a. A new landscape for Cultural Heritage Management: characterisation as a management tool. In L. Lozny (ed.), *Landscapes under Pressure: Theory and Practice of Cultural Heritage Research and Preservation*, 55–74. New York: Springer.

Fairclough, G.J. 2006b. Our place in the landscape? An archaeologist's ideology of landscape perception and management. In T. Meier (ed.), *Landscape Ideologies*, Archaeolingua, Budapest.

Fairclough, G.J. 2006c: Large Scale, long duration and broad perceptions: scale issues in Historic Landscape Characterisation. In G. Lock and B. Molyneaux (eds), *Confronting Scale in Archaeology: Issues of Theory and Practice*. Dordrecht: Kluwer Academic Publishers. pp. 203–215

Fairclough, G.J. 2006d: From assessment to characterisation. In J. Hunter and I. Ralston (eds), *Archaeological Resource Management in the UK, Second Edition*, 250–270. Stroud: Sutton.

Fairclough, G.J. 2007. L'histoire et le temps: gérer paysage et ses peceptions (History, time and change: managing landscape and perception). In M. Berlan-Darque, D. Terrasson, and Y. Luginbuhl (eds). *Paysage: de la connaissance à l'action* (*Landscapes: from knowledge to action*). Paris: Editions Quae.

Fairclough, G.J. and Rippon, S.J. (eds) 2002. *Europe's Cultural Landscape: archaeologists and the management of change*, EAC Occasional Paper no 2, Europae Archaeologiae Consilium and English Heritage, Brussels and London.

Fairclough, G.J. and Sarlöv Herlin, I. 2005: The meaning of countryside: what are we trying to sustain?, in D. McCollin and J.J. Jackson (eds): *Planning, People and Practice – The landscape ecology of sustainable landscapes*, Procs of 13th IALE(UK) Conference, IALE(UK), Northampton, pp. 11–19.

Fairclough, G.J. and Wigley, A. 2005. Historic Landscape Characterisation: an English approach to landscape understanding and the management of change. In M. Ruiz del Árbol and A. Orejas (eds), *Landscapes as Cultural Heritage in the European Research: Proceedings of COST A27 Workshop, Madrid 2004*, 87–106. Madrid: CSIC.

Gwyn, D., 2002. 'Associative Landscape in a Welsh Context', chapter 21 in Fairclough and Rippon (eds), 187–192.

Historic Scotland, 2002. *Passed to the Future: policy for the sustainable management of Scotland's historic environment*, Edinburgh.

INRAP 2006: http://www.inrap.fr/site/fr/page.php?id=32&p=Accueil%20FR&r= (accessed 14 November 2006).

Lake, J. and Edwards, B. 2006a. Farmsteads and Landscape: Towards an Integrated View, *Landscapes*, 7(1): pp. 1–36.

Lake J. and Edwards, B. 2006b. Buildings and Place: Farmsteads and the Mapping of Change, *Vernacular Architecture*, 3: pp. 33–49.

National Trust and accenture, 2006. Demonstrating the Public Value of Heritage, National Trust: Swindon.

Olwig, K.R. 2004: 'This is not a landscape': circulating reference and land shaping. In H. Palang, H. Sooväli, M. Antrop and G. Setten (eds), *European Rural Landscapes: Persistence and Change in a Globalising Environment*, 41–65. Dordrecht: Kluwer Academic Publishers.

Palang, H. and Fry, G., (eds), *Landscape Interfaces: Cultural Heritage in Changing Landscapes*, Landscape Series 1, Dordrecht: Kluwer Academic Publishers.

Ruiz del Árbol, M. and Orejas, A. 2005. *Landscapes as Cultural Heritage in the European Research: Proceedings of the Open Workshop, Madrid 29th October 2004*. Madrid: CSIC.

Sarlöv Herlin, I. 2004. New challenges in the field of spatial planning: landscapes. *Landscape Research*, 29(4), 399–411.

Selman, P. 2006. *Planning at Landscape Scale*. London: Routledge.

Startin, B. 1993. 'The Assessment of Fields Remains', in Hunter, J. and Ralston, I, (eds), 1993: *Archaeological Resource Management in the UK, An Introduction*, 1st Edition, Routledge: London, 184–196.

Stoumann, I, 2002: Archaeology and the cultural environment: an example from the Danish Wadden Sea Region, chapter 7 in Fairclough and Rippon (eds), pp. 61–68

van de Stoep, H. and van den Brink, A. 2005: Heritage Management and Spatial Planning: the case of Stolwijksluis, Wageningen.

http://library.wur.nl/way/bestanden/clc/stolwijkersluis/presentatie-data/data/pdf/-vdStoep-paperAesop05Vienna.pdf (accessed 14 November 2006).

Tress, B., Tress, G. and Fry, G., 2005. Defining concepts and the process of knowledge production in integrative research. In Tress *et al.* (eds) 2005, 13–26.

Tress, B., Tress, G., Fry, G., Opdam, P. (eds), 2005. *From landscape research to landscape planning: aspects of integration, education and application*, Wageningen UR Frontis Series, no. 12.

Teutonico, JM. and Matero, F., (eds) 2003. *Managing Change: Sustainable approaches to the Conservation of the Built Environment*, Proceedings of the 4th Annual US/ICOMOS International Symposium, Philadelphia, Pennsylvania, April 2001. Los Angeles: The Getty Conservation Institute.

Turner, S. 2006. 'Historic Landscape Characterisation: a landscape archaeology for research, management and planning', *Landscape Research* 31 pp. 385–398.

Turner, S. and Fairclough, G.J. 2007. Common Culture: Time Depth and Landscape Character in European Archaeology. In D. Hicks, L. McAtackney and G.J. Fairclough (eds). *Envisioning Landscape, Situations and Standpoints in Archaeology and Heritage*; WAC; One World Archaeology 52, Left Coast Press Inc, Walnut Creek Ca.

Chapter 22

Sustaining the Historic Environment
New perspectives on the future

English Heritage

Past and future

This discussion document, *Sustaining the Historic Environment*, is concerned with archaeology and the built heritage, in all its forms from hillforts to industrial archaeology, from historic townscapes to gardens or hedges, from great houses to farm buildings. But it is not about the past – it is about the present day and the future. It tries to broaden our appreciation of the historic environment which forms a backdrop to everyday life, and above all it looks to the future, in seeking to use an understanding and appreciation of the past to influence our children's environment.

Nor is this document simply about monuments and buildings. Like the idea of sustainability itself, it is about people. Our archaeology, historic buildings and gardens, towns and historic landscape, were all created by people in the past, but in addition this heritage owes its present value and significance to people's perceptions and opinions, or in other words to their personal beliefs and values.

In the case of other facets of the environment, such as nature conservation, we are also readier to acknowledge objective truths and intrinsic worth, although human perception is still important in determining value. So, for example, we protect wildlife for its own sake, because we recognise that the animals have in some degree their own right to survive; we protect air and water for an even more global good, the survival of all life. Our reasons for protecting the cultural heritage, however, are less absolute. People believe that it is important to keep sight of the past for personal reasons, and because it gives them a sense of belonging, defines their identities at national and local scale, and provides depth and character for their working and living environment. In particular, we value the legacy of the past, our archaeology and buildings, because it tells us in an immediate way about who we are, and because it is the principal evidence and record of our history.

Keeping in touch with the past, and preserving the best for our grandchildren, is not an optional extra, especially at a time in history when we have an unprecedented capacity to change and destroy what has gone before. It is one of the touchstones of society and community. The historic environment in particular, because it reminds us of our origins and is essentially traditional in its appeal, plays a particularly significant part in our view of quality of life. At the heart of a sustainable approach is the idea that we should conserve or improve the quality of life for both present and future generations. We should also recognise, however, that sustainability is a process, not always an end-product: it is as much concerned with *how* we manage change as with what we achieve. We need to conserve and enhance the whole environment, and to adopt a much longer-term view than normal, both of the environment and of the effects of our actions on it.

This will not be an easy task, nor one achieved rapidly, not least because it is only worth doing if it has high levels of public involvement. There is still much work to do on translating ideas into practice. This document, therefore, is a starting point. It sets out our current views, in order to stimulate ideas and contribute to a wider debate.

Sustainability

The central idea of sustainability is that we should achieve an acceptable quality of life, where necessary through growth, without disinheriting our grandchildren or mortgaging their future. Put at its simplest, sustainability is about ensuring that the activities that we have to carry out to meet our range of needs can be continued indefinitely. To do this, we must ensure that these activities, whether they are power generation, farming, waste disposal or tourism, do not irreversibly damage the environment or its assets. We need to take a balanced view of the need for development, reconciling growth with the requirement to stay within environmental thresholds of change and loss. Sustainability has to be founded on a long-term and broadly-based view of society's needs. There is no future in justifying damaging development purely for short-term economic gains.

The idea of sustainability has great resonance and potential. We do not seek the static preservation of our heritage, because sustainability offers us something more important, the chance to create a wide-ranging debate, not only with our usual partners but with a wider public, and not only about the minority of 'best' sites but about our whole historic environment. This is why we see sustainability as a process as well as a goal.

The pursuit of sustainability encourages active individual participation in land use decisions and in planning. It also requires from specialists and experts in any given field an acceptance of the value of local perception and a recognition of other people's non-expert values. It calls for a long-term view, certainly much longer than the 5- or 10-year life of local development plans, in which the future consequences as well as the immediate benefits of development and exploitation are considered; we aim to ensure that our grandchildren will be able to enjoy the heritage that we pass on to them, and to study and appreciate for themselves their origins and culture at first hand, not merely through books or film. But at the same time, sustainability is firmly rooted in the present, and in quality of life and local distinctiveness, to both of which the historic environment makes a major contribution.

Understanding the whole environment

Conservation usually concentrates on the parts of the heritage that are thought to be most important. Many of our finest buildings and archaeological sites are carefully protected and managed, but there has been much less emphasis on understanding and protecting all the other aspects of the historic environment which give the key sites their context and meaning. Most attention has focused on nationally designated sites or areas such as scheduled monuments, listed buildings, conservation areas and registered Parks and Gardens. Much less attention has been given to the heritage outside such special areas and sites, sometimes to the detriment of the setting of the important buildings as well as of the overall environment. Conversely, within designated areas there is a tendency to regard value and character as being uniform, and for diversity within these areas to be overlooked. A much more finely tuned characterisation of the whole historic resource is required.

Very often too the historic environment is thought of as simply being made up of individual historic buildings, archaeological sites or other quite specific areas such as historic gardens or conservation areas. These sites are often of very great individual importance, which justifies their careful protection by designation. But it is too easy to look only at separate sites, and to ignore the fact that the whole of our environment has been shaped and created by people and their work. The past, and its impact on the landscape, can be appreciated in every part of the country, not necessarily because of particular buildings or monuments but because of the detail, the fundamental grain and the basic character of the landscape in its entirety. Focusing only on parts of this whole removes history from its context and ignores the sum of all the parts.

It is also the more ordinary features that create 'local distinctiveness'. They often have as much if not greater significance for people's day-to-day lives as the nationally significant earthworks or buildings. The features which shape local environments and create the distinctive culture and meaning of a particular area are all too easily overlooked in our concentration on the nationally special sites. More local values frequently go unrecognised until actually threatened with loss, and everyday historic buildings, landscape features, archaeological sites, and gardens often remain undervalued and unprotected.

A focus on the 'finest assets' on their own therefore provides an incomplete picture of what the past can offer the future, and will not on its own allow us to sustain our heritage properly. At the heart of a sustainable approach is the acceptance that, to a greater or lesser extent, the whole environment is historic. A major part of English Heritage's job is about helping people to develop an understanding of the whole of their historic environment so they can contribute their own perspectives to the debate about what is important and what should be conserved or changed.

The concept of character is proving to be central to this aspect of sustainability. For example, English Heritage promotes conservation area appraisals designed to define and establish the special interest, character, and appearance of conservation areas, in order to underpin their designation and guide planning and management policies. We have also been developing character-based approaches to assessing and understanding the historic landscape, taking a holistic view of the whole landscape in preference to selective designations. Full-scale historic landscape maps have been prepared in a number of counties and are proving to be a valuable framework for developing conservation policies.

In addition, English Heritage work on mapping at national level the pattern and diversity of settlement and field patterns will complement the Countryside Character Map prepared by English Nature and the Countryside Commission with our assistance. Finally, in relation to individual sites or buildings, both the English Heritage Monuments Protection Programme and Thematic List Reviews have for some years now approached areas of the heritage (for instance the legacy of historic industry) by means of characterising the whole resource at strategic level before considering individual examples. Ideas on characterisation as being the key methodology of sustainability are being developed further as part of current work carried out by English Heritage in collaboration with the Countryside Commission, English Nature, and the Environment Agency.

Valuing the historic environment: a broader perspective

It is an essential first step in this wider understanding to acknowledge that different elements of the historic environment are valued in different ways, for different reasons, and by different people. We wish, therefore, to understand why a particular site or area is important and to whom and for what reasons. The list of 'heritage values' indicates some of the principal reasons why people value their environment for its historic interest:

- **Cultural values:** the historic environment helps to define a sense of place and provides a context for everyday life. Its appreciation and conservation fosters distinctiveness at local, regional, and national levels. It reflects the roots of our society and records its evolution.
- **Educational and academic values:** the historic environment is a major source of information about our ancestors, the evolution of their society and the characteristics of past environments. It provides a means for new generations to understand the past and their own culture. We can also use archaelogy to learn about the long-term impact (and sustainability or otherwise) of past human activity and development, and to use this knowledge when planning our future.
- **Economic values:** the historic environment can make a significant contribution to economic development by encouraging tourism, but more generally it also supports viable communities by creating good environments where people will prefer to live and work.
- **Resource values:** longer-lived buildings usually make better use of the energy and resources that were used during their construction, and reuse is usually more economic than demolition and redevelopment. Conservation is inherently sustainable.
- **Recreational values:** the historic environment plays a very significant role in providing for people's recreation and enjoyment. Increasingly, the past and its remains in the present are a vital part of people's everyday life and experiences.
- **Aesthetic values:** archaeology and historic buildings make a major contribution to the aesthetic quality of townscapes and landscapes, enhancing the familiar scene of our historic towns and villages and giving historic depth and interest to our countryside.

The importance of these different values will vary for different aspects of the historic environment. Most will also vary depending on peoples' individual judgement and needs. They will also have differing importance at local, regional, and national levels.

In addition, of course, we should aim not to separate the environment's very great historic qualities from its significance in other fields, notably, its ecological or scenic character. These other aspects demonstrably owe their existence in their current form to historical processes and human action in the past, since little in England is genuinely and entirely 'natural'. More than this, however, it is important to recognise that when we speak of wildlife or nature conservation, of archaeological value or scenic beauty, we are merely adopting different perspectives, not necessarily claiming greater importance for one or other of these aspects. It is essential both to keep a clear awareness of the different values, and to integrate our approach to their conservation and enjoyment.

Participation and involvement

Sustainability for the historic environment, therefore, depends on taking a comprehensive and integrated view of the environment and accepting that the values ascribed to the historic environment include personal perspectives and perceptions. One of its central aims is, therefore, to take account of who makes the value judgements involved: experts, local residents, politicians, or business people?

Until very recently, planning and managing the historic environment was often seen as exclusively a job for the expert. Involvement by ordinary people has often been limited.

This has begun to change, not least through the growth of wider environmental awareness and the work of groups like Common Ground, but formal conservation mechanisms such as designation still only partially reflect the wide range of 'heritage values' just described. In particular, little attention is given at national level to the identification and appropriate conservation of the 'locally important' heritage.

It is all too easy to allow a gap to grow between public understanding and awareness of the historic environment on the one hand, and the occasionally more specialist concerns and priorities of those who are responsible for managing it. We need to avoid this by helping professional conservationists to reflect the concerns and values of the rest of society, and at the same time helping everyone to appreciate from a scientific or academic perspective why a particular heritage asset is important from a national viewpoint.

Developing an understanding of local historic environments can be an effective and powerful way of increasing public awareness and involvement. Everyone has a local scene, which throughout England is coloured by the past. Not every locality has a listed building or a scheduled monument, but apparently more humdrum local features such as field patterns, road alignments, boundaries, and buildings all reflect many centuries of history and social and economic development. They reveal the thousands of years of interplay between nature and human activity, demonstrating the enormous extent to which England is a cultivated, nurtured landscape. Such features also provide easily accessible and easily understood links with a community's past. They are an echo of our predecessors' lives and actions.

A range of techniques will be needed to achieve greater public involvement. Key interest groups and their special concerns need to be identified to involve them throughout the process. Such participation itself can help foster a sense of local ownership of the historic environment, providing a powerful form of protection in its own right. It also allows wider debate about what is important and how we all wish to see the landscape change in future.

Working for sustainability

Sustainability is about the continuous *process* of conservation rather than achieving any particular final position, and although we can choose to take sustainable decisions, we will never achieve a final state of sustainability because there will always be a need for further change. Above all, however, we need to allow our descendants to have their own opportunity to decide their own future, and to do this we must avoid preempting thei options. A first step is to leave a healthy and viable historic environment for later generations.

At the same time, most people acknowledge that we must also live for the present day, and that our generation has a valid and understandable wish to leave its own mark on the environment. Just as we have inherited historic resources (whether areas, landscapes, buildings, archaeology, or historic parks) from previous generations, so future generations will inherit from us the 'new' assets that we choose to conserve. We also have an obligation to pass on a better, and more widely spread, understanding of the historic environment and of the various disciplines and sciences which allow us to explore our past. For this reason, there is a need to use parts of the historic resource, for example, by exploiting archaeological sites through excavation for research purposes, in order to justify conservation and sustainability decisions. We must get the right balance between new and old, and between keeping and using the historic and archaeological resource, but we should not be afraid of creating tomorrow's historic environment, or of using our historic and archaeological resources for the benefit of the present, as long as we do so wisely.

If we choose not to conserve important parts of our historic environment, we will make it harder for future generations to understand and appreciate their past, and we will impoverish their quality of life. On the other hand, preserving too much would risk 'freezing' the historic environment at a single point in time, denying it the continuing change which allows life to go on while reflecting our evolving culture, interests, and fashions. The historic environment that we have inherited is the product of long centuries, even millennia, of change, and even if it were possible, it would be wrong to deny future change. There has always been change; indeed, without change in the past there would be no historic environment and the past would be identical to the present. It is true, however, that the scale of modern changes, and the pace at which they occur, can sweep everything away if we do not think ahead and plan well, and our generation must define the balance with particular care. Our task is probably greater and more difficult than that of earlier generations. A sustainable approach, based on a thorough understanding of the historic environment and the options for its management, is where the best chance lies of a practical, proper balance between past and future.

It is not proving easy to put sustainability theory into practice. The framework for action is becoming clearer, however. In particular, following a series of clearly identified steps will help to ensure that we can achieve the aims of sustainability – that is, to meet the needs of current generations without compromising the ability of future generations to meet theirs. Some suggested steps, are as follows:

i   improve understanding and appreciation of the historic environment and its values, for instance by well judged exploitation and presentation of the resource as well as its protection; characterisation is proving to be one of the most useful tools available;
ii   identify the present and likely future forces for change affecting the resource;
iii make informed judgements, for example by the use of environmental indicators, about the level of change or activity that it can accommodate without unacceptable damage or risk to viability;
iv   use this information to set objectives for managing and planning the historic environment, notably the identification of acceptable thresholds or limits for change;
v   match these priorities (by means of strategic assessment of the consequences of action) to the most appropriate implementation mechanisms;
vi   define and implement a sustainability strategy including overall plans, policies, and the assessment of specific proposals for change;
vii monitor the character and condition of the historic environment to determine the effectiveness of policy mechanisms, also monitoring any new trends or forces for change and feeding back to adjust strategies and policy mechanisms as necessary.

By understanding the historic environment and our perceptions of its value, the essential first step, we can begin to decide which parts of it we wish to conserve and in what form, which parts may be less important, and which parts we may wish actively to change and enhance. Discussion of these questions has tended to use metaphors framed in specialist jargon that has been drawn from financial terminology, and it is not easy to escape from inaccessible language. In brief, three broad categories of 'historic environmental capital' have been defined.

In the past, environmental resources (whether wildlife habitats, buildings or archaeological sites) have been labelled wholly as either 'critical' or 'constant' assets. The implication of this has sometimes been that no change can be accepted for a critical resource, whereas any change would be justified for the constant assets. Although this may be appropriate for some aspects of the physical and natural environment, it is rarely so for the cultural environment. We are therefore adopting the tripartite classification that recognises that some aspects of the heritage may be 'critical' and others 'tradable' but that in between there is a much larger body of assets, which we are calling 'constant', which will change but which should not be entirely destroyed. It is in this area that past and present will be reconciled to create tomorrow's heritage.

For example, a fairly ordinary house may make an important contribution to the character of a conservation area; an unconverted field barn may be important as part of a shrinking population of such buildings. Some degree of change may be acceptable within these groups of assets provided that the overall character of the area or population is maintained. Indeed, change in this sphere is both acceptable and inevitable, particularly as we do not want to see a sterile, unchanging heritage. Change of some sort, not necessarily new buildings but, for example, the different use or adaptation of historic buildings, is just as vital to healthy life as the need to have an understanding of the past or to retain good quality of environmental life.

Any particular heritage asset can be valued in different ways or by different people. These multiple values cannot necessarily be applied as a one-off choice, however. The cultural and academic aspects of an archaeological site, for example, might be regarded as being of critical importance, with its economic and recreational aspects being much less important in the 'constant' or 'tradable' categories. Other values need to be taken into account, too, for example, nature conservation and visual landscape. We should, therefore, apply the critical/constant/tradable categories, not to a heritage asset as a whole, but to aspects or specific values of that asset. This will allow a more finely turned management of change.

Furthermore, different scales of importance should be taken into account. It might, for instance, be agreed that 'nationally critical' resources should be sacrificed only in response to benefits that are demonstrated to be of international importance. Similarly, 'local critical' resources might be sacrificed only where regional, national, or international benefits are likely. Under such a system, there would be a clear onus to demonstrate the nature and degree of benefit of new development, for example.

Much additional work, some of which is in hand, is needed to develop robust methodologies for using the ideas of environmental capital.

Living within the capacity of the environment

The historic environment, like the natural environment, can only accommodate a certain level of activity, or rate of change, before it is damaged permanently and loses its character or value. Examples include the physical impact of very high numbers of visitors on archaeological sites, the effects of air pollution and vibration from traffic on historic buildings, the effect on historic town centres of out-of-town retail, the requirement for gravel extraction for road programmes, non-traditional intensive farming methods, or the impact on the wider environment of encouraging visitors and tourism at historic sites. A sustainable approach requires that activities are managed so that valuable aspects of the environment are not damaged in this way. If 'supply' (i.e. the historic environment with all its values, vulnerability, and limited tolerance to change) cannot meet demand, then it becomes necessary to look for ways to reduce demand, or in some other way to manage it.

We can start to do this by defining 'environmental capacity'; that is, the capacity of the environment to absorb or accommodate activity or change without irreversible or unacceptable damage. Capacity may be expressed in a number of different ways, for instance the number of visitors or vehicles that can safely be accommodated without permanent physical damage, the rate of demolition and new development that can be sustained without losing the character of a historic town, or the point at which agricultural change (for example, ill-judged woodland creation, hedgerow removal, and intensification, or for that matter diversification) will create a new, rather than a historic, landscape.

The point at which the level of activity approaches the resource's capacity is usually termed the 'environmental threshold'. Beyond this point, the activity becomes unsustainable and very likely to result in permanent environmental damage, for example, to the historic character of an area, or the integrity of a building or ancient monument. The response should be to consider whether to 'alter course' as a threshold is approached; in other words, to take a view of wider priorities. One option at that stage is to manage demand more carefully, for instance by reducing the need for new mineral extraction by stopping new road building. At the very least, this approach allows decisions to be taken in the full knowledge of the consequences. If parts of the historic environment are to be lost, we could at least plan alternative action such as recording before loss.

The economic viability of a historic resource is one form of environmental threshold. A building's survival may be put at risk if conservation controls make its ongoing use uneconomic, as a certain level of economic viability is normally required before a building's future can be assured. For some types of historic asset, economic viability can, therefore, be an important threshold in itself.

It is important to note that neither environmental capacity nor thresholds are rigidly scientific concepts. They should be based on a consensus view of why a resource is important and what levels of damage or loss can be accepted. This consensus can only be reached after thorough understanding of the resource, and by involving those people and groups who have an interest in the resource in question. This might include academic experts, local residents, landowners, or potential investors, at appropriate local, regional, or national levels.

In practice, environmental management often makes use of 'environmental indicators' which in conjunction with long-term views can act as a proxy for the health of the environment as a whole. Examples might include the length and condition of historic field boundaries, the level of erosion at archaeological sites, or the numbers of converted or unconverted field barns in a particular area. These can act as signals to indicate when a broader environmental threshold or capacity limit is starting to be reached, preferably at a sufficiently early stage for action to be possible.

Dealing with uncertainty

One of the principal aims of a sustainable approach to environmental management is ensuring that decisions are made on the basis of the best possible information. By its nature, however, we cannot always know everything about the historic environment, particularly in the use of archaeological sites. There may be circumstances, therefore, where the precise effects of a particular proposal on the historic environment are unknown, although we can guess that they will be serious. Where this is the case, it makes sense to err on the side of caution. This approach is generally known to planners as the 'precautionary principle'. It is of particular relevance to the historic environment, where the full significance of many sites or areas is hidden or unknown.

The precautionary principle should not become an excuse for inaction, however. Doubt about the effect of a proposed action should be countered by attempts to reduce uncertainty so that a better decision can be made. There will be some instances (particularly in relation to archaeological sites) where the research needed to reduce uncertainty could itself be unacceptably damaging.

Moving forward

Sustainable development is not an easy option. Its theories and aspirations do not offer an instant solution to conservation problems, ideas in this discussion paper do, however, give us an opportunity to readjust our way of thinking about the role of the past in the present, and of how we should aim to pass on a viable historic environment to future generations.

This initial English Heritage document, therefore, does not conclude with a full set of answers, or even with a list of action points. It is intended to generate a much wider-ranging debate on the implications of the issues which our consideration of sustainability has raised. Predominant among these are:

- How to create stronger public participation in conservation debates, and to ensure that the past takes its proper place in the present.
- How to develop the conservation of locally valued and less scientifically valued historic and archaeological remains, in particular, how to protect and enhance local distinctiveness.
- How to use the distinctions between 'constant capital' and its 'critical/tradable' sub-categories to influence development and land management policies without falling into the trap of trying to protect everything.
- How to keep alive the sense of discovery which should accompany any exploration of our past. Historic remains should form part of our understanding of our origins and history, of cultural identity and of our quality of life; they should not merely be part of the unnoticed backdrop of everyday life.
- How can we set appropriate limits for acceptable change, the balance between new and old? Equally, what mechanism can be put in place to ensure that we change direction when limits are approached?

The best starting point for sustainability is for ideas for action to grow out of a popular consensus, drawing in landowners and planners, local communities, and individuals as well as experts.

Chapter 23

The Conservation Plan

James Semple Kerr

A new approach to an old concept

The Conservation Plan is a process that seeks to guide the future development of a place through an understanding of its significance. The objective is to evolve policies to guide work that is feasible as well as compatible with the retention, reinforcement, and even revelation of significance. These twin concepts of compatibility and feasibility are the bases on which the policies are built.

While there may be nothing new in this concept, its presentation in a co-ordinated written document has been extraordinarily useful. First, the policies, their supporting arguments, and evidence can be reviewed, tested, and adjusted. It is surprising how quickly woolly thinking can be exposed when committed to paper. Second, because the Conservation Plan policies have been tailored to a particular place, it not only provides useful guidance when planning new work, but also simplifies the process of assessing the impact of proposals that affect the place. Both are of immediate benefit to the client and reassuring to any funding body involved.

As an example I have tabled a copy of the Sydney Opera House Conservation Plan (Kerr 1996b) and a copy of an assessment of proposed work based on that Conservation Plan. The latter is sub-titled 'statement of the heritage impact of the proposed Broadwalk Studio redevelopment intended to provide an assembly area for the concert hall, a venue for "new music" and associated access and facilities'. It demonstrates just how strongly the impact assessment is based on the Conservation Plan and how much time and money is saved by the existence of the Conservation Plan.

A Conservation Plan is something of a paradox. It must have a scholarly basis yet be prepared in a commercial context using finite resources – and whatever techniques and sources of information are most appropriate, expeditious, and economical. As well as developing policies based on an understanding of the place, it should so engage the reader that the policies evolved become persuasive as well as practicable. There is, therefore, an underlying marketing objective, which must be tempered by the integrity of the practitioner.

Instead of focusing on the mechanics of the Plan, this talk is about the virtues which help rescue Conservation Plans from oblivion:

- flexibility rather than standardisations;
- co-ordination rather than disciplinary demarcation;
- simplicity, clarity, and relevance rather than bulk, density, complexity, fragmentation, and esoteric jargon.

The objective is to make the Plan readable rather than impenetrable and to offer ways of solving relevant problems.

Sequence, integrity, and confidentiality

Irrespective of the nature of the place and its problems, there is a basic sequence appropriate to the preparation of a Conservation Plan. The first stage is an assessment of significance based on an adequate understanding of the place through a co-ordinated analysis of relevant documentary, oral, and physical evidence. The second stage contains the policies to guide the future treatment of the place. It takes into consideration the practical issues that bear on the place as well as an understanding of the nature and, where necessary, the levels of significance.

This separation has its uses: it allows assessment of significance to be made away from extraneous pressures and thus helps preserve the integrity of the process. Anyone who has worked in the conservation trade for any length of time will be aware of the occasional pressures to understate (or overstate) the level of significance of a particular item. Such pressure may be subtle or blatant, but the intention is almost always to render the assessment compatible with an intended proposal, or even an objection to a proposal. The reverse sequence is obligatory: that is, making the proposal compatible with the retention of significance.

There is a further value in maintaining a distinct separation of the two stages. It was nicely illustrated by an Australian Department of the Environment campaign in 1978, which defined Heritage as 'things we want to keep'. The campaign helped to muddle assessment and management issues, and to polarise attitudes to conservation.

Heritage is what we inherit. It includes things we do, and do not, want to keep as well as things we want to modify or develop further – urban disaster as well as architectural masterpieces, surface salination as well as surviving old forest, and genetic predisposition to certain diseases as well as creative talent. To illustrate: the 'circle' or 'bullring' at Parramatta Gaol was a heritage structure of exceptional significance. The proposed continuation of the gaol in its original use, however, made the demolition in 1985 of the circle both a social necessity and an acceptable heritage option.

My reservation about the use of the seemingly innocent phrase 'things that we want to keep' stems from the erroneous but real public perception that when a thing is heritage it must be kept. An unintended result has been a stiffening of institutional resistance to any assessment process, and particularly listing, for fear of inflexible consequences. Developer-inspired excisions from the city of Sydney list confirm the point. Such difficulties reinforce the value of a two-stage Conservation Plan in which assessments of significance may be seen to be untainted by expediency. A flexible second stage can then provide an opportunity for all aspects to be considered before developing policies.

Assessments should not be confidential. What is done openly is more likely to be done with integrity – and more competently. Government agencies and developers are inclined to include confidentiality clauses in their standard contracts for Conservation

Plans. In the case of the agencies this is due to habit and precedent rather than necessity, and it is my experience that such clauses are easily removed. Sensitive defence installations and high-security prisons can be an exception. The Conservation Plans for two such prisons that I was commissioned to do at Goulburn and Parramatta (in 1994 and 1995) were published immediately on completion – simple and non-technical plans or diagrams being adequate for the report.

Commercial developers are somewhat different. There can be reasons for short-term confidentiality, but it should only be for a stated time. The more experienced developers tend to choose conservation practitioners with reputations for competence and integrity who are likely to have the respect of the approving authority. Some others prefer more amenable creatures who will give them what they want. The latter submissions necessitate a time-consuming review process by the relevant authority.

The sequence of the Conservation Plan preceding the concept stage of development proposal is ideal but not common. Most Conservation Plans down under are still commissioned in response to a proposal or premature political decision and are carried out to a tight schedule. The Capitol in Sydney's Haymarket was an example. The Conservation Plan (Kerr 1992) for this last reasonably intact atmospheric cinema or 'picture palace' in Australia was prepared at the same time as a revised application to local government for the development of the block in which it was situated.

I had the pleasure of simultaneously investigating and assessing significance and enunciating policy, at the weekly prayer meeting of the 14 sub-consultants engaged by the project architects, Peddle Thorp. The revised development application and the Conservation Plan were submitted in tandem. It was a process that makes me doubly appreciative of your Heritage Lottery Fund, which presumably allows a less hurried approach to conservation planning – at least in theory. Doubtless, market forces and short-term political expediency are not entirely absent even in your relatively utopian situation.

Flexibility

Model 'briefs' and 'templates' for Conservation Plans all rightly emphasise the need to adapt them to 'your requirements and the needs of your particular site'. Retaining such flexibility is an essential part of the process of structuring and presenting a Conservation Plan. It applies equally to assessment and policy sections and enables the report to be presented in as brief, clear, and simple a way as the complexity of the place permits.

Beware the mania for standardisation: standard briefs, standard criteria for assessment, and standard structures for Conservation Plans. Where they have been enforced, the results have mostly been depressingly repetitive and long-winded. Instead, all aspects of the Plan should be tailored to fit the nature, complexities, and problems of the particular place. It is the opposite approach to that of compiling and storing a list or inventory. In the latter case, standard criteria can be tolerated and even useful for their computer-friendly and accessible characteristics.

Similarly, there should be no standard way to set out the important link between policy and the data and argument on which it is based. The link may be presented in terms of traditional 'issues and opportunities', or as factors to be taken into consideration, as described in *The Conservation Plan* (Kerr 1996a), or even in terms of the vulnerability of the place. Whatever is most simple, direct, and easy to follow is appropriate.

Parramatta Gaol was the oldest and longest serving penal establishment in Australia when its Conservation Plan was completed in 1995. It was a major complex, including 50 to 60 penal, industrial, and residential structures both above and below ground together with landscaped and specimen-planted riverlands. Its policy section was kept simple by incorporating evidence, argument, policy, and any qualification or implementation of policy under each aspect or element of the place. The policy for the removal of intrusive elements is a basic example (Kerr 1995).

> **Removal of intrusive elements**
> A number of elements have been identified as intrusive in this policy section. Examples include the additions to the former female hospital, upper verandah additions to the 1901 governor's and gaoler's house.
>
> Policy 8.1 *Elements identified as intrusive in this conservation plan should be removed or modified.*
>
> Where the element is necessary to the function of the establishment, action may be deferred until new developments or change of use make the element redundant or suitable for modification. Occasionally, intrusive elements are also significant . . .

Being a former administrator, I understand the apparent advantages of standardisation, but I believe its disadvantages heavily outweigh its advantages.

Co-ordination

Most places or sites require a multi-disciplinary approach. However, the more disciplines and people involved, the more difficult it is to evolve a coherent product. The most useless Plans are those that are virtually a collection of separate analyses or essays by persons from every conceivably applicable discipline. Antipodean cellars are full of them. There has to be a balance.

> The objective should be . . . to engage the minimum number of persons having the necessary range of skills between them directly relevant to the assessment of the particular place. Whatever the arrangement, multiple contributions will need to be co-ordinated.
>
> (Kerr 1996a, 18)

In these days of cross-disciplinary education, relevant skills are not confined to traditional disciplines and increasing numbers of practitioners within those disciplines are multi-skilled. This can mean that careful selection will result in teams shrinking rather than expanding – making the whole process less unwieldy. If this is also becoming true of the United Kingdom, it may mean some reduction in time and cost for Conservation Plan work.

It is a truth universally acknowledged that the number of experts needed for any job directly corresponds to the funds available. Happily, there are solutions, regardless of the size of your cast. The first is the team system which espouses the multi-disciplinary team and emphasises the role of the co-ordinator – 'someone with the breadth of experience and imagination to understand the various issues and to pull them together in a balanced way' (English Heritage 1997a, 2).

The same draft added a zealous note:

> no one – not even an experienced conservation architect – can write a Conservation Plan by themselves. It is a team effort, and might well include:
>
> an architectural historian . . .
> archaeologist . . .
> architect . . .

landscape architect/archaeologist . . .
specialists . . .
engineer . . .
planner . . .
operations manager/director.

The writer was quite properly reacting to those Plans that are limited in their vision to a single aspect of a site, for example, the architectural fabric. Nevertheless, care is needed to prevent this laudable approach being translated into a level of resource utilisation, fragmentation, and detail, which is more likely to produce a fat pup than a lean running dog. Team selection is a matter of flexibility, balance, and choosing the right people with the right skills – not necessarily the 'right' disciplines.

There is an alternative model of equal strengths and weaknesses. It might be called the star system, as it involves complete control of all aspects by a single experienced person who draws on such expert assistance as is necessary to fill gaps and who writes the entire Plan. Its advantages are easy co-ordination, economy, complete continuity, and quality control. Accurate acknowledgement of all assistance is essential to both systems.

Of my 14 published assessments and Conservation Plans, only one, Yungaba Immigration Barracks in Queensland (Kerr 1993), was basically a team effort. As I never met the other team members, it was a very odd example. The other 13 reports were classic star-system jobs. Starting with a specialist knowledge of prisons and asylums, I gradually extended my range. For example, before tackling nineteenth-century fortifications, I spent time in the Royal Engineer Corps Library, Brompton, the Royal Artillery Institution Library and Museum, Woolwich, the Public Record Office, Kew, and the United Services Institution Library, Sydney. As I had earlier been a gunnery rating in the Navy, it was like the proverbial duckling taking to water and a fine basis for work on Sydney Harbour fortifications.

Where neither time nor interest permitted such preparations, as in the assessment of the riverlands west of Australia's longest serving gaol at Parramatta, I prepared a base map and worked over the area with a botanical expert. This filled out a sufficient understanding of structures above and below ground as well as remnant natural vegetation and exotic plantings of the late nineteenth century.

The obvious difference between 'team' and 'star' is that the former is multi-disciplinary and the latter cross-disciplinary. Cross-disciplinary only works if you have people who have built up the breadth of knowledge and techniques but who remain aware of their areas of ignorance and hence know when to seek help – and then to acknowledge all assistance fully. As all respected authors know, acknowledging sources not only retains friends and self-respect, but it also fingers the culprit if that part of the exercise has flaws. Whether 'team' or 'star', many a Conservation Plan has foundered on the time-honoured public service principle of never putting your name to anything, especially your own work.

When a Conservation Plan is a team effort, effective co-ordination is vital. This is nowhere more apparent than in the interpretation and analysis of evidence. In this modern age historians, architectural historians, and architects involved in the investigation of a place who are not trained to recognise and 'read' physical fabrics (and graphic images) as core documents are condemned to being a few bob short of a pound.

As well as Nikolaus Pevsner's famous pronouncement about cathedrals being architecture unlike bicycle sheds, some of you may remember his more laudable emphasis on the physical fabric of a place as a document to be 'read' and interpreted. It was his practice to deposit his mixed bag of students at an undisclosed, unknown, and complex building at sparrow fart on a Saturday morning and to require an analysis of its building history by nightfall. Lunch had to be carried and no one was to leave the site. Pevsner himself prowled round to encourage diligent application and discourage truancy. The evidence had to be located and analysed without intervention and it gave his students a great respect for the reliability of the actual fabric as primary evidence as well as a sharp awareness that it could be incomplete. It also emphasised how useful prior documentary research would have been in helping with interpretation.

Where documentary, oral, and physical evidence is not analysed by a single person, it is essential that those involved work as a team and feed off one another in the interpretation of that evidence. For example, an architect of the Sydney School trained in 'aesthetics' and 'gut feelings' might be unimpressed by Gladesville Psychiatric Hospital's dovecot made out of salvaged timber. An accompanying documentary researcher would take one look at the prickly Doric column and recall the complaint of the keeper of the Gladesville (then Tarban Creek) Asylum following its opening in 1838:

> the patients shin up the verandah posts of the airing yards and escape over the roof.
> (Digby to Colonial Secretary, 29.1.1844 and 21.3.1844, ML, MSS 20/1)

Colonial Architect Mortimer Lewis responded by having the posts (or rather columns) 'studded with tenterhooks' as a discouragement (ibid.), information which throws new light on both the dovecot as a fabric for interpretation and as a source of otherwise vanished evidence of the precise nature of the verandah columns.

Neglect of the written word can be equally deleterious to the work of engineers. Before commencing the redevelopment of the south-western part of Parramatta Gaol, a geo-technical investigation was commissioned. It involved boring test holes to understand sub-surface strata before determining the type of structure that could be appropriately superimposed. The holes delivered divergent results and presented a somewhat incomprehensible picture. The documentary research required for a Conservation Plan would have revealed the early location of a deep pool, an underground tank, and an erratic escarpment base, all covered by a process of cut and fill. This knowledge would have permitted boreholes to be located to give maximum relevant data and a clearer overall picture.

The reason I so strongly emphasise co-ordination is the defective structure of so many current Conservation Plans. They contain a section on documentary history by an historian, an analysis of the fabric by an architect, and, depending on the thematic complexity of the place, a range of separate specialised inputs from other disciplines. Without a combined analysis of evidence, it is a half-baked approach, which delivers reports of almost useless volume rather than a succinct understanding of the place.

As mentioned, optimum results are obtained by involving the fewest persons having the relevant skills for the job and by ensuring that evidence from all sources is analysed in a combined operation and set out in a co-ordinated narrative.

Consultation and the resolution of conflict

One of the major benefits of the Conservation Plan process is its potential for the resolution or, at least, reduction of conflict by consultation with, and involvement of, interested parties. The process can be effective at both assessment and policy stages if the parties are listened to attentively and their suggestions either worked into the text or acknowledged by an argument which sets out clearly why one of several alternative solutions may be preferable. It is an informal process by which a competent and experienced practitioner becomes both conciliator and arbitrator.

Regardless of relative reputation and expertise, the practitioner must be listener and negotiator, not dictator. Once he or she assumes the mantle of Moses handing down the tablets to the children of Israel, he or she is a dead duck – and so, most likely, is the Plan.

At least four and perhaps six of my Conservation Plans were commissioned because the client saw it as an opportunity for resolving awkward local situations. The first was the Governor General's residence in Sydney, Admiralty House, where there was a polite dispute over responsibility and jurisdiction. Both the house and the Commonwealth Public Works Department had received a mauling from a Governor General's wife, and officers from the Works Department sought a rational argument to protect the house and give them appropriate jurisdiction (Kerr 1987).

Different, but similarly awkward, situations had arisen at Sydney Observatory, Tamworth Gaol, the Sydney Opera House, and Juniper Hall – the last being the aptly named 1824 home of a convict who made his pile distilling gin. It follows that those who draft Conservation Plans should display a nice balance of integrity and diplomacy as well as knowledge and experience. It is important to work at getting the tone right. Partisan, dogmatic, or naive passages can irritate to the point where the draft never reaches the public eye. After all, the client has ultimate control over the Conservation Plan and can not only ignore it but also commission a replacement.

Fremantle Prison was a case in point. The complex is now part of a proposed serial World Heritage listing of Australian convict sites. It was disestablished in November 1991 after nearly 150 years of occupation as a purpose-built gaol (erected by its inmates). In the previous three years so many reports had been written by so many experts that I received a late-night distress call: 'If we send them all to you, will you write a policy for the place?' They arrived airfreight two days later and weighed 16.75 kg.

The policy development process at Fremantle was made difficult by conflicting demands of potential and established users, local and state government agencies, and watchdog societies – most of whom were represented on a very large steering committee. A process of individual consultation and policy adjustment resulted in the full committee endorsing the final draft without dissension and without losing the thrust of the policies. It was published within a month and the 1100 or so copies sold out in nice time to make way for the revised version, which was published in June (Kerr 1998). All my Conservation Plans recommend periodic revision – and this one was needed after six years of changed use as a tourist attraction and leased premises.

Conservation Plan revision need not be expensive. It usually only involves the policy stage. In 1992, Fremantle Prison, for example, required a fee of about £7600 and expenses of £2000. The 1998 revision fee was £2200, with expenses unchanged. The expenses are due to the fact that Fremantle is as far from Sydney as Moscow is from Oxford.

Three months is an average time for the preparation of a Conservation Plan. Large complexes such as Parramatta Gaol and associated lands may take five or six. Plans that extend past six months are usually no longer Conservation Plans.

Irrespective of the processes and parties involved in the preparation of a Conservation Plan, it is finally the practitioner (or team co-ordinator) who must shape and take responsibility for its content. If approached without a preconceived agenda, evolved with skill, acquired contextual knowledge, and integrity, and drafted with precision and clarity, the Plan will make a strong and positive contribution to the future of the place.

As the most interested party, the client should be kept in touch with the progress of the Plan and should be involved in its evolution. Springing a completed Plan on a client may lead to nasty surprises for both practitioner and client. The provision of drafts of both the first and second stages of a Plan for discussion and comment is a basic requirement. It is also my practice to provide drafts of key policies for informal comment. In this way policies can be improved and their relevance sharpened. Acceptance of the final draft can then become a formality.

A word of caution: the client contact for a practitioner should be an individual of some ability, understanding of the client's requirements, and adequate seniority. I have seen many projects go astray because the client has not taken reasonable care in choosing its representative.

The brief and commissioning process

Inadequate or muddled briefs and contractual agreements will disable a Conservation Plan. The worst of these pests is the detailed standard brief designed to cover a multitude of situations and often applicable to none. Like criteria for significance, each brief and agreement should be tailored to cover the issues relevant to the particular place and circumstances.

Where a client has an established working relationship with a practitioner, and knows from previous experience what will be produced, the relevant issues can be covered in a single page. The Parramatta Correctional Centre letter of agreement provides a suitable example. It covered:

> role of the practitioner,
> role of the client,
> practitioner's contact,
> schedule of work,
> remuneration,
> publication and copyright,
> indemnity of client,
> status of practitioner.

Contracts between less familiar parties, or which are going to tender, will need to be more precise in setting out the scope and intensity of the work expected. They should not, however, prescribe structures or criteria to be adopted in the report unless able to be designed with a precise knowledge of the particular place and issues involved.

Selecting the lowest tender for a Conservation Plan (even from a select list) frequently produces dismal results. Two of my recent jobs were directly commissioned by clients after such an experience. It effectively doubled their cost and the time taken to complete the work. A carefully prepared brief directly relevant to the place, and interviews with the persons actually doing the work, are necessary preliminaries to reducing the risk of tendering.

Dissemination, publication, and costs

The preparation of a Conservation Plan usually involves a limited number of people, yet it is important for the future care of the place that the Plan is widely disseminated and, where appropriate, published. Apart from the fact that it can both interest and instruct all persons involved in the use and care of the place, publication of seminal Plans plays an important part in advancing skills and typological knowledge of practitioners (and students) in the industry. It is in the interest of government and local government agencies and other funding bodies to advance the quality of conservation practitioners and hence Conservation Plans. Perhaps the situation is better in England but at home Conservation Plans range from abysmal to good. It is, however, much better than it was a decade ago and access to examples of what is done well has made a distinct impact.

The Conservation Plan as a story

You can read about the mechanics of preparation in *The Conservation Plan* (Kerr 1996a). The concept I want to leave you with today is that of the Conservation Plan as a story. It is a story that reveals the cultural values and character of the participants and the way these have shaped the fabric and function of the place. In one respect, however, it exceeds the traditional story-line – as well as telling of past development and present significance, it goes on to propose how the story should be continued in the future.

While the techniques and knowledge of all relevant disciplines should be brought to bear on the contents of the Plan, it is the traditional skills of story-telling that will convey its message to the reader and user. Continuity of structure, clarity of style, precision and economy of words, and, because of the need to include some relatively indigestible material, variations of pace are all necessary attributes. The whole is made immediate and comprehensible by the intimate relationship of text and supporting graphics. The production of a Conservation Plan in comic strip form remains my unrealised (and perhaps unrealisable) ideal.

Finally, as a Conservation Plan is a guide to the future, it is a beginning – not an end. It is vital that Plans make provision for the continuation of conservation advice and informed supervision of work. The Molong (New South Wales) mason, John Cotter, strikingly illustrated the need for future supervision when he carved his own gravestone, leaving a space for the date of his death and his age. His assistant or successor faithfully carried out the accompanying instruction and inscribed on the stone:

WHAT WAS HIS AGE
WHEN HE DIED
IN YEARS MONTHS
WEEKS AND DAYS

References

Nearly a decade has passed since this talk was delivered and most of the documents I refer to in the text have been revised and improved. Therefore I suggest you use "The Sixth Edition of the Conservation Plan" 2004 (not the 1998 edition), the 3rd edition of the Sydney Opera House Conservation Plan 2003 (not the 1993 1st edition) and the revised 2nd edition of the Yungaba Plan 2001 (not the 1993 edition). Full details of all publications appear in "The Sixth Edition of the Conservation Plan" as an appendix.

English Heritage, 1997a *Conservation Plans: a brief introduction*, London.

Kerr, J S, 1987 *Admiralty House: a Conservation Plan prepared for the Department of Housing and Construction*, The National Trust of Australia (NSW), Sydney.

Kerr, J S, 1992 *The Haymarket and the Capitol: a Conservation Plan for the area bounded by George, Campbell, Pitt and Hay Streets, Sydney*, 2nd impression, for Ipoh Garden (Australia) Limited, The National Trust of Australia (NSW), Sydney.

Kerr, J S, 1993 *Yungaba Immigration Depôt: a plan for its conservation*, Q-Build Project Services, Brisbane.

Kerr, J S, 1996a *The Conservation Plan: a guide to the preparation of Conservation Plans for places of European cultural significance*, 4th edition, The National Trust of Australia (NSW), Sydney.

Kerr, J S, 1996b *The Sydney Opera House: an interim plan for the conservation of the Sydney Opera House and its site*, 2nd impression, commissioned by New South Wales Public Works for the Sydney Opera House Trust.

Kerr, J S, 1995 *Parramatta Correctional Centre: its past development and future care*, commissioned by New South Wales Public Works for the Department of Corrective Services, Sydney.

Kerr, J S, 1998 *Fremantle Prison: a policy for its conservation*, 2nd edition, Department of Contract and Management Services for the Fremantle Prison Trust Advisory Committee, Perth.

Chapter 24

Commemorative Integrity and Cultural Landscapes
Two national historic sites in British Columbia

Lyle Dick

Commemorative integrity provides a methodology for identifying heritage values and objectives for the management of cultural landscapes which comprise great variety in the nature and extent of their features and present particular challenges in management. For this chapter, the use of the term "cultural landscape" follows the definition in Parks Canada's policies: "any geographical area that has been modified, influenced, or given special meaning by people."[1] What these landscapes share in common is that they tend to comprise a complex set of cultural resources that are distributed over a larger surface area than are such heritage sites as individual buildings or monuments. To manage these landscapes properly, managers confront a range of challenges in terms of identifying their heritage elements, determining their historic value, and then protecting and presenting them so that they may survive into the future.

This chapter discusses the concept of commemorative integrity as it relates to the identification, planning, and management of cultural landscapes. It can be applied to many different kinds of sites; for the purpose of illustration, however, two national historic sites in British Columbia – Vancouver's Stanley Park and Hatley Park near Victoria – will be highlighted. The chapter will explore ways in which commemorative integrity can facilitate the work of cultural resource management by enabling the setting of priorities according to historic values.

Parks Canada is the agency charged with administering Canada's national commemorative program. Although commemorative integrity is a relatively new concept for this agency, it is at the core of its mandate. Parks Canada's Guiding Principles and Operational Policies (p71) state that the program's objectives for national historic sites are as follows:

- To foster knowledge and appreciation of Canada's past through a national program of historical commemoration.
- To ensure the commemorative integrity of national historic sites; by protecting and presenting them for the benefit, education, and enjoyment of this and future generations, in a manner that respects the significant and irreplaceable legacy represented by these places and their associated resources.
- To encourage and support the protection and presentation by others of places of national historic significance that are not administered by Parks Canada.

This chapter will look primarily at the second and third objectives for national historic sites. By policy, the agency is committed to developing commemorative integrity statements for each of the 145 national historic sites that it administers, including those managed through lease arrangements. Stanley Park and a significant component of Hatley Park are managed by third parties outside of the federal structure. To manage these cultural landscapes effectively, the federal government is obliged to work with other agencies or institutions to foster the desired level of protection and presentation of their nationally significant values.

Commemorative integrity is defined as "the health and wholeness of a national historic site." The medical analogy may be appropriate if we consider that with cultural resources, as with the human body, it is important to identify threats or impairments before major problems are evident. The basic tool is the commemorative integrity statement, which defines the heritage values of the national historic site and sets forth objectives for its management. Typically, these statements are developed in a workshop setting by site managers, stakeholders, and specialists, who pool their knowledge to identify the elements of national historic significance, aspects of local importance, and other heritage values. Based on the identification of values, the resulting statement will provide benchmarks for the achievement of commemorative integrity through a concrete cultural resource regimen for the site.

The two cultural landscapes to be examined share a number of similarities. They are both of considerable size: Stanley Park is about 1,000 acres and Hatley Park comprises 650 acres. Both sites incorporate elements of coastal forest, historical buildings, gardens, roads, and pathways, and both are, at least some of the time, open to the public for recreational use. The federal government owns both sites, and they are managed through long-term leases by third-party custodians. Both are also outstanding heritage places that have been commemorated as national historic sites by the Government of Canada.

Historical background: Stanley Park

Established in 1888, Stanley Park is one of the outstanding urban parks of Canada. Its integration of natural and cultural features and the diversity of its evolving cultural landscape exemplify many of the key trends in the philosophy and spatial development of the country's major urban parks over the past one hundred years. Situated in Vancouver, British Columbia, the park is located on a forested peninsula that is surrounded on three sides by the Pacific Ocean; it abuts the central part of the city on its southeast periphery.[2]

Since 1888 the Vancouver Board of Parks and Recreation and assorted stakeholders have undertaken many initiatives to develop the park into one of Canada's premier playgrounds. In the first 25 years of the park's existence, the Park Board struck a middle course between the business elite, who advocated leaving Stanley Park in a quasi-wilderness state, and members of the city's working class, who pressed for the development of recreational facilities in the park. The compromises between these forces and their succeeding counterparts have produced a natural and cultural hybrid landscape of significance to all Canadians.[3]

Between 1913 and 1936 the park was managed by W.S. Rawlings, the superintendent of Vancouver's park system. Rawlings guided the development of a park landscape with strong British antecedents, including the redevelopment of areas of blowdown or cleared forest to create English park landscapes of lawn, trees, and ornamental shrubs. During his tenure many of the gardens and designed park landscapes were also laid out, and park recreational facilities were developed. The building of park structures in the rustic style, using natural materials such as timber or stone to build park facilities that would blend with their natural surroundings was a key trend.[4]

From the park's establishment in 1888, the natural forest environment has been an integral component of Stanley Park. Despite selective logging for Douglas fir from 1860 to

1880, there remain three-hundred-year-old coniferous stands with "old-growth" attributes. Another important feature is Beaver Lake, a shallow marsh in the central area of the park. Since both cultural and natural landscapes, as well as their balanced relationship, are of national historic significance, transitional areas defining the interface of these landscapes are important to the commemorative integrity of the designated place. Over the years, park authorities have devoted attention to planting deciduous and ornamental coniferous tree species in these transitional zones, and the planting program has served to soften the interface between the artificial and natural landscapes. In addition to the cultural resources relating directly to the history of the park, Stanley Park possesses a number of additional cultural resources associated with other activities including First Nations sites, the light station at Brockton Point, and military installations of the First and Second World Wars.

Historical background: Hatley Park

Hatley Park is another cultural landscape that illustrates well the interaction between human and natural forces. Situated in Colwood, British Columbia, it occupies a tract of land bordered by the Esquimalt Lagoon, a saltwater body connected to the Strait of Juan de Fuca. Other natural features include Colwood Creek, which flows through the central areas of the property, and an extensive tract of coastal forest, much of which survives to the present.

Human use of Hatley Park extends back several thousand years, when the Lekwammen, a Coast Salish people, lived in villages along or adjacent to Esquimalt Lagoon and utilized the rich marine and terrestrial resources of the area.[5] With the arrival of Europeans, land use changed from marine to forest extraction, as these lands were selectively logged, beginning in the 1860s. Around 1905, a British settler sold the property to businessman James Dunsmuir, then lieutenant-governor of the province and heir to the immense fortune of Robert Dunsmuir, a coal baron. In 1908 Dunsmuir purchased an additional 250 acres, adding another 300 acres in 1910. His lands included an extensive stretch of shoreland and large tracts of forest on three sides of the property.[6] With this land base in place, he embarked on an ambitious plan to convert these lands into a grandiose Edwardian estate, first engaging Samuel Maclure, a noted British Columbia architect, to design a manor house in the Tudor Revival style.[7] Dunsmuir also hired American landscape architects Franklin Brett and George D. Hall of Boston, students of Frederick Law Olmsted, to develop a landscape plan for the entire site. They prepared a classic design for an Edwardian park encompassing the entire property, designed several of the gardens and lawns, manipulated water courses to create a series of artificial lakes, and arranged the setting of several existing and new buildings.[8]

Overall, the plan carefully organized the landscape into four zones that progressed from a series of gardens near the manor house, to recreational spaces, to agricultural lands, and finally to the forest surrounding the estate. When complete, the estate incorporated a series of nine garden "rooms." In addition to three terraced garden spaces in front of the house, these garden "rooms" included the Neptune garden, organized around a processional staircase descending to the north entrance of the Castle; an Italian garden; a Japanese garden; a naturalistic English garden; a rose garden; and a glen garden in the forest.

A feature of the recreational zone was the transformation of nature to serve as James Dunsmuir's private hunting and fishing preserve. The artificial lakes were stocked with fish and equipped with fish ladders linked to Esquimalt Lagoon that enabled spawning species to reach them, while the forest was largely left intact and stocked with deer. In the agricultural zone, fields were laid out, and a stable, dairy barn, slaughter house, and smokehouse were built to realize the Dunsmuirs' vision of a self-sufficient estate. Several of these buildings were designed in the half-timbered Tudor Revival style to complement the castle. James Dunsmuir died in 1920 and his widow, Laura, in 1937. Soon afterwards their heirs sold the estate to the federal government, which from the 1940s established here the Royal Roads Military College whose management since has continued to maintain the extensive Dunsmuir gardens, enabling them to achieve the mature appearance they present today.[9]

As with Stanley Park, Hatley Park has a number of important features associated with the cultural landscape that are beyond its commemorated values. These include the ecological values of both the forest and Esquimalt Lagoon, a protected area under provincial legislation and an important habitat for marine life and birds. In addition, a number of First Nations sites, such as a shell midden on the shores of the lagoon, document thousands of years of occupation and land use by Coast Salish peoples.[10]

Commemorative integrity as applied to Stanley Park and Hatley Park

To aid in the management of the cultural values of these outstanding landscapes, commemorative integrity statements were developed for each site. A commemorative integrity statement incorporates three elements. A site is said to possess integrity when the resources that symbolize or represent its national historic significance are not impaired or are under threat, when the reasons for its commemoration are effectively communicated to the public, and when the site's heritage values are respected by all whose decisions or actions affect the site.

In developing the document, the first step is to craft a Statement of Commemorative Intent, which is a capsule summary of the reasons for the commemoration, as articulated in the minutes of the meetings of the Historic Sites and Monuments Board of Canada. This short statement of significance is the linchpin for much of the commemorative integrity statement that follows it. In contexts other than national historic sites, heritage managers could easily take a similar approach by developing a statement of historical significance for any heritage place, based on the input of knowledgeable professionals and stakeholders. In the case of Stanley Park, the actual words of the Historic Sites and Monuments Board of Canada were integrated into the following Statement of Commemorative Intent:

> Stanley Park is nationally significant because, in its splendid setting and in the relationship of its natural environment and cultural elements which developed over time, it epitomizes the large urban park in Canada.

Another essential early step is to define the designated place, so that its areal boundaries and what the resources it encompasses are clearly defined and understood by all persons with a relationship to the site. Workshop participants then apply the meaning of the designation in evaluating the site's cultural resources. Resources directly related to the commemorative intent of the site are deemed to be Level 1 cultural resources. Features that have not been commemorated but are nevertheless considered to have historic value are deemed to be Level 2 cultural resources, which also require objectives for the protection and presentation of their values.

First element: protection of nationally significant resources

The first element of commemorative integrity deals with the protection of a range of Level 1 cultural resources and typically includes such components as the designated place, buildings and structures, component landscapes and their features, and in situ archaeological resources. The "designated place" is the term used to describe the overall place encompassed by the commemoration. Since the whole of a cultural landscape is generally greater than the sum of the parts, it is considered important to define the heritage values of the entire site. A holistic approach can help avert incremental impairments to commemorative integrity, the "death of a thousand cuts." In the case of Stanley Park, the designated place is easily established as it

encompasses the peninsular lands encompassed by the park lease with the federal government, combined with a tract added to the park by the city of Vancouver in 1910. This is the
area that must be managed with integrity according to its historic values.

To protect the designated place, physical and associative values of the cultural resources
of the site are enumerated, and objectives are established for their future management. For
example, the nationally significant values of the site as a whole can readily be drawn out of the
Statement of Commemorative Intent and summarized in bullet format, as follows:

Designated Place: Level 1 Values
• An assemblage of natural and cultural elements;
• The balanced relationships of natural and cultural elements;
• The evolved character of the commemorated environment.

To help ensure that these nationally-significant values are maintained, objectives or
indicators are established for each enumerated value to guide future decision-making
processes. In the case of the designated place, the following objectives were specified:

Designated Place: Level 1 Objectives
• The cultural elements are inventoried, preserved, maintained, and monitored;
• Natural landscape and ecological features are inventoried, maintained, and monitored;
• The balanced relationships of natural and cultural elements are maintained.

As is suggested in the first two objectives, if the resources have not been fully documented, the Commemorative Integrity Statement should indicate the need for such studies
to be compiled. Since the commemorated environment of Stanley Park required cultural
values for both elements, as in the following objectives:

Cultural Elements of the Commemorated Environment: Objectives
• New construction of buildings and facilities in areas of the designed landscapes
  should he compatible with the historic character of these landscapes and the balanced relationships of cultural and natural elements;
• Facilities and corresponding activities should support and respect the heritage
  character and role of the park as it has evolved.

These objectives were drafted to provide general guidance to help protect the heritage
values of the cultural landscape, while recognizing that, as an operating urban park, Stanley
Park will necessarily continue to change and evolve. While these objectives will need to be
interpreted in specific contexts, they imply that new facilities should be of an appropriate
scale, materials, and finishes so as to blend in with the existing cultural and natural elements,
including buildings, gardens, the forest, and other features of Level 1 value. At the very least,
these objectives would oblige planners and managers to take the heritage character of the cultural landscape into account when formulating development plans.

Similar objectives were developed for the natural elements of the commemorated
environment, including the identified need for an inventory of natural forest values. They
also set out resource protection strategies to foster the continued integrity of the natural
environment, including the forest, shore, wildlife habitats, and physiographic features.
Generally, the objectives should be sufficiently detailed so that, if followed, the Level 1
values of the commemorated environment would not he impaired or be under threat. At
the same time, the objectives should not be too prescriptive in terms of how these objectives are to be carried out, leaving specific determinations of required actions to a future
management or cultural resource plan, which would take its general direction from the
Commemorative Integrity Statement.

Second element: presentation of the site's national historic significance

The next stage of the commemorative integrity process is to identify the Level 1 messages, that is, the reasons of national historic significance for which the site was commemorated and which should be communicated to convey its importance to Canadians. The importance of communicating the messages relates to the dual mandate of Parks Canada, that is. "to protect and present significant examples of Canada's natural and cultural heritage in ways that encourage public understanding, appreciation, and enjoyment of this heritage..." As with the first element dealing with resource protection, the second element relating to protection flows directly from the Statement on Commemorative Intent. Taking Hatley Park as an example, the commemorative intent was derived from the recommendations for this site of the Historic Sites and Monuments Board of Canada:

> Hatley Park has been designated a National Historic Site of Canada because:
>
> - its distinctiveness as an evolved cultural landscape defines its national historic significance;
> - it is a superb example of an Edwardian park;
> - the institutional imprint of Royal Roads Military College is apparent and complementary.[11]

In applying the commemorative intent to the second element, key messages are drawn out and reinforced with contextual messages that help communicate the elements of national significance. For example, the first key message relates to the evolved cultural landscape, while several contextual messages are identified so that the full meaning of the key message can be appreciated. In this case, the key message is that Hatley Park is a distinctive evolved cultural landscape of national historic significance.

> Context Messages
>
> - The integration of architecture and landscape, with Hatley Castle at its centre.
> - The roles of Samuel Maclure and Brett and Hall in designing, developing, and integrating the major features.
> - The contribution of individual components (e.g. gardens, forest, and agricultural lands) to the sense of place.
> - An estate that evolved over 80 years and continued to evolve during the Royal Roads Military College occupancy.

As with the Level 1 cultural resources, the nationally-significant messages need to be accompanied by objectives to ensure that they are effectively communicated to the public. For Hatley Park and other national historic sites, general objectives have been identified to indicate the goals of message delivery toward which site managers should be striving:

> Messages: General Objectives
>
> - Canadians and visitors understand the key components of commemorative intent.
> - The messages of national historic significance are not overwhelmed by other messages.
> - Appropriate means have been identified for delivery of the messages to target audiences.

It is recognized that other agencies managing federal sites may not be as concerned with heritage presentation as Parks Canada; however, this element is considered as important as resource protection strategies to achieving the health and wholeness of the site. If the public understands the nationally significant values of the site, the potential to generate the necessary support to ensure its protection will be enhanced. In this regard, Royal Roads University is already delivering some important messages through walking tours of the grounds and a recently established museum on the history of Royal Roads, both carried out in partnership with the Friends of Hatley Castle, a not-for-profit heritage group. Other potential avenues of delivery might include publications and the university's web site.

Third element: the site's heritage values are respected

Finally, every Commemorative Integrity Statement is required to address the third element of commemorative integrity, defined as the other heritage values that need to be respected by all persons whose decisions or actions affect the national historic site. These include the identification of cultural resources and messages considered to be of value but not directly related to the reasons for designation.

In this regard, an important value for both sites is the presence of archaeological sites of former First Nations villages and culturally-modified trees on these properties. To address the protection of these resources at Hatley Park, values of the Aboriginal archaeological sites were enumerated, including their documentation of land use by the Lekwammen (i.e. through faunal remains, such as bone, shell, artifacts, fire features, and culturally modified trees). These values were then accompanied by objectives to ensure that the values are appropriately respected in future decision-making, including an identified need for consultation with First Nations with a declared interest in the site. As with the Level 1 features, Parks Canada's Cultural Resource Management Policy provides specific guidance for the appropriate protection and presentation of the Level 2 cultural resources.[12]

Conclusion

The concept of commemorative integrity provides a holistic methodology for identifying values for cultural landscapes and their relative priority, as well as for establishing objectives for the future protection and presentation of those values. If a team charged with developing a Commemorative Integrity Statement is faithful to the commemorative intent, they should find that it provides a useful methodology for identifying the values of highest significance and, therefore, a way to set priorities for the management of these properties.

Does commemorative integrity work in actuality? When Parks Canada is the custodial federal agency and it directly manages the site, its policy requires that commemorative integrity guides the range of management instruments and activities for a national historic site, including planning, research, development, day-to-day maintenance, and monitoring. Commemorative integrity is written into the sites' management plans and since 1997 has been the basis of accountability through the State of the Parks Report, the biannual report to Parliament by the chief executive officer for Parks Canada. When a national historic site managed by others is recommended for cost-sharing for protection and/or presentation, the site's owners must agree to the implementation of commemorative integrity as a precondition of contribution funding.

In the case of national historic sites such as Stanley Park and Hatley Park, which are administered through lease arrangements, implementation of commemorative integrity is a more complex issue. For Stanley Park, Parks Canada administers the property through a long-term lease with the city of Vancouver but the property is actually managed by the Vancouver Board of Parks and Recreation. At Hatley Park, the Department of National

Defence is the custodial department, but the core components of the site are leased to Royal Roads University. Under these circumstances, it is essential that all site managers understand the process and take an active role in its implementation. To this end, Parks Canada worked with the Department of National Defence and Royal Roads University to develop a Commemorative Integrity Statement for Hatley Park, and with the Vancouver Park Board to develop a CIS for Stanley Park.

For these sites, some concern has been expressed that commemorative integrity might unduly restrict the development of new facilities. In both cases, the commemorative integrity objectives take into account the fact that these are functioning, evolving landscapes. Since the evolutionary character of these sites is itself an identified value, the objective is not to preserve a fossil or relic landscape but rather to protect their heritage character in the context of change. As with the sites managed by Parks Canada, strategies to protect and present their heritage values will necessarily be implemented gradually, enabling the identified planning, conservation and presentation requirements, and associated costs to be spread out over a period of years.

Perhaps the most useful application of commemorative integrity is that it provides a basis for undertaking an analysis of the current state of a cultural landscape, enabling priorities to be established for future actions to protect and enhance its integrity. Normally, a situation analysis would take into account any threats or impairments requiring particular attention and specify the need for remedial action. These might include the development of a conservation plan, cultural or natural resource inventories, or a monitoring regimen, leading to specific intervention strategies to protect the resources, commensurate with the objectives outlined in the commemorative integrity statement. It is intended that these statements will form a key component of the management plans to be prepared for each of these sites.

It is acknowledged that a number of issues remain to be resolved regarding the future management of these two sites. While the Stanley Park Commemorative Integrity Statement has now been approved by the Park Board, Parks Canada as the custodial federal agency is obliged by policy to work its counterparts to encourage its implementation. At Hatley Park the process is farther advanced, as federal administrators have indicated their commitment to address commemorative integrity in the context of third-party instruments to manage the site. The precise means by which commemorative integrity will be carried out at these sites remains to be established, but its application to national historic sites managed by Parks Canada provides some models for discussion with the third-party managers. Given that commemorative integrity is a fairly new concept, Parks Canada's responsibility is to build a more general awareness of this methodology and its potential to help protect and present heritage places of national historic significance. The qualities that make Stanley Park one of the world's favorite urban parks or that give Hatley Park its appeal as an outstanding campus are values that have been articulated in the Commemorative Integrity Statements for these sites. The challenge is to build a consensus among all parties, not to freeze these cultural landscapes in time but to ensure that change is managed so that these heritage places continue to represent the values for which they have justifiably achieved national recognition. Commemorative integrity provides a methodology for achieving that goal.

Acknowledgments

The editorial and critical comments of Ron Frohwerk, John McCormick, Marty Magne, and two anonymous peer reviewers for the *APT Bulletin* on the earlier draft of this paper are gratefully acknowledged. Sincere thanks are due to Susan Buggey, who first proposed the preparation of this paper for the APT Conference in Banff, Alberta in October 1999. I would also like to acknowledge the contribution of Joanne Latremouille, whose insightful analysis of the Edwardian design of Hatley Park has informed this discussion.

Note to this edition

This chapter has been slightly revised from the original version, which appeared in the *APT Bulletin*, Volume 31, No. 4 (2000), 29–36. It is being republished courtesy of Mount Ida Press, 152 Washington Avenue, Albany, New York 12210, USA <mtida@albany.net> Readers wishing to view historical images of various cultural resources referenced in this chapter are referred to the earlier article.

Notes

1   Parks Canada, 1994: *Guiding Principles and Operational Policies*, Ottawa: Department of Canadian Heritage, 119. I have also followed the framework of the World Heritage classification of landscapes into designed, evolved (both relict and continuing), and associative landscapes. Evolved landscapes divide further into relict and continuing landscapes. See UNESCO, 1996: *Criteria for the Inclusion of Cultural Properties in the World Heritage List*, Operational Guidelines for the Implementation of the World Heritage Convention, Paris: UNESCO.

2   On the general history of Stanley Park, see Richard M. Steele, 1985: *The Stanley Park Explorer*, Vancouver: Whitecap Books; Richard (Mike) Steele, 1988: *The Vancouver Board of Park and Recreation: The First Hundred Years: An Illustrated Celebration*, Vancouver: Vancouver Board of Parks and Recreation; Lynn Vardemann and Freda Carr, 1973: *A Guide to StanleyPark*, Vancouver: Seaside Publications; R. A. Hood, 1929: *By Shore and Trail in Stanley Park,* Toronto: McClelland and Stewart; Catherine Mae MacLennan, 1993: *Roaming Around Stanley Park*, Toronto: Ryerson Press.

3   Robert A. J. McDonald, 1984: " 'Holy Retreat' or Practical Breathing Spot? Class Perceptions of Vancouver's Stanley Park, 1910–1913," *Canadian Historical Review* 65 (1984): 127–153, 5.

4   Sally Coutts, 1988: "Stanley Park, Vancouver, British Columbia," National Historic Sites Directorate, Parks Canada, Ottawa (unpublished paper).

5   Cindy English, 1996: "Traditional Use Study, Victoria Approaches, Vancouver Island Highway Project," report prepared by the Songhees First Nation for the BC Ministry of Transportation and Highways.

6   Terry Reksten, 1991: *The Dunsmuir Saga*, Vancouver: Douglas and McIntyre, 220–221.

7   Martin Segger, n.d. "Building Hatley Castle: The Architect," in *Hatley Park: An Illustrated Anthology*, 61–66.

8   Leslie Maitland, 1995: *Hatley Park/Royal Roads Military College, Colwood, British Columbia*, unpublished research report, National Historic Sites Directorate, Parks Canada, Hull, Quebec; Parks Canada 2000: *Commemorative Integrity Statement for Hatley Park*, copy filed with the Western and Northern Service Centre, Parks Canada, Vancouver. The landscape analysis was provided by Joanne Latremouille, Conservation Landscape Architect, Historic Conservation Services, Public Works and Government Services, Gatineau.

9   Peter J. S. Dunnett, 1990: *Royal Roads Military College, 1940–1990; A Pictorial Retrospect*, Victoria: Royal Roads Military College, 37–49, 82.

10 Millennia Research, 1997: *Archaeological Baseline Study, Royal Roads*, unpublished report prepared for Public Works and Government Services Canada and Parks Canada, Victoria, BC.

11 Historic Sites and Monuments Board of Canada, 1995: Minutes, Spring 1995, Parks Canada, National Historic Sites Directorate, Ottawa.

12 Parks Canada, 1994: *Guiding Principles and Operational Policies*, 99–115.

Chapter 25

Explaining LARA

The Lincoln Archaeological Research Assessment in its policy context

David Stocker

Introduction

LARA, the Lincoln Archaeological Research Assessment, is an attempt both to summarise the archaeological debate on the City of Lincoln to date and to chart an agreed course for future work, which will continue that debate. It rides on the top of the collection, classification and analysis of archaeological data for the city achieved by the Urban Archaeological Database (UAD) and, in that respect, it can be seen as an extended 'discussion' similar to sections found at the end of site reports. But because LARA aims to assess the archaeological potential of the entire District Council area and to discuss the research agenda for areas which have never been investigated archaeologically, it is also legitimately described as a form of *characterisation* of the city from an archaeological perspective.

LARA also fits within a wider framework – the exercise has emerged from national English Heritage programmes of Urban Archaeological Assessment which themselves are rooted in developing concepts of both planning and archaeology. Urban Assessments (like all high level evaluation, assessment and characterisation work) are located right at the point at which academic debate meets the development planning and development control system and here, at this hinge, we need to bring together qualities and perceptions from both academic archaeology and planning skills and concerns. This is where academic archaeology meets the real world and it is therefore an indispensable step in 'informed conservation' in Lincoln.

Archaeological theory

We now live in a somewhat different theoretical environment from that in which some of us grew up. Thirty years ago archaeology was keen to define itself as a science, imitating the empirical method and insisting that all theorising had to be based on extensive experimentation (i.e. excavation). We all thought that few conclusions could be drawn from archaeological data without extensive experimentation first. In this 1970s world, the most important task of the archaeologist working in the context of urban redevelopment was to identify where he thought there might be archaeology surviving and then argue for the funds to excavate before destruction to find out what the archaeology 'really' comprised.

This mind-set never dominated the whole of archaeology (it never really caught on in landscape archaeology for example), and it has lost ground steadily over the last three decades to more discursive approaches. Increasingly field archaeologists have been asked to do more than identify undifferentiated archaeology, which requires excavation before it can be discussed. It is no longer helpful for the archaeologist simply to point to an area where archaeology may exist and then ask for funding (either from a developer or from another funding agency) to find out what the archaeology consists of. Archaeologists are now expected, first, to attempt to predict what lies below the ground, to extrapolate from knowledge of similar sites and contexts, and to interpret and synthesise existing understanding far more broadly. Second, archaeological curators, funding bodies and indeed the general public, look for a pre-defined research framework within which an investigation can take place.

Planning theory

A major trend in Planning in the last ten years has been a shift away from the *ad hoc* decision-making that emerged during the 1980s back towards plan-led development more in keeping with some of the original aims of the Town and Country Planning Acts. Rather than making decisions on an *ad hoc* basis when the planning application is made, we are moving back towards a situation where planning negotiations should be conducted on the basis of agreed aims and objectives which have already been spelled out in the Local Plan, in advance, and given legitimacy through democratic consultation and political approval. The LARA methodology was developed to express archaeological concerns in such a way that they could be easily deployed as part of planning negotiations conducted through plan-led development strategies. Put briefly, the archaeologists in Lincoln have spelt out, in an accessible way, what we want to achieve through future archaeological work, using plan-led planning strategies.

In the world of developer funding for archaeology that has been emerging for the past 15 years or so, we might also argue that the funders, usually developers, have a right to ask why they are being asked to pay for archaeology. It is sometimes clear why they are being made to pay for many environmental and other subsidiary aspects of their development – in Lincoln, for example, that is all laid down in the Local Plan (and will be in its successors) – but the detailed reason why they are asked to pay for any particular piece of archaeology has often, in Lincoln, been left undefined. The broad reasons are defined clearly enough in national planning guidance (PPG16) (retrieval of evidence before destruction; destruction in effect being seen as pollution; hence the polluter pays) but in reference to specific development proposals detailed justification is unusual. Beyond the bald statement that 'archaeology' is present, there is rarely any explanation in the Local Plan, or in Supplementary Planning Guidance, available to the developer, to explain why he/she is required to pay for an excavation on a particular site, or how the community as a whole hopes to benefit from their investment.

The present position

Current negotiating stances

Currently, most developer funded archaeological research is undertaken because the developer is told by national planning policy guidance that it is a requirement for obtaining planning permission. In practice this results in debates between the developer (or developer's consultant) and the curator being conducted with few visible rules. For the curator in most planning authorities it is not clear what would constitute a successful outcome – frequently it is nothing more than the mere presence of an archaeological phase in the development and the implementation of a written scheme of investigation. The curator has nothing against which to measure the success or failure of a planning condition imposed in this way. Worse still, for the developer, there is little positive to be taken away from the process. The less additional cost the archaeology brings the better, but nothing positive is offered by the planning authority to show that the developer's contribution might be valuable or might have a public benefit. At present the parameters for excavations set by some planning authorities are not expressed in terms of an increase in knowledge. Archaeological requirements are often indicated negatively, in terms of the preservation of unrecorded deposits, rather than positively, in terms of the gains in knowledge aimed at in dealing with deposits which are to be removed.

Research agendas or frameworks

Partly this lack of defined aims and targets is because much of the archaeology profession has been too busy excavating individual sites to stand back and apply (or even to review) what they have learnt in a general sense. Excavation reports still focus on the presentation of excavated evidence rather than on the broader lessons for the city or region as a whole. And it is to try and rectify this that English Heritage has in recent years promoted programmes of research aiming to draw together conclusions from individual sites and surveys – the so called 'Research Frameworks Programme'. LARA should also be seen as a facet of this work, as well as an example of an Urban Assessment project and as an example of urban characterisation used as a way of helping to manage change.

Proposed improvements in the Lincoln case?

The Lincoln Urban Archaeological Database (UAD)

The work of pulling together the data on Lincoln's archaeology (the UAD completed six years ago) should be seen as part of this Research Frameworks process. This chapter does not discuss the Lincoln UAD, but its construction should be recognised as the first step in a process of making the archaeological case. It can be conceptualised as the base of a pyramid (see Figure 25.1) – the material from which interpretation and ideas can be drawn, and on which policy and action can be built thereafter.

The next step in the pyramid towards making the archaeological case, is to make this data more readily comprehensible to the public. This is the purpose of LARA, a stepping stone from data (the UAD) towards policy (the Local Plan and/or its successors).

From UAD to local plan: the role of LARA

Characterisation

Getting from the UAD to the Local Plan is not straightforward. Many authorities have simply referred to their databases (or similar documents) in their Local Plan, but this is a very limited response and in Lincoln it was felt to be inadequate. Although it helps to make this data publicly available in this way, the data on all UADs needs sophisticated

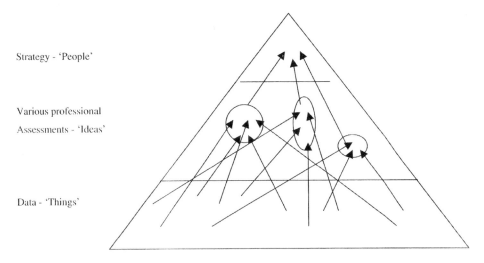

Strategy - 'People'

Various professional
Assessments - 'Ideas'

Data - 'Things'

Figure 25.1   The hierarchy of tasks in holistic environmental planning.

interpretation before it can be understood. Furthermore it cannot be given the force of a Local Plan policy, (except in the most general terms – "Lincoln is a large archaeological site and we will ensure that archaeology is done"). No, we need an intermediate stage, where the data is interpreted more broadly, by professionals, and the current best guess as to the type of archaeology that will be found in any given spot, will be explained. In English Heritage this sort of work on an archaeological data-set is seen as one of the central elements of the process of characterisation. LARA, then, is also a characterisation of Lincoln.

In the abstract, then, we have clear aims for the archaeological assessment process and in LARA we have tried to put this theory into practice. The Lincoln methodology aims to characterise urban deposits in a way which is both acceptable professionally and which can also be used as the basis for Local Plan statements about our archaeological ambitions in every area of the city.

Results

LARA, then, is an attempt to express our understanding of the city's archaeology in a holistic, interconnected, way. Another way to describe LARA is to outline its beneficial results. Following the completion of LARA, rather than merely saying to the developer (or to the school teacher/pupil, or other interested party), that there is archaeology here and we want to excavate it. LARA says instead:

– We have done a lot of previous work in Lincoln, and the results of that work are summarised here in an easily accessible form, filtered through wider up-to-date interpretations of the past.
– All this previous work allows us to see that any given part of the City Council Area has a specific archaeological character. LARA has defined this character – and this is what we can now say/predict about the particular site in which you are interested.
– Based on our current understanding we need you, in your contribution, to address a range of specific questions about the history of the city in your work on your particular patch – and LARA provides a list of them.

Methodology

So how are we going to characterise the archaeology of Lincoln? Well, for any meaningful characterisation we presumed that we should start by dividing up the city both geographically into character areas as in Historic Landscape Characterisation (Fairclough 2002). Furthermore, because Lincoln is a place with great time-depth (very well-known through 30 years of large scale excavation) it is possible to do this chronologically for several different periods of history. This process has created geographical and chronological units held on a simple GIS and relational database for each of seven broad periods into which we have broken up the history of the city. We have called these period Eras. 'Eras' are periods of time of markedly different lengths during which it seemed to the LARA team that there was a broad continuity in the city's material culture. Some of these Eras are highly debatable, of course, especially, perhaps, the way in which we have divided up the medieval and early modern periods. What is more, they will be different for different cities, but for Lincoln they are:

1–4 Not assigned,
5   Prehistoric settlement in the immediate vicinity of Lincoln,
6   The Roman Military Era (*c*.43AD–*c*.90AD),
7   The Roman Colonia Era (*c*.90AD–*c*.400),
8   The Early Medieval Era (*c*.400–*c*.850),
9   The High Medieval Era (*c*.850–*c*.1350),
10 The Early Modern Era (*c*.1350–*c*.1750),
11 The Industrial Era (*c*.1750–*c*.1945).

Within each Era, LARA seeks to identify sets of character areas, geographical components based on, but not defined by, buried archaeological structures, urban plan-form, building groups or past landscape and townscape. We were clear that we could not use the 'monuments' identified in the UAD as the basis for the geographical characterisation as there were far too few of them, they only covered a very small percentage of the District, and the boundaries of many of them were unknown. Consequently we devised a method for defining areas on the ground within which specified archaeological research questions could be addressed. We have therefore called LARA's geographical and chronological units RAZs, *Research Agenda Zones* and we have managed to define a total of some 550 across the entire District, from the Mesolithic to 1945.

Boundaries of these RAZs (which are always contiguous or overlapping – there is no 'white space', no unclassified areas) were decided through a small panel of Lincoln specialists considering which research questions should be asked within each Era at each point on the map. Texts were then generated and subject to further discussion and agreement. However, it is recognised that these individual research agendas represent the view of a limited group at a single moment in time and so, in the coming years, the City Archaeologist will seek views of many external specialists and continually improve the research agendas offered.

Some of the RAZs are single building complexes while others are large areas of land. For each of these RAZ components in each Era on the map there is a short text on the linked database. This means that for any given location in the District there will be a minimum of seven statements explaining, within each Era, what research questions archaeologists would like to see answered in future research at that point. Access via the GIS is very simple; you simply place the cursor at any point within the District boundary and it automatically provides the seven (or more) database entries, the RAZ texts.

Each RAZ text has four parts:

—   a brief statement about the physical character of the component,
—   a statement about the relative archaeological significance of the component,

- a statement about how we wish to explore it in future, and
- a statement about how we have defined the boundary of the component – whether it is clearly defined or vague, whether it is known or guesswork.

In this way, then, we have encapsulated the archaeology of the city, and we have provided a clear statement of the research questions we wish to see addressed in future work. Although LARA's primary function is as an active GIS database, the complete RAZ texts and the maps, which go with them, can be abstracted and presented in hard copy to provide the City and the public with a comprehensive Research Agenda for any part of it at any given moment.

Using LARA

LARA was completed early in 2002 and is proving to be of enormous practical use. It structures the archaeological component within the daily development control process and has placed the archaeologists and heritage managers at the centre of the planning team.

Lincoln now has full documentation of our archaeological understanding in a format that allows our knowledge to be used within the Local Plan process, and as the basis for Supplementary Planning Guidance (SPG) in support of innovative Local Plan Policies. This sort of *characterisation* can be used in the same way that Conservation Area Statements can be used to conserve Conservation Areas, because the Council can judge any proposals against the characterisation statement and agree that it works towards the aims presented there, or not.

This is straying into a third stage of work, however. The drafting of holistic Local Plan Policies which encapsulate not just the Archaeological Research Assessment, but also those produced by other professional groupings (such as ecologists and townscape planners) was beyond LARA's brief. This is the uppermost stage in the pyramid shown in the figure. However, LARA does ensure that the archaeological case is both well-organised and easily accessible when it needs to be combined with parallel assessments by these other interest groups in Plans for wider environmental management. Traditionally, we have called this tertiary phase the 'Strategy' phase and, in Lincoln we are currently drafting the specifications for such work aimed at bringing together the various professional assessments of the City into a single environmental plan.

Review of LARA

Finally, it is important that we do not regard LARA as set in stone. It is merely a snapshot of the current state of archaeological understanding of the city. Next month, next year, new excavations and other discoveries will make aspects of the RAZ texts in each era obsolete. That is as it should be, and will be a sign of the success of the LARA approach. And coping with these continual changes should be no different from coping with change in any other aspect of Plan production. The Plan review cycles sweep up any new information in other professional fields and incorporate it into the revised documentation, and archaeology should simply be another part of that process. In each review cycle the Lincoln City Archaeologist will be faced with reconsidering LARA and redrafting it where appropriate.

Among all these other things, then, LARA is also a benchmarking exercise; providing the structure and the preliminary statement for a cyclical process that will provide Lincoln with a practical management tool for its archaeology into the foreseeable future.

Chapter 26

Assessing Public Perception of Landscape
The LANDMAP experience

Alister Scott

Assessing public perception of landscape continues to be both an academic and a policy challenge. The involvement of the public in landscape matters has been and continues to be both controversial and problematic. Constraints of time and resources, together with a reluctance to delegate responsibility to the public, have generally limited the scope and influence of much participation to conventional reactive strategies. The potential of a new methodology to identify public perception of landscape in Denbighshire is assessed. Forming part of a wider initiative known as LANDMAP, a technique adopted by the Countryside Council for Wales for identifying distinctive landscape areas, household questionnaires and focus groups have been used to evaluate public perception in response to carefully selected photographic media. The results afford important insights into public perception and allow particular landscape types to be evaluated in both quantitative and qualitative terms. Analysis of the results for two selected areas shows that the public has strong attachments to managed rural landscapes in general, and wishes to see more integrative and participative strategies for landscape protection and management. Such attitudes challenge planners and policy makers to rethink their approaches towards conventional landscape management strategies and planning.

Introduction

This chapter presents a new methodology developed for measuring and mapping public perception of landscape in Wales.[1] Two fundamental questions posed by Appleton (1975) – What is it we like about landscape and why? – have long pre-occupied academic researchers and provide the main inspiration to the research reported here. In addition, there is a further question relating to the extent that public perception should influence landscape policy.

The principal focus of this chapter relates to a pilot study of mapping public perception in Denbighshire in 1999 (Scott, 1999).[2] Forming part of LANDMAP, a new landscape resource assessment technique devised by the Countryside Council for Wales (CCW), public perception is identified as one of eight factors contributing to a multi-dimensional assessment of landscape (CCW, 1999, 2001).

The chapter proceeds with a critical review of factors influencing, and past approaches to measuring, landscape perception and the allied problem of securing effective public participation. It then considers the methodological approach employed within LANDMAP using two landscape studies from the Denbighshire study to highlight the potential and application of the approach.

Landscape perception and the public

Public perception of landscape is playing an increasingly important role in contemporary rural Britain. The psychology of seeing, and attaching value and meaning, to a landscape influences where people choose to live, how and where they work, their sense of well being and their sense of place (Appleton, 1996; Countryside Commission, 1993). Perceptions can also influence subjective judgements at a sub-conscious level, so shaping reactions to, and feelings about, certain landscapes, features or developments. Consequently, the visual appearance and perception of our surroundings continue, as in the past, to be important (Moore-Colyer, 1999). Certain landscapes are valued for their character, features and patterns, and people are often resistant to significant changes in the visual appearance of familiar or local landscapes (Council for the Protection of Rural England (CPRE), 1999; Gourlay & Slee, 1998; House & Fordham, 1997; Shucksmith et al., 1993). Gold and Burgess quote the pre-occupation with 'high culture environments' (1982, p. 2) and question the daily environments that are taken for granted by policy makers, academics and inhabitants, where the strength of attachment to ordinary places and landscapes frequently only emerges when they are threatened by change. Indeed, familiarity with landscape has long been an important factor identified in perception studies by Burgess et al. (1988) and Penning-Rowsell (1982). As Tapsell (1995) acknowledges, the most valued open areas are often the familiar ones which play a part in people's daily lives.

Consequently, perception does not depend just on the physical landscape components, but also on the values, past experiences and socio-cultural conditioning of the observer (Brabyn, 1996). Landscape responses are therefore viewed as a product of the interaction of people with the physical and cultural environments at particular times (Emmelin, 1996; Muir, 1999). Appleton (1994) speculates that positive responses to landscape are derived from the totality of the landscape, and not only from the particular features and elements contained within it.

When landscapes change at varying paces according to the relative rate of land-use change, technological development and the needs of society, a clear tension is created between differing sectors of the public that value particular landscapes. The relationship between perception and participation is complex and brings into consideration issues of equity, accountability and democracy, and questions the way that the wider public interest is represented and implemented in landscape management terms.

The town and country planning system is the principal mechanism invoked to address and resolve such matters, balancing the sometimes competing views and needs of private individuals with the wider public interest (Cullingworth & Nadin, 2001). Since perception of the landscape is an important component of planning practice and policy, it is important to understand the multiple factors shaping that perception.

The CCW captures the essence of the multi-dimensional nature of landscape within the following summary:

> Landscape may be thought of as the environment perceived predominantly visually but also with all the other senses. Sight, smell and sound all contribute

to landscape appreciation. Our experience of landscape is also affected by cultural background and personal and professional interests. For CCW's purposes landscape is defined as the sum of all these components.

(CCW, 1999, Appendix 1, p. 4)

Clearly, public perception is complex and idiosyncratic, rendering simple analysis or generalization problematic. The resulting variability and subjectivity arising from human responses to particular 'landscapes', therefore, are both elusive and conditional. Indeed, research has demonstrated that people can exhibit different perceptions of the same landscape (Brabyn, 1996). These findings lend support to those who argue that such views are incapable of meaningful interpretation and are often cited as reasons why the public should not be directly involved in landscape matters (Nicholls & Sclater, 1993). This reluctance is not just confined to practitioners, but is also evident in the academic literature, where various commentators have argued for a professionally led approach, relying on those trained in design to express judgements of scenic quality in order to interpret the aesthetic values of society in a consistent manner (Jacques, 1980; Kaplan & Kaplan, 1982, Chapter 4; University of Manchester, 1976; Sanoff, 1991).

This genre of landscape studies, evident in the work of Linton (1968), Crofts (1975) and the CCW (1999), has essentially involved a multivariate and spatial type analysis. The most striking example is found in the work of the Coventry-Solihull-Warwickshire Sub-Regional Planning Group (1971), which identified three factors as principal determinants of a landscape's value (land-form, land use and land features). The subsequent creation of maps using calculated indices of landscape value and inter-visibility produced an expert-led and so-called 'objective' measure of landscape value. Studies of this type have attracted considerable academic debate and criticism, primarily relating to the aggregation of synthetic landscapes from pre-selected components and from the biases inherent in the values and preferences of experts involved in subjective assessments in the field (Duffield & Coppock, 1975; Gold, 1980). Appleton (1994) presents a powerful polemic against the use of such techniques where, in particular, the 1975 Manchester Landscape Evaluation Research Project is shown as an example of the extent to which subjective and relatively arbitrary assumptions are built into the system. Similarly, Kaplan (quoted in Nasar, 1988) noted that although experts are invaluable when used appropriately, they are unreliable as objective judges of what people care about in the landscape.

Consequently, a number of authors have endorsed the value of public perception and preference approaches, particularly as it is the public who will ultimately experience the developments in question (Kent, 1993; Penning-Rowsell, 1982; Seddon, 1986). In a similar vein, House & Fordham (1997) warn against the danger of bypassing the views of the 'ordinary person'. In 1976, research carried out by the US Department of Agriculture highlighted the importance of listening to the perceptions of the public when a Forest Service National Recreation Strategy was being formulated. Henson (1990) argued that it was the people, not the framework, that were the vital element of the programme.

Today, there is a growing, if seemingly reluctant, recognition among decision makers and affected parties addressing landscape problems that traditional top-down strategies are insufficient. Expert-led approaches can readily bypass local and anecdotal knowledge of places and circumstances and risk producing outcomes that are incompetent, irrelevant or unworkable (Roberts, 1998). Consequently, a more citizen-led philosophy has been widely promulgated within a new rhetoric of empowerment and local action, strongly associated with the advent of Agenda 21 strategies and their corresponding Local Agenda 21 plans (Edwards, 1998). This 'bottom-up' approach has been characterized by a range of responses and initiatives aimed at improving local landscapes and quality of life. Parish maps celebrate local identity and distinctiveness using a variety of visual forms (Clifford & King, 1993; Crouch & Matless, 1996; Greeves, 1987), whilst village appraisals have led to a range of landscape and other community improvements (Francis & Henderson, 1992; Greeves & Taylor, 1987). More recently, village design statements have emerged as powerful supplementary planning tools (Owen, 1999).

Notwithstanding these advances, assessing public perception *per se* continues to be a problematic task. Studies of perception by Burgess *et al.* (1988) and Lee (1982) and the landscape assessment studies of Fines (1968), Penning-Rowsell (1981, 1989) and Penning-Rowsell & Hardy (1973), in particular, highlight the difficulties in ascertaining meaningful interpretations of landscapes and public perception. Similarly, in work by Lee (1990) on perception of forestry landscapes, the principal difficulty occurred with the measurement and transference of preference into landscape planning policies.

Although the academic contribution has undergone significant evolution and refinement, partly as a result of the problems identified above, it has yet to produce a universally accepted approach. Pioneering quantitative-based methodologies are evident in the work of Penning-Rowsell (1974) with semantic rating scales in the Wye Valley Area of Outstanding Natural Beauty (AONB) and Shafer and Brush's (1977) research into utilizing photographs in public-perception research. Byrne (1979) also used photographs in conjunction with a questionnaire in order to assess public perception of the Land's End Peninsula, where it was felt that such surveys had the potential to be a useful tool in landscape appraisal and development control matters. Significantly, Dunn's work helped to confirm the validity of substituting photographs as a means of identifying landscape perception (Dunn, 1976). However, Rieser (1972) sounds a note of caution in the use of photographs as landscape surrogates with their emphasis on the visual component and their overall subjectivity. More recently, approaches have utilized new technologies where Internet and geographical information system (GIS) applications have flourished (Brabyn, 1996; Wherrett, 2000). An interesting project for virtual decision incorporating Planning for Real with Internet applications has been developed for the village of Slaithwaite at Leeds University (Kingston *et al.*, 1999). Despite all these developments, their effective translation into policy still seems elusive. Nevertheless, some interesting work is evident in the use of scenario-based studies, where the public respond to a series of visual representations of possible future landscapes in a more proactive and policy-oriented process (Tress & Tress, 2000; Yorkshire Dales National Park, 1992).

Such difficulties have resulted in a significant shift towards more experiential research utilizing more qualitative-based methodologies where, in particular, the use of focus groups has mushroomed in applied landscape research (Burgess, 1996). Indeed, pioneering work by Burgess on fear in community woodlands demonstrated the value of focus groups which provided a valuable discourse on a subject when time for field research was constrained and policy recommendations were needed quickly by decision makers (Burgess, 1996; Burgess *et al.*, 1988). Furthermore, small-group discourse allows debate, argument and values to come to the fore, thereby supplementing the more established quantitative methods of enquiry (Burgess, 1999; Penning-Rowsell, 1982). However, Burgess, while advocating qualitative methodologies, felt it crucial to back up these studies with quantitative evidence. Indeed, this partnership approach is central to the methodological development of the present study.

Public perception and LANDMAP

The research on public perception reported here forms a constituent part of the LANDMAP approach in Wales. This is an expert-led technique for landscape resource assessment which identifies and maps landscape according to a range of combined criteria. The process was introduced and devised by the CCW and the Welsh Landscape Partnership Group in 1996 (CCW, 1999, 2001).[3] LANDMAP uses a multivariate approach to landscape based on composite geographical areas, known as 'landscape character areas'.

These are based on seven factors, which produce 12 separate layers of information, as follows:

- geology and geomorphology (three layers),
- visual, sensory and spiritual (one layer),
- biodiversity (one layer),
- historic (one layer),
- cultural associations (two layers),
- settlement and development (one layer),
- rural land use (three layers).

The last two are included as contextual information only, to provide additional insight for decision makers, and not for the identification of character areas.

Each character area is identified and evaluated by nominated 'experts' who work to set templates provided by the LANDMAP advisory service (Parker, 2000, pers. comm.). Data is built up from the superimposition of different layers of information in the process incorporating contextual information and evaluative aspects.

Through this combined approach, LANDMAP sets out to bring together the many facets of landscape into a single, multi-purpose assessment that surpasses simple visual assessment. LANDMAP's flexibility in integrating the various layers of information through GIS and remote sensing applications has the potential to allow informed decisions to be made at a variety of scales. Such an approach has a major role in influencing the content of landscape plans and providing a spatial framework for local planning matters. Indeed, LANDMAP is now the favoured approach to landscape assessment throughout local authorities in Wales and has been favourably received by planning inspectors at public inquiry, particularly in the development of local authority managed designations (Special Landscape Areas).

The public-perception aspect, whilst not a 'character area' as such, has been incorporated into the overall methodology. The responsibility for devising the methodology lay with the present author, in conjunction with other staff at the Welsh Institute of Rural Studies.[4]

Methodology

The study in Denbighshire was the first to involve this overall methodological stance. A key requirement would be to provide some summary public-perception data to accord with the template and GIS applications of character areas.[5] Given that public-perception research occurs towards the end of the LANDMAP process after the composite character areas have been identified and mapped, the experts critically shape and influence the process. This compromise is important, as the public perception is operationalized within the boundaries and technical knowledge of professionals. This top-down approach is seen as necessary given the nature of the exercise, but it does condition and generalize perception to fit in with 'expert' notions of character areas. This is both its strength and its potential weakness: strength because it focuses the public on certain landscapes; weakness because it constrains the comments to constructed landscapes rather than local landscapes and concerns. This has been addressed, in part, in the handbook, with the development of a more ambitious, long-term bottom-up methodology (CCW, 2001).

A combination methodology was adopted in the present study, utilizing both conventional household questionnaires and focus groups following the recommendations of Lee (1990) and Burgess (1996). The principal objects focused on by the public-perception study were the photographic media, and the researchers sought to select images which were more representative than had been the case in previous studies.[6]

The LANDMAP process in Denbighshire resulted in the identification of 10 'landscape character' areas (Rees, Principal Countryside Officer, Denbighshire Countryside Service, 1999, pers. comm.). The strategy employed was to select three 'representative' landscape photographs from within each of these areas to be used for the study. The Principal Countryside Officer took a large number of photographs from each area, during a three-week period. The use of a 'local expert' was critical in attempting to obtain the best representation of photographs; to minimize bias all photographs were taken in similar light and weather conditions and were devoid of people. The final choice of photographs was then decided by a team involving the public-perception consultants and the Denbighshire Countryside Service.[7] However, there is a problem in reconciling the multi-dimensional assessment of landscape as employed by the experts in devising the character areas with the mono-dimensional response obtained from the public responding to the photographs, where the visual component clearly dominates the assessment. Methodologically, however, given the constraints of time and resources, there seemed little alternative to this approach.

The following question areas pertaining to each of the 10 'landscapes' were systematically addressed in the household questionnaires and focus groups:

- landscape appreciation (likes and dislikes) with justification;
- features important to conserve with justification;
- features important to change/enhance with justification.

'Open' questions were used throughout so as not to pre-judge responses. These were later coded for tabular display from the questionnaire or subjected to discourse analysis for the focus groups.

Respondents employed in the household questionnaire were chosen at random from the electoral register. The reliability of the sample was improved by selecting respondents from specific ward clusters according to various economic, social and rural/urban factors (Office for National Statistics, 1991). In addition, the sample was stratified by age and gender statistics. This modification of the sample was critical given the relatively small sample size within the study area (100 respondents).

The results from six focus groups provided the qualitative material to complement the data collected from the household questionnaire. Crucially, it allowed the views of groups in the community not normally elicited in conventional survey approaches to be identified and explained, as well as facilitating a more detailed discourse into people's attitudes and feelings towards local landscapes (Gibbs, 2001; Scott & Jones, 1998).

A facilitator was used for all sessions, which were taped to enable transcripts to be made of the interviews. Welsh or English was used as dictated by the groups' wishes. The groups used in the research were as follows:

- Children
- Youth (aged 13–17)
- Special Needs
- Unemployed
- Visitors
- Rural Land Use.

Selection was based on a purposive approach, adapting the stakeholder groupings identified by the former Local Government Management Board (1994) for Local Agenda 21 plans. Normally groups were constructed by targeting appropriate organizations – a primary school for 'Children', a youth club for 'Youth' and so on. No attempt was made to be representative, as that was the preserve of the household questionnaire. Exceptions to this method included the composite Rural Land Use and Visitor groups, which demanded a more individual approach to secure the necessary 9–12 participants.[8]

Results and mapping

Once the survey results and focus-group responses were coded and analysed, it was possible to build a general picture of public perceptions to particular landscape types.[9] The data were then transferred into a Microsoft Access database for incorporation and use within other aspects of the LANDMAP process. In this way, public perception forms an integral part of LANDMAP and the results form one layer of information in the resultant GIS application. These results may potentially feed into future landscape management policies such as the All Wales Agri-Environmental Scheme (Tir Gofal) and Unitary Development Plans (UDPs), both of which utilize GIS applications. For the first time, it will be possible to incorporate detailed public-perception data into landscape management proposals. The emphasis, however, lies with the policy maker, but there does seem a readiness to present material from the public-perception study as supplementary planning guidance for the UDP process.

Application of the methodology in practice

This section shows the detailed operation of the methodology in two landscape character areas from the Denbighshire study (Deep Valley and Vale Farmland). The results from the household questionnaire and focus groups are highlighted and discussed, and the implications for landscape management strategies examined (Scott, 1999).

Deep Valley

Positive factors. The household questionnaire confirms the importance of particular landscape features, characteristics and sense of place. The water feature (stream) was a strong positive attractor (50%), with trees also contributing to the attraction (22%). Interestingly, the influence of colour was also significant and largely unexpected by the project sponsors (28%) (Rees, 1999). However, 28% of the responses also referred to the value of the 'overall landscape'. The reasons for this high positive assessment focus primarily on the perceived beauty of the scene (46%) and its naturalness (29%). Significantly, this landscape attracted the highest individual rating for beauty across the 10 landscapes. Other attributes such as 'inviting' (17%) and 'managed' (11%) were also evident.

The focus-group responses help explain and contextualize the strong attraction to this landscape. Most contributions support the contention that this landscape is valued holistically, rather than based on the contribution of individual factors. Landscape complexity and diversity condition positive responses, with the interplay of landform, topography and colour acting as contributory factors.

> There's so much more in the landscape.
>
> (Youth)

> Like it because it's got everything; sheep, trees and mountains . . . because of the colours and the stream.
>
> (Children)

Plenty of colours and lows and highs, lots of trees and would like to walk in that landscape. The diversity is important.

(Visitor)

The more managed aspect to the countryside was also recognized and appreciated.

It's obviously not rough and tumble; it's tidy, that's how the country-side should be.

(Special Needs)

Negative factors. The high positive assessment for this landscape is reinforced by the muted profile of negative responses. In total 61% of respondents registered no dislikes. Minor criticisms related to the trees, together comprising 11%. The principal reasons for this was the antipathy towards conifers which created discord in the landscape (10%).

The focus-group responses exhibit a similar profile, with few negative comments recorded. The visitor-group comment encapsulates the main source of criticism relating to the management of woodland and the unwelcome introduction of alien species.

A bit overcontrolled. Trees look like they have been plonked in a very unnatural way.

(Visitor)

Landscape conservation and change. Given the high positive rating afforded to this landscape it was not surprising that it was seen as important to conserve the landscape in its entirety (48%). Particular features also merited special attention, reflecting the importance of water features (33%) and trees in this landscape (14%), as previously identified.

Changes to the landscape were not deemed particularly necessary, with the majority of responses advocating the *status quo*. Changes deemed desirable related primarily to modifying the balance between conifers and deciduous trees, placing greater emphasis on deciduous trees (10%).

Within the focus groups, the conservation message clearly supported wholesale conservation of the entire landscape.

The present ownership is doing a good job; leave them alone.

(Rural Land Use)

In terms of changes desired, the only significant comments related to more countryside furniture (Youth and Special Needs) and removal of conifers (Unemployed and Visitor).

It's all very well for active people but is there any way for disabled people to access this landscape?

(Special Needs)

I do not like the way these alien conifers dominate the scene; they look out of place.

(Visitor)

Vale Farmland

Positive factors. This landscape elicits a range of positive responses from the household questionnaire. These tend to revolve around the inherent qualities of a predominantly rural and agricultural landscape where, in particular, the field pattern is highly influential. As with the previous landscape, the impact of colours is also highly significant. Reasons for the positive assessment reflect the perceived beauty (25%) and 'naturalness' (15%) of the scene; management of the agricultural land also featured (13%). It is also significant to record that 12% of responses found this landscape inviting, reflecting a desire actively to engage with the landscape.

The focus-group responses accord with the household survey results. The productive and fertile farmland of Denbighshire elicited a strong positive response, reflecting the high regard felt by the public for agricultural landscapes in terms of both their productive and their aesthetic potential.

> Boring when you look at it from a distance but good when you are actually in it and see the crops growing.
>
> (Unemployed)

> Looks like a giant chess board. Like a patchwork. I like the pattern and colours.
>
> (Children)

> Someone has been working very hard there.
>
> (Visitor)

The impact of landform on the area, with the contrast between the plain and adjoining hills, also contributes to the positive scene. In addition, the unique value of the landscape is recognized as important.

> The lovely red soil of the vale has a beauty all of its own. That red colour is different from elsewhere in Denbighshire.
>
> (Rural Land Use)

> The contrast between this and the slopes that gives it such great appeal. It would be different if this was just a ten mile plain.
>
> (Rural Land Use)

It was interesting to note the very strong set of positive responses from the focus groups. Consistently, responses praised the harmonious relationship between farming and the landscape and how farming was of primary importance in the rural economy of Denbighshire.

> Farming is very important here. This is a natural landscape. I think we are spoilt living in this area.
>
> (Special Needs)

Negative factors. The predominantly positive assessment is reinforced by the lack of criticism relating to the landscape (31%). Concern was evident, however, over the potential threats that could manifest themselves in the landscape. For example, new houses (21%) and the encroachment of urban influences on the landscape were seen as important (12%). Clearly, this landscape was perceived as one under threat of development, although significant new development was not in evidence in the photographs. This suggests that the landscape provoked a response based on associated negative personal experiences in similar landscapes elsewhere in the county, which was confirmed in the subsequent discussion.

Other, more minor criticisms related to the perception that the landscape was cluttered (11%), personal distaste (9%), ugliness (9%) and artificiality (8%).

Within the focus groups too, there was a similarly low number of negative comments. However, there were some neutral responses that recognized farmland as a functional, but not particularly attractive landscape. A few comments went beyond this, focusing around the rather dull and uninspiring aspect to the landscape (Youth, Visitor, Unemployed).

> It's ok but does not really affect me in any way.
>
> (Visitor)

> The land has to be worked but it hardly can be described as beautiful.
>
> (Unemployed)

> You can't make an intensively farmed landscape turn me on.
>
> (Youth)

Landscape conservation and change. The responses for landscape conservation confirm the value afforded to this farmed landscape, with one-fifth of respondents wanting 'everything' to be conserved. Specific features high-lighted were the fields (18%), farmland (15%), rural settlement (14%), trees (13%) and hedgerows (10%).

In terms of change, there was a general reluctance to intervene, with 24% wanting no changes. The principal change advocated involved the settlement pattern: a decline in density and curtailment of the urban influences on what was an essentially rural landscape.

The focus-group responses produced a clear consensus on the importance of protecting farmland and agricultural landscapes as a whole. Significantly, there were no comments opposing this view, even from the Youth and Children!

> Farming; it is important to protect us not just the wildlife.
>
> (Rural Land Use)

> The agricultural landscape is in need of protection, it may not be attractive but it provides us with food. Let us not forget this.
>
> (Unemployed)

> You cannot split this up into features; you must conserve it all or lose its character.
>
> (Special Needs)

Similarly, across all groups, there was general resistance to landscape change and improvement, albeit with one crucial exception. Comments from the Visitor group suggested the need for more hedges to help break up the impact of the larger ploughed fields, while the Rural Land Use group did not want to preclude the need for more 'balanced' development in the landscape. This typifies the classic tension apparent in contemporary rural perceptions.

> We cannot keep places in a time warp. The future of rural areas depends on the people who live and work in them.
>
> (Rural Land Use)

> Keep it as it is. It is so beautiful; this is our heritage; do not spoil it by development.
>
> (Special Needs)

Interpreting the public perceptions

> Nobody ever listens to what we say anyway.
>
> (Special Needs)

The household survey and focus groups showed a remarkable and surprising degree of convergence in the views expressed and, in so doing, afford a comprehensive and valuable insight into understanding the value of the two landscape types. Whereas Appleton (1975) sought answers to his questions from John Dewey and the writings of 18th-century philosophers, the Denbighshire study allows a contemporary consumer-led response.

The 'Deep Valley' and 'Vale Farmland' landscape examples highlight the positive role that diversity, contrast and colour play in landscape appreciation. Indeed, such complexity and contrasts within landscapes match Appleton's postulations for the highest-order landscapes. They also support Brabyn's (1996) contention that the interaction of components is more important than the components themselves. While specific landscape features such as the stream and the intimate pattern of farm fields are also positively evaluated, the focus-group responses reveal that people see the landscape as a whole; they rarely dissect the landscape into its constituent parts and features, as do policy makers and professionals.

In terms of seeking an explanation of why these landscapes are liked, 'beauty', 'naturalness', 'inviting' and 'managed' are the terms most commonly encountered within the questionnaire. There appears to be an element of contradiction here in the expression of 'naturalness' and 'managed' for the same landscape. Appleton (1994) notes a similar use of terms and views it as a 'meaningless cliché'. Nevertheless, these results have featured in many other public-perception studies across Wales (Bullen et al., 1998a, 1999) and suggest closer inspection of what is actually meant in contemporary terms by the term 'natural'. It is postulated by the author that it is significant and laden with symbolism, requiring professionals to adopt a more liberal interpretation of the term towards a more idyllic vision on behalf of the respondents; i.e. how nature should be, which does not conflict with 'managed' (Scott, 1999). The use of the term 'beauty' is seen as complementary to this sentiment. It is not coincidental that the terms are generally used together in the household survey responses. The positive statement alluding to a 'tidy landscape . . . that is as it should be' (Special Needs) further develops this idyllic theme. The prevalence of the term 'inviting' adds a further dimension to perception, suggesting that responses to valued landscapes are more than just aesthetic; people want to interact with the landscape in a more direct and explicit manner. This raises the importance of accessibility to particular landscapes and its correlation with positive value, introducing a new factor of landscape intercourse.

The 'management' response is also important and serves notice that people appreciate the way farmers and landowners manage landscapes. Indeed, the results show a strong predilection towards agriculture, both in terms of landscape aesthetics and in terms of its economic function in the landscape to produce food. Again, this was an unexpected result, yet one which was also obtained in six other perception studies undertaken in Wales. The expressed comments and prevalence for a tidy and managed landscape may not equate with conservation objectives, particularly for biodiversity, where areas perceived as neglected and overgrown are less valued (Scott, 1999).

The results show a real antipathy towards new or alien developments, even when they are merely potential threats to the landscape, as typified in the Vale Farmland landscape example. Here, the depicted landscape triggered a response to personal experiences involving the loss of valued landscape. Moreover, such perceptions are nothing new. Moore-Colyer's (1999) illuminating paper on the urban–rural divide in inter-war Britain contains many parallels with the findings of this research. He documents the public outcry surrounding new developments in the countryside where both the quantity and quality of buildings were criticized. Citing A.G. Street, he states there are 'Hideous rows of glaring slums, of flaring red, unlovely grey and sickly repulsive ochre' (p. 106), a comment not out of place with the results from the concerns over the Vale Farmland landscape. The Deep Valley example shows significant concern over conifers in the landscape, again with strong symbolism attached to the introduction of something alien or new. More specifically, the straight-line geometry and darkness of conifers are seen as out of place in a landscape which is more naturally associated with random features.

The value of the mapping methodology

The methodology presented in this chapter effects a direct relationship between the components that make up a landscape assessment in the LANDMAP process and public perception in a relatively new and innovative way. As far as the public-perception study is concerned, the landscape professionals are intimately and exclusively involved in formulating information about, and evaluations of, the seven aspect areas into 12 layers of mapped information. These different layers are then generalized into a composite landscape classification of 'character areas', which form the basis of the public-perception study. However, subjective judgements are required to select photographs as accurate representations of these areas. Rieser's (1972) concerns regarding photographic selection are equally valid here. However, there is a distinct process shaping the identification of character areas within which photographs are selected that increases the overall validity and rigour, albeit within the constraints of an essentially visual component.

A significant weakness in this largely reactive technique is exposed in the inability of people to appreciate what kind of change in the landscape might be acceptable. The methodology uses a current photographic representation of a landscape with no attempt to present visual images of change with which the respondent could agree or disagree. Rather, the respondents are required to assess, based on their own experience and knowledge, the capacity of the landscape to absorb change. Scenario-based research, in which artists' representations (cf. Yorkshire Dales National Park, 1992) or computer simulations (e.g. Tress & Tress, 2000) are used to convey alternative landscape futures, points the way to obtaining more reliable responses to the dynamics of landscape change and conservation.

There is a further weakness in that the methodology proceeds to treat the perceptions obtained from the photographs as indicative of general responses to a particular landscape type. However, the familiarity and accessibility of a landscape will undoubtedly influence its perceived value, yet these will be bypassed in most photographs. Hence we are left with a relatively crude generalization, but one that is both practical and meaningful for LANDMAP purposes, where data on public perception for specific landscape types are accessible in separate windows in GIS applications alongside biodiversity and visual impact.

While the results highlighted in this chapter provide useful information, it is the author's contention that it is not the true representation of public perception of landscape that has been measured but public perception of LANDMAP character areas. This is both its greatest strength and its greatest weakness. It is a strength because the results are ingrained into the LANDMAP process, but a weakness because the results may not be directly transferable outside the process itself and may bypass important perceptions about particular localities. Indeed, the author has recognized this with the development of a phase 2 methodology in the LANDMAP handbook, which has been termed the 'bottom-up' approach and which focuses on perception-type studies in community council areas that collectively form a jigsaw of perception.[10]

The criticisms first advanced by Duffield and Coppock in 1975 in response to quantitative models for measuring and evaluating landscapes are also applicable in this instance and present a powerful criticism of the LANDMAP process itself (Duffield & Coppock, 1975). Expert led, over a relatively short time scale, using relatively crude information and fieldwork, the method inevitably generates a false sense of objectivity. Nevertheless, this approach has the benefit of allowing public perception to be comparable with other aspect areas that comprise a composite landscape assessment. This is highly significant given that the approach taken by the English Countryside Agency deliberately excluded public perception from their Countryside Character Initiative, which is based primarily on visual components. It is the author's contention that, as complex and problematic as public perception is, it cannot be ignored or bolted on to landscape tools. There is a need for methodologies to incorporate public perception explicitly into the policy-making process in a more proactive and innovative way. The research reported here has attempted to meet that challenge. The problems of policy implementation still remain, but now that policy makers have the views of the public accessible and assessable in the LANDMAP results, significant progress has been made. The ultimate test is the extent to which such information is used and applied in landscape policy. There is emerging evidence that the public-perception study is emerging as powerful supplementary planning guidance. The prospects as revealed in this chapter appear hopeful.

Acknowledgements

The author would like to thank Countryside Council for Wales for supporting the research reported in this chapter. The views expressed in the chapter are the author's own, and do not necessarily reflect those of the CCW.

Notes

1   This research was undertaken for the Countryside Council for Wales and the researchers (Scott and Bullen) developed the resultant methodology now employed throughout Wales and described in the LANDMAP handbook (CCW, 2001).

2   Other public-perception studies had been undertaken before across Wales, however, this was the first time that this approach was used.

3   The initial methodology for LANDMAP did not include a public-perception component. This was added to the process after some debate and the author, under contract and in collaboration with J.M. Bullen, was responsible for its methodological development.

4   Previous public-perception studies were undertaken by J.M. Bullen, E.M. Jones and A.J. Scott (Bullen et al., 1988a,b, 1999). They were more general and as such did not allow the results to be readily incorporated into the GIS product.

5   Indeed, this represents the culmination of two years of methodological experiments and evaluations involving the author and the LANDMAP advisory service.

6   The photographic selection method was developed by the author and is now available in the LANDMAP handbook (CCW, 2001).

7   The recommendations for selection of photographic media were devised by Bullen and Scott and appear in the LANDMAP handbook (CCW, 2001).

8   The Visitor group involved approaching people at random in Loggerheads Country Park to ascertain that they were visitors and seek their involvement. The Rural Land Use group was selected from a countryside forum umbrella group within Denbighshire. A representative sample of interests was approached.

9   In order to keep the database manageable, focus-group comments were selected to be illustrative of the various viewpoints proffered. Full transcripts were made available within the appendices of the report.

10   This approach involves a long-term process whereby individual community council areas undertake a form of parish appraisal highlighting particular landscapes that are valued or disliked. Over time a full public-perception study can be made available at a more local level. However, this process is still under development and is likely to be an extremely long-term venture.

References

Appleton, J. (1975) *The Experience of Landscape* (London, Wiley).

Appleton, J. (1990) *The Symbolism of Habitat* (Washington, University of Washington Press).

Appleton, J. (1994) Running before we can walk: are we ready to map 'beauty'?, *Landscape Research*, 19(3), pp. 112–119.

Appleton, J. (1996) *The Experience of Landscape*, 2nd edn (Chichester, Wiley).

Bernaldez, F.G., Gallardo, D. & Abello, R.P. (1995) Children's landscape preferences: from rejection to attraction, in: Sinha, A. (Ed.) *Landscape Perception*, pp. 11–18 (London, Academic Press).

Brabyn, L. (1996) Landscape classification using GIS and national digital databases, *Landscape Research*, 21(3), pp. 277–299.

Bullen, J.M., Jones, E.M. & Scott, A.J. (1998a) *LANDMAP Pilot: public perception of landscape*, Unpublished report to Countryside Council for Wales (Bangor, Countryside Council for Wales).

Bullen, J.M., Jones, E.M. & Scott, A.J. (1998b) *LANDMAP: public perception of the Gwynedd landscape*, Unpublished report to Gwynedd County Council (Caernarfon, Gwynedd County Council).

Bullen, J.M., Jones, E.M. & Scott, A.J. (1999) *LANDMAP: public perception of the Cardiff landscape*, Unpublished report to Cardiff County Council (Cardiff, Cardiff County Council).

Burgess, J. (1996) Focusing on fear: the use of focus groups in a project for the Community Forest Unit, Countryside Commission, *Area*, 28(2), pp. 130–135.

Burgess, J. (1999) The genesis of in-depth discussion groups: a response to Liz Bondi, *Professional Geographer*, 51(3), pp. 458–460.

Burgess, J., Harrison, C. & Limb, M. (1988) Exploring environmental values through the medium of small groups, *Environment and Planning A*, 20, pp. 309–326.

Byrne, S.M. (1979) Perception of the landscape in the Land's End Peninsula, *Landscape Research*, 5(1), pp. 21–24.

Clifford, S. & King, A. (Ed.) (1993) *Local Distinctiveness: place, particularity and identity* (London, Common Ground).

Council for the Protection of Rural England (1999) *Rural Renaissance* (London, Council for the Protection of Rural England).

Countryside Commission (1993) *Landscape Assessment Guidance CCP423* (Cheltenham, Countryside Commission).

Countryside Council for Wales (1996) *The Welsh Landscape: our inheritance and its future protection and enhancement*, CCC16 (Bangor, Countryside Council for Wales).

Countryside Council for Wales (1999) *LANDMAP (the landscape assessment and decision making process)*, initial draft handbook (Bangor, Countryside Council for Wales).

Countryside Council for Wales (2001) *The LANDMAP Information System* (Bangor, Countryside Council for Wales).

Coventry-Solihull-Warwickshire Sub-Regional Planning Study Group (1971) *A Strategy for the Sub-region, Supplementary Report 5 'Countryside'* (Coventry, Warwickshire County Council).

Crofts, R.S. (1975) The landscape component approach to landscape evaluation, *Transactions of the Institute of British Geographers*, 66, pp. 124–129.

Crouch, D. & Matless, D. (1996) Reconfiguring geography: parish maps and common ground, *Transactions of the British Geographers*, NS 21(1), pp. 236–255.

Cullingworth, B. & Nadin, V. (2001) *Town and Country Planning in the UK* (13th edn) (London, Routledge).

Darvill, T. (1998) Landscapes: myth or reality?, in: Jones, M. & Rotherham, I. (Eds) *Landscapes Perception, Recognition and Management: reconciling the impossible*, pp. 8–16 (Sheffield, Wildtrack Publishing).

Dewey, J. (1934) *Art as Experience* (New York, Capricorn).

Duffield, B.S. & Coppock, J.T. (1975) The delineation of recreational landscapes: the role of a computer based information system, *Transactions of the Institute of British Geographers*, 66, pp. 141–148.

Dunn, M.C. (1976) Landscape with photographs: testing the preference approach to landscape evaluation, *Journal of Environmental Management*, 4, pp. 15–26.

Edwards, W.J. (1998) Charting the discourse of community action: perspectives from practice in rural Wales, *Journal of Rural Studies*, 14(1), pp. 63–77.

Emmelin, L. (1996) Landscape impact analysis: a systematic approach to landscape impacts policy, *Landscape Research*, 21(1), pp. 13–35.

Fines, K.D. (1968) Landscape evaluation: a research project in East Sussex, *Regional Studies*, 2, pp. 41–55.

Francis, D. & Henderson, P. (1992) *Working with Rural Communities* (Macmillan, London).

Gibbs, A. (2001) Focus groups social research update <http://www.soc.surrey.ac.uk/sru/SRU19.html>, University of Surrey, accessed 30 October 2001.

Gold, J.R. (1980) *An Introduction to Behavioural Geography* (London, Oxford University Press).

Gold, J.R. & Burgess J. (Eds) (1982) *Valued Environments* (London, George Allen & Unwin).

Gourlay, D. & Slee, B. (1998) Public preferences for landscape features: a case study of two Scottish environmentally sensitive areas, *Journal of Rural Studies*, 14(2), pp. 249–263.

Greeves, T. (1987) *Parish Maps: celebrating and looking after your place* (London, Common Ground).

Greeves, T. & Taylor, R. (1987) *The Local Jigsaw: an information pack on village appraisals and parish maps* (Cheltenham, Countryside Commission/Rural Development Commission).

Henson, L. (1990) The US forest service recreation strategy: bringing the great outdoors to the American people, in: Talbot, H. (Ed.) *People, Trees and Woods*, pp. 7–13, Proceedings of the 1989 Countryside Recreation Conference, organised by the Countryside Recreation Research Advisory Group, Heriot-Watt University, Edinburgh, 19–21 September (Bristol, CRRAG).

Hitchmough, J.D. & Bonugli, A.M. (1997) Attitudes of residents of a medium-sized town in South West Scotland to street trees, *Landscape Research*, 22(3), pp. 327–337.

Hodgson, R.W. & Thayer, R.L. (1980) Implied human influence reduces landscape beauty, *Landscape Planning*, 7, pp. 171–179.

House, M. & Fordham, M. (1997) Public perception of river corridors and attitudes towards river works, *Landscape Research*, 22(1), pp. 25–44.

Hull, R.B. & Revell, G.R.B. (1995) Cross-cultural comparison of landscape scenic beauty evaluations: a case study in Bali, in: Sinha, A. (Ed.) *Landscape Perception*, pp. 83–98 (London, Academic Press).

Jacques, D.L. (1980) Landscape appraisal: the case for a subjective theory, *Journal of Environmental Management*, 10, pp. 107–113.

Kaplan, S. & Kaplan, R. (1982) *Cognition and Environment: functioning in an uncertain world* (New York, Praeger).

Kent, R.L. (1993) Attributes, features and reasons for enjoyment of scenic routes: a comparison of experts, residents and citizens, *Landscape Research*, 18(2), pp. 92–102.

Kingston, R., Carver, S., Evans, A. & Turton, I. (1999) Virtual Decision Making in Spatial Planning: web-based geographical information systems for public participation in environmental decision making, Paper presented at the International Conference on Public Participation and Information Technology, Lisbon, October 1999.

Lee (1982) The value of the local area, in: Gold, J.R. & Burgess, J. (Eds) *Valued Environments*, p. 168 (London, George Allen & Unwin).

Lee, T. (1990) What kind of woodland and forest do people prefer, in: Talbot, H. (Ed.) *People, Trees and Woods*, pp. 37–51, Proceedings of the 1989 Countryside Recreation Conference, organised by the Countryside Recreation Research Advisory Group, Heriot-Watt University, Edinburgh, 19–21 September (Bristol, CRRAG).

Linton, D.L. (1968) The assessment of scenery as a natural resource, *Scottish Geographical Magazine*, 84, pp. 219–238.

Local Government Management Board (1994) Community participation in Local Agenda 21, in: *Local Agenda 21 Roundtable Guidance*, pp. 1–7 (Luton, Local Government Management Board).

Moore-Colyer, R. (1999) From Great Wen to Toad Hall: aspects of the urban–rural divide in inter-war Britain, *Rural History*, 10(1), pp. 105–124.

Muir, R. (1999) *Approaches to Landscape* (London, Macmillan).

Nasar, J.L. (1988) (Ed.) *Environmental Aesthetics: theory, research and applications* (Cambridge, Cambridge University Press).

Nicholls, D. & Schlater, A. (1993) Cutting quality down to scale, *Landscape Design*, 218, pp. 39–41.

Office for National Statistics (1991) *ONS Classification of Wards in Great Britain (Local Government Version)*, produced for the Local Government Management Board (Luton, Local Government Management Board).

Office for National Statistics (1994) Welsh Ward Survey, Unpublished data supplied to Welsh County Councils (London, Office for National Statistics).

Owen, S. (1999) Village design statements: some aspects of the evolution of a planning tool in the UK, *Town Planning Review*, 70(1), pp. 41–59.

Penning-Rowsell, E.C. (1974) Landscape evaluation for development plans, *Journal of the Royal Town Planning Institute*, 60, pp. 930–934.

Penning-Rowsell, E.C. (1981) Assessing the validity of landscape evaluations, *Landscape Research*, 6(2), pp. 22–24.

Penning-Rowsell, E.C. (1982) A public preference evaluation of landscape quality, *Regional Studies*, 16(2), pp. 97–112.

Penning-Rowsell, E.C. (1989) Landscape evaluation in practice: a survey of local authorities, *Landscape Research*, 14(2), pp. 35–37.

Penning-Rowsell, E.C. & Hardy, D.I. (1973) Landscape evaluation and planning policy: a comparative survey in the Wye Valley Area of Outstanding Natural Beauty, *Regional Studies*, 16(2), pp. 97–112.

Rieser, R. (1972) *Urban Spatial Images: an appraisal of the choice of respondents and measurement situation*, Discussion Paper 42 (London, London School of Economics).

Roberts, T. (1998) The seven lamps of planning, Paper given to Town and Country Planning Summer School, September <www.planning.haynet.com>

Sanoff, H. (1991) *Visual Research Methods in Design* (New York, Van Nostrand Reinhold).

Scott, A.J. (1999) *Public Perception of Landscape in Denbighshire: results of household survey and focus groups*, Technical report to Denbighshire County Council (Aberystwyth, Welsh Institute of Rural Studies).

Scott, A.J. & Jones, E.M. (1998) *Focus Groups*, Technical briefing sheet to Jigso, Welsh Council for Voluntary Action, Aberystwyth.

Seddon, A. (1986) Landscape planning: a conceptual perspective, *Landscape and Urban Planning*, 13, pp. 335–347.

Shafer, E.L. & Brush, R.O. (1977) How to measure preferences for photographs of natural landscapes, *Landscape Planning*, 4, pp. 237–256.

Shucksmith M., Watkins, L. & Henderson, M. (1993) Attitudes towards residential develop-
     ment in the Scottish Countryside, *Journal of Rural Studies*, 9(3), pp. 243–255.
Tapsell, S.M. (1995) River restoration: what are we restoring to? A case study of the Ravens-
     bourne River London, *Landscape Research*, 20(3), pp. 98–111.
Tress, B. & Tress, G. (2000) Scenarios for the multifunctional use of landscapes in Denmark,
     http://www.tress.cc/scenario.html, accessed 20 September 2000, Centre for Land-
     scape Research, Roskilde.
University of Manchester, Landscape Evaluation Research Project (1976) *Landscape Evaluation:
     a report of the Landscape Evaluation Research Project* (Manchester, University of Manches-
     ter).
Wellman, J.D. & Buhyhoff, G.J. (1980) Effects of regional familiarity on landscape prefer-
     ences, *Journal of Environmental Management*, 11, pp. 105–110.
Wherett, J.R. (2000) Landscape preference questionnaire, Macaulay Land Use Research Insti-
     tute, Aberdeen <http://www.mluri.sari.ac.uk/~mi550/landscape.html>, accessed 12
     May 2000.
Yorkshire Dales National Park (1992) *Landscapes for Tomorrow* (Grassington, Yorkshire Dales
     National Park).

Chapter 27

Cultural Heritage and Resources

Richard Stoffle

A Native Americans Social Impact Assessment (SIA) is virtually unique because it is negotiated rather than just conducted. In SIA projects the study evaluates the potential impacts of a proposed action on human social, cultural and economic values. The study may be stratified by an ethnic group, but even so there is little expectation that somehow the study will stimulate a permanent connection between the involved ethnic groups, the project and the Federal regulatory agency that is overseeing the project decision. Exceptions to this are long-term projects that contain continual community monitoring. On the other hand, virtually all Native Americans SIAs will leave the regulatory agency, the project and the involved tribes as future partners. For this reason, this chapter talks about conducting Indian SIAs with an eye on past and future relationships between the tribes, the Federal agency and even the SIA team.

SIA projects potentially impact Native Americans in many ways (Geisler, Green, Usner and West, 1982). Indian tribes, communities and individuals experience all of the same impacts that other people do (Stea and Buge, 1982:190–4), and the analysis of such impacts should proceed along standard lines as suggested in the Guidelines and Principles for Social Impact Assessment (National Oceanic and Atmospheric Administration, 1994). When Indian people write about these issues they define themselves as specially impacted because their communities have already lost most of their traditional productive base, have lost large percentages of traditional populations, and are recovering from the pressures of a dominant society that sought to rationalize conquest by denigrating traditional languages, culture and social organization. The Federal policy of forced acculturation was rejected and apologized for by the United States Congress in the American Indian Religious Freedom Action of 1978. This event alone set up Indian people as special in future agency actions and in SIAs (CEQ NEPA – regulations Federal Register Vol. 43 No. 230:44978–56007). Indian tribes are further recognized as the aboriginal land holders of the territorial United States and thus are considered to be dependent nations within the United States (Deloria and Lytle, 1984). Today, Indian concerns tend to be highlighted throughout various sections of environmental impact study (EIS) documents. Whole new sections, such as Environmental Justice, specially address Indian issues. Still, when we think of Indian SIA studies, cultural issues come to mind.

Native American cultural resources

Indian SIAs are complex because they are protected by specific Federal laws, congressional actions and presidential orders. Sometimes Indian SIA studies are glossed by a term that refers to a single type of study. In fact, even though a Federal agency has selected one law as the specific driver for an Indian SIA study, all of the various laws still apply and should be considered in the EIS. The five types of studies are:

1   Cultural landscapes – National Register Bulletin 30.
2   Traditional cultural properties – National Register Bulletin 38.
3   Sacred sites – Executive Order 13007.
4   Native American Graves Protection and Repatriation – 1989, 43 CFR 10.
5   American Indian Freedom Act – 1978, 92 Stat. 469.

It is important to remember that each type of study considers different aspects of Indian culture. Choosing the most appropriate ones will critically impact the outcomes of the study and the willingness of the Indian tribes to participate.

Indian cultural resources are complex because Indian people have lived so long on their traditional lands. This is a simple process of human adaptation (Rappaport, 1990). As a general rule of thumb, the longer a human group lives in a place, the more it comes to know about the place and to translate this knowledge into increasingly abstract culture phenomena (Bennett, 1976:265–305). Today, we call the spatial aspects of this cultural cognition of the environment a 'cultural landscape', and it has both physical and spiritual dimensions. Cultural landscapes involve, from the most to the least abstract (a) holy lands; (b) song and story scapes; (c) regional landscapes; (d) ecoscapes; (e) landmarks (Stoffle, Halmo, and Austin, 1997).

Our study team has selected the concept of cultural landscapes as the overarching analytical frame in an Indian SIA because it best reflects how Indian people view their cultural resources (Dewey-Hefley, Zedeno, Stoffle, and Pittaluga, 1998:15). This frame permits the assessment of impacts on the relationships between places and objects (Zedeno, Austin and Stoffle, 1997:125–7). Often SIA research ends with the identification of objects and places and their potential project impacts. If the SIA team uses a cultural landscape frame, then both types of impacts are assessed. This has important implications for the Record of Decision as well as for mitigation and monitoring.

Local cultural resource studies consider identification and assessment of impacts to the following:

- archaeology sites;
- petroglyphs;
- human burials;
- plants;
- animals;
- minerals;
- water.

The air as a living organism has recently been identified in a major EIS as a variable to be assessed (Department of Energy, 1996). Cultural resource studies also can consider impacts to Native American cultural practices (like a traditional healing ceremony) that are not tied to specific places. Ideally, each of these cultural resources should become the subject of a separate study so that native groups can send persons with special knowledge about the topic. In practice, they tend to be folded into a single study thus challenging the SIA team and the Indian people to do it all at once.

Our study team has responded to the challenge of doing all types of Indian cultural resource studies at once by developing a series of data collection forms each with a specific purpose. In addition, we qualify our SIA text with the understanding that Indian cultural resources are more complex than our narrowly defined SIA efforts can reveal. All of our data collection forms emerged out of studies where data were gathered through open-ended interviews. The forms were created because Indian people told us later that they felt constrained by the presence of other people around during the interviews. The forms are a practical solution to conducting simultaneous interviews at the same location, and permit the systematic collection of data with each tribal representative having a private interview. We have found it optimal to have two Indian people for every one SIA interviewer.

At this time our SIA team has developed unique forms for the study of plants, animals, archaeology sites and petroglyphs. In addition, we have developed forms for the study of places and cultural landscapes. The forms have been refined in response to comments by Indian people. Federal agencies, and the academic community. Some forms have been used dozens of times, so have become really quite useful. Other forms are very much in process, and we are looking for better ideas for how to collect complex data. Forms are printed as an appendix to each SIA report and are available for use and review by other SIA teams.

Location is critical in interviews. Sitting in people's homes and talking about things far away in space and time is a bad idea. Early SIAs were conducted with this type of interview, but today our SIA team would reject a study design that totally relies on this procedure. If you want to talk about something or some place, the SIA interviewer and the Indian person must be looking at the thing or sitting at the place. This is easy to achieve for plants, water, archaeology sites, petroglyphs and landmarks, but difficult if studying animals and isolated caves.

Consulting with Native Americans

Formally working with Native American tribes is called consultation, and here is presented a model for that consultation. The model describes nine ideal steps for developing a consultation relationship with Native Americans who are culturally affiliated with lands being studied. These steps are suggested on the basis of the past experiences of the SIA team and on the analysis of other consultation relationships. Examples of relationships between Native Americans and Federal agencies are used throughout so the model will be as instructive as possible. These steps suggest how a process might occur, but they need not always be followed in order to achieve an acceptable consultation. Instead, the nine steps suggest a logical sequence of decisions and actions that normally would be involved in developing a consultation relationship. It is important that the SIA study team work with the involved Indian tribes to design a consultation relationship that reflects their needs, the needs of the responsible Federal agency and the protection requirements of the cultural resources under consideration. The ideal steps (of which only the first two are discussed in this abbreviated version of the paper) are:

1   Defining consultation.
2   Establishing cultural affiliation.
3   Contacting the tribes.
4   Having an orientation meeting.
5   Forming a consultation committee.
6   Conducting site visits.
7   Developing mitigation recommendations.
8   Maintaining ongoing interactions and monitoring.
9   Terminating consultation.

Defining consultation

Federal land managers have a stewardship responsibility to consult with Native American people regarding cultural resources found on Federal lands and on other lands affected by a Federal activity. The Federal government requires that all of the lands held by its various agencies be managed in certain ways; some ways defined by legal obligations, others defined by treaties, and still others reflecting the desire of the Federal agency to involve Native people in the management of their ancestral resources. Increasingly Native Americans have been asked to identify their cultural resources located on these lands and to suggest culturally appropriate management practices.

'Consultation' is a term that is commonly used to describe a process by which Native American peoples with traditional ties are identified and brought into discussions about cultural resources on Federal or Federal-activity-affected lands. Consultation involves a fundamental decision on the part of the Federal land agency to share some decision making with Native Americans. Native people are asked to share in the decision to identify resources needing protection, the decision to prioritize which cultural resources will be protected first, and the decision to select from among a variety of management practices those that most appropriately protect the cultural resources in the context of other resource uses. Native peoples are asked to share in the long-range planning and monitoring of these cultural resources and the lands that hold them.

According to scholars who study consultation (Cernea, 1991; Dobyns, 1951; Parenteau, 1988:5–10), the quality and success of the consultation process depends directly on the degree to which decision-making power is shared. Arnstein's (1969) studies demonstrate that any consultation process can be characterized as falling on a scale from 1–8 where participation without shared power is called 'manipulation' and where sharing power even to the point of negotiating with the agency is called 'partnership'. The primary decision that a Federal agency must make is how much decision-making power can be and will be shared with Native people. Once the range of decision-making sharing is established, it should be clearly identified at the outset of the consultation so that it can become a part of the Native people's decision to participate in the consultation.

General Consultation   More and more Federal agencies are becoming involved in general consultation with Native Americans. This establishes a permanent relationship with Native American groups who have cultural ties to the lands and resources managed or affected by the actions of a Federal agency. General consultation should be based on extensive research concerning cultural resources that Native groups identify as being located on lands of concern. General consultation should be based on a strong information foundation.

A major advantage of general consultation is that it can occur in the absence of a specific project proposal, which is evaluated under specific laws usually as part of an NEPA. Often the laws that govern specific project studies add third parties to discussions between the Federal land managers and Native people, which can confuse and limit discussions. General consulatation occurs when it is desired by the Federal land manager and the Native people and is neither limited by time nor issue. It is the perfect social environment for discussing a complex relationship designed to protect cultural items of greatest significance. Another advantage of general consultation is that it produces a strong information base for identifying cultural resources for both the Federal agency and for Native people.

Through various cultural studies, the Native people build a set of recommendations that suggest how to best manage these resources. Most Native American cultural resources located on Federal lands or effected by the Federal actions will become known through the process of general consultation. This will reduce the number of times that Federal actions will have to be stopped and modified because of unanticipated discoveries of cultural resources. If Federal actions activities were to impact cultural resources not previously identified, procedures would be in place for informing the Native people about the discovery and those Native people would have procedures for helping the Federal agency minimize adverse impacts on the newly discovered cultural resources.

General consultation is the only way to build true and stable partnerships between Federal agencies and Native American people. Often project-driven SIAs bring Federal agencies and Native people together for the first time, and afterwards they decide to move to general consultation as a means of resolving problems before projects precipitate specific cultural resource decisions. The initial SIA team can be retained to facilitate these further studies.

Native people approach cultural resource management from what has been termed 'holistic conservation' (Stoffle and Evans, 1990). They respond positively to holistic studies that bring into consideration as many factors as possible, so the Federal agency can better understand the complex interrelationship between cultural resources and other aspects of Native life ways. Interestingly, the new Federal initiative for ecosystem management closely reflects the philosophical orientation of Native peoples. According to Gore (1993:300) '. . . some people now define themselves in terms of an ecological criterion rather than a political subdivision'. For example, the people of the Aral Sea and the Amazonian Rain Forest define themselves in terms of these all-important ecosystems. In March 1994, eighteen United States federal agencies demonstrated their ecosystem management activities to the United States Congress (Morrissey, Zinn and Corn, 1994). By 1994. (Yaffee, Phillips, Frentz, Hardy, Maleki and Thorpe, 1996), there were hundreds of ecosystems projects most involving extensive SIA components. Native people have responded in a positive way to Federal agencies that are willing to consider cultural resources from an ecosystem perspective.

Specific Consultation   There is always the need to conduct specific consultation regarding cultural-resource issues associated with actions on Federal lands. For example, when general consultation has identified all types of cultural resources, ground-disturbing activities may unexpectedly unearth a human burial or an object of great Native ceremonial significance. The Federal agency may wish to use some portion of their reserve lands for an activity that was not considered during general consultation. Also, the United States Congress may pass new laws regarding the management of cultural resources that potentially would alter the existing relationship between the Native people and the Federal agency. One such law is the Native American Graves Protection and Repatriation Act (NAGPRA), which specifically requires certain types of information to flow between the Federal land managers and Native American people.

Specific consultation is limited by the scope of the specific law that is being complied with and the proposed activity that is being evaluated. Native people often are frustrated by specific consultations because they are limited to those project-specific issues and cultural resources that are being assessed. The Federal agency's responses are too often limited by third parties that legally participate in the assessment. None-the-less, a series of SIA consultations can produce the base from which to build general consultation.

Establishing cultural affiliation

There are many ways that Native American peoples have established cultural affiliations to lands held or affected by a Federal agency. At the most general level Native Americans established these ties because they lived on the land long enough for a culturally shared connection to occur. So the basic question asked in cultural affiliation is, 'What Native American people or ethnic groups lived here?'

The nature of the relationship between Native American people and the land is cultural. The concept of culture (LeVine, 1984:68, 72, 79) implies that a phenomenon is shared in that it represents a consensus on a wide variety of meanings among members of an interaction community; that it is connected and ultimately comprehensible only as a part of a larger organization of beliefs, norms and values; that people who share a culture make sense of new information in terms of a cultural rationale which is founded on a single collective formula. Simply put, the connection between Native Americans and lands held or affected by a Federal agency is abstract, complex and non-trivial. Assessing this relationship is best accomplished by professionals trained in the study of cultural systems, in consultation with potentially culturally affiliated Native American people.

Most laws, regulations and guidelines that cause Federal land-holding agencies to consult with Native Americans do not define what is meant by the term 'cultural affiliation'. Some laws do define this concept: for example, the term is defined very specifically by the NAGPRA. It is important to note that when a Federal agency adopts a broad definition of cultural affiliation for most kinds of cultural resource studies they can still narrow the consultation process when needed for NAGPRA and then resume Native American interactions based on the broader definition. Flexibility is needed when establishing consulation relationship with Native Americans.

How long must a people have lived on the land in order to establish a cultural affiliation? The length of time. Native Americans have spent on the land will vary from groups who perceive they have lived there since the beginning of creation to groups who have had a brief but culturally significant experience on the land. Native American cultural affiliations are created by the supernatural at the beginning of time and by historic events such as a military battle that lasted only a day. When periods of time are chosen as the frames for viewing cultural affiliation, three broad divisions emerge:

1   Traditional period.
2   Aboriginal period.
3   Historic period.

It is important to remember that Native Americans may use other definitions of time – including a pre-human time, which is without measure and is thus time-less.

Traditional-period Affiliation   Native American people have lived on the North American continent for at least 14,000 years according to some scholars (Dincauze, 1991; Haynes, 1987) and as much as 30,000 years according to other scientists (Dillehay, 1991; Grayson, 1988; Meltzer, 1989: Whitley and Dorn, 1993). Despite various scientific interpretations of their origins, most Native Americans believe they were created as a people in North America given birthright ties to a holy land. Often Native American people have a specific cave, spring, valley or mountain where they were created. Similarly, the people of Polynesia, including Hawaiians, emerged from an earlier people known as the Lapita, who spread eastward into the Pacific from their homelands in northwestern Melanesia. The Lapita people were a marine people who began their eastern journey to new islands about 1600 BC and arrived in the Hawaiian islands about AD 300 (Abbott, 1992:1–4; Cuddihy and Stone, 1990).

Native American peoples have lived in many locations during the thousands of years that the Americas have been occupied. Because native peoples moved or were moved, most portions of their traditional land have been occupied by peoples of different cultures. When such movements have been retained in the memory of the living native people, they often have cultural attachments to places where they no longer live. Oral history can accurately convey certain types of information over thousands of years, as illustrated by the Hebrew and Islamic peoples of the Middle East. Like other peoples with oral traditions, Native Americans retain their attachments to sacred places over long periods.

Aboriginal-period Affiliation   The term 'aboriginal' is used here to refer to those people who are recognized by the United States government as having possession of land at the time it was lost to the United States. For many Native American groups, this transfer involved a treaty negotiated between their people and the government of the United States. For many other Native American people, however, they simply were moved away from their aboriginal lands without formal transference of title. These two unique processes of land-loss produced two types of aboriginal period cultural affiliations for Native Americans, which are termed here treatytribes and land-claim tribes.

'Tribe' is used here to refer to the aboriginal inhabitants of territory lost to the United States Federal government. The term tribe is commonly used as a gloss for a variety of Native American social structures that existed aboriginally. Actually, few aboriginal Native American peoples were organized as a tribe, if the technical meaning of this term is used. Most cultural anthropologists would call aboriginal Native American people an 'ethnic group'. In the following discussion the term 'tribe' is used as meaning something like an ethnic group. It is important to make this distinction because not all of the people from any particular Native American ethnic group participated in the 'tribalization process'. Representatives of the United States government often organized Native American ethnic groups by region, a process that often occurred without the full participation of the people. Normally some ethnic group members were left without any tribal membership. Today, there are many Native people who do not belong to a formally recognized tribe or Native organization. These people are usually referred to as not 'federally acknowledged' peoples; none-the-less, they remain Native peoples. Some of these Native people are seeking federal acknowledgement and others are not. The cultural concerns of not 'federally acknowledged' people need to be considered during most types of Native American consultation.

1   **Treaty-tribes.** Native Americans who lost control over some or all of the lands they occupied at the beginning of the historic period to the United States government are called here 'treaty-tribes'. The term is a useful distinction for Federal agencies seeking to understand cultural affiliation because there are a variety of primary references listing United States federal treaties, specifying the lands considered under the treaty, and identifying the Native American group involved in the treaty. While it is relatively easy to identify treaty lands and tribes. most aboriginal lands were not transferred to the United States by treaty.

2   **Land-claims tribes.** Most Native American people can be classified as land-claims tribes, because they lost control over their lands to Euroamericans, but no treaty was ever signed. In most cases, these Native Americans simply were moved off aboriginal lands by force and non-Indian settlers (Sutton, 1985) occupied the lands. The United States Federal government created the Indian Claims Commission (ICC) in 1946 (60 Stat. 1049) charging it with adjudicating the claims of Native Americans for lands lost. After three decades of legal action, a map was prepared that listed the lands considered and the associated Native American people. The ICC produced a multicoloured foldout map entitled 'Indian Land Area Judicially Established' as part of its final report (ICC, 1978; Sutton, 1985:12–13). This ICC map is a useful (but not definitive) tool for identifying the cultural affiliation for most Native Americans to aboriginal lands.

To summarize, both treaty and ICC documents can be used to begin to determine which Native American ethnic groups occupied certain lands when these were lost to Euroamerican society through encroachment or to the Federal government through treaty. It must be remembered, however, that both treaties and ICC processes only establish which Native American group lived on a segment of land at the time it was lost to non-Indian peoples, and do not identify pre-existing Native groups who lived on the land. Furthermore, few land areas were covered by treaty and few treaty lands were surveyed to make reference maps geographically accurate. The ICC process also did not address lands jointly used or claimed by more than one Indian ethnic group, so that many lands were not designated as belonging to any Indian ethnic group (Sutton, 1985:112). Finally, treaties and ICC claims rarely specified the contemporary Native American group or tribe who would be culturally affiliated with the land in question. Given these limitations, the process of establishing cultural affiliation should include a search of treaties and ICC documents, but it should not be limited to Native ethnic groups found in these documents.

Historic-period Affiliation Probably the time of greatest movement for Native American peoples was during the historic period when the Euroamerican frontier expanded into lands held by Native Americans. The historic period began at different times for different Native American groups and the encroachment on Native lands resulted in both total dislocation and gradual dislocation. In many instances, however, when Euroamericans arrived in a place the Native peoples moved. After forced relocation, Native people retained cultural attachments to their aboriginal lands, while culturally re-establishing their way of life in new lands. In the new lands they gathered plants, killed animals, planted crops, gathered clay for pottery, had babies and died. In other words they continued to live as coherent cultural groups. When they interacted with the new lands through traditional ceremony they formed new cultural affiliations.

Native people often were repeatedly relocated; thus they became culturally affiliated with many places. The Shawnee people, for example, were moved from southern Michigan to Ohio where they lived and died; then they moved near to Kansas City, Kansas, where they lived and died; then they moved to Oklahoma where they live today. When asked about cultural affiliation to places where they had lived in Kansas, Ohio and Michigan, the Shawnee tribal council expressed concerns for these and other places where they had resided during their forced migrations (Stoffle, 1990), because in these places their ancestors are buried and the places represent critical junctures in Shawnee cultural history.

Some Navajo people were relocated in the 1950s, in response to pressure from the United States government, to the Colorado River Indian Tribes reservation, which is located on the lower Colorado River in the Mohave Desert. Two generations later, descendants of these Navajo people had attached themselves to these lands that were the aboriginal lands of both the Mohave and the Chemehuevi Southern Paiute. During recent SIAs, these Navajo people expressed concerns for places in the Mohave Desert that were made sacred when they worked there as railroad workers (Drover, 1985) and for plants in the Mohave Desert now used in medicinal ceremony and rug weaving (Cultural Systems Research, 1987:129–31). Navajo people only used these places and plants after being relocated to the lower Colorado River, but the places and plants were used by the Navajo people in a traditional way, thus qualifying as sacred items under the National Historic Preservation Act.

Perhaps one of the most complex cultural resource issues that emerged during the historic period occured when one native ethnic group was relocated to lands formerly occupied by another native ethnic group. This process was not restricted to the historic period, but it seems to have occurred most often then. A recent study of petroglyph sites in Wyoming and Montana (Francis, Loendorf and Dorn, 1994) used chemical dating techniques to show that over thousands of years different native peoples made petroglyphs on the same rock panel. The Navajo Nation expresses claims to prehistoric Pueblo sites because the sites are used by Navajo medicine men to gather arrowheads, pottery, rattles, and even the skin and bones from pueblo burials for use in Navajo ceremonies (McPherson, 1992:105–22). Some Navajo people express claims to prehistoric Pueblo sites because the Navajo people believe they are biologically and culturally related to these Pueblo people. These cases of sequential use and cultural affiliation demonstrate that places, artefacts and even bodies can have multiple and even conflicting native cultural affiliations.

References

Abbott, I.A. (1992), *La'au Hawai'i: Traditional Hawaiian Uses of Plants*, Manoa, HI: Bishop Museum Press.

Arnstein, S.R. (1969), 'A Ladder of Citizen Participation', *Journal of the American Institute of Planners*, 216–24.

Bennett, J. (1976), *The Ecological Transition: Cultural Anthropology and Human Adaptation*, New York: Pergamon Press.

Cernea, M. (ed.) (1991), *Putting People First: Sociological Variables in Rural Development*, New York: Oxford University Press.

Cuddihy, L.W. and Stone, C.P. (1990), *Alteration of Native Hawaiian Vegetation: Effects of Humans, Their Activities and Introductions*, Honolulu: University of Hawaii Cooperative National Park Resources Studies Unit.

Cultural Systems Research, Inc. (1987), *Cultural Resources Surveying: Ethnographic Resources Candidate Site Selection Phase*, California Low-Level Radioactive Waste Disposal Project, prepared for United States Ecology, Inc., Menlo Park, CA: Cultural Systems Research, Incorporated.

Deloria, V. Jr. and Lytle, C. (1984), *The Nations Within: The Past and Future of American Indian Sovereignty*, New York: Pantheon Books.

Department of Energy (DOE) (1996), *Final Environmental Impact Statement for the Nevada Test Site and Off-Site Locations in the State of Nevada*, Vol. 1 Appendix G: American Indian Assessment, Las Vegas. Nevada: United States Department of Energy, Nevada Operations Office.

Dewey-Hefley, G., Zedeno, N., Stoffle, R. and Pittaluga, F. (1998), 'Piecing the Puzzle', *Common Ground* (Winter/Spring): 15.

Dillehay, T.D. (1991), 'Disease Ecology and Initial Human Migration', in T.D. Dillehay and D.J. Meltzer (eds), *The First Americans: Search and Research*, Boca Raton, FL: CRC Press, 231–66.

Dincauze, D.F. (1991), 'Review of Monte Verde. A Late Pleistocene Settlement in Chile, by T. Dillehay', *Journal of Field Archaeology*, 18:116–19.

Dobyns, H. (1951), Blunders with Bolsas, *Human Organization*, vol. 10: pp. 25–32.

Drover, C.E. (1985), 'Navajo Settlement and Architecture in Southeastern California', *Journal of California and Great Basin Anthropology*, 7(1):46–57.

Francis, J., Loendorf, L. and Dorn, R. (1994), 'AMS Radiocarbon and Cation-Ratio Dating of Rock Art in the Bighorn Basin of Wyoming and Montana', *American Antiquity*, 58(4):711–37.

Geisler, C., Green, R., Usner, D. and West, P. (1982), *Indian SIA: The Social Impact Assessment of Rapid Resource Development on Native Peoples*, Monograph No. 3, Ann Arbor, MI: The University of Michigan, Natural Resource Sociology Research Lab.

Gore, A. (1993), *Earth in the Balance: Ecology and the Human Spirit*, New York: Plume.

Grayson, D.K. (1988), 'Perspectives on the First Americans', in R. Carlisle (ed.), *Americans Before Columbus: Ice Age Origins*, Ethnology Monographs No. 12, Pittsburgh, PA: Department of Anthropology, University of Pittsburgh, pp. 107–23

Haynes, C.V. Jr. (1987), 'Clovis Origin Update', *The Kiva*, 52:83–93.

Indian Claims Commission (ICC) (1978), *Indian Claims Judicially Established*, Washington, DC: The Commission.

LeVine, R. (1984), 'Properties of Culture: An Ethnographic View', in R. Shweder and R. LeVine (eds), *Culture Theory: Essays on Mind, Self, and Emotion*, Cambridge, England: Cambridge University Press, pp. 67–87.

McPherson, R. (1992), *Sacred Land Sacred View: Navajo Perceptions of the Four-Corners Region*, Provo, Utah: Brigham Young University.

Meltzer, D.J. (1989), 'Why Don't We Know When the First People Came to North America?', *American Antiquity*, 54:471–90.

Morrissey, W.A., Zinn, J.A. and Corn, M. (1994), 'Ecosystem Management, Federal Agency Activities', in *CRS Report for Congress*, Washington, DC: The Library of Congress.

National Oceanic and Atmospheric Administration (NOAA) (1994), Guidelines and Principles for Social Impact Assessment, *National Marine Fisheries Service*, prepared by the Interorganizational Committee on Guidelines and Principles for Social Impact Assessment. NOAA Tech. Memo, NMFS-F/SPO-16, 29pp.

Parenteau, R. (1988), *Public Participation in Environmental Decision-Making*, Montreal: University of Montreal Press.

Rappaport, R. (1990), 'Ecosystems, Populations and People', in E. Moran (ed.), *The Ecosystem Approach in Anthropology*, Ann Arbor, MI: The University of Michigan Press.

Stea, D. and Buge, C. (1982), 'Cultural Impact Assessment on Native American Reservations: Two Case Studies', in C. Geisler *et al.* (eds), *Indian SIA*, Monograph No. 3, Ann Arbor, MI: The University of Michigan, Natural Resource Sociology Research Lab, pp. 177–99.

Stoffle, R.W. (ed.) (1990), *Cultural and Paleontological Effects of Siting a Low-Level Radioactive Waste Storage Facility in Michigan: Candidate Area Analysis Phase*, Michigan, MI: Institute for Social Research, The University of Michigan.

Stoffle, R.W. and Evans, M.J. (1990), 'Holistic Conservation and Cultural Triage: American Indian Perspectives on Cultural Resources', *Human Organization*, 49(2): 91–9.

Stoffle, R.W., Halmo, D. and Austin, D. (1997), 'Cultural Landscapes and Traditional Cultural Properties: A Southern Paiute View of the Grand Canyon and Colorado River', *The American Indian Quarterly*, 21(2):229–49.

Sutton, I. (ed.) (1985), *Irredeemable America: The Indians' Estate and Land Claims*, Albuquerque, MI: Native American Studies, University of New Mexico Press.

Whitley, D.S. and Dorn, R.I. (1993), 'New Perspectives on the Clovis Versus Pre-Clovis Controversy', *American Antiquity*, 58(4):626–47.

Yaffee, S., Phillips, A., Frentz, I., Hardy, P., Maleki, S. and Thorpe, B. (1996), *Ecosystem Management in the United States: An Assessment of Current Experience*, Washington, DC: Island Press.

Zedeno, N., Austin, D. and Stoffle, R. (1997), 'Landmark and Landscape: A Contextual Approach to the Management of American Indian Resources', *Culture and Agriculture*, 19(3):123–29.

Editors' note

For the different context of the present book, this chapter has been significantly abbreviated and two appendices removed.

Chapter 28

Cultural Connections to the Land
A Canadian example

Ellen Lee

The concept of cultural landscapes is widely used today, under a broad range of circumstances, from the very general to the very specific. It is a convenient term for integrating the cultural and natural values of a place and for conveying the wholeness of a place, rather than just the sum of its elements. In order to evaluate and manage cultural landscapes we must find some culturally-appropriate way to understand it. However, some kinds of cultural landscapes can be difficult to define in concrete physical terms because of their intangible cultural values. This chapter discusses some of the issues surrounding the identification, evaluation and management of cultural landscapes associated with the history of Aboriginal peoples in Canada, in particular suggesting an approach that integrates the intangible and the tangible, with the cultural with the natural.

Introduction

In general, in western terms, cultural resources are defined as having a specific physical nature and fall into specific categories, such as buildings and structures, archaeological sites, artefacts and so forth. These categories are seen as more or less mutually exclusive, primarily in terms of the academic disciplines best suited to study them. However, as a category of cultural resource, the term 'cultural landscape' is not so exclusively defined. It tends to be used to lump rather than to split, to unite rather than divide, and to integrate the cultural with the natural world in a way that other categories of cultural resource do not. The quintessential nature of the use of the term cultural landscape is that its definition and meaning are in the eye of the beholder. The same area of land can therefore be looked upon as several different versions of cultural landscape depending on the cultural or disciplinary filters and values of the person who is doing the looking, even within a group of western scientists with the same cultural background. The meaning of a landscape to a botanist is different than the meaning of the same landscape to a forester, a wildlife biologist, a farmer, a cottage owner, an ornithologist, a miner, an engineer and so on.

Parks Canada is a Canadian federal government agency, which manages the national historic sites programme and the national parks programme. In these two programmes places of national significance for their historic/cultural values and/or for their natural values are identified, evaluated, designated, in some cases set aside as protected areas, and presented to the public. Fitting cultural landscapes into this process of identification, evaluation, designation and protection presents some significant challenges.

Two of the challenges we face in this exercise are to:

• develop approaches to identifying, categorising and evaluating the significance of cultural landscapes in an appropriate comparative context while respecting holistic cultural perspectives and values;
• find ways to protect these sites in a context of limited legal mechanisms for protected areas, which often artificially separate natural and cultural values.

Places associated with the history and culture of the Aboriginal peoples of Canada present particular challenges. The Aboriginal peoples of Canada fall into three diverse groups, each with its own complex histories, traditional territories and interrelationships – First Nations, Inuit and *Metis* (the latter, for those not familiar with the term, refers to the people resulting from intermarriage between First Nations or Inuit people and Canadians of European ancestry, particularly French and Scottish). In a recent report, the Royal Commission on Aboriginal peoples discussed the diversity of Aboriginal peoples in Canada and described them in terms of over 60 language groups (56 First Nations, 4 Inuit and the Metis).

Approaches to identifying, categorising and evaluating Aboriginal cultural landscapes

In order to develop approaches to identifying, categorising and evaluating the significance of Aboriginal cultural landscapes in an appropriate comparative context, while respecting holistic cultural perspectives and values, several steps are required.

Identification

First of all, there is the process of identification – an Aboriginal group looks at its traditional territory and identifies which site(s) it would like to have protected and presented. This identification is based primarily on cultural values, which may or may not be articulated or shared outside the group. This process in itself may be alien to traditional ways of operating. Many elders find it difficult to select specific sites for special consideration – often all the land is considered sacred. Depending on the cultural group, however, this may sometimes be a fairly straightforward process, as traditional villages, hunting, fishing or plant collection sites, seasonal gathering places, landscape features with associative value or places of spiritual power can be identified.

Identifying sites within a cultural group relies on internal or *emic* approaches to describing and categorising the sites within the internal meaning systems of the group. However, once these sites begin to be discussed and examined outside the cultural group with people of other cultures, the places are often given new meanings and names by these outsiders, which are not necessarily congruent with their original meanings and values.

Categorisation or classification

The names that these places acquired then fall into *etic* or external categories or terminology. Even the words used to describe places identified by Aboriginal groups – 'traditional villages, hunting, fishing or plant collection sites, seasonal gathering places, landscape features with associative value or places of spiritual power' – are external words which reflect western anthropological and archaeological training. They are not the words that any given group would necessarily use to describe their specific sites. So when I talk about these sites from my Euro-Canadian, anthropological perspective, I am adding layers or filters of meaning to the sites and obscuring the rich individual values, experiences and stories that are connected to the place by the cultural occupants who gave the place its original meaning.

Evaluation using the concept of cultural landscapes

Once sites have been identified the next step is to evaluate them according to some explicit criteria, which will help to determine their relative significance. This process can be problematic for several reasons. First, what should be the comparative context within which sites should be evaluated? Should a rock art site associated with one language group in a maritime environment on the east coast of Canada be compared and evaluated relative to a rock art site associated with a very different language group in a maritime environment on the west coast of Canada? Should a Caribou hunting site associated with the autumn Caribou hunt of the Inuit in the Kivalliq area of Nunavut be compared and evaluated relative to a Caribou hunting site of the Vuntut Gwich'in in northern Yukon, more than a thousand miles away and associated with a different Aboriginal group with a significantly different history and language?

The important question to address at this point is 'What is the purpose of the comparison?' That should help to determine whether the comparison is appropriate. In this case, the purpose of the comparison is to determine whether the site should be considered of national historic significance. Should sites be compared within site types or categories, and if so, whose categories, or should they be compared within their own cultural context, which is what gives them meaning?

Slotting or pigeon-holing sites within a particular set of themes or types can be problematic, as generally most sites, especially cultural landscapes, have many layers of meaning. Trying to develop site types or categories to use across cultural boundaries is very tricky. We may look at a particular site and say 'from our perspective, that is a fishing site – therefore it will get compared to other fishing sites to determine whether it is of national significance or not'. However, by doing so we make it very difficult to give adequate consideration to the other layers of value that the site may have, which may not be present in the fishing sites from other cultural areas to which we wish to compare it.

The concept of 'national' significance – political versus cultural definitions

The next question to address, is how to approach the concept of 'national' significance. Western researchers tend to see site designation as a positive, non-political act. However, Aboriginal Canadians do not necessarily see it that way. The term 'First Nations' has been developing as a political concept in Canada over several decades. The history of how the original, independent, sovereign Aboriginal peoples of what is now Canada came to be subject to the laws of the Canadian nation state and part of the geographical entity of Canada continues to be the subject of a considerable amount of study and legal debate. On-going land claim and treaty negotiations and precedent setting legal cases demonstrate that the relationship between Aboriginal peoples and the Canadian government continues to evolve.

Cultural connections to the land

The approach we are developing is to do some pilot projects using the concept of the Aboriginal nation as the comparative context. When a community expresses an interest in having one of their sites considered, Parks staff work with them to prepare a descriptive report on the site using a set of explicit guidelines, which will help in the evaluation process. The report gives the cultural, geographical and historical context of the Aboriginal Nation or group and describes their traditional territory. It positions the specific site as a *cultural landscape*, representing or illustrating important aspects of the larger cultural landscape of the traditional territory of the Nation or group. The concept of Aboriginal cultural landscapes has been further developed through the preparation of *An Approach to Aboriginal Cultural Landscapes* (Buggey 1999a).

> The aim was to provide the Board with a framework that could encompass the traditional values of Aboriginal peoples, including spiritual values, cosmic views of the natural world, and the associative values in the land, while still being understandable to Board members whose world views are typically based in western historical scholarship.
>
> (Buggey 1999b)

The following definition of Aboriginal cultural landscapes is proposed:

> An Aboriginal cultural landscape is a place valued by an Aboriginal group (or groups) because of their long and complex relationship with that land. It expresses their unity with the natural and spiritual environment. It embodies their traditional knowledge of spirits, places, land uses, and ecology. Material remains of the association may be prominent, but will often be minimal or absent.
>
> (Buggey 1999a)

Criteria or indicators

The evaluation of a site involves describing both its cultural and natural values. This is where elements related to biodiversity can be identified. Often if resource extraction is one of the main characteristics of the site (a fishing site or a Caribou hunting site, for example), natural elements play an important role in making the place significant for cultural reasons. In one case, a Sahtu Dene elder described a cultural area they want protected in the following way: 'it has everything you need to live (fish, small game, Caribou, etc.)'. Sometimes the site is a place where oral traditions indicate that a particular species of animal originates, through a connection between the underworld and this world. However, in the description of the values of this place, the scientific version of the values in terms of biodiversity is not always described.

The following principles for identifying and evaluating Aboriginal cultural landscapes are proposed:

- The long associated Aboriginal group or groups have participated in the identification of the place and its significance, concur in the selection of the place to commemorate their culture/history and support designation.

- Spiritual, cultural, economic, social and environmental aspects of the group's association with the identified place, including continuity and traditions, illustrate its historical significance.
- The interrelated cultural and natural attributes of the identified place make it a significant cultural landscape.
- The cultural and natural attributes that embody the significance of the place are identified through traditional knowledge of the associated Aboriginal group(s).
- The cultural and natural attributes that embody the significance of the place may be additionally comprehended by the results of academic scholarship (Buggey 1999a).

Some of the evaluation criteria include the following:

- the site's ability to represent the cultural and historical values within the traditional territory and cultural expression of the group;
- the site's ability to express the group's attachment to the land;
- the site's integrity (both cultural and natural);
- the site's importance to cultural survival;
- the site's importance to the understanding of the complexity and diversity of Canadian history;
- the potential public benefit related to the site's protection.

Protection of cultural landscapes

The second major issue is the challenge of finding ways to protect these sites in a context of limited legal mechanisms for protected areas, which often artificially separate natural and cultural values. In Canada, most legislation providing for the establishment of protected areas focuses on natural values. In fact, National Parks are seen by many as wilderness areas, with as little human impact as possible. However, in the last decade or so, partly as a result of the influence of northern Aboriginal groups in the settlement of land claims, this has begun to change and the cultural values of National Parks are beginning to be recognised. However, it is still the case that the identification of areas for consideration of National Parks uses natural criteria identified by Euro-Canadian scientists for determining what areas should be protected. Minor consideration may be given to boundary adjustments to include important archaeological sites, and once the natural area is identified, its cultural values are then determined. However, cultural values are still seen as secondary in this process.

On the other side of the coin, most cultural heritage legislation focuses on the identification and designation of cultural heritage sites, and is particularly suited to dealing with built heritage such as buildings and archaeological sites. Natural values are rarely considered in the initial identification stages, and then are considered to be secondary only as complementary to or a subset of the cultural values. Most National Parks are large geographic areas. Most cultural heritage sites are small geographic areas. In both cases the legislative and policy process for the establishment and management of these parks and sites reflect this reality. So what happens when we try to identify places with both cultural and natural values, giving their cultural and natural elements equal attention? We get cultural landscapes, some of which are quite large, by traditional historic site standards whose characteristics do not fit very well with the sets of legislative and policy processes and mechanisms for either National Parks or cultural heritage sites.

This can put considerable stress on communities who would like to have their special places recognised and protected from inappropriate development and bureaucrats who are faced with trying to fit park or site proposals into legislative or policy moulds which are not really meant for the purpose at hand. This is made worse in a situation where Aboriginal communities do not have adequate access to land ownership to protect these places themselves. On the other hand, governments who have land management responsibilities have to answer to many constituencies, including the heritage and environmental lobbies, as well as development and industrial sectors whose main interest is resource extraction, such as lumbering and mining or hydroelectric development.

Historic treaties/comprehensive land claims

Aboriginal ownership or control of land in Canada or lack thereof, is at the root of the difficulty here. Historically, the way Aboriginal groups have gained control of specific pieces of land has been through the process of the establishment of reserves created as a result of historic treaties. These reserves generally are very small relative to the original traditional territories of the particular group. Also, in the eastern part of the country, where early 'Peace and Friendship' treaties did not deal with land rights, very little land was reserved for Aboriginal communities. In some historic treaty areas, not all reserves promised have been established. Modern land claim and treaty making deals in large part with how much and which land will become Aboriginal land within the traditional territory of the group or Nation. However, generally speaking, the amount of land that is available for selection is limited, and in the end because of survival needs, the criteria for selection ends up being economic potential, with heritage and environmental concerns receiving minimal consideration.

A recent legal ruling by the Supreme Court of Canada in the Delgamuukw case may have a major impact on the question of Aboriginal land ownership (Supreme Court of Canada 1997). In this case, the court ruled that where it has not been extinguished through treaty, Aboriginal title could co-exist with Crown title. It also indicates that Aboriginal title does not just mean rights to use, but also proprietary rights. The full implications of this decision have yet to be determined, but they could be very significant.

Fitting heritages places into a protected area strategy – an example from the Canadian North

An interesting exercise is proceeding in the Northwest Territories (NWT) with regard to protected areas. As a result of the environmental assessment process in response to major mining activities in the area, a commitment has been made by government to develop a Protected Area Strategy (PAS) for these areas. Work on this strategy is currently underway, with community consultation being one of the major parts of the exercise. The focus of the exercise from the government perspective is on natural or environmental values, but communities have the potential to add a significant cultural component. Two of the relevant guiding principles are to 'recognise the importance of linkages between Aboriginal peoples and the land, and respect and use traditional and scientific knowledge' (NWT Protected Areas Strategy Advisory Committee 1999).

At the same time, a working group established by the Sahtu Dene and Metis Land Claim Agreement (for the Sahtu region, an area within the NWT), has developed a list of heritage places and sites which it has recommended for protection through a range of available mechanisms. This group included three representatives appointed by the Sahtu Secretariat Inc. (the Aboriginal organisation established to implement the land claim on behalf of the Sahtu Dene and Metis) and two representatives appointed by government.

The list of places developed includes a range of types including:

- sacred mountains and other landscape and water features with associated stories (Figure 22.4),
- homelands of specific family groupings,
- places where specific historic events took place and places of medicine power,
- places where supernatural events occurred to create the landscape as it is today,
- the place where a supernatural hero killed the giant beaver (which existed in the area at the end of the Pleistocene) to make the area safe for the Dene people,
- meeting places where yearly gatherings occurred,
- whirlpools,
- burial sites,
- fishing lakes,
- important trails,
- water transportation routes.

Some of these places are large, some are small, some are round or globular and some are linear corridors. Some are places to preserve species, some are places to interpret and present history and culture, and some are places where people should not go because of the dangerous power of the place.

The heritage-working group itself has no power to determine how these places will be managed. Its role was to make recommendations to the appropriate government department and to the Sahtu Secretariat Inc. regarding these heritage places and sites. In addition to developing a list of sites and describing their cultural values, the heritage-working group has identified the kind of protective mechanisms, which might be appropriate to manage these sites.

The mechanisms recommended, sometimes alone, sometimes in combination, include:

- National Historic Site,
- Transfer to Commissioner's land,
- Territorial Historic Park,
- Critical Wildlife Area,
- Migratory Bird Sanctuary,
- Caribou Protection Measures,
- Identification for protection under the Archaeological Sites Regulations,
- Identification for special consideration by land management authorities,
- To be determined after further inventory and evaluation,
- Subsurface protection,
- Heritage River.

Although specific, explicit criteria were not developed by the working group to determine which mechanisms would be the most appropriate for which site, some patterns can be observed in the results. For example, generally sacred sites which have Medicine Power or landforms created by 'supernatural events' have values that are not just manifested on the surface of the land, but have a more three-dimensional expression. For these places, the group recommended subsurface as well as surface protection. Three of these places are very large, averaging roughly 3,000 km^2. Obtaining subsurface protection for such places will be very difficult because of the legislation and regulations governing access for mineral extraction.

Discussions between this heritage working group and those working on the protected area strategy may lead to a better integration of cultural values into the protected area strategy. One of the simple ways of integration is to add cultural information to the Geographic Information System used to map the natural/environmental values used by the regional renewable resources staff to manage fish and wildlife resources in the area and to feed information into the land use planning process. This has the potential to be a breakthrough in the integration of cultural and natural values in determining protected area regimes, and hopefully it can be a model for use in other areas.

The challenge to all of this is to bring a variety of interests together to deal with a common, overlapping issue. Sometimes integrating technical information can lead to a change in the perceptions of the users of this information, to broaden their way of looking at the landscape, and recognising that their way of seeing the world is not strictly objective but has cultural filters. Recognising your own cultural filters can sometimes lead to a more enlightened perception of other peoples' cultural values and perspectives, and lead to a more holistic approach to dealing with the environment and landscape.

The Report of the Sahtu Heritage Places and Sites Joint Working Group has been released, and the NWT Protected Areas Strategy has been finalised and approved and is ready for implementation (Rakeké Gok'é Godi 2000). The implementation of these two reports will be the test of the commitment of all parties to move forward and take some creative steps to resolve some of these issues.

Conclusions

Recent initiatives of the World Commission on Protected Areas of the International Union for the Conservation of Nature promote a more integrative approach to the development of protected areas management categories (IUCN World Commission on Protected Areas 1999). One of the purposes of these new approaches is to encourage the involvement of local people in the management of protected areas. In order for this to be effective, the cultural understanding of the landscapes of the protected areas of these local peoples must be integrated into the approach to identifying, evaluating and managing the protected areas. Work that is currently being done in Australia on the development of Indigenous Protected Areas appears to be an innovative approach to integrating natural and cultural values in protected areas (Biodiversity Group, Environment Australia 1998).

Both of these initiatives are encouraging signs that international efforts in the establishment of protected areas are moving to more integrative and creative arrangements. To conclude, I would like to focus on where I think we need to go to begin to resolve some of the challenges that I have identified. First of all, I think we need to further develop the concept of a cultural landscape as a protected area. To do that, we need to work at developing a more holistic approach to integrating natural and cultural values of special places. We need to look at the entire landscape as a whole, and identify the diverse elements within it, rather than just focussing on individual elements or sites. Finally, I think we need to work on developing new legislative or statutory mechanisms, which will meet the needs of protecting a cultural landscape for all of its inherent values. This will go a long way to increasing both the protection of biodiversity and the cultural survival of threatened indigenous groups on this planet.

References

Buggey, S. 1999a: *An Approach to Aboriginal Cultural Landscapes*. Agenda paper for the Historic Sites and Monuments Board of Canada. Hull, Quebec.

Buggey, S. 1999b: *An Approach to Aboriginal Cultural Landscapes*. Website, Parks Canada, www.parkscanada/aborig/main_e.htm

Biodiversity Group, Environment Australia 1998: *Indigenous Protected Areas: A New Approach to Biodiversity Conservation in Land and Sea Country*. Biodiversity Group, Environment Australia, Canberra.

IUCN World Commission on Protected Areas (WPCA) 1999: *Short Term Action Plan 1999–2002*. IUCN WPCA, http://wcpa.iucn.org/pubs/publications.html#wcpa

NWT Protected Areas Strategy Advisory Committee 1999: *Northwest Territories Protected Areas Strategy: A Balanced Approach to Establishing Protected Areas in the Northwest Territories*, prepared by the NWT Protected Areas Strategy Advisory Committee, February 15, 1999. Website, Department of Resources, Wildlife and Economic Development, Yellowknife, Northwest Territories, Canada, http://www.gov.nt.ca/RWED/pas/index.htm

Rakeké Gok'é Godi 2000: *Places We Take Care Of*. Report of the Sahtu Heritage Places and Sites Joint Working Group, January 2000. Parks Canada, Ottawa.

Supreme Court of Canada 1997: Delgamuukw versus British Columbia: *Supreme Court of Canada Ruling, December 11, 1997*.

This article is a reworked, updated version of a presentation entitled 'Sacred places, cultural landscapes and protected areas: A Canadian perspective', presented at National Sacred Sites and Cultural Diversity and Biodiversity, an international symposium sponsored by UNESCO, CNRS, MNHN, September 22–25, 1998.

Chapter 29

'An Emu in the Hole'

Exploring the link between biodiversity and Aboriginal cultural heritage in New South Wales, Australia

Anthony English

Introduction

In New South Wales (NSW), Aboriginal heritage has been defined as having a focus on pre-contact sites such as middens and rock art. This focus has dominated both off-park Environmental Impact Assessment and the management of Aboriginal heritage in protected areas. The continued importance of biodiversity and environmental health to the identity and lifestyle of Aboriginal communities has been largely ignored. The dynamic nature of Aboriginal people's culture which has included strategies designed to allow continued contact with the land has been hidden by this emphasis on relics and pre-contact Aboriginal sites.

This has resulted in an array of Aboriginal social values being neglected in environmental management. This chapter looks at the values associated with the use of wild foods and resources and the role this activity plays in the transmission of cultural knowledge and in binding Aboriginal families together. The extent of such activity in NSW is little understood and its importance to Aboriginal communities is rarely considered when assessing the impacts of a proposed development on Aboriginal heritage values. Similarly, Aboriginal people's involvement in park management has been largely restricted to the conservation of sites and physical remains.

The NSW National Parks and Wildlife Service (NPWS) has been working with two Aboriginal communities to explore the continued cultural importance of biodiversity and to develop mechanisms which can build associated cultural values into environmental management in NSW.

Over the last two years, the NSW NPWS has been talking with Aboriginal people about the ways in which they value land and biodiversity. This process has formed part of the Aboriginal People and Biodiversity Project which seeks to assess whether these values are taken into account during off-park Environmental Impact Assessment (EIA) and protected area management.

The project has revealed that biodiversity is valued by Aboriginal people in NSW for many reasons. This may come as a surprise to wider society in NSW which has little understanding of the manner in which Aboriginal people have adapted and developed their cultural identity throughout 200 years of immense upheaval and change. The opinions and knowledge that Aboriginal people have shared with us during the project demonstrate the strength of indigenous people's capacity to retain links with their country and to utilise and pass on cultural knowledge despite the effects of dispossession.

The project also revealed that this aspect of contemporary Aboriginal life is not encompassed by the notion of 'Aboriginal heritage' as it is applied in EIA and protected area management. Instead, the term has been defined as primarily relating to 'Aboriginal sites' or the material remains of pre-invasion occupation of the land by Aboriginal people. Rock art, middens, burials and stone artefact scatters and not the dynamic nature of living people's culture are the focus of heritage management in NSW.

This chapter looks in detail at this issue and uses the outcomes of interviews with Muruwuri and Gumbaingirr people about the importance of utilising wild resources to critically assess the current approach to Aboriginal heritage management in NSW. Wild resources are defined here to include native and introduced species of flora and fauna utilised for food, medicine and materials. It also includes the land and sea where these species are obtained. For example, this could include a beach, a pathway through the forest or a stand of trees.

I have approached this situation as an archaeologist who works for the NPWS. This chapter therefore represents a non-Aboriginal person's interpretation of these issues but it is based on close collaboration with Aboriginal people in two areas of NSW.

The Aboriginal People and Biodiversity Project

Background

As an archaeologist with the NPWS, I have been regularly involved in surveying newly created protected areas for Aboriginal sites (English, 1997b and English et al., 1997). These surveys have been conducted in collaboration with local Aboriginal people, many of whom talked about how they still utilised wild foods and medicines as part of their daily life. People pointed out plants and animals during these surveys which they valued and in some cases stated they were finding increasingly difficult to access due to the effects of clearing and cropping and landowner objection to Aboriginal people coming onto their land.

It became obvious that by recording the physical remains of past Aboriginal occupation on the land now within park boundaries, the NPWS was recognising only a fraction of the cultural values that Aboriginal people attached to these landscapes. Of more importance however was the fact that the failure to understand contemporary values associated with the environment was limiting the scale and form of Aboriginal people's involvement in environmental management and effectively barring them from expressing their interest in accessing wild resources within the park system and on non-reserved lands.

The emphasis on relics and their protection in NSW reflects a particular view of Aboriginal history and culture which is now openly brought into question by events such as the passage of the *Native Title Act 1993* (Cth.). Byrne argues that it reflects a desire on the part of the State to acquire a 'deep' history which it could not otherwise obtain. He also points out that it is symptomatic of the European perspective that Aboriginal culture in NSW was corrupted through Aboriginal people's contact with Europeans. Artefacts and the archaeological remains became viewed as being a "benchmark of authentic Aboriginality" (Byrne, 1998).

One of the outcomes of this situation has been a tendency for government to represent Aboriginal communities in NSW as "products of colonial history which have left their members, whether as passive victims or resistance fighters, dislocated and implicitly bereft of their cultural traditions" (MacDonald, 1997). By focusing on pre-contact sites in park management plans, NPWS has been unconsciously creating an impression that Aboriginal heritage is tangible only where it is directly associated with the period before European invasion. This has rendered invisible what Byrne (1998) describes as "dynamic and adaptive forms of Aboriginality."

This is not to say that sites associated with pre- and post-contact occupation are not important to Aboriginal people. On the contrary, they are highly valued and represent a depth of connection with the landscape that cannot be underestimated. Sites, however, represent only one facet of Aboriginal heritage. Contemporary land use and the transmission and adaptation of cultural knowledge are another, yet they are generally left out of the heritage equation.

Building on change within the NPWS

While being aware of the perspectives described above, the project was aided by the fact that in the late 1990s, the NPWS was beginning to shift slightly in its approach to working with Aboriginal communities to manage their heritage. First, in 1996, legislation was passed which allowed the joint management of protected areas with Aboriginal people where those parks were of cultural significance (English, 1997a). This represented a strong recognition of the continued importance of land and wildlife to Aboriginal people in NSW. A handful of reserves have now been identified for joint management.

Second, in 1998, the NPWS embarked on the Visions Symposium that was modelled on the Vail Symposium held in 1997 in the United States. The Visions Symposium report recommended a radical change in the NPWS's approach to defining 'Aboriginal heritage' values. It recommended that traditional and contemporary associations with the land be recognised and that the indivisibility of the environment's natural and cultural values should form the basis for working with Aboriginal people (Report of the Steering Committee, 1998).

The NPWS needed to better understand how to put this approach into practice. The majority of staff in the agency at the field management, policy and research levels have been operating in a system that has seen little linkage between those involved in what have been termed 'natural' and 'cultural' heritage management. The Aboriginal People and Biodiversity Project has been designed to help address the agency's limited experience in working with Aboriginal people to understand how they value land and biodiversity. Prior to this there has been little or no consideration by the NPWS of the Aboriginal cultural values associated with biodiversity.

Methodology

The project has been based on the close involvement of two Aboriginal communities. The first involved working with the Muruwari people in the semiarid north-western part of the State. These people live in a number of towns such as Bourke, Brewarrina, Lightning Ridge and Weilmoringle. The second case study with the Gumbaingirr people, was conducted on the mid-north coast at Corindi Beach. Both case studies allowed us to compare and contrast people's experience in two areas with vastly different environments as well as different European and Aboriginal land use histories.

Importantly, the work was not designed as a dry academic exercise that sought to create lists of people's ecological knowledge. Rather, it has been issues-based and has focused on seeking people's responses to a set of key questions in taped interviews and in informal trips out into the bush. The scope of the work was designed collaboratively with the two communities who retain ownership of all of the information shared with the NPWS during the project.

The interviews were conducted with both sexes and across a wide range of age groups. This allowed us to assess and understand people's experiences over the last 50 years.

We asked people to discuss a number of key questions with us. These included:

1   Has using the beach and bush been important to you?
2   If so, has your ability to access wild resources changed over time?
3   What has caused a change in levels of access?
4   Has environmental change and development affected your ability to utilise the land and sea?
5   Does using the land and sea have cultural meaning to you as an Aboriginal person?
6   What are your feelings about how Aboriginal people are involved in EIA and the management of National Parks?

These questions interweave in complex ways. They required us to understand the life history of the interviewees and the changes in land use and land access which have occurred in both areas of the State where these people live.

Preliminary case study results

Both the Muruwuri and Gumbaingirr people involved in the project have retained their connections with the land since European settlement. After periods of violence in the mid-19th Century involving massacre and dispossession, people used a variety of strategies to locate themselves physically on land that was important to them. These included gaining employment on farms and occupying pastoral camps and vacant Crown land. Members of both communities were able to avoid being congregated onto Missions in this way. Some Muruwuri people were moved to a large Mission at Brewarrina but even here they retained links with the land through the continued use of wild foods and the passing on of stories and knowledge throughout the Mission era, which extended into the second half of the 20th Century.

The people we interviewed in both communities explained that utilising wild foods and medicines remains an important part of their lifestyle. Apart from being delicious, wild food collection and consumption brings families and communities together. Learned rules about sustainable use, sharing and the seasonal availability of resources are passed from one generation to the next. This activity is viewed as being an important means of expressing one's identity and connection with the land. The experience for successive generations has been different, but underlying the effects of social change is a continued commitment to the value of wild resource utilisation, which spans different age groups.

The case study from Corindi Beach is discussed here in more detail. The experience of the Muruwuri people has been made into a documentary titled 'Muruwuri Voices' as part of this project.

Case study at Corindi Beach

Corindi Beach is a small settlement located on the NSW north coast, 30 km north of the regional centre of Coffs Harbour. Prior to European settlement of the region in the 1840s, the Gumbaingirr people occupied a resource-rich environment, which encompassed the coast and the immediate hinterland. In the Corindi Beach area, people were initially forcefully displaced but a small group of families returned and occupied farming land with the permission of a landowner in the late 1890s. Following this, the families moved to occupy vacant Crown land adjacent to the beach where they remained until the late 1980s under the terms of a permissive occupancy (Cane, 1988; Morris, 1992). Occupation was focused on a freshwater lake which lies behind the dunes.

Today, the community resides on land within the township close to the lake. They were moved away from the lake itself when the permissive occupancy was revoked to allow the land to be managed for coastal recreation and conservation.

We interviewed people ranging in age from 58 to 19. It became clear that a number of factors had operated to reduce people's access to land since the 1950s and their level of reliance on wild foods.

These included:

1   Environmental change caused by residential development and pollution which has destroyed areas used for wild food collection.
2   Change in landowner attitudes to Aboriginal people having access to their land from the late 1960s onward.
3   The emergence of environmental laws which prohibited or restricted the taking of some wild foods.
4   Changes in lifestyle and improved access to bought foods and products.

During the 1950s and 1960s Aboriginal people living at Corindi Beach were still relying on wild foods for subsistence. Low-income levels and sporadic work opportunities meant that kangaroo, wallaby, echidna, fish and an array of plant foods were obtained on a daily basis. This activity allowed a level of independence and ensured that knowledge about the land was used and passed on. One Elder explained that this situation created a strongly-knit community:

> Everyone had to do something. Like today, you can write an order out and one person can go into the supermarket while other people are just sitting around. They're not going to do anything. They don't know nothing. Because you had to know – you were part of a team, in a group, that you had to go out next morning. There might be three or four different groups that had to go and collect stuff, you know. Because you had no money it was no good sitting at home. You had to keep going. Share it around.

Today, people are able to access only a small area of bushland and Corindi Beach itself if they wish to obtain wild resources such as fish, shellfish and plant foods and medicines. The lake was polluted in the 1970s by urban runoff and pollution at a time when many families were still relying on it for food. One Elder explained the effects of this on people and pointed out that it is still polluted today:

> Oh, I think they ruined that lake. All that murky water come down from that big drain near the shop there. All run into the swamp there and from the swamp out into the lake. So we hardly don't take anything from the lake now, clouded up like that . . . I don't know how the turtles are getting on in the swamp hole, where they go to, because it runs straight into the swamp and from the swamp straight out to the lake, big lake. All of it's polluted.

Despite the fact that wild foods are no longer relied on for subsistence, wild food collection still forms an important part of many old and young people's lifestyle. Different generations have a different perspective on this. The Elders talk with nostalgia about accessing places which are now barred to them and obtaining foods which are now either prohibited by law or unavailable due to a lack of access to land. People interviewed who were born during and after the 1960s see their use of the beach and bush as being an expression of their Aboriginality and wish to expand their use of wild foods under the tutelage of the Elders. Where wild foods are gathered today, such activity is valued by the younger generations as a means of binding families together. One interviewee aged 30 explained:

> We had a really big pipi gathering day here and we had everybody down there. We had them down from the camp, and Mum and Dad. We had everyone down on the beach and it was really good. It's a good feeling to have everybody doing it and talking while you're doing it, trading stories. People start remembering the old days and what their Mum would have said or what they would have done when they were living. That's how its passed on. It's very important. I want to be able to teach my kids about it as well. I mean, I'm never going to stop learning about bush tucker. I'm never going to stop learning about who I am. But I want my kids to have that feeling as well . . . When I grew up I was made to feel ashamed that I was black and I mean you hate that. You feel like you don't belong anywhere.

Today, the community at Corindi Beach is actively seeking to negotiate access to land and resources in State forests and on Crown land. They are also seeking to play a greater role in environmental management to ensure that the land is protected from overdevelopment.

These desires are currently not recognised as forming an element of Aboriginal people's heritage due to a focus by government on sites and relics. As an Elder at Corindi Beach explained, this is not enough:

> I know sites are very important, but sites are only part of the land. That's how it works. The land is the base of your culture; your tradition and your culture. That's where your food source is. It could be a swamp but it's very valuable. The site may be a very important place, but without a land base you can't teach anything.

Implications for land and heritage management

Off-park EIA

At present, the social values associated with Aboriginal people's continuing use of wild foods and the land are rarely considered as part of the EIA process. Cultural heritage assessment is largely restricted to archaeological surveys. The assessment of potential impacts on the environment is restricted to fauna and flora surveys which take no account of the link between the environment and contemporary Aboriginal people's lifestyle and values.

As an example, in north-western NSW near the township of Goodooga, the last quandong tree accessible on foot by Muruwuri people was destroyed by a road development that had been designed to ensure avoidance of archaeological sites. This left people reliant on access to vehicles and farming land at much greater distances from the town if they wanted to obtain the fruit from the quandong tree. In a town where people have sporadic access to vehicles and limited money for petrol, the loss of the tree was noted by the community as a real impact.

Another scenario common to coastal NSW can be used to illustrate this issue. A housing development is proposed for a headland overlooking a beach. Behind the beach, a swamp feeds a creek that empties into the sea. The beach, creek and swamp are used by local Aboriginal people for fishing and collecting plant foods and medicines. These foods and medicines supplement people's diet and allow those on limited incomes to have a level of economic independence.

Under the current approach to EIA, archaeological sites in the area would be identified and managed as part of the development process. Threatened species of flora and fauna would also be identified. No assessment of the possible impact of the development on contemporary Aboriginal use of the beach, swamp and bush would occur. This is not dealt with by the NPWS's approach to development consent.

This needs to be rectified. We need to be asking a range of questions about developments. Does a development have the potential to impact on the extent and accessibility of resources currently utilised by Aboriginal people, such as fish in rivers and foods in estuarine environments? Might these impacts manifest themselves outside a development's boundaries and affect areas used by the community due to the detrimental effect of the development on surrounding ecosystems? Could these impacts extend to lands which are either claimable under the *Aboriginal Land Rights Act 1983* (NSW) or the *Native Title Act 1993* (Cth)? Is the development going to create access problems for Aboriginal people when they are travelling to an area they use?

Building such considerations into EIA would require restructuring Aboriginal heritage management. Archaeologists currently dominate cultural heritage assessment in EIA but the sorts of considerations listed above could not be assessed by archaeologists. There needs to be a multi-disciplinary approach to assessing Aboriginal heritage values and a greater role for Aboriginal people in identifying and articulating potential cultural impacts and management options.

One approach that needs greater consideration in NSW is the application of Social Impact Assessment (SIA). SIA relating to Aboriginal people has been neglected in NSW both in formal EIA, regional planning and reserve selection despite its ability to empower Aboriginal people. SIA is supposed to involve the assessment of a development's potential impacts on a community's well being (BBC Consulting Planners, 1994).

Examples of SIA being applied can be found in many countries, including Australia where its treatment of indigenous issues appears to have been restricted largely to large-scale mining developments in the Northern Territory and Cape York, Queensland (Gagnon *et al.*, 1993). In some cases, the SIAs have been commissioned by indigenous groups who have employed consultants who are provided with all of the data feeding into the EIA. Impacts, which have been dealt with under these projects, have included the effects of an influx of construction workers and alcohol on remote communities, loss of land and resources and the effects of pollution on surrounding country utilised by the community.

SIA does not appear to have been adopted however in broad scale EIA in States like NSW. While SIA is not without methodological problems, elements of SIA could at least be applied as a requirement of the development approval process. This could be given a legislative foundation by utilising the broad definition of the 'environment' provided in the *Environmental Planning and Assessment Act 1979* (NSW) (EPAA) to require the consideration of a development's social and cultural impacts. This Act defines the environment as including "all aspects of the surroundings of man whether affecting him as an individual or in his social groupings." This wording is very similar to that used in the American National Environmental Policy Act (1969) which has been used to support the application of SIA as part of the development approval process. Such wording should conceivably allow indigenous social values attached to the environment to be a relevant consideration in EIA.

An instructive example of the poor consideration of Aboriginal cultural values associated with the environment in NSW is provided by the Commission of Inquiry report on a proposed mineral sands mine in an area valued by Aboriginal people on the mid-north coast (Cleland and Carelton, 1992). This represented a higher level of scrutiny than generally occurs in EIA and was prompted by the fact that the land had also been flagged by the NPWS as being suitable for reservation.

The Aboriginal cultural importance of the Saltwater area was identified during a Heritage Study of the Taree Council area and not during a specific EIA project. The community indicated that the area had been utilised for wild food collection and camping since the 1890s and acted as a place where people could go to escape the restrictions of the Mission system. The Purfleet-Taree Local Aboriginal Land Council requested that the area be gazetted as an Aboriginal Place under the National Parks and Wildlife Act 1974 (NSW) to protect the "traditional cultural values inherent in the open beach and Khappinghat estuary, and to preserve an existing use" (Cleland and Carelton, 1992).

Despite this information, which was repeated at the Commission of Inquiry, the Commission argued that mining of the area should be allowed with the provision that known Aboriginal sites (relics) not be impacted. No statement is made about the effects of the development on contemporary Aboriginal land use.

The question can be asked, why cannot people seek to use the existing development assessment process to raise their concerns? Certainly, non-indigenous people who wish to ensure their rights to a clean environment or to protect a threatened species from a housing development have used planning law to their advantage. Standing rights provided by the EPAA allow anyone in the community to question an EIA decision by responding to documents such as Development Applications and Environmental Impact Statements. If this fails to achieve a desired outcome then litigation may follow, sometimes as class actions. To a large extent however, the success of these actions is dependent on the scope and strength of related statutes such as wildlife protection legislation. Court action is also an expensive and adversarial process which members of the public may be poorly-resourced to undertake.

Aboriginal people have access to these same rights yet they face further restrictions. The ability of an Aboriginal group to argue that cultural values might be impacted by a development is greatly muted by the restricted approach to defining Aboriginal heritage values in heritage law and EIA and by the absence in planning law of specific reference to indigenous social values as being a consideration in land use planning. A restricted approach to environmental assessment has become entrenched in NSW and the potential linkage between planning and heritage law has been largely condensed to an archaeological question. The Saltwater case is a good example of this.

It is important to emphasise that the cultural foundation of Aboriginal concern about environmental management is not explicitly supported by planning legislation. This can be seen by contrasting NSW with New Zealand where planning laws such as the *Resource Management Act 1991* have been revised to incorporate Maori values and concerns into the land use planning process (English, 1996). In NSW, the cultural impacts of loss of biodiversity, restricted access to resources or limited involvement in land use planning is not presented as a potential consideration of EIA. This remains to be argued in court using an interpretation of the EPAA and addressed by more enlightened government policy. The project report (English, 2000) is recommending that the NPWS use its consent role in EIA to develop standards and guidelines for assessing social and cultural impacts relating to Aboriginal community values.

A preliminary attempt has been made to identify criteria that could be used to assist the assessment of Aboriginal cultural values associated with biodiversity and contemporary land use during the EIA process. These are under the headings of 'use of wild foods and resounds', the 'Passing on of Cultural Knowledge', and 'Community Health'. It is recommended that the term 'cultural heritage assessment' be replaced with 'cultural environment assessment' to promote a more inclusive approach to the identification of social values.

The NPWS

The Aboriginal People and Biodiversity Project also argues for a number of changes in the way in which the NPWS manages the reserve system and carries out regional planning and biodiversity survey and research. At present there is little or no Aboriginal community involvement in biodiversity survey and research and no consideration of the social impacts that can occur to Aboriginal communities through the inclusion of land and resources within the reserve system.

The NPWS does not fully recognise the link between Aboriginal people's involvement in environmental management and the sense of playing a custodial role over culturally significant land. Outside the handful of reserves flagged for joint management, reserve Plans of Management provide for only limited involvement in site management.

The NPWS also has no policy on Aboriginal utilisation of wild foods and this is restricting Aboriginal communities from understanding their rights at law. For example, communities are largely unaware of the possibility of using the wildlife licensing system managed by the NPWS to their benefit (English, 1997a).

A variety of changes in NPWS policy and practice are being recommended as part of the Aboriginal People and Biodiversity Project. These argue that the NPWS should, among other things:

1   develop mechanisms for Aboriginal community involvement in pest species and fire management programmes in protected areas;
2   develop projects that facilitate co-operative approaches to wildlife management on Aboriginal lands and in the reserve system;
3   integrate Aboriginal community concerns, values and knowledge into regional planning exercises;
4   develop protocols on Aboriginal involvement in programmes and projects covering issues such as intellectual property rights, training, consultation and employment;
5   actively build SIA in relation to Aboriginal people into the reserve design and selection process;
6   expand the role of Aboriginal staff within the agency to allow them to assist Aboriginal communities to identify concerns about land management and access to wild resources within the reserve system and as part of the off-park EIA process.

The project has already inserted many of these recommendations into reviews of NPWS Field Management Policy and the NPWS's response to the NSW Biodiversity Strategy.

Conclusion

The utilisation of wild resources in NSW remains an important element of many Aboriginal people's lives. It represents the continuation of traditions and practices that have been adapted and maintained by Aboriginal communities throughout the period since European settlement, and remains highly valued by people of different age groups.

This aspect of contemporary Aboriginal life is not encompassed by current approaches to recognising and managing Aboriginal heritage in NSW. It is neglected in both off-park EIA and regional planning as well as in protected area management. A focus on relic or site protection is obscuring the dynamic nature of Aboriginal people's culture and addresses only part of the concerns felt by Aboriginal people.

The Aboriginal People and Biodiversity Project has allowed the NPWS to work with two communities to better understand the continuing cultural value of land and biodiversity. It is hoped that the projects recommendations for change will have an effect on the policy and practice of environmental management in NSW.

References

BBC Consulting Planners. 1994. Review of Commonwealth EIA-Social Impact Assessment. Prepared for the Assessment Policy and Coordination Section, Commonwealth Environment Protection Agency, Canberra.

Byrne, D. 1998. Deep nation: Australia's acquisition of an indigenous past. *Aboriginal History* 20:82–107.

Cane, S. 1988. The Red Rock Mob. Aboriginal relationships with the Red Rock–Corindi Area, NSW. Report to the Grafton Lands Office.

Cleland, K. and Carelton, M. 1992. Mineral Sands Mine. Proposed by Mineral Deposits Limited, Saltwater, City of Greater Taree. Report by the Commissioners of Inquiry for Environment and Planning to the Honourable Robert Webster, Minister for Planning and Minister for Housing.

English, A.J. 1996. Legislative and policy frameworks for indigenous involvement in cultural heritage management in New Zealand and New South Wales. *Environment and Planning Law Journal* 13(2):103–119.

English, A.J. 1997a. Terrestrial hunting and gathering by Aboriginal people in New South Wales: an assessment of law and policy. *Environmental and Planning Law Journal* 14(6): 437–455.

English, A.J. 1997b. Archaeological Survey of Culgoa National Park, North Western New South Wales. Unpublished report to the NSW National Parks and Wildlife Service and the Muruwuri Tribal Council.

English, A.J. 2000. What does the land mean to you? Contemporary Aboriginal landuse and cultural heritage management in NSW. Unpublished report to the NSW National Parks and Wildlife Service, the Yarrawarra Aboriginal Corporation and the Muruwuri Tribal Council.

English, A.J., Erskine, J., Veale, S. and Robinson, J. 1997. Cultural Heritage Assessment of Goobang National Park, Central Western New South Wales. Unpublished report to the NSW National Parks and Wildlife Service and Peak Hill, Dubbo and Wellington Local Aboriginal Land Councils.

Gagnon, C., Hirsch, P. and Howitt, R. 1993. Can social impact assessment empower communities? *Environmental Impact Assessment Review* 13:229–253.

MacDonald, G. 1997. Recognition and justice: the traditional/historical contradiction in NSW. In Smith, C. and Finlayson, R. (eds) *Fighting Over Country*. CAEPR Australian National University Research Monograph 12: 65–82.

Report of the Steering Committee. 1998. Visions for the new millennium. Report of the Steering Committee to the Minister for the Environment.

Chapter 30

Social Sustainability
People, history, and values

Setha M. Low

My interest in social sustainability grows out of personal as well as professional reflections on the meaning of the built environment for defining who we are – as individuals and as groups. To discuss these concerns, however, I need to shift the unit of analysis from considerations of economics and cultural landscapes to individual histories, needs, and values, and focus on how we can sustain the social relations and meanings that make up our complex life-world. I begin with my own experiences and research.

As I drive Interstate 10 from Palm Springs to West Los Angeles, my personal history passes by inscribed in places, institutions, and cultural markers. I am reminded of where I went to college, where I spent my summers as a child, and where I got my first job. These physical reminders provide a sense of place attachment, continuity, and connectedness that we are rarely aware of but that play a significant role in our psychological development as individuals and in our "place identity" or "cultural identity" as families or ethnic and cultural groups (Low and Altman 1992).[1]

But what happens when your places are not marked, or even more to the point, when your personal or cultural history is erased – removed by physical destruction and omitted from historical texts? The redevelopment of Paris by Baron Haussmann and removal of buildings around Notre Dame in the nineteenth century are a classic example of the erasure of a working-class and poor people's history (Halloran 1998). In the United States we have been more subtle. For instance, the contextually complex, residential streets of Bunker Hill were lost in the modernist redevelopment of downtown Los Angeles (Louksitou-Sideris and Dansbury 1995–96), and Robert Moses obliterated entire working-class neighborhoods to make way for the Cross-Bronx Expressway in New York City.

At Independence National Historical Park in Philadelphia, there is no record of the people who built the buildings (African Americans), or financed the Revolution (Jewish Americans), or fed the soldiers (women, mothers, and wives). The processes of historic preservation, planning and development, and park interpretation re-created the colonial period as a white, male space. Even the documentation of lost buildings and physical context is missing from the histories of minority people during colonial times.

African Americans in Philadelphia, though, are fighting to reclaim their history by supporting research and setting up archives to ensure that their history and culturally significant sites are included. The African American community in New York was successful in contesting the federal government's claims to the African American Burying Ground, demanding its commemoration and preservation, but was less successful in preserving the Audubon Ballroom, where Malcolm X was shot. Thus even as histories are erased, they are re-searched and rediscovered so that they can be commemorated.

Ellis Island, only four hundred meters from the New Jersey shore, is inaccessible to the residents of surrounding neighborhoods. Their lack of economic resources makes the cost of the ferry ride prohibitive, especially for large family outings. Residents want a bridge from Ellis Island to Liberty State Park to provide free access for their community, but historic preservationists argue that a bridge will destroy visitors' experience of arriving by water. Conflicting values derived from distinct social needs and assumptions often produce these kinds of conservation and heritage site problems but can be resolved through a better understanding of those values and their meanings for local populations. Here I address the problem of how to incorporate conflicting cultural values and diverse cultural histories at heritage sites to enhance their social sustainability.

Definitions

What do we mean by "social sustainability"? Following Throsby (1995), sustainability refers to the evolutionary or lasting qualities of the phenomena, avoidance of short-term or temporary solutions, and a concern with the self-generating or self-perpetuating characteristics of a system.[2] Drawing a parallel with natural ecosystems that support and maintain the "natural balance," "cultural ecosystems" support and maintain cultural life and human civilization (Throsby 1999). Sustainable development is the preservation and enhancement of the enviroment through the maintenance of natural ecosystems, whereas culturally sustainable development refers to the preservation of arts and society's attitudes, practices, and beliefs.

Social sustainability is a subset of cultural sustainability; it includes the maintenance and preservation of social relations and meanings that reinforce cultural systems. Specifically, it refers to maintaining and enhancing the diverse histories, values, and relationships of contemporary populations. To understand social sustainability – at the level of individuals and groups – I need to expand Throsby's analysis by adding three critical dimensions:

1   Cultural ecosystems are located in time and space: for a cultural ecosystem to be maintained or conserved, its place(s) must be preserved (Low 1987). Cultural conservation and sustainability require place preservation. This rather obvious point is crucial when dealing with the material environment and issues of cultural representation at heritage sites.

2   Anthropologists employ a variety of theories of how cultural ecosystems work in particular places over time. For example, anthropologists have studied the ecological dynamics of natural systems to understand sociopolitical changes in the cultural ecosystems of farmers and have developed cultural evolutionary schemes to predict settlement patterns and sociocultural development in the third world. Many of these cultural ecology theories were subject to historical critiques; nonetheless, the dynamic and predictive aspects of cultural ecosystem models are useful when examining social change at a particular site.

The case of the historic Parque Central in San José, Costa Rica, illustrates this point. Until 1992, Parque Central was a well-established, spatially organized, cultural ecosystem made up of shoeshine men on the northeast corner, pensioners on the southwest corner, vendors and religious practitioners on the northwest corner, and prostitutes and workmen on the center inner circle. The established cultural ecosystem, however, was disrupted in 1993 when the municipality closed the park and redesigned the historic space to remove users perceived as unattractive to tourists and the middle class (Low 2000).

The redesign destroyed the "natural balance." A new social group, a gang of young men, took over the public space, creating an even more dangerous and undesirable enviroment, and young Nicaraguans, rather than Costa Ricans, became the main inhabitants on Sunday. This case illustrates the fragility of existing cultural ecosystems (and its diverse niches); when the sociospatial niches (places) are destroyed, the system may not be able to maintain itself.

3   The third important dimension is cultural diversity. Biodiversity, so critical to the physical enviroment as a genetic repository and pool of adaptive evolutionary strategies, has its social counterpart in cultural diversity. Cultural diversity became a "politically correct" catchphrase during the 1980s in the United States, but it has not been addressed in planning and design – much less, sustainable development – practice. While sustainable development includes maintaining cultural diversity as a conceptual goal, there is little agreement, much less research, on what it means. But cultural diversity provides a way to evaluate cultural and social sustainability.

For example, I have been studying patterns of cultural use in large, urban parks and heritage sites over the past ten years. Based on this research, the Public Space Research Group has developed a series of principles that encourage, support, and maintain cultural diversity – and, I would argue, social sustainability (Low *et al.* 2002). These principles are similar to William H. Whyte's rules for small urban spaces that promote their social viability, but in this case, the rules promote and/or maintain cultural diversity. Among their directives are the following:

- If people are not represented in historical national parks and monuments and, more important, if their histories are erased, they will not use the park.
- Access is as much about economics and cultural patterns of park use as circulation and transportation. Thus income and visitation patterns must be taken into consideration when providing access for all social groups.
- The social interaction of diverse groups can be maintained and enhanced by providing safe, spatially adequate "territories" for everyone within the larger space of the overall site.
- Accommodating the differences in the ways social class and ethnic groups use and value public sites is essential to making decisions that result in sustaining cultural and social diversity.
- Contemporary historic preservation should not concentrate on restoring the scenic features without also restoring the facilities and diversions that attract people to the park.
- Symbolic ways of communicating cultural meaning are an important dimension of place attachment that can be fostered to promote cultural diversity.
- A large site can be designed and managed to offer spaces that foster local neighborhood community life and activity, and at the same time provide special spaces and activities to attract culturally diverse users from a broader geographic area.

These social sustainability principles for urban parks and heritage sites are just a beginning. More research is required to understand the importance and difficulties of maintaining cultural diversity. But at the very least, they demonstrate how cultural diversity can be an essential component of evaluating the success of a cultural ecosystem. Cultural diversity is one observable outcome of the continuity of human groups in culturally significant places – an important aspect of social sustainability.

This modified cultural ecosystem – diversity model – provides an effective theoretical basis for defining social sustainability. *But social sustainability encompasses more than understanding cultural ecosystems and diversity. It implies a moral and political stance vis-à-vis sociocultural systems – maintaining them, supporting them, and, in some cases, improving them.* And it is in this sense that a new series of questions must be asked. Is social sustainability applicable to all populations? We have been assuming that human ecosystems do not compete with each other, but of course they do. A successful cultural system can overrun another. Is this what we mean by sustainability, natural selection of cultural ecosystems and the survival of the fittest based on an evolutionary or a sociobiological model? Or should we be protecting weaker groups, systems, and urban niches from stronger ones? And who is "we"? These are moral and political questions that must be addressed in our discussions of application and practice. For the moment, though, I will assume that "we" refers to conservation practitioners and social scientists who are involved in site analysis and that our goal is to sustain cultural groups on or near a heritage site and for whom the site is significant.

Ultimately, we need to address issues of social sustainability at various scales: the local, the regional, and the global. Social sustainability at the local scale has been illustrated by the examples I have presented so far, that is, understanding the cultural dynamics of a place so that specific individuals and their histories and values are sustained at or near the heritage site, across generations, over time. At the regional scale, social sustainability might be better conceptualized through a regional plan that supports not only individuals but also neighborhoods, communities, churches, associations, and the institutional infrastructure necessary for the survival of cultural values and places of larger groups throughout history. Dolores Hayden's *Power of Place* (1995) provides a vision of documenting and commemorating cultural histories of minorities and women that go beyond the local and sustain larger elements of society. Social sustainability at the global scale moves closer to where we began, with David Throsby's "sustainable development" based on intergenerational, and, I would add, cultural, equity and environmental justice.

But other work covers this ground. Instead I would like to offer a research strategy, Rapid Ethnographic Assessment Procedures (REAPs), for incorporating diverse cultural histories and values and enhancing social sustainability at the local scale. I present two cases, Independence National Historical Park and Ellis Island, as examples of how REAPs help us to understand the histories, values, and relationships on a site, a first step toward enhancing their social sustainability.

Rapid Ethnographic Assessment Procedures

Background

The intent of a Rapid Ethnographic Assessment Procedure is to provide ethnographic information on local populations in order to "evaluate alternatives and assess planning impacts on ethnographic resources and associated user groups" (National Park Service 2000:196). Ethnography is concerned with the people associated with parks, with their cultural systems or ways of life, and with the related sites, structures, material features, and natural resources. Cultural and ethnic systems include expressive elements that celebrate or record significant events, and many carry considerable symbolic and emotional importance for local cultural groups (National Park Service 2000:165).

The National Park Service (NPS) first employed ethnographic research in connection with western Native American communities having long-standing associations with certain parklands. These lands – natural resources and, in the case of objects and structures, cultural resources – are required by Native Americans or other local communities for their continued cultural identity and survival. The NPS calls these lands "ethnographic resources," and the peoples associated with them "traditionally," "park-associated" peoples (Crespi 1987). In providing systematic data on local lifeways, applied ethnographic research is intended to enhance the relationships between park management and local communities whose histories and associations with park cultural resources are unknown or poorly understood (Bean and Vane 1987; Crespi 1987; Joseph 1997). In many newer national parks, the NPS shares jurisdiction with other federal agencies, state and local governments, and Indian nations or other culturally distinctive communities. The resulting complexity of planning tasks makes ethnographic research with affected communities especially helpful (Mitchell 1987).

The literature points to several kinds of benefits from ethnographic research. One is in the area of conflict management, for example, where local communities anticipate adverse impacts from new park or heritage site designations or changes to existing parks. Wolf (1987) describes the contribution made by ethnographic research to community relations in the difficult process of establishing a National Historic Park around sites in Atlanta associated with the life of Martin Luther King, Jr. Ethnographic knowledge helped management to identify opportunities for compromise and potential mitigating measures (Wolf 1987). The process of ethnographic research with culturally distinctive communities affected by construction projects can give a certain credibility to agency decision making (Liebow 1987).

Community empowerment is another benefit in that relationships established create a dialogue between officials and local neighborhood and cultural groups who would not otherwise have a voice in the planning process. Joseph (1997) stresses the collaborative nature of the applied ethnographic research done by the NPS, wherein ordinary citizens and community leaders participate alongside elected officials, park managers, and the researchers. I have suggested that most preservation problems in cultural landscapes, especially vandalism, underutilization, and neglect, could be prevented with more dialogue between the community and the governmental agency (Low 1987).

A third important benefit of ethnographic research is that it presents and represents the cultural heritage of local communities within the overall programming of site resources. Ethnographic information is useful in presentation, particularly for heritage sites such as Minuteman, in Massachusetts, that include existing communities within their borders. Minuteman has endeavored to restore and preserve farming as a traditional cultural practice within the historic environment the park preserves and interprets. Information that may be uncovered only through ethnography, such as the gendered division of labor on family farms, may be crucial to the continued effective management of a generations-old practice (Joseph 1997). Where the presentation of historic objects is concerned, ethnographic information, gained from living members of the associated cultural group, can reveal uses and meanings not apparent in the objects themselves (Brugge 1987).

"Most cultural landscapes are identified solely in terms of their historical rather than contemporary importance to the community" (Low 1987:31), privileging historical meanings over those of the geographically and/or culturally associated communities. This oversight often promotes friction and local disagreements that can be solved through the knowledge produced by a REAP. Social sustainability of these sites cannot be maintained without the cooperation of local populations, which means supporting their needs and values while at the same time preserving the historical qualities of the heritage site.

Methodology

In a REAP, a number of methods are selected to produce different types of data from diverse sources that can be triangulated to provide a comprehensive analysis of the site. A brief description of each method is presented below.

1   *Historical and Archival Documents.* The collection of historical documents and review of relevant archives, newspapers, and magazines begins the REAP process. At historically significant sites, this process may be quite extensive, especially if secondary sources do not exist. This method of data collection is very important, as it is through a thorough understanding of the history of the site that areas of cooperation and conflict often become clear and identifiable.

2   *Physical Traces Mapping.* Physical traces maps record the presence of liquor bottles, needles, trash, clothing, erosion of planting, and other traces of human activities. These maps are completed based on data collected early in the morning at each site. Records of physical evidence of human activity and presence provide indirect clues as to what goes on at these sites during the night. Physical traces mapping assumes that there is a base map of resources and basic features available that can be used to locate the physical traces. Otherwise, part of the task is to create such a map, both for the physical traces and for the behavioral maps. At many archaeological sites a base map might not be available, adding another step to the research process.

3   *Behavioral Maps.* Behavioral maps record people and their activities located in time and space. These maps arrange data in a way that permits planning and design analyses of the site and are very useful in developing familiarity with the everyday activities at the site and its problems. They are most effectively used in limited park areas with a variety of social and economic uses where the researcher can return repeatedly to the various social spaces during the day.

4   *Transect Walks.* A transect walk is a record of what a community consultant describes and comments on during a guided walk of the site. The idea is to include one or two community members in the research team, to learn about the site from their point of view. In most REAPs local consultants work with the researcher as collaborators. In the transect walk, however, this is especially important in that the method is dependent on the quality of the relationship between the collaborator and the researcher.

5   *Individual Interviews.* Individual interviews are collected from the identified populations. The sampling strategy, interview schedule, and number of interviews vary from site to site. In most cases on-site users and residents who live near the site are interviewed, but in specific situations interviews might be collected more broadly.

6   *Expert Interviews.* Expert interviews are collected from those people identified as having special expertise to comment on the area and its residents and users, such as the head of the vendors' association, neighborhood association presidents, the head of the planning board, teachers in local schools, ministers of local churches, principals of local schools, and representatives from local parks and institutions.

7   *Impromptu Group Interviews.* Impromptu group interviews are conducted where people gather outside public places or at special meetings set up with church or school groups. The goal of group interviews (as opposed to individual interviews or focus groups) is to collect data in a group context as well as to provide an educational opportunity for the community. Impromptu group interviews are open-ended and experimental and include any community members who are interested in joining the discussion group.

8   *Focus Groups.* Focus groups are set up with those people who are important in terms of understanding the park site and local population. As opposed to the large, open

group interviews, the focus groups consist of six to ten individuals selected to represent especially vulnerable populations, such as schoolchildren, seniors, and the physically challenged. The discussions are conducted in the language of the group
directed by a facilitator and are tape recorded.

9   *Participant Observation.* The researchers maintain field journals that record their
observations and impressions of everyday life in the park. They also keep records of
their experiences as they interact with users and communities. Participant observation is a valuable adjunct to the behavioral maps and interviews. It provides contextual information and data that can be compared to what is seen and said to enable
accurate data interpretation.

10   *Analysis.* Interview data are organized by coding all responses and then content analyzed by cultural-ethnic group and study question. Transect walks, tours, and interviews are used to produce cultural resource maps for each group. Focus groups
determine the extent of cultural knowledge in the community and identify the areas
of conflict and disagreement within the community. Mapping, transect walks, individual and expert interviews, and focus groups provide independent bodies of data
that can be compared and contrasted, thus improving the validity and reliability of
data collected from a relatively small sample. As in all ethnographic research, interviews, observation, and field notes, as well as knowledge of the cultural group patterns and local politics, are used to help interpret the data collected.

A number of procedures are used to analyze the data. First, the resource maps are
produced by an overlay method that combines the behavioral maps, physical traces, and
participant observation notes. These maps are descriptive in that they summarize activities
and disruptions on site. Second, a research meeting is held in which each participant sum-
marizes what they have found in their interviews. These are general observations that
guide the research team (or researcher) as they begin to develop more precise coding
strategies. This synthetic stage provides a place to start thinking about what has been
found. The "general summaries" are used to explore theoretical approaches and prioritize
the coding procedure.

Third, each generalization is broken down into a set of codes that can be used to
analyze the field notes. Once this is completed, the interview questions are reviewed and a
similar coding scheme is developed. The interview coding relies on the findings of the
maps, the field notes, and the structure of the questions themselves. This is the lengthy
part of the analysis process and requires discussion between the research team and the
client and, in some cases, individual stake-holders. Some coding schemes may require
multidimensional scaling and a quantitative analysis, although qualitative content analysis is
usually adequate in a REAP. Because a REAP is a "rapid" procedure, there are usually
fewer than one hundred and fifty interviews, and therefore they can be analyzed by hand.
The advantage of a qualitative analysis procedure is that the data are not abstracted from
their context and, therefore, retain their validity and detail. Fourth, the various analyses
are triangulated, and common elements, patterns of behaviors, and areas of conflict and
differences, both in the nature of the data and in the group themselves, are identified.

Rapid ethnographic assessment procedures for heritage conservation sites

Two National Park Service projects, one at Independence National Historical Park, focusing on the importance of ethnicity and cultural representation in park use, and the other at
Ellis Island, evaluating access alternatives, are discussed here. The issues involved – identifying the stake-holders, community, and local users, eliciting their cultural values, under-

standing the meanings that the site holds for various groups, and giving voice to their concerns and perspectives – are similar to those considered by a conservation professional whose task is to evaluate a site for its social sustainability.

Independence National Historical Park: ethnicity, use, and cultural representation

In 1994 Independence National Historical Park began developing a general management plan that would set forth basic management philosophy and provide strategies for addressing issues and objectives over the next ten to fifteen years. The planning process included extensive public participation, including a series of public meetings, televised town meetings, community tours, and planning workshops. As part of this community outreach effort, the park wanted to work cooperatively with local ethnic communities to find ways to interpret their diverse cultural heritages in the park's portrayal of the American experience. The study, therefore, was designed to provide a general overview of park-associated ethnic groups, including an analysis of their values and the identification of cultural and natural resources used by and/or culturally meaningful to the various groups.

The research team spent considerable time interviewing cultural experts and surveying the neighborhoods located near Independence National Historical Park. Based on these interviews and observations, four local neighborhoods were selected for study: Southwark for African Americans, Little Saigon for Asians and Asian Americans, the Italian Market area for Italian Americans, and Norris Square for Latinos. These neighborhoods were selected based on the following criteria: (1) they were within walking distance of the park (excluding Norris Square); (2) they had visible spatial and social integrity; and (3) there were culturally targeted stores, restaurants, religious organizations, and social services available to residents, reinforcing their cultural identity. The Jewish community could not be identified with a spatial community in the downtown area; therefore, members of both Conservative and Orthodox synagogues in the Society Hill area were interviewed as a "community of interest" rather than as a physically integrated area. In thirty-six days of fieldwork, 135 people were consulted in the form of individual and expert interviews, transect walks, and focus groups.

The data were coded and analyzed by cultural group and study question. All places in and around the park having personal and cultural associations for our research participants were recorded on cultural resource maps. One map was prepared for each cultural group.

Relevant findings: cultural representation

Many participants were concerned with issues of cultural representation. Some assimilated Italian Americans and Jews were ambivalent about presenting themselves as distinct from other Americans. African Americans, on the other hand, saw a lack of material and cultural representation in the park's historical interpretation. For some, the park represented the uneven distribution of public goods: "So much for them [tourists, white people] and so little for us [African Americans, working-class neighborhood residents]." Asian Americans and Latinos favored a curatorial approach less focused on national independence and integrating their immigration stories and colonial struggles into a more generalized representation of liberty and freedom within the American experience. Italian Americans, too, were interested in a more inclusive representation – not ending park interpretation in 1782 or 1800 but continuing to the present.

Three of the cultural groups – African Americans, Latinos, and Jews – mentioned places they would like to see commemorated or markers they would like to see installed to bring attention to their cultural presence within the park boundaries. Many participants

– particularly Latinos, African Americans, and Asians – saw the need for more programming for children and activities for families. Unlike the visual, pictorial experience the tourist seeks, residents in general were interested in the park's recreational potential, its sociable open spaces where one can get food, relax, and sit on the grass, or as a place for civic and cultural celebrations. These residents wanted the park to be a more relaxed, fun, lively place. As a group, Latinos made the most use of the park for recreational purposes in their leisure time. Latinos were particularly interested in developing the recreational potential of the park, but their sentiments were echoed by at least a few consultants in each of the other ethnic groups.

Relevant findings: cultural values

The REAP demonstrated that the park holds multiple values for Philadelphians that are often overlooked because of management's emphasis on accommodating visitors. "Visitors" was a problematic term, as residents who use the park do not see themselves as visitors. Treating everyone as a visitor (read "tourist") neglects an important sense of territoriality. The resident incorporates the park into her home territory; the visitor knows she is a visitor. To the resident, the park is symbolically and functionally part of the larger landscape of the city and the neighborhood. The resident likes being surrounded by familiar sights and places, follows her own rhythm in moving around the city, and enjoys a proprietary right of access. Those sensibilities are offended by crowds of tourists, by the denial of free access to historic sites (that is, when not part of a tour), and perhaps by an emphasis on official interpretations. The more the park sets its landmarks off from the surrounding city, reducing everyday contact with residents, the more the objects and places lose their meaning for residents.

The REAP of Independence National Historical Park is an example of issues of ethnicity and culture corresponding with either use or nonuse. Identifying relevant cultural-ethnic groups as constituencies that live in the local neighborhood, or that traditionally have a relationship to the park, and then learning about those groups and neighborhoods through the REAP methods provides a quick but complete snapshot of the community and its diverse values, meanings, and sense of cultural representation. Further, this REAP was able to distinguish between conflicting visitor and resident values and suggest possible solutions. The space the park occupies – who gets to use it and whose identity is reflected in it – is as symbolic for local people as Independence Hall and the Liberty Bell are for tourists (Taplin, Scheld, and Low 2002).

Ellis Island access alternatives: conflicting cultural values

The research goal was to provide commentary from an ethnographic perspective on four alternative scenarios (bridge, subsidized ferry, elevated rail, and tunnel) proposed in *A Progress Report: Ellis Island Bridge and Access Alternatives*. For the purposes of this project, the culturally appropriate populations included the local users of Battery Park and Liberty State Park; local providers of services at Battery Park and Liberty State Park, including vendors and small-scale tourist services; residents of the Jersey City neighborhoods adjacent to Liberty State Park; special populations such as children, the elderly, and the physically challenged; and "traditional cultural groups," those people whose families entered through Ellis Island or who are themselves immigrants with identities and aspirations connected symbolically to Ellis Island.

The research focused on constituency groups; further into the project, however, when constituency analysis did not provide statistically significant clustering of similar people and points of view, a values orientation-based analysis was incorporated. The constituency groups provided a guide to sampling the users and residents on the three sites – Battery Park, Liberty State Park, and the Jersey City neighborhoods surrounding Liberty State Park (Lafayette, Van Vorst, and Paulus Hook) – who were consulted concerning their perceptions of possible positive or negative impacts of each of the proposed access alternatives. Their attitudes and concerns were collected through a series of REAP data collection methods including behavioral maps, transect walks, individual interviews, expert interviews, impromptu group interviews, and focus groups completed at the various field sites. A total of 318 people were consulted: 117 through individual interviews in the two parks, 113 through impromptu group interviews in neighborhood gathering places, and 88 in focus groups both in the parks and in neighborhood churches and institutions.

The data were analyzed by coding all responses from the interviews and focus groups and then compared by constituency group. Constituency groups were defined as groups of people who share cultural beliefs and values and who are likely to be affected by the proposed access alternatives in a similar way. Correlational, content, and value orientation analyses were used to present the various positions held by consultants across the subgroups studied in this project.

Relevant findings: interests and attitudes

In Battery Park, the people who were the most concerned about the negative impact of a bridge were the service managers, city employees, park employees, ferry representative, can collector, and tour bus driver, that is, those constituencies with a vested interest in the success and profitability of Battery Park. The greatest differences in attitudes about the proposed bridge were found between people who were there for recreation versus those who were working in Battery Park – the former were more positive, the latter more negative – and between people who were immigrants and those who were native born – the immigrants were more positive, the native born more negative. Overall, Battery Park users were most concerned about the economic consequences of the proposed access alternatives, but there were a number of people who were concerned about access to Ellis Island or who questioned the social priorities of the bridge alternative.

In Liberty State Park, constituency groups were not predictive of attitudes toward the alternatives, with the one notable exception of such vested interests as Liberty State Park officials and workers, who were overwhelmingly against the proposed bridge. The active recreation users, such as walkers and cyclists, were more in favor of the bridge than were the passive user groups and organized group leaders. There was also a sharp distinction between Latino and non-Latino consultants: the Latino consultants were very positive about the access alternatives compared to non-Latino groups. The same differences in attitude between user type (work-related use versus recreational use) and place of origin (immigrant versus native born) found in Battery Park were found in Liberty State Park. The two most frequently cited value orientations were health and recreation and park quality – quite a contrast from the economic findings in Battery Park – followed by aesthetic concerns and concerns about improved access.

The residents of the various neighborhoods surrounding Liberty State Park were generally in favor of the proposed bridge and less interested in the other alternatives, yet each neighborhood had a slightly different perspective on the issue. Paulus Hook residents had very mixed opinions about the proposed bridge and were concerned about potential problems, such as increased traffic or limited parking. Van Vorst residents were more positive and considered the proposed bridge a way to increase democratic access to Ellis Island. They saw the recreational benefits of the bridge as improving their neighborhood.

Lafayette residents were the most positive about the proposed bridge because it would allow them to visit Ellis Island without paying the ferry fare that was perceived as too high for families and groups of children to afford in this low-income area. They, too, saw the bridge as an amenity that would add to the beauty and recreational potential of Liberty State Park and their local community.

Relevant findings: value orientations

Comparing the value orientations across the parks and neighborhood reveals that each area has slightly different priorities and concerns. Battery Park workers and users are not at all concerned about the cost of the ferry or the bridge but instead are concerned about the possible economic consequences of the proposed access alternatives. Liberty State Park workers and users, on the other hand, are concerned about the health and recreation advantages and park quality disadvantages of the access alternatives. The residents of Lafayette, Van Vorst, and Paulus Hook are most concerned with the cost of the ferry or proposed access alternative. Cost, access, park quality, and economics were the most frequently mentioned concerns for all groups.

Conclusion

The practice of historic preservation and restoration can disrupt a local community's sense of place attachment and disturb expressions of cultural identity for local populations. New ethnic and immigrant groups can be excluded from a site, because of a lack of sensitivity to cultural values, nonverbal cues from architecture and furnishings, and symbols of cultural representation. Cultural diversity and indigenous cultural ecosystems are difficult to sustain, especially within the constraints of creating, managing, or maintaining a heritage site. Creative forms of cultural representation and a deeper understanding of cultural values are fundamental to cooperative, ongoing use and maintenance by contemporary groups.

   Social sustainability, as a subset of cultural sustainability, is dependent on the maintenance of the existing cultural ecosystem and cultural diversity but can be more easily studied at the site level. REAPs can be used to elicit the histories, values, and relationships of local populations who are often overlooked at heritage sites. Understanding these populations' social relations and meanings enhances our ability to promote social sustainability. Resolving value conflicts and developing more inclusive cultural representations are just two of many possible solutions for promoting more successful local identification with the site.

Acknowledgments

I would like to thank the members of the Public Space Research Group – Dana Taplin, Suzanne Scheld, Tracy Fisher, and Kate Brower – for their participation in these research projects. I have gained insight from their discussions, publications, and analyses. Maria Luisa Achino-Loeb and Joel Lefkowitz discussed the concept of sustainability with me; the conclusions, however, are my own.

Notes

1 Anthropologists spend much of their lives arguing about the categories "ethnicity" and "culture." "Ethnicity" is a slippery term that evokes different meanings when used by the informant as an identity marker (e.g. I am ethnically Jewish, or I am a WASP) and when used as an analytic category by an anthropologist or census taker (e.g. The informant appears to be Asian American or an African American). "Culture" is equally problematic. The term "culture" (lowercase *c*) often refers to local traditions or practices that might define an ethnic group, whereas "Culture" (capital *C*) refers to an analytic category with overarching meanings. Further, ethnicity and culture covary with nationality and other political designations. Here I use "ethnic group" and "cultural group" interchangeably and do not try to untangle the multiple intellectual histories of the terms. I prefer "cultural group" as it is clearer in terms of the traditions and histories that I am discussing. On the other hand, Italian Americans and Puerto Ricans can be considered ethnic groups, since ethnicity is colloquially understood as biological or derived from immigrant group status in the United States, and culture usually refers to the arts.

2 Throsby (1999) examines sustainability in the context of the environment, linking the term "sustainable" with the word "development." *Sustainable development* marries the ideas of sustainable *economic* development with *ecological* sustainability, "meaning the preservation and enhancement of a range of environmental values through the maintenance of ecosystems in the natural world" (Throsby 1999:15). Throsby employs the concepts of distributive justice and intergenerational equity to evaluate fairness in the distribution of welfare, utility, or resources over time.

References

Bean, L. J. and S. B. Vane. 1987. Ethnography and the NPS: Opportunities and obligations. *CRM Bulletin* 10(1):36–44.
Beebe, J. 1995. Basic concepts and techniques of rapid appraisal. *Human Organization* 54:42–51.
Brugge, D. M. 1987. Cultural use and meaning of artifacts. *CRM Bulletin* 10(1):14–16.
Crespi, M. 1987. Ethnography and the NPS: A growing partnership. *CRM Bulletin* 10(1):1–4.
Ervin, A. M. 1997. Trying the impossible: Relatively "rapid" methods in a city-wide needs assessment. *Human Organization* 56:379–387.
Halloran, M. 1998. *Boston's "Changeful Times": The Origins of Preservation and Planning in America*. Baltimore, Md.: Johns Hopkins University Press.
Hayden, D. 1995. *The Power of Place*. Cambridge, Mass.: MIT Press.
Joseph, R. 1997. Cranberry bogs to parks: Ethnography and women's history. *CRM Bulletin* 20:20–24.
Liebow, E. 1987. Social impact assessment. *CRM Bulletin* 10(1):23–26.
Louksitou-Sideris, A. and G. Dansbury. 1995–96. Lost streets of Bunker Hill. *California History* 74(4):394–407, 448–449.
Low, S. M. 1987. A cultural landscapes mandate for action. *CRM Bulletin* 10(1):30–33.
Low, S. M. 2000. *On the Plaza: The Politics of Public Space and Culture*. Austin, Tex.: University of Texas Press.
Low, S. M. and I. Altman. 1992. *Place Attachment*. New York: Plenum.
Low, S. M., D. Taplin, S. Scheld, and T. Fisher, 2002. Recapturing erased histories: Ethnicity, design and cultural representation. *Journal of Architectural and Planning Research* 19(4):282–299.
Mitchell, J. 1987. Planning at Canyon de Chelly National Monument. *CRM Bulletin* 10(1):27–29.

National Park Service. 2000. Applied Ethnography Program. NPS web site http://www.cr.
    nps.gov/aad/appeth.htm.
Taplin, D., S. Scheld, and S. Low. 2002. REAP in urban parks: A case study of Independence
    National Historical Park. *Human Organization* 61(1):80–93.
Throsby, D. 1995. Culture, economics, and sustainability. *Journal of Cultural Economics*
    19:199–206.
Throsby, D. 1999. Cultural capital. *Journal of Cultural Economics* 23:3–12.
Wolf, J. C. 1987. Martin Luther King, Jr. *CRM Bulletin* 10(1):12–13.

Chapter 31

European Landscape Convention
An Extract

Preamble

The member States of the Council of Europe signatory hereto,

. . .

Noting that the landscape has an important public interest role in the cultural, ecological, environmental and social fields, and constitutes a resource favourable to economic activity and whose protection, management and planning can contribute to job creation;

Aware that the landscape contributes to the formation of local cultures and that it is a basic component of the European natural and cultural heritage, contributing to human well-being and consolidation of the European identity;

Acknowledging that the landscape is an important part of the quality of life for people everywhere: in urban areas and in the countryside, in degraded areas as well as in areas of high quality, in areas recognised as being of outstanding beauty as well as everyday areas;

. . .

Wishing to respond to the public's wish to enjoy high quality landscapes and to play an active part in the development of landscapes;

Believing that the landscape is a key element of individual and social well-being and that its protection, management and planning entail rights and responsibilities for everyone;

. . .

Acknowledging that the quality and diversity of European landscapes constitute a common resource, and that it is important to co-operate towards its protection, management and planning;

Wishing to provide a new instrument devoted exclusively to the protection, management and planning of all landscapes in Europe,

Have agreed as follows:

Chapter I – General provisions

Article 1 – Definitions

For the purposes of the Convention:

a   "Landscape" means an area, as perceived by people, whose character is the result of the action and interaction of natural and/or human factors;

b   "Landscape policy" means an expression by the competent public authorities of general principles, strategies and guidelines that permit the taking of specific measures aimed at the protection, management and planning of landscapes;

c   "Landscape quality objective" means, for a specific landscape, the formulation by the competent public authorities of the aspirations of the public with regard to the landscape features of their surroundings;

d   "Landscape protection" means actions to conserve and maintain the significant or characteristic features of a landscape, justified by its heritage value derived from its natural configuration and/or from human activity;

e   "Landscape management" means action, from a perspective of sustainable development, to ensure the regular upkeep of a landscape, so as to guide and harmonise changes which are brought about by social, economic and environmental processes;

f   "Landscape planning" means strong forward-looking action to enhance, restore or create landscapes.

Article 2 – Scope

Subject to the provisions contained in Article 15, this Convention applies to the entire territory of the Parties and covers natural, rural, urban and peri-urban areas. It includes land, inland water and marine areas. It concerns landscapes that might be considered outstanding as well as everyday or degraded landscapes.

Article 3 – Aims

The aims of this Convention are to promote landscape protection, management and planning, and to organise European co-operation on landscape issues.

Chapter II – National measures

Article 5 – General measures

Each Party undertakes:

a   to recognise landscapes in law as an essential component of people's surroundings, an expression of the diversity of their shared cultural and natural heritage, and a foundation of their identity;

b   to establish and implement landscape policies aimed at landscape protection, management and planning through the adoption of the specific measures set out in Article 6;

c   to establish procedures for the participation of the general public, local and regional authorities, and other parties with an interest in the definition and implementation of the landscape policies mentioned in paragraph *b* above;

d   to integrate landscape into its regional and town planning policies and in its cultural, environmental, agricultural, social and economic policies, as well as in any other policies with possible direct or indirect impact on landscape.

Article 6 – Specific measures

A Awareness-raising

Each Party undertakes to increase awareness among the civil society, private organisations and public authorities of the value of landscapes, their role and changes to them.

B Training and education

Each Party undertakes to promote:

a   training for specialists in landscape appraisal and operations;
b   multidisciplinary training programmes in landscape policy, protection, management and planning, for professionals in the private and public sectors and for associations concerned;
c   school and university courses which, in the relevant subject areas, address the values attaching to landscapes and the issues raised by their protection, management and planning.

C Identification and assessment

1   With the active participation of the interested parties, as stipulated in Article 5.c, and with a view to improving knowledge of its landscapes, each Party undertakes:

    a   i   to identify its own landscapes throughout its territory;
        ii   to analyse their characteristics and the forces and pressures transforming them;
        iii to take note of changes;
    b   to assess the landscapes thus identified, taking into account the particular values assigned to them by the interested parties and the population concerned.

2   These identification and assessment procedures shall be guided by the exchanges of experience and methodology, organised between the Parties at European level pursuant to Article 8.

D Landscape quality objectives

Each Party undertakes to define landscape quality objectives for the landscapes identified and assessed, after public consultation in accordance with Article 5.c.

E Implementation

To put landscape policies into effect, each Party undertakes to introduce instruments aimed at protecting, managing and/or planning the landscape.

Chapter 32

'The Long Chain'

Archaeology, historical landscape characterization and time depth in the landscape

Graham Fairclough

> . . . think for a moment of the long chain of iron or gold, of thorns or flowers, that
> would never have bound you, but for the formation of the first link . . .
>
> Charles Dickens, Great Expectations (1860–61)

1 Ways of seeing landscape: characterizing the historic depth of landscape

Landscape Assessment in England in its modern sense has origins in the late 1980s, following unsuccessful attempts to produce objective, quantified methods (Countryside Commission 1987, 1993; Countryside Agency & Scottish Natural Heritage 2002). More
broadly, the method can be carried back to the 1940s and 1950s and the creation of the
first UK protected areas, known in UK legislation as National Parks and Areas of Outstanding Natural Beauty using criteria of 'specialness', perceived naturalness and aesthetic
quality. Going back further, there is a long English tradition of landscape assessment based
on the aesthetic values of landscape; this included interest in consciously designed high
status ornamental landscape. For some heritage managers and planners, 'landscape' still
seems to mean only 'natural' or 'designed' landscape.

Scenic and visual criteria still stand close to the heart of English landscape assessment,
with some added concern for geology and topography, and a few concessions to history.
There is, however, limited recognition of the human processes by which environment has
been modified. Most importantly, there is an underestimation of the importance of the
interaction of people and nature over very long periods of history, and of the long-term
sequence of change and continuity that creates so much of the landscape's character. It
does not fully accept that historic human impact on the environment is fundamental in creating landscape, and that few landscapes can be classed as natural.

This chapter describes an attempt to redress some of these shortcomings in a heritage
management context in England under the general banner of *Historic Landscape Characterization* (HLC), a technique developed to help people understand time depth in the landscape (Fairclough 2002e; English Heritage 2003a). As will become clear, HLC also

addresses one of the shortcomings of heritage management itself, its limited engagement with heritage at landscape scale.

During the 1990s, archaeology and ecology both began to develop additional methods of understanding and assessing landscapes that properly reflected human cultural process (Macinnes & Wickham-Jones 1992). In particular they pursued the idea that landscape is the sum of all its parts – natural, cultural, ecological, archaeological, historic, aesthetic, social and mental – and that multidisciplinary approaches are necessary to do full justice to it.

Archaeologists understand the present-day landscape by means of long-term narratives and explanations rooted in social, political and economic historic processes. The main archaeological contribution to landscape is an understanding of time-depth, placing change at the centre of landscape history and character, and indeed celebrating its effects (Fairclough et al. 1999), a perspective that encourages interest in the sustainable management of future change (Fairclough 2002d).

The basis of all today's cultural landscape, however, was created in the past, and is an equal concern for archaeologists. The cultural landscape can be regarded as one of our richest historical records, containing an archive of how human communities shaped, destroyed or created their environment over many hundreds or even thousands of years. It is an archive that exists both for prehistory long before documents illuminate the past, and even in historic periods it touches on areas of ordinary life rarely documented. It even enables us to know a little about our predecessors' cognitive landscapes. Historic landscape characterization, this chapter's main subject, was thus developed to use this physical archive to forge an archaeological perception of the present-day landscape.

HLC adopts the idea that *landscape* is not quite the same as *environment*. There is a need for archaeological and historical understanding of past environments, but the concept of landscape is seen to be something more than a mere description of the physical traces of the past. This additional factor, which changes environment into landscape, is the existence of an observer who constructs what we call landscape from the material environment. Because of such modern methods as air photographs, satellites and virtual-reality modelling, we no longer need to be constrained by the original definition of the word landscape as an area of land, a prospect, taken in by a viewer at a single viewpoint. We are also able to move away from seeing observation as merely a visual act, and to accept that landscape, whilst in the eye of the beholder, is also more importantly in the intellect, mind, heart and senses of its observer. All 'beholders' possess mixed as well as personal viewpoints, and thus an infinite multiplicity of responses and perceptions. This is what makes landscape such a powerful concept.

Landscape is in fact doubly cultural. Its components ('ingredients') within the environment are the product of hundreds, sometimes thousands, of years of human, cultural actions. At the same time, however, the landscape as a whole is cultural because it is created only in the present-day by our own cultural and social attitudes – it is not the same as environment but an intellectual construct.

HLC differs from landscape history in both method and sources. The two disciplines may as a result produce different 'stories', but in their different ways both are valid interpretations of their own data. History studies the past through old documents, and in the case of landscape, is essentially a documentary study of maps and documents related to landscape. Archaeology studies the past more directly, through material remains in the present. In the case of landscape, it is the landscape itself and the environment 'beneath' that are its main sources, even if sometimes they are studied through the proxy of maps and documents used in a supporting role. Historians discover meaning in documents, archaeologists attribute meaning to material culture as well as using it as 'document'.

HLC shares with landscape ecology a concern for historic processes in the landscape. It looks for example at the mechanisms that create the pattern of field and woodland, town and farmland, hedge and wall that sit at the heart of most people's perceptions of land-scape. HLC probably recognizes a greater depth of time in these processes than landscape ecology, because, whenever it can, archaeology uses past material remains that survive in the modern world to look at longer time-frames. These often go beyond oral and even documentary history, and are taken beyond tradition and custom if possible.

Causal sequences that have led from one landscape pattern to another are equally rele-vant. They may not always appear directly to affect the present form of the land, but they are nevertheless important parts of the chain between then and now, a part of how we perceive and 'read' landscape in the way that we do. This is what Charles Dickens (*Great Expectations*) described in the slightly different context of human rather than landscape biography: "the long chain of iron or gold, of thorns or flowers, that would never have bound you, but for the formation of the first link".

2 Deeper roots and a broader spread – 'whole landscape' and sustainability

In addition to its aim of helping people to understand the historic depth of landscape, HLC also had other origins and aims, largely growing out of the explosion of interest in sustain-ability in the 1990s (Fairclough 1995; English Heritage 1997). One aim was to provide an archaeological understanding of landscape that other landscape workers could easily absorb, understand and use. Greater integration between all these is needed, but all the separate strands need to be pursued first until they are sufficiently well understood. An integrative agenda is, therefore, at the core of HLC. Initially, this means using a spatial and landscape-based approach to create a common language so that ideas can transcend bound-aries between disciplines. HLC, therefore, adopted landscape assessment approaches, but adapted them to an archaeological perspective in order to tell us about the past as well as the present, and to help shape a future.

HLC is also part of a trend to expanding archaeological and heritage resource manage-ment from individual sites to the whole environment. Landscape is an ideal vehicle for this. Historic significance can be read by archaeologists, not merely in those places where archaeological deposits can be excavated, but also in features whose simple existence and interrelationship tells us why we have inherited the landscape that we have. HLC can embrace the patterns of trees, hedges and woodland, the distribution of land cover such as moor or heath, or the patterning of settlement and township boundaries. It has no chrono-logical cut-off, being interested in remains of all periods, modern as well as ancient.

Working at landscape scale is also more accessible to public participation. People relate to landscape in more ways than they relate, for example, to wildlife, archaeological sites or fine buildings; as *the European Landscape Convention's* preamble insists, landscape is everyone's common heritage. Everyone 'owns' landscape, in memory and in daily life, everyone has roots in at least one landscape somewhere. Landscape connects people to their concerns about protecting sense of place and local character, and about the increased importance of local distinctiveness in the face of globalization. Almost any common measure of a place's distinctiveness mentions history, archaeology and the cultural processes that created and nurtured landscape.

A landscape viewpoint is also one of the most effective ways of delivering sustainabil-ity. Rare species cannot be preserved without keeping the wider landscapes – habitat, ter-ritory – that sustains them, and so too with cultural heritage. Archaeological sites without appropriate (not necessarily 'authentic') landscape contexts lose some significance, visibil-ity and relevance to everyday life.

In Europe, all of these ideas, and more, have been brought together in a new aspira-tional instrument, *the European Landscape Convention* (Council of Europe 2000; Desjeants-

Pons 2002; Naturopa 2002). This was opened for signature by its sponsor the Council of Europe in Florence in October 2000, and came into force having been ratified by ten states in 2004. It is the first Convention in Europe, and perhaps the world, devoted exclusively to landscape. It covers not just special, attractive, or 'natural' landscapes but all areas of landscape, everywhere, no matter how cultural. It calls for equal integration of natural and cultural values, defining landscape as the perceived interaction of nature and culture. It sets these ideas into an explicit framework of sustainability, democratization, common popular heritage and public participation.

In England, HLC is also part of a shift from protecting the past at special places ('designation') to managing change across the whole historic environment in broader, more socially embedded, ways that relate to all places, in all aspects. As such, is has been endorsed by recent UK Government policy for the historic environment, *The Historic Environment: A Force for Our Future* (DCMS & DETR 2001; for Scotland see HS 2002). The aim is to ensure that the entire historic environment is taken into account when changes are proposed, but this requires an acceptance that the goal is informed management of change rather than protection (Clark 2001; Bloemers 2002; Fairclough 2003).

Selective protection by designation of special places has been effective in the UK for over a century, but during the 1980s and 1990s opinion grew that additional approaches were needed to recognize that all aspects of the historic environment had significancce. These ideas came from various quarters, such as the local distinctiveness movement, landscape assessment and archaeological resource management. Other conservation and environmental disciplines, notably ecologists, made the same transition from site-centered to area-based perceptions, recognizing that sustainable countryside management required more than the protection of nesting sites. Paradoxically, given their origins in the European Union's *Common Agricultural Policy* which is widely regarded as one of the most destructive agents of change to the cultural landscape, there emerged between 1986 and 1994 the beginnings of national, comprehensive incentive schemes to help farmers manage the land more sensitively. But it was sustainable development that gave this movement its greatest impetus, underlining the need to consider all parts of the historic environment when planning the future (English Heritage 1997).

3 Inclusive, modern and flexible – characterization as a new habitat for heritage and landscape managers

Characterization is one of the principal vehicles for putting these ideas into practice, with HLC, like landscape assessment, as a pioneer of the approach. It adopts a generalized understanding of large areas, noting their diversity and complexity but focusing on their essential overall character – in other words, a method for creating a comprehensive but generalized, neutral and interpretative description of the historic character of an area. It is a context for other information, and a framework for decision-making about change and management. Its main focus is on supporting conservation and historic environment resource management, but it also creates new understanding for a variety of uses, including research.

The task of creating contexts and frameworks for understanding and managing change is perhaps most important. It allows characterization to be enabling and capacity-building because it can open up more public debate about significance, rather than closing them with definite black and white answers from experts. It can encourage participation by informing anyone's decision-making without usurping decision making from communities of place or of interest. It is integrative, combining and synthesizing existing research and knowledge; and connecting different types of environmental management.

This approach supports a more diverse and flexible approach to the management of change than designation alone does. It recognizes that we preserve our past for our sake not for its sake, a recognition that can equally apply to protecting natural resources such as wildlife. These ideas accept that change should not be stopped, especially where landscape is concerned, but it should whenever possible (and wherever possible) be guided into sustainable and historically sensitive directions.

Alongside these ideas is a growing recognition of the need to manage change more broadly than protecting a sample of special sites or buildings. Traditional methods of monument preservation (essentially a 19th-century approach) were until recently the only significant theory in historic conservation, but they worked well during the 20th century, albeit at the price of great selectivity and exclusion. Recent years have seen the approach more or less successfully expanded to other 'new' types of heritage, but such expansions cannot go on forever without changing approaches: not everything can be protected in that way, and recognition of everything is the goal, especially in landscape management.

Saying this is not meant to challenge the need for designation-based systems. These successful and effective methods have not suddenly failed, or become obsolete; rather it is society's ambitions for protecting and utilizing the historic environment that are changing, so that additional methods are now needed to work alongside the old tried and tested methods. These additional methods should ensure that all aspects of the historic environment (and other dimensions of the environment) are taken into account in planning change for the future, and that multiple ways of valuing are recognized. This is the aim that methods under the generic heading of 'characterization' are trying to achieve, particularly when dealing with the big picture of landscape character and processes.

There is, however, a trade-off at the heart of this concept as mentioned above. Characterization broadens the heritage canvas, so to speak, and gives a wider view that potentially includes everything, but it must paint a different picture on this new canvas. Characterization suggests that everything in the historic environment deserves to be taken into account in some way, however, local or ordinary, rather than only ever fighting to keep a few places largely unchanged while often all around may change. There will be compromise and debate, with greater inclusiveness and participation, to seek the best achievable new development and the highest practical levels of historic preservation. Giving new weight to local context might mean for example that it is not always the nationally important things that matter most. Characterization aims at a different mentality to be applied everywhere, by planners and developers as well as by conservationists. It is a way of starting to ensure that the historic environment plays a fuller role – its proper role – in modern life.

To do this, the process of characterization has to be essentially neutral in the first instance. It does not in itself define relative significance, nor does it give easy answers to the question of what to keep from the past. Instead, it provides knowledge, interpretation and understanding to allow decisions to be made at the appropriate time, when heritage significance can be matched to the proposed change rather than judged in a social vacuum. It has multiple uses in the planning process, in agri-environmental and rural development policy, in urban regeneration and in conservation, and its users will come to include heritage and conservation agencies, government at local, regional and national levels, owners, developers and business, and of course among the wider public.

As an approach that seeks to use different ways of seeing and understanding in order to help manage change, characterization can be used at many different scales, from local through regional to national and beyond, as long as when used its perceptions are matched correctly to the level of decisions-taking. It works for townscape as well rural landscape, and for topics or thematically as well as geographically. It seems to work best at larger scales, however, being well suited to a landscape-scale. The most developed approach as far as the historic environment in England is concerned has been for the historic dimension of the rural (and now urban) landscape, through HLC.

3.1 Historic landscape characterization (HLC)

HLC was invented and developed in England, and first used in Cornwall, during the 1990s. There was at that time wide consensus that landscape is the sum of all its parts and that assessment was needed (Brown & Berry 1995). But it is only possible to integrate ideas and information that exists, and we did not have genuinely landscape-led understanding of the historic environment to supplement landscape assessment. HLC was designed to fill this gap, with future integration in mind (Fairclough et al. 1999). English HLC now takes the form of a national programme that is over half-complete, promoted at county level by English Heritage (the government agency responsible for leading the protection, management and sustainable use of the historic environment, in both town and country) in partnership with local government archaeological services. It allows the time-depth of the landscape, its historic and archaeological dimension, to be read (Fairclough et al. 1999; Darlington 2002; Fairclough et al. 2002; Dyson-Bruce 2002; Fairclough 2002a; Hampshire County Council website). HLC techniques have begun to be adapted to urban as well as rural contexts, and is being used or tested in other countries in the UK, for example in Scotland (Dyson-Bruce et al. 1999; Macinnes 2002; Dixon & Hingley 2002), and further afield in other parts of Europe, such as Ireland (ERM 2000) and Sweden in the context of a Culture 2000 programme called European Pathways to the Cultural Landscape (www.pcl-eu.de; Nord Paulsson 2002; Nord Paulsson & Fairclough 2002).

The information and understanding that HLC creates can be used in very many different ways. First, most straightforwardly, it adds landscape knowledge to traditional Site and Monument Records, to strengthen their contribution to development planning, development control, Environmental Impact Assessment, designation, land management policy and agri-environmental programmes and hedgerow protection. It adds an understanding of time-depth and human actions to aesthetic-based visual landscape assessment and to the land management insights of landscape ecology.

In terms of research, HLC provides a new context for site-specific data, and it can be used as a predictive tool, or to identify gaps and weaknesses in existing knowledge, or to define research agendas. An HLC project carried out in 2003 can also be a benchmark for future change in the landscape and change in our knowledge and perception.

HLC also offers the potential for closer links to public awareness, encouraging 'democratization'. As suggested earlier, landscape is perhaps uniquely accessible to the public, particularly when assessed in ways that recognize that landscape is ubiquitous, everywhere and on everybody's doorstep, and that it can carry multiple not only specialist values. It has links to local identity and common heritage, and methods like this, therefore, as The European Landscape Convention recognizes, offer one way of enabling wider social participation in decision-making, both about the landscape's significance and about its future management and sustainability.

3.2 The philosophy of HLC

All these considerations combine to create a series of principles that support HLC. They are closely connected with The European Landscape Convention's commendably straightforward definition of landscape as: "an area, as perceived by people, whose character is the result of the action and interaction of natural and/or human factors". For convenience, this chapter presents the summary version of these principles that was drawn up for the landscape network European Pathways to the Cultural Landscape (funded by the European Union Culture 2000 programme; www.pcl-eu.de). They summarise what HLC is setting out to achieve, and what distinguishes this approach from other methods of understanding and assessing landscape:

– a concentration on present-day landscape character, not past landscape; today's landscape as material culture – the main object of study and protection by HLC is the present-day landscape, as created by human action and perception;

– history not geography – the most important characteristic of landscape for the purposes of HLC is its time-depth, the way that earlier landscape and change can still be seen in the present-day landscape;

– area not point data – HLC-based research and understanding is concerned with landscape not sites; it is not a process of mapping find-spots and monument distributions;

– all areas and aspects of the landscape, no matter how modern or ordinary, for example, are treated as part of landscape character; not just 'special' areas;

– landscape is a human construct – semi-natural and living features (woodland, land cover, hedges etc.) are as much a part of landscape character as archaeological features; biodiversity is a cultural phenomenon;

– landscape is different to environment – a characterization of landscape is a matter of interpretation not record, perception not facts; 'landscape' is an idea not a thing, constructed by our minds and emotions from the combination and inter-relationship of physical objects;

– peoples' views – an important aspect of landscape character in HLC will be collective and public perceptions laid alongside more expert views.

The most important of these, perhaps, are those which concern time and human agency (Fairclough 1994, 1999a). These concerns most define HLC's unique and special contribution to the wider integrative project of knowing the landscape by coordinating all the several ways of defining landscape character, including landscape ecology and landscape architecture as well as HLC.

The role of the passage of time is very important in HLC, which is most of all concerned to trace the imprint of the past on landscape, its time-depth. This can involve defining the survival of past environments at landscape scale, or looking for the deeper structures, such as long-established communications systems or deeply embedded field and settlement patterns that our landscape has inherited from the past. A particular concern is how these landscape components have either changed through time or survived through continuity.

Changes through time in this concept of landscape are caused mainly by human action, human 'agency'. HLC emphasizes the role of people in landscape creation, both in the past through physical activity and in the present through perception. Like landscape ecology, HLC recognizes the critical role of human land management practices on landscape character. It is particularly defined by its description of the interaction of humans and nature through the filter of social and historic processes (e.g. prehistoric woodland clearance, privatization of land in the late middle ages, fenland and coastal land reclamation). It works above the level of simple geological or climatic determinants to explore the more subtle nuances of human responses, some of the most significant of landscape's cultural attributes.

English HLC presently operates mainly at county level. This level allows generalization without being too distant from local distinctiveness; it also happens to match the level at which archaeological resource management operates. It is, however, only one of the levels at which HLC can work, and county HLC already fit into two national frameworks: *The Countryside Character Map* (Countryside Commission 1998; Countryside Agency 1999) and *English Heritage's Settlement Atlas* (Roberts & Wrathmell 2000, 2002). There have also been successful experiments in doing HLC more locally, and in producing higher-level regional views. The ultimate aim is for county HLC to be part of a 'ladder' of characterization rising from ultra-local small studies, through county and regional assessments, to national and international overviews. At each step, different aspects of the landscape can be considered, with greater or lesser generalization, to answer appropriate research and management questions and needs.

The HLC method takes an inclusive view of what are the 'building blocks' or ingredients of landscape. They must have a historic or an archaeological aspect, and they must operate to influence perception at landscape-scale, but beyond that there are no limits. HLC does not restrict itself to 'monuments', conventional archaeological sites or historic buildings, which actually form only a very small part of HLC. It encompasses semi-natural components (hedgerow, woodland, heath), more abstract aspects such as the pattern of land use (arable, pasture, woodland), their inter-relationship to each other and to settlement patterns, roads and track-ways, or coastal movement.

Even the things often thought to be most natural have cultural depth. Wetlands in NW Europe have long-forgotten (except through archaeology) religious and ritual meaning, while rock outcrops anchored cognitive, mental maps to the real environment at many dates in deep prehistory. Less tangible aspects such as the historical processes that underlie the material record of the spatial and territorial patterns of estates, or town-lands are also part of the pattern of HLC. Importantly, it is not these elements in isolation that make HLC what it is, but the connection between them, both in space (geographical patterns) and in time (time-depth, successive layers, the rich palimpsest of the whole present-day landscape); most of all, HLC is about patterns.

Because HLC methodology concentrates on present-day historic landscape character before earlier layers and horizons, in England it tends to emphasize landscape character of the most recent few centuries. The focus on recent periods is also quite useful, representing part of a wider move away from site-based conservation, and from a single period focus, so it also reflects a wider growth of interest in 'new' heritage, even of the late 20th century.

Additionally, even the most 'shallow' HLC-based assessment of time-depth will spread backwards across several centuries, which is significantly deeper than most non-historical landscape characterization that sometimes seems to minimize human impact of any date in favor of contemporary or supposedly 'ageless' natural explanations. It is also worth commenting that the first historic landscape characterization of an area is also only a starting point to which greater time-depth can be added, later and in localized areas if need be, within an overarching framework that is anchored in the present-day. Indeed, a critical review of HLC would draw attention to the limitations inherent in current methods because of its choice of county scale. Further methodological development should focus on applying the principle of HLC both at a more detailed local level, and at higher levels. Regional overviews are planned in England, which will produce different but scale-valid interpretations. In its present manifestation, HLC's planning and management outputs are mainly linked to strategic and spatial planning, and the setting of priorities for agri-environmental schemes. Applications for development control (e.g. using it to contextualize very local aspects of landscape character) still remain to be developed.

As practiced within English Heritage's national programme, HLC has also been tailored to types of landscape common in England. It reflects that country's dense and diverse, chronologically rich and morphologically varied patterns of hedge- and wall-bounded fields, closely linked to different types of settlement pattern and to a particularly fine-grained type of landscape. Where similar landscape exists – in NW France perhaps – the method could probably be used largely unchanged. It would be much less easy to use in more open unenclosed landscapes, such as parts of Portugal or in areas of Sweden heavily remodelled in the 18th or 19th century, which by and large lack visible marks of land division. Nor might it be easily used, for different reasons, in landscapes that on the surface appear to be overwhelmingly modern, such as those of the Netherlands. In such places, modification would be needed. The part of HLC that is most transferable is its general theoretical framework and its principles, notably those concerned with time-depth, the importance of change, the focus on human agency and the determination to characterize the present-day landscape historically rather than to study past landscapes.

3.3 How HLC is carried out – methods and uses

A detailed description of the HLC method is not necessary here, and several are published elsewhere (e.g. Herring 1998; Fairclough 1999; Fairclough et al. 1999; Dyson-Bruce 2002; Fairclough 2002a; Fairclough et al. 2002; Darlington 2002; English Heritage 2002; Aldred & Fairclough 2003. In summary, HLC uses area-based generalizations within a GIS environment to produce an overview of an area's broad landscape character. It is a desk-based vertical assessment of pattern, process and function in the landscape. It uses maps (modern but also historic), vertical air photographs and other datasets such as land cover, land use or ecological data, to define areas of land – created as polygons in the GIS – that have similar characteristics, described by attributes and data contained in related data-bases. These descriptive attributes allow complex modelling and classification to be carried out, and the result is a sophisticated spatial database that produces not just one simple HLC map but the ability for almost endless interrogation, analysis and thematic mapping.

The HLC method creates a continuous patchwork of small areas, each of which is a separate data-holding unit in the GIS (polygons). Polygons are defined subjectively, because of a general broad similarity within their boundaries, or because they share domi-nant characteristics (e.g. regular fields, fields cut out of woodland, ancient or new wood-land, unenclosed heath, major industrial areas, or urban areas). The character of each area (or GIS polygon) is not normally homogenous, as that approach would become too detailed and tell us little other than that every piece of land is unique. What HLC seeks to do is to identify similarity and general patterns. It is not an environmental database, but a way of mapping interpretations.

The detailed attributes attached to each polygon provide the basic means to describe present-day historic landscape character. They allow identification of time-depth and other historic aspects, such as the shape and nature of field boundaries and the historic, social and economic processes that created them. They might also include indicators of past his-toric landscape character that explain present-day character, such as relicts of medieval open fields, the exixtence of diagnostic types of buildings, field ponds or indicative field or place-names. In urban landscape, HLC attributes reflect date, function (e.g. housing, industrial, civic space) or form (terrace versus semi-detached versus detached housing, for example) of buildings, or variations in plan form of streets and spaces. HLC can also look below the modern town to characterize the pre-urban landscape, to show how this often still shapes the course of modern streets or the distribution of building types.

Many different classifications can be produced from these attributes, and maps can be made that reflect either the generality or some of the detail of the historic landscape. Themes can be addressed, previous past landscape character can be modelled; pie-charts and histograms can be used to analyse and compare the particular character of areas such as parishes and townships. Analysis of the distribution and particular types of historic land-scape or areas that share similar combinations of attributes is also possible, as is the pro-duction of historically informed models of past or possible future landscape.

The use for which HLC was primarily designed (Herring 1998; Fairclough et al. 1999) is as a tool for conservation and historic environment management (Clark et al. 2004). Simply, it provides new information to guide decisions about proposed change to the environment. Understanding is a prerequisite for taking sensible conservation and devel-opment decisions, as part of a process known as *Informed Conservation or Applied Archaeology*

(Clark 2001; Bloemers 2002). The most significant results of HLC are when it changes perceptions and understanding of the landscape. It can encourage people to review their assumptions (such as that a particular landscape is 'unchanged', 'natural' or 'age-old') by drawing attention to time-depth and human agency. Conversely it can demonstrate that even in very modern, or recently greatly changed, landscapes there are still traces of the more distant past that are important contributors to landscape character, sense of place or local distinctiveness.

Which fields in the countryside, for example, are the oldest or the rarest or provide particularly significant archaeological evidence for history? Which type and areas of field are likely to have been cleared and enclosed from medieval enclosure of woods and forests, and therefore what is the likely previous extent of woodland? Which fields, though perhaps modified, are the genetic descendants of prehistoric or early medieval patterns, which tell us most about the past, which contribute most to the landscape's historic character? Which types are most sensitive to change, or which can absorb change whilst keeping their essential historic character? Which areas have seen several successive layers of change, being dynamic zones where further change might seem most appropriate, and which are zones of longer-term continuity that we might argue should remain largely unchanged? Why does woodland have particular locations, and a particular mix of trees? What are the human management systems that have made woodland, and woodland biodiversity? Such types of knowledge about the history of the landscape's historic character are essential for the sustainable planning of the future landscape.

In relation to English conservation and spatial planning, the types of new understanding that HLC provides are wide-ranging. Because HLC uses sophisticated GIS and spatial databases, it can produce an almost endless series of interrogations, analysis and thematic maps. Many different combinations of polygon attributes can be created, and many different maps, whether selective, synthetic or interpretative, can be made in response to different priorities and policies. Past landscape character can be modelled, change and activity can be charted, and benchmarks and baselines can be set for monitoring future change. Analysis of HLC in comparison with other archaeological, ecological or architectural datasets can help to explain the patterns and biases of existing knowledge, highlighting gaps and illuminating factors of survival and condition. New research agendas can be created using HLC's insights, so that the process of understanding becomes iterative and ongoing.

4 Reflections – a wider landscape of landscape management

As discussed earlier, landscape can be regarded as 'merely' a construct of perception and interpretation. This means it is not the same as environment, even if is forged from the raw materials of the environment. Seen in this way, landscape is a product of cultural ideas, historic processes and change in many different ways. Of all heritage or conservation values and significances, those attached to 'landscape' are among the hardest to capture, and the most difficult to define. But for almost the same reasons, landscape is the most democratic, ubiquitous and socially-relevant aspect of heritage; at some level, it not only includes everything else, but it also allows everyone to be involved in appreciating and caring for it.

How we perceive landscape constantly changes, just as its component parts change through time. What people value in landscape, what they wish to preserve, why they wish to preserve it or manage it – all these change, all of the time. Our understanding evolves, and what we think is significant or worth keeping develops. All these changes are furthermore refracted through the autobiography, knowledge and aims of any observer. Finally, there is future change, the ever-present potential for more change and all the decisions and valuations that precede and accompany it.

Change takes many forms – slow long-term change or rapid change; recent change, with the immediate consequences of which we must deal; current change that can be mitigated or encouraged. In fact, if any one characteristic most deserves to be singled out as an essential defining feature of cultural landscape, it is surely its dynamism, the fact that it changes all the time, and the legibility or visibility of change within its fabric. The aim is surely to manage the physical and perceptual aspects of the cultural landscape, and at the same time to preserve the dynamism that characterizes landscape and makes it live into the future. To do this, landscape heritage management will require more sophisticated and nuanced methods than the straightforward ones that are effective to manage sites and monuments.

For landscape, conservation or heritage management cannot be an activity at the edges of society, standing on the sidelines and intervening only reactively. It should be a constructive proactive process, concerned to shape the future, not merely to keep fragments of the past. It needs to be more of an activity at the heart of society and politics, a way of living not a pastime. This is the ultimate implication of accepting the need for sustainable development – a full integration of all three factors of sustainability – the environmental with the social and economic.

This chapter has tried to demonstrate that better understanding of the historic dimension of landscape – of what has created it and of what has survived from the past, time-depth in short – is needed if the future landscape is to continue meaningfully to reflect its past. Having roots in a landscape or place, visible everyday connections to history, tends to create better quality of life than when dislocated from any past, and an inclusive approach to understanding landscape and place is likely to be part of the way to achieve this. In an English framework, the programme of landscape characterization described above – HLC – attempts to begin to meet some of these needs by providing many different tools. Methods like HLC can measure long-term change and help to understand why the landscape has evolved to be like it is. They are, therefore, well placed to help with shaping the landscape of tomorrow, and many other European countries have research programmes on this theme. *The European Landscape Convention*, even though not yet in force, is already heightening this trend.

HLC's central aims are to increase understanding, and to use landscape as a vehicle to bring together disconnected information and different disciplines. It teaches a great deal about the historic depth of the present-day landscape, and equally important it puts this into formats that are more accessible to other landscape disciplines. In addition, it tells us a lot about the sites and monuments within the landscape, providing for them a wider meaning. It offers predictive tools that allow us to see where our knowledge is inadequate, where we may have looked with the wrong methods, where new archaeological sites might be found. More, it answers questions about landscape's historic character, helps to write new agenda for research, and asks new and better questions.

Looking forward in time, HLC will provide a benchmark for monitoring change, so in years to come we can see how the environment itself and landscape perceptions have both changed. The current search to define indicators to monitor and shape change (in the UK at least but more widely) is proving difficult, and it may be a mistake to measure them too quantitatively. Perhaps what we should be measuring as an indicator is the much more subjective idea of landscape character, what people think about landscape rather than what it is.

If landscape is truly personal, as argued above, it is also therefore ever changing, as people change. At a very crude level, in the UK, it is many years since most people worked on the land – a century since more than 10% worked the land (Fairclough 2002), and current figures suggest perhaps only 1% in many parts of the country. This means of course that the land is being used differently and looks different, but more subtly, and equally inevitably, it means that most peoples' perception of landscape, and opinions about its value, are not the same as those of their grandparents. Almost everyone now sees the rural landscape as to some degree a conservation landscape, a leisure landscape, a backdrop for life, an ecological necessity perhaps, the raw material of the tourism industry, a place to have a second home or to build new better houses. For most people in the UK today, food production is not very high on the list of what landscape is actually *for*. So what matters most now in agri-politics – the view from the tractor or the view through the passing car windscreen?

The pace of change in peoples' perceptions is matched by the dynamism of the environment itself, which raises other issues of perception. We think the rate and type of change in the modern landscape is faster or worse than at any time in the past, but is this true? Comparison of present-day changes to false ideas of past 'timelessness' can say more about our values, and our response to change, indeed our dislike of change, than about the degree of change itself. Archaeology can highlight such issues by showing the scale of change in the past, and the degree to which the environment, and hence the landscape we create, is the product of change not continuity. It can also show how many times in the past people have damaged the ecosystem, and how they had done this.

HLC rarely creates prescriptions or presumptions (e.g. in favour of keeping something unchanged) and does not necessarily dictate protection. Instead it provides better information to support proper discussion and sustainable decision-taking between all those involved in deciding change (hopefully through a democratic inclusive approach). The overall aim is to ensure that historic character is not lost through ignorance, but only by conscious decisions that weigh all factors. Methods like HLC aim to extend consideration of the impact of change and development (e.g. urban regeneration, agricultural environmental policies) beyond a few special sites to everything within the environment, everywhere. The environment cannot be treated as a new empty page on which to write the future. We have to reuse the same page. Landscape is an old document, a palimpsest showing centuries of human remains, the human habitat we have engineered for ourselves. The past cannot be swept away without thought to make way for new development. If it were treated like that, as English experience in the 1950s and 1960s shows, the result is usually unsustainable and unsatisfactory, notably in quality of life terms; instead new development has to be fitted smoothly into old.

Studying and trying to characterize the historic dimension of the whole landscape through HLC shows what we have inherited in the landscape and the patterns of change and survival that lead to the present-day landscape, and it explains the human processes that make landscapes work. It therefore gives information to help us decide what could be preserved and passed on to the future as part of the next stage of landscape evolution. In the past, the drivers of landscape change have mainly been matters such as food production, shelter, political control, profits or industrial production. While these will doubtless continue to be important in future change to the landscape of the 21st century, there will also be newer drivers of change.

Public and political concerns about sustainability, and the pressures of increasing population and development, suggest that some of these newer factors will – and already do – fall under the heading of 'conservation', 'resource management' or 'local identity'. Landscape management like other areas of environmental management could become more proactive, with a larger share in deciding the sort of landscape we make for our descendants. The control of landscape change in the past was conscious, whether by farmer or by landscape architect, and to use a conservation and heritage ethos to take conscious decisions about the landscape is just a modern version of this. It does not make the resultant landscape change any less 'natural' or any more 'artificial', simply admits that conservation, or sustainability, is in itself a force for change not merely a constraint on change.

This is perhaps already to be seen in the concept of paying farmers to be custodians of the landscape as well as (and perhaps soon instead of) to produce food producers. It is also seen in the modern enthusiasm for 'recreating' lost habitats such as heath or woodland, even if this is not always in support of landscape character as opposed to creating new bio-diversity, which are not the same thing of course. If these trends accelerate, it may be that landscape protection and management will become a mainstream part of the social processes that shape human interaction with use of the environment, and determine how people perceive the landscapes in which they live and work. In this sense, landscape has already changed. Most people in England for example now see landscape not as a place of work but as a sort of nature reserve, holiday location or pretty backdrop to everyday urban lifestyles. As the motivation for changing landscape becomes more conservation-led, and as traditional methods of land management fades from memory, we will need more and more knowledge and understanding of the landscape's historic aspects to help us take sustainable decisions.

It will remain difficult to come to terms with landscape change. Landscape has always changed, as all students of landscape accept, and studying that change is an important part of understanding our history: the landscape itself offers evidence of our past that is at least as important as historic documents. It can be argued that recent or current levels of change in relation to the *fabric* of the landscape are no greater or faster than they have been at other dates in the past. Without going back more than a few hundred years, the rapid re-structuring of the English landscape through Enclosure, or on Scania by the land reform shifts of the early 19th century were major upheavals greater than most witnessed in the past 50 years. The removal by human actions of all significant woodland in midland England by about 1000 AD was a remarkable change, as was the creation of upland and lowland heaths – now greatly valued for their 'wildness' – by over-intensive farming during prehistoric times. Such examples can be multiplied across the world.

What is perhaps different now is the accompanying loss of the *processes* that sustain particular types of landscape. Agricultural incentive schemes or consciously archaic methods of land management are having some success in replacing modern intensive agri-culture with new, more environmentally sensitive methods that are not necessarily his-toric or traditional. On the whole, however, traditional land-management processes such as wood pasture land use, hay making, upland sheep grazing, cork production are vanish-ing, to be replaced by intensive monocultures, new energy crops, golf courses, new nature reserves or untended land. In areas of depopulation or demographic desertification, the landscape that they created will be difficult or impossible to maintain, but little of cul-tural (as opposed to natural, unmanaged) value will be put in its place.

It is particularly difficult, as mentioned above, to protect and manage landscape charac-ter where the activities that created it – notably traditional types of farming and land use – no longer take place. Is society prepared to create an artificial rural economy, for example, continuing to subsidize hill-sheep farming in order to preserve the present appearance of upland landscapes, even though there is no economic demand for the lamb or wool? When do we accept that historic processes have stopped, and recognize that we need to create a new environment with new character? In some parts of Europe (southern France, Spain and Portugal, the Western Isles of Scotland, upland England and Wales) the problem of disap-pearing farming is, or threatens very soon, to change the character of cultural landscape very severely. Archaeologists have an option of simply accepting this as the continuance of the change that is archaeology's main subject matter, and welcoming it as the creation of 'new' historic landscapes for us to study and protect at a future date. Alternatively, we could offer an archaeological understanding of the present-day landscape to help society create tomorrow's landscape in ways that reflect or grow out of yesterday's, and allow future generations to enjoy the evidence of their long history in the way that we can.

A good starting point is to recognize that the protection of cultural landscapes is not first and foremost about preventing change but about managing it, living with it. Historic landscape character (perhaps more so than other types of landscape character) cannot survive without appropriate land use, and cannot be held in stasis. Because it so complex, it is perhaps not susceptible to the sort of artificial management that can maintain some aspects of biodiversity in isolation from cultural processes. Landscape has never been static during human history, despite the impression we sometimes think we have of timeless, unchanging aeons, especially in rural contexts when viewed with a post-industrial detachment from the land, a romanticized view of the past that has little justification. To try to keep the cultural landscape as a sort of unchanging fossil of itself or (worse) as a fossil of some mythical 'golden age' or 'rural idyll' (Fairclough 1996b), will remove one of the things that create landscape character and makes it so valuable: the visibility of change and the evidence for past human actions.

Accepting change, however, need not lead to fatalistic acceptance of any or all change. Decisions are still there to be made, unless we are prepared not to interfere at all but simply to allow natural human processes to take over, in the 21st century largely the workings of the global marketplace: change could just be 'allowed to happen'. Or we could try to steer it in various directions, preferably respecting historic patterns and traditional trajectories of change. There is a need for some clarity on why we make changes to the landscape. In the past it was usually clear enough – to grow more food, or to obtain timber, for example – but now? We need to explore more carefully our current motives for restoring field boundaries, replanting woodland or recreating wetlands. Such activities are sometimes said to be re-creating the past, or replacing lost biodiversity, but this is not really the case, not just because a replaced hedge, for example, cannot be truly authentic, but because more fundamentally the reasons and processes of creation are different. It is better to regard such landscape changes as attempts to produce new biodiversity (all biodiversity is cultural as well as natural) for people to enjoy looking at, or simply as the creation of new layers in the sequence of landscape history, not as a return to a better past. All landscape management is forward-looking; it can make new landscapes, but it cannot re-make old ones.

But we can take decisions about what new landscape should contain, based on understanding of what makes landscape, what has shaped it in the past, how it works and fits together, what is sustainable. A key aim of landscape management should be a balance between continuity and change. Significant features of the landscape can be preserved, so that people may continue to identify and celebrate the work of their predecessors, in ways that allow a landscape feature to have a new use. We best protect what we value by giving it an appropriate (not necessarily its original) use, and this is true of the landscape as much as of an historic building. We should strive to pass on the ability to understand the past, by keeping its traces and imprints, by making time-depth and historic character.

Our goal, then, might not be to pass on to those who follow us the things that *we* think they will value, but rather to give them options by bequeathing a landscape that retains enough historic and archaeological depth for them to 'read' and study it afresh for themselves. This would be a living landscape in a new sense, that of being alive as a document that renews itself continuously, both because it is being changed and added to, and because age and experience normally makes re-reading a book worthwhile and productive of new meaning and understanding. In this way, the landscape can be read and re-read, each time surrendering up new meaning to new questions. This may ultimately be seen as more important than trying to pass on particular things that we value, in the hope that our descendants will agree.

References

Aldred, O. & Fairclough, G.J. 2003. *Historic Landscape Characterisation: Taking Stock of the Method – The National HLC Method Review*. English Heritage and Somerset County Council: London. www.english-heritage.org.uk/characterisation<landscape

Bloemers, J.H.F. (2002). Past- and future-oriented archaeology: protecting and developing the archaeological-historical landscape of the Netherlands. In G.J. Fairclough & S.J. Rippon (eds) *Europe's Cultural Landscape: Archaeologists and the Management of Change* (pp. 89–96). EAC Occasional Paper no. 2, Europae Archaeologiae Consilium and English Heritage, Brussels and London.

Brown, I.W. & Berry, A.R. (eds) (1995). *Managing Ancient Monuments: An Integrated Approach*, Association of County Archaeology Officers/Clwyd County Council, Mold.

Castro *et al.* (2002). Archaeology in the south east of the Iberian Peninsula: a bridge between past and future social spaces. In G.J. Fairclough & S.J. Rippon (eds) *Europe's Cultural Landscape: Archaeologists and the Management of Change*, EAC Occasional Paper no. 2 (pp. 133–142), Europae Archaeologiae Consilium and English Heritage, Brussels and London.

Clark, J., Darlington, J. & Fairclough, G.J. 2004. *Using Historic Landscape Characterisation, English Heritage Review of HLC Applications, 2002–3.* English Heritage and Lancashire County Council, Preston. www.english-heritage.org.uk/characterisation<landscape.

Clark, K. (2001). *Informed Conservation: Understanding Historic Buildings and their Landscapes for Conservation*, English Heritage, London.

Council of Europe (2000). *European Landscape Convention*, Florence, European Treaty Series – No. 176; www.coe.int/T/E/cultural-co-operation/Environment/Landscape.

Council of Europe (2002). *The European Landscape Convention,* Naturopa Issue 98/2002 European Landscape Convention, Strasbourg.

Countryside Agency (1999). Countryside Character volumes: vol. 4 *East Midlands* (CA10), vol. 5. *West Midlands* (CA11), vol. 6 *The East* (CA12), vol. 7 *South East* (CA13), vol. 8 *South West* (CA14), Cheltenham. www.countryside.gov.uk/cci

Countryside Agency & Scottish Natural Heritage (2002). *Landscape Character Assessment: Guidance for England and Scotland*, CAX 84. www.countryside.gov.uk/cci/guidance.

Countryside Commission (1987). *Landscape Assessment – A Countryside Commission Approach*, CCD18, Cheltenham.

Countryside Commission (1993). *Landscape Assessment Guidance*, CCP423, Cheltenham.

Countryside Commission, (1998). Countryside Character volumes: vol. 1 *North East* (CCP535), vol. 2 *North West* (CCP536), vol. 3 *Yorkshire and the Humber* (CCP536), Cheltenham. www.countryside.gov.uk/cci.

Darlington, J. (2002). Mapping Lancashire's historic landscape: the Lancashire HLC programme (pp. 97–105). In G.J. Fairclough & S.J. Rippon (eds) *Europe's Cultural Landscape: Archaeologists and the Management of Change*, EAC Occasional Paper no. 2, Europae Archaeologiae Consilium and English Heritage, Brussels and London.

Déjeant-Pons, M. (2002). The European Landscape Convention, Florence. In G.J. Fairclough & S.J. Rippon (eds) *Europe's Cultural Landscape: Archaeologists and the Management of Change* (pp. 13–24), EAC Occasional Paper no. 2, Europae Archaeologiae Consilium and English Heritage, Brussels and London.

Department of Culture, Media and Sport & DTLR (2002). The Historic Environment: A Force for Our Future, PP378, Department for Culture, Media and Sport & Department of Transport, Local Government and the Regions, London, www.culture.gov.uk/heritage.

Department of the Environment & Department of National Heritage, (1994). *Planning and the Historic Environment, Planning Policy Guidance (PPG) 15*, HMSO.

Dixon, P & Hingley, R. (2002). Historic land-use assessment in Scotland. In G.J. Fairclough & S.J. Rippon (eds) *Europe's Cultural Landscape: Archaeologists and the Management of Change* (pp. 85–88), EAC Occasional Paper no. 2, Europae Archaeologiae Consilium and English Heritage, Brussels and London.

Dyson-Bruce, L. (2002). Historic Landscape Assessment – the East of England experience, in G. Burenhult (ed.) *Archaeological Informatics: Pushing the Envelope*, Computer Applications and Quantitative Methods in Archaeology, Proceedings of the 29th Conference, Gotland, April 2001, BAR International Series 1016, (pp. 35–42). Archaeopress.

Dyson-Bruce, L., Dixon, P., Hingley, R. & Stevenson, J. (1999). *Historic Landuse Assessment (HLA): Development and Potential of a Technique for Assessing Historic Landscape Patterns, Report of the Pilot Project 1996–98*, Historic Scotland, RCHMS, Edinburgh.

Ede, J. & Darlington, J. (2002). *The Lancashire Historic Landscape Characterisation Programme*, Lancashire County Council/English Heritage, Preston.

English Heritage (1997). *Sustaining the Historic Environment*, London.

English Heritage (2002). *Historic Landscape Characterisation: Template Project Design for EH-Funded County Level Projects*, English Heritage, London.

ERM & ERA (2000). *Pilot Study on Landscape Characterisation in County Clare*, Oxford, Dublin and Kilkenny: Environmental Resource Management and ERA-Maptec Ltd for the Heritage Council (Ireland).

Ermischer, G. (2002). Spessart goes Europe: the historic landscape characterisation of a German upland region. In G.J. Fairclough & S.J. Rippon (eds) *Europe's Cultural Landscape: Archaeologists and the Management of Change* (pp. 157–168). EAC Occasional Paper no. 2, Europae Archaeologiae Consilium and English Heritage, Brussels and London.

Fairclough, G.J. (1994). Landscapes from the past – only human nature. In P. Selman, *The Ecology and Management of Cultural Landscapes* (pp. 64–72) (Proceedings of an IALE UK Conference at Cheltenham 1993 published – Landscape Issues vol. 11 no. 1).

Fairclough, G.J. (1995). *The Sum of All Its Parts: An Overview of the Politics of Integrated Management in England*. In Brown & Berry, (pp. 17–28).

Fairclough, G.J. (1999a). Protecting time and space: understanding historic landscape for conservation in England. In P.J. Ucko & R. Layton (eds). *The Archaeology and Anthropology of Landscape: Shaping your Landscape*. One World Archaeology 30 (pp. 119–134). London: Routledge.

Fairclough, G.J. (1999b). Protecting the cultural landscape – national designations and local character. In J. Grenville (ed.) *Managing the Historic Rural Environment* (pp. 27–39). Routledge/English Heritage, London.

Fairclough, G.J. (2002a). Cultural landscape, computers and characterisation. In G. Burenhult (ed.) *Archaeological Informatics: Pushing the Envelope*, Computer Applications and Quantitative Methods in Archaeology, Proceedings of the 29th Conference, Gotland, April 2001, BAR International Series 1016, Archaeopress (pp. 277–294).

Fairclough, G.J. (2002b). Cultural landscape and spatial planning. In *'Historic Environments of the North Sea'*, Proceedings of an InterReg II Conference, March 2001, South Shields.

Fairclough, G.J. (2002c). Europe's landscape: archaeology, sustainability and agriculture. In G.J. Fairclough & S.J.Rippon (eds) *Europe's Cultural Landscape: Archaeologists and the Management of Change* (pp. 1–12). EAC Occasional Paper no. 2, Europae Archaeologiae Consilium and English Heritage, Brussels and London.

Fairclough, G.J. (2002d) Archaeologists and the European Landscape Convention. In G.J. Fairclough & S.J. Rippon (eds) *Europe's Cultural Landscape: archaeologists and the management of change* (pp. 25–37), EAC Occasional Paper no. 2, Europae Archaeologiae Consilium and English Heritage, Brussels and London.

Fairclough, G.J. (2002e). Steps towards the integrated management of a changing landscape: Historic Landscape Characterisation in England. In G. Swensen (ed.) *Cultural Heritage on the Urban Fringe, Nannetsad Workshop Report March 2002*, NIKU 126, (pp. 29–39). Oslo: Norsk Institut for kulturminneforskning.

Fairclough, G.J. (2003). Cultural landscape, sustainability and living with change? In J.-M. Teutonico (ed.) *Managing Change: Sustainable Approaches to the Conservation of the Built Environment*. The Proceedings of the US/ICOMOS 4th International Symposium, April 5–8, 2001, Philadelphia.

Fairclough, G.J. (ed.) (1999). *Historic Landscape Characterisation* (Papers presented at an English

Heritage seminar held at the Society of Antiquaries, 11 December 1998), English Heritage, London.

Fairclough, G.J., Lambrick, G. & McNab, A. (1999). *Yesterday's World, Tomorrow's Landscape* (The English Heritage Historic Landscape Project 1992–94), London: English Heritage.

Fairclough, G.J., Lambrick, G. & Hopkins, D. (2002). Historic Landscape Characterisation in England and a Hampshire case study. In G.J. Fairclough & S.J. Rippon (eds) *Europe's Cultural Landscape: Archaeologists and the Management of Change* (pp. 69–83). EAC Occasional Paper no. 2, Europae Archaeologiae Consilium and English Heritage, Brussels and London.

Fairclough, G.J. & Rippon, S.J. (eds) (2002). *Europe's Cultural Landscape: Archaeologists and the Management of Change*. EAC Occasional Paper no. 2, Europae Archaeologiae Consilium and English Heritage, Brussels and London.

Herring, P. (1998). *Cornwall's Historic Landscape. Presenting a Method of Historic Landscape Character Assessment*, Cornwall Archaeology Unit and English Heritage, Cornwall County Council, Truro.

Historic Scotland (2002). *Past to the Future: Historic Scotland's Policy for the Sustainable Management of the Historic Environment*, Historic Scotland, Edinburgh.

Macinnes, L. (2002). Examples of current national approaches – Scotland. In G.J. Fairclough & S.J. Rippon (eds) *Europe's Cultural Landscape: Archaeologists and the Management of Change* (pp. 171–174). EAC Occasional Paper no. 2, Europae Archaeologiae Consilium and English Heritage, Brussels and London.

Macinnes, L. & Wickham-Jones, C.R. (1992). *All Natural Things: archaeology and the Green Debate*. Oxford, Oxbow Monograph 11.

Nord Paulsson, J. (2002). Raising awareness and managing change: the cultural landscape of the Bjäre Peninsular, Sweden. In G.J. Fairclough & S.J. Rippon (eds) *Europe's Cultural Landscape: Archaeologists and the Management of Change* (pp. 143–148). EAC Occasional Paper no. 2, Europae Archaeologiae Consilium and English Heritage, Brussels and London.

Nord Paulsson, J. & Fairclough, G.J. (2002). Bjare and Bowland: computer applications. In *European Pathways to Cultural Landscapes*, a Culture 2000 programme. In G. Burenhult (ed.) *Archaeological Informatics: Pushing the Envelope*, Computer Applications and Quantitative Methods in Archaeology, Proceedings of the 29th Conference, Gotland, April 2001, BAR International Series 1016, Archaeopress (pp. 551–557).

Roberts, B.K. & Wrathmell, S. (2000). *An Atlas of Rural Settlement in England*. London: English Heritage.

Roberts, B.K. & Wrathmell, S. (2002). *Region and Place, Rural Settlement in England*. London: English Heritage.

www.hants.gov.uk/landscape: Hampshire County Council website for its Historic Landscape Characterisation.

www.pcl-eu.de, the website of the European Pathways to the Cultural Landscape Culture 2000 network.

SECTION FOUR

Interpretation and communication

Chapter 33

Presenting Archaeology to the Public, Then and Now

An introduction

John H. Jameson, Jr, US National Park Service

[National parks and heritage sites] are more than physical resources. They are the delicate strands of nature and culture that bond generation to generation.
George B. Hartzog, Jr, former Director, US National Park Service

History of public interpretation practice and philosophy

The public presentation of archaeology in the United States and many Western countries can be traced to the historic preservation and conservation movements of the 19th and 20th centuries, an intensity of conservation and environmental concerns after World War II, and expanded activities in educational archaeology since the 1980s. Another pattern has been the increased attention and access to information since the 1960s afforded to indigenous cultures. Challenges to management such as site protection, looting, and crises in curation and storage continue to dominate attention and resources, sometimes detracting from personnel and monies dedicated to public interpretation and educational archaeology (Jameson 2004a).

As a specialty within the sphere of public archaeology and cultural heritage management, the public interpretation of archaeological and cultural sites has come to be recognized as an essential component in the conservation and protection of cultural resources and sites and in fostering public stewardship around the world. In the United States, the development of resource protection legislation and cultural resource management (CRM) strategies in the 1960s and 1970s, and the resultant very rapid accumulation of archaeological and historical site information and collected artifacts, led to concerns for inclusiveness and sensitivity to heritage values of multidimensional constituents or "stakeholders" (Jameson 2004a).

The decades between the 1970s and the early 1990s were a time when many in the archaeology profession came to the realization that they could no longer afford to be detached from mechanisms and programs that attempt to convey archaeological information to the lay public. Although notable efforts had occurred previously (South 1997), they were isolated occurrences and rarely made it beyond the gray literature of archaeologists and educators. In the face of an increasing public interest and demand for information, archaeologists have increasingly collaborated with historians, museum curators, exhibit designers, Web designers, and other cultural resource specialists to devise the best strategies for translating an explosion of archaeological information for the public. The 1980s and 1990s saw a great proliferation of efforts to meet this demand, with varying degrees of success (Jameson 2000).

The republished articles presented in this section by McManamon (2000) and McDavid (2002) are exemplary pieces that address the need for multivocality of archaeological messages and for collaboration of archaeologists with their public communication partners such as teachers and multimedia specialists, and designers of exhibits and Web sites.

Notable international achievements in effective presentation have been outlined in articles and edited books by Peter Stone in the UK and his involvement with the management of Stonehenge World Heritage Site has affected that monument's role as an international icon for management and interpretation in archaeology (Stone 2006, republished in Chapter 38, this volume). Philosophical movements in Australasia toward inclusiveness of indigenous perspectives has set an example for other countries. Standards and models for heritage interpretation in Australia were proposed in the late 1990s that emphasized effective access to the cultural resources ". . . through appropriate technologies and the responsible stimulation of ideas, feelings and opinions . . . that promote public stewardship" (Nethery 1999). Jameson (1997) summarized the philosophy, definition, and status of public interpretation through the mid 1990s with international examples.

More recently, forums for discussion and available literature on this topic have provided discussions and publications that are beginning to fill the informational and case-study gap. Although many success stories in educational archaeology remain to be publicly discussed or written, the last two decades have seen a significant improvement in the number of public and professional forums and a few notable publications have been produced, including: Stone and Mackenzie 1990; Stone and Molyneaux 1994; Jameson 1997; Stone 1999; McManamon and Hatton 2000; Smardz and Smith 2000; Bender and Smith 2000; Little 2002; Jameson 2004; Jameson and Scott-Ireton 2007; and Jameson and Baugher 2007. Discussions have also taken place at international forums such as the World Archaeological Congress, the European Archaeological Association, and International Council on Monuments and Sites (ICOMOS) international forums.

In the United States, professional societies, notably the Society for American Archaeology (SAA), the Archaeological Institute of America (AIA), and the Society for Historical Archaeology (SHA), plus state and local groups, have played important roles in providing leadership and inspiration in public interpretation and outreach. An exemplary recent project was SHA's *Unlocking the Past: Celebrating Historical Archaeology in North America*, a multi-year public outreach and education initiative. This project produced a generously illustrated book (De Cunzo and Jameson 2005) and a complementary Web site that stresses educational links (SEAC 2006). Both the book and Web site introduce general readers to the archaeology of North America's history beginning with the early contacts between Europeans and Native Americans. Contributors to the volume shared their findings to engage readers and encourage them to join the "experts" in preserving and studying cultural heritage. They also explained why historical archaeology is important in providing objectively derived context as well as filling information gaps in the historical record. The *Unlocking* material was designed to appeal to a wide general audience of young readers as well as adults interested in archaeology, North American history, and historic preservation.

Exemplary government programs in the United States at federal, state, and local government levels have taken the lead in promoting education and outreach: Jameson (1997); Smardz and Smith (2000); Derry and Malloy (2003); and Jameson and Baugher

(2007). The National Park Service (NPS) has traditionally taken the lead in promoting education and outreach activities at the federal level. A major emphasis has been in promoting partnerships and initiatives both within and outside the government. In recent years, a number of NPS publications have been produced that support archaeology education and outreach. An exemplary publication at the federal level is *Common Ground*, a quarterly magazine distributed to over 12,000 members of the public as well as archaeologists, land managers, preservation officers, museum professionals, Native Americans, law enforcement agents, and educators. An interdisciplinary course of study was developed by NPS that can be used in cross-training employees in the three career fields of archaeology, interpretation, and education. Specialists in these fields are trained together in the skills and abilities (shared competencies) needed to carry out a successful public interpretation program. Among the main precepts of the curriculum are the needs for interdisciplinary communication and for sensitive interpretation to multicultural audiences. The NPS Southeast Archaeological Center (SEAC) in Tallahassee, Florida, has provided leadership by promoting the objectives of public interpretation and communication of cultural heritage values by helping to develop heritage-related curricula, both in formal school settings and at more informal settings such as national parks and museums. Activities have included the organization and coordination of public-oriented publications, academic symposia, workshops, and training sessions presented in a variety of professional and public venues.

Many private and public institutions and universities, archaeology and anthropology departments, and museums in the United States have launched effective public interpretation and outreach programs in recent years. One example is Sonoma State University's Anthropological Studies Center (ASC) which has placed special emphasis on education and outreach in the production of publications and activities for teachers, local civic organizations, archaeology groups, and continuing education programs. ASC's award-winning publications have included public awareness slide shows and videos. A leader and innovator among natural and historical museums is the Chicago Field Museum which provides outstanding public-oriented educational programs. The museum programs focus on cultural diversity as well as the contents of its collections. More than 250,000 students visit the museum and over 10,000 teachers take advantage of the museum's resources for professional development (Field Museum 2006). A large number of private CHM contracting firms have provided leadership in promoting educational opportunities for volunteers and students. An example is the establishment of a full-time public programs division by Statistical Research, Inc. (SRI) in Tucson, Arizona. At SRI, public programs are structured into compliance and noncompliance projects as well as being funded by stand-alone contracts dedicated to public outreach. Since the 1990s, SRI has produced the US Forest Service's "Passport in Time" *PIT Traveler* publication that advertises nationwide programs and volunteer opportunities. The US Bureau of Land Management, which manages over 300 million acres of public land, has developed *Project Archaeology*, a national program that uses archaeological and cultural heritage inquiry to foster understanding of past and present cultures, improve social studies and science education, and enhance citizenship education to help preserve our rich cultural heritage (BLM 2006).

Recent developments in public interpretation and presentation standards

Values-based management schemes

The development and adoption of values-based management strategies has resulted in more democratic and far ranging treatments of cultural heritage involving comprehensive assessments based on input from a broad range of stakeholders. Values-based management approaches have aided inclusiveness in interpretation by providing mechanisms for accountability of the totality of values and significance attributed to a site or cultural landscape. "Values" in this sense relate to tangibles and intangibles that define what is important to people. In all societies a sense of well being is associated with the need to connect with and appreciate heritage values. An understanding of how and why the past affects both the present and the future contributes to people's sense of well being. In heritage management, we articulate "values" as attributes given to sites, objects, and resources, and associated intellectual and emotional connections that make them important and define their significance for a person, group, or community. Uzzell and Ballantyne's 1999 article, republished in this section, was one of the first publications to point out the serious mistake of excluding or downplaying emotional values and content in interpretations of cultural heritage sites.

Practitioners of values-based management strive to identify and take these values into account in planning, physical treatments, and public interpretation efforts. In theory, values-based management, if thoroughly and impartially executed, will result in more democratic and inclusive interpretations by accounting for the values of all stakeholders. This is the ideal. Some notable examples of values-based management were published in a series of studies sponsored by the Getty Institute in 2003. And there are many more examples from the United States and elsewhere: Chaco Canyon National Historic Park in the United States; Port Arthur World Heritage Site, Tasmania, Australia; and Hadrian's Wall World Heritage Site in the UK (Mason *et al.* 2003a; Mason *et al.* 2003b; MacLean *et al.* 2003).

Although differing ethnic groups will not agree on the meaning of, or share the same perspective toward, concepts of value, all people who ascribe meaning and significance for a site will relate to concepts of value in some significant way. Perhaps an extension of the values-based approach that can facilitate interpretation that is more inclusive is to develop mechanisms of identifying more broadly defined value categories. More broadly, defined concepts of value would aid inclusiveness in interpretation by making meanings accessible and relevant to wider communities of stakeholders. It seems that many of the contested issues surrounding values assessments are rooted in divergent concepts of authenticity. Authenticity involves factors that ascribe values or meanings that make something real and not an imitation; they ascribe concepts of "truth" or legitimacy for a society, group, community, or individual.

For many cultural heritage specialists, "value sets" are changing from traditional definitions for the historic, archaeological, and scientific, to incorporate intangibles such as aesthetic, artistic, spiritual, and other values stemming from introspection. This involves an expansion and broadening of the content of "archaeological knowledge" to be more inclusive and accepting and less authoritative, that is, a broadening of the meaning of "expert." One important development is the emergence of the interpretive narrative approach in archaeological interpretation, a post-processual approach where archaeologists actively participate in structuring a compelling story instead of just presenting sets of derived data. The narrative is used as a vehicle for understanding and communicating, *a sharing as well as an imparting* of archaeological values within the interpretation process. Compelling arguments for this approach are contained in two republished articles in this section by John McCarthy (2003): "More Than Just 'Telling the Story': Interpretive Narrative Archaeology" and James Gibb (2003): "The Archaeologist as Playwright."

This trend will result in profound ramifications for definitions of significance in heritage management deliberations and what is ultimately classified, conserved, and maintained. It will change the role we play and the values we present in historic preservation and education. It will affect our strategies for conducting research and the public interpretation of that research. The challenge for archaeologists, cultural historians, and other resource stewards is to educate ourselves on the requisite knowledge, skills, and abilities to deal with these developments. Paramount for educators and interpreters is to ensure that our audiences connect with and understand cultural heritage values, the tangibles and intangibles that define what is important to people.

Market versus non-market value assessments

Joan Poor, a cultural economist, has shown (Poor 2007) that values assessments and analyses at cultural heritage sites can draw from the social science of economics. She defines "economics" as the social science of choice, where decisions are made by weighing the benefits versus the costs of moving from the status quo. Natural and environmental resource economists have been studying decision-making regarding public goods [values] for decades, and much of this research can be applied to archaeological and cultural heritage studies. Poor portends that we can consider archaeological resources as public or quasi-public goods, such that they are characterized to some extent as being non-exclusive to members of society. If we assume archaeological resources possess public goods characteristics, then "we cannot solely rely on 'market-based' valuation analyses to estimate the true value of these resources to society." Typically omitted non-market values, she says, include a wide variety of value categories, including historic and archaeological values. If we omit such values, Poor says, "making management decisions for society at large is not only difficult, the resultant decisions are likely to be inefficient and in many cases can be very controversial."

For example, in the context of heritage tourism, making decisions about the management and interpretation of archaeological sites based solely on tourism or other market-based analyses will often result in controversy. Using 'Non-market Valuation' studies we can begin to manage archaeological resources to minimize the conflicting interests between market-based tourism interests and the non-market based preservation benefits [values] that these sites provide to society. It is necessary, Poor says, "to know – evaluate or estimate – an archaeological resource's Total Value in terms of both market (tourism) value and non-market (preservation) value in order to make effective management decisions and preservation policies" (Poor 2007).

Peter Stone, in chapter 38 on the management dilemmas faced at the Stonehenge World Heritage Site, addresses the need to use newly developed, more inclusive, and more accurate cost–benefit analyses that take into account non-market values, "the reasons why people wish to change the current management scheme [public values] and other heritage benefits [values] associated with the site."

Emphasis on inclusiveness

Our interpretations of the meaning of sites are inherently important to the conservation process and, therefore, play a defining role in conservation/tourism interactions (see discussion of heritage tourism below). We strive in these endeavors to develop more holistic interpretations, in which the values of sustainable environment and heritage are inextricably linked. We have recognized that multidisciplinary and inclusive approaches are the most effective. The sites we deal with are no longer limited to great iconic monuments and places, but now include millions of places of importance to sectors of society that were once invisible or intentionally ignored. These sites can play an important role in fostering peaceful multi-cultural societies, maintaining communal or ethnic identities, and serving as the indispensable theater in which the ancient traditions that make each culture a unique treasure are performed periodically, even daily. The values of these previously ignored and heretofore low priority sites and features are often not readily obvious in the material fabric or surrounding geography, but they must be identified and require a narrative for the fullness of their meaning to be properly conveyed to locals, site visitors, and the public at large. This is accomplished through processes of public interpretation and education (US/ICOMOS 2004).

Interdisciplinary training standards

The NPS Interpretive Development Program (IDP)

The US National Park Service (NPS) has been a leader in North America in developing interdisciplinary and more holistic approaches to public interpretation of heritage. The agency regards interpretation as a distinct profession encompassing a philosophical framework that combines the essence of the past with the dynamism of the present to shape the future.

The Interpretive Development Program, conceived by NPS in the mid 1990s, encourages the stewardship of park resources by facilitating meaningful, memorable visitor experiences. The program is based on the philosophy that people will care for what they first care about. This is accomplished by aiming for the highest standards of professionalism in interpretation. It provides for mission-based training and development curriculum, field-developed national standards for interpretive effectiveness, a peer review certification program, and developmental tools and resources. It is designed to foster accountability and professionalism in interpretation, facilitate meaningful and memorable experiences for visitors, result in a higher level of public stewardship for park resources, and facilitate learner-driven skill development (NPS 2005; Larsen 2003).

Before the mid 1990s, training for new NPS interpreters included a detailed introduction to significant names, dates, and references to important books. Often this introduction was coupled with an exercise in writing a personal definition of interpretation. The current approach incorporates many important aspects of the former with a strengthened sense of individual responsibility. Professional interpreters are expected to search for understanding of the process of interpretation, its roots, its purpose in fostering resource stewardship, and the direction that they will take both as individuals and as professionals. They must also be able to articulate the outcomes of interpretation so they can make personal choices in approach and establish the relevance of interpretation for managers making resource decisions. The interpreter needs a clear understanding that interpretation moves beyond a recitation of scientific data, historical chronologies, and descriptions. For the NPS, the ultimate role of interpretation is to support conservation by facilitating public recognition and support of resource stewardship (NPS 2005).

The NPS interpretation formula is expressed as "(KR + KA) × AT = IO" (Knowledge of the Resource + Knowledge of the Audience × Appropriate Techniques = Interpretive Opportunities). The interpretive equation applies to all interpretive activities. It is important to keep the equation elements in balance. Interpretation in this scheme embraces a discussion of multiple points of view incorporating related human values, conflicts, ideas, tragedies, achievements, ambiguities, and triumphs. The ultimate goal of interpretation, then, is to facilitate opportunities for visitors to forge linkages with resource meanings and thereby develop a stewardship ethic. The credo is "Interpretation is a seed, not a tree" (NPS 2005).

IDP attempts to define the *art* and *skill* of interpretation, effective interpretation techniques, and modes of delivery. The techniques and modes used are tailored to the backgrounds and identities of target audiences and communities, as well as other constituent stakeholders. To date, twelve training modules for interpretation have been developed, expressed here in ascending degrees of specialty and employee development (NPS 2005):

- Module 101: Fulfilling the NPS Mission: The Process of Interpretation;
- Module 102: Informal Visitor Contacts;
- Module 103: Prepare and Present an Interpretive Talk;
- Module 210: Prepare and Present a Conducted Activity;
- Module 220: Prepare and Present an Interpretive Demonstration or Illustrated Program;
- Module 230: Effective Interpretive Writing;
- Module 270: Present an Effective Curriculum-Based Program;
- Module 310: Planning Park Interpretation;
- Module 311: Interpretive Media Development;
- Module 330: Leading Interpreters: Training and Coaching;
- Module 340: Interpretive Research and Resource Liaison;
- Module 440: Effective Interpretation of Archeological Resources.

These specialties relate to a set of competencies developed by NPS for national standards in interpretation. They stand as a goal to foster interpretive excellence nationwide in NPS areas at every stage of an employee's career. The standard rubric for each competency is used by peer review certifiers in measuring whether a specific product demonstrates the elements of success in that area, at a point in time. Employees use the rubric as a guide for self-assessment and to determine whether they need to work on skills or complete other preparation before attempting to meet the certification standards. The basic or core assessment rubric is expressed in two connected parts:

- successful as a catalyst in creating opportunities for the audience to form their own intellectual and emotional connections with meanings/significance inherent in the resource; and
- appropriate for the audience, and provides a clear focus for their connection with the resource(s) by demonstrating the cohesive development of a relevant idea or ideas, rather than relying primarily on a recital of a chronological narrative or a series of related facts.

Module 440 "Effective Interpretation of Archeological Resources" Training Module

Modern public interpretation programs seek to present a variety of perspectives to multicultural audiences that result in a greater understanding and appreciation of past human behavior and activities. In these settings, archaeologists, interpreters, educators, and site managers collaborate and use their knowledge and skills to create opportunities for the audience to form intellectual and emotional connections to the meanings and significance of archaeological records and the peoples who created them.

In the late 1990s, an interdisciplinary task group created a training module within IDP that strengthens the relationships between archaeology and public interpretation. The goal of the training is to make public archaeological presentation and interpretation more accurate and effective. The course of study calls for archaeologists, interpreters, educators, and others to be trained together in the skills and abilities (shared competencies) needed to carry out a successful interpretation program. It stems from a NPS-wide push to improve training and development of its employees and to promote better methods for interpreting archaeological resources. Courses and workshops are designed to improve interdisciplinary communication for a team approach to developing and carrying out effective public interpretation programs and projects. They utilize the universal standards and principals of public interpretation developed and promoted by the US National Park

Service and are designed for cross-cultural and international relevancy. Interpreters and educators gain knowledge of archaeology for developing presentations and media about archaeological resources. Archaeologists gain the foundation of knowledge and skills in interpretation necessary to develop interpretive presentations and media about cultural resources. All groups gain knowledge and skills through increased dialogue and interactions between archaeologists and interpreters for joint development of effective interpretation of archaeology. Two major goals of courses and workshops are to create opportunities for audiences to (1) learn about archaeological interpretations and how they are made, and (2) to ascribe their own meanings (values) to archaeological resources, helping to increase public understanding and concern for preservation and protection of archaeological values. The target audience for training workshops typically includes interpreters, park guides, education specialists, museum specialists, site managers, and archaeologists. The module is being applied at training courses and workshops at national park sites throughout the United States.

The "ICOMOS Charter for the Interpretation and Presentation of Cultural Heritage Sites" (Ename Charter) Initiative

This ICOMOS Charter for the Interpretation and Presentation of Cultural Heritage Sites (Current Draft, Appendix 1) drafted under the auspices of ICOMOS International and sponsored by Flemish governmental authorities, seeks to establish scientific, ethical, and public guidelines for the public interpretation of cultural heritage. Its aim is to "define the basic objectives and principles of site interpretation in relation to authenticity, intellectual integrity, social responsibility, and respect for cultural significance and context." It recognizes "that the interpretation of cultural heritage sites can be contentious and should acknowledge conflicting perspectives." The need for the charter stems from the recognition that the existing and extensive international charters, declarations, and guidelines that address conservation and restoration of the physical fabric of historic sites and places do not adequately define standards for interpretive and presentation treatments. With the steadily increasing investment by regional governments, municipalities, tourist authorities, private firms, and international organizations in expensive and technologically advanced presentation systems as a spur to tourist development, the need for the charter was clear (Ename Center 2005).

The main premise of the Draft Charter is that "Interpretation of the meaning of sites is an integral part of the conservation process" (Ename Center 2005). Prequelitus to the ICOMOS Ename Charter were a number of important international charters, declarations, and guidelines, including the Nara Document on Authenticity of 1994, the Burra Charter of 1999, and the International Charter on Cultural Tourism of 1999, that make some reference to interpretation. The Nara Document on Authenticity (1994) was composed by a consortium of representatives from the Japanese Agency for Cultural Affairs, UNESCO, ICCROM (International Centre for the Study of the Preservation and Restoration of Cultural Property), and ICOMOS. It stated that conservation of cultural heritage in all its forms and historical periods is rooted in the values attributed to the heritage, and that an understanding of these values depends, in part, on the degree to which information sources about these values can be understood as credible or truthful. The Burra Charter, initiated in Burra Burra, Australia, provided a roadmap for conservation and management best practices, recognizing the tangibles and intangibles of cultural heritage inclusive of indigenous cultural heritage. A key objective of the International Cultural Tourism Charter was to facilitate and encourage the tourism industry to promote and manage tourism in ways that respect and enhance the heritage and living cultures of host communities. All of theses previous charters had emphasized the fundamental role of sensitive and effective interpretation in heritage conservation (ICOMOS ICIP 2006a).

The November 2006 draft of the charter is a simplification of previous drafts' attempts to offer internationally relevant and acceptable definitions and principles. For the purposes of the charter, *interpretation* is defined as the full range of activities intended to heighten public awareness and enhance understanding of cultural heritage sites. Activities can include public lectures, formal and informal educational programs, community activities, as well as on-going research, training, and evaluation of the interpretation process itself. *Presentation* is distinguished from interpretation by more specifically denoting the carefully planned communication of interpretive content through the arrangement of interpretive information and physical access at a cultural heritage site. Presentation can be conveyed through a variety of technical means, including informational panels, museum displays, formalized walking tours, lectures, and multimedia applications. The draft charter defines *interpretive infrastructure* as all physical installations, facilities, and areas at a cultural heritage site utilized for the purposes of interpretation and presentation. *Site interpreters* are staff or volunteers at a cultural heritage site who are permanently or temporarily engaged in the public communication of information relating to the values and significance of the site (Ename Center 2006).

The charter *Principles* (Ename Center 2006) place emphasis on the essential roles of public communication and education in heritage preservation and are presented under seven general headings:

- Principle #1: Access and Understanding: Interpretation and presentation programmes should facilitate broad physical and intellectual access by the public to cultural heritage sites.
- Principle #2: Information Sources: Interpretation and presentation should be based on evidence gathered through accepted scientific and scholarly methods as well as from living cultural traditions.
- Principle #3: Context and Setting: The interpretation and presentation of cultural heritage sites should relate to their wider social, cultural, historical, and natural contexts and settings.
- Principle #4: Authenticity: The interpretation and presentation of cultural heritage sites must respect the basic tenets of authenticity in the spirit of the Nara Document (1994).
- Principle #5: Sustainability: The interpretive plan for a cultural heritage site must be sensitive to its natural and cultural environment, with social, financial, and environmental sustainability among its central goals.
- Principle #6: Inclusiveness: The interpretation and presentation of cultural heritage sites must actively involve the participation of associated communities and other stakeholders, recognizing the validity of diverse perspectives and interests while encouraging tolerance and mutual respect.
- Principle #7, Research, Evaluation, and Training: Continuing research, training, and evaluation are essential components of the interpretation of a cultural heritage site.

Subheadings under each principle provide elaboration and give examples and guidelines on how each principle should be internationally applied. On the surface, the principles are generally commonsensical in terms of conditions and prescriptions for effective public interpretation. Just *how* the principles are articulated, however, will determine how well they are received in international circles and whether they will be considered desirable, practical, and feasible. In countries with fragile or questionable human rights histories or poorly developed infrastructure, practical applications could be problematic.

The US/ICOMOS Charleston Declaration of 2005

International dialogue and reaction spurred by the ICOMOS Ename Charter initiative led ICOMOS to expand global discussions using the ICOMOS Ename Charter as a stimulus to guide and inform the process. In May 2005, in recognition of high public interest and the effects of mass tourism, the connections to current heritage management practices, and technological advancements, US/ICOMOS held a conference in Charleston, South Carolina, to better articulate a consensus on internationally applicable public interpretation principles. The main outcome of the conference was the Charleston Declaration on Heritage Interpretation (Appendix 2), issued on 7 May 2005. This document reiterated the importance and purpose of establishing a set of internationally relevant principles for interpretation and called for further international dialogue. The Declaration pointed out that additional clarifications were needed before the adoption of a doctrinal document on interpretation at the ICOMOS General Assembly in Quebec in 2008:

- defining mechanisms for incorporating stakeholder perceptions and values;
- providing guidance for interpretation of religious and sacred sites, places of contested significance, and sites of conscience or "painful memory;"
- defining the concept and role of "authenticity;" and
- determining how the categorization of heritage sites and the circumstances that surround them affect opposition or support among cultures and communities as well as the level of interpretation.

The newly formed (2006) ICOMOS International Scientific Committee for Interpretation and Presentation (ICIP) underlines the ICOMOS commitment to taking on the challenges of developing internationally relevant standards and definitions. The main task of the committee is to study the evolving methods, techniques, and technologies of public interpretation and presentation, evaluating their potential to enrich contemporary historical discourse and to heighten sensitivity to the universal values and particular modes of human expression embodied in cultural heritage sites. The work of the committee explicitly focuses on the experiential dimension of visits to cultural heritage sites, particularly by means of various media and methods of public communication. One major focus is to evaluate and revise the Ename Charter in preparation for its adoption as a doctrinal document by the ICOMOS General Assembly in 2008 (ICIP 2006).

The ICOMOS Ename Charter and the Charleston Declaration are important in that they address international standards of public interpretation through conservation and stewardship messages that relate to cultural heritage values. The use in the Charter of such terms as "responsibly" and "appropriateness" calls for careful scrutiny in how certain terms and expressions are worded and how well the Charter is ultimately accepted internationally.

Challenges for the present and future directions

The controversial concept and principle of "authenticity"

As is reflected in the Charleston Declaration, further discussions are needed on the concept and meaning of "authenticity" in interpretation. Traditional attitudes that focus on static, material authenticity will need to be replaced with more conditional and contextual definitions shaped by acknowledgement of dynamic processes of cultural change and diversity rather than judgments based on fixed criteria. Definitions of authenticity must be tempered or guided by local and community-based, inclusive, analyses. McDavid (2002;

chapter 37, this volume), for example, points out the importance of an inclusive, community-based approach in her discussion of archaeologists and local citizens who collaborated to create a Web site about politically and emotionally charged cultural heritage of an 18th-century sugar plantation. Any analysis model for authenticity should reflect and represent multiple perspectives on what is authentic or "true" about a site or place and should provide a roadmap for practical solutions. The nature and qualifications of "experts" on authenticity should reflect the diversity of cultural affiliations and values attributed to the site, which, in turn, should be periodically reviewed and reassessed.

Interpretation as a mechanism for resource sustainability

Many of the established principles for interpretation in the United States, as well as internationally, stem from the writing and philosophy of Freeman Tilden (Tilden 1957). Tilden defined interpretation as an educational activity that aims to reveal meanings and relationships through the use of original objects by firsthand experience and illustrative media, rather than to simply communicate factual information. Freeman's six principles emphasized relevance to the experience of the audience and interpretation as a teachable art form. According to Tilden, the chief aim of interpretation is not instruction, but provocation, and must address itself to the whole person rather than any phase. Tilden advocated what we would describe today as a "layered" approach to interpretation that takes into account the perspectives of a variety of audiences differentiated by age, socio-cultural background, and other factors.

Later advocates have built on the foundations of Tilden and applied post-modern theoretical approaches. Jon Kohl (2003), for example, defines interpretation in terms of a "paradigm," a deeply embedded set of beliefs that together form a story or worldview. Jon Kohl (2003), for example, defines interpretation in terms of a "paradigm or deeply embedded set of beliefs that together form a story or worldview." To Kohl, each culture has a story that explains its people's creation, significance, and destiny. This set of beliefs directs how they relate to resources. Kohl advocates expanding the scope and ultimate goal of interpretation beyond conservation goals toward an integration of "deep stories" that "carry it across the divide to conservation in the short term and sustainability of natural and cultural resources in the long." For interpreters, he says, these changes will first be felt in conservation, a sector of sustainable resource management, and then later for sustainability issues in general.

Kohl (2003) believes that effective interpretation in the future will involve a paradigm shift that re-writes the worldview script by interpreting new ideas and meanings in order to move society toward sustainability. The interpretation profession, he says, is the field closest to the theater stage, closer than filmmakers, educators, clergy, or even actors. It . . . "belongs to a broader family of persuasive communication tools such as rhetoric, social marketing, and environmental education." Interpreters in the future, he says, will be communication strategists targeting leverage points in society to help move its worldview toward sustainability. They will expand their focus beyond site-specific resource protection to the larger system of information and beliefs that affect how civilization treats natural and cultural entities. They will no longer, he contends, refer to other species as "resources" for humans.

Heritage and tourism

Heritage management in the West is increasingly focused on preservation (especially resource integrity), public interpretation issues, and on developing analytical and technological competencies. Because of the increasingly diverse and multicultural nature of audiences, training programs are shifting in emphasis from an academic to an increasingly applied focus. Professional or formal training of local staff is necessary to ensure that high standards are maintained and are, for many regions, internationally portable. The challenge is to ensure that high standards of skill and competency are accepted, welcomed, and valued at local and community levels (US/ICOMOS 2004).

In many developing countries, heritage management is emerging as a critical component of national economies to promote tourism and to structure development initiatives. Development schemes focus on sustainable concepts that encourage both the preservation of resources and the recognition of socio-economic values of local people. And, hopefully, these schemes involve participative decision-making and learning processes attuned to the culture and traditions (i.e. values) of the people affected (US/ICOMOS 2004).

It has been said that tourists are alienated people seeking authenticity as a form of fulfillment (MacCannell 1973). At heritage sites, authenticity is offered through presentation of information and by experts along with physical and sensory trappings such as exhibits, 3-D reconstruction, audio-visuals sounds, smells, and special effects. The terms "authenticity" and "integrity" are often linked in meaning in that the latter can mean unspoiled or unadulterated authentic materials. "Authenticity" and "integrity" as terms can be seen as representing the values of preservationists, such as archaeologists and architectural historians.

Globalization is changing our world in ways that we are just beginning to understand. Heritage tourism, with its ties to the currents of rapidly evolving global economies, is causing increasing needs and demands for cross-cultural and international communication and interdisciplinary training. Emphasis is on transferable skills such as the application of interdisciplinary approaches, writing for both academic and non-academic audiences, oral presentation, and experience with multimedia packages.

We should keep in mind that one effect of globalization is that prescriptions for authenticity, integrity, and most concepts associated with modern and standardized definitions of historic preservation originated in Western systems of classification and ranking, that is, the notion that heritage is an *inclusive possession of all humanity* belonging to no one individual. Concepts such as "world heritage site," "national park," and other forms of commemoration developed within Western philosophical traditions. Who is in charge at heritage sites? They are usually Western or Western-trained. In the United States, for the most part, they are found in government and museums. What values in society do they reflect?

As mentioned above in the discussion of values-based management schemes, the use of non-market valuation studies can help us manage and interpret heritage resources to minimize the conflicts between market-based tourism interests and non-market-based preservation values. Identification of a heritage site's total value in terms of both market (tourism) value and non-market (preservation) value will enable decision makers to enact more accurate and effective management decisions and policies. This approach can be especially useful in high profile, complex, and controversial management settings such as the Stonehenge World Heritage Site in the UK.

It is important for those of us who manage, study, and present the past to be aware of how the past is understood within the context of socio-economic and political agendas and how that influences what is taught, and how it is valued, protected, authenticated, and used. We must understand the philosophical, political, and economic forces that affect how sites and parks are managed. We know that archaeological resources, as well as the built environment, are being affected. Dwindling budgets and reductions in personnel are exacerbating the problem. Political currents are threatening to weaken long-standing principles, standards, and commitments to public stewardship. Heritage tourism pressures have become important elements of interpretive messages at parks, historic sites, and museums.

Continuing debates on the values of reconstruction versus preservation-in-place

A lingering source of controversy in CHM since the 1930s has been the debate over the pros and cons of reconstructions versus preservation-in-place. The main focus of discussion for archaeologists has been on the appropriate level of archaeological investigations and knowledge needed prior to on-site reconstructions and whether reconstructions of *any* nature are appropriate when *in situ* materials will be damaged or destroyed.

The philosophical arguments for and against the practice of reconstructing historical and archaeological sites can be traced to developments of the conservation movement of the 19th and early 20th centuries. Other developments, such as the opening of Colonial Williamsburg by the Rockefeller foundation in 1933, helped focus public attention on the values of historic preservation. At Colonial Williamsburg, a reconstructed historic community of the 1770s was based on detailed historical and limited archaeological research. These reconstructions proved to be immensely popular with the public. The reconstruction technique at Colonial Williamsburg involved recreating over 450 buildings in an effort to completely restore the town. Lack of specific information on a particular building presented no problem to project designers and architects, who relied on architectural precedents and an examination of surviving colonial buildings in the region to invent building types based on general architectural practices of the period (in this case, the middle to late 18th-century). These planners and architects saw life in 18th-century Virginia as more homogenous and genteel than do historians today. This popular, yet conjectural, technique became the standard applied to hundreds of reconstructions in the United States for decades to come. It pervaded and guided the work of the National Park Service and other federal agencies in scores of New Deal public works projects carried out in the years preceding World War II. By the late 1940s and 1950s, historic preservation as the commemoration of sites and structures associated with famous people and events had entered the mainstream of public consciousness. The resulting collection of national and state historic sites, monuments, and parks, as well as an abundance of privately administered buildings and sites, became standard fare for an increasingly mobile American public (Jameson 2004).

In the National Park Service, the US government's leading preservation agency, policies for reconstruction have always been a source of controversy among staff professionals. This policy calls for reconstructions to occur only after thorough archaeological investigations have been carried out. Archaeological research provides details of architectural design not available in existing records and contributes further information on the uses and cultural contexts of architectural features and material objects. NPS defines "reconstructions" as measures to preserve any remaining prehistoric or historic materials, features, and spatial relationships. It is based on the accurate duplication of features documented through archaeology, archival research, or physical evidence, rather than on conjectural designs. In most cases, methodology is not restricted to the technology of the period. By inference, reconstructions may include the use of modern materials and tools only if these do not conflict with the purpose of "replicating its appearance." Reconstructions differ from restorations in that they involve *new* construction of various components of the cultural landscape, such as buildings, huts, towns or villages, earthworks, living areas, trails, and roads (Jameson 2004; Jameson and Hunt 1999).

The international nature of the debates on the pros and cons of reconstructions were featured in an international colloquium at Beziers, France, in 2005. This conference was organized by the French Center of the National Monuments (MONUM), French Ministry for Culture and Communication, and examined international definitions and standards for reconstructions in Europe (emphasis reconstructed on Roman ruins) and North America (Jameson 2006).

In the United States as elsewhere, the "value" of reconstructions often goes beyond

any scientific, educational, or conservation considerations to premeditated or desired outcomes that are also influenced by a blend of other factors such as societal morality, politics, local economy, and tourism. In a representative democracy such as the United States,
the determining factors for creating any given national park unit revolve around these
issues. Despite agency policies that have generally discouraged the use of reconstructions
as public interpretation tools, a wide variance in the National Park System has developed
between sites that have virtually no reconstructions, such as at Jamestown, Virginia, to
parks that depend almost entirely on reconstructions in their public programs, such as Fort
Vancouver National Historic Site, Washington, which has a reconstructed stockade and
five major buildings (Jameson 2004; Stone 1999).

Archaeology as inspiration through art and imagery

Many archaeologists today are not content to rely solely on traditional methodologies and
analytical techniques in their attempts to reconstruct human history and bring it to life for
the public. They want to venture beyond utilitarian explanations and explore the interpretive potential of cognitive imagery that archaeological information and objects can inspire.
They realize the value and power of artistic expression in helping to convey archaeological
information to the public. Archaeologists are increasingly concerned with how the past is
presented to, and consumed by, non-specialists. They want to examine new ways of communicating archaeological information in educational venues such as national parks,
museums, popular literature, film and television, music, and various multimedia formats
(Jameson et al. 2003).

In order to provide a richer conceptual imagery to the accounts of prehistoric lifeways
and to augment the large collection of available photographs, the authors of *Beneath These
Waters*, the award-winning popular history account set in rural South Carolina and Georgia,
made use of original paintings commissioned by the National Park Service from an artist. The
two original oil paintings produced as illustrations greatly enhanced the attractiveness of the
volume and also provide iconic imagery for use in educational Web sites, public awareness
posters, and other publications. The paintings depict prehistoric scenes based on published
archaeological findings, adding an entertaining, yet informative dimension not commonly
seen in government-sponsored popular accounts (Figures 33.1 and 33.2).

Archaeology and archaeologically derived information and objects have inspired a
wide variety of artistic expressions ranging from straightforward computer-generated
reconstructions and traditional artists' conceptions to other art forms such as poetry and
opera. Although some level of conjecture will always be present in these works, they are
often no less conjectural than technical interpretations and have the benefit of providing
visual and conceptual imagery that can communicate contexts and settings in compelling
ways. Two such interpretive formats, two-dimensional paintings and popular history
writing, are used by the National Park Service as public interpretation and education tools
(Jameson 1999, 2000).

Archaeology in popular history writing

Too often, among the flood of reports and artifacts that have come from CRM studies,
archaeologists lose sight of the real purpose of the compliance process: to provide public
enjoyment and appreciation for the rich diversity of past human experiences. An important, and some would say the *most* important, outcome of CRM mitigation programs is the
production of publications, programs, and exhibits that provide public access to research
findings.

Figure 33.1   Sara's Ridge Archaic Site, oil painting by Martin Pate. Courtesy, Southeast Archaeological Center, National Park Service.

Figure 33.2   Rucker's Bottom Prehistoric Village, oil painting by Martin Pate. Courtesy, Southeast Archaeological Center, National Park Service.

It is generally accepted today, among cultural heritage mangers and specialists that *both* quality research and the public interpretation of research findings are indispensable outcomes of their work. After all, is not the ultimate value of archaeological studies not only to inform but also ultimately to improve the public's appreciation of the nature and relevance of cultural history? This improved appreciation results in enhanced public stewardship and improved quality of life for people.

Exhibits and popular history writing are two of the most effective communication modes for public interpretation of archaeology. To be successful, both techniques must not only inform but entertain. The goals are to connect, engage, inform, and inspire, resulting in a lasting and improved appreciation of the resource.

One of the most prolific and effective writers of popular histories in cultural heritage has been Professor Brian Fagan of the University of California, Santa Barbara. Now retired from the university, Fagan has an impressive track record in archaeological and cultural heritage popular writing. His books have covered wide ranging topics in prehistory that allow public audiences to connect emotionally and intellectually to past eras. In *The Little Ice Age* (2000), for example, Fagan takes advantage of the public's preoccupation with the concept of global warming. He spins an interesting tale of how changing sea temperatures caused English and Basque fishermen to follow concentrations of cod fish all the way to the New World; how English efforts to improve farm productivity in the face of a deteriorating climate helped pave the way for the Industrial Revolution and our modern dilemma of global warming. In *Fish on Friday* (2006), Fagan gives us a thought-provoking, well-researched explanation for early European exploration: navigational innovations were motivated by ordinary seamen seeking fish, a preservable commodity that was considered a delicacy in Europe during the Middle Ages. With a compelling analysis of the various claims regarding who reached the New World first, Fagan adds to his engaging writing style by sprinkling the text with fish recipes through time.

Fagan has said that modern archaeologists too often have fallen under the influence of the publish or perish syndrome in academia that encourages overspecialization, "We also lack people who have an expertise as generalists, who look at the bigger picture and are willing to . . . share our enthusiasm and science with the broadest possible audience from grade school onwards. Archaeologists," Fagan says, "have a responsibility both to share their results with the local people *and* help in training future generations of *local* professionals: publication in *American Antiquity* is *not* sufficient. Archaeologists, he says, "will increasingly become involved with CRM, to the point it will be the dominant activity. I think that in academic terms, there will be more and more laboratory research, as collections are curated and reanalyzed." Fagan espouses ". . . a new marriage between archaeologists and tourism – one of the great neglected areas of archaeology" (SCA 2002; ref. above discussion of heritage tourism).

In another example, an important outcome of the Richard B. Russell (RBR) CRM program in the southeastern United States was the production of publications and exhibits that would provide public access to the findings of the RBR studies. In 1985, the US Army Corps of Engineers established an on-site public exhibit and brochure derived from the results of the RBR Cultural Resources Mitigation Program. The exhibit continues to be maintained at the Richard B. Russell Project Office near Elberton, Georgia. In the production of the Richard B. Russell popular history volume, *Beneath These Waters*, the National Park Service and the US Army Corps of Engineers placed heavy emphasis on producing a popular account that is both informative and entertaining. The resulting exhibits and publications, when coupled with the technical work, make the Richard B. Russell Cultural Resources Mitigation Program an exemplary model on a global scale, both in providing high quality research and public access to research findings.

In preparing *Beneath These Waters*, the National Park Service chose a team of professional writers adept at the art of effectively translating technical information for the lay public. Contract writers Sharyn Kane and Richard Keeton, because they were not formally trained archaeologists or historians and were unfamiliar with the world of federal contracting, faced distinct disadvantages in taking on the task of writing these books. However, as they poured over the various technical archaeology and history reports, they realized that this estrangement from technical know-how had given them an important advantage in writing the RBR popular history: nearly complete objectivity in viewing the overall project and its results, unencumbered by the predictable baggage of professional biases, cultivated styles, and emotions attached to a project of this magnitude and importance. The authors' task was to take the results of these two decades of research, strip them down to the essentials, and reclothe them in a fashion readily acceptable to a general audience without losing the fundamental integrity of the original material (Kane *et al.* 1994). The universal praise of *Beneath These Waters* from the educational, scientific, and local communities attests to the book's success in providing informative and inspirational access to research findings.

Conclusions

The last decades have witnessed a dynamic period of evolving standards and philosophy in public archaeology and heritage interpretation. Philosophical approaches and techniques exemplified by the US National Park Service's IDP program have formed a basis for the development of international definitions, standards, and approaches that lead to more effective strategies for site protection and conservation through enhanced public stewardship. Discussions on issues such as authenticity and inclusiveness will continue to dominate international debates about the significance and proper use of sites. The challenges for international relevance and application posed by the ICOMOS Ename Charter initiative will form the center of future debates and deliberations. The goal of more inclusive interpretations will require an acceptance of divergent definitions of authenticity that depend on a level of tolerance of multiple definitions of significance with concomitant, objectively derived, assigned and ascribed heritage values. Cost–benefit analyses for site management and interpretation schemes should be carried out and include the identification and consideration of both market and non-market values. We can hope that these efforts lead to the recognition of the full array of public values that are reflected in heritage tourism practices, as well as site commemoration and protection decisions by controlling authorities.

References

Baxter, I. and Chippindale, C. 2002. From 'national disgrace' to flagship monument: recent attempts to manage the future of Stonehenge. *Conservation and Management of Archaeological Sites 5*, 151–184.

BLM (Bureau of Land Management) 2006. *Project Archaeology*, http://www.projectarchaeology.org/.

DeCunzo, Luann, and Jameson, John H., Jr (eds) 2005. *Unlocking the Past: Celebrating Historical Archaeology in North America*, Gainesville: University Press of Florida.

De la Torre, Marta 2003. *Assessing the Values of Cultural Heritage*. The Getty Conservation Institute, Los Angeles: The J. Paul Getty Trust.

De la Torre, Marta, MacLean, Margaret G., and Myers, David 2003. *Chaco Culture National Historical Park, U.S. National Park Service, a Case Study*. The Getty Conservation Institute, Los Angeles: The J. Paul Getty Trust.

Derry, Linda and Malloy, Maureen 2003. *Archaeologists and Local Communities: Partners in Exploring the Past*. Washington, DC: Society for American Archaeology.

Fagan, Brian M. 2000. *The Little Ice Age: How Climate Made History, 1300–1850*, New York: Basic Books.

Fagan, Brian M. 2006. *Fish on Friday: Feasting, Fasting and the Discovery of the New World*, New York: Basic Books.

Field Museum 2006. Education, http://www.fieldmuseum.org/education/default.htm.

Gibb, James G. 2003. The Archaeologist as Playwright. In *Ancient Muses: Archaeology and the Arts*. John H. Jameson, Jr, John E. Ehrenhard, and Christine A. Finn (eds). Tuscaloosa: University of Alabama Press.

ICOMOS ICIP 2006. Interpretation and Presentation of Cultural Heritage Sites, http://icip.icomos.org/ENG/home.html.

ICOMOS ICIP 2006. Mission Statement, http://icip.icomos.org/ENG/about_missionstatement.html

ICOMOS ICIP 2006. The ICOMOS Charter for the Interpretation and Presentation of Cultural Heritage Sites, Fifth Draft, Revised under the Auspices of the ICOMOS International Scientific Committee on Interpretation and Presentation, 1 November.

Jameson, John H., Jr 2000. Public Interpretation, Education and Outreach: The Growing Predominance in American Archaeology. In *Cultural Resource Management in Contemporary Society, One World Archaeology 33*, Francis P. McManamon, and Alf Hatton (eds). Routledge: London and New York.

Jameson, John H., Jr 2003. Purveyors of the Past: Education and Outreach as Ethical Imperatives in Archaeology. In *Ethical Issues in Archaeology*, Larry Zimmerman, Julie Hollowell-Zimmer and Karen Vitelli (eds). Walnut Creek: AltaMira Press.

Jameson, J.H., Jr 2006. The Reconstructed Past: Glories, Perils, and Dilemmas. Revision of paper originally presented during "Restitution in archaeology and presentation with the public" international colloquium, Enséruné/Béziers, Herault, France, October 2005. Copy on file at the Southeast Archeological Center, National Park Service, Tallahassee, Florida.

Jameson, John H., Jr (ed.) 1997. *Presenting Archaeology to the Public: Digging for Truths* . Walnut Creek: AltaMira Press.

Jameson, John H., Jr (ed.) 1999. *Archaeology and the National Park Idea: Challenges for Management and Interpretation*. The George Wright Forum 16 (4).

Jameson, John H., Jr 2004a. Public Archaeology in the United States. In *Public Archaeology*, Nick Merriman (ed.). Routledge: New York and London, pp. 21–58.

Jameson, John H., Jr (ed.) 2004b. *The Reconstructed Past: Reconstructions in the Public Interpretation of Archaeology and History*. Walnut Creek: AltaMira Press.

Jameson, John H., Jr, Ehrenhard, John E., and Finn, Christine A. (eds) 2003. *Ancient Muses: Archaeology and the Arts*. Tuscaloosa: University of Alabama Press.

Jameson, John H., Jr and Baugher, Sherene 2007. *Past Meets Present: Archaeologists Partnering with Museum Curators, Teachers and Community Groups*. New York: Springer.

Jameson, John H., Jr and Hunt, William J. 1999. Reconstruction vs. Preservation-in-place in the National Park Service. In *The Constructed Past: Experimental Archaeology, Education and the Public, One World Archaeology 36*, Peter G. Stone (ed.). Routledge: London and New York.

Jameson, John H., Jr and Scott-Ireton, Della 2007. *Out of the Blue: Public Interpretation of Maritime Cultural Resources*. New York: Springer.

Jeppson, P.L. 1997. Levelling the Playing Field in the Contested Hhistory of the South African Past: A 'Public' Versus a 'People's' Form of Historical Archaeology Outreach. *Historical Archaeology* 31, 65–83.

Kane, Sharyn and Keeton, Richard 1993. *Beneath these Waters: Archeological and Historical Studies of 11,500 Years Along the Savannah River*. Atlanta: Interagency Archeological Services Division, Southeast Region, US National Park Service, and Savannah: US Army Corps of Engineers, Savannah District.

Kane Sharyn, Keeton, Richard, and John H. Jameson, Jr 1994. A Publication for the Public

The Richard B. Russell Cultural Investigations Popular Volume, online article dated April 20, 1994, http://www.cr.nps.gov/seac/beneath.htm, 2006.

Kohl, Jon 2003. *Interpreters and the Big Story, Parts 1–3. Legacy* (July–December), National Association for Interpretation, Fort Collins, Colorado. Online text at URL: http://www.jonkohl.com/publications/legacy-pubs/article1.htm, http://www.jonkohl.com/publications/legacy-pubs/article2.htm, and http://www.jonkohl.com/publications/-legacy-pubs/article31.htm, accessed 22 June 2005.

Larsen, David L. (ed.) 2003. Meaningful Interpretation: How to Connect Hearts and Minds to Places, Objects and Other Resources. Fort Washington: Eastern National.

Little, Barbara J. 2002. *Public Benefits of Archaeology*. Gainesville: University Press of Florida.

Little, Barbara J. 2004. Is the medium the message? The art of interpreting archaeology in the U.S. National Parks. In *Marketing Heritage: Archaeology and the Consumption of the Past*, Yorke Rowan and Uzi Baram (eds). Walnut Creek: AltaMira Press.

MacLean, Margaret G.H. and Myers, David 2003. *Grosse Île and the Irish Memorial National Historic Site, Parks Canada, A Case Study*. The Getty Conservation Institute. Los Angeles: The J. Paul Getty Trust.

Mason, Randall, Myers, David, and de la Torre, Marta 2003a. *Port Arthur Historic Site, Port Arthur Historic Site Management Authority, A Case Study*. The Getty Conservation Institute. Los Angeles: The J. Paul Getty Trust.

Mason, Randall, MacLean, Margaret G.H., and de la Torre, Marta 2003b. *Hadrian's Wall World Heritage Site, A Case Study*. The Getty Conservation Institute. Los Angeles: The J. Paul Getty Trust.

McCarthy, John P. 2003. More than Just "Telling the Story": Interpretive Narrative Archaeology. In *Ancient Muses: Archaeology and the Arts*, John H. Jameson, Jr, John E. Ehrenhard, and Christine A. Finn (eds). Tuscaloosa: University of Alabama Press.

McDavid, C. 2002. Archaeologies that Hurt: Descendents that Matter: A Pragmatic Approach to Collaboration in the Public Interpretation of African-American Heritage. *World Archaeology* 34 (2), 303–314.

McManamon, F. 2000. Archaeological Messages and Messengers. *Public Archaeology 1*. Reply by Holtorf and response by McManamon.

McManamon, Francis P. and Hatton, Alf (eds) 2000. *Cultural Resource Management in Contemporary Society, One World Archaeology 33*. London and New York: Routledge.

NAI (National Assciation for Interpretation) 2005. National Association for Interpretation: Mission, Vision, and Core Values. http://www.interpnet.com/about_nai/mission.shtml.

Nethery, W.H. 1999. Beyond Compliance: Things and Places, Hearts and Minds. Paper delivered at the NPWS Heritage Interpretation and Education Program Development Workshop, 19 October.

NPS (US National Park Service) 2005. Module 440: Effective Interpretation of Archeological Resources, http://www.nps.gov/idp/interp/440/module.htm.

NPS IDP (US National Park Service, Interpretive Development Program) 2006. The Interpretive Development Program, Aiming for High Ground, http://www.nps.gov/idp/interp/, accessed on June 15.

Poor, P. Joan 2007. The Economics of Archaeological Resource Management. Paper delivered at a forum organized by the Advisory Council on Historic Preservation, entitled "Heritage Tourism and Archaeology – Challenges and Opportunities," Annual Meeting of the Society for Historical Archaeology, Williamsburg, Virginia.

Potter, Parker B. 1997. The Archaeological Site as an Interpretive Environment. In *Presenting Archaeology to the Public: Digging for Truths*, John H. Jameson, Jr. (ed.). Walnut Creek: AltaMira Press.

SCA (Society for California Archaeology) 2002. Brian Fagan Interview, http://www.scahome. org/educational_resources/2002_Fagan.html.

SEAC (Southeast Archeological Center, US National Park Service) 2006. *Unlocking the Past: Celebrating Historical Archaeology in North America: A Public Outreach Project of the Society for Historical Archaeology*, http://www.cr.nps.gov/seac/Unlocking-web/index.htm.

Smardz, Karolyn 1997. The Past Through Tomorrow: Interpreting Toronto's Heritage to a Multicultural Public. In *Presenting Archaeology to the Public: Digging for Truths*, John H. Jameson, Jr (ed.). Walnut Creek: AltaMira Press.

Smardz, Karolyn and Smith, Shelley (eds) 2000. *Sharing Archaeology with Kids: A Handbook of Strategies, Issues, and Resources in Archaeology Education*. Walnut Creek: AltaMira Press.

South, Stanley 1997. Generalized Versus Literal Interpretation. In *Presenting Archaeology to the Public: Digging for Truths*, John H. Jameson, Jr (ed.). Walnut Creek: AltaMira Press.

Stone, Peter G. and Mackenzie R. (eds) 1990. *The Excluded Past: Archaeology in Education, One World Archaeology 17*. Routledge: London and New York.

Stone, Peter G. and Brian L. Molyneaux (eds) 1994. *The Presented Past: Heritage, Museums, and Education, One World Archaeology 25*. Routledge: London and New York.

Stone, Peter G. and Phillippe G. Planel (eds) 1999. *The Constructed Past: Experimental Archaeology, Education and the Public, One World Archaeology 36*. Routledge: London and New York.

Stone, P.G. 2006. Stonehenge – a final solution?, *Public Archaeology* 5 (2).

Tilden, Freeman 1957. *Interpreting Our Heritage: Principles and Practices for Visitor Services in Parks, Museums, and Historic Places*. New York: Van Rees Press.

US/ICOMOS (2004). 8th Annual US/ICOMOS International Symposium on 'Heritage Interpretation Call for Papers', http://www.icomos.org/usicomos/Symposium/Call for Abstracts.htm.

Uzzell, D. and Ballantyne, R. 1999. Heritage that Hurts: Interpretation in a Postmodern World. In *Contemporary Issues in Heritage and Environmental Management*, D. Uzzell and R. Ballantyne (eds) 152–171. The Stationery Office.

Appendix 1: The ICOMOS Charter for the Interpretation and Presentation of Cultural Heritage Sites (2006 Draft)

FIFTH DRAFT
Revised under the Auspices of
the ICOMOS International Scientific Committee
on Interpretation and Presentation

12 December 2006

Preamble
Definitions
Objectives
Principles

Preamble

Since its establishment in 1965 as a worldwide organization of heritage professionals dedicated to the study, documentation, and protection of cultural heritage sites, ICOMOS has strived to promote the conservation ethic and to help enhance public appreciation of humanity's material heritage in all its forms and diversity.

As noted in the Charter of Venice (1964) "It is essential that the principles guiding the preservation and restoration of ancient buildings should be agreed and be laid down on an international basis, with each country being responsible for applying the plan within the framework of its own culture and traditions." Subsequent ICOMOS charters have taken up that mission, establishing professional guidelines for specific conservation challenges and encouraging effective communication about the importance of heritage conservation in every region of the world.

These earlier ICOMOS charters stress the importance of public communication as an essential part of the larger conservation process (variously describing it as "dissemination," "popularization," "presentation," and "interpretation"). They implicitly acknowledge that every act of heritage conservation – within all the world's cultural traditions – is by its nature a communicative act.

For the vast range of surviving material remains of past communities and civilizations, the choice of what to preserve, how to preserve it, and how it is to be presented to the public are all elements of site interpretation. They represent every generation's vision of what is significant, what is important, and why material remains from the past should be passed on to generations yet to come.

The need for a clear rationale, standardized terminology, and accepted professional principles for Interpretation and Presentation (see definitions below) is evident. In recent years, the dramatic expansion of interpretive activities at many cultural heritage sites and the introduction of elaborate interpretive technologies and new economic strategies for the marketing and management of cultural heritage sites have created new complexities and aroused basic questions that are central to the goals of both conservation and the public appreciation of cultural heritage sites throughout the world:

- What are the accepted and acceptable goals for the Interpretation and Presentation of cultural heritage sites?
- What principles should help determine which technical means and methods are appropriate in particular cultural and heritage contexts?
- What ethical and professional considerations should help shape Interpretation and Presentation regardless of its specific forms and techniques?

The purpose of this Charter is therefore to define the basic principles of Interpretation and Presentation as essential components of heritage conservation efforts and as a means of enhancing public appreciation and understanding of cultural heritage sites.[1]

Definitions

For the purposes of the present Charter,

Interpretation refers to the full range of potential activities intended to heighten public awareness and enhance understanding of cultural heritage sites. These can include professional and popular publications, public lectures, on-site installations, formal and informal educational programmes; community activities; and ongoing research, training, and evaluation of the interpretation process itself.

Presentation more specifically denotes the carefully planned communication of interpretive content through the arrangement of interpretive information, physical access, and interpretive infrastructure at a cultural heritage site. It can be conveyed through a variety of technical means, including, yet not requiring, such elements as informational panels, museum-type displays, formalized walking tours, lectures and guided tours, and multimedia applications.

Interpretive infrastructure refers to physical installations, facilities, and areas at a cultural heritage site that may be specifically utilized for the purposes of interpretation and presentation.

Site interpreters refers to staff or volunteers at a cultural heritage site who are permanently or temporarily engaged in the public communication of information relating to the values and significance of the site.

Cultural Heritage Site refers to a locality, natural landscape, settlement area, architectural complex, archaeological site, or standing structure that is recognized and often legally protected as a place of historical and cultural significance.

Objectives

In recognizing that interpretation and presentation are part of the overall process of cultural heritage conservation and management, this Charter seeks to establish seven cardinal principles, upon which Interpretation and Presentation – in whatever form or medium is deemed appropriate in specific circumstances – should be based.

Principle 1: Access and Understanding
Principle 2: Soundness of Information Sources
Principle 3: Attention to Setting and Context
Principle 4: Preservation of Authenticity
Principle 5: Planning for Sustainability
Principle 6: Concern for Inclusiveness
Principle 7: Importance of Research, Evaluation, and Training

Following on from these seven principles, the objectives of this Charter are to:

1   **Facilitate understanding and appreciation** of cultural heritage sites and foster public awareness of the need for their protection and conservation.
2   **Communicate the meaning** of cultural heritage sites through careful, documented recognition of their significance, through accepted scientific and scholarly methods as well as from living cultural traditions.
3   **Safeguard the tangible and intangible values** of cultural heritage sites in their natural and cultural settings and social context.
4   **Respect the authenticity** of cultural heritage sites, by communicating the significance of their historic fabric and cultural values and protecting them from the adverse impact of intrusive interpretive infrastructure.
5   **Contribute to the sustainable conservation** of cultural heritage sites, through promoting public understanding of ongoing conservation efforts and ensuring long-term maintenance and updating of the interpretive infrastructure.
6   **Encourage inclusiveness** in the interpretation of cultural heritage sites, by facilitating the involvement of stakeholders and associated communities in the development and implementation of interpretive programs.
7   **Develop technical and professional standards** for heritage interpretation and presentation, including technologies, research, and training. These standards must be appropriate and sustainable in their social contexts.

Principles

Principle 1: Access and Understanding

Interpretation and presentation programs, in whatever form deemed appropriate and sustainable, should facilitate physical and intellectual access by the public to cultural heritage sites.

1.1   Effective interpretation and presentation should enhance experience, increase public respect and understanding, and communicate the importance of the conservation of cultural heritage sites.

1.2   Interpretation and presentation should encourage individuals and communities to reflect on their own perceptions of a site and establish a meaningful connection to it by providing insights – as well as facts. The aim should be to stimulate further interest and learning.

1.3   Interpretation and presentation programs should identify and assess their audiences demographically and culturally. Every effort should be made to communicate the site's values and significance to its varied audiences.

1.4   The diversity of language among visitors and associated communities connected with a heritage site should be reflected in the interpretive infrastructure.

1.5   Interpretation and presentation activities should also be physically accessible to the public, in all its variety.

1.6   In cases where physical access to a cultural heritage site is restricted due to conservation concerns, cultural sensitivities, adaptive re-use, or safety issues, interpretation and presentation should be provided off-site.

Principle 2: Information Sources

Interpretation and presentation should be based on evidence gathered through accepted scientific and scholarly methods as well as from living cultural traditions.

2.1   Interpretation should show the range of oral and written information, material remains, traditions, and meanings attributed to a site. It should also clearly identify the sources of this information.

2.2   Interpretation should be based on a well researched, multidisciplinary study of the site and its surroundings, but should also acknowledge that meaningful interpretation also necessarily includes reflection on alternative historical hypotheses, local myths, and stories.

2.3   At cultural heritage sites where traditional storytelling or memories of historical participants provide an important source of information about the significance of the site, interpretive programs should incorporate these oral testimonies – either indirectly, through the facilities of the interpretive infrastructure, or directly, through the active participation of members of associated communities as on-site interpreters.

2.4   Visual reconstructions, whether by artists, architects, or computer modelers, should be based upon detailed and systematic analysis of environmental, archaeological, architectural, and historical data, including analysis of written, oral and iconographic sources, and photography. The information sources on which such visual renderings are based should be clearly documented and alternative reconstructions based on the same evidence, when available, should be provided for comparison.

2.5   Interpretation and presentation activities and the research and information sources on which they are based should be documented and archived for future reference and reflection.

Principle 3: Context and Setting

The Interpretation and Presentation of cultural heritage sites should relate to their wider social, cultural, historical, and natural contexts and settings.

3.1   Interpretation should explore the significance of a site in its multi-faceted historical, political, spiritual, and artistic contexts. It should consider all aspects of the site's cultural, social, and environmental significance.

3.2   The public interpretation of a cultural heritage site should always clearly distinguish and date the successive phases and influences in its evolution. The contributions of all periods to the significance of a site should be respected.

3.3   Interpretation should also take into account all groups that have contributed to the historical and cultural significance of the site.

3.4   The surrounding landscape, natural environment, and geographical setting are all integral parts of a site's historical and cultural significance, and, as such, should be taken into account in its interpretation.

3.5   Intangible elements of a site's heritage such as cultural and spiritual traditions, stories, music, dance, theater, literature, visual arts, personal customs and cuisine should be noted and included in its interpretation.

3.6   The cross-cultural significance of heritage sites, as well as the range of perspectives about them based on scholarly research, ancient records, and living traditions, should be considered in the formulation of interpretive programs.

Principle 4: Authenticity

The Interpretation and presentation of cultural heritage sites must respect the basic tenets of authenticity in the spirit of the Nara Document (1994).

4.1   Authenticity is a concern relevant to human communities as well as material remains. The design of a heritage interpretation program should respect the traditional social functions of the site and the cultural practices and dignity of local residents and associated communities.

4.2   Interpretation and presentation should contribute to the conservation of the authenticity of a cultural heritage site by communicating its significance without adversely impacting its cultural values or irreversibly altering its fabric.

4.3   All visible interpretive infrastructure (such as kiosks, walking paths, and information panels), when deemed appropriate and necessary must be sensitive to the character, setting and the cultural and natural significance of the site, while remaining easily identifiable.

4.4   On-site concerts, dramatic performances, and other interpretive activities – when deemed appropriate and sensitive to the character of the site – must be carefully planned to minimize disturbance to the local residents and to the physical surroundings of the site.

Principle 5: Sustainability

The interpretive plan for a cultural heritage site must be sensitive to its natural and cultural environment, with social, financial, and environmental sustainability among its central goals.

5.1   The development and implementation of interpretation and presentation programs should be an integral part of the overall planning, budgeting, and management process of cultural heritage sites.

5.2 The potential effect of interpretive infrastructure and visitor numbers on the cultural value, physical characteristics, integrity, and natural environment of the site must be fully considered in heritage impact assessment studies.

5.3 Interpretation and presentation should serve a wide range of educational and cultural objectives. The success of an interpretive program should not be judged solely on the basis of visitor attendance figures or revenue.

5.4 Interpretation and presentation should be an integral part of the conservation process, enhancing the public's awareness of specific conservation problems encountered at the site and explaining the efforts being taken to protect the site's physical integrity.

5.5 Any technical or technological elements selected to become a permanent part of a site's interpretive infrastructure should be designed and constructed in a manner that will ensure effective and regular maintenance.

5.6 Interpretive activities should aim to provide equitable and sustainable economic, social, and cultural benefits to the host community at all levels, through education, training, and the creation of economic opportunities. To that end, the training and employment of site interpreters from the host community should be encouraged.

Principle 6: Inclusiveness

The Interpretation and Presentation of cultural heritage sites must be the result of meaningful collaboration between heritage professionals, associated communities, and other stakeholders.

6.1 The multidisciplinary expertise of scholars, conservation experts, governmental authorities, site managers, tourism operators, and other professionals should be integrated in the formulation of interpretation and presentation programs.

6.2 The traditional rights, responsibilities, and interests of property owners, nearby residents, and associated communities should be noted and respected in the planning of site interpretation and presentation programs.

6.3 Plans for expansion or revision of interpretation and presentation programs should be open for public comment and involvement. It is the right and responsibility of all to make their opinions and perspectives known.

6.4 Because the question of intellectual property and traditional cultural rights is especially relevant to the interpretation process and its expression in various communication media (such as on-site multimedia presentations, digital media, and printed materials), legal ownership and right to use images, texts, and other interpretive materials should be discussed and clarified in the planning process.

Principle 7: Research, Evaluation and Training

Continuing research, training, and evaluation are essential components of the interpretation of a cultural heritage site.

7.1 The interpretation of a cultural heritage site should not be considered to be completed with the completion of a specific interpretive infrastructure. Continuing research and consultation are important to furthering the understanding and appreciation of a site's significance and should be integral elements in every heritage interpretation program.

7.2   The interpretive program and infrastructure should be designed and constructed in a way that ensures periodic content revision and/or expansion.

7.3   Interpretation and presentation programs and their physical impact on a site should be continuously monitored and evaluated, and periodic changes made on the basis of both scientific and scholarly analysis and public feedback. Visitors and members of associated communities as well as heritage professionals should be involved in this evaluation process.

7.4   Every interpretation program should be seen as an educational resource and its design should take into account its possible use in school curricula, communications and information media, special activities, events, and seasonal volunteer involvement.

7.5   The training of qualified professionals in the specialized fields of heritage interpretation and presentation, such as content creation, management, technology, guiding, and education, is a crucial objective. In addition, basic academic conservation programmes should include a component on interpretation and presentation in their courses of study.

7.6   On-site training programs and courses should be developed with the objective of updating and informing heritage and interpretation staff of all levels and associated and host communities of recent developments and innovations in the field.

7.7   International cooperation and sharing of experience are essential to developing and maintaining standards in interpretation methods and technologies. To that end, international conferences, workshops and exchanges of professional staff as well as national and regional meetings should be encouraged. These will provide an opportunity for the regular sharing of information about the diversity of interpretive approaches and experiences in various regions and cultures.

Note to Appendix 1

1   Although the principles and objectives of this Charter may equally apply to off-site interpretation, its main focus is interpretation and presentation at, or in the immediate vicinity of, cultural heritage sites.

Appendix 2: The Charleston Declaration on Heritage Interpretation (2005)

Charleston Declaration on Heritage Interpretation
7 May 2005
Charleston, South Carolina, USA

On the occasion of the 8th International Symposium of US/ICOMOS, "HERITAGE INTERPRETATION, Expressing Heritage Sites Values to Foster Conservation, Promote Community Development, and Educate the Public," approximately 200 delegates from all over the United States, more than a dozen nations and several disciplines met in Charleston, South Carolina, from 5 to 8 May 2005, to share experience, draw lessons and address issues surrounding the public interpretation of cultural heritage sites.

The symposium benefited from continuing scholarly and professional discussion of the methods and philosophy of heritage interpretation in many regions of the world and the ongoing review and revision process of the ICOMOS Ename Charter on the Interpretation of Cultural Heritage sites, drafted under the scientific auspices of ICOMOS and sponsored by the government of the Province of East-Flanders and the Flemish Community of Belgium. This document seeks to establish an international consensus on the scientific, ethical, and educational principles for the public presentation and interpretation of cultural heritage.

US/ICOMOS, the Ename Center, and other organizations and individuals are embarking on a multi-year program of activities connected with the charter initiative, in order to facilitate the development of site interpretation principles and techniques. Although the objectives and principles of this Charter deal primarily with interpretation at, or in the immediate vicinity of cultural heritage sites, they may equally apply to off-site interpretation.

The need for such a document has become clear in recent years, as regional governments, municipalities, tourist authorities, private firms, and international organizations have become increasingly concerned with the importance of communicating heritage values and information to the general public, investing in expensive and technologically advanced presentation systems as a spur to tourist development. Yet while there are a large number of international charters, declarations, and guidelines to maintain the quality of the conservation of the physical fabric of ancient monuments and the management of cultural heritage sites, there is no generalized international consensus on the methods and quality standards of public interpretation.

In the current draft of the charter, reviewed by the International Scientific and National Committees of ICOMOS, principles of cultural heritage interpretation were formulated in order to:

- Facilitate understanding and appreciation of cultural heritage sites and foster public awareness of the need for their conservation. The effective interpretation of a wide range of heritage sites across the world can be an important medium for intercultural and intergenerational exchange and mutual understanding.
- Communicate the meaning of cultural heritage sites through careful, documented recognition of their significance, including their tangible and intangible values, natural and cultural setting, social context, and physical fabric.
- Respect the authenticity of cultural heritage sites, by protecting their natural and cultural values and significant fabric from the adverse impact of physical alterations or intrusive interpretive infrastructure.
- Contribute to the sustainable conservation of cultural heritage sites, through effective financial planning and/or the encouragement of economic activities that safeguard conservation efforts, enhance the quality of life of the host community, and ensure long-term maintenance and updating of the interpretive infrastructure.
- Ensure inclusiveness in the interpretation of cultural heritage sites, by fostering the productive involvement of all stakeholders and associated communities in the development and implementation of interpretive programs.
- Develop technical and professional standards for heritage interpretation, including technologies, research, and training. These standards must be appropriate and sustainable in their social contexts.
- The aim of the ICOMOS Ename Charter is thus to define the basic objectives and principles of site interpretation in relation to authenticity, intellectual integrity, social responsibility, and respect for cultural significance and context. It further recognizes that the interpretation of cultural heritage sites can be contentious and should acknowledge conflicting perspectives.
- Based on the proceedings of this conference, we propose the following definition and recognition of the conceptual and operational difference between "Presentation" and "Interpretation":

"Presentation" denotes the carefully planned arrangement of information and physical access to a cultural heritage site, usually by scholars, design firms, and heritage professionals. As such, it is largely a one-way mode of communication. "Interpretation," on the other hand, denotes the totality of activity, reflection, research, and creativity stimulated by a cultural heritage site. The input and involvement of visitors, local and associated community groups, and other stakeholders of various ages and educational backgrounds is essential to interpretation and the transformation of cultural heritage sites from static monuments into places and sources of learning and reflection about the past, as well as valuable resources for sustainable community development and intercultural and intergenerational dialogue.

We also recognize that there is still much to do. The following are major areas where clarification and consensus are still needed, and to which special attention is needed:

- Incorporating stakeholder perceptions and values in interpretation programs remains a challenge.
- The interpretation of religious and sacred sites, places of contested significance, and sites of conscience or "painful memory" needs further analysis in terms of establishing acceptable boundaries and better guidance as to their interpretation.
- In spite of years of expert discussion, the concept of "authenticity" continues to be elusive. Additional research and discussion is needed to define its nature and role in heritage interpretation.
- Certain cultures and communities oppose or prefer alternative methods for the public interpretation of their cultural heritage sites. This requires a continuing dialogue and analysis of how heritage site categories and the circumstances that surround them should influence the decision to interpret as well as the level of interpretation.
- These fundamental areas of inquiry will be the focus of discussion and other activities in the coming three years. By approaching the topic of interpretation from many geographic, cultural, and professional directions, we believe that a consensus can be reached that may serve as a source of guidance in the proper interpretation of heritage sites.

Proposed at the US/ICOMOS 8th International Symposium at Charleston, South Carolina, 7 May 2005

Appendix 3: Selected Reprints

The following chapters in Section Four are a collection of exemplary and key works that attempt to provide case studies that are geographically diverse. Taken in conjunction with this introductory chapter, they represent a combination of established principles and new thinking in public interpretation that have emerged since the 1980s. Two broad themes that crosscut these presentations are developments in effective engagement with audiences and communities and a trend toward inclusiveness in providing multivocal interpretations that connect to wider-ranging public audiences.

Chapter 34. McManamon, F. 2000. Archaeological messages and messengers. *Public Archaeology* 1. Reply by Holtorf and response by McManamon.

This seminal piece and accompanying discussions published in 2000 outline the importance of outreach as part of the presentation of archaeology and archaeological resources that also promotes public stewardship. Another important message in these discussions is the recognition of the validity of multivocality and of multicultural and multidimensional values in archaeological messages. The article also stresses the need for archaeologist practitioners to collaborate with their public communication colleagues in parks, museums, and schools.

Chapter 35. Jeppson, P.L. 1997. Levelling the playing field in the contested history of the South African past: a "public" versus a "people's" form of historical archaeology outreach. Historical Archaeology 31, 65–83.

Patti Jeppson was one of the first public archaeologists to espouse the importance of public engagement and methods to achieve inclusiveness in interpretations. She presents an overview of the complex and changing research context in South Africa and its implications for a historical archaeology study of South African frontier identity. Research and "public" archaeology efforts concerning material and mythical perspectives of ethnicity are discussed. Employed in a cross-context comparison with African-American research, this study highlights the need for decolonized historical archaeology outreach. The paper argues that historical archaeology can provide both a methodology and raw materials which South Africans can use to form their own interpretations of their past, helping, in turn, to engender pride through a historical consciousness emancipated from colonial and apartheid ideology.

Chapter 36. Uzzell, D. and Ballantyne, R. 1998. Heritage that hurts: interpretation in a postmodern world. In D. Uzzell and R. Ballantyne (eds), *Contemporary Issues in Heritage and Environmental Management*, 152–171. The Stationery Office.

The authors use examples from Europe, Africa, and Australia to demonstrate what they term as "hot interpretation" and the degree to which emotions color memories and experience. The article is notable in that it was among the first publications to rebuke the common misconception that emotion, and emotional connections to resource meanings, should be deemphasized in public interpretation programs and exhibits at cultural heritage sites. Especially if one substitutes the word "hot" for "emotion" or "emotional," the text suits modern interpretation standards terminology perfectly.

Chapter 37. McDavid, C. 2002. Archaeologies that hurt; descendents that matter: a pragmatic approach to collaboration in the public interpretation of African-American heritage. *World Archaeology* 34 (2), 303–314.

This article examines a community-based project in Barzoria, Texas, in which archaeologists and local citizens have collaborated to create a Web site to discuss the politically and emotionally charged archaeologies and histories of an 18th-century sugar plantation. It concludes with a discussion on whether post-processual strategies (multivocality, interactivity, reflexivity, contextuality) were effective in creating an open, relevant, democratic, and multivocal discourse about archaeology.

Chapter 38. Baxter, I. and Chippindale, C. 2002. From "national disgrace" to flagship monument: recent attempts to manage the future of Stonehenge. *Conservation and Management of Archaeological Sites 5*, 151–184.

Baxter and Chippindale provide a thorough overview of the attempts to improve public presentation at Stonehenge. The paper identifies seven enduring essentials of the Stonehenge problem along with three obstacles to progress. The present provision is described, and four schemes for transformation are then reported and analyzed. The story of the history and plethora of social and political complexities and management dilemmas involved at the site and its associated cultural landscape is a textbook case. This discussion can be compared to Peter Stone's (2006) "Stonehenge – a final solution?" article that reiterates, and to some extent updates, the descriptions and dilemmas associated with Stonehenge as perhaps the world's most renowned, iconic, and challenging of managed heritage sites. Stone describes four newer alternative options for management that may lead to a final "unfortunate" decision on how the World Heritage site will be managed.

Chapter 39. McCarthy, John P. 2003. More than Just "Telling the Story": Interpretive Narrative Archaeology. In *Ancient Muses: Archaeology and the Arts*. Tuscaloosa: University of Alabama Press.

This article is important in that it articulates the proposition that "archaeological knowledge" is expanding and broadening to be more inclusive and accepting and less authoritative – a broadening of the meaning of "expert." One important development is the emergence of the interpretive narrative approach in archaeological interpretation, where archaeologists actively participant in structuring a compelling story instead of just presenting sets of derived data. McCarthy describes the modern trend of archaeologists to use a narrative approach in presenting and interpreting data, and making it meaningful to broader audiences. Sometimes described as simple story telling, this interpretive approach often uses the third person with a goal of making the results of archaeological research more relevant and meaningful to the members of the public in whose interests such work is undertaken. These narratives are strongly grounded in archaeological and historical data, but generally follow a "microhistory" approach in which broad social patterns are described through the detailed study of specific events and individual experiences. McCarthy describes this trend toward narrative, places it in context, and assesses its potential to fundamentally change how archaeologists think about and conduct research.

Chapter 40. Gibb, James G. 2003. The Archaeologist as Playwright. In *Ancient Muses: Archaeology and the Arts*. Tuscaloosa: University of Alabama Press.

James Gibb follows McCarthy in the 2003 *Ancient Muses* volume, further illuminating the modern trend in archaeological interpretation toward narrative using the example of playwriting. Gibb starts by explaining that stage plays can teach through aesthetic experience, creating settings in which facts, figures, and historical relationships are depicted in an integrated, meaningful manner. Plays also can serve as tools for exploring the past, the archaeologist–playwright experimenting with interactions among individual roles and larger historical events, first on paper and then in production. The use of interpretive historical fiction in general, and playwriting specifically, acknowledges the limitations of mainstream theoretical approaches, but does not reject them: on the contrary, the imaginative use of drama elicits insights into the actions and motivations of past peoples, and their use of artifacts, that may be testable through more conventional approaches. Gibb illustrates this approach with a discussion of two plays that he wrote and produced at the London Town historic site in Edgewater, Maryland.

Chapter 34

Archaeological Messages and Messengers

Francis P. McManamon

Archaeological resources include important places and objects of commemoration and remembrance. Properly investigated, they provide interpretations of pasts that are often inaccessible otherwise. Although there seems to be an inherent public curiosity about and interest in archaeology and archaeological resources, the nature of these are not well understood. Also, we know very little about how the public absorbs information about archaeology. Information on both of these topics is being accumulated, but much remains to be learned and utilised. Public outreach should be, and increasingly is, in fact, an important consideration in all professional archeological studies. Professional archaeologists in all branches of the discipline should engage in public outreach according to their abilities and opportunities. They also should support such efforts by their colleagues.

Introduction

Archaeological resources are non-renewable and unique remains that, with proper investigation and study, can inform us about what happened in the past. If studied carefully and cleverly enough, archaeological remains can give us ideas about why things happened as they did. Because they are non-renewable and unique, these remains must be used frugally. The greatest benefit of archaeological resources is what we can learn about the past from them and the links they have as material remains to important past events, individuals or historical processes. The examples and specifics discussed in this article relate to the United States; however, the issues considered are similar to those confronted in many nations around the globe, as suggested by examples in articles in recent collections of international scope (Cleere 1989; Stone and MacKenzie 1989; Stone and Molyneaux 1994; McManamon and Hatton 2000).

Many Americans are interested in archaeology and the connection it can make with the past. For some this interest takes the form of intellectual curiosity, an affinity with a particular place or time that connects them with the past or a cultural connection. For others, fortunately only a relative few, it has to do with personal or financial exploitation.

Those concerned about the accurate interpretation of the archaeological record and its long-term preservation and use must recognise these different interests. They also should work to improve public access to archaeology and the understanding of its interpretive and preservation goals.

Too many professional archaeologists are still uninterested in public education and outreach. They are unwilling to devote more of their own professional activity to it or to set higher priorities for it among the activities of the institutions where they work (Smith 1993; McManamon 1998; Sabloff 1998). Brian Fagan (1993) has justifiably lashed out at such 'arrogant archaeologists' and their lamentably myopic inattention. The contemporary mistreatment of archaeological sites and the distortion of archaeological interpretation by looters, misdirected hobbyists, some developers and different kinds of charlatans is a great concern to all in the field.

Rather than inattention and neglect, archaeologists and others interested in archaeological interpretation and preservation need to devote more professional energy to public education and outreach. Doing so requires a better understanding of what and how non-archaeologists think about archaeology, archaeological resources, and the benefits they provide. A great deal has been accomplished, especially during the last decade, yet much remains to be done and most of what is underway requires continued efforts (e.g. McManamon 1991a; 1994b; Jameson 1997; Lerner and Hoffman 2000). We must develop effective means of spreading accurate interpretations of the ancient, historic and recent past based upon scientific archaeology. We must show more persuasively the benefits of these insights and this perspective. Education and outreach activities for the general public need to be diverse to accommodate the range of interests and levels of knowledge about archaeology. These efforts need to be undertaken nationally, regionally, statewide and in local communities (McManamon 1998).

Why is public outreach important?

Providing a tangible, accessible return through interpretation products and programmes in order to maintain or build public support is often given as the justification for public education and outreach in archaeology. Yet other important reasons exist for these efforts. Fundamentally, we must realise that the interpretation of the archaeological record for general audiences, as well as its protection, is simply too important to leave to others. The interests of some others, e.g. looters and treasure hunters, after all, involve the commercial exploitation of the archaeological record or its wanton destruction by other means (Herscher and McManamon 1995; Lynott and Wylie 1995, 28; Sabloff 1998, 871–874).

This same problem exists in the broader context of public understanding, or misunderstanding, of science. In his 1993 President's Lecture to the American Association for the Advancement of Science, F. Sherwood Rowland (1993; 1571) addressed this topic:

> We live in the midst of massive information flow, but those items connected with science itself are often badly garbled, sometimes with potentially serious negative consequences.

The results of poor understanding range from simple cases of inconsequential ignorance or misinformation, to large and costly errors of judgement, to widespread misunderstanding or deceit such that:

> the scientific community . . . [has] lost control of what gets described as science. The designation 'scientific' often is applied as a kind of public rela-

tions cover for projects whose true origin is in economic activity unable to prosper on its own merits.

(op cit., 1575)

Surely archaeologists can recall archaeological examples that fit this range of misunder-standings? Archaeology, in fact, may be more susceptible to public misunderstanding and misinterpretation, as examples from ancient astronauts to Indiana Jones testify. These public misconceptions are sometimes harmless, such as the common misunderstanding that prehistoric humans and dinosaurs coexisted. With some forethought and skill, the interest that non-archaeologists have about archaeology can help correct such misunder-standings and be used to enhance the interest.

More serious and potentially damaging are pseudo-archaeologists, or individuals per-ceived by an under-informed public as carrying out archaeological investigations (Sabloff 1998, 872–873). Von Daniken, Barry Fell and Mel Fisher come to mind in this context. Feder (1990; 1998), Wauchope (1962) and Williams (1988; 1991) have described in detail many historic and current examples of such misguided interpretations.

The recent lack of political support in the United States for the scientific investigation of the archaeological record has been startling. This has been most noticeable in the face of claims by some Native Americans for control over all or parts of archaeological sites. Con-trast this with the substantial political support, even initiative, from influential national legislators during the mid- and late 1970s. At that time, substantial legal protection for archaeological resources and the need for archaeological investigations as part of planning for public undertakings were recognised as important. Legislation was sponsored and sup-ported actively by Representatives and Senators from many parts of the country. Frank Moss, Charles Bennett, Pete Domenici, Jeff Bingaman and Mo Udall were only the most active and prominent supporters. At that time the threats to the archaeological record were from wanton destruction in the face of Federal construction projects and from rapa-cious looters (Davis 1972; Friedman 1985; McGimsey 1985; 1989; McManamon 1991b).

Today's challenges, some of them legitimate and supported by many archaeologists (e.g. Klesert 1992; McManamon 1994a), are not necessarily equivalent to those of the 1970s. Yet the recent absence of political acknowledgement that scientific study of the archaeological record is important, beneficial and in the nation's interest, is disconcerting. Clearly, more cultivation of interest and support among the political portion of the Ameri-can public is warranted.

The implicit or explicit political power of interpretations of the past (see Lowenthal 1985; 1996), including those based upon archaeological information, establish an impor-tance in public interpretation beyond funding and support. Advocates of this perspective emphasise that archaeologists must not only provide interpretations, but also explain how they are constructed in order that the informed public comes to understand not only the past, but also its use in the present (e.g. Leone and Potter 1992; Leone and Preucel 1992; Potter 1994).

Another major justification for public education programmes is that actions by indi-viduals often decide whether individual archaeological sites are preserved or destroyed. Law-abiding and conscientious citizens will not vandalise or loot sites if they can be con-vinced that these actions are often illegal and diminish the cultural heritage left to all people. Through their own public outreach efforts, archaeologists must be among those spreading these messages. Some people are even willing to work actively to promote site protection and preservation by helping to monitor the existing condition of archaeological sites through regular observation and reporting to preservation authorities about site con-dition (e.g. Davis 1990, 1; 1991; Hoffman 1991).

It is not only from looting and vandalism that archaeological sites must be protected. Individuals and groups of concerned citizens are among the most effective means of working for the protection of sites in local development schemes and land use plans. Individuals among the general public can serve as the eyes and ears of local, state or even national officials who are responsible for archaeological preservation. Certainly, there are not enough trained archaeologists in the United States to serve such a widespread monitoring function, nor will there ever be.

Despite all the challenges presented to those who want to improve public understanding and appreciation of archaeology and the preservation of archaeological sites, archaeology is a subject with apparently inherent public appeal. Brian Fagan, an archaeologist both prolific and successful in educating the public, noted this based upon his own experience and provided a succinct rationale for why this inherent public interest must be cultivated actively:

> Archaeology is almost unique among the sciences in having an interested public following. In this time of eroding archaeological records, wholesale looting, vandalism, and social condoning of pot hunting, good press relations are a basic responsibility of any late 20th century archaeologist.
>
> (Fagan 1991, 18)

This inherent interest might provide fertile ground, but it must be cultivated. An active, informed public, supportive of archaeology and archaeological preservation can serve as an invaluable source of political, voluntary and economic backing. If archaeological sites are to be preserved for the very long term, and if archaeological administration, planning, investigations, reporting and curation are to be supported for the long term, more and better public education must become an actively pursued and highly regarded part of the discipline of archaeology.

What are the public benefits of archaeology?

There are two kinds of benefits derived from archaeological sites and interpretations of the past based upon archaeological data. These benefits are realised both by individuals and by groups or communities. The first benefit results from the fact that archaeological sites are places associated with specific people and events. These associations sometimes result in sites being used in the commemoration of the individual(s), events or general pattern that the site is related to. The second benefit is derived from the fact that archaeological sites are sources of information about specific events and general cultural and historical patterns, derived through proper study of their contents, structure and locations.

Associative and commemorative value

Archaeological sites are real places where real events took place. Knowing about these places and having a sense of what happened at them provide an important temporal context for modern life. Such places and knowledge about them plan an essential role in 'sustaining the American heritage and the American community' (Kennedy 1997, 33).

The historian David Lowenthal (1985, xxiii), commenting on this appreciation of archaeological and historical places, has noted that:

> memory and history both derive and gain emphasis from physical remains. Tangible survivals provide a vivid immediacy that helps to assure us there really was a past. Physical remains have their limitations as informants, to be sure; they are themselves mute, requiring interpretation; their continual but

differential erosion and demolition skews the record; and their substantial survival conjures up a past more static than could have been the case. But however depleted by time and use, relics remain essential bridges between then and now. They confirm or deny what we think of it, symbolise or memorialise communal links over time, and provide archaeological metaphors that illumine the processes of history and memory.

These associations are derived by individuals who use the archaeological and historical context provided by places to evaluate their own family, career or other personal conditions. In some situations these associations benefit modern communities, by enhancing social cohesion through the bond of a shared historical context. Members of a modern city or town may associate themselves with the deep archaeological, cultural or historical roots of their habitat, using this connection to build a spirit of community involvement.

Tourism is another benefit that sometimes results from archaeological and historical sites. This benefit, which typically is mixed with costs, is derived when people from elsewhere visit a place to enjoy the archaeological or historical sites in or near the community, enhancing the local economy in the process.

That Americans recognise and appreciate the association of archaeological sites and their commemorative benefit is proven by the large number of such places identified as national, state, regional and local parks and sites throughout the nation. Some archaeological places are associated with specific events or individuals, such as Franklin Court in Philadelphia, Jamestown National Historical Site (NHS), Little Big Horn NHS, Monticello and Mount Vernon. Others commemorate broader historical patterns or periods in American history and prehistory, such as Saugus Ironworks NHS in Massachusetts, Hopewell Culture National Historic Park (NHP) and Serpent Mound State Memorial in Ohio, Etowah Indian Mounds State Historic Site in Georgia, Moundville State Monument in Alabama, Cahokia Mounds State Historic Site in Illinois, Pecos NHP and the Pueblo of Acoma in New Mexico, and Casa Grande Ruins National Monument and Pueblo Grande City Park in Arizona. These brief listings mention only a very few of the rich national assortment of archaeological and historic places that draw tourists intent upon visiting them and other nearby sites and parks. More lengthy lists with informative summaries can be found in Folsom and Folsom (1993) and Thomas (1994).

Tourism interest in archaeological and historic sites is substantial. Millions of Americans and foreign visitors tour these sites and museums displaying and interpreting United States history and prehistory yearly. National guidebooks for archaeological sites and museums have been produced (Folsom and Folsom 1993; Thomas 1994) listing hundreds of historic and prehistoric sites that can be visited in the United States and Canada. Periodically, *National Geographic* magazine also provides such a listing and a map to go with it, most recently in the October 1991 issue as part of its commemoration of the Colombian Quincentennial. Annually in the May–June issue *Archaeology* magazine lists dozens of archaeological sites and active excavations in North, Middle, and South America that can be visited or that accept volunteer workers. Regional archaeological travel guides also have been published, for example for the southwest (Noble 1991), for the Ohio Valley (Woodward and McDonald 1986) and, for the Atlantic Coast (McDonald and Woodward 1987). Information about public sites to visit can be found on websites associated with many archaeological organisations (e.g. in the 'Ancient Architects of the Lower Mississippi' pages at www.cr.nps.gov/aad/feature, and for many archaeological sites in the southeast at www.cr.nps.gov/seac/seac.htm).

The associative benefit of archaeological and historical places for individuals and communities also has an economic aspect. Visitors spend dollars during their visits. The state of New Mexico, for example, reports that $293 million flow directly into the state from visitors coming to visit cultural resources or take part in cultural activities, such as performing arts events, festivals and fairs. This tourism infusion leads to $1.6 billion in overall spending (New Mexico 1995). The number of visitors who come to the state to visit the archaeological and historic sites, museums and Indian reservations is 8.2 million of the estimated 19 million visitors who come to the state for appreciation of cultural activities of one sort or another.

In addition to the potential economic benefits, archaeology enriches communities by focusing energy and enthusiasm. Spin-offs from individual projects have rippled through communities touching public schools, museums, neighbourhood actions, street names and the design of public places. Baltimore (Peters *et al.* 1987), Alexandria, Virginia (Cressey 1987), Pensacola (Bense 1991; 1995), St Augustine (Smith and Piatek 1993), Tucson (Ellick 1991), Flagstaff (Phagan and Pilles 1989) and other parts of Arizona (Hoffman 1991) are only a few examples of local archaeological programmes with community involvement at their core. Pam Cressey, City Archaeologist for Alexandria, Virginia, was not exaggerating when she wrote:

> every community in America has an archaeological heritage that, if managed properly as a public resource, can help us recognise and celebrate the accomplishments of our predecessors. Archaeology brings the American legacy to life.
>
> (Cressey 1987, 6)

All archaeology, like politics, is local. In a few instances, archaeological discoveries have national or international import, but they always have local interest.

> Few archaeologists will ever find a pharaoh's tomb or buried gold . . . most finds are of purely local, or perhaps regional, importance, even sometimes, frankly dull. But the information that comes from them is of more than passing local significance and educational value. This is where archaeologists can work miracles with public relations, provided they develop close links with the local media.
>
> (Fagan 1991, 18)

Here is another important rationale for local focus in archaeological programmes and projects. Good relationships with local broadcasters and reporters are important and the means of developing and fostering these kinds of relationships are not secret. Archaeologists in many places have discovered how to do this and have published advice for all to read and use (e.g. Potter and Leone 1987; DeCicco 1988; Hoffman and Lerner 1988; Potter 1990; Lerner 1991; Potter 1994).

In addition to personal considerations and reflections, the commemorative benefit of archaeological places may act on a wider social scale. For example, the ancient monumental architecture found in the midwestern and southeastern United States, from the upper Mississippi and Ohio valleys to the Gulf Coast, might provide inspiration for broader social harmony. Roger Kennedy (1994, 1–6) notes that these prehistoric examples of engineering and complex human social organisation ought to give modern Americans a greater appreciation of the achievements and potential of non-Western cultures and their modern descendants. From such an enhanced appreciation might come increased tolerance.

It is important to recognise that many people may have views of the past and places associated with it that differ substantially from those held by archaeologists or historians with their research-based knowledge. Using such public perceptions about heritage effectively may be crucial for site preservation and obviously must be dealt with in order to ensure accurate interpretation programmes.

For Native Americans, the cultural associations with ancient archaeological sites are more direct. These links hold special commemorative value associated with ancient histories of creation, special events and epic journeys. Links between traditional histories and archaeological sites provide opportunities for archaeologists to work directly with Native Americans to examine the ways that their different approaches to understanding the past are complimentary (e.g. Deloria 1992; Reid 1992a; 1992b; Echo-Hawk 1993; 1997; Klesert and Downer 1990). Pyburn and Wilk (1995) urge archaeologists and native people to take advantage of this challenge and opportunity:

> Archaeology can be used in the service of native people by reconstructing some of the heritage that has been lost through conquest and deprivation. Archaeologists can also offer real support for developing tourism, jobs, crafts industries, self-respect, education, and public awareness. It is absolutely crucial that archaeological reconstructions not be framed as 'gifts from the archaeologists', but as the results of scientific research, which is a technique of understanding that is useful and available to anyone.
>
> (Pyburn and Wilk 1995, 72)

In order for this to work effectively, however, each side must not only respect the position of the other, but also be able and willing to be effective advocates of their own perspective. The benefits of an archaeological approach to investigations and understanding the past must be pressed by its supporters (McManamon 1994a, 19).

Cultural associations also are possible for other groups of Americans in relation to historic period sites. Jamestown in Virginia, early European settlement sites in Canada, New England, the southeast and the southwest hold cultural associations for Americans of European background. African Americans recently experienced a cultural connection with the unexpected discovery, investigation, and after some controversy, commemoration of the African Burial Ground in lower Manhattan, New York City.

Lowenthal (1996, x–xiii) distinguishes between the personal or community associations with places that commemorate the past and historical or archaeological knowledge about the past. He uses the term 'heritage' to describe the latter and 'history' for the former. His point and distinction is important because it illuminates how individuals and communities actually use the past, both places that commemorate it and information about it.

> In domesticating the past we enlist it for present purposes. Legends of origin and endurance, of victory or calamity, project the present back, the past forward; they align us with forebears whose virtues we share and whose vices we shun. We are apt to call such communion history, but it actually is heritage. The distinction is vital. History [and archaeology] explore and explain pasts grown ever more opaque over time; heritage clarifies pasts so as to infuse them with present purposes.
>
> (Lowenthal 1996, xi)

Educational and information value

The second major benefit of archaeological resources is the more general information that can be learned about the past through the proper investigations. This information helps us to understand larger patterns of the past, for example, the development of human settlement or land use over a large area, or the development of agriculture or a certain kind of technology. Lipe (1996, 23) has noted that its ability to provide information about the past is the principal benefit of archaeology:

the primary social contribution of archaeology . . . [is] the production and dissemination of new information about the past based on the systematic study of the archaeological record . . . most sites in fact gain their primary social value because they have the potential to contribute new information about the past when subjected to archaeological study.

The value of information about the past that can be learned from the resources of course overlaps with the associative and commemorative benefit already described. Sense of place and historical context are enhanced by interpretations derived from archaeological investigations. The importance of the scientific investigation of archaeological sites for information about the past, rather than haphazard, individual collecting of artefacts, was established as public policy in the United States by the Antiquities Act of 1906 (Lee 1970; McManamon 1996). This statute stated that the public benefits of the information and artefacts recovered were the primary reasons for allowing archaeological investigations on the public lands controlled by the national government.

Educators, and by extension their students, have discovered that archaeology can provide stimulating subject matter for teaching a wide range of subjects (Rogge and Bell 1989; Stone and MacKenzie 1989; articles in Smith and McManamon 1991; Stone and Molyneaux 1994; Smith and Smardz in press). Fay Metcalf, a distinguished American educator, experienced and familiar with issues at the local, state and national levels, recognises the excitement and intrigue that archaeological approaches and information can bring to formal education. She points out that using material culture, its spatial context and archaeological methodology promotes complex thinking skills involving the evaluation of data, the construction of inferences and the flexibility of interpretations (Metcalf 1992).

National and international archaeological organisations, like the Archaeological Institute of America, the Society for American Archaeology and the Society for Historical Archaeology, all have active committees working on integrating archaeology into formal educational systems (e.g. anonymous 1991; Smith 1993; Messenger 1994; Few *et al.* 1995; Messenger 1995; Society for American Archaeology 1995; O'Brien and Cullen 1996; Smith 1998). Several specialised newsletters and web pages have been created focusing on teaching of archaeology and anthropology in elementary and secondary schools. One of the most useful for teachers seeking background information on anthropological and archaeological topics is *Anthro Notes*, published by the Department of Anthropology, National Museum of Natural History, the Smithsonian Institution (Selig and London 1998). The National Park Service (www.cr.nps/aad/teach.html), the Public Education Committee of the Society for American Archaeology (Smith 1998; www.saa.org/Education/education.html), and the Archaeological Institute of America (O'Brien and Cullen 1996; www.archaeology.org) are among the national organisations that have compiled and published on the web educational information for teachers to use in developing classroom information about archaeology. In the United States, many public agencies at all levels of government also have recognised the utility of this approach and have active programmes with formal educational systems (e.g. articles in Hawkins 1988; Charles and Walden 1989; Williams 1989; Ellick 1991; Butler 1992; Smith *et al.* 1992; Jameson 2000; Lerner and Hoffman 2000).

Teaching archaeology has obvious connections with history, geography and social studies (e.g. Selig 1991; Metcalf 1992; Shull and Hunter 1992; MacDonald 1995; Smith 1995; Lavin 1996). All American schoolchildren learn United States history, state history and ancient history at least twice during a normal 12-year exposure to elementary and secondary education. Information from archaeological investigations can address United States prehistory, early contact between Native Americans and European colonists, and later periods of US history (e.g. MacDonald 1995). Along with classic texts and ancient writings, archaeology is one basic source of information about ancient civilisations. Many teachers have found that incorporation of archaeological information and discussions of how the investigation of material remains, can illuminate aspects of history, stimulates student interest. Archaeological examples also can provide intriguing introductions to topics in biology, chemistry and physics. For example, radiocarbon dating is a practical and interesting application with which to launch a discussion of general atomic structure; two and three dimension coordinate geometry can be explored using standard archaeological horizontal and vertical recording of artefacts and features.

The public's understanding of archaeology

Archaeologists' knowledge about the kinds of archaeological subjects that are of most interest to the public, how well the public understands archaeological interpretations and most other aspects of the public's understanding of archaeology, is practically non-existent. Understanding the levels of knowledge and views of the general public about archaeology is an important component of effective public outreach. Only a few public surveys have been carried out to date and these have been of limited geographical scope. For example, public surveys of different groups of students at Central Connecticut State University and a sample of households in Vancouver, British Columbia, have been reported (Feder 1984; Feder 1987; Pokotylo and Mason 1991; Feder 1995; Pokotylo and Guppy 1999).

By and large the results have shown that there is not a very clear understanding by non-archaeologists of archaeological facts, or a clear distinction between scientifically derived inferences and fanciful interpretations offered by promoters of ancient space alien contacts or literal readings of the Bible. Feder's (1995) investigation in this area is particularly interesting because he was able to compare two similar samples of college students at a ten-year interval. His interpretation of the results is sobering. He found no substantial difference between the two groups of students, separated by ten years, in their knowledge about general archaeological interpretations. Feder concluded that, despite the substantial amount of energy devoted to public education and outreach by the archaeological community in the past decade, noticeable improvement could not be detected in the responses from his recent sample of students.

Pokotylo and Mason (1991) found similar confusion about archaeological facts in their survey of 550 households in Vancouver, British Columbia. For example, over half the respondents, included 'fossils, such as dinosaurs', among objects studied by archaeologists. A more encouraging result of the Vancouver survey is the high degree of interest or potential interest in archaeology expressed by the respondents. Ninety-three per cent of them had visited a museum that had archaeological exhibits and 61% had visited a historic or archaeological site. Eighty-four per cent responded that archaeology was relevant to modern society and 67% indicated that they wanted more information about archaeology made available to the public. David Pokotylo and his colleagues have continued their public survey efforts. A recent report affirms the general observations made in their past investigations and provides additional details (Pokotylo and Guppy 1999)

These results are comparable to public surveys from the late 1980s in Great Britain and the United States concerning interest and 'literacy' in science (Culliton 1988; Hively 1988; Durant et al. 1989). These surveys suggest that only about 5% of Americans are truly scientifically literate, about 25% are informed or interested in science and the remaining 70% are not well-informed or knowledgeable about scientific topics. Lawler (1996) reported more recently on a United States survey with very similar results. The good news from this public attitude research is that a large majority of the public has a positive view of science and is supportive of scientific endeavours in general. If these survey results are reasonable approximations of actual attitudes and potential public interest regarding archaeology, they suggest fertile ground for effective public education about archaeology. But, the ground must be cultivated to achieve fruitful results.

A recent public survey funded by The History Channel and conducted by Roper and Starch, an American public opinion polling firm, provides a closer analogue for gauging general public interest in archaeology (Roper and Starch 1995). This survey used telephone interviews to poll a national cross-section of 1,004 adult Americans. The results are encouraging for archaeologists, if, as seems reasonable, it is legitimate to infer interest in archaeology from results focused mostly on history. A plurality (42%) of the general public indicated an above average interest in historical topics. About one in five (22%) said they were extremely interested in history and another 20% said that they were very interested in historical topics. A very large majority (84%) were dissatisfied with their own knowledge of history, suggesting an interest in learning more, or differently, about the past.

The History Channel survey also asked about interest in 16 different historical time periods or topics. Among the top half of categories ranked as of above average interest were three closely or directly linked with archaeology:

* topic (1), the most popular topic, 'the history of science or technology' (46%);
* topic (3), 'ancient civilizations and archaeology' (38%);
* topic (7), 'other ethnic history, such as Native American or Hispanic history' (34%).

The connection between science and technology and archaeology exists at two levels. Archaeology frequently is used to describe the technological developments during prehistoric and historic times; the development of agriculture, or domestication, or metallurgy, for example. Archaeology also uses scientific methods and techniques as part of its investigations. Applications of scientific techniques, such as radiocarbon daring, remote sensing or chemical analysis of organic materials are frequently as interesting to the public as the archaeological subject being studied. The third ranked interest in ancient civilisations and archaeology is perhaps the most direct measurement of general opinion about archaeology that has yet been made and it indicates substantial public interest. The relatively high ranking for ethnic histories, such as Native American history, also suggests substantial public interest in information about one of the primary topics of American archaeology, the history and prehistory of American Indians.

These survey results affirm that the information value of archaeological resources and archaeological studies is an important public benefit. In order to improve understanding of public knowledge and attitudes about archaeology a public opinion survey that focused on specifically archaeological topics would be useful. To provide at least a baseline of information on these topics, a group of national archaeological organisations based in the United States and federal agencies with substantial responsibilities for archaeological resources are cooperating in an investigation of public attitudes and knowledge about archaeology. This investigation, underway at the time of writing (August 1999), will investigate what non-archaeologists know about archaeology, where they get their information about archaeology and what they think about how archaeological resources should be treated (McManamon 1999). Included in the study is a public survey being conducted by a national public opinion polling firm.

It is hoped that the results of this first national effort at understanding will help to focus efforts already underway to improve public understanding and appreciation of archaeology and archaeological resources. One way of improving effectiveness would be to target messages and means of delivery on different portions of the general public (Lerner 1991; McManamon 1991a; Shields 1991; McManamon 1994b, 65–73). Focused messages are more likely to achieve the most positive and lasting effect by dividing the public in terms of varied knowledge of or interests in archaeology. Experts in marketing,

advertising and public relations may be needed to develop effective means of communication. There are possibilities for making a positive impression on the mass audience in such
approaches.

Public attitudes and understanding need to be better known. Then, more effective
means can be devised for communicating with these people about archaeology in an understandable way.

Archaeological messages

There is no single archaeological message for archaeologists to aim at the public. In his
insightful comment on archaeology and public outreach, Potter (1990) echoes Fagan, as
quoted above, and the useful, practical advice provided by DeCicco (1988) in his public
outreach printer.

> The most significant and meaningful messages are not 'one size fits all'.
> Instead, they are local. Different communities have different pasts and need to
> know specific things about those pasts.
>
> (Potter 1990, 610)

Potter urges archaeologists to explore and discover what the public knows, thinks about or
uses from the past as part of the effort to construct interesting, useful messages. From the
perspective of critical analysis, reflection upon the modern context in which archaeology is
being done is essential (e.g. Leone *et al.* 1987). Certainly, from a practical perspective in
education and outreach, this is good advice. It is emphasised by others in their own work
and experience from working with local media (Peters *et al.* 1987; DeCicco 1988; Fagan
1991, 19).

One of the archaeological messages in any public outreach activity must include some
local focus and be sufficiently interesting to attract individuals with no special archaeological training. This might include information about how people lived in the local area at
some point in the past, an unexpected event, an unusual kind of feature or a special artefact found locally. Communication with the public should also, directly or indirectly,
make general points related to the value of archaeological resources, the care that must be
used when studying these resources, the necessary effort to curate artefacts and records
following excavations, and the non-renewable, often fragile, nature of archaeological
remains (e.g. Stuart and McManamon 1996). General points such as these were identified
as important messages to be used in educational, voluntary and other public outreach programmes designed to work over the long term on the prevention of archaeological looting
and vandalism (Lerner 1991, 103).

One of the most important distinctions to make in public outreach is the difference
between scientific archaeology and destructive looting or vandalism of the archaeological
record. Contrasts between these two approaches are numerous, including how the activities are planned, how artefacts are uncovered and removed, the extent of recording of
information about the archaeological context, description and analysis of the work, interpretation of the results, reporting of the results and the ultimate treatment of the artefacts, data and other material recovered. These differences need to be pointed out clearly
and in plain language.

There are a few basic messages that public outreach efforts should aim to incorporate.
These might be passed along in relation to specific local resources or interpretations, or
they might be included as general points. One message is that interesting and useful knowledge can be learned from archaeological remains *if they are properly studied*. Another is that
the proper study of archaeological remains is careful, painstaking investigation including

field work, lab work, report preparation and distribution and, ultimately, the curation of collections and records. Finally, it should be clear that archaeological remains are often fragile, always non-renewable, and ought not to be destroyed wantonly. Much archaeological research involves consumption and destruction of the *in situ* archaeological record. So, messages about archaeology and archaeological interpretations need to discourage individual excursions into archaeological fieldwork by enthusiasts.

The successful transmission of these general messages is an important goal of public education and outreach. A public with the appreciation for and understanding of archaeology and archaeological resources would be a public that abhorred site destruction and supported scientific archaeological activities and preservation. Only a small percentage of the public explicitly holds these beliefs at present. Yet, working to increase that percentage is both an important and a worthwhile goal (McManamon 1994b, 65; Sabloff 1998).

Archaeological messengers

These specific and general messages need effective messengers. Archaeologists ought not to be alone in communicating the messages. Educators, reporters, film makers and a host of others are already enlisted in these efforts. However, archaeologists of all sorts should have some role in public education and outreach, even if only as cheerleaders and supporters for those who actively take on this challenge (Fagan 1984; 1993; McManamon 1998; Sabloff 1998, 873–874; McManamon in press). So says *Principle No. 4: Public Education and Outreach* in the 'Principles of Archaeological Ethics' of the Society for American Archaeology (Herscher and McManamon 1995):

> Archaeologists should reach out to, and participate in cooperative efforts with, others interested in the archaeological record with the aim of improving the preservation, protection, and interpretation of the record. In particular, archaeologists should undertake to: (1) enlist public support for the stewardship of the archaeological record; (2) explain and promote the use of archaeological methods and techniques in understanding human behaviour and culture; and (3) communicate archaeological interpretations of the past. Many publics exist for archaeology including students and teachers; Native Americans and other ethnic, religious, and cultural groups who find in the archaeological record important aspects of their cultural heritage; lawmakers and government officials; reporters, journalists, and others involved in the media; and, the general public. Archaeologists who are unable to undertake public education and outreach directly should encourage and support the efforts of others in these activities.
>
> (Society for American Archaeology 1996, 452)

There are various kinds of jobs that professional archaeologists hold. Among the most common places of employment are academic research and teaching, conducting investigations as consultants in the planning and conduct of public projects, working for public agencies that manage lands, programmes or resources and in museum curation, interpretation, and research. In each of these areas of employment, many opportunities exist to include public education and outreach as a part of professional activities. An increasing number of references describing public outreach projects and programmes are available to provide examples and guide the unfamiliar in this area (e.g. Peters *et al.* 1987; Potter and Leone 1987; DeCicco 1988; Bense 1991; Ellick 1991; Fagan 1991; Milamich 1991; Potter 1994; Bense 1995; articles in Jameson 1997; Jameson 1999; Lerner and Hoffman 1999; Chiarulli and Hawkins 2000; Hawkins 2000).

When addressing general audiences, new students or smaller groups of non-archaeologists, archaeologists should endeavour to talk and write clearly and simply. Altamira Press (Allen 1995) suggests ten rules as guidance whether one is speaking or writing for non-specialised audiences:

1 find a hook
2 tell a story
3 include yourself
4 avoid jargon
5 talk to a single reader
6 names are important
7 determine the data you need
8 present the data visually
9 emphasise theory and methods
10 always think audience.

All archaeologists should promote archaeology. They can act locally, regionally or nationally, using newspapers, magazines, radio and television to feature archaeological activities, events and news. Individual archaeologists, no matter which part of the field they work in, should be willing to speak at elementary and secondary local schools, civic organisations and for local archaeological, historical, preservation and conservation organisations. Professional archaeologists must be willing to work with avocational archaeological societies. They need not lead these societies, although some do, but willingness to take part is appropriate recognition of the important work that such volunteer organisations can accomplish (Davis 1991; Hoffman 1991).

There are exceptions, of course. Some professional archaeologists, like certain experts in other fields, are not particularly suited by ability, personality or skills for effective public outreach. Still, these professionals can support outreach efforts by their colleagues. Professional education needs to emphasise more the importance of interaction with non-archaeologists and teach the skills needed for these activities. As young professionals learn firsthand of the importance of such public activities and increasingly take them on, the frequency of professionals ill-equipped for public outreach will lessen.

There are local activities that archaeologists, as individual citizens, can undertake or support to enhance a local archaeology programme, a local environmental ordinance or historic zoning restrictions that interpret or preserve local archaeology. Having a professional degree and job do not absolve individuals of civic responsibilities or prevent them from actively working on public issues or supporting public initiatives that improve the support for, preservation of or public concern about archaeology. Individual archaeologists can and should work with local community governments, local service organisations, local libraries and other educational services.

Within their professional jobs, archaeologists working for public agencies at all levels, national, regional, state and local, have opportunities to enhance public education and outreach. During the last decade, public agencies at all levels have taken the lead in presenting archaeology to the public (e.g. Cressey 1987; Hawkins 1988; Osborn and Peters 1991; Brook 1992; Smith *et al.* 1992; Jameson 2000; Lerner and Hoffman 2000). This has been so in formal educational settings, especially primary and secondary public schools, as well as in outreach for the general public. These kinds of programmes often provide substantial rewards for the public agencies that undertake them. Many have become regular features of agency programmes and should remain as such.

Archaeologists working for consulting firms also have accomplished much with public education and outreach. Many medium- and large-size archaeological projects, for example, for highways, power lines or water control projects, produce brochures, public lectures, 'open house' days at sites and displays. Project sponsors often see these products as tangible public benefits for which they can take credit. The positive public relations obtained make them willing to sponsor these kinds of programmes as outcomes of the archaeological investigations they fund (e.g. Rogge and Montgomery 1988; Redman 1989; Bense 1991; 1995). These kinds of activities should be supported by the archaeological community and encouraged by those who design and scope proposals for public projects.

Archaeologists teaching introductory or general survey courses usually will be the only ones that most people personally encounter during their lives. For most of the students these classes will be the most extended presentation about archaeology that they ever hear. It is imperative, therefore, that the professionals teaching these courses use them as effectively as possible to inculcate in their audiences an appreciation and understanding of archaeology. These classes present a unique and important opportunity to create a supportive, well-informed, educated public. Those teaching adult education courses on archaeological topics have the same opportunities and obligations for creating public advocates and supporters. Professors educating graduate students, those individuals who eventually will replace contemporary practitioners and become the professional corps of archaeologists ought to provide their students with experience working with the general public through schools, mass media print and electronic publications and local communities (Smith 1993; Sabloff 1998).

Archaeologists in every part of the profession need to serve as messengers for and about archaeology. Self-interest is one reason for this, but preserving some portion of the past is the greater goal. Communication efforts are essential if accurate information is to be shared widely with others. Certainly the desire to share what we have learned from our archaeological investigations is at least part of the motivation driving most archaeologists. We need effective messages delivered effectively by dedicated messengers.

Acknowledgements

All my colleagues concerned about public education and outreach at the National Park Service, in other public agencies, in academic settings and in the private sector have contributed to the ideas and suggestions in this article. I am especially grateful to S. Terry Childs, Hester Davis, John Jameson, Jr, and Barbara Little for specific comments on earlier drafts. I hope they see in the final version the improvements I have made based upon their suggestions. This chapter began life as a commentary in one of the sessions at the conference on the public benefits of archaeology held in November 1995, in Santa Fe, New Mexico.

Francis P. McManamon is the Chief Archeologist of the United States National Park Service based in Washington DC. He also serves as Departmental Consulting Archeologist, carrying out responsibilities assigned by United States law and regulations to the Secretary of the Interior. He oversees the Archeology and Ethnography Program of the Service's National Center for Cultural Resource Stewardship and Partnerships in Washington, DC. His formal education includes: BA, Colgate University, 1973, MA (1975) and PhD (1984). His areas of professional expertise include Eastern and Northeastern North American prehistory; public archeology and cultural resource management; archeological education and outreach; and, archeological methods and techniques. Contact address: Francis P. McManamon, Archeology and Ethnography Program (Suite NC340), National Park Service, 1849 C Street NW, Washington, DC 20240 USA Tel: +1 (202) 343 4101; Fax: +1 (202) 343 6250; email: fp_mcmanamon@nps.gov.

References

Allen, M. *Altamira's Rules for the Archaeological Writer*. Distributed at the Public Benefits of Archaeology Conference, Santa Fe, NM, November (1995).

Anonymous. A sampling of creative initiatives. *Archaeology* **44**(1) (1991) 40–43.

Bense, J. A. The Pensacola model of public archaeology. In: Smith, K. C. and McManamon, F. P. (eds) *Archaeology and Education: The Classroom and Beyond*. Archaeological Assistance Study Number 2. National Park Service, Washington, DC (1991) 9–12.

Bense, J. A. Putting Pensacola on the map! Archeotourism in West Florida. *AnthroNotes* **17**(1/2) (1995) 17–21.

Brook, R. A. Adventures in the past. *Federal Archaeology Report* **5**(1) (1992) 1–4.

Butler, W. B. (ed.) *State Archaeological Education Programs*. Interagency Archaeological Services, Division of National Preservation Programs. Rocky Mountain Regional Office, National Park Service, Denver, CO (1992).

Charles, T. and Walden, M. B. *Can You Dig It? A Classroom Guide to South Carolina Archaeology*. South Carolina Department of Education, Columbia, SC (1989).

Cressey, P. J. Community archaeology in Alexandria, Virginia. *Conserve Neighborhoods* **69** (1987) National Trust for Historic Preservation, Washington, DC 1–7.

Cleere, H. Introduction: the rationale of archaeological heritage management. In: Cleere, H. (ed.) *Archaeological Heritage Management in the Modern World*, Unwin Hyman, London (1989) 1–19.

Chiarulli, B. and Hawkins, N. Programs that educate: two successful archaeology education efforts provide models for up-and-coming programs. *Archaeology and Public Education* **8**(3) (1998) 6.

Culliton, B. J. The dismal state of scientific literacy. *Science* **243** (1988) 600.

Davis, H. A. The crisis in American archaeology. *Science* **175** (1972) 267–272.

Davis, H. A. *Training and Using Volunteers in Archaeology: A Case Study from Arkansas*. Archaeological Assistance Program Technical Brief 9. National Park Service, Washington, DC (1990) www.cr.nps.gov/aad/aepubs.htm.

Davis, H. A. Avocational archaeology groups: A secret weapon for site protection. In: Smith, G. C. and Ehrenhard, J. E. (eds) *Protecting the Past*, CRC Press, Boca Raton, FL (1991) 175–180.

DeCicco, G. A public relations primer. *American Antiquity* 53 (1988) 840–856.

Deloria, V., Jr Indians, archaeologists, and the future. *American Antiquity* **57**(4) (1992) 595–598.

Durant, J. R., Evans, G. A. and Thomas, G. P. The public understanding of science. *Nature* **340** (1989) 11–14.

Echo-Hawk, R. Working together: exploring ancient worlds. *Society for American Archaeology Bulletin* **11**(4) (1993) 5–6.

Echo-Hawk, R. Forging a new ancient history for Native America. In: Swidler, N., Dongoske, K. E., Anyon, R. and Downer, A. S. (eds) *Native Americans and Archaeologists: Stepping Stones to Common Ground*, Altamira Press, Walnut Creek, CA (1997) 88–102.

Ellick, C. Archaeology is more than a dig: educating children about the past saves sites for the future. In: Smith, K. C. and McManamon, F. P. (ed.) *Archaeology and Education: The Classroom and Beyond*, Archaeological Assistance Study Number 2. Archaeological Assistance Program, National Park Service, Washington, DC (1991) 27–32.

Fagan, B. M. The past as news. *CRM* **14**(1) (1991) 17–19.

Fagan, B. M. The arrogant archaeologist. *Archaeology* **46**(6) (1993) 14–16.

Fagan, B. M. Archaeology and the wider audience. In: Green, E. L. (ed.) *Ethics and Values in Archaeology*, The Free Press, New York (1984).

Feder, K. L. Irrationality and popular archaeology. *American Antianity* **49** (1984) 525–541.

Feder, K. L. Cult archaeology and creationism: a coordinated research project. In: Harrold,

F. B. and Eve, R. A. (eds) *Cult Archaeology and Creationism: Understanding Pseudoscientific Beliefs About the Past*, University of Iowa Press, Iowa City, IA (1987) 34–48.

Feder, K. L. *Frauds, Myths, and Mysteries: Science and Pseudoscience in Archaeology*. Mayfield Publishing, Mountain View, CA (1990).

Feder, K. L. Ten years after: surveying misconceptions about the human past. *CRM* **18**(3) (1995) 10–14.

Feder, K. L. *Frauds, Myths, and Mysteries: Science and Pseudoscience in Archaeology*. 4th edition. Mayfield Publishing, Mountain View, CA (1998).

Few, J., Hawkins, N., Hooge, P., MacDonald, C., Smith, K. C. and Smith, S. *Teaching Archaeology: A Sampler for Grades 3 to 12*. Public Education Committee, Society for American Archaeology, Washington, DC (1995).

Folsom, F. and Folsom, M. E. *America's Ancient Treasures*. Fourth revised and enlarged edition. University of New Mexico Press, Albuquerque, NM (1993).

Friedman, J. L. (ed.) A history of the archaeological resources protection act: law and regulations. *American Archaeology* **5**(2) (1985) 82–119.

Hawkins, N. W. *Classroom Archaeology: A Curriculum Guide for Teachers*. Division of Archaeology, Department of Culture, Recreation, and Tourism, Baton Rouge, LA (1988).

Hawkins, N. W. To dig or not to dig? *Archaeology and Public Education* **8**(3) (1998) 10–11.

Herscher, E. and McManamon, F. P. Public education and outreach: The obligation to educate. In: Lynott, M. J. and Wylie, A. (eds) *Ethics in American Archaeology: Challenges for the 1990s*, Society for American Archaeology, Washington, DC (1995) 42–44.

Hively, W. Science observer: How much science does the public understand? *American Scientist* **76** (1988) 439–444.

Hoffman, T. L. Stewards of the past: preserving Arizona's archaeological resources through positive public involvement. In: Smith, G. C. and Ehrenhard, J. E. (eds) *Protecting the Past*, CRC Press, Boca Raton, FL (1991) 253–259.

Hoffman, T. L. and Lerner, S. *Arizona Archaeology Week: Promoting the Past to the Public*. Archaeological Assistance Program Technical Brief No. 2. National Park Service, Washington, DC (1998) www.cr.nps.gov/aad/aepubs.htm.

Jameson, J. H., Jr Public interpretation, education, and outreach: The growing predominance in American archaeology. In: McManamon, F. P. and Hatton, A. (eds) *Cultural Resource Management in Contemporary Society: Perspectives on Managing and Presenting the Past*, One World Archaeology, Number 33. Routledge, London and New York (2000) 288–289.

Jameson, J. H., Jr (ed.) *Presenting Archaeology to the Public: Digging for Truths*. Altamira Press, Walnut Creek, CA (1997).

Kennedy, R. G. *Hidden Cities: The Discovery and Loss of Ancient North American Civilization*. The Free Press, New York (1994).

Kennedy, R. G. Conservation, preservation, and the cause conservative. *Preservation Forum* **11**(2) (1997) 33–41.

Klesert, A. L. A view from Navajoland on the reconciliation of anthropologists and Native Americans. *Human Organization* **51**(1) (1992) 17–22.

Klesert, A. L. and Downer, A. S. (eds) *Preservation on the Reservation: Native Americans, Native American Lands, and Archaeology*. Navajo Nation Papers in Anthropology Number 26. Navajo Nation Archaeology Department, Navajo Nation Historic Preservation Department. Shiprock, AZ (1990).

Lavin, M. B. So, you're still not sure about archaeology and eighth graders? *Archaeology and Public Education* **6**(2) (1996) 4–5, 14.

Lawler, A. Support for science stays strong. *Science* **272** (1996) 1256.

Lee, R. F. *The Antiquities Act of 1906*. National Park Service, Washington, DC (1970).

Leone, M. P., Potter, P. B. Jr and Shackel, P. A. Toward a critical archaeology. *Current Anthropology* **28**(3) (1987) 283–302.

Leone, M. P. and Potter, P. B., Jr Legitimization and the classification of archaeological sites. *American Antiquity* **57**(1) (1992) 137–145.

Leone, M. P. and Preucel, R. W. Archaeology in a democratic society: a critical theory perspective. In: Wandsnider, L. (ed.) *Quandaries and Quests: Visions of Archaeology's Future*, Centers for Archaeological Investigations, occasional paper No. 20, Southern Illinois University, Carbondale, IL (1992) 115–135.

Lerner, S. Saving sites: preservation and education. In: Smith, G. C. and Ehrenhard, J. E. (eds) *Protecting the Past*, CRC Press, Boca Raton, FL (1991) 103–108.

Lerner, S. and Hoffman, T. L. Bringing archaeology to the public: programs in the southwestern United States. In: McManamon, F. P. and Hatton, A. (eds) *Cultural Resource Management in Contemporary Society: Perspectives on Managing and Presenting the Past*, One World Archaeology, Number 33. Routledge, London and New York (2000) 231–246.

Lipe, W. D. In defense of digging: archaeological preservation as a means, not an end. *CRM* **19**(7) (1996) 23–27.

Lowenthal, D. *The Past is a Foreign Country*. Cambridge University Press, Cambridge (1985).

Lowenthal, D. *Possessed by the Past: The Heritage Crusade and the Spoils of History*. The Free Press, New York (1996).

Lynott, M. J. and Wylie, A. Stewardship: the central principle of archaeological ethics. In: Lynott, M. J. and Wylie, A. (eds) *Ethics in American Archaeology: Challenges for the 1990s*, Society for American Archaeology, Washington, DC (1995) 28–32.

McDonald, J. N. and Woodward, S. L. *Indian Mounds of the Atlantic Coast: A Guide to Sites from Maine to Florida*. The McDonald and Woodward Publishing Company, Newark, OH (1987).

McGimsey, C. R., III 'This, too, will pass': Moss-Bennett in perspective. *American Antiquity* **50**(2) (1985) 326–331.

McGimsey, C. R., III Perceptions of the past: public archaeology and Moss-Bennett – then and now. *Southeastern Archaeology* **8**(1) (1989) 72–75.

McManamon, F. P. The many publics for archaeology. *American Antiquity* **56**(1) (1991a) 121–130.

McManamon, F. P. The federal government's recent response to archaeological looting. In: Smith, G. C. and Ehrenhard, J. E. (eds) *Protecting the Past*, CRC Press, Boca Raton, FL (1991b) 261–269.

McManamon, F. P. Changing relationships between Native Americans and archaeologists. *Historic Preservation Forum* **8**(2) (1994a) 15–20.

McManamon, F. P. Presenting archaeology to the public in the USA. In: Stone, P. G. and Molyneaux, B. L. (eds) *The Presented Past: Heritage, Museums, and Education*, Routledge Publishers, London and New York (1994b) 61–81.

McManamon, F. P. The Antiquities Act – setting basic preservation policies. *CRM* **19**(7) (1996) 18–23.

McManamon, F. P. Public archaeology: a professional obligation. *Archaeology and Public Education* **8**(3) (1998) 3, 13.

McManamon, F. P. Understanding the public's understanding of archaeology. *Common Ground* **4**(2) (1999) 3.

McManamon, F. P. Public education: a part of archaeological professionalism. In: Smith, S. and Smardz, K. (eds) *The Archaeological Education Handbook: Sharing the Past with Kids*, Altamira Press, Walnut Creek, CA (in press).

McManamon, F. P. and Hatton, A. (eds) *Cultural Resource Management in Contemporary Society: Perspectives on Managing and Presenting the Past*. One World Archaeology, Number 33. Routledge, London and New York (2000).

MacDonald, C. Historical archaeology meshes learning experiences for kids. *Archaeology and Public Education* **6**(1) (1995) 5.

Messenger, P. The future of the past: SAA maps a long-term strategy. *Archaeology and Public Education* **5**(2) (1994) 1, 3, 11.

Messenger, P. Public education and outreach. In: Lynott, M. J. and Wylie, A. (eds) *Ethics in American Archaeology: Challenges for the 1990s*, Society for American Archaeology, Washington, DC (1995) 68–70.

Metcalf, F. Knife River: early village life on the Plains. A 'Teaching with Historic Places' supplement. *Social Education* **56**(5) (1992) 312 ff.

Milanich, J. T. Archaeology in the sunshine: grass roots education through the media and public involvement. In: Smith, G. C. and Ehrenhard, J. E. (eds) *Protecting the Past*, CRC Press, Boca Raton, FL (1991).

New Mexico, Office of Cultural Affairs *On Fertile Ground: Assessing and Cultivating New Mexico's Cultural Resources*. New Mexico Office of Cultural Affairs, Santa Fe, NM (1995).

Noble, D. G. *Ancient Ruins of the Southwest: An Archaeological Guide*, revised edition. Northland Publishing, Flagstaff, AZ (1991).

O'Brien, W. and Cullen, T. *Archaeology in the Classroom: A Resource Guide for Teachers and Parents*. Archaeological Institute of America, Boston and New York. Kendall/Hunt Publishing Company, Dubuque, IA (1996).

Osborn, J. A. and Peters, G. Passport in time. *Federal Archaeology Report* **4**(3) (1991) 1–6.

Peters, K. S., Comer, E. A. and Kelly, R. *Captivating the Public Through the Media While Digging the Past*. Technical Series No. 1. Baltimore Center for Urban Archaeology, Baltimore, MD (1987).

Phagan, C. J. and Pilles, P. J., Jr Public participation archaeology at Elden Pueblo. In: Rogge, A. E. and Montgomery, J. (eds) *Fighting Indiana Jones in Arizona: American Society for Conservation Archaeology*, 1988 Proceedings, American Society for Conservation Archaeology, Portales, NM (1989) 13–16.

Pokotylo, D. L. and Mason, A. R. Public attitudes towards archaeological resources and their management. In: Smith, G. C. and Ehrenhard, J. E. (eds) *Protecting the Past*, CRC Press, Boca Raton, FL (1991) 9–18.

Pokotylo, D. L. and Guppy, N. Public opinion and archaeological heritage: views from outside the profession. *American Antiquity* **64** (1999) 400–416.

Potter, P. B., Jr The 'what' and 'why' of public relations for archaeology: a postscript to DeCicco's Public Relations Primer. *American Antiquity* **55** (1990) 608–613.

Potter, P. B., Jr *Public Archaeology in Annapolis: A Critical Approach to History in Maryland's Ancient City*. Smithsonian Institution Press, Washington, DC (1994).

Potter, P. B., Jr and Leone, M. P. Archaeology in public in Annapolis: four seasons, six sites, seven tours, and 32,000 visitors. *American Archaeology* **6**(1) (1987) 51–61.

Pyburn, K. A. and Wilk, R. R. Responsible archaeology is applied anthropology. In: Lynott, M. J. and Wylie, A. (eds) *Ethics in American Archaeology: Challenges for the 1990s*, Society for American Archaeology, Washington, DC (1995) 71–76.

Redman, C.L. Revitalizing archaeology through public outreach. In: Rogge, A. E. and Montgomery, J. (eds) *Fighting Indiana Jones in Arizona: American Society for Conservation Archaeology*, 1988 Proceedings, American Society for Conservation Archaeology, Portales, NM (1989) 25–27.

Reid, J. J. Editor's corner: recent findings on North American prehistory. *American Antiquity* **57**(2) (1992a) 195–196.

Reid, J. J. Editor's corner: Quincentennial truths and consequences. *American Antiquity* **57**(4) (1992b) 583.

Rogge, A. E. and Bell, P. *Archaeology in the Classroom Case Study from Arizona*. Archaeological Assistance Program Technical Brief No. 4. National Park Service, Washington, DC (1989).

Rogge, A. E. and Montgomery, J. (eds) *Fighting Indiana Jones in Arizona: American Society for Conservation Archaeology*, 1988 Proceedings, American Society for Conservation Archaeology, Portales, NM (1989).

Roper and Starch *Americans' Attitudes Toward History*. Conducted for The History Channel, New York (1995).

Rowland, F. S. President's Lecture: the need for scientific communication with the public. *Science* **260** (1993) 1571–1576.

SAA Executive Board Society for American Archaeology Principles of Archaeological Ethics. *American Antiquity* **61**(3) (1996) 451–452.

Sabloff, J. A. Distinguished lecture in archaeology: communication and the future of American archaeology. *American Anthropologist* **100**(4) (1998) 869–875.

Selig, R. Anthropology in public schools: Why should we care? *Anthropology Newsletter* (February 1989) 28.

Selig, R. Teacher training programs in anthropology: the multiplier effect in the classroom. In: Smith, K. C. and McManamon, F. P. (eds) *Archaeology and Education: The Classroom and Beyond*, Archaeological Assistance Study No. 2, National Park Service, Washington, DC (1991).

Selig, R. O. and London, M. R. (eds) *Anthropology Explored: The Best of Anthro Notes*. Smithsonian Institution Press, Washington, DC and London (1998).

Shields, H.M. Marketing archaeological resource protection. In: Smith, G. C. and Ehrenhard, J. E. (eds) *Protecting the Past*, CRC Press, Boca Raton, FL (1991) 167–173.

Shull, C. D. and Hunter, K. Teaching with historic places. *Social Education* **56**(5) (1992) 312.

Smith, B. A new goal for academia. *Archaeology and Public Education* **3**(3) (1993) 1.

Smith, K. C. Picture this: using photographs to study the past. *Archaeology and Public Education* **6**(1) (1995) 6–8.

Smith, K.C. One era ends, another begins. *Archaeology and Public Education* **8**(3) (1998) 2, 15.

Smith, K. C. and McManamon, F. P. (eds) *Archaeology and Education: The Classroom and Beyond*. Archaeological Assistance Study No. 2, National Park Service, Washington, DC (1991).

Smith, K. C. and Piatek, B. J. New discoveries in the oldest city. *Archaeology and Public Education* **4**(2) (1993) 7–8.

Smith, S., Moe, J., Letts, K. and Paterson, D. *Intrigue of the Past, Investigating Archaeology: A Teachers Activity Guide for Fourth Through Seventh Grades*. Utah Interagency Task Force on Cultural Resources, Bureau of Land Management, Utah State Office, Salt Lake City, UT (1992).

Smith, S. and Smardz, K. (eds) *The Archaeological Education Handbook: Sharing the Past with Kids*. Altamira Press, Walnut Creek, CA (in press).

Society for American Archaeology *Guidelines for the Evaluation of Archaeology Education Materials*. Prepared by the Formal Education Subcommittee, Public Education Committee, Society for American Archaeology, Washington, DC (1995).

Society for American Archaeology Society for American Archaeology Principles of Archaeological Ethics. *American Antiquity* **61**(3) (1996) 451–452.

Stone, P. G. and MacKenzie, R. (eds) *The Excluded Past: Archaeology in Education*. Unwin Hyman, London (1989).

Stone, P. G. and Molyneaux, B. L. (eds) *The Presented Past: Heritage, Museums, and Education*. Routledge Publishers, London and New York (1994).

Stuart, G. E. and McManamon, F. P. *Archaeology and You*. Society for American Archaeology, Washington, DC (1996).

Thomas, D. H. *Exploring Ancient Native America: An Archaeological Guide*. MacMillan, New York (1994).

Wauchope, R. *Lost Tribes and Sunken Continents: Myths and Method in the Study of American Indians*. University of Chicago Press, Chicago, IL (1962).

Williams, J. A. *Illinois Archaeological Resource Materials with Annotated Bibliography for Teachers*. Illinois Historic Preservation Agency, Springfield, IL (1989).

Williams, S. Some fantastic messages from the past. *Archaeology* **41**(5) (1988) 62–70.

Williams, S. *Fantastic Archaeology: The Wild Side of North American Prehistory*. University of Pennsylvania Press, Philadelphia, PA (1991).

Woodward, S. L. and McDonald, J. N. *Indian Mounds of the Middle Ohio Valley: A Guide to Adena and Ohio Hopewell*. McDonald and Woodward Publishing Company, Blacksburg, VA (1986).

Appendix 1: Engaging with multiple pasts, reply to Francis McManamon

Cornelius Holtorf

Francis McManamon's passionate plea for improved public outreach by professional archaeologists is laudable in so far as archaeology's role in society continues to be an issue in need of discussion and critique (McManamon 2000). But these discussions and critiques should not be pre-empted by senior professionals who assert their own perspective as that of all archaeologists. Passages in McManamon's essay and similar literature (e.g. Feder 1984) come across as rather prescriptive to his colleagues, and just a mite uncharitable to his fellow citizens: 'One way of improving effectiveness would be to target messages and means of delivery on different portions of the general public ... There are possibilities for making a positive impression on the mass audience in such approaches'; 'It is imperative, therefore, that the professionals teaching these [introductory or general survey] courses use them as effectively as possible to inculcate in their audiences an appreciation and understanding of archaeology'; 'Individuals among the general public can serve as the eyes and ears of local, state or even national officials who are responsible for archaeological preservation' (McManamon 2000, 13,16, 7). This language frightens me.

I am challenging the principal assertion that all archaeologists ought to share McManamon's concerns. In my experience, archaeologists are not all willing to transmit the same 'messages' to their audiences, nor do they necessarily see themselves as 'messengers' at all. Several important questions and issues that remain unresolved in McManamon's essay need to be raised.

(1) What exactly is a 'mistreatment' of archaeological sites? Who says what can and cannot be done with archaeological sites? Is destruction any less serious when conducted by archaeologists? What distinguishes an unpublished excavation from a looted site? Even widespread assumptions such as the alleged non-renewability of archaeological resources and the urgency of 'rescuing' sites from developers can be challenged: they rely largely on an essentialist notion of authenticity and on unconfirmed beliefs about the social reality of historical understanding and consciousness (Holtorf forthcoming). The issues of looting, illicit antiquities trade and collecting are very complex too and deserve a better appreciation than the very one-sided polemics some people sometimes get engaged in (cf. 'The Good Collector' Forum pieces in *Public Archaeology* 1[1] and this issue). All such questions deserve as comprehensive and sophisticated a discussion as possible, among archaeologists and others; this will not harm but strengthen archaeology's role in the context of our (post) modern society. To my mind, ideologically sound declarations that proclaim definitive 'answers' and aim for discursive closure are not helpful.

(2) What exactly is a 'distortion' of archaeological interpretation, or a 'damaging' and 'fanciful' interpretation, as opposed to one based on the 'proper' study of archaeological remains and resulting in 'accurate' information about the past? On what authority does McManamon divide up his fellow Americans as 'charlatans', 'misdirected hobbyists', 'pseudo-archaeologists' and 'conscientious citizens', among others? Surely such judgements are socially negotiable and subject to change over time. Kenneth Feder's recent study of 'misconceptions' of the past, undertaken a decade after a first such survey, can serve as an example for the arbitrariness that divides 'pseudo-science' from 'real science' (Feder 1995). Feder asked undergraduate students to rate statements about the human past. In 1983, one such statement read 'Human beings biologically just like us have been around for about 40,000 years', and anyone disagreeing with this was considered misinformed and influenced by pseudo- or non-scientific approaches to the past rather than by the results of 'real' archaeology. In 1994, in the light of a changing consensus among archaeologists, the same question had to be revised to 'Human beings biologically just like us have been around for more than 100,000 years'. As a result,

some 'misinformed' students in 1983 would now be considered as 'informed', as long as they gave the same answer as before. (Feder assumes, perhaps correctly, that most people disagreeing with either version may do so because they think modern humans are *younger* than both figures quoted, but this does not invalidate my point.)

The alternative I am proposing here is not one of an unbound relativism according to which any position would be as good as any other (cf. Lampeter Archaeology Workshop 1997). I propose instead a commitment to multiple approaches and values brought to bear on archaeological sites and objects. Clearly, every past is a construct of the present. Different logics and conceptions of the past correspond to different contemporary discourses and contexts. Neither students nor other audiences ought to be indoctrinated with a particular version of the past or approach to its management in the present. If anything, people might be informed about the very mechanisms that make some accounts and policies locally more meaningful and influential than others (see Michlovic 1990). Only informed dialogue can bring about mutual understanding and willingness to compromise, thus helping to avoid unnecessary confrontations.

Professional archaeologists differ from amateurs in so far as they carry out a profession which is socially valued, whether that means administering a museum collection, managing rescue excavations or teaching students, among other occupations. No further crusades are required in order to make a positive contribution to society. Archaeologists share their commitment to, and fascination by the distant past and its remains with many others, especially a considerable number of amateur enthusiasts. I can see no good reason why non-professionals should not be welcomed and indeed be encouraged and supported in their own encounters with archaeology, whether these may closely resemble professional attitudes or not (for positive examples, see Faulkner 2000; Field *et al.* 2000).

Critical understanding and dialogue, not dismissive polemics, are the appropriate ways to engage with the multiple pasts and alternative archaeologies we encounter in our society (cf. Michlovic 1990; Trubshaw 1996). To me, this is what makes both public archaeology and *Public Archaeology* challenging and ultimately worthwhile.

References to Appendix 1

Faulkner, N. Archaeology from below. *Public Archaeology* **1** (2000) 21–33.

Feder, K. L. Irrationality and popular archaeology. *American Antiquity* **49** (1984) 525–541.

Feder, K. L. Ten years after surveying misconceptions about the human past. *CRM* **3** (1995) 10–14.

Field, J., Barker, J., Barker, R., Coffey, E., Coffey, L., Crawford, E., Darcy, L. Fields, T., Lord, G., Steadman, B. and Colley, S. Coming back: Aborigines and archaeologists at Cuddie Springs. *Public Archaeology* **1** (2000) 35–48.

Holtorf, C. Is the past a non-renewable resource? In: Layton, R., Stone, P. and Thomas, J. (eds) *The Destruction and Conservation of Cultural Property*. One World Archaeology Series. Routledge, London (forthcoming).

Lampeter Archaeology Workshop Relativism, objectivity and the politics of the past. *Archaeological Dialogues* **4** (1997) 164–198.

McManamon, F. Archaeological messages and messengers. *Public Archaeology* **1**(1) (2000) 5–22.

Michlovic, M. G. Folk Archaeology in anthropological perspective. *Current Anthropology* **31** (1990) 103–107.

Trubshaw, R. Who's fringe now? *Assemblage* 1. http://www.shef.ac.uk/~assem/1/trub2.html (1996).

Appendix 2: Promoting an archaeological perspective, a response to Cornelius Holtorf

Francis P. McManamon

In his thoughtful comment on my article, 'Archaeological messages and messengers', which appeared in the first issue of this journal, Cornelius Holtorf takes me to task for spouting 'dismissive polemics' and being possessed of a singular view of archaeological interpretation that would exclude all except 'professionals' from the practice of the discipline, or the right to their own interpretations of the archaeological record. I believe this is a misinterpretation of my article. I hope this response, following on Holtorf's comment, will give greater clarity to the points I was trying to make in the original article.

The main point of 'Archaeological messages and messengers' is that professional archaeologists and others who believe that historical and scientific archaeological methods and techniques provide an informative and valuable view of the past need to promote this point of view more avidly. Archaeological data rarely are accessible or understandable to untrained observers. Archaeological sites more often than not are invisible or very difficult to discern. Archaeological methods, techniques and interpretations based upon them usually are not readily apparent or understandable to one and all. So, it is not surprising that people without archaeological training need some help via an archaeological perspective in order to understand the past. In addition, translations of professional concepts, quantitative and scientific analysis often are necessary.

Even the visual appearance of archaeological resources typically requires interpretation. Nearly 20 years ago, I was involved in the excavation of a prehistoric ossuary, a multiple, secondary burial in which were interred the remains of over 50 individuals. This feature was found by accident in a small construction site on Cape Cod, Massachusetts, hundreds of miles from known archaeological sites of the same sort (McManamon et al. 1986; McManamon and Bradley 1988). The public became actively engaged in observing the excavation, for this unexpected discovery occurred in the midst of a bustling summer residential community during August. Many residents and vacationers visited the site and voiced their own initial interpretations about it, the site of a bloody massacre, a pile of plague victims hurriedly buried, that sort of interpretation.

The professional team that excavated the burial feature was itself unfamiliar with this kind of interment. After all, such burial features had not been found in any other locations in southern New England. Only after comparative information from published investigations in the Chesapeake Bay and eastern Great Lakes regions was located and referred to did the interpretation of the bone patterns and cremated remains become clear. Archaeological study of the bone and the burial population characteristics were essential to explaining the cultural pattern that created the burial feature. In this case from the ancient past, an archaeological perspective was not one among a number of equally likely interpretations: rather, without the archaeological recovery and analysis, the actual events that created the burial would be unknown.

Many archaeologists recognise that there are different perspectives on the past and other views regarding the value of archaeological sites than the one informed by an archaeological perspective. Although it is only one among a number of perspectives, those of us who have spent years or decades learning and improving the methods and techniques of archaeology feel that it is the best way of interpreting the physical remains we refer to as the archaeological record. I do not suggest that we dismiss all other perspectives as uninteresting, uninformative or unworthy. Indeed, as Holtorf notes, other perspectives need not be inconsistent with an archaeological perspective. A number of them in fact either are or have the potential to be complementary. On the other hand, we must recognise that some of the other views indeed are unworthy, even dangerous.

Holtorf finds some of my statements 'frightening'. He characterises three different phrases, composed of four sentences, in the original article by this term. Readers should note that in the original article, these sentences are spread over ten pages of text. One might respond simply that Holtorf has taken these sentences and thoughts out of context and constructed what he considers to be a scary polemic. However, let me examine each example separately to more completely establish their context and try to explain these sentences and the thoughts behind them more clearly.

(1) 'One way of improving effectiveness would be to target messages and means of delivery on different portions of the general public ... There are possibilities for making a positive impression on the mass audience in such approaches' (McManamon 2000, 13). Part of Holtorf's complaint is that my article called for a single dogmatic archaeological message. However, these sentences illustrate a recognition of many publics, each with a different perspective on archaeology. I suggest that different portions of the public have different concerns and backgrounds that influence how they understand and appreciate archaeology (McManamon 1991).

Recent investigations of public attitudes regarding archaeology show that people assign different values to archaeological resources (Harris 2000, 22–26; Pokotylo and Guppy 1999). Similarly, people learn about archaeology and archaeological resources in different ways. Television, magazines and newspapers all are major sources of archaeological news for most people. Books, secondary schools and colleges also serve as a means by which people learn about archaeology (Harris 2000; 16–17). Isn't it logical, then, that information organised and presented in order to make a positive impression about archaeology and archaeological resources should be focused on particular audiences? Good lecturers or writers, no matter what their subject, mould their material to the audience they are addressing. Archaeological messages and messengers need to do the same in order to be effective.

(2) 'It is imperative, therefore, that the professionals teaching these [introductory or general survey] courses use them as effectively as possible to inculcate in their audiences an appreciation and understanding of archaeology' (McManamon 2000, 16). Like many scientific methods and techniques, archaeological approaches to understanding the past are not necessarily self-evident. In a recent essay on science and society, Boyce Rensberger, director of the Knight Science Journalism Fellowships programme at the Massachusetts Institute of Technology and former science reporter for *The New York Times* and *Washington Post*, pointed out that scientists frequently need to 'translate' their findings for journalists and their readers. Journalists, he also argued, need to better understand the method and techniques of science so they can convey these effectively to a public audience that is interested, but not so well versed in the nature of scientific inquiry as to evaluate or understand results without some assistance (Rensberger 2000, 61). We ought not to find anything sinister or frightening in similar discussions or explanations of archaeological method, technique or interpretations. We know that introductory college courses on archaeology are the most detailed exposure that many individuals will have to the topic. Each of these courses is an opportunity to gain public support of an archaeological perspective.

Alternative interpretations of archaeological data, such as those promulgated by Eric Van Daniken (of extraterrestrial interventions in human developments and history) or Barry Fell (of extraordinary ancient migrations or voyages) need to be evaluated critically. Holtorf declares that he is not proposing 'an unbound relativism according to which any position would be as good as any other'. Instead, he proposes, 'a commitment to multiple approaches and value brought to bear on archaeological sites and objects'. I agree with Holtorf that there are multiple views of the past. In my article, I extended this topic further and also attempted to describe some alternative views that were unsupportable.

Archaeologists must recognise that some of these views stand directly in opposition to an archaeological perspective. In some situations, such alternative views need to be challenged and opposed actively. For example, there are some who view and value archaeological sites and collections as sources of objects for sale, rather than as sources of information about the past or of commemorative or heritage value. Almost always the commercial activities associated with this particular alternative perspective destroys archaeological resources (e.g. Meyer 1973; Elia 1997; McManamon and Morton 2000). It is a perspective that should be struggled against by all those who value archaeological preservation.

Another perspective is one that so undervalues scientific approaches to the investigation of archaeological sites that its proponents object to any such study and work actively to block such investigations. Unfortunately, some aboriginal people in some parts of the world have adopted this perspective, although others actively pursue archaeological investigations and support archaeological programmes. All those who wish to learn about the past using archaeological data and investigations should be prepared to object to this alternative perspective.

(3) 'Individuals among the general public can serve as the eyes and ears of local, state or even national officials who are responsible for archaeological preservation' (McManamon 2000, 7). There are cooperative volunteer activities that can implement national, state, tribal or local archaeological protection laws. Where such programmes exist, for example, the Site Stewards programmes in Arizona and Texas, they involve non-professional volunteers monitoring site conditions and reporting any signs of looting or vandalism with coordination and subsequent formal reporting by a small professional staff (e.g. Hoffman 1991). I was not implying or proposing to initiate a 'big brother' system of archaeological oversight. Rather, my point is to emphasize that archaeological sites are often in remote locations and may be looted by unscrupulous or misguided individuals. In parts of the United States, volunteer 'site steward' programmes have provided a very valuable means of helping to provide site protection. These individuals value archaeological resources and have been willing to donate their time and energy for the public good.

I want to thank Holtorf for his careful reading of my article. There is no greater compliment from one colleague to another than a serious reading of one's work. I thank him for raising the issues that concerned him and hope that this response allays his fears and enables him to see the importance of valuing an archaeological perspective enough to be an advocate for it, especially when alternative views threaten the archaeological record.

Acknowledgements to Appendix 2

I thank Cornelius Holtorf for sending me a copy of his comment in advance and Neal Ascherson for the opportunity to include my response in the same issue of *Public Archaeology*. Terry Childs and Barbara Little of the Archeology and Ethnography Program, National Park Service, discussed the topic with me and offered some suggestions. I hope they agree with how I have taken this information and used it in this response, for which I alone am responsible.

References to Appendix 2

Elia, R. Looting, collecting, and the destruction of archaeological resources. *Non-renewable Resources* **6**(2) (1997) 85–98.

Harris, Interactive, *Exploring Public Perceptions and Attitudes about Archaeology*. Society for American Archaeology, Washington, DC (2000) (available at www.saa.org).

Hoffman, T. L. Stewards of the past: preserving Arizona's archaeological resources through positive public involvement. In: Smith, G. S. and Ehrenhard, J. E. (eds), *Protecting the Past*. CRC Press, Boca Raton, FL (1991) 253–259.

McManamon, F. P. The many publics for archaeology. *American Antiquity* **56**(1) (1991) 121–130.

McManamon, F. P. Archaeological messages and messengers. *Public Archaeology* **1**(1) (2000) 5–20.

McManamon, F. P., Bradley, J. W. and Magennis, A. L. *The Indian Neck Ossuary. Chapters in the Archeology of Cape Cod, V.* Cultural Resources Management Study, No. 17. North Atlantic Regional Office, National Park Service, Boston, MA (1986).

McManamon, F. P. and Bradley, J. W. The Indian Neck Ossuary. *Scientific American* **258**(5) (1988) 98–105.

McManamon, F. P. and Morton, S. D. Reducing the illegal trafficking in antiquities. In: McManamon, F. P. and Hatton, A. (eds) *Cultural Resource Management in Contemporary Society: Perspectives on Managing and Presenting the Past.* Routledge, London (2000) 247–275.

Meyer, K. *The Plundered Past: The Story of Illegal International Traffic in Works of Art.* Atheneum, New York.

Pokotylo, D. L. and Guppy, N. Public opinion and archaeological heritage: views from outside the profession. *American Antiquity* **64** (1999) 400–416.

Rensberger, B. The nature of evidence. *Science* **289**(5476) (2000) 61.

"Leveling the Playing Field" in the Contested Territory of the South African Past

A "public" versus a "people's" form of historical archaeology outreach

Patrice L. Jeppson

In South Africa, the legacy of colonialism and apartheid includes a history of partisan concepts of ethnic and social identity. The long charged, sociopolitical context has also affected research questions, as well as public interpretations, about the past. Today, there are calls for a new past for the new South Africa. Historical archaeology can provide both a methodology and raw materials which South Africans can use to form their own interpretations of their past, helping, in turn, to engender pride through a historical consciousness emancipated from colonial and apartheid ideology. This chapter presents an overview of this complex and changing research context and its implications for an historical archaeology study of South African frontier identity. Research and "public" archaeology efforts concerning material and mythical perspectives of ethnicity are discussed. Employed in a cross-context comparison with African American research, this study highlights the need for decolonized historical archaeology outreach.

Introduction

Formal calls to incorporate the voice and the needs of "the other" in historical interpretations have become commonplace within North American archaeology and within the field of anthropology in general (e.g. Tilley 1989; Pinsky and Wylie 1989). In historical archaeology, this concern falls within the spheres of critical archaeology (e.g. Leone *et al.* 1987; Handsman and Leone 1989; Potter 1994) and archaeology in the public interest. South African archaeological practice has similar public responsibility concerns. However, within this regional tradition, a distinction is clearly drawn between a public archaeology which popularizes knowledge about the past and a people's archaeology based on democratizing knowledge. As Ritchie (1990:31) explains it, "a popularizing archaeology brings to light aspects of the past excluded in dominant or elitist history" while a people's archaeology "defines instead the different processes through which knowledge about the past is produced."

This difference in outreach orientation became important during the People's Education for People's Power campaign initiated in the 1980s in the fight to end Nationalist Party government rule and establish a democratic South African society (Kruss 1988; Odendaal 1991). By promoting "the values of democracy, nonracialism, collective work, and active participation" (Callinicos 1991:262), this campaign sought to create an alternative to state-directed history interpretations. In line with this need, the principle objective of a people's archaeology became "to empower communities so that they may develop the ability to produce knowledge and establish for themselves a popular memory" (Ritchie 1990:32).

The contrast between these two forms of archaeological responsibility has bearing on material culture studies of ethnicity and on historical archaeology's potential for challenging ethnic stereotypes, be it in South Africa or elsewhere. A "public" archaeology type of outreach involves cracking open the door of the past a little wider in order to incorporate "other voices" for a richer, fuller, story of the past. This endeavor also involves sharing history constructions more broadly with an audience beyond that found in the academic arena. The focus of this activity rests on exposing to the public the archaeologist's role as a caretaker of the common heritage, and this understanding, in turn, assists in archaeology's need to secure both heritage resources as well as the practice of archaeology itself. Alternatively, a people's archaeology type of outreach advocates a change in the power relations involved in the control of history interpretation and history resources. This outreach form takes the position that the art and activity of constructing the past must itself be shared. In this focus, the archaeologist's role as the authoritative voice in the practice of history interpretation is surrendered.

A look at historical archaeology research and outreach in the realm of South African politics helps to distinguish the contributions produced by these two options and highlights why historical archaeology's responsibility to the public should be based not just on archaeology's needs but on archaeology's need to meet the needs of the public.

Background

To consider this topic more fully, its context within the study of the 19th-century South African frontier and within anthropology in apartheid South Africa is addressed.

The 19th-century South African frontier: history, ethnicity, historiography, and historicity

Few would be surprised to learn that understandings about the past in South Africa are found wanting. The existing history interpretations, whether scholarly or public, are generally Eurocentric in their orientation, their intellectual tradition, and the source data on which they are based. For a discussion on South African historiography see, among others, Smith (1988) and Saunders (1988). History written about black South Africans, and black contributions to traditional Occidental history, has always been limited. Prior to colonial contact, indigenous Southern Africans chronicled their histories orally leaving no written documents for Western-style history construction. Later, during the colonial and apartheid eras, blacks were restricted both in their access to Western forms of education and in what they could be taught in Western educational institutions (Kallaway 1984).

An absent or static perception of the indigenous population in historical interpretations, and a Eurocentric concern for important people, places, and events, is not an unusual occurrence in histories produced in a post-colonial setting. But, in South Africa, the historical memory has been additionally compromised by the development of, and the opposition to, Afrikaner Nationalism and, in particular, the political historical myths constructed to support the policy of apartheid.

The place and potency of Afrikaner Nationalism in South African society and its history is easily demonstrated by the Voortrekker Monument, a prominent example of Afrikaner material culture located on a hillside outside the city of Pretoria (Figure 35.1). This artifact of Afrikanerdom dates to the urbanizing and industrial changes occurring in the country during the first half of the 20th century. In particular, British capitalist imperialism and increasing competition from black migrant workers led to a minority political separatist action involving mainly rural white inhabitants (Le Cordeur 1981). This faction of society created a social group consciousness through such activities as a language movement, the creation of a new national anthem, new stamp and coin decoration, and a new flag (Moodie 1975; Adam and Gilomee 1979; Thompson 1985; Gilomee 1989). This ethnic affirmation response became crystallized in the historical myth of the Great Trek and the memorial to it, the Voortrekker Monument (Du Toit 1984).

In brief, the Great Trek story involves a Genesis-like history of frontier migration. It details the movement of Dutch colonial farmers who trekked northwards during the 1830s from the Colony of the Cape of Good Hope into the interior of Africa. The myth rests on a belief that these migrants, redefined as *Afrikaner Voortrekkers*, were a chosen people summoned by God to spread civilization and Christianity into the heart of the continent. This saga and its commemorating structure have long served as a rallying point for the descendant Afrikaner people or *volk*.

The monument's architectural features, its interior furnishings and external landscaping, and its function as a historic landmark and gathering place are reflective of, and act to fulfill, an understanding of this Afrikaner unity. The concentric-ring pattern on the interior main floor is suggestive of ripples in a pond into which a stone has been cast, and signifies to the visitor the spirit of Afrikaner sacrifice spreading throughout the country (*Sentrale Volksmonumente-Komitee En Die Sentrale Voortrekker Eeufeeskomitee* (SVE) 1938). A marble frieze adorning the nearby interior walls depicts the frontier migration story helping to indoctrinate the thousands of people who have viewed it over the past half century (*SVE* 1938). An oil lamp, reputedly used on the Great Trek, burns as an eternal flame (Bond 1949). Near to this lies a cenotaph commemorating the life of the unknown, martyred, Afrikaner soldier. This crypt is illuminated one day each year, noon on 16 December, by a ray of sunlight guided through an astronomically positioned roof aperture (Heymans 1986:7). This yearly event marks a date in Afrikaner political historical myth on which the Voortrekkers made a covenant with God.

On the outside, the fortress-like monument with its gun slit window openings and encircling wagon-train decorated wall, is reminiscent of a defensive ring encampment, or *laager* (*SVE* 1938; Heymans 1986). Beyond this wall, the hillside is richly landscaped with indigenous African plants. The various trek routes which the immigrants followed into the

Figure 35.1 The Voortrekker Monument, 1990, view looking north (photograph by the author).

African interior are recreated in miniature in this "wild garden" using a landscape map model. Along these paths are markers symbolizing the obstacles and events which the Voortrekkers encountered during their journey. This configuration allows visitors to the monument to relive the Trek experience for themselves.

This Afrikaner ideology of "a sacred mission and calling for providence" was wedded, with the sanctioning of the official state church (Dutch Reformed), to the idea of a human racial taxonomy (Moodie 1975:265). In this world view, members of the human species are perceived as separated into stable, bounded entities, each with distinctive cultural and physical characteristics. This understanding, in turn, held that the Afrikaner "people" should be separate from all others in order to maintain their position in a hierarchy of ethnic and cultural difference (Moodie 1975:265; Schutte 1989). Thus, while crucial to establishing the identity of the Afrikaner, the Genesis ideology also formed a larger social context that provided the logic for a system of ethnic segregation.

This understading of South African society and its history became sacrosanct and ultimately formed the substructure for a "civil religion" (Moodie 1975:296) that served for over half a century as the ideological basis for apartheid, the Afrikaner Nationalist policy of "Separate Development." Under this logic, racial and/or ethnic culture groups or populations were perceived as unassimilable and incompatible, each with its own character, its own potential, and its own destiny – Zulu, Afrikaner, English, Sotho, Xhosa, Venda, and so on (Thompson 1985). Legislation enforced and, in turn, justified these ethnic-based separations. These separations were furthermore supported and maintained through retroactively constructed, discrete ethnic histories (Dubow in Hall 1990:65).

For the past 50 years, until the recent political transformations, these segregated pasts were propagated through Nationalist bureaucratic rule making their way into everyday experience through school books (Auerbach 1966; Adam and Gilomee 1979; Cornevin 1980; du Preez 1983; Thompson 1985; Ashley 1989), national monuments and museums (Wright and Mazel 1987; Peires 1989; Davison 1991), and popular heroic tales (Moodie 1975; Thompson 1985; Naidoo 1989). These political histories have helped to sever the black African from a past that provides a stabilizing and positive sense of identity: the black South African heritage has itself been colonized:

> If a ruling minority can enslave the minds of the people, control their ideas and their whole way of thinking, they have found an even more efficient weapon for subjugating them than the use of force, the military and the police. For then the people themselves assist in their own enslavement. If the rulers can make the people believe that they are inferior, wipe out their past history or present it in such a way that they feel, not pride but shame, then they create the conditions that make it easy to dominate the people.
>
> (Majeke 1952:Introduction)

This apartheid history point of reference remains active, residual, and latent in much of the South African public consciousness helping keep apartheid history interpretations institutionally and mentally ingrained even while political transformations have occurred. As such, the apartheid created past unconsciously, consciously, and covertly continues to shape both the South African present and its future (Kallaway 1991; Mare 1993).

Anthropology in apartheid South Africa

One result of the apartheid and colonial heritage is that there has been a tainting of major anthropological analytical concepts including, among others, ethnicity, community, culture, and tradition, in South African based anthropological and archaeological research

(Gluckman 1975; Sharp 1980a; Whisson 1981; Hall 1990, 1993). Under the social and political context of apartheid, studies that employed these constructs were perceived as representing a colonialist stance and/or collusion with the "White Regime" (Hall 1983, 1984). This represented a valid concern in this context because talking about ethnicity could create or reinforce the ethnic divisions of apartheid and colonialism (Boonzaier and Sharp 1988; Kuper 1988:50; Horowitz 1991:28–29). This "opposition" was also a response to specific disciplinary developments unique to South Africa.

Within South Africa's charged sociopolitical setting, the local anthropology tradition underwent a split into two contrasting camps, that of a British-style social anthropology in English-speaking universities, and a discipline called *Volkekunde* found at Afrikaans speaking universities, several homeland universities, and in government agencies such as the Bureau for Racial Affairs and the South African Defense force (Sharp 1980a, 1980b; Booyens and van Rensburg 1980; Pauw 1980; Sharp 1981; Kuper 1983, 1986, 1988; Gordon and Spiegel 1993). For the past 30-some years, South African anthropological research has "normally been formulated in terms of one or other of these anthropology traditions, and, as often as not, the efforts have been judged in political terms as much as by academic criteria" (Kuper 1986:4).

Liberal-thinking South Africans have commonly believed that *Volkekunde* and its practitioners were, by and large, committed to the Nationalist movement and that the discipline was the deliberate development of the intellectual underpinnings of apartheid (Moodie 1975:245; Kuper 1983:104, 1988:35). This belief was based on the particular use and understanding of ethnicity in *Volkekunde* known as "ethnos theory." This theoretical understanding divides humankind into *volke (nations,* people) each with its own particular culture (Booyens and van Rensburg 1980; Sharp 1980a, 1981:19; Kuper 1983:33; Voorster *et al.* 1986). *Volkekunde*, according to a University of South Africa course study guide, involves the study of: "a) peoples as cultural groups, b) culture as the product of peoples, c) psychological features of peoples of all times as the cause or result of culture, and d) physical features of peoples of all times as the cause or result of culture" (Voorster *et al.* 1986:97–98). This central concern with ethnos also underlay the *volk* mythology of Afrikanerdom, and, in its practice, *Volkekunde* essentially extended the core conception of the Afrikaner *volk* to other ethnos (Moodie 1975; Sharp 1981:28; Butler 1989; Gilomee 1989). As a result, *Volkekunde* can be conceived of as anthropology constructed in terms of an intellectual paradigm conducive to Afrikaner consciousness (Kuper 1988:35).

The tendency toward a divergence into these two camps became marked in the 1940s with the arrival of Afrikaner Christian Nationalist rule (Sharp 1981). With this Nationalist Party victory over British imperial interests, Afrikaner intellectuals appropriated institutions to enforce the *volk* ideal (Moodie 1975; Adam and Gilomee 1979; Smith 1988:4; Pityana 1995). University of Pretoria anthropology professor W. M. Eiselen, for example, was a major architect of "separate development," serving as an administrator of apartheid policy under the new Afrikaner government (Moodie 1975:73). Other *Volkekunde* anthropologists served the government on the Committee for Bantu Affairs, in the Department of Cooperation and Development, and in the Defense Force which had an ethnological section. *Volkekunde* departments, meanwhile, offered "service courses" that prepared students for civil service sector jobs in which they functioned to enforce and justify the policy of apartheid and the homelands system (Sharp 1981:5).

During this period, many South African social anthropologists strongly sought to distance themselves from the ethnos theory approach of their *Volkekunde* colleagues. Several of these individuals were also politically active in opposing apartheid that several became targets and victims of the government, suffering actions ranging from harassment to even murder – including the assassinations of Ruth First and University of the Witwatersrand anthropologist, David Webster. The South African social anthropologists formally renounced apartheid by professionally stating a political position supporting a democratic society (Association for South African Anthropology in Southern Africa (AASA) 1988; Fry 1992:230).

By the time I began my own research (Jeppson [1998]), this branch of South African anthropology had come to define analytical concepts such as ethnicity, culture, and tradition as aspects of political nationalism which held no anthropological relevancy. Ethnicity was considered a "dirty word," and culture was a concept regarded, as by necessity, racist, a point I discovered during one of my early talks. I found that negative critiques haunted American anthropology, particularly the work of Melville Herskovits – also the father of American African Studies – whom *Volkekunde* studies heavily adopted from, and Alfred Kroeber, because of his (later retracted) paper on the "Superorganic" (Sharp 1980a, 1981:36). This anti-cultural anthropology sentiment condemned the holistic, four-field approach and assessed American cultural anthropology as not just inferior but immoral. As a result of this guilt by association, visiting American cultural anthropologists were sometimes avoided by local social anthropologists and, every so often, I even heard the name of Herskovits "demonized" and invoked as an epithet.

This avoidance of "culture," as a term and concept, in this regional tradition also stemmed, in part, from social anthropology's theoretical positioning – "the reluctance of the Radcliffe-Brown school to allow an independent explanatory role to cultural factors" (Kuper 1983:48; Gluckman 1975) – and a Marxist paradigm favored for the last two decades in the radical branches of South African history, sociology, anthropology, and archaeology. Moreover, the anti-culture stance was reinforced and supported by black consciousness politics, by the mass democratic processes striving for national unity, and by a black nationalist position within South African anthropology that promoted the judging of research efforts on the basis of the "contribution to a national identity" (Kuper 1986:2). Adding to the equation was South Africa's isolation from metropolitan anthropology and its ideas due to its extreme geographical position, located on the southern tip of the continent, and to global politics – specifically, the decades of national economic decline and therefore loss of university funding, and the years of academic boycotts, all of which limited the information flow normally available through academic journals and scholarly exchanges (Gordon and Spiegel 1993).

A historical archaeology study of 19th-century frontier identity: reassessing ethnicity in the search for a new South African past

The methods and theory behind this historical archaeology research are addressed below along with the outreach practices and resulting responses.

Method and theory

So how does a historical archaeology study conducted in the American anthropological tradition effectively incorporate, and become incorporated into, such a research context? Ethnicity as a cultural term does have a complex history, a variety of meanings, and a number of uses and abuses both inside and outside South Africa. The approach I take in my investigation of the South African frontier is to illustrate the value of ethnicity and identity concepts in the study of South African society and its history (Jeppson 1993, 1995a, 1996a, [1998]). Specifically, I use excavated objects and documentary evidence from four frontier sites – a mission, a fort, a hinterland domestic site, and a colonial town site – to investigate the nature and role of material culture in frontier social dynamics: using a cross-cultural approach, I investigate how Industrial Age, mass-produced British goods are involved in the construction, reproduction, and transformation of shared cultural beliefs and values during a time of contact, conflict, and culture change (Jeppson 1987, 1988b, 1988c, 1988e, 1988f, 1990a, 1990c, 1991a, 1991b, [1998]). The recovered evidence suggests that material culture functions in 19th-century frontier society as symbols in social interaction, reflecting and actively communicating information about the making and marking of social group identities. I argue, both in the research and in related public outreach activities, that a concern with the definition and self-definition of frontier social groupings, and the relationship of these definitions to history, is integral for an understanding of the South African past, present, and future.

Unlike apartheid's hegemonic ideology and the responding impetus to ignore ethnicity and culture, much academic and public emphasis in American society and history is concerned with questions of self-identity and collective self-consciousness, and the circumstances under which self-perceptions yield to the will of a democratic majority (Appleby et al. 1994). In the ideological understanding of the United States, studies of social group identity – ethnicity, nationalism – play an increasing part. Furthermore, while ethnicity in South Africa has long remained associated with "tribe," American anthropology long ago jettisoned this understanding, aligning with metropolitan anthropology's interest in multicultural, multiethnic, and interactive contexts. Within this research context, my investigation of South African frontier ethnicity embraces epistemological features fundamental to these paradigms and postures, that is, that ethnicity is non-isolated, contemporary, and universally applicable; that it is subjectivist, or both objectivist and subjectivist; that it exists as a unit only in relation to others; and that it has shifting boundaries and varying degrees of "systemic" quality (Cohen 1978:384–385).

Such issues of classification in cognition – social group identity, ethnicity, and nationalism – are also a central focus of an "anthropology of knowledge"; the anthropological concern for culture "as a process of acquiring and displaying knowledge" – of rules, values, and beliefs – including how it is that people learn about and create social consciousness (Crick 1982:287). Such knowledge includes how social identities come into existence, what resources may be employed in the process, what roles material culture may play in their social reproduction, and why the social identifications might be mobilized (Shennan 1989:16). An understanding of how such cultural histories and ethnic origins are experienced, remembered, and created is a relevant enterprise both in South Africa and in the modern world in general, plagued as it is by racial schisms, ethnicity factionalism, and rival nationalisms.

The study of ethnicity similarly plays an important role in the development of North America historical archaeology as an academic enterprise (e.g. Deetz 1977; Schuyler 1980). Unlike the social science conducted in the apartheid context, historical archaeology studies of ethnicity are undertaken within a social and political setting that favors a multicultural heritage approach as a way to reach a more accurate understanding of the American past and present. For a discussion of this context see, among others, Takaki (1987) and Appleby et al. (1994). An interest in ethnicity is a logical outgrowth of American historical archaeology's goal of "writing the history of the inarticulate" (Ascher 1974:10). The descendants of enslaved Africans, Chinese laborers, and other American immigrants, as well as First Nations people, have strong ethnic heritage interests which form a common point for contemporary popular and political organization and definition (Glazer and Moynihan 1963).

The theoretical underpinnings of current historical archaeology ethnicity research, described elsewhere by, among others, McGuire (1982) and McKee (1984), is foreign to that found in Volkekunde and that long feared by the South African social anthropologists. American historical archaeologists routinely propose an adaptive nature for tradition and identity. In this approach, ethnicity is seen as something that people themselves create, as something that grows and changes. The emphasis in this understanding is placed on process, or on the consciousness that forms the starting point for the construction and maintenance of social group boundaries (Earth 1970). These boundaries are often imposed or reinforced using symbols, including material culture, putting them within the purview of historical archaeology.

Research, outreach, and response in the South African context

While I propose that issues of classification and cognition should not be ignored in the study of the South African past, it has not always been the case that these interests are welcome. South Africa's turbulent social and political context presents perplexing issues for a material culture investigation of cultural identity at every stage of the research process: at the point of determining categories for data analysis, in the methodological practice of archaeological comparison, in defining the theoretical concepts of anthropology knowledge, and in the public outreach related to the research. I touch on two such examples here.

Preliminary documentary research conducted on the Wesleyan Mission Station of Farmerfield (established 1839) indicates that a complex social landscape comprised of discrete ethnic villages once existed at this site (*Graham's Town Journal* 2 April 1840:4; Wesleyan Missionary Society 1840, 1847, 1853:13–14; Merriman in Varley and Matthew 1957 [17 August 1850]:125; Shaw 1860 [July 1850]). A church building, the Catechist's home, and the common pasture lands were reputed to be surrounded by three hamlets or villages located contiguous to each other: one hamlet inhabited by individuals formerly enslaved by European colonists, another occupied by farmer-herders indigenous to the area (amaXhosa), and a third inhabited by farmer-herders from the north (Sotho). This structured residential setting constitutes one of the earliest episodes of a segregated South African landscape although the reported social divisions could have been imposed or reflected acknowledged emic differences – linguistic, racialistic, ethnic – or could have even been nonexistent.

These historically perceived, discrete, village locations make for an ideal archaeological opportunity for investigating questions of social distinctions marked by material culture variations. However, when these historically defined social groupings were juxtaposed with one another for artifact analysis and interpretation, the response among many local liberal and radical academics, those with whom I eagerly desired to share this research, was overwhelmingly negative. Among other things, I was told categorically that culture groups did not exist in the past, or the present, but were only figments of the South African Christian National frame of reference. When I presented artifact pattern evidence and oral history testimony that could be indicative of possible "social groupings," it was suggested to me that perhaps I "could substitute the word ethnicity with a Latin or German term that sounded scientific," or perhaps I could "find a French term that had flair" (audience remarks, South African Association of Anthropologists conference 1988). I found that inquiries about the culture, tradition, and/or ethnicity of the inhabitants at Farmerfield constituted research that was "inherently racist" (audience remarks, Archaeology Department guest lectures, University of the Witwatersrand 1987, 1992).

As my research became crowded by the South African social and political context, it became obvious to me that the difficulties harbored valuable clues into how the past served as a resource in current South African society. Once I recognized the dominant ideologies of the research context, and their components, I found I could deal with the research context anthropologically and not as simply a situation that had to be correct or corrected for. The focus of my artifact study and the related outreach efforts shifted to include the practice of culture as a historical experience: the problematic relationship between history, ethnicity, historiography, and historicity became part of the story of investigating identity definitions and the relations of these definitions to history. In brief, I propose in this research and outreach that frontier material culture differences reflect self-generated as well as externally imposed social designations formed in response to, and partly in opposition to, the new or changing environment and encountered "others." As such, the recovered symbolic markers, and the social divisions of difference and sameness they mirror and mark, are products of intra- and inter-group relations, representing cultural resource grounded in a shared historical experience.

In this process-oriented interpretation, social identity constructs are assessed as fluid entities based on shifting, concurrent, common interests. As social categories, such classifications do not define all of a person, nor even all of a collective. Moreover, I do not perceive such material reflections of identity to be simply a matter of maintained cultural background or tradition represented by "survival" markers. They are, in fact, distinguished from social categorizations based on mere spatial variation in material remains. I do not ascribe site specific assemblages to static ethnic or cultural stereotypes as "archaeological cultures." Rather, any discovered social group identifications refer instead to self-conscious identifications that are anchored internally in experience and externally in the contingent situation, or setting, involving the mobilizing identity. Thus, while the South African frontier identities may, in their making, be in part derived from a sense of a deeper cultural past, the relationship between these colonial-era residents and their heritage of cultural beliefs and practices is not an uninterrupted one.

I suggest with this research that the borders and nature of frontier social groupings change according to the needs and social circumstances developing in culture contact and conflict. In their use as a symbol of identity definition and boundary maintenance, the material culture expressions of identity represent a form of knowledge. This knowledge is not just about social meaning alone but is also knowledge about how it is that these symbols themselves are formed and maintained (Crick 1982). Such knowledge is significant because, as Comaroff (1982:50) explains elsewhere, "in a world of marking relations, of denoting identities, it isn't the contents of those identities alone that is important but the processes of marking them, establishing with them a sociological chain of being." It is the interpreting of these boundaries and identities, providing the how and why for these material record patterns, that returns those "forgotten" to South African history in a two-directional process of culture change.

In the end, the social identities translated from the frontier material record are presented as non-static cultural entities that only can be understood in historical perspective. This situationally defined and historically contextualized concept of identity formation helps to expose as fallacy the notions of primordial, bounded ethnicities that have shaped the South African segregated historical consciousness. I argue that once there is an understanding of the situationalness of identity formation, the imposed, self-defined, and adopted social definitions found in apartheid South Africa can be evaluated. Employed with this aim, the frontier past constructed with historical archaeology evidence is used to challenge the present. It becomes a resource that is more effective for the general public: historical archaeology research on frontier society holds a promise of empowerment for those whose contributions to the past and to the present have been denied, or for those who have assimilated into their self-identity the static, negative, handicapping representations created by others.

In the archaeological outreach related to this dissertation study (Jeppson 1988a, 1988c, 1989a, 1989b, 1989c, 1989e, 1990a, 1990b, 1990d, 1990e, 1991c, 1992, 1995a 1995b) I have attempted to illuminate the interconnectedness of the colonizer and colonized in frontier experience and the contingency of social othering. I combined these points with an emphasis on critical thinking skills to form a recurring theme in both public and people's types of archaeology outreach – including site tours, field and lab work with students and public volunteers, school-based presentations, public and in-house museum lectures, research-related museum exhibits, and museum education program aids.

Among my various archaeology outreach efforts is a traveling museum exhibit case that I constructed during research at the British military site of Fort Double Drift (established 1836). This exhibit case, discussed elsewhere (Jeppson 1988a, 1988d, 1989b, 1989c, 1989d, 1989e, 1995a, 1995b), was designed as a remote educational aid for the Mobile Museum Education Service at the Albany Museum in Grahamstown. This liberal-leaning institution embraced historical archaeology in the late 1980s, serving as host to numerous projects (cf. Hardwick 1989; Scott and Deetz 1990; Winer and Deetz 1990; Deetz 1993; Jeppson [1998]). The museum kindly supported the construction of this educational aid lending me materials, equipment, and the assistance of their Displays Department staff.

This exhibit, comprised of a display case and work booklet, is designed to compare and contrast history information sources — documents and excavated artifacts — and to include, within one scenario, all those present on the frontier landscape — San, Khoi, Xhosa, British settler, and British military. It is hoped that the comparison of history information sources will encourage an awareness of how interpretations about the past come about in a "method as message" approach. This approach, detailed elsewhere by Leone (1983:46), uses the concept of "how do we know what we know" to illustrate the "process of knowing." As Leone (1983:46) states, "method displays provide the public with the ability to assess and the possibility of challenging conventional conclusions about the past."

For a South African public armed with such critical thinking skills (Tunmer 1988; van Zyl 1988), apartheid history constructions, and even presently held beliefs, can come to be recognized as part of a historical process and thus be removed from a state of inviolate fact. In this manner, history no longer remains something that is static but rather becomes part of the ongoing process of making the past. Importantly, in this approach to the study of the South African frontier there is no "absolving of activities of the past" and no "correcting past history constructs" (Leone 1983:46). Likewise there is "no encouragement of a state of historical amnesia" (Leone 1983:46). In this outreach activity, the critical thinking skills used in the study of the past become important as educational messages themselves, and these skills, in turn, can be taken beyond the exhibit exercise, out into general life experience. In contrast to apartheid and colonial history constructs, this history interpretation is useful for citizens of the new South Africa. The relations between past and present and between history and modern society are exposed raising the possibility for an understanding of the conditions of modern life (Potter 1991, 1992, 1994).

It is also my hope that the broader based picture of the frontier, made possible with archaeologically recovered evidence, can help, in one small measure, to free South Africans to move beyond the ideological impasse of Nationalist and colonial interpretations and preconceptions by uniting the history of Europeans with the history of the indigenous. The interpretation of the frontier portrayed in this educational exhibit is not of an elite, a majority, or a dominant history, nor a history of only those forgotten. It is a presentation of a past that both of these partake of and help create. Such "integrating" of the past can help create potential scaffolding for a new historical social reality (see McDavid, chapter 37, this volume). The historical archaeology data and interpretations, and the methods and methodology for their recovery, are resources available for a new socialization of people into knowledge (Peponis and Hedin 1982).

This educational exhibit received positive evaluations from, among others, the curator of the Africana Museum (Nagelgast 1990), a university historian in a Teaching Credential program, museum educators at the South African National Gallery and the South African Museum (audience comments, South African Museum Associations Education Conference IX 1989), and staff at both local, then segregated, black and white elementary and high schools who were desperate to circumvent or amend government produced history texts. Despite these positive reviews, in the final analysis this educational exhibit could not be accessioned into the museum's Education Department. Not only did it not fit with the state-mandated school syllabus which formed the basis for the mobile museum service, but it also conflicted with the ideological structure of South African museums.

This ideological structure during the final years of apartheid was mandated by the Nationalist government's "Own Affairs/General Affairs" policy (Smith 1987; Owen and Holleman 1989; Webb 1989). "Own Affairs," as defined in the 1983 constitution, concerned "matters which specially or differentially affect a population group in relation to the maintenance of its identity and the upholding and furtherance of its way of life, culture, traditions, and customs" – any concerns beyond the unit of the "population group" were part of "General Affairs." Under the choke hold of this ideology and bureaucracy, museum scholarship, social space, and funding were divided into discrete domains: the disciplines of cultural history and *kulture geskeidens* were concerned with the history of the English colonists, their descendants and the Afrikaners; anthropology departments – also referred to as ethnology or, as a distancing measure from *Volkekunde*, ethnography – performed study on black lifeways; and archaeology departments concerned themselves with pre-contact indigenous history such as that of the deep Iron Age and the Stone Age (Davison 1991).

The multicultural, multidisciplinary museum educational exhibit "confused" these commonly held, official notions of segregated South African history, and so, in essence, the exhibit could not find a home – it is, however, used by the Archaeology Department staff. As a "critical thinking"-based display, it also presented an alternative methodology to the one-sided and distorted Nationalist history narrative. In this sense, it challenged the authority of the state which was, in part, divinely sanctioned through ideological schooling and which required loyalty and obedience from its students (Ashley 1989:23). South African museums, long a tool of apartheid with their ideological history interpretations, still remained at this time, regardless of individual sentiments within the institutions, a victim of apartheid ideology and bureaucracy and the exhibit outreach effort became, in turn, a victim of this.

Conclusion

Today, a rejection of the existing historical interpretations by the majority of the South African populace, an abandonment of Afrikaner Nationalist politicized history practice, and a spate of history revisions related to the changing discourse of African and South African politics marks the state of anthropology research in South Africa and South African history construction. At the same time, the continuing ethnic strife in South Africa's Kwazulu/Natal Province has helped it become readily apparent that ethnicity cannot be washed or wished away as a factor in explaining prevailing South African social relations (Mare 1993). Now, as enforced separations between South Africans disappear, ethnicity is reemerging as a valid topic in a surge of post-Resistance activity (Fry 1992; Gordon and Spiegel 1993). This move complements the many calls made for useful histories for a changing South Africa and holds promise for anthropological historical archaeology research.

The "masses," speaking through social organizations, trade unions, political platforms, and now political leaders in departments of ministry, have specifically "demanded" an end to histories characterized by domination and by a lack of common national unity and purpose. Such requirements strike at the heart of the segregated and static ethnic histories that have formed the core of much public history and apartheid ideology, and that have long supported dehumanizing domination. The expressed desire is for a history that supports liberation and transformation from colonial and apartheid oppression and that restores a sense of historical consciousness (Ashley 1989; Kallaway 1991).

Because the past in South Africa has been a site of oppression – one reinforced through a pervasive, repressive, historical ideology – any social rather than only structural change towards a new society must include a handing over of the reins of power. This surrender must specifically include the power of the historical frame of reference, particularly that of "social group identity" which is linked to culture pride and self worth. This will free the population from the fear of difference instituted under the apartheid construction of knowledge.

Historical archaeology can contribute toward the creation of a historical past of common national unity and restored pride in heritage relevant to today's post-apartheid South Africa. The raw data recovered in such research, and the resulting broader based history interpretations, can add testimony needed for a reevaluation of self- and national identity for a new South African society. In contributing to such alternative history interpretations, historical archaeology studies of ethnicity can also make transparent the ideological realities of colonialism and apartheid oppression, helping to maintain a vigilance against their continuation in postapartheid life.

Beyond this regional contribution, when considered at a global level scale of comparison, historical archaeology in the realm of South African politics can also serve as a case study example against which to examine public outreach issues in African American archaeology. The analysis of another culture is an effective way to open up areas of one's own culture in which notions of the past and cultural integrity are created and remain largely unexamined (Thornton 1988). This comparison of two, "colonial brother," nation-states helps highlight contradictions that exist in global-wide historical archaeology research contexts and, therefore, in its practices and goals. The comparison reveals, for example, how a concern for poly-vocality in North America "could" describe an Americancentric need and focus. This follows an understanding that "the knowledge we formulate about 'the other' is refracted through the knowledge we have built to define ourselves" (Crick 1982:293).

Viewed within the larger, modern world context, the segregation ideology of apartheid South Africa remains unique among the ideological unity credos that evolved in other heavily European populated, post-colonial, nation states, such as Brazil, Australia, and Mexico, or even in the European "mother countries" which were formed or transformed as a result of colonial expansion and conquest. It stands, for example, as an antithesis to the American ideology of *e pluribus unum* – "one out of many" – where diversity is perceived as a source of identity and unity: a syncretic, evolving, commonality in civil culture (Fuchs 1991; Appleby *et al.* 1994). Whereas the concept of "multiculturalism" serves as a basis and reaffirmation of an American national identity, the Afrikaner "united as one" ideology alternatively represents one ethos – Afrikaner culture – against, and above, all others (Moodie 1975).

The "multicultural" understanding of American collective identity represents a recent national meta-narrative. Based on the last quarter-century of social history scholarship, this understanding challenges the older order of Anglo-American leadership supported by objectivist science paradigms that were themselves reworked from earlier notions of manifest destiny and social progress (Appleby *et al.* 1994). Like those believed in before it, this defining sense of national identity gives cohesion to an aggregation of people missing a common, shared folk culture. This use of multiculturalism as an understanding for American national identity (context) is reflected in the calls for poly-vocality in history interpretations and in the responses to this need found in historical archaeology research and archaeology outreach. This national identity also endorses the inclusiveness of an open society while falling short of creating one in practice. As a result, extreme adherents of multiculturalism advocate a fragmented "identity politics," not dissimilar in structure and emphasis to apartheid politics.

The importation into South Africa of the North American concept of multiculturalism has several implications for national consciousness of which the historical archaeologist would want to be aware. In this setting, the term has been put to various context-specific uses. During the recent political transitions, multiculturalism has served a Nationalist Party political strategy in "a plan for a continued plural society with group rights" (Kallaway 1991). Used in this sense, multicultural history, or poly-vocality, would mean the continuation of special privileges and rights for particular culture groups in the new South Africa. This term-sans-concept adoption follows two earlier consequences of "relative usage" or "the penetration of [South African] intellectual culture by otherwise commonly used international, scientific ideas" (Kuper 1988:50). Decades ago, apartheid rulers tried to gain legitimacy for their policy by replacing the term "race" with the metropolitan term "culture" and replaced the apartheid term "pluralism" with "segregation." These apartheid-type uses were incompatible with an American or nationalist black majority emphasis on national heritage. More recently, in the election of a transitional government of national unity with Nelson Mandela as president, multiculturalism in South Africa was celebrated as "one nation, many cultures." This understanding encourages an appreciation of culture difference. "Unity in Diversity" forms the basis for building a "rainbow nation" identity for the new South Africa (African National Congress Information Services, 22 April 1996).

Similarly, in a cross-context comparison, the anti-American cultural anthropology sentiment once found among South African social anthropologists appears paradoxical when juxtaposed with the rhetoric of the prominent conservative wing of US society, which rails against affirmative action, multiculturalism, and a broader based set of history standards (Appleby *et al.* 1994). Meanwhile, the most extreme rightwing factions frequently attack the "liberal scholarship" of American anthropology as the root cause for (what they perceive to be) America's social ills. For example, a member of the National Alliance – a patriot movement-aligned neo-Nazi group that shares sentiments with the Freemen, Christian Identity, some militias, and the Ku Klux Klan – said the following on a recent radio broadcast: "Herskovits . . . and other students of the cultural anthropology school headed by the communist Boas [including] Ashley Montagu, Raymond Pearl, Herbert Seligman, Otto Klineberg, Gene Weltfish, Amram Scheinfeld, Ruth Benedict, L. C. Dunn, Isador Chein, and Margaret Mead . . . propagandized the public and subverted the govenment with that foundation and wellspring of liberalism . . . the fraudulent doctrine of universal human equality" (McKinney 1995a, 1995b).

Transcripts of this and similar discussions are widely available on the AM dial, FM dial, and shortwave radio (e.g. the National Alliance radio broadcast, *American Dissident Voices Weekly*), in publications (e.g. the National Alliance's publication, *National Vanguard*), and on Internet Radio (National Alliance's *FreeSpeech* at http://www.natvan.com). In this rhetoric, the position is that "liberalism" is based on an anthropology-linked sociopolitical agenda responsible for "fifty years of liberal and alien subversion of our government and institutions, the moral decay, the decline of the public school system, the out-of-control immigration, the explosion of non-white crime, [and] the other consequences of diversity" (McKinney 1995b). Anthropologists have furthermore "brainwashed" the public about "the study of race": the "modern religion of equalitarianism" is presented as the Boas school's attempt to "distort and falsify science" conducted on race (McKinney 1995a). In these media forums, books such as *The Bell Curve* (Hernstein and Murray 1994) are cited extensively as "scientific" sources that valiantly attempt to expose this anthropological "brainwashing."

A comparison of historical archaeology in the realms of South African and African American politics exposes context-specific assumptions that could potentially affect practices and goals. Edward Said (1989:210–211), among others, has cautioned about the imperialistic aspects of decolonialism in the field of anthropology, stating that "even as we strive to decolonize anthropology, with much theoretical work on textuality and discourse, American imperialism remains a factor affecting theoretical discussion. To practice anthropology in the U.S. is not just to be investigating 'otherness' and 'difference' in a large country; it is to be discussing them in an enormously influential and powerful State whose global role is that of a superpower."

This same caution is relevant for the role of poly-vocality, depending on its use and definition, in historical archaeology. A comparison of research contexts helps to make known how historical archaeology is part of itself, how any statement about culture is a statement about historical archaeology and how any practice of archaeology outreach is therefore a cultural decision involving power relations.

Once the goals and practices that exist in differing research contexts are identified, they can be reflected upon and can be fed back into historical archaeology, ultimately enriching the field of study as a whole. The resulting decolonized research will add to ongoing discussions within general, or metropolitan, anthropology and archaeology about how people define and shape their world and the approaches useful for identifying and understanding such world views.

Acknowledgements

I thank the Albany Museum, the Department of Archaeology and the Oppenheimer Centre for African Studies at the University of Cape Town, the Institute for Social and Economic Research at Rhodes University, and the National Monuments Council of South Africa for facilitating various phases of this research. Anna Papp and Stephen Welz kindly donated materials, and Gerard Marx graciously provided artistic advice for the display case. Headmistress Qaba, Mr Mfino, Ms Qama, the students at Farmerfield School, Headmistress Lehr, Keith James, Virginia Burrage, George Brauer, and especially Mr Cecil Nonqane helped with outreach activities. I owe my gratitude to Antonia Malan, Gabrielle Ritchie, Edwin O. Hanish, Simon Hall, Patrick McAllister, and Robert Thornton for helping me to refine my understanding of South African disciplinary traditions. I thank Robert Schuyler and James Deetz for their advice, support, and direction with this research. Carol McDavid made several helpful suggestions concerning this chapter.

References

Adam, Herbert, and Hermann Gilomee 1979 *The Rise and Crisis of Afrikaner Power*. David Philip, Cape Town, South Africa.

African National Congress Information Services 1996 Freedom Day Celebrations: "Unity in Diversity." South African Communications Services, 22 April 1996. Johannesburg, South Africa. <http://WWW.scas.org.za/cgi-bin/vdkw_cgi>.

American Dissidentvoicesweekly 1991 – Radio program hosted by William Pierce and the 1996 National Alliance. Shortwave 15420 and 7355 kHz; Satellite G7 Channel 14; 7.56 MHz audio; AM radio dial Q 100 (Florida); AM 760, 890 (Alabama); AM 1230,1180 (Texas); 1190,490 (Arkansas); AM 1090 (Midwest and Gulf South US); AM 1540 (Upper Midwest and Northern Mountain US); AM 990 (Northeast); Q FM 94.3 (Texas), ADV Internet Radio on-line <http://www.natall.com/radio.html>. Hillsboro, VA.

Appleby, Joyce, Lyn Hunt, and Margaret Jacob 1994 *Telling the Truth about History*. W. W. Norton, New York.

Ascher, Robert 1974 Tin Can Archaeology. *Historical Archaeology* 8:1–16.

Ashley, Michael 1989 *Ideologies and Schooling in South Africa*. Pioneer Press, Mowbray, South Africa.

Association for Anthropology in Southern Africa (AASA) 1988 Ethical Guidelines for South African Anthropologists (as approved by the Association for Anthropology in Southern

Africa at its 1987 conference). Presented to the Membership at the Annual Meeting of the Association for Anthropology in Southern Africa Conference, Grahamstown, South Africa.

Auerbach, Franz 1966 *The Power and Prejudice in South African Education: An Enquiry into History Textbooks and Syllabuses in the Transvaal High Schools of South Africa*. Balema, Cape Town, South Africa.

Barth, Frederick 1970 *Ethnic Groups and Boundaries*. Little, Brown, New York.

Bond, J. J. 1949 The Saga of the Great Trek. *The Star*, 16 December: Insert. Johannesburg, South Africa.

Boonzaier, Emile, and John Sharp 1988 *South African Keywords: The Uses and Abuses of Political Concepts*. David Philip, Cape Town, South Africa.

Booyens, J. H. and N. S. Jansen Van Rensburg 1980 Reply from Potchefstroom, Anthropology in South Africa. *Royal Anthropology Institute Newsletter* 31:3–4.

Butler, Jeffrey 1989 Afrikaner Women and the Creation of Ethnicity in a Small South African Town, 1902–1950. In *The Creation of Tribalism in Southern Africa*, edited by Leroy Vail, pp. 55–81. James Currey, London.

Callinicos, Luli 1991 Popular History in the Eighties. In *History from South Africa*, edited by Joshua Brown, Patrick Manning, Karin Shapiro, Jon Wiener, Belinda Bozzoli, and Peter Delius, pp. 257–268. Temple University, Philadelphia, PA.

Cohen, Ronald 1978 Ethnicity: Problem and Focus in Anthropology. *Annual Review of Anthropology* 7:379–403.

Comaroff, John 1982 Dialectical Systems, History and Anthropology: Units of Study and Questions of Theory. *Journal of Southern African Studies* 8:143–172.

Cornevin, Marianne 1980 *Apartheid Power and History Falsification*, UNESCO, Paris.

Crick, Malcolm 1982 Anthropology of Knowledge. *Annual Review of Anthropology* 11:287–313.

Davison, Patricia 1991 Material Culture, Context and Meaning: A Critical Investigation of Museum Practice with Particular Reference to the South African Museum. Unpublished PhD thesis, Department of Archaeology, University of Cape Town, Cape Town, South Africa.

Deetz, James 1977 *In Small Things Forgotten, The Archeology of Early American Life*. Anchor Press/Doubleday, New York. 1993 *Flowerdew Hundred: The Archaeology of a Virginia Plantation, 1619–1864*. University of Virginia, Charlottesville, VA.

Dupreez, J. M. 1983 *Africana Afrikaner Meestersimbole in Suid-Afrikaanse Skoolhandboeke*. Librarius, Alberton, South Africa.

Du Toit, Andre 1984 Captive to the Nationalist Paradigm: Prof. F. A. van Jaarsveld and the Historical Evidence for the Afrikaner's Ideas on His Calling and Mission. *South African Historical Journal* 16:49–78.

FREESPEECH 1995 Monthly Newsletter for Supporters of American Dissident Voices. <http://www.natall.com/FREESP/FSDIR.html> National Alliance, Hillsboro, WV.

Fry, Peter 1992 Anthropology in Southern Africa. *Current Anthropology* 33(2):230–231.

Fuchs, Lawrence H. 1991 *The American Kaleidoscope: Race, Ethnicity and the Civic Culture*. Wesleyan University, Middletown, CT.

Gilomee, Hermann 1989 The Beginnings of Afrikaner Ethnic Consciousness. In *The Creation of Tribalism in Southern Africa*, edited by Leroy Vail, pp. 21–54. James Currey, London.

Glazer, Robert and Daniel P. Moynihan 1963 *Beyond the Melting Pot*. MIT Press, Cambridge, MA.

Gluckman, Max 1975 Anthropology and Apartheid: The Work of South African Anthropologists. In *Studies in South African Anthropology*, edited by Miles Fortes and S. Patterson, pp. 21–39. Academic Press, London.

Gordon, Robert, and Andrew D. Spiegel 1993 Southern Africa Revisited. *Annual Review of Anthropology* 22:83–105.

Graham's Town Journal [Grahamstown, South Africa] 1840 Wesleyan Missions in South Africa: Extracts from the Report for 1839–1840. *Graham's Town Journal*, 2 April 1840:4.

Hall, Martin 1983 Tribes, Traditions and Numbers: The American Model in Southern African Iron Age Ceramic Studies. In *South African Archaeological Bulletin* 38:51–57.

—— 1984 The Burden of Tribalism: The Social Context of Southern African Iron Age Studies. *American Antiquity* 49:445–467.

—— 1990 "Hidden History": Iron Age Archaeology in Southern Africa. In *A History of African Archaeology*, edited by Peter Robertshaw, pp. 59–77. Currey, London.

—— 1993 The Archaeology of Colonial Settlement in Southern Africa. *Annual Review of Anthropology* 22:177–200.

Handsman, Russell G. and Mark Leone 1989 Living History and Critical Archaeology in the Reconstruction of the Past. In *Critical Traditions in Contemporary Archaeology*, edited by Rebecca Pinsky and Alison Wylie, pp. 117–135. Cambridge University Press, Cambridge, UK.

Hardwick, J. J. 1989 A Comparative Study of Staffordshire Ceramics of the Nineteenth Century in America and South Africa. Unpublished BA Honors thesis, Department of Anthropology, University of California, Berkeley, CA.

Hernstein, Richard J. and Charles Murray 1994 *The Bell Curve: Intelligence and Class Structure in American Life*. Free Press, New York.

Heymans, Riana 1986 *The Voortrekker Monument*. Board of Control of the Voortrekker Monument, Pretoria, South Africa.

Horowitz, Donald L. 1991 *A Democratic South Africa? Constitutional Engineering in a Divided Society*. University of California, Berkeley, CA.

Jeppson, Patrice L. 1987 Research Report. *Martevaan II, Cape Historical Archaeology Association Newsletter*. Antonia Malan, Newsletter Editor. University of Cape Town, Cape Town, South Africa.

—— 1988a Getting the Research Out. *Martevaan IV, Cape Historical Archaeology Association Newsletter*. Antonia Malan, Newsletter Editor. University of Cape Town, Cape Town, South Africa.

—— 1988b Historical Archaeology at Farmerfield Mission Station: Method and Theory. Paper presented at the Annual Meeting of the Southern African Association of Anthropologists, Grahamstown, South Africa.

—— 1988c Historical Archaeology in the Eastern Cape: Introduction to the Research Design. Paper presented at the Southern African Archaeology Association Biennial Conference, Johannesburg, South Africa.

—— 1988d Historical Archaeology in the Eastern Cape. Paper presented at the South African Museum Association, Eastern Cape Regional Conference, East London, South Africa.

—— 1988e Research Report. *Martevaan HI, Cape Historical Archaeology Association Newsletter*. Antonia Malan, Newsletter Editor. University of Cape Town, Cape Town, South Africa.

—— 1988f South African Historical Archaeology Report. *The Society for Historical Archaeology Newsletter* 21(3):45.

—— 1989a Ceramics as History or Ceramics as Objects? Paper presented at the South African Museum Association Eastern Cape Regional Conference, Cradock, South Africa.

—— 1989b Historical Archaeology and Alternative Cultural History Interpretations. Paper presented at the South African Museum Association Educational Conference IX, Cape Town, South Africa.

—— 1989c Historical Archaeology and Method, Alternative Cultural History Interpretations in South African Museums. Paper presented at the Joint South African Museum Association/Cape Historical Association Symposium, Cape Town, South Africa.

—— 1989d Historical Archaeology, History and Archaeology of a Frontier Fort: Methods Used in the Study of the Past. Booklet prepared for Albany Museum, Mobile Museum Education Box, on file, Archaeology Department, Albany Museum, Grahamstown, South Africa.

—— 1989e History in a Case. *The Elephant's Child*, Newsletter of the Albany Museum, Grahamstown, South Africa.

—— 1990a 19th-century Ceramics as Clues to Social Identity in the Eastern Cape Colony of South Africa. Paper presented at the Annual Meeting of The Society for Historical Archaeology Conference on Historical and Underwater Archaeology, Tucson, AZ.

—— 1990b Bridging the Gap – Shamans, Bains and Pembe: Archaeology as an Integrating Force in Cultural History Museums. Paper presented at the Southern African Archaeology Association Conference, Kimberly, South Africa.

—— 1990c Ceramics as Clues to 19th-Century Social Organization in the Eastern Cape. Paper presented at the Southern African Association of Archaeologists Biennial Conference, Kimberly, South Africa.

—— 1990d Historical Archaeology in South African Museums. Invited plenary session paper presented at the South African Museum Association History Sectional Meeting, Pretoria, South Africa.

—— 1990e The Way We See It: Images of Eastern Cape History – The History Behind, Within, and Outside a New Culture History Display. Report submitted to the Albany Museum, Grahamstown, South Africa.

—— 1991a Colonial Systems and Indigenous Response: Material Expressions Discovered at Farmerfield Mission Station. Paper presented at the Institute for Social and Economic Research Seminar Series, Rhodes University, Grahamstown, South Africa.

—— 1991b Colonial Systems and Indigenous Responses: Black Material Culture at a 19th-Century, British, Methodist Mission in South Africa. Paper presented at the Annual Meeting of The Society for Historical Archaeology Conference on Historical and Underwater Archaeology, Richmond, VA.

—— 1991c Shaman, Bain's and Pembe: The Material Culture Approach in South African Museums. Paper presented at the South African Museum Association Annual Conference, Cape Town, South Africa.

—— 1992 Archaeology Is a Strange Concept: Problems Encountered Teaching Archaeology at the University of Venda. Paper presented at the Archaeology and Education Workshop, conducted by Edwin Hanisch and Patrice L. Jeppson, at the Southern African Association of Archaeologists Conference, Cape Town, South Africa.

—— 1993 Material Culture Expressions of Ethnicity and Identity on the Nineteenth-Century Eastern Cape Frontier. Paper presented at the Sociology and Anthropology Colloquium Series, California State University, Bakersfield.

—— 1995a Archaeology in the Public Interest: Applied Historical Archaeology in a South African Museum Educational Exhibit. Paper presented at the Chacmool Conference, University of Calgary, Canada.

—— 1995b Historical Archaeology and Alternative History Interpretations in a South African Museum Education Exhibit. Paper presented at the Annual Meeting of The Society for Historical Archaeology Conference on Historical and Underwater Archaeology, Washington, DC.

—— 1996a "Leveling the Playing Field" in the Contested Territory of the South African Past: Prospects for Public Archaeology. Paper presented at the Annual Meeting of the Society for Historical Archaeology Conference on Historical and Underwater Archaeology, Cincinnati, OH.

—— [1998] Mythical and Material Perspectives of Ethnicity on the 19th-century South African Frontier. Unpublished PhD dissertation, Program in Historical Archaeology, University of Pennsylvania, Philadelphia.

Kallaway, Peter 1984 *Apartheid and Education*. Raven Press, Johannesburg, South Africa.

—— 1991 Education and Nation Building in South Africa in the 1990s: Reforming History Education for the Post Apartheid Era. Paper presented at the Comparative and International Education Society Conference, Pittsburgh, PA.

Kruss, Glenda 1981 *People's Education: An Examination of the Concept*. Cape Town, South Africa.

Kuper, Adam 1983 *Anthropology and Anthropologists*. Routledge and Kegan Paul, London.

—— 1986 The Anthropologist's Vocation in South Africa. *African Studies* 45(1).

—— 1988 Anthropology and Apartheid. In *South Africa in Question*, edited by John Lonsdale, pp. 33–52. University of Cambridge African Studies Centre, Cambridge University Press, Cambridge, UK.

Lecordeur, Basil 1981 *The Politics of Eastern Cape Separatism: 1820–1854*. Cape Town, South Africa.

Leone, Mark P. 1983 Method as Message. *Museum News* 62:34–41.

—— 1992 "Epilogue": The Productive Nature of Material Culture and Archaeology. In *Meanings and Uses of Material Culture*, edited by Barbara Little and Paul Shackel. pp. 130–133. California, PA.

Leone, Mark P., Parker B. Potter, and Paul Shackel 1987 Towards a Critical Archaeology. *Current Anthropology* 28(3):283–302.

Majeke, Nosipho [Nora Taylor] 1952 *The Role of the Missionaries in Conquest*. Cumberwood, South Africa.

Mare, Gerhard 1993 *Ethnicity and Politics in South Africa*. Zed Books, London.

McGuire, Randall 1982 The Study of Ethnicity in Historical Archaeology. *Journal of Anthropological Archaeology* 1(2): 159–178.

McKee, Larry W. 1984 Delineating Ethnicity from the Garbage of Early Virginians: The Faunal Remains from the Kingsmill Plantation Slave Quarter. Paper presented at the Annual Meeting of The Society for Historical Archaeology Conference on Historical and Underwater Archaeology, Williamsburg, VA.

McKinney, Ian 1995a The Long March. *American Dissident Radio*, National Alliance Radio broadcast, 1 July 1995. Hillsboro, WV.

—— 1995b The Long March. *FreeSpeech* 1(8). Monthly Newsletter for Supporters of American Dissident Voices. William Pierce, Newsletter Editor. National Alliance, on-line <http:www.natall.com./FREESP/FSDIR.html> Hillsboro, WV.

Moodie, T. Dunbar 1975 *The Rise of Afrikanerdom: Power, Apartheid, and the Afrikaner Civil Religion*. University of California Press, Berkeley, CA.

Nagelgast, E. B. 1990 Letter from Africana Museum Curator requesting information concerning "the philosophy behind, and the construction and function of, the traveling exhibit by Jeppson." Submitted 11 November 1990 to Brian Wilmot, Director, Albany Museum, Grahamstown, South Africa.

Naidoo, Jay 1989 *Tracking Down Historical Myths*. A. D. Donker, Johannesburg, South Africa.

National Vanguard 1993 – Publication of the National Alliance, on-line <http://1996 www/natall.com/NATVAN/NATDIR.html>. Hillsboro, WV.

Odendaal, Andre 1991 Developments in Popular History in the Western Cape in the 1980s. In *History from South Africa: Alternative Visions and Practices*, edited by Joshua Brown, Patrick Manning, Karin Shapiro, Jon Wiener, Belinda Bozzoli and Peter Delius. Temple University Press, Philadelphia, PA.

Owen, D. and W. Holleman 1989 Grey History: A Pox on General and Own Affairs. Paper presented at the South African Museum Association Annual Conference, Bloemfontein, South Africa.

Pauw, B. A. 1980 Recent South African Anthropology. In *Annual Review of Anthropology* 9:315–338.

Peires, Jeff 1989 Ethnicity and Pseudo-Ethnicity in the Ciskei. In *The Creation of Tribalism in Southern Africa*, edited by Leroy Vail, pp. 395–113. James Currey, London.

Peponis, J. and J. Hedin 1982 The Layout of Theories in the Natural History Museum. *NineH* 3:2\–25. London.

Pinsky, Valerie and Alison Wylie 1989 *Critical Traditions in Contemporary Archaeology*. Cambridge University Press, Cambridge, UK.

Pityana, Sipho Mila 1995 HSRC's Revolution from Above. *Weekly Mail and Guardian* 6–12 January:8. Johannesburg, South Africa.

Potter, Parker B., Jr. 1991 What Is the Use of Plantation Archaeology? *Historical Archaeology* 25(3):94–107.

—— 1992 Critical Archaeology: In the Ground and on the Street. *Historical Archaeology* 26(3): 117–129.

—— 1994 *Public Archaeology in Annapolis: A Critical Approach to History in Maryland's Ancient City*. Smithsonian Institution Press, Washington, DC.

Ritchie, Gabrielle 1990 Dig the Herders/Display the Hottentots: The Production and Presentation of Knowledge about the Past. Unpublished MA thesis, African Studies Department, University of Cape Town, South Africa.

Said, Edward W. 1989 Representing the Colonized: Anthropology's Interlocutors. *Critical Inquiry* 15:205–225.

Saunders, Christopher 1988 *The Making of the South African Past: Major Historians on Race and Class*. Cape Town, South Africa.

Schutte, Gerhard 1989 Afrikaner Historiography and the Decline of Apartheid: Ethnic Self-reconstruction in Times of Crisis. In *History and Ethnicity*, edited by Elizabeth Tonkin, Maryon McDonald, and Malcolm Chapman. *Association of Social Anthropology Monographs* 27:216–231. Routledge, London.

Schuyler, Robert 1980 *Archaeological Perspectives on Ethnicity in America*. Baywood, Farmingdale, NY.

Scott, Patricia E. and James Deetz 1990 The Transformation of British Culture in the Eastern Cape, 1820–1860. *Social Dynamics* 16(1):55–75. Cape Town, South Africa.

Senirale Volksmonumente-Komiteeen Diesenirale Voortrekker Eeufeeskomitee (SVE) 1938 *Sentrale Voortrekker-Eufees, 1838–1938*. Pretoria, South Africa.

Sharp, John 1980a Can We Study Ethnicity? A Critique of Fields of Study in South African Anthropology. *Social Dynamics* 6(1):1–16. Cape Town, South Africa.

—— 1980b Two Separate Developments, Anthropology in South Africa. *Royal Anthropology Institute Newsletter* 36:4–6.

—— 1981 The Roots and Development of Volkekunde in South Africa. *Journal of South African Studies* 8(1):16–36.

Shaw, William 1860 *The Story of My Mission in South Eastern Africa*. Hamilton Adams, London.

Shennan, Stephen 1989 *Archaeological Approaches to Cultural Identity*. Unwin Hyman, London.

Smith, Andrew 1987 Museums in a Changing and Divided Society. Paper presented at Africa Seminar, Centre for African Studies, University of Cape Town, South Africa.

Smith, Ken 1988 *The Changing Past: Trends in South African Historical Writing*. Ohio University Press, Athens.

Takaki, Ronald 1987 *From Different Shores: Perspectives on Race and Ethnicity in America*. Oxford University Press, New York.

Thompson, Leonard 1985 *The Political Mythology of Apartheid*. Yale University Press, New Haven, CT.

Thornton, Robert 1988 Culture. In *South African Keywords*, edited by Elaine Boonzaier and John Sharp, pp. 17–28. Philip, Cape Town, South Africa.

Tilley, Christopher 1989 Archaeology as Socio-Political Action in the Present. In *Critical Traditions in Contemporary Archaeology*, edited by Margaret Conkey and Christine Hastorf, pp. 3–84. Cambridge University Press, Cambridge, UK.

Tunmer, Roy 1988 Museum Education as Skills Education. *South African Museum Association Bulletin* 18(4):12–16.

Vanzyl, Silvia 1988 Guest Editorial: Museum Education within the Overall Framework of South African Education. *South African Museum Association Bulletin* 18(4):1.

Varley, C. H. and H. M. Matthew 1957 *The Cape Journals of Archdeacon N. J. Merriman 1848–1855*. Van Riebeeck Society, Cape Town, South Africa.

Voorster, R., R. Hambrock-Uken, and F. C. De Beer 1986 *Anthropology Study Guide SKA-301–6*. University of South Africa, Cape Town.

Webb, Denver 1989 The Cheshire Cat's Advice and the Problems of History in Museums.

Paper presented at the South African Museum Association Annual Conference, Bloemfontein, South Africa.

Wesleyan Missionary Society (WMS) 1840 Missions in South Africa. *Wesleyan Missionary
Notices, &c.* (September) 1(21):22–23. James Nichols, Hoxton-Square, London.

—— 1847 Wesleyan Mission at Farmerfield, South Africa. *Wesleyan Missionary Notices, &c.*
(December) 5(110):206–208. James Nichols, Hoxton-Square, London.

—— 1853 *Report on the Auxiliary Wesleyan Mission Society for the Albany and Kaffraria District for
the Year Ending May 1853*. Godlonton, White, Grahamstown.

Whisson, Michael 1981 Anthropological Research in Contemporary South Africa. In *Apartheid
and Social Research*, edited by John Rex. UNESCO Press/Unipub, Lanham, MD.

Winer, Margot and James Deetz 1990 The Transformation of British Culture in the Eastern
Cape, 1820–1860. *Social Dynamics* 16(1):55–75. Cape Town, South Africa.

Wright, John and Aaron Mazel 1987 Bastions of Ideology: The Depiction of Precolonial
History in the Museums of Natal and KwaZulu. In *South African Museum Association Bulletin* 17:301–310.

Chapter 36

Heritage that Hurts

Interpretation in a postmodern world

David Uzzell and Roy Ballantyne

Concept of hot interpretation

The term 'hot interpretation' was introduced to the field of heritage interpretation in 1988 (Uzzell 1989). The concept arose as a response to the failure of many interpretive designers and providers to acknowledge that visitors to heritage sites do not experience heritage simply as a cognitive experience. The principle behind hot interpretation is that although a detached, cool and objective approach to the presentation and assessment of information and subsequent decision-making is seen as highly desirable in our society, there are many decisions that we make in both our private and public lives where a purely rational Vulcan-like approach to the world is difficult, impossible or even undesirable. Whenever we are presented with choices, we rarely stand by as disinterested observers. Of course, we hope our judgements will be thought through carefully having drawn on as much information as possible and weighing up all the pros and cons of alternative options. However, our feelings, emotional instincts and reactions play an important role in our decision-making.

Emotions colour our memories and experiences and thus our selective attention to information. Our minds are not virgin territories and our past experiences and decisions influence our future actions. This applies to all areas of our lives whether concerning career, marriage, consumerism or health. To deny the emotional side of our understanding and appreciation of the world and our relationships is to deny the very humanity that makes us part of the human race. This should not be interpreted as if there were two types of thinking which exist independently of one another – cool and dispassionate, and hot and emotional. Neither are we arguing that the latter has priority over the former. What is suggested, however, is that issues which involve personal values, beliefs, interests and memories will excite a degree of emotional arousal which needs to be recognised and addressed in interpretation.

These ideas are not new to interpretation. 'Good' interpretation has always reflected this. Tilden (1957:8) defined interpretation as 'an educational activity which aims to reveal meanings and relationships through the use of original objects, by firsthand experience, and by illustrative media, rather than simply to communicate factual information'. Meanings and relationships necessarily have an emotional dimension yet these have often been excluded from interpretation. This may have something to do with the scientific and academic background to most interpretation where emotion is seen as contrary to objectivity. Two of the six principles of interpretation put forward by Freeman Tilden over forty years ago surely presumed an affective component. Tilden (1957:9) argued that 'the chief aim of interpretation is not instruction but provocation'. How better to provoke than through addressing the affective side of the visitor's personality? He also advocated that interpretation must 'address itself to the whole man rather than any phase' (Tilden 1957:9). This must include people's feelings and emotions. A reading of Tilden's book forcefully reminds one that interpretation is about kindling a spiritual awakening in visitors to the wonder of the world around them. For Tilden then, interpretation which does not lead to an emotional experience of the world is deficient in some important respect.

There are some areas in heritage interpretation which have a strong affective and emotional impact on people. This might be because the interpretation touches on personal memories: for instance, at battlefield sites where loved ones were killed. Interpretation could equally have resonance at a collective level such as at a site where a nation achieved its independence from a colonial power or where a pressure group won a famous battle to protect a threatened landscape. Likewise, emotional responses could be fired through interpretation related to issues which evoke strong ideological beliefs and convictions such as the protection of a rare bird or plant species or opposition to non-renewable energy sources such as nuclear power.

Interpretation that appreciates the need for and injects an affective component into its subject matter, where appropriate, is 'hot interpretation'. Hot interpretation accepts that we are subject to a full repertoire of emotional responses – the palette is very varied, more varied than is typically acknowledged, anticipated or encouraged through interpretation. Furthermore, there are strong theoretical grounds for believing that we will not be as effective as we could be as communicators and people in the business of changing attitudes and behaviours in respect of serious environmental issues if we exclude an affective dimension in interpretation. If the affective element required for effective attitude change is absent then interpretation is unlikely to achieve its objectives (McGuire 1985).

It would be strange if heritage did not have an effect upon us. This surely is the point about heritage – it is value laden. Of course, we can value things which are old simply because they are old, but when our perceptions are coloured by thoughts about their origins, their construction, their context and who used them, it would be an insensitive and insensible person who claims that heritage does not provide the spark of an emotional charge. Heritage resonates for us because it not only relates to our past but is an important part of our present and future. This is not meant in the sense of 'having' but rather in the sense of 'being'.

Emotional engagement with the heritage

The resonance of heritage applies equally to the natural and cultural landscapes and artefacts. It can emerge out of the heritage itself or can be mediated by interpretation. The function of interpretation in this case is to make links, to remind us, to make us aware. The degree to which interpretation 'works on us' and the strength of the affect will be conditioned by a number of factors. Five such factors have been identified here which serve to influence our emotional engagement with either the heritage itself or its interpretation: time, distance, experiencing places, the degree of abstraction and management.

Time

The issue of time and meaning in the context of interpretation is addressed elsewhere in (Uzzell and Ballantyne 1998). However, there are some issues related to time that have a particular bearing on hot interpretation. Uzzell (1989) has demonstrated how the meaning and resonance of events from the past changes as time separates us from those events. Three examples of the interpretation of war and conflict were described, ranging from events which happened fifty, eighty and seven hundred years ago.

The first case study related to the massacre by the Nazis of virtually all the men, women and children from the village of Oradour-Sur-Glane near Limoges in France in May 1944. Suspected of harbouring resistance fighters who had a few days earlier ambushed a German patrol, all the men of the village were taken to various houses, garages and public spaces and summarily executed. Following this, all the women and children were rounded up and taken to the church. They were barricaded in and grenades were thrown into the building which was then torched. Over 640 villagers were killed and the village destroyed. It was decided after the war that the village should not be rebuilt, but a new one should be constructed on the outskirts. The old village was turned into a national memorial by the French Government as a permanent reminder of what had happened.

Today it is possible to visit the village and walk down the destroyed streets and into the shell of the church. In the mid 1980s a guide, related to one of the villagers who had been killed, took visitors around the town and explained in detail the chronology of events. It is also possible to buy various guidebooks and leaflets which graphically depict with contemporary photographs what happened. There is additional interpretation in the form of a small museum which contains the personal effects of those who were immolated. Returning to the village several years later it seemed that there is a subtly different atmosphere. Maybe it is the tourist detritus that could be found on the ground, or maybe it is the presence of more young families. Whatever the cause, the place itself seemed to have changed from being a memorial and a place of remembrance to a tourist attraction. As Oradour-Sur-Glane moves from being a memorial to a day-trip destination, it may also move from being an affective to a cognitive experience. For many French people (and non-French too) who had experienced the war, the name Oradour-Sur-Glane would have a powerful resonance and retain its place in the French collective memory. Clearly this is not the case for all visitors. Although the French authorities originally decided that visitors should not be spared the horror of what happened, one suspects that the anger and anguish will slowly be muted. The numbers for whom Oradour-Sur-Glane provides a cathartic experience are declining.

The second example of the way in which time affects the emphasis which is placed by interpreters on events and consequently what those events are made to mean to us is illustrated by reference to a major conflict just over eighty years ago. The presentation and interpretation of World War I displays at the Imperial War Museum recently came in for criticism because it seemed that war was reduced simply to being a story about the application of technological and industrial developments to the slaughtering of millions, as if the most significant aspect was the military technology. This museum was not alone in this kind of presentation – quite the contrary, it was the norm. However, the displays have now been transformed in a successful attempt to interpret the 'meaning and significance' of the war in its many dimensions. But there are still many museums around the world where the sartorial elegance of the soldiery and the impressiveness of the instruments of war assumes as much if not more significance than their purpose and effect. As we go back in time we seem to be more willing to ignore suffering and treat events in a more disinterested way as if they are from a 'foreign country' (Hartley 1953).

The third example illustrates that as we progress in time not only are the emphases of history changed but history can become rewritten or forgotten altogether. At the time when the first study was written, the interpretation of Clifford's Tower in York did not just minimise the history but failed even to tell the story of the 'ethnic cleansing' of the Jewish population of that city in a wave of anti-Semiticriots which occurred in various parts of the country after the Crusades, some 700 years ago. The interpretation of the Tower's history focused on who had lived there, its changing role over the centuries and its building materials, but no mention was made of the fact that the Jews of York were corralled into the Tower and, when faced with annihilation, committed suicide. Those who did not die at their own hands were tricked into opening the Tower's gates on the promise of clemency, but were then slaughtered. In the case of Clifford's Tower, it was not a case so much of history being rewritten, but rather history being forgotten. The displays at Clifford's Tower have since been changed by English Heritage. However, how many other heritage sites exist where shameful events of our past are forgotten altogether because they are seen to be so temporally distant that it is expedient to forget their occurrence.

Experiencing places

When we talk about experiencing place and events, especially in terms of our emotional reactions, it is difficult to know to what degree other people share similar feelings. Even more problematic, of course, is specifying what we mean when we talk about a place or an event having a particular atmosphere. Where is this atmosphere? It is hardly 'out there' like a magic ingredient which has been added to the oxygen, nitrogen, argon, carbon dioxide and water vapour (not counting, of course, the carbon monoxide, sulphur dioxide and lead). If it is not out there, then clearly it is some form of projection from ourselves; we impose our feelings and emotions onto the scene. This can be illustrated by a consideration of the atmosphere in London in the week following the death of Diana, Princess of Wales.

Many thousands of people travelled to London to pay their last respects by signing the books of condolences at St James's Palace and leaving flowers outside both St James's and Buckingham Palace. This was reported daily on TV, radio and in the press. TV reporters stood in front of the carpet of flowers or alongside the quarter-mile-long queue of mourners and tried to share the experience with the nation by commenting that 'there is a muted and melancholic atmosphere here in The Mall'. A picture was painted of clothes-rending mourners queuing under a pall of gloom and sadness. Yes, the occasion was sad like any untimely death, perhaps especially so in the case of someone who meant so much for all sorts of reasons to so many people. But when one of us walked down The Mall on the Wednesday following Diana's death, I cannot say that there was a tangible atmosphere – not for me anyway. This should not be taken to mean that I did not feel something about the tragedy that had happened in the early hours of the previous Sunday morning, neither does it imply that such 'atmospheres' do not exist. They clearly do, but they are not a ubiquitous experience for all people, all of the time, in every situation.

Space is endowed with 'atmosphere' according to activities and memories of what has occurred there. For instance, a person walking up The Mall a few days previously would have relied on other past events and memories to create 'an atmosphere'. Similarly, for some visitors with memories of World War II, Oradour-Sur-Glane is undoubtedly a highly provocative environment generating an emotive 'atmosphere', while for others perhaps this is not the case. What are the implications for interpretation? Should hot interpreters be trying to create an 'atmosphere'? Who is the target audience – those with first-hand experience of the situation or general visitors? The answers to such questions are important in designing hot interpretation. As seen later in this chapter, the nature of hot interpretation of Aboriginal cultural heritage is greatly influenced by responses to questions relating to target audience (tourists or Aboriginal communities) which impact upon the purpose of the interpretation.

As time separates us from past events our emotional engagement is reduced. Does the time period separating events affect our decisions regarding the presentation of information, emotional reaction and issues of taste? A few examples of recent events are discussed below, promoting reflection on the impact that distance, in terms of time from 'hot' events, has upon interpretation decision-making. These examples raise questions about what should be interpreted, how it should be interpreted and when. They also illustrate the relative nature of visitor emotional engagement, a consideration of which impacts upon decisions regarding the choice of interpretive techniques needed to make historic hot events and places 'live' for those who have little empathy or connection with such events and places.

Late in the evening of the 22 December 1988, the BBC was due to show the film *Fear is the Key*, but the continuity announcer came on and said that due to the crash of Pan Am Flight 103 over Lockerbie, it had been decided that it would be inappropriate and distressing for some viewers and therefore the film would be shown at a later date. Of course, one can understand this decision and arguably it was the appropriate and most sensitive thing to do. But why should it be more acceptable to show the film at a later date – would not the elements which potentially made the film distressing still be present? What will have changed over the intervening period? In the case of news we seem to be prepared to forget quite quickly, while this is not so with recent history. This may present interpreters with particular problems.

The recency of hot events can make interpretation difficult as they cannot easily be placed in a larger historical continuity and context. But it is also problematic for a reason associated with the issue of hot interpretation. We have seen that war loses its emotional sting with the passing of years. Both we as providers of interpretive events and visitors as their consumers, appear to feel no twinge of conscience or unease at sitting down to watch two warring factions pretend to slaughter each other in an historical re-enactment of a Civil War skirmish. But why should the passing of time make this almost voyeuristic behaviour an acceptable form of entertainment when applied to an event 100 or 200 years ago, but not acceptable in the context of re-enactment of a battle fought ten years ago? Would we consider it appropriate and 'tasteful' to see a re-enactment between interpreters dressed as Serbs and Bosnians engaging in 'ethnic cleansing' or street fighting from Sarajevo?

The difficulties of interpreting recent hot issues are clearly illustrated by events occurring at the Port Arthur Historic Site in Tasmania, Australia. Port Arthur served as a prison to over 12,000 convicts transported to Australia from Britain between 1831 and the 1870s. Tragically, in 1996 it became the site of Australia's worst massacre as Martin Bryant, armed with an automatic rifle, first entered the Blue Arrow Café and opened fire on visitors before roaming around the 40-hectare site of historic buildings indiscriminately shooting people. Prior to the massacre, the site was very popular with visitors who 'enjoyed' the interpretation and stories of the hard life and characters who inhabited the Model Prison, worked and died at the site and were buried on the Isle of the Dead. The Ghost Tour, which recounted all the strange and horrible events that occurred there, was very popular with visitors. After the massacre, interpreters were left reflecting upon the nature of their interpretation of the site and whether distance in terms of time had led to the 'gentrification' of both the buildings and the stories of what was a feared and terrible place for so many. Did the interpretation exploit the horror and misery of being a convict at Port Arthur? What attracts people to come and pay to be entertained at such a site? Should such a site be interpreted – what would the convicts imprisoned there have thought?

It is interesting to contemplate that the site was ordered to be destroyed once transportation was stopped, but the order was never carried out. Why would people at the time want it destroyed? Were they too close to the experience of what life was like there – would interpretation have been viewed as tasteless?

Interestingly, a similar situation has now developed; the Blue Arrow Café, where most of the victims lost their lives, may be demolished. Is the Blue Arrow Café any more a reminder of horrific events and sorrow than the Model Prison building or others on the site? This was after all a place where convicts were so traumatised that they would draw straws to determine who would murder whom (as suicide was considered an unforgivable sin) so that both the murderer (who would be hanged) and the murdered would escape forever. Should not the Blue Arrow Café be considered as a future exhibit on the Ghost Tour? Our attitudes towards the recent past and the way in which it engages our emotions are interesting issues that need to be addressed by those responsible for interpretation.

Abstraction

Another factor which impinges on our emotional reaction to interpretive experiences concerns the degree of abstraction of the heritage being interpreted. Again this interacts with time, suggesting that the relationship between time and emotional involvement is not necessarily linear or negatively correlated. The interpretation of the Cold War presents an interesting example as it is both a recent event and, as the name suggests in the context of this chapter, not perhaps particularly promising in terms of hot interpretation.

The Cold War was unlike any previous war; it was a placeless war. There were, of course, sites which were strategically critical and place bound such as Fylingdales and as much in the 'front line' as any trench on the Somme. But the Cold War was also everywhere, as well as nowhere. While for many people it was real and costly, it was also an attitude of mind as two ideologies clashed in propaganda battles. It was not so overtly situated as previous wars. It extended across continents, although it did find visible expression where the two ideologies met at the borders of the countries separated by the Iron Curtain. The Cold War was as much about threat and potential harm, albeit on a cataclysmic scale, as about conventional death and destruction. Finally, the Cold War was also both a highly public and a highly secret war. All these factors make its interpretation problematic for those more used to dealing with plaques and audio-visual guides than to battlefield sites.

Cold War sites are different from other war sites inasmuch as they are often not the scenes of actual conflict and death. Their importance and value lie in what they represent and what they could have been. War sites visited by the public are invariably either where battles took place or exceptionally from where war was managed, like the Cabinet War Rooms in London. In the case of Cold War sites, while everything about them certainly meant business, they were at the same time about not being used. They are silent and cerebral in contrast to what most visitors assume and look for on a battlefield site – the noise, the clamour and the tangible. It is ironic that Janis and Mann (1979) chose to emphasise the argument that even if dispassionate objectivity were possible in our decision-making with regard to personal or societal issues, it is questionable whether it is desirable – by reference to one of the most memorable satirical films of the Cold War era: 'A world dominated by Dr. Strangelove and like-minded cost accountants might soon become devoid of acts of affection, conscience and humanity, as well as passion' (Janis and Mann 1979:45).

Distance

The third factor that relates to our emotional engagement and response to heritage, and interacts with both time and abstraction, is distance. Both physical and psychological distance from people, places, events and artefacts can accentuate or moderate one's emotional involvement as well as one's knowledge, concern and, of course, action. This is well illustrated by some research we have undertaken over a number of years to examine the awareness and attitudes of the public to global environmental problems (Uzzell, in preparation).

A large sample of environmental science, environmental education and geography students studying in the UK, Slovakia and Australia were asked to rate the seriousness of seven environmental problems (water pollution, atmospheric pollution, noise pollution, acid rain, deforestation, global warming, ozone holes). The problems were rated on a five-point scale varying from 1 (extremely serious) to 5 (not serious at all) as they were perceived to affect individuals, their town, country, continent and finally the world. It was decided to use a sample of environmental studies students as it was felt that they would probably be well informed about environmental problems and, therefore, a yardstick against which one could measure other populations.

Overall, it was found that there was a statistically significant difference in the way that students perceived environmental problems at the five areal levels. Environmental problems were considered to be more serious as geographical distance from the perceiver increased. The effects of environmental problems on the world were perceived as more serious than their effects at the continental, country, town or individual level. Similarly, problems at the continental level were viewed as more serious than at the country, town or individual level, and so on. This trend held true for all three national groups, with a minor exception in the case of the Australian sample who, for understandable reasons, made no distinction between the severity of environmental problems at 'country' and 'continent' areal levels, presumably as a consequence of the sheer size of Australia. One interesting paradox revealed by this research is that students from the UK thought that the most serious evidence of global environmental problems would be found at the other end of the world (i.e. Australia), while Australian students believed that the most serious evidence of global environmental problems would be found at an antipodean distance (i.e. the UK).

The research went on to ask students in each country who they perceived as being responsible for addressing and solving environmental problems. It was generally found that students saw themselves as being responsible for local problems but felt that governments and agencies should be responsible for problems at the national and international scales. This finding is intersting, however, as students do not perceive local environmental problems to be particularly significant compared with global problems. This allows them to abrogate their need to deal with environmental issues by passing the responsibility on to governments and international agencies.

The relevance of this for hot interpretation is twofold. It is suggested that the amount of mass media attention given to global environmental issues may actually mean that they are more salient for people at a global rather than local level. The amount of television and newspaper coverage given to global warming and consequential sea level rises, destruction of the ozone layer through the emission of CFC's, cutting down of rain forests and species depletion has placed global environmental problems near the top of the public's environmental agenda. The maxim 'Think globally – act locally' was coined many years ago in an attempt to overcome the phenomenon whereby the public becomes highly aware, largely through mass media images, of the destruction of ecosystems and wildlife, but fails to appreciate that the same destructive processes operate on their own doorsteps. Events such as Rio only serve to emphasise the seriousness of global as opposed to local or even national environmental problems, despite follow-up initiatives such as Local Agenda 21.

Second, processes of global environmental change operate across considerable spatial and temporal social distances (Pawlik 1991). It is often the case with environmental problems that they are 'exported' from one region to another. Thus, an individual who receives the benefits of an environmentally damaging action is not likely to suffer its consequences. As social learning is facilitated by the interpersonal proximity of the individuals involved (Bandura 1977), learning through feelings of responsibility and/or empathy with the 'victim' will thus be inhibited (Pawlik 1991). Because of these processes we are less likely to have an emotional engagement with the 'victims' of the environmental damage we cause.

How should interpreters respond when faced with the knowledge that personal responsibility decreases with distance and that environmental winners and losers are generally separated by large distances? Surely, they need to ensure that the interpretation of environmental issues helps to make people aware of local actions on national and global 'others'. Attention should be paid to interpreting links between environmental winners and losers. A hot interpretive approach would be valuable in this regard, engaging visitors emotionally and helping them to identify with and acknowledge responsibility for environmental problems. In this way interpretation could enhance mutual understanding and appreciation and promote personal action facilitating environmentally sustainable practice at different spatial scales.

Management

The final factor which is important in influencing the affective impact of interpretation concerns the interpretive media itself. As a factor it is very much related to the promotion, marketing and management of an interpretive site, as discussed in the previous section. The pen may be mightier than the sword, but all the evidence suggests that when it comes to interpretive media the public prefer historical re-enactments, first person interpretation and demonstrations. Of course, the word can be powerful and effective such as the letter home from the front or the interpreted list of species lost this century through the destruction of the environment, but visitors can relate to people-based interpretation precisely because it invariably contains the full human response – the affective as well as the cognitive. Interpreters have long known this. But perhaps what they have not considered is the question: Does people-based interpretation lead to a particular or a restricted set of emotions and feelings being portrayed? The French film director, François Truffaut, once said that it is not possible to make an anti-war movie because all war movies, with their energy and sense of adventure, end up making combat look fun. This is an oversimplification and contradicted by evidence (for example *Platoon* and *Saving Private Ryan*), but the point being made is that it may well be that certain types of presentation lead to certain types of interpretation.

Those responsible for interpreting and managing battlefield sites face a particular dilemma. On the one hand there is a desire to tell the story, to convey not only an accurate technical, logistic and strategic account of the conflict, but also to capture what the conflict meant at a human level for those involved so that the story told is as complete and 'truthful' as possible. But the truth can be nasty. In wars people get injured, maimed and killed in the most appalling ways. Children are orphaned and spouses are widowed. This is part of the truth. On the other hand, the owners and managers of battlefield sites are also required to attract as many visitors as possible and provide them with an 'entertaining day out for all the family'. These two objectives may not be compatible. It is a dilemma which is not easily resolved. Many managers take the line of least resistance and present a sanitised form of truth which will not upset, offend or challenge. If there is an attempt to engage the visitors' emotions, it may be restricted to superficial feelings which do not last beyond the visit. More often than not no emotional response is called for or encouraged.

What is the use of hot interpretation?

Hot interpretation as a concept has been discussed here largely in relation to the interpretation of war. This is because war tends to be a rather emotional subject which excites a strong affective response. But it has equal application to the many different subjects for which interpreters are responsible such as environmental destruction and pollution; species depletion; religious, sexual and racial intolerance and discrimination; class and caste issues; social reforms and differential access to health, welfare and education. It is not a coincidence that hot interpretation should have particular relevance and application to the interpretation of war and conflict. The reason for this is that conflicts between people are invariably emotional affairs. Therefore, wherever we find conflict between people there ought to be a role for hot interpretation and, arguably, the interpretation will be incomplete without this element.

We believe that the function of hot interpretation is twofold. First, interpretation that has an affective dimension will more adequately convey the meaning and significance of the heritage of the people, places, events and artefacts. In a sense, this is the touristic function of hot interpretation. Hot interpretation can, however, be used pro-actively and politically. This is the community development function of hot interpretation.

One example of this community development function is described in Ballantyne and Uzzell's (1993) paper concerning the role of hot interpretation in facilitating community healing in post-apartheid South Africa. As South Africa emerges from the trauma of its racial past, interpretation of the apartheid system and its city structures can help promote the process of reconciliation and nation building. In this regard, a hot interpretation approach is an ideal vehicle to promote community reconciliation in relation to forced removals. The effect of the Group Areas Act 1950, which led to the legal separation and forced uprooting of large numbers of the population, has left a legacy of deep bitterness. Removals were, and still are, a very 'hot' issue which the community needs to address. Of all the many forced removal areas in South Africa, District Six in Cape Town is perhaps the most infamous. Any visitor to Cape Town cannot escape noticing the 'scar' on the side of Table Mountain and inhabitants of the city well know the emotional impact of that space:

> Today the bare, scarred earth, and the hate and anger which its destruction generated have created a special kind of monument. On the one hand it bears witness to the crude, inhuman and ruthless vandalistic spirit of the South African ruling class and its equally crude and hateful race mythologies and policies, as well as its arrogance and violence with which it pursues its policies.
>
> (Dudley 1990: 197)

Such a 'hot' monument to apartheid cannot be interpreted without acknowledging and dealing with the emotional aspects which surround it – to to ignore the 'heat' in its interpretation would be to fail the community. This does not mean that a hot interpretation of District Six should be used to whip up further hate against those who were responsible for and profited from the removals. Rather, it is argued, that a hot interpretation of the history of District Six and its peoples should be designed to promote a healing of the anger and facilitate reconciliation in the community. A hot interpretation approach could help bring about Jeppie and Soudien's (1990:16) vision for District Six to become 'a healing symbol for a new and reconciled South Africa'.

The establishment of the District Six Museum in Buitenkant Street, Cape Town, in 1992 has gone part of the way towards achieving some of the aims of a hot interpretive approach. It is truly a 'people's' museum and has been established through the goodwill of the community. Housed in the old Central Methodist Church, which in the days of apartheid was the venue for protest meetings, prayer vigils and a sanctuary for those physically and psychologically injured by police during protest actions, the museum has been very successful in attracting Cape Town community members and tourists through its doors. Exhibitions have focused upon community 'memories' of living in the area. Methods of interpretation have generally been hot in nature as exhibits encourage people to remember or imagine the impact of removals upon people of the area. Past members of District Six are normally around to personalise the visitor experience. The impact of visitor interaction with those who lived the experience can be quite dramatic as personal experience and stories are related. People who 'watched' the removals and those who were moved often become engaged in conversation and leave with a greater understanding of what happened there.

The District Six Museum does not have flashy exhibits and the presentation of material is easily criticised. However, like the Checkpoint Charlie Museum in Berlin, the visitor is emotionally engaged by the significance and reality of the stories of the area and its people (Uzzell 1989). Although research needs to be undertaken to assess the impact of the museum and its interpretation, observation suggests that, like visiting a holocaust museum, people are profoundly affected.

Another example of the way in which hot interpretation could be used to bring about community development is described in a paper by Ballantyne (1995) which investigated conceptions of Aboriginal heritage and their implications for interpretive practice. In this study, interviews with interpreters of Australian Aboriginal heritage identified two ways of conceiving it with implications for the aims, content and strategies of interpretive programmes. Simply put, Aboriginal heritage can be understood to be either 'a thing of the past' or as 'evolving and contemporary'. It is suggested that a hot interpretive approach is suitable for addressing a number of issues involving contemporary, post-contact, Aboriginal heritage: for example, the positive role played by Aboriginals in Australian society, the nature of cultural beliefs and practices today, landrights, massacre sites, life on mission stations and the 'stolen generation'. Due to the cultural context within which such interpretation is to be presented, it is important that the interpreter adopts a sensitive, consultative approach and undertakes interpretation 'for' the community.

Those undertaking a hot interpretation of Aboriginal heritage should aim to interpret with, rather than about, Aboriginal people. Undertaking Aboriginal interpretation is at the best of times fraught with difficulties. Many well-meaning interpreters have found to their cost that what and how they have interpreted has not found favour with the Aboriginal community. An example of this would be the interpretation of Aboriginal heritage at the Ayers Rock Resort Visitor Centre in central Australia. In Aboriginal communities there are a number of 'mens', 'womens' and community stories and secrets which mean that what and how heritage is interpreted must be negotiated and at the discretion of the community.

A hot interpretation of post-contact heritage issues could play an important role in helping Aboriginal communities to tell their stories, as well as foster an understanding on the part of their fellow Australians about the history of the impact of European settlement upon Aboriginal peoples and their culture. As one Aboriginal interpreter suggested, it could play a role in helping people:

> to mature and come to terms with facts instead of covering up lies. Look at the Jews in Germany – they got wiped out, the same thing happened here and yet they tell us to forget about it, it's in the past. How can we forget about it? We know that our grandfather's father was beheaded over there . . . to teach us a lesson. We can't forget about it.
>
> (Ballantyne 1995: 16)

Conclusion

Why are interpreters wary of employing hot interpretive techniques? Some are concerned that hot interpretation will be used simply for cheap shock value – the touristic equivalent of our more prurient and basic tabloid newspapers. Looking at some 'heritage' sites and facilities one has sympathy with their concern. But often these places actually have little to do with heritage, history and least of all education. Hot interpretation has to be under-taken responsibly if it is not to be merely sensational.

Interpreters are generally willing to claim credit when visitors leave a heritage site having had a stimulating and enjoyable educational experience. Should they not also take responsibility for other effects, particularly those which are intended? How does one cater for those for whom the interpretation provides a powerful, evocative and emotional experience? What responsibility do interpreters have for the reactions of people who may have found the interpretation moving or even traumatic? Such visitors need to be catered for, as well as those for whom a place or experience is simply an intellectual encounter with the past – one which evokes little or no emotional connection.

Some may be concerned that hot interpretation might be used for propaganda pur-poses – to indoctrinate ideas, reinforce stereotypes, incite and encourage fear. This is not being advocated here. Hot interpretation, like all interpretation, should present perspec-tives on the world which encourage visitors to question and explore different understand-ings, values and viewpoints. Truth is, after all, contestable. Is it the fact that hot interpretation openly admits that information is by its nature value laden and attempts to engage the whole person, rather than restricting itself to a knowledge-based approach, which opens it to the criticism of not being 'objective' or 'balanced'? Surely, however, no interpretation is values free? For instance, simply to ignore the emotions and ethical issues surrounding armed conflict or to fail to represent the impact of air pollution on people's health and development is to exhibit a very real values position. It might be hidden from the visitor, but it clearly represents a values standpoint. It could be argued that at least a hot interpretation approach alerts the visitor to the critical approach and stance being employed. One is reminded of the words of Martin Luther King:

> History will have to record that the greatest tragedy of this period of social transition was not the vitriolic words and violent actions of the bad people but the appalling silence and indifference of the good people.

Surely we are not questioning whether interpreters should nail their colours to the mast and 'shout' a warning to society on certain issues. This was Tilden's motivation, after all. The issue is not whether, but how. For this reason, we have argued that hot interpretation has potentially positive roles to play in society. In particular, we have outlined by two examples, how, when used as part of community development, it can bring peoples together rather than be used as an instrument of division.

References

Ballantyne, R. R. (1995) 'Interpreters' conceptions of Australian Aboriginal culture and heritage: implications for interpretive practice', *Journal of Environmental Education*, 26(4): 11–17.

Ballantyne, R. R. and Uzzell, D. L. (1993) 'Environmental mediation and hot interpretation: a case study of District Six, Cape Town', *Journal of Environmental Education*, 24(3): 4–7.

Bandura, A. (1997) *Social Learning Theory*, Englewood Cliffs, NJ: Prentice Hall.

Dudley, R. (1990) 'Forced removals: the essential meanings of District Six', in S. Jeppie and C. Soudien (eds) *The Struggle for District Six – Past and Present*, Cape Town: Buchu Books.

Hartley, L. P. (1953) *The Go-Between*, Harmondsworth: Penguin.

Janis, I. L. and Mann, L. (1979) *Decision-Making: A Psychological Analysis of Conflict, Choice and Commitment*, New York: Free Press.

Jeppie, S. and Soudien, C. (1990) *The Struggle for District Six – Past and Present*, Cape Town: Buchu Books.

McGuire, W. J. (1985) 'Attitudes and attitude change', in G. Lindzey and E. Aronson (eds) *Handbook of Social Psychology*, vol. 2, 3rd edn, New York: Random House, pp. 233–346.

Pawlik, K. (1991) 'The psychology of global environmental change: some basic data and an agenda for co-operative international research', *International Journal of Psychology*, 26(5): 547–563.

Tilden, F. (1957) *Interpreting Our Heritage*, Chapel Hill, NC: University of North Carolina Press.

Uzzell, D. L. (1989) 'The hot interpretation of war and conflict' in D. L. Uzzell (ed.) *Heritage Interpretation: Volume 1: The Natural and Built Environment*, London: Belhaven, pp. 33–47.

Uzzell, D. L. (in preparation) 'The psycho-spatial dimension to global environmental problems'.

Uzzell, D. and Ballantyne (eds) 1998. Contemporary Issues in Heritage and Environmental Management. London: The Stationary Office.

Chapter 37

Archaeologies that Hurt; Descendants that Matter

A pragmatic approach to collaboration in the public interpretation of African-American archaeology

Carol McDavid

Abstract

Pragmatism's anti-essentialist emphasis on contingency and plurality and its notion of truth-as-created (not discovered) have important implications for the interpretation of archaeological data, and for the 'public presentation' of archaeological research. This chapter will examine a pragmatically oriented project in Brazoria, Texas, USA, in which archaeologists and local citizens (including site descendants) have collaborated to create an Internet website to discuss the politically and emotionally charged archaeologies and histories of an eighteenth-century sugar plantation. It will discuss ways in which a pragmatic philosophical framework has given archaeologists new ways of approaching and 'conversing' about their data, and new ways of dealing, openly and non-hierarchically, with the communities most affected by their research. It will also discuss ways in which elements of post-processual archaeological theory – multivocality, interactivity, reflexivity and contextuality – were incorporated within both the content and delivery of the website, and will close with a short discussion about whether these strategies were effective in creating an open, relevant, democratic and multivocal discourse about archaeology.

Introduction

In this chapter, I shall discuss the Levi Jordan Plantation Website Project, in which archaeologists and local citizens have collaborated to create an Internet website to present and discuss the archaeologies and histories of plantation life in the southern United States. The geographical context of this project is the small, rural community of Brazoria, Texas, located about one hour's drive south of Houston, Texas. Excavations at the Jordan Plantation have been under way for sixteen years, under the direction of Kenneth L. Brown at the University of Houston, and have focused primarily on the slaves and tenants quarters (Brown and Cooper 1990; Brown 1994) of the plantation. The Jordan Website Project, for which I function as public archaeologist and 'project leader', is currently the primary public interpretative activity for the archaeological excavations. As such, it represents an

attempt to see whether 'the Net' can provide a way for the descendants of the original residents of this plantation (both African-American and European-American) to conduct critical dialogues with archaeologists, with each other, with people elsewhere – and with 'the
past' (McDavid 1999). My collaborators include Kenneth Brown, his graduate students,
plantation descendants and other community members – all of whom provided content for
the site (http://www.webarchaeology.com).

The project also formed the basis of my doctoral research at the University of Cambridge, where I used the Jordan website as a case study to examine whether Internet websites are effective communicative media for archaeologists to interact with their publics in
open, democratic, multivocal and relevant ways, particularly when the archaeological
interpretations themselves are 'sensitive' and 'charged' in contemporary social and political contexts. To examine this, I employed what has been termed a 'self-reflexive post-
processual methodology' in 'real-site' (as opposed to 'website') excavation contexts
(Hodder 1997). That is, I (and we, in the sense that the creation of the website was a collaborative effort) attempted to incorporate elements of multivocality, interactivity, reflexivity and contextuality in the basic structure of both the content and delivery of the
website. This chapter will describe some of the specific strategies employed to do this –
both on the screen and behind the scenes. It will close with some preliminary conclusions
about whether these strategies were effective in 'opening' and 'democratizing' archaeological discourse.

I should offer some background information before continuing. Even though the
Jordan archaeological project began in 1986, there was no public component until much
later. For a variety of reasons (McDavid 2004), in the 1990s it became necessary to create
an active 'public' component for the Jordan archaeological project. One could argue (in
retrospect) that the public should have been involved in the Jordan project from its beginning – but collaborative public archaeology projects were very uncommon in America at
that time, and were only beginning to emerge as accepted subjects for academic historical
archaeological research. In any event, in 1992 I was recruited by Kenneth Brown to
develop the public dimensions of the Jordan archaeological research. My first project, conducted while I was a graduate student in anthropology at the University of Houston, was
to conduct ethnographic research to learn if it would be feasible to locate public interpretations of this archaeology within the local community surrounding the plantation. It was
unknown at that point whether these interpretations would be in the form of a museum,
site tours or something else. I – we – needed to learn about the 'interests and conflicts'
(Leone et al. 1987) that formed the social and political landscape of Brazoria, and to determine whether people in the community would support a project which would, necessarily, require them to deal publicly with some rather uncomfortable aspects of their
community's history. That research (McDavid 1996; summarized in McDavid 1997b) led
to the website project described here. Therefore, my work with the Brazoria community
is ongoing, and includes many activities not related to the work described here.

Philosophical context

One philosophical approach has proved particularly useful as we worked together to create
this website – American pragmatism, especially as expressed in the philosophical writings
of Richard Rorty, Cornel West, John Dewey and William James (see, for example, Rorty
1991; West 1993; Dewey 1916; James 1996). One important idea borrowed from pragmatism is the idea that all human interaction can be conceived of as historically situated,
contingent, pluralistic *conversation*. In pragmatist thought, particularly that of Richard
Rorty, the 'conversational' metaphor goes far beyond the linguistic. Some human interactions – such as wars and social movements – are seen as meta-conversations in which 'we'

humans decide, over time and distance, how to direct our lives. Pragmatists share an anti-essentialist, anti-foundationalist and pluralist point of view towards truth, and are keenly aware of the contingency of historically and socially constructed categories and practices. While pragmatists do *not* believe that one truth is as good as another, they do believe that humans can and will be able to discover, over time, which truths are more meaningful and useful. In Rortian terms, humans can learn which truths will help 'us' to be less cruel, and which will help us to understand each other better. It is a very optimistic approach, though not a nihilistically relativistic one: pragmatists may have a profound belief in the capacities of humans to determine their own fates – to 'figure it out' – but they also demand that each human speak up, loudly, to express his or her own voice in social, cultural and political life.

In our case, as archaeologists taking part in the 'conversation' of creating public interpretation of archaeology, this idea was enacted as we attempted to make our archaeological truth claims forcefully and creatively (Hodder *et al.* 1995: 28) embracing science (but not scientism) as our tool-of-trade – operating within a pragmatic realism that did not lead to relativism or scepticism (Goodman 1995: 4). At the same time, we sought opportunities for other ways of understanding the past to be expressed – such as oral history, folklore, genealogy and others. All of these 'ways of knowing' are represented on the Jordan website. As is true with archaeology at most (if not all) African-American sites in the United States, the story being told necessarily deals with human acts of oppression and cruelty (see McDavid and Babson 1997 for other examples) – acts which are acknowledged and dealt with in different ways by different groups of site descendants. In order to allow space for these different 'ways of understanding' to emerge, and to deal with this potentially hurtful archaeology, the Levi Jordan website project was conceived of as a contingent, historically situated *conversation*. It was not conceived of as a 'presentation', nor was it regarded as an effort to 'educate' (though there are elements of both on the site). Most public interpretations of archaeology operate as one of these and, because of this, most have an unavoidably authoritative, hierarchical flavour. They do not lend themselves easily to open discourse, disagreement or challenge, and tend to stop 'conversation' before it starts. In addition, both 'presentation' and 'education' do not fit as comfortably into the associative, multi-linear logic of the Internet. The Levi Jordan website was designed with the specific intent of decentring the archaeologist as *the* expert about the multiple pasts of one community – archaeology was seen as one important voice, but one of many.

The notion that finding truths about the past is a result of our continuing experience with each other is something that, on one level, is taken for granted by the individuals I work with – many of whom had ancestors who owned, and were owned by, each other. Indeed, they are very matter-of-fact about the notion that 'what happened' for a slave was obviously different from 'what happened' for an enslaver. This issue was stated explicitly very early in our work together, in the Mission Statement and Statement of Goals written by members of the Levi Jordan Plantation Historical Society (LJPHS), the non-profit organization that runs the plantation (http://www.webarchaeology.com/html/about.htm). This organization is composed of archaeologists, African-American and European-American descendants and other community members. What was not taken for granted, by them or by me, in the beginning of our acquaintance was the idea that *my* point of view, as academic, archaeologist, white, female, urban and so on was just as contingent. When I began to present myself – and, more importantly, to *see* myself – as only one actor in a conversation which allowed space for alternative truth claims, not as someone with a privileged, exclusive way of understanding the past, I began to have more credibility in the community, not less. As I continued to assure people that 'we' archaeologists regarded other ways of looking at history as legitimate, they began to trust us with more family stories, documents, pictures and so on than they had before. This obviously had a direct and positive effect on the content we were able to include in the Jordan website, but it also had a positive effect on the research itself. The principal investigator, Kenneth Brown, began to incorporate these local understandings into his research questions, as well as his interpretations of the archaeological and historical data (Brown 2000). Over time, this decentred, 'conversational' approach has had a very real and concrete effect on both the way the archaeology was done and the way it is being publicly interpreted.

Creating the website: process and structuring principles

Continuing my collaboration with the Brazoria community, in the summer of 1997 I began the process of creating, or 'weaving', this website, and, first, met with members of the LJPHS to obtain their support and initial input. At this point they approved the original website proposal, and began to contribute content for the site and make decisions about some of the more 'sensitive' content components. Working with these people and others (including Kenneth Brown and his students), I began to assemble various content components – data, texts, images and so on. By the end of the summer of 1997 we had published a prototype site, which I then asked my collaborators to comment upon. I spent the spring and summer of 1998 revising the prototype site based on the critiques received, and adding more archaeological, anthropological and historical data. At this point I added a variety of on-line interactive elements to the website, including an on-line discussion forum, feedback forms and a questionnaire. The final evaluation of this project (McDavid 2002b) includes analysis of the development process, as well as analysis of questionnaire, discussion, feedback form and e-mail data. Even though that evaluation is complete, the website will remain, and we shall continue to change it based on what I (and we) learned during the evaluation period.

Strategies

I shall now discuss some of the strategies we employed to be reflexive, interactive, multivocal and contextual. I should emphasize that the website does not purport to *be* reflexive, multivocal and so on, but, rather, to employ some degree of all four elements in varying degrees in different parts of the site: there is certainly material on the site that is decidedly non-reflexive and univocal, although we do attempt to use even this material in a reflexive, transparent way.

I should first clarify terms. By *reflexivity* I mean that we hoped to reveal something about our own assumptions and 'taken-for-granteds', and that we attempted to be critical of these assumptions as we decided what sorts of content to include. Being reflexive also required that we be aware of what these assumptions revealed about our own ideologies, and that we be aware how our ideologies came into play as we dealt with each other. By *multivocality* I mean simply that we wanted to ensure that a diversity of people had the opportunity to participate in the 'conversation' of the website – in both content development and on-line phases of the project. This includes people who do not own and do not intend to use computers, and I shall discuss that further below. By *interactive* I mean that we wanted to provide ways for people to question our archaeological interpretations, and ways for them to approach the material from a variety of angles – using different disciplines and different ways of evaluating truth claims. It also means that we had to provide ways for us to respond to their questions and challenges. Finally, by being *contextual* we wanted to communicate how this archaeology depends on history, on ethnography, on genealogy and on the continuities and conflicts between past and present. These four elements, which came to operate as structuring principles for the website, overlapped and occasionally merged, as the examples here will illustrate.

I shall first discuss interactivity and multivocality. In 'webspeak', interactivity generally refers to buttons to push, video clips to see, sound bites to hear, feedback forms to submit and (less often) on-line discussion forums to participate in – what I tend to call the 'bells and whistles'. In developing this website, however, we conceived of interactivity somewhat differently – as part of the ongoing process of communication between members of descendant communities and others collaboratively to create website content. This interactively developed content *then* became part of the interactive on-line environment, in which we did bring in some of the technological 'bells and whistles' mentioned above.

Likewise, multivocality here was not just the passive presentation of 'different voices', but the ongoing, active involvement of many diverse people in determining what ultimately shows up on the screen. Most importantly, we needed to find ways to include the voices of people who do not use and do not plan to use computers. I work with many descendants whose voices are an important part of both past and present in these communities. These descendants include the elders, and many of them have little or no interest in purchasing or using computers. Even so, we needed to find ways for their voices to appear on the website – a website that some of them will never see (though their children and grandchildren will). I shall discuss two strategies that have proved useful in doing this.

First, we met with several of these key individuals and conducted oral history interviews. I and, usually, at least one other family member conducted the interviews. Frequently the family members were the ones asking most of the questions, and these interviews sometimes led to more inter-family discussions about history, genealogy, etc. Transcripts of the interviews were given to the family members involved, and subsequent meetings were held to clarify information, approve the interview segments used for the website, obtain pictures and the like. Portions of these transcripts were included on the website, with links to other parts of the website that were discussed during these off-line conversations.

Second, we adopted a policy of 'asking permission' to put certain kinds of information on the website – even when we did not have to, legally speaking. Much of the material we wanted to use was from public records – genealogical information, in particular, came from census records and public births, deaths and marriage records. We wanted to include it, but we decided not to without explicit permission from at least some of the family's descendants. Doing this had two positive results. First, it assured descendants that we respected their privacy and their families' privacy, and reinforced our position as collaborators, not authorities with some 'right' to use and 'converse about' their families' histories. Second, it opened avenues for additional information about the lives of the people who lived on this plantation. This information has not only enhanced our understanding of the past, but it has also helped contemporary people to see their ancestors in ways they had not before.

For example, it was during one of these 'asking permission' interviews with an African-American descendant that we learned something that has turned out to be very important to some of the European-American descendants we work with. It had to do with McWillie Martin, the person who owned the plantation when the quarters area was suddenly abandoned, and who had been very involved in white supremacist activities in the late nineteenth century. Both archaeological and historical research have indicated that Martin had a lot to do with why the tenants left the plantation suddenly, leaving so many things behind to be excavated today.

We learned that Martin apparently regretted the actions of his youth – to the point that, according to the person who volunteered the information, he 'repented' these actions before his death. We learned of this from a descendant of the family of George Holmes, a person who had been enslaved on the plantation, as we met to discuss the possibility of putting some of the Holmes family's genealogical records on the website. As far as we know, this explicitly expressed regret was unknown to any of Martin's descendants, many of whom continue to struggle with the harsh reality of their ancestors' actions. This new information was included on the website, and serves to put earlier historical information about Martin's life in a more long-range historical context. More importantly, it serves to reinforce the ways that people's lives, identities and knowledge about each other overlapped (and continue to overlap) in sometimes unexpected ways.

Along with the two strategies above, used to develop *content* interactively and multivocally with people who may not own computers, we also attempted to find ways for people without computers to see and use the website. To this end, I held a series of on-line Internet workshops in the computer labs of local schools – they took place in junior and high school history, social studies and other classes. The data gathered from these workshops was part of what was used to evaluate whether the site succeeded in terms of openness, relevance, multivocality and democracy; as stated earlier, the conclusion to this chapter will offer some of these findings.

I should point out that the website does not include many of the features that are usually regarded, by website designers, as pathways to *so-called* interactivity – such as Java applets, videos, audios and the like. We made a conscious decision to avoid many of those features because of the long download times they require, and because they demand the latest, fastest software and hardware – in a word, because of *access* (McDavid 2003). We have also avoided large images and some other technological features for the same reason. Our priority has been to enable people to see and enjoy the site with a minimum of frustration – even people with slower computers and slower modems. We aimed most of our time and effort at developing *content* interactively and multivocally, rather than just relying on the technology to create an interactive environment.

A final note on multivocality – we also developed a 'participants' section of the website. This includes short biographies of descendants, academics, students, other participants, as well as links to information they wish to put on the site under their own names. Whenever possible, the biographies are written by the individual participants, and sometimes they have used their own pages to publicize information about various community causes. This not only allows more local voices to be represented on the website, but it also highlights our collaborative approach. On these participant pages, archaeological and local agendas merge in mutually empowering, reciprocal ways, and the website project becomes more firmly situated within the social context of the local community – even though it is accessible to people all over the world.

I shall also comment briefly on some of the ways in which we attempted to incorporate reflexivity and contextuality. In terms of reflexivity, we felt it was important to reveal something about the assumptions of the individual archaeologists involved in the project. When the site was first created, most of the archaeological information on the site had been taken directly from published scholarly sources (Brown and Cooper 1990; Brown 1994). It tended, not surprisingly, to be very non-reflexive, authoritative and static. We did want to use this material, but to find ways to use it more reflexively and transparently. Therefore, I conducted interviews with Kenneth Brown and some of his research students. During these interviews, we discussed how they developed their interpretations – how they went back and forth between ideas, theories and data, how they used various sorts of ethnographic and historical data, how they looked at artefacts and artefact contexts in terms of that data, and so on. After being taped and transcribed, portions of these interviews (reviewed and edited by the archaeologists who were interviewed) were then included on the website. We then added links from these interview segments to materials that were discussed during the interviews (diaries, ethnographic material, photos of artefacts, tables, documents, etc.). We also linked the interviews to the original scholarly documents, which are still on the website, to situate both sorts of documents as specific kinds of historical artefacts – as products of specific, and different, modes of knowledge production.

Finally, hypertext links within the website itself have proved the most useful way to reveal the contextuality of archaeological knowledge. I should also point out that our choices about which hyperlinks to use, and where to insert them, had a number of rhetorical and political implications, and revealed a great deal about our own assumptions, theoretical and otherwise (see McDavid (1999) for a more detailed discussion of these implications). On the main 'archaeology' page, for example, there are links to history pages, ethnography pages and links back to oral histories written by family members. These link in turn to family genealogies, church histories and other documents. There are excerpts from a diary written (during and after the Civil War) by the plantation owner's granddaughter, linked to an analysis of the diary by a linguistic anthropologist. There are links from this diary to information about people who lived and worked on the plantation, along with links to archaeological interpretations that have been informed by certain passages in the diary. There is oral history information from the African-American descendant community, linked to church histories, linked in turn to genealogical information about individual families. This is linked to and from archaeological data concerning African religious and healing practices – linked to information about burial traditions within the community, linked back to the oral history data that discusses those traditions. There is also information about the social and political contexts in which the people on this plantation lived (and in which their descendants continue to live), linked to archaeological data which resulted from those contexts. The idea of context – that everything depends on everything else – was enacted in the links we chose to make between various parts of the website's content.

Conclusions

Earlier I stated that the Jordan Plantation website had two purposes – to serve as an important component of an ongoing community public archaeology project, and to examine some more general questions about the Internet and archaeological practice. I shall conclude this chapter by offering a glimpse of the data gathered in aid of the second agenda. To restate, the primary purpose of my individual research was to investigate whether Internet websites could be an effective medium for archaeologists to communicate with diverse publics in open, democratic and relevant ways, and to see whether they could provide opportunities for multiple and contested understandings of past and present to emerge. In order to evaluate these questions, I examined several different types of data: qualitative data gathered during the course of creating the Levi Jordan Plantation Website; qualitative and quantitative data gathered from questionnaires, e-mails and feedback forms submitted by people who visited it; and quantitative visitor data gathered from automated software (about numbers of visitors, etc.). The full results of this evaluation appear in more detail in McDavid (2002), but I summarize them below.

First, it would appear that the Jordan Plantation Website was successful in being *open* to its visitors; feedback form and e-mail data made it clear that people perceived our desire for input, argument and challenge. People seemed to have responded to the site's openness *to the degree that they wished to do so*. This is an important qualification, as the following remarks will indicate. Second, it was apparent that my experiment with creating a space for *democratic* communication space was not as successful – even though the process of designing the site, described above, was extremely democratic. Unfortunately, website visitors did not tend to question the authority of archaeological findings or the authority of individual archaeologists or other people who provided content. They were, as would perhaps be expected given the positive results to the 'openness' question, quite willing to send compliments and to ask for additional information. They were not as willing to engage in meaningful, prolonged conversation about archaeology or history, with me or other project participants – either via e-mail or in the discussion forum.

Third, the experiment with *relevance* had mixed results: it succeeded insofar as certain groups of respondents are concerned, but did not with respect to others. Educators did find the site to be particularly relevant: they seemed to enjoy having their students use the site and in this way the site was able to reach members of some minority groups more effectively. As would be expected, the site also appeared to be relevant and interesting to people interested in history and archaeology; for example, many people interested in genealogy, as one form of history, did find and use the site. This had the effect of exposing archaeological information to those who might not necessarily have attempted to engage with it otherwise – they 'entered' the site through searches for genealogical information. However, I also wanted to reach *and engage* other 'sorts' of people – not just those interested in archaeology.

Fourth, our attempt to achieve *multivocal* communication was least successful. Although the design of the site did provide space for dissent (or, at least, comment) to emerge, for the most part visitors did not take the opportunities provided. It could be that my authority – or, rather, the authority of being part of a 'scientific' discipline – was simply too embedded in visitors' minds for them to contest the findings of that discipline. People may have been reluctant to break established norms – one of which would be the idea that archaeological science can provide The Truth about the past. It could also be that my partial success in being relevant, and my attempt to be democratic and multivocal with regard to archaeology versus other ways of knowing worked against any tendency people might have had to argue. Multiple different types of content were *already* provided on the site, and it is possible that providing uni-dimensional content would have elicited more comment from people from different cultural groups. It is also possible that multivocality, as a goal, is simply not seen as important by many of the site's visitors – that is, it may have been my agenda, but not theirs.

This may relate to my 'liberal' assumptions of what multivocality should look like. Whereas I define it as the idea of allowing *dissenting* points of view to emerge, others may see it as something simpler – they may take for granted the idea that different people see the past in different ways. Certainly my experience working collaboratively in the Brazoria community would support this. My collaborators have always operated in a multivocal way, and, as mentioned earlier, graciously and unselfconsciously accepted – and lived – the idea of 'multiple truths, through multiple lenses'. It may be that site descendants (and members of other publics) do not need a 'critical dialogue' with archaeologists about their pasts and their relationships with it. It may even be arrogant of archaeologists to suggest that they do. If this is true, does that mean that multivocality is *not* a Good Thing? I think it is still a worthy pursuit, although I do think archaeologists should continue to look at the concept critically and reflexively.

Archaeology as a multivocal (and democratic and open) exercise is new: typically, archaeological information has been presented in authoritative ways by archaeologists who want to promote archaeological agendas. The Jordan Website is working against a long history of public archaeological discourse which has not encouraged debate and critique. Perhaps it is too early for archaeologists who do want to engage more openly, democratically, and so on, with the public to expect enthusiastic responses – at least in terms of large numbers of people. It could be that as more and more models of this sort exist, the average member of the public will develop the experience and knowledge to challenge archaeological and academic authority. This is by no means clear, however; almost 50 per cent of my questionnaire respondents already had some prior knowledge about archaeology and history. Presumably they had the understanding to express opinions, dissent, etc. – and they did not.

Before I conclude, it should be noted that, while some of the results described here are somewhat negative, each time I read over the e-mails, feedback forms and question-naires I received, my impression is that our efforts to be open and relevant (and, even, to be democratic and multivocal) were appreciated by a good many people. This would be true even if the project had not been undertaken as part of an academic research project. As one local descendant put it recently, 'Even if we never do anything else with this archaeology, doing the website will have been worth it'. In pragmatic terms, the project had 'cash value' for this individual (James 1995:56) – as, I believe, it did for others. Truly interactive sites which have attempted to do what I (we) did are unusual, and the people who might benefit most may be those who are least acquainted with the Internet. There-fore, even though in some respects our experiments failed, each one taught us valuable lessons about how to improve, next time.

One intent of the Levi Jordan Website Project has been to help create a more demo-cratic, socially relevant archaeology. Indeed, that is probably a major objective for *any* community archaeology, as the rest of this issue will no doubt demonstrate. It is import-ant, however, to take that project farther, past the concerns of a 'democratic archaeology' into a larger arena, where citizens can actively attempt to use archaeology to create a more democratic *society* (Jeppson 2001). By creating a truly collaborative, diverse, non-hierarchical public archaeological project, what I have referred to here as a 'conversation' (McDavid 1997a) about the past, we are not only working towards the first objective, but, we hope, the second one as well.

This project represents one of the first times that members of both African-American and European-American descendant communities came together with archaeologists, in a setting of shared power and responsibility, to decide how to tell the stories of plantation life in the American South. This collaborative effort has been aimed at talking about the histories of both enslavers and enslaved, without doing either at the expense of the other, through the multiple lenses of history, archaeology, folklore, genealogy and other 'ways of knowing'. By using the Internet to expand our local conversations to worldwide ones, we may be able to use archaeology to help create a more relevant, democratic world, where we all can discover what 'truths' about our pasts – and our presents – are most meaningful and relevant.

References

Brown, K. L. 1994. Material culture and community structure: the slave and tenant commun-ity at Levi Jordan's Plantation, 1848–1892. In *Working Toward Freedom: Slave Society and Domestic Economy in the American South* (ed. L. E. Hudson, Jr). Rochester, NY: University of Rochester Press, pp. 95–118.

Brown, K. L. 2000. From archaeological interpretation to public interpretation: collaboration within the discipline for a better public archaeology (phase one). Paper presented at the 65th Annual Meeting of the Society for American Archaeology, Philadelphia, Pennsylva-nia.

Brown, K. L. and Cooper, D. C. 1990. Structural continuity in an African-American slave and tenant community. In *Historical Archaeology on Southern Plantations and Farms, Historical Archaeology*, special issue of *Historical Archaeology* (ed. Charles E. Orser, Jr), 24(4): 7–19.

Dewey, J. 1916. Does reality possess a practical character? In *Essays, Philosophical and Psycholog-ical, in Honor of William James*. New York: Longmans, Green, pp. 49–62.

Goodman, R. B. (ed.) 1995. *Pragmatism: A Contemporary Reader*. New York and London: Routledge.

Hodder, I. 1997. Towards a reflexive excavation methodology. *Antiquity*, 71(273): 691–700.

Hodder, I., Shanks, M., Alexandri, A., Buchli, V., Carman, J., Last, J. and Lucas, G. (eds) 1995. *Interpreting Archaeology: Finding Meaning in the Past*. London and New York: Routledge.

James, W. 1995. Pragmatism. In *Pragmatism: A Contemporary Reader* (ed. R. B. Goodman). New York and London: Routledge, pp. 53–75.

James, W. 1996. *A Pluralistic Universe*. Lincoln and London: University of Nebraska Press; originally published New York: Longmans, Green, 1909.

Jeppson, P. L. 2001. Pitfalls, pratfalls, and pragmatism in public archaeology. Paper presented at the Annual Meetings of the Society for Historical and Underwater Archaeology, Long Beach, California.

Leone, M. P., Potter, P. B., Jr and Shackel, P. A. 1987. Toward a critical archaeology. *Current Anthropology*, 28(3): 283–302.

McDavid, C. 1996. The Levi Jordan Plantation: from archaeological interpretation to public interpretation. Master's thesis, Department of Archaeology, University of Houston, Texas.

McDavid, C. 1997a. Archaeology as cultural critique: a pragmatic framework for community collaboration in the public interpretation of the archaeology of a Southern plantation. Paper presented at the Annual Meetings of the American Anthropology Association, Washington, DC.

McDavid, C. 1997b. Descendants, decisions, and power: the public interpretation of the archaeology of the Levi Jordan Plantation. In *In the Realm of Politics: Prospects for Public Participation in African-American Archaeology*, special issue of *Historical Archaeology* (eds C. McDavid and D. Babson), 31(3): 114–131.

McDavid, C. 1999. From real space to cyberspace: contemporary conversations about the archaeology of slavery and tenancy. *Internet Archaeology (Special Theme: Digital Publication)*, 6. URL: http://intarch.ac.uk/journal/issue6/mcdavid_toc.html.

McDavid, C. 2002. From real space to cyberspace: the Internet and public archaeological practice. Doctoral dissertation. Department of Archaeology, University of Cambridge, Cambridge.

McDavid, C. 2004. From 'traditional' archaeology to public archaeology to community action: the Levi Jordan Plantation Project. In *Places in Mind: Archaeology as Applied Anthropology* (eds P. Shackel and E. Chambers).

McDavid, C. 2003 forthcoming. Towards a more democratic archaeology? The Internet and public archaeological practice. In *Public Archaeology* (eds N. Merriman and T. Shadla-Hall). London: Routledge.

McDavid, C. and Babson, D. (eds) 1997. *In the Realm of Politics: Prospects for Public Participation in African-American Archaeology*, special issue of *Historical Archaeology*, 31(3).

Rorty, R. 1989. *Contingency, Irony and Solidarity*. Cambridge: Cambridge University Press.

Rorty, R. 1991. *Objectivity, Relativism, and Truth: Philosophical Papers*, Vol. 1. Cambridge: Cambridge University Press.

West, C. 1993. *Keeping Faith: Philosophy and Race in America*. New York and London: Routledge.

Chapter 38

Stonehenge – A Final Solution?

Peter Stone

Introduction

Stonehenge is one of the world's iconic prehistoric sites and was inscribed as part of a wider prehistoric landscape as the World Heritage Site of *Stonehenge, Avebury and Associated Sites* in 1986. However, the landscape is dissected by two roads that cut through this part of the World Heritage Site and pass within metres of the stone circle. Over the last 20 years some 50 different options for the upgrading and/or removal of these roads have been discussed. The UK Government is on the verge of making a final decision about the roads that will affect the site for ever. Some argue that this decision will be made without taking either the wider responsibilities enshrined in the 1972 *Convention Concerning the Protection of the World Cultural and Natural Heritage* or the full economic implications of the decision into full consideration.

> Stonehenge is the finest achievement of megalithic architecture in England . . . Together with the associated sites and monuments, the Stones contribute to a wider archaeological landscape *without parallel in the world*.
> (*Stonehenge World Heritage Site Management Plan*, English Heritage, 2000a: Part 2:5, my emphasis)

Stonehenge, one of the world's iconic prehistoric sites, was inscribed on the World Heritage List in 1986. The landscape immediately surrounding Stonehenge is dissected by two busy roads that intrude on the landscape, shattering its tranquillity, and pass within metres of the stone circle. Over the last 20 years some 50 different options for the removal of these roads have been discussed. After a lengthy Public Inquiry in 2004 the Inspector recommended that one be closed and the other placed in a 2.1-km bored tunnel. However, a year later, in the light of increased costs not available at the time of the Inquiry, the Government has decided that this recommendation, which it had supported, is too expensive. It has therefore put forward four other much cheaper options to consultation and is now on the verge of making a crucial, final decision that will radically affect Stonehenge and its surroundings for ever. It appears, unfortunately, that this decision will be made

(a)

(b)

Figure 38.1   (a) Stonehenge from the south; (b) Stonehenge from the south after tunnel.

without taking either the wider responsibilities enshrined in the 1972 World Heritage Convention or the full economic implications of the decision into due consideration. Some argue that these omissions mean that the site should be put on the *List of World Heritage in Danger*.

This decision is to be made not by an archaeologist, 'heritage manager' or any other who might normally be regarded as an 'interested party', but rather by the Secretary of State for Transport. It will be this Minister (following consultation with the Secretary of State at the Department for Culture, Media and Sport), who will make a decision not only symbolizing the Stonehenge that this generation 'deserves' (to echo Jaquetta Hawkes, 1967: 174), but also creating for real the Stonehenge that future generations will inherit, whatever they deserve.

Context

The UK Government became a State Party to UNESCO's 1972 *Convention Concerning the Protection of the World Cultural and Natural Heritage* in 1984 and Stonehenge was inscribed under Criteria (i), (ii) and (iii), as part of a Site that has as its full title: *Stonehenge, Avebury and Associated Sites* (UNESCO, 2006a). It is worth reminding ourselves of the details of these criteria to re-emphasize the importance with which Stonehenge was regarded by those involved in its inscription. According to the inscription Stonehenge:

i   Represent[s] a masterpiece of creative human genius
ii   Exhibit[s] an important interchange of human values, over a span of time or within a cultural area of the world, on developments in architecture or technology, monumental arts, town-planning, or landscape design
iii Bear[s] a unique or at least exceptional testimony to a cultural tradition or to a civilisation which is living or which has disappeared (UNESCO, 2005: 19).

It is also worth taking time to understand the implications for any government of becoming a State Party to the 1972 Convention. Apart from the understanding that States Parties to the Convention will only nominate sites that exhibit 'Outstanding universal value, authenticity, and integrity', Article 4 of the Convention states that:

> Each State Party to this Convention recognizes that the duty of ensuring the identification, protection, conservation, presentation and transmission to future generations of the cultural and natural heritage referred to in Articles 1 and 2 and situated on its territory, belongs primarily to that State. *It will do all it can to this end, to the utmost of its own resources* and, where appropriate, with *any international assistance and co-operation*, in particular, financial, artistic, scientific and technical, which it may be able to obtain.
> (English Heritage, 2000a, my emphasis – see below)

Article 5 continues that States Parties are required 'To ensure that effective and active measures are taken for the protection, conservation and presentation of the cultural and natural heritage situated on its territory'. In practice this means that all sites on the List should have an appropriate management system in place. The UK government interprets this to mean each site should have a management plan (Stonehenge's was published in 2000: English Heritage, 2000a); a clear reporting structure to UNESCO (in England via the Department of Culture, Media and Sport with the expert advice of English Heritage and the UK National Commission for UNESCO); adequate legal protection (for Stonehenge through the 1979 *Ancient Monuments and Archaeological Areas Act* supported, as a

World Heritage Site, by *Planning Policy Guidance Note 15*, which requires Local Authorities to '. . . formulate specific planning policies . . . [for protection]'); and at least some form of presentation and interpretation policy in place (at present delivered by English Heritage and the National Trust). It is relatively safe to argue, therefore, that UNESCO views the UK Government as satisfying all of its responsibilities with respect to the conservation and protection aspects of the Convention relating to Stonehenge. The UK's commitment to the Convention and its implications is actually emphasized in the Stonehenge Management Plan (English Heritage, 2000a: Part 2:3) when it states:

> The UK is a strong supporter of the Convention and the Government has an international obligation to identify, protect, conserve, present and transmit to future generations the cultural World Heritage values of its inscribed Sites.

Under the commitment the UK has kept the World Heritage Committee briefed on the long saga regarding the intrusive roads at Stonehenge and the poor quality of the visitor facilities. However, while no-one has questioned the validity of these briefings, concern has been raised that they have emphasized only the positive aspects of proposed solutions, and certainly have not revealed the extent to which they might be argued to frustrate the longer-term aspirations of the Site's Management Plan, thereby highlighting the conflict of interest within governments of States Parties as to their roles as both developer and protector. These concerns aside, the Committee has considered Stonehenge on no less than 14 occasions since 1986 – certainly not a record of interest in any one Site under its jurisdiction, but a level of attention that emphasizes both the State Party's and the Committee's major commitment to finding a solution to the present *impasse*.

The 1972 Convention is usually argued to be the most successful of all UNESCO's international conventions, with 181 States Parties to it and 812 cultural and natural sites inscribed on the List in April 2006. The Convention is overseen by a World Heritage Committee comprising representatives from 21 member states, elected from the 181 States Parties for a period of up to six years. The Committee's main responsibilities are to (a) ensure the proper implementation of the Convention; (b) inscribe (or not) sites nominated by States Parties after expert advice (for cultural sites from the International Council on Monuments and Sites (ICOMOS) and, on occasion, the International Centre for the Study of the Preservation and Restoration of Cultural Property (ICCROM)); and (c) react to problems and threats facing inscribed Sites. If a World Heritage Site is identified as being under threat, the Committee usually reacts by seeking detailed information concerning the perceived threat. It then offers advice or assistance – frequently after a visit by an expert mission and, on occasion, additional funding to help remove or at least mitigate the threat. If, after such efforts, the Site is still perceived by the Committee to be under threat, the Committee may, after careful consideration, place the Site on the *List of World Heritage in Danger* (Article 11.4). Such extreme action is usually intended to support the State Party but can be used to put international pressure on a State Party to fulfil its obligations under the Convention or to raise international awareness of the threat to the Site in an attempt to mobilize an international response. *In extremis* the Committee can remove a Site from the World Heritage List if it believes that the Site has lost the characteristics that originally gave it a place on the List. To date, no Site has been removed from the List and at the last meeting of the World Heritage Committee (Durban, July 2005) only 31 Sites were on the *In Danger List*. It is worth quoting the part of the Convention that identifies the type of threats that might be regarded as good reason for inclusion on the *In Danger List*:

> The list may include only such property forming part of the cultural and natural heritage as is threatened by serious and specific dangers, such as the threat of disappearance caused by accelerated deterioration, *large-scale public or*

> *private projects or rapid urban or tourist development projects*; destruction caused by changes in the use or ownership of the land; major alterations due to unknown causes; abandonment for any reason whatsoever; the outbreak or the threat of an armed conflict; calamities and cataclysms; serious fires, earthquakes, landslides; volcanic eruptions; changes in water level, floods and tidal waves.
>
> (World Heritage Committee: Article 11, my emphasis)

While few World Heritage Sites have actually been identified as 'In danger' many do suffer from pressures over and above those normally expected at heritage sites. For example, at *Uluru-Kata Tjuta*, in Australia, the Government has to deal with issues that are remarkably similar to those that face the UK Government at Stonehenge. A small visitor centre, set within the World Heritage Site, barely copes with visitor numbers, while car and coach parks specifically created for sunrise and sunset are frequently overfull and present significant traffic dangers. Unregulated car parking also poses significant problems for safety and proper site management. Visitors stray away from designated routes and continually stretch the patience and goodwill of the host Aboriginal community. In Sweden, at the World Heritage Site of *Tanum*, plans for a single lane road to be up-graded have been discussed for over a decade but lack of agreement between highways and heritage agencies has meant that no solution has been found as yet (Larsson-Modin, personal communication, 15 May 2006). In Egypt, the Site of *Memphis and Its Necropolis — the Pyramid Fields from Giza to Dahshur*, was threatened in the late 1990s by plans for the Cairo Ring Road to pass within close proximity. The World Heritage Committee sent an expert mission to help identify a different route for the road and all appeared to be safe. However, in the years since the original threat the remainder of the ring road has been constructed without this section, with the two ends of the new road pointing menacingly at each other across the Giza Plain, essentially fixing as the only possible route for completion one that puts a finished ring road in clear sight of, and in close proximity to, the Pyramids (Veronique Dauge, personal communication, 30 March 2006).

A tangent(?): the broader agenda

It is frequently overlooked that the 1972 Convention is much more than a list of hundreds of special sites. It encompasses many of the overarching aspirations of UNESCO to work 'to create the conditions for genuine dialogue based upon respect for shared values and the dignity of each civilization and culture' (UNESCO, 2006b). For example, Article 27 of the Convention states that:

> The States Parties to this Convention shall endeavour by all appropriate means, and in particular by educational and information programmes, to strengthen appreciation and respect by their peoples of the cultural and natural heritage defined in Articles 1 and 2 of the Convention.

To this end, in 1994, UNESCO launched the 'Young People's Participation in World Heritage Preservation and Promotion' Project to 'encourage and enable tomorrow's decision-makers to participate in heritage conservation' (UNESCO, 2006c). The programme has a number of elements including the production of an educational Resource Kit entitled 'World Heritage in Young Hands'. This Kit, now published in over 20 languages and adapted to fit national curricula in over 130 countries, has five main strands: the Convention; Identity; Environment; Tourism; and a Culture of Peace.

These are huge, brave, worthy topics but they are also difficult to engage with, and thus easy to ignore. Perhaps more problematic still for many governments is that each of these strands aims to 'develop knowledge, provide skills, and change attitudes' (UNESCO, 1998: 59). While the development of knowledge and provision of skills are, usually, seen as positive aspects of education, many of those involved in the organization of education at a national level become more uncomfortable when the aspiration of education becomes overtly to change attitudes. Such an aspiration is frequently seen by governments (unless, of course, instigated by government) as an overtly uncomfortable idea; one with which it is frequently difficult to engage, regarded even as potentially dangerous: an aspiration easy to commit to but as easily overlooked and ignored as States Parties concentrate on the conservation and management of sites on the *World Heritage List*. Conservation and management of sites is, obviously, a necessary and basic foundation for their long-term survival – and for their exploitation as stimuli for local and national economies. However, through such overconcentration on conservation and physical management States Parties open themselves to the potential of overlooking the more fundamental and wide-ranging aspirations of the Convention.

The present situation

Everyone agrees that the present situation at Stonehenge is a very long way from satisfactory – the 'national disgrace' of the House of Commons Public Accounts Committee report of 1993. The A344 passes within a few metres of the Heel Stone and cuts the Stone Circle from its associated sites in the landscape to the north, most notably the Avenue, seen by most archaeologists as the main ceremonial approach to the Stones. The A303 passes within a few hundred metres of the Stone Circle and divides it from its associated sites to the south. Both roads combine to create an accident black-spot in Stonehenge bottom, and an aural and visual intrusion that dissects the World Heritage Site into three, essentially separate, areas, thereby significantly undermining any potential for real holistic management, presentation or interpretation. It is a Site that, if not in danger, is certainly in crisis. To echo the English Heritage/National Trust campaign of the 1990s *something must be done*. But what?

A 1995 planning conference achieved a consensus on a long bored-tunnel solution but this was quickly deemed to be too expensive; numerous cheaper surface routes and shorter tunnels have been explored and all dismissed as being detrimental to the World Heritage Site. The present 'Stonehenge Project' (English Heritage, 2006) aims to achieve a significant number of the Management Plan objectives by hiding the A303 as viewed from Stonehenge in a tunnel; closing the A344 where it passes the site; building a new Visitor Centre outside the World Heritage Site near Countess Roundabout; removing the existing facilities near the centre circle; and restoring much of the core area of the World Heritage Site to grass. Most accept that the existing visitor facilities are far from adequate for the numbers who visit; are a million miles away from what would normally be expected of a World Heritage Site; and go against all international heritage advice in that they are situated within the confines of the Site (see Feilden and Jokilehto, 1993: 97–104; ICOMOS, 1999).

If any decision were to be taken solely with respect to the commitments made by UK Government under the 1972 Convention, the solution to the roads issue would be simplicity itself: both roads would be removed immediately and entirely from the whole of the World Heritage Site. The nomination of the Site in 1986 focused exclusively on the prehistoric elements of the landscape and thus, even if anyone were to argue that the area was important as a palimpsest cultural landscape, including features from prehistory to the twenty-first century, and even if someone wanted to argue (a somewhat extreme if not downright eccentric viewpoint) that even the roads were an integral element of such a palimpsest landscape, their argument would have no legal standing, given the 1986 reasons for nomination and inscription.

On the occasion of the inscription of Stonehenge as a World Heritage Site in 1986, the World Heritage Committee noted 'with satisfaction' '. . . the assurances provided by the authorities of the United Kingdom that the closure of the road [A344] which crosses the Avenue at Stonehenge was receiving serious consideration'. *Where* the roads should be moved to is really nothing to do with UNESCO and the organization would be within its rights to make this point strongly. Unfortunately, we do not live in a simple world and the UK Government, along with all States Parties to the Convention, has to balance a wide variety of pressures, obligations and responsibilities – a balancing act fully understood and appreciated by UNESCO and the World Heritage Committee.

One factor that impinges upon this whole issue is, of course, the boundary of the World Heritage Site (or at least the Stonehenge part of the whole Site). Anecdotal evidence suggests that the present boundaries are the result of a decision in 1985 to ensure that the first group of sites to be nominated by the UK would pass through a level of international bureaucracy, with an unknown degree of scrutiny, with as much ease as possible. The boundaries of the Stonehenge part of the World Heritage Site were therefore identified by the route of three roads and a river that enabled the majority of the major scheduled ancient monuments in the area to be included (Malone, personal communication, 13 April 2006). For better or worse, this is the only part of the wider landscape of this area to be identified as World Heritage. It is not, of course, the only part of the landscape to host significant and important prehistoric remains – for example the western boundary, identified by the A360, passes directly through a Bronze Age barrow cemetery, actually cutting one barrow in half, thereby valuing one part of the cemetery – one part of the barrow – as heritage of 'outstanding universal value' and leaving the rest as only an, albeit nationally important, Scheduled Ancient Monument. An application for nomination, showing the boundaries based on what are effectively modern intrusions into an earlier landscape, would almost certainly be rejected now by the Committee. This supposition apart, the current reality is that the World Heritage Site is ringed by an area full of important prehistoric remains, so that any movement of the roads within the immediate vicinity would impact on these remains and almost certainly result in significant damage to important buried archaeology. The implication of this is that we must accept, as noted above, that the only acceptable road solution, based solely on heritage criteria, is to remove both roads not only from within the confines but also from within the *immediate vicinity* of the World Heritage Site. Perhaps an unrealistic aspiration.

However, it should not be forgotten that some of the proposed southern routes, rejected on cost and/or environmental grounds, do very largely achieve this. Some parts of the heritage sector believe that the 'best' solution discussed to date has been the removal of the A344 and the transfer of the A303 into a 4.3-km-long bore tunnel, almost entirely removing it also from the surface of the World Heritage Site. Others believe – even more strongly now that cost estimates for tunnelling options have risen – that solutions outside the World Heritage Site have never been adequately explored in the context of the level of budget now being mentioned. The Department for Transport and the Highways Agency have long maintained that any long bore tunnel would be too expensive (current guesstimates go as high as £1 billion). They now argue that the shorter 2.1-km bore tunnel (a length that would mean that the road would not be visible from Stonehenge itself) as jointly promoted by the state heritage and highways agencies though a hotly contested Public Inquiry would also be too expensive (current estimates £500 million). Government Ministers have, therefore, asked for four other, cheaper, routes to be considered. It appears that one of these, a *c*.2.1-km cut-and-cover tunnel, has already been rejected by English Heritage, the National Trust and other heritage bodies as being unacceptable: not only does it put even more unknown buried archaeology at risk within the World Heritage Site, but it also significantly changes the topography of the landscape in Stonehenge Bottom and essentially destroys forever any potential for increased landscape understanding of the relationship between the Stone Circle and the Avenue. Such intrusion and impact on the Site would almost certainly result in a questioning of the UK Government's commitment to the 1972 Convention and, some have suggested, *could* lead to the site being put onto the *In Danger List*, and possibly, although unlikely, the removal of the Site from the World Heritage List altogether. A surface route to the south of the present line of the A303 was also firmly previously rejected as unacceptable by Government and voluntary heritage bodies since it cuts through a hitherto essentially undisturbed area of the World Heritage Site and its choice should elicit a similar, if not more damning, response from UNESCO (it would also impact on areas of the World Heritage Site important for environmental and natural reasons). A suggested northerly route potentially has an equally threatening impact on unknown buried archaeology and the setting of important monuments, and appears in any case to be an unlikely choice given its proximity to Ministry of Defence land at Larkhill (especially as the army is currently refurbishing and expanding the Larkhill site in readiness for the redeployment of the British Army of the Rhine to the UK). The final 'new' option in the present consultation is the so-called 'Partial Solution' that provides for a bypass for Winterbourne Stoke to the West; a flyover at Countess Roundabout to the East that would enable traffic to move Westwards uninterrupted by those wishing to go to a relocated Visitor Centre off the Countess Roundabout; and the closure of the A344. This would leave the present single carriageway A303 on the surface within the World Heritage Site. This is perhaps the most innocuous, yet perhaps the most dangerous, of all of the options. The Department for Transport and the Highways Agency have commented frequently that there would be no consideration of any tunnel schemes were it not for the World Heritage status of Stonehenge: if it were not for this status the A303 would simply be turned into a surface dual carriageway. The Partial Solution effectively fixes the entry and exit points of the A303 with respect to the World Heritage Site, just as the ends of the Cairo ring road constructed so far appear to ensure that the only way for the ring road to be finished is to let it pass over the Giza Plain. Assuming that this option were chosen, how long would it be before the section of the A303 passing through the World Heritage Site was the only section of this important trunk road to be single carriageway and, as road deaths would inevitably climb as frustrated drivers took impossible risks, how long would the heritage community be able to argue against the modification of the A303 into a surface dual carriageway passing within a few hundred metres of the Stone Circle? If we lose tunnel options now, there is no guarantee of returning to them in the future. It has been suggested that there is a sound argument, effectively supported in the Site's Management Plan, to take the first basic steps now of closing the A344 and improving traffic flow at junctions while a much more serious consideration is given to a more complete long-term solution. This Partial Solution, it is argued, actually achieves significant benefits by closing the A344 and easing congestion; it does not cost a great deal; it allows further action in the future; and, perhaps more importantly from a political standpoint, it puts off any costly 'final' decision for some considerable time. However, this 'Giza option' is fraught with danger; some argue that it is too dangerous an option to consider and the heritage community must consciously decide, if it so wishes, to put the Site into such medium-term danger or must accept one of the other routes on offer outlined above. An unpalatable choice, but we cannot sleepwalk into accepting the 'Partial Solution' without consciously accepting what some see as its almost inevitable consequences.

   If government statements about making a final decision concerning the roads this summer are delivered, we appear to be on the edge of a momentous decision. The decision will be informed to a significant degree by available funding. The Department for Transport and the Highways Agency say they cannot afford the only solution (the long bored tunnel) that has limited consensus support among the heritage community. And yet, the 1972 Convention declares that all States Parties have a 'duty of ensuring the identification, protection, conservation, presentation and transmission to future generations of the cultural and natural heritage [on the List] . . . *to the utmost of its own resources* . . .' To be very simplistic, £1 billion might sound far too high a price when the money could be used to alleviate hunger in the Developing World or even within the UK National Health Service; it may seem to some to be a more reasonable amount if it could be pruned from the defence budget. However, the figure is not too dissimilar to that paid out to develop, and then prop up, the London Millennium Dome (National Audit Office, 2000) and actually almost matches the UK's bi-annual expenditure on Easter Eggs! (Catholic Agency for Overseas Development (CAFOD), 2006).

The expenditure would be, essentially, a one-off cost. The money would be spent within the confines of a project lasting a year or so that would provide a solution for at least 150 years or more – meaning an annual cost of somewhere just over £6.5 million over 150 years or £5 million over 200 years. Put this way, is there an argument that says such expenditure is economically justifiable? In 1997 the Parliamentary Office of Science and Technology (POST, 1997: 21) suggested that the economic value of driving a tunnel under a mythical *Twyburyhenge*, a site that bore remarkable similarities to Stonehenge, was 'good value'. Results of further work on the economic value of different road options for Stonehenge (Maddison and Mourato, 1998, 2002) were less clear but certainly provided evidence to show that the heritage benefits (that is the benefits to the British public) alone justified the cost of the bored tunnel investigated at that time (with the heritage benefit identified as £149 million). Expenditure needs to be put into a context. The Highways Agency has carried out a conventional cost–benefit analysis with respect to the options regarding the A303 but, in the words of the economist Professor David Maddison speaking at the 2004 Public Inquiry, such an analysis '. . . overlook[s] the main reason why people wish to change the current layout' and '. . . it therefore represents something of a missed opportunity' as the analysis does not include all (if any) of the heritage benefits. The 'missed opportunity' is exacerbated by the fact that the Highways Agency has failed to use more robust methods developed since the 1998 work carried out by Maddison and Mourato that better measure the economic value of heritage than attempt to include/measure all benefits. This is despite the Treasury recommending that the use of valuation techniques be extended as far as possible (Economics for the Environment Consultancy (EETEC), 2005: preface) and it could be argued that the Highways Agency is failing to carry out government requirements by not carrying out a full cost–benefit analysis. In his evidence to the Public Inquiry, Maddison pointed to '. . . literally hundreds of other applications of environmental valuation methodologies [relating to new quarries; the preservation of biodiversity; the recreational uses of forests; changes in agricultural techniques that might have an effect on the landscape and so on] which monetise environmental impacts'. The use of these environmental techniques, and in particular contingent valuation studies, has been fully explored in courts in the USA (perhaps the most testing environment to which such a new methodology could be exposed) as the result of the Exxon Valdez disaster in Alaska, and their use and validity are now fully accepted. These valuation techniques have also received some endorsement from a panel of Nobel Prize-winning economists in the USA. Similar work has been discussed and promoted through expert meetings instigated by the Getty Conservation Institute (Getty Conservation Institute, 1998) and large cultural institutions have used such methods to place a monetary value on their non-marketed services to justify government funding, for example, the British Library (Pung *et al.*, 2004). Some of these techniques could have been used by the Highways Agency to better assess the true economic value of the various road options at Stonehenge and Maddison commented '. . . perplexingly the Highways Agency has not used these techniques so far'. Indeed, some economists (for example, Throsby, 2001) argue that heritage assets generate both an economic *and* a cultural value, thereby adding an additional, yet undeterminable, value to any given asset. Part of this additional value stems from a site's uniqueness and its inability to be replaced or replicated: a concept that brings us firmly back to the ideology surrounding the original reason for inscription on the World Heritage List. The 1998 work by Maddison and Mourato was the first study in the UK to use non-market valuation methodologies to monetize the environmental impacts of road transport on an actual site and it appears to be still the only study to address road development in this way. This is a staggeringly negligent position. Maddison concluded his evidence by stating:

> . . . Stonehenge is such an important site that it surely merits doing an addi-tional valuation study, using all the techniques and all the advances which have occurred in the last six or seven years since we did the [1998] study . . . valua-tion techniques have improved markedly; given the importance of the site I think we would be well-advised to do the study again, just to check some of the perhaps, with hindsight, unreasonable assumptions that I made during the course of the study and also were forced on me by the people who were handling me during the course of the work.

The last point presumably relates to the fact that Maddison and Mourato were not asked to evaluate a long bore tunnel option. In principle the importance of heritage to the economy is well recognized by Government and its agencies. English Heritage's publication, *The Heritage Dividend* (for example, English Heritage, 1999) is deliberately intended to demon-strate and emphasize this link, as does the Heritage Lottery Fund's (2004) *New Life: Her-itage and Regeneration*; it was stressed in both *Power of Place* (English Heritage, 2000b) and *A Force for Our Future* (Department for Culture Media and Sport/Department for Transport, Local Government and the Regions (DCMS/DTLR), 2001), and Government was instru-mental in organizing, and played a large part in, the recent conference *Capturing the Public Value of Heritage* (London, January 2006). Given this understanding, it seems incredible and impossible that the Government is about to make a decision that fails to take into account the full potential economic value of Stonehenge by neglecting to assess all of the benefits produced by the different options. Indeed, this point has been made already by the World Archaeological Congress (WAC) in a report submitted to the UK Government in 1999 in which WAC explicitly called on the UK Government to '. . . commission an independent assessment of the cost and benefits of a long-bore tunnel for the A303' (Layton and Thomas, 1999). Nevertheless, despite the intent that the whole project should be exceptional in setting new standards, it appears to have been allowed to remain obstinately hidebound by an outdated, long-since discredited method for analysing the most crucial issue of all – what is worth spending to safeguard one of the world's greatest monuments for not just one, but countless more future generations.

Considerable effort has already gone into trying to cut the Gordian Knot of Stone-henge – indeed, some estimates suggest that over £20 million has already been spent. Nevertheless, at the very least, such failure to assess all the options would, almost without question, leave the Government open to a charge of failing to fulfil its duty under the 1972 Convention, if not its own Treasury guidelines. However, in the present economic-led system, it could be argued that an even greater criticism is that Government might be failing to reap the potential economic rewards of its premier World Heritage Site. Might a one-off payment of £1 billion not actually be a sound economic investment as well as a strong signal to the international community that the UK aspires to lead the world in her-itage conservation and interpretation, and that it treasures and values its heritage as an integral part of its national estate and resource? Some argue that the point about safeguard-ing the Stonehenge part of this World Heritage Site *properly*, rather than in the partial ways being variously proposed by the UK Government and its advisers, is that such huge invest-ment will actually be cost-effective. The investment will not only provide a return over the 30 years usually allowed by Treasury for roads to prove their worth in traffic terms, but will benefit countless generations. That, so the argument goes, is the point about Stonehenge and the monuments that were so carefully set in the landscape around it: they have already been appreciated for several millennia and will continue to be so for the foreseeable future. The benefits of removing the roads completely from the World Heritage Site will far outlast the passing of the motor car and open up possibilities of enjoyment and appreciation, of which we have not even thought. Despite these arguments, the likelihood of such investment taking place appears negligible.

In some respects the real issue at stake here is not whether these two roads and visitor facilities are removed or not from within the World Heritage Site. The real issue is whether States Parties can be allowed to effectively pick and choose which articles of an international (in this case UNESCO) Convention they choose to put into practice and which they do not; and, once this choice has been made, how far they go in fulfilling their obligations with respect to those articles they choose to put into practice. If, in this example, the UK Government chose to do so, it could remove both roads and the visitor facilities from the World Heritage Site altogether. Such dramatic and radical action would be sending a message, not only that the UK is willing to lead the international community in the conservation and preservation of the world's cultural and natural heritage, but also that it is willing to engage with the wider implications enshrined within the 1972 Convention, beginning the process of 'changing attitudes'.

As there is little evidence of government taking such a bold stance, we must ask has Stonehenge missed the boat? We must ask, have we, as the heritage community, allowed Stonehenge to miss the boat? Who is going to accept the responsibilities under the 1972 World Heritage Convention? Responsibilities to the site; to World Heritage, and through this to setting an example to the international community of best practice; 'to developing knowledge, providing skills and to changing attitudes'; perhaps even to those who have gone before, to the builders of Stonehenge, who understood its meaning, who knew its value, who must have valued its presence; and to those who are still buried within its hinterland.

Stonehenge is a site 'without parallel in the world'. We must grasp the opportunity to convince Government of the economic value of Stonehenge to the UK; to accept our obligations and responsibilities under the 1972 Convention; to take a lead in World Heritage preservation, management and interpretation; to use Stonehenge to show the next generation that heritage matters; to change attitudes. If we do not, no-one else will. Or do we accept failure and begin to plan for Stonehenge to be placed on the *List of World Heritage in Danger*. Will we seize the day, or let future generations rue the day you and I could have done something, but failed?

Acknowledgments

Thanks to Naomi Kinghorn, George Lambrick, Genevieve Stone and Christopher Young for reading and commenting on earlier versions of this article, despite not necessarily agreeing with what I have written here. All mistakes are my own.

References

Catholic Agency for Overseas Development (CAFOD). *Buying World Gifts instead of Easter Eggs*. http://www.cafod.org.uk/news_and_events/news/buying_world_gifts_2006_03_22 (accessed 6 June 2006) (2006).
Department for Culture Media and Sport/Department for Transport, Local Government and

the Regions (DCMS/DTLR). *The Historic Environment: A Force for our Future.* DCMS/DTLR, London (2001).

Economics for the Environment Consultancy (EFTEC). *Valuation of the Historic Environment – the Scope for Using Results of Valuation Studies in the Appraisal and Assessment of Heritage-related Projects and Programmes, Executive Summary.* Report to English Heritage, the Heritage Lottery Fund, the Department for Culture, Media and Sport and the Department for Transport. EFTEC, London (2005).

English Heritage. *The Heritage Dividend: Measuring the Results of English Heritage Regeneration, 1994–1999.* English Heritage, London (1999).

English Heritage. *Stonehenge World Heritage Site Management Plan.* English Heritage, London (2000a).

English Heritage. *Power of Place: the Future of the Historic Environment.* English Heritage, London (2000b).

English Heritage. *The Stonehenge Project.* http://www.thestonehengeproject.org/) (accessed 12 May 2006) (2006).

Feilden, B. and Jokilehto, J. *Management Guidelines for World Cultural Sites.* ICCROM, Rome (1993).

Getty Conservation Institute. *Economics and Heritage Conservation: A Meeting Organised by the Getty Conservation Institute.* Getty Center, Los Angeles (1998).

Hawkes, J. God in the machine. *Antiquity,* **41** (1967) 174–80.

Heritage Lottery Fund. *New Life: Heritage and Regeneration.* London, Heritage Lottery Fund (2004).

ICOMOS *International Cultural Tourism Charter: Managing Tourism at Places of Heritage Significance.* International Council on Monuments and Sites, http://www.international. icomos.org/charters/tourism_e.htm (accessed 12 May 2006) (1999).

Layton, R. and Thomas, J. Proposals for a Tunnel at Stonehenge: An Assessment of the Alternatives. Unpublished report to the Executive of the World Archaeological Congress (and submitted to the UK Government) (1999).

Maddison, D. and Mourato, S. Valuing Different Road Options for the A303 (The Stonehenge Study). Unpublished report to English Heritage (1998).

Maddison, D. and Mourato, S. Valuing Different Road Options for Stonehenge. In: S. Navrud and R. Ready (eds) *Valuing Cultural Heritage: Applying Environmental Valuation Techniques to Historic Buildings, Monuments and Artefacts.* Edward Elgar, Cheltenham (2002).

National Audit Office. *The Millennium Dome: Report by the Comptroller and Auditor General.* HC 936 Session 1999–2000; 9 November 2000 (2000).

Parliamentary Office of Science and Technology (POST). *Tunnel Vision? The Future Role of Tunnels in Transport Infrastructure.* POST, London (1997).

Pung, C., Clarke, A., and Patten, L. Measuring the Economic Impact of the British Library. *New Review of Academic Librarianship,* **10** (2004) 79–102.

Throsby, D. *Economics and Culture.* Cambridge University Press, Cambridge (2001).

UNESCO. *World Heritage in Young Hands: To Know, Cherish and Act.* UNESCO, Paris (1998).

UNESCO. *Operational Guidelines for the Implementation of the World Heritage Convention.* http://whc.unesco.org/achive/opguide05-en.pdf (accessed 18 May 2006) (2005).

UNESCO. *The World Heritage List: Stonehenge, Avebury and Associated Sites.* http://whc. unesco.org/en/list/373 (accessed 18 May 2006) (2006a).

UNESCO. *About UNESCO.* http://portal.unesco.org/en/ev.phpURL_ID = 3328 & URL_DO=DO_ TOPIC&URL_SECTION=201.html (accessed 18 May 2006) (2006b).

UNESCO. *Youth Education: World Heritage in Young Hands Programme.* http://whc.unesco.org/ en/initiatives/28/ (accessed 12 May 2006) (2006c).

Chapter 39

More Than Just "Telling the Story"

Interpretive narrative archaeology

John P. McCarthy

Introduction

An increasing number of American archaeologists are turning to a narrative approach in presenting and interpreting data. This trend has sometimes been described as simple "storytelling," usually, but not always, in the third person. Its goal is to make the results of archaeological research more relevant and more meaningful to the members of the public in whose interests such work is undertaken. In other cases, it is a first-person attempt to personalize, contextualize, and demystify the research process. In a few cases, it is a combination of both. In all cases, when well done, it is an art form.

These narratives are strongly grounded in archaeological and historical data, although in some cases this is difficult to assess. The narratives generally follow an approach described by some historians as "microhistory," in which broad social patterns are described through the detailed study of specific events and individual experiences (e.g. Wood 1994). This chapter describes this trend toward narrative, places it in context, and assesses its potential to fundamentally change how American archaeologists think about and conduct research. I will argue that this new focus on narrative is more than just "telling the story." It recasts interpretation at the center of the archaeological enterprise, and for this reason I will be referring to this approach as "interpretive narrative archaeology."

Interpretive narratives

At the January 1997 meeting of the Society for Historical Archaeology in Corpus Christi, Texas, I attended a session called "Archaeologists as Storytellers." I did this in part because a number of my close friends and colleagues were participants and I wanted to be supportive of their efforts. However, I also attended because I was curious about what they were going to do and, frankly, how it would affect what I, as an archaeological practitioner, do. I was treated to more than ten papers presenting diverse narratives. Some of them were presented in the first person and focused on how the excavation was conducted and the data interpreted. Some were presented in the third person and discussed the everyday lives of the people who once inhabited the sites, using artifacts and other site data to "flesh out" the description. The most unusual papers, however, were presented in the first person and told the fictionalized story of an event or events in a past life as informed by archaeological data. The papers were entertaining as well as informative. Following the conference I began to think about what I had heard and what it really meant. The "problem," as I had come to think of it, of these narratives was reinforced when volume 32, number 1, of the journal *Historical Archaeology* arrived on my desk just over a year later. It contained nine of the papers presented in the session.

The "Archaeologists as Storytellers" session was not the first instance of an interpretive narrative approach in American archaeology. James Deetz made use of short, fictionalized narratives for introductory purposes in his volumes *In Small Things Forgotten* (1977) and *Flowerdrew Hundred* (1993). However, neither of these volumes was truly "interpretive" in focus or intent in the sense that I am using the concept here.

This recent trend toward interpretive narrative has it roots in two complementary trends in American archaeology. First, there has been a growing realization that the public could not understand and did not care about the "narratives" that archaeologists were producing, even though the archaeological endeavor increasingly relies on public support and financing (e.g. Klein 1999). At the same time, increasing disenchantment with the scientific paradigm of the New Archaeology led to the growing influence of postmodern theoretical perspectives that emphasize understanding over objective description and that recognize constructed and contingent aspects of the nature of knowledge (e.g. Beaudry *et al.* 1991; Leone *et al.* 1987).

During the first half of the 1990s, several monographs appeared introducing first-person narration of archaeological enquiry. Notable among these were Leland Furguson's (1992) *Uncommon Ground*, which focused on the importance and origins of Colonoware, an African-American pottery tradition found throughout the slave South; Janet Spector's (1993) *What This Awl Means: Feminist Archaeology at Wahpeton Dakota Village*, which discusses how she undertook the investigation of a nineteenth-century Dakota settlement in Minnesota, made contact with descendants of the inhabitants of the site, and then made considerable use of informant information to interpret the site; and Anne Yentsch's (1994) volume on the eighteenth-century Calvert family of Maryland and their slaves, titled *A Chesapeake Family and Their Slaves*.

Perhaps the first, and certainly the most influential, use of first-person "fictionalized" interpretive narrative, however, is found in Carmel Shrire's (1995) *Digging through Darkness*. Shrire, a native South African, teaches at Rutgers University, and I know from conversations that *Digging* had considerable impact on some of the participants in the "Archaeologists as Storytellers" session.

The "Archeologists as Storytellers" session was important, not because it broke entirely new ground, but because it represented a breakthrough from isolated academic production of interpretive narratives to the wider "mainstream" of archaeological practitioners. Most archaeologists in the United States (60 to 70 percent) are employed in cultural resources management (CRM), a broad category of applied practice that includes the public and private sectors and that relies on legislation requiring the identification, evaluation, and management of archaeological resources (Elston 1997). Four participants were full-time CRM consultants, three were academics who spent at least a portion of their time involved in CRM activities, and only two were academics not actively involved in CRM work, although one had been a full-time practitioner earlier in her career and the other has been involved in CRM projects from time to time.

Each of the papers that appeared in volume 32, number 1, represented an act of archaeological interpretation that gave form and meaning to lifeless and often dull archaeological and historical data. As Rebecca Yamin (1998:85), author of the paper on the notorious Five Points area in New York City, stated, "The stories are a kind of hermeneutic exercise in drawing . . . strands of information into a coherent whole. The construction of a narrative vignette provides a methodological beginning point." Yamin here draws on Hodder's (1991) notion of "coherence" as the explanation that makes the most sense of the most data. However, while Hodder (1989a) argued that the narrative report should be a process of argument, Yamin (2002) uses narrative as a process of understanding and communicating.

Each of the authors focused on telling a story rather than presenting data; in so doing, they moved the interpretive process to center stage. More traditional forms of archaeological discourse focus on data and their presentation, leaving interpretation to last – and too often least – priority. The narratives were personal, impressionistic essays and were definitely not science as traditionally understood. The papers and the movement they reflect, in fact, constitute an explicit rejection of objective, positivist science. To understand this turn of events, we need to place it in context and examine the nature of science and scientific reasoning in archaeology.

Context: the development of historical archaeology

In North America, historical archaeology has it roots in the 1930s with the restoration archaeology of the National Park Service at Jamestown (Cotter 1958) and other sites (e.g. Harrington 1957) and of the Colonial Williamsburg Foundation (Hume 1994). These investigations were undertaken to support the restoration and re-creation of historic structures on a massive scale. At this time, historical archaeology was seen as an adjunct to history, specifically architectural history (Harrington 1955). Archaeological undertakings at this time were site-specific and humanistic in their focus if informed by theory at all. A typical research question in this period might have been, "Is there any evidence documenting the size, shape, and stairway configuration of the porch that documentary sources suggest was built on the east side of the building sometime between 1750 and 1780?"

The 1960s saw the increasing application of "hard science" techniques to archaeological problems. This, coupled with an increasing emphasis on the mechanisms of social processes and cultural change (e.g. Binford 1962; Willey and Philips 1958), was the New Archaeology, a more technically and methodologically sophisticated and productive approach (Trigger 1989). By the 1970s, the New Archaeology seemed to have succeeded in changing everything: we were scientists, archaeology was anthropology or it was nothing, and historical archaeology was going along for the ride (e.g. Schulyer 1970). In 1977, Stanley South's *Method and Theory in Historical Archaeology* introduced quantitative functional analysis of artifact assemblages and study of quantitative patterns reflecting cultural "universals." One was to develop formal hypotheses to be tested with our formally organized and presented data sets. Unfortunately, these data were all to often left to "speak for themselves" when no law-like, "nomothetic" statements were forthcoming (e.g. Otto 1977). Even when forthcoming, these statements were banal and obvious statements of the human condition. Although this approach came to be criticized for a wide range of reasons (e.g. Meltzer 1979; Trigger 1978), its basis in a flawed understanding of science is of significance to this discussion.

Science and objectivity in archaeology

Popular notions of science privilege the "scientific" as being based in proven, true, objective knowledge. Science is believed superior to other forms of inquiry based on this assertion. Yet in practice, science is usually based on the collection of facts based on minor inductive predictions of limited applicability. A number of critiques of science have developed from various postmodern viewpoints, including feminism (e.g. Harding 1991; Martin 1993). While these analyses present some interesting arguments – attacking, for example, notions of objectivity and rationalism – the most powerful critiques are found among philosophers of science.

Bhasker (1978) argues that science cannot be limited simply to showing relationships between sets of events. In seeking to explain what the world is really like, scientists make generalizing statements that are tested experimentally. However, such experiments are closed systems in which some variables are isolated while others are frozen or removed. Although the purpose of this approach is ostensibly to allow underlying laws to show themselves, in this sense experiments are not "true," objective representations of reality are specially constructed for particular purposes. Although replicable, they tell us nothing, in themselves, about the reality of nature.

A further problem exists in science's understanding of lived reality, which Chalmers (1982:168) has attempted to address in what he terms "unrepresentative realism." This construction allows a theory to be assessed from the point of view of the extent to which it successfully comes to grips with some aspect of the world, whereby rejection of correspondent truths is possible. Hence, Newton's laws of motion can be used in a wide variety of circumstances, but they can be equally rejected in favor of relativity theory to the extent that it applies elsewhere. Light can have the properties of both a particle and a wave.

Archaeology is not an experimental science. It deals with complex phenomena. Sites are unique manifestations of past behavior, and replication of results is rarely possible. Although archaeology is based in a material reality that represents an objective record of past events, the discipline of archaeology is socially constructed. Investigators' biases color not only the questions asked of the record but also what data are observed, recorded, and interpreted. Perceptions are subtly colored by preconceptions of reality that may preclude an awareness of the full range of data and possible interpretations (Trigger 1989:382–384).

As archaeologists have become aware of the contingent and limited nature of science and the socially constructed nature of all knowledge, the positivist paradigm of processual archaeology has been increasingly eroded. In this process, deductive reasoning is being abandoned in favor of inductive reasoning.

Deductive and inductive reasoning in archaeology

The term "deductive reasoning" refers to the process of concluding that something must be true because it is a special case of a general principle that is known to be true. For example, if you know the general principle that the sum of the angles in any triangle is always 180 degrees, and you have a particular triangle in mind, you can then conclude that the sum of the angles in your triangle is 180 degrees. Deductive reasoning is always logically valid, and it is the main means by which science advances.

In the context of archaeology, deductive reasoning applies concepts known to be true to interpret a site, region, and so forth. Thus, for example, stratigraphic superposition and the ways that humans interact with the natural environment are applied to deduce conclusions about the site, region, or other factors being considered. This has been the main approach of American processual archaeology. In my view, this fact represents the principal reason why truly nomothetic results did not emerge very often or were trivial if forthcoming at all. The production of generalizing statements from the specific case ran counter to the structure of the thought processes used to analyze the specific case in the first place.

Further, the quality and validity ("soundness" in rhetorical terms) of a conclusion are wholly dependent on the soundness of the premises from which it was deduced. Hence problems with the structure or content of a premise can produce any of a number of deductive fallacies, resulting in an unsound conclusion.

"Inductive reasoning" (not to be confused with "mathematical induction") is the process of reasoning that a general principle is true because the special cases you have seen are true. For example, if all the archaeologists you have ever met have been very strange, you might then conclude that "all archaeologists are strange." That is inductive reasoning: constructing a general principle from special cases. Conceptually, this process "goes" in the opposite direction from deductive reasoning.

While inductive reasoning is empirical and is based on experience and observation, it is not necessarily logically valid. The fact that all the archaeologists *you* happen to have met were strange is no guarantee that *all* archaeologists are strange. Yet, reasoning from the data available to you, you may legitimately develop the *theory* that all archaeologists are strange. Thus, inductive reasoning leads to conclusions in which an observer may have a high level of confidence but not absolute certainty.

Historical archaeologists seem to have been comfortable with inductive thinking. In fact, many had never really embraced the New Archaeology's deductive approach beyond the most superficial level. Working within a post-processualist framework, many of my colleagues found they were addressing broad sociocultural phenomena (e.g. slavery, industrialism, capitalism, etc.) through the detailed study of specific events and individuals. This is essentially what many social historians have been doing for years under the rubric "microhistory" (e.g. Wood 1994).

Some implications

The trend toward an interpretive narrative archaeology raises a number of fundamental issues about what archaeology is and how it is to be done. I briefly consider three of these here: (1) the potential for archaeology that is relevant and meaningful to the public; (2) implications for our understanding of archaeological significance; and (3) the implications for narrative "truth."

Public relevance

As noted above, the majority of archaeologists in the United States work in the field of cultural resources management, not in academic posts. This work is done in the public interest and often with public dollars. For too long archaeologists have written for their professional colleagues and only rarely for anyone else. Clearly, some archaeologists writing more accessible interpretive narratives have been motivated by the need to carry public favor and raise support for archaeology in times of regulatory reform and increasingly tight budgets inadequate to society's many conflicting priorities. Others regard public interpretation as a professional responsibility no less important than any other, and some find such efforts personally rewarding (see, e.g. chapter 2 in this volume).

The public thirsts for reliable, credible information about the past and often satisfies that thirst through heritage tourism. Heritage tourism is on its way to being a leading sector of the economy, not only in the United States but internationally as well. Archaeology is particularly well suited to telling compelling stories, supported by material evidence that allows a tangible connection to the human past that no other discipline can match. While there is a danger that we engage in the creation of some kind of *Archaeology for Dummies*, this need not be the case. The public is smarter and more willing to listen to complex stories than academics generally imagine, as the success of Ken Burn's multipart television documentary *The Civil War* attests. However, the stories must be compelling and they must be well told.

Site significance

My colleague Terry H. Klein (1999) has argued that the most important issue facing American archaeology is that of site significance. This characteristic influences where we perform an archaeological survey, what methods we use for the survey, how we investigate the sites we identify, and how we treat the sites (once we find them) in terms of excavation, analysis, and management.

Archaeological significance is generally defined under provisions of federal law and regulation as the quality of having yielded, or being likely to yield, "information important in prehistory or history" (Title 36, US Code of Federal Regulations, Section 60). Klein (1999) noted that this conception of significance and National Park Service guidance regarding how this criterion is to be applied are inherently and explicitly positivist, requiring that sites have the ability to "test hypotheses about events, groups, or processes in the past that bear on important research questions in the social or natural sciences or the humanities; or corroborate or amplify currently available information suggesting that a hypothesis is either true or false" (National Park Service 1991:21).

Klein (1999) has also noted that the trend toward archaeological narrative infuses the archaeological enterprise with new criteria. These new criteria focus on the people who lived on a site and the site's potential to support the development of narratives to tell the stories of those people. This trend has the potential to affect how the bulk of American archaeologists – the majority of whom still practice some form of processual archaeology – look at the archaeological record and order their survey, evaluation, and excavation priorities.

Narrative "truth"

As with archaeology in general, there is a danger that the stories told may be more a reflection of the archaeologist than of the historic period, site, or artifacts. While Trigger (1989) has argued that there are limits to what a practitioner can honestly believe is true based on the archaeological record, our various weaknesses as human actors in a particular sociocultural context can radically affect our ability to observe, record, and interpret the objective reality of the past that the record offers. There is also the possibility that archaeological narratives will be used for purposes other than those intended by the archaeologist. Silberman (1989), for example, has vividly shown how archaeology has been manipulated to serve nationalists' ends in the Middle East, and Kohl and Fawcett (1995) have broadly analyzed the political uses of archaeology.

Interpretive narrative archaeology provides a way to try to explain the things that we, as archaeologists, *feel* are true about a site, the people who lived there, and the times in which they lived. The use of the techniques of fiction – plot, setting, character, and so forth – to tell a story in either the first or third person suggests the potential to "overcome" limits inherent in data. However, use of fictional techniques also suggests the possibility that any and all fictionalized accounts of the past, or the present for that matter, may be equally valued and held valid.

As James Gibb (2003) suggests in the following chapter, we need to be aware of the distinctions between historical fiction and interpretive historical fiction. Carnes has also addressed the dynamic difference between historical fiction and historical narrative, noting that the fictive account allows translation of events of the past in a way that may speak more powerfully to our needs and concerns in the present than facts alone may be able to. He writes: "Novel history, like alchemy, is an inaccessible science and elusive art, but to readers who seek understanding of themselves and the world, its riches are real" (2001:25).

If we have, for example, the goal of empowering historically, socially, or economically disadvantaged communities, then we may deem it acceptable to sacrifice aspects of the "truth" suggested by the data, or overcome inadequacies in the data, in order to address a conceivably "higher" goal through historical fiction. Any such effort must be undertaken only with the utmost care and with explicit statements of the liberties taken.

However, as archaeologists we stand on the firmest ground when we remain true to our data and the facts as we understand them in the creation of our narratives. It is our unique and privileged position to discover the material past and make it meaningful in the present, and we do a disservice to the archaeological record when, or if, we lose touch with that fact. Our professional ethics should require that our narratives remain firmly grounded in historical and archaeological data.

Finally, this approach cannot become a refuge for those practitioners unable or unwilling to organize and present their data coherently. The data upon which our narratives are based must be available for independent review and reinterpretation by others, even if only relegated to fine-print appendices at the back of the report.

Notwithstanding any of the above, the future of the interpretive narrative in archaeology appears bright. I look forward to reading many more interpretive narratives and to trying, myself, to make the past come more alive through this technique.

Acknowledgements

This chapter is based on an essay originally presented in the session "Narrative Archaeology" at the 1999 meeting of the Theoretical Archaeology Group, Cardiff University. I would like to thank John Jameson for the invitation to submit a chapter to this volume. I was greatly assisted by comments by and discussions with the following in the refinement of my thoughts on this subject: Anna Agbe-Davis of the Colonial Williamsburg Foundation; John Beech of Coventry University School of Business; Elaine Elinson, novelist, of San Franciso, California; James Gibb of Annapolis, Maryland, independent archaeological consultant; Robert Hedin, director of the Anderson Center for Interdisciplinary Studies in Red Wing, Minnesota; Leslie "Skip" Stewart-Abernathy of the Arkansas Archaeological Survey at Arkansas Technical University; Rebecca Yamin of John Milner Associates, Inc., Philadelphia; and the mother of my children, Jeanne Ward of Applied Archaeology and History Associates, Inc. I am especially indebted to Terry Kline of URS Corporation for his analysis of the implications of narrative archaeology for assessing site significance. Any errors of fact or interpretation, of course, are solely my responsibility.

References

Beaudry, M.C., L.J. Cook, and S.A. Mrozowski. 1991. Artifacts and Active Voices: Material Culture as Social Discourse. In *The Archaeology of Inequality*, R.H. McGuire and R. Paynter (eds), pp. 150–191. Oxford: Basil Blackwell Ltd.

Bhaskar, R. 1978. *A Realist Theory of Science*. Brighton: Harvester.

Binford, L.R. 1962. Archaeology as Anthropology. *American Antiquity* 28:217–25.

Carnes, M.C. 2001. Introduction. In *Novel History: Historians and Novelists Confront America's Past (and Each Other)*, M.C. Carnes (ed.), pp. 1–25. New York: Simon & Schuster.

Cotter, J. 1958. Archaeological Excavations at Jamestown Colonial National Historical Park and Jamestown National Historic Site, Virginia. *Archaeological Research Series No. 4*. Washington: US Department of the Interior, National Park Service.

Deetz, J. 1977. *In Small Things Forgotten: The Archaeology of Early American Life*. Garden City: Anchor Press.

Deetz, J. 1993. *Flowerdew Hundred: The Archaeology of a Virginia Plantation, 1619–1864*. Charlottesville: University Press of Virginia.

Gibb, J.G. 2003. The Archaeologist as Playwright. In *Ancient Muses: Archaeology and the Arts*, J.H. Jameson, Jr, J.E. Ehrenhard, and C.A Finn (eds). Tuscaloosa: University of Alabama Press, pp. 25–39.

Elston, R.G. 1997. Issues Concerning Consulting Archaeologists in the United States. *Society for American Archaeology Bulletin* 15(5):20–24.

Furguson, L. 1992. *Uncommon Ground: Archaeology and Early African America, 1650–1800*. Washington: Smithsonian Institution Press.

Harding, S. 1991. *Whose Science? Whose Knowledge?* Ithaca: Cornell University Press.

Harrington, J.C.1955. Archaeology as an Auxiliary Science to American History. *American Anthropologist* 57(6): 1121–1130.

Harrington, J.C. 1957. *New Light on Washington's Fort Necessity*. Richmond: Eastern National Parks and Monuments Association.

Hodder, I. 1989. Writing Archaeology Site Reports in Context. *Antiquity* 63:268–274.

Hodder, I. 1991. Interpretive Archaeology. *American Antiquity* 56(1):7–18.

Hume, I.N. 1994. *Here Lies Virginia: An Archaeologists View of Colonial Life & History* (Revised Edition). Charlottesville: University Press of Virginia.

Klein, T.H. 1999. The Problem and Promise of Cultural Resource Management in the United States. Paper presented at the World Archaeological Congress 4, Cape Town, South Africa.

Kohl, P.L. and C. Fawcett. 1995. Archaeology in the Service of the State: Theoretical Considerations. In *Nationalism, Politics, and the Practice of Archaeology*, P.L. Kohl and C. Fawcett (eds), pp. 3–18. Cambridge: Cambridge University Press.

Leone, M.P., P.B. Potter, Jr, and P.A. Shackel 1987. Toward a Critical Archaeology. *Current Anthropology* 28(3):283–302.

Martin, B. 1993. The Critique of Science Becomes Academic. *Science, Technology, and Human Values* 18(2):247–259.

Meltzer, D.J. 1979. Paradigms and the Nature of Change in American Archaeology. *American Antiquity* 44(3): 644–657.

National Park Service 1991. *National Register Bulletin 15: How to Apply the National Register Criteria for Evaluation*. Washington: US Department of the Interior, National Park Service.

Otto, J.S. 1977. Artifacts and Status Differences – A Comparison of Ceramics from Planter, Overseer, and Slave Sites on an Antebellum Plantation. In *Research Strategies in Historical Archaeology*, S. South (ed.), pp. 91–118. New York: Academic Press.

Schuyler, R.L. 1970. Historical and Historic Sites Archaeology as Anthropology: Basic Definitions and Relationships. *Historical Archaeology* 4:83–89.

Shrire, C. 1995. *Digging through Darkness: Chronicles of an Archaeologist*. Charlottesville: University Press of Virginia.

Silberman, N.A. 1989. *Between Past and Present: Archaeology, Ideology, and Nationalism in the Modern Middle East*. New York: Anchor Press.

South, S. 1977. *Method and Theory in Historical Archaeology*. New York: Academic Press.

Spector, J. 1993. *What this Awl Means: Feminist Archaeology at Dakota Village*. St. Paul: Minnesota Historical Society Press.

Trigger, B. 1978. *Time and Traditions: Essays in Archaeological Interpretation*. New York: Columbia University Press.

Trigger, B. 1989. *A History of Archaeological Thought*. Cambridge: Cambridge University Press.

Willey, G.R. and P. Phillips 1958. *Method and Theory in American Archaeology*. Chicago: University of Chicago Press.

Wood, G.S. 1994. The Wandering Jewish Prophet of New York. A Review of *The Kingdom of Matthias: A Story of Sex and Salvation in 19th-Century America* by Paul E Johnson and Sean Wilentz. *The New York Review of Books*, pp 56–58.

Yamin, R. 1998. Lurid Tales and Homely Stories of New York's Notorious Five Points. *Historical Archaeology* 32(1):74–85.

Yamin, R. 2002. New York City's five points. In *The Archaeology of Urban Landscapes,* A. Mayne and T. Murray (eds). Cambridge: Cambridge University Press.

Yentsch, A.E. 1994. *A Chesapeake Family and Their Slaves: A Study in Historical Archaeology.* Cambridge: Cambridge University Press.

Chapter 40

The Archaeologist as Playwright

James G. Gibb

Introduction

Stage plays can teach through aesthetic experience, creating settings in which facts, figures, and historical relationships are depicted in an integrated, meaningful manner. Plays also can serve as tools for exploring the past, the archaeologist-playwright experimenting with interactions among individual roles and larger historical events, first on paper and then in production. The use of interpretive historical fiction in general, and play writing specifically, acknowledges the limitations of mainstream theoretical approaches, but it does not reject them; on the contrary, the imaginative use of drama elicits insights into the actions and motivations of past peoples that may be testable through more conventional approaches. In this chapter, I illustrate this approach with a discussion of two plays I wrote and produced at the London Town historic site in Edgewater, Maryland.

Archaeologists as playwrights

A report of some five hundred pages bound in plastic spiral binding, on top of a spreading pile of books and note-filled binders, occupies the right corner of a desk. A tablet with several pages covered in scribbled notes and quotations, many with accompanying marginalia, lies on the left corner and forms a small ramp to an overflowing stack of inbox/outbox trays. In the middle is a computer, its screen full of carefully worded comments and enumerated points. This is my desk, and my thoughts are equally jumbled. Years of university training ingrained in me the idea that archaeological research, inadequately reported, isn't archaeology. And yet, here on my desk lies perhaps the most scrupulously documented and fussily organized technical report I had ever read, much less peer reviewed, and reading it has made me none the more knowledgeable about anything I regard as worth knowing. The few insights garnered from the notes and books sliding eastward across the desk add little of consequence to the investigator's observations and results.

Critical deposits at the site were recently disturbed (I can take a perverse sense of comfort in that), and an underdeveloped research design foreshadowed disappointment.

But even exemplary reports on well-preserved sites – replete with testable questions, detailed descriptions of appropriate methods and findings, and rigorous analyses – often hit a blank wall and fall in heaps next to earlier reports of greater and lesser quality. There is little or no real advancement in knowledge and understanding and, worse yet, no view of what may lie beyond the wall. What wall? The wall we have created, occasionally modify, and generally maintain through the questions and methods that compose contemporary archaeology and science in general. The formulation of non-overlapping categories of phenomena and the rigorous collection and analyses of data, although essential to the development of a reputable field of inquiry, create their own artifacts – walls, if you will – that impede further development. Art can help us scale the wall without permanently abandoning the firmament.

Scientists of all sorts resort to imagination, and science without creativity probably isn't science. But science has limits more constraining than those of art. Taking a somewhat conservative view, I see what Ehrenhard and Bullard (2003) characterize as an intersection of science, humanities research, and art, where art transcends experience. I argue, however, that art also creates experience that can be subject to analysis. Art produces not data but perceptions of reality for which scholars can generate expectations of the archaeological and documentary records. Archaeologists can draw together disparate data from artifacts (including, among other things, buildings, music, poetry, and paintings), archaeological deposits, and conventional historical documents and, through drama, posit relationships and processes that they can then test through more conventional archaeological methods. Play writing may not allow archaeologists to leap over the wall, but it might provide a glimpse over the top to see what lies beyond.

Play writing

Play writing and science can be inspired, but in the end, both grow out of what we know, or want to know, and what we want to share. And the idea I want to explore and share is that stage plays not only can convey what we have learned through science but can be part of the scientific process itself, a means of constructing and refining hypotheses about people, places, and events and how each shaped the other. The argument does not dismiss the power of archaeology and history to provide inspiration for artistic expression and to explore our common humanity: several of the chapters in this volume demonstrate that very well (e.g. chapters 3, 7, 16, and 17). Nor does this argument overlook interpretive art's very considerable potential for education and public interpretation (see chapters 4 and 5); rather, it recognizes that archaeologists and historians are as much a part of the public as individuals in any other occupation. We too can learn from the plays we write and, we hope, see produced, and then we can bring what we have learned back to our research.

Few archaeologists have ever considered writing a play, fewer have actually written one, and fewer still have had a play produced. One might argue that, given the apparent lack of training and interest in the art, we might best devote our time and energy to artifact studies and becoming more comfortable with non-parametric testing. But here's the rub: there are lots of writers and producers and directors and actors – professional and avocational – involved in historical plays. Some manage not just to get the facts right but also to accurately portray the behaviors and motivations and attitudes of a past people. Most don't, and many, in my judgment, don't try. The usual results: bad history well told and lost opportunities to explore the past. I am convinced that many archaeologists and historians have the ability to write good plays, and I know that many historic sites have the interest and resources to support the production of such works.

I don't expect to turn most of my readers into playwrights: our first responsibility is timely production of detailed technical reports, the data and analyses of which provide the raw material for what I have termed "interpretive historical fiction" (Gibb 2000a, 2000b). For those who choose to write plays, I offer a few suggestions. For those who choose not to, I hope to convince you that some of the suggestions may prove useful in analyzing plays for insights into the past. I briefly discuss play writing and offer suggestions by way of an example: an original play in two acts written and produced to interpret reactions in the provincial port town of London, Maryland, to events in Lexington and Concord in April 1775.

Plays as experiments

Many writers have mined the past for plots, scenes, and characters that best suited their interests in a particular problem or aspect of humanity. Canadian playwright Robertson Davies (1913–1995), for example, set his *At My Heart's Core* (1950) in the forests of Upper Canada (now Ontario Province) during Mackenzie's 1837 rebellion. Armed conflict in the province drew many of the "gentlemen" homesteaders to York, now Toronto, to defend the provincial government, and many families sent their children to distant towns where they might be better defended. This dispersal aggravated the social and intellectual isolation of three women who remained on their homesteads, surrounded, in the case of Frances Stewart, by good-quality furniture in a log house, itself surrounded by a recent clearing in the midst of the forest primeval. Each succumbed, at least in part, to discontent, tempted by a visitor with remembrances of what they left behind in Dublin and London.

There is nothing in *At My Heart's Core* to indicate that Davies was trying to elicit a greater understanding of pioneer Canadian women; indeed, a review of his oeuvre suggests a tendency to use Canada's rural past allegorically. Davies was more interested in the struggle of the individual spirit in the face of intellectual starvation. But he was a teacher and a man of letters, not a scientist. Like many other writers, he mined the past for literary material to put in the service of the present. Reversing this relationship, scientists can use literature to understand the past.

Think of a play as a well-planned experiment: the writer selects a setting, one or more characters, and possibly a specific time and place, then allows the people, places, and events to interact – each to a greater or lesser extent shaping the others, often with one asserting considerable influence over the others (see chapter 1 on the limitations of conventional hypothesis testing). Although not quantitative, this sounds a bit like hypothesis testing, identifying dependent and independent variables, holding some variables constant to see how the others react. And that is as good a way as any to think about it.

The use of "interpretive art" (see chapter 5) in science requires imagination but is not purely imaginative. Archaeology and archival research establish the time, place, and historical context of the action to be portrayed (see chapter 3). Archival research provides the characters, some well documented, others distillations or stereotypes drawn from period literature. Documents provide specific historical events as well as the perspectives of some characters at the time of each event. (Whether as technical writers or fiction writers, we owe it to our subjects to ask them what they thought they were doing and why, and it is the writer's responsibility to consult and critique at least a representative sample of pertinent surviving documents.) Architectural and archaeological analyses establish the setting and identify the props. Each of these fields – archaeology, architectural history, general history and its constituent subfields, and even literary theory and criticism – provides the questions or issues around which a play revolves. They also provide the methods and techniques of scholarly analysis.

I have written two short historical plays, not as experiments, but because the marketing director of the London Town Foundation asked me to (Gibb 1998, 1999). She saw the plays as fund-raisers and as educational programs. Each work incorporated archaeological and archival data from a multiyear research program in London, Maryland, an active port town in the eighteenth century. I filled gaps in the research, particularly concerning attitudes and motivations, with material from the works of novelists Daniel Defoe and Samuel Richardson in much the way that Robertson Davies borrowed from nineteenth-century Canadian writers, including at least one of the principal female characters in *At My Heart's Core*, novelist Susanna Moodie. In some instances I lifted blocks of dialogue wholesale from period documents and a poem, editing for clarity, brevity, and dramatic intensity.

I designed each act in each play to convey up to three ideas, including different perspectives of colonists and modern scholars. In one act, for example, an archaeologist stands in front of a partially excavated tavern cellar, interpreting the findings for the audience. Ghosts of the tavern owners (it was a Halloween play) engage both the archaeologist and the audience. The archaeologist demonstrates how careful archival research and excavation allowed the project team to identify the tavern's owners and clientele and to document the appearance of the building and how it changed. The ghosts confirm some of the observations, but they are incensed by the suggestion that they habitually threw kitchen trash into their cellar, a critical assumption in the archaeological interpretation of the site and its assemblage:

ARCHAEOLOGIST: The Rumneys dumped *broken* artifacts under the floorboards of their tavern, the abandoned cellar hole also providing a convenient place to dump oyster shells and bones from fish, poultry, deer, pigs, sheep, and cattle. Needless to say, the trash reeked, and the tavern probably smelt bad.

To which tavern keeper Elinor Rumney responds:

ELINOR: If ya don't like it here, try the tavern down the road, there y'll see filth. And there y'll sit with the servants. [Sassily] Ah, but what am I saying, ya needed shovels to find my tavern, can you find the road? [Elinor leaves the scene in a huff.]

Earlier in the act, the issue of cultural diversity arises, the pith of which appears in these few lines between the tavern owners and the archaeologist:

ELINOR: I don't begrudge him for spending so much time about his boats and ferries, but I think the man spends more time talking to travelers than movin' them.
EDWARD: Hold your tongue there, Mrs. Rumney. Who moves them barrels of ale for ya and who kept digging out this damnable cellar after every rain! And . . .
ELINOR: Settle, Mr. Rumney, settle, I didn't . . .
EDWARD: Ya calt me a skellum . . . a blethering, blustering, drunken blellum!

The archaeologist has no idea what this line, lifted from a Robert Burns poem, means. Elinor Rumney explains:

ELINOR: He says I've called him a worthless drunken fool! And, as you can see, he can't speak His Majesty's English.
EDWARD: Damn you English and your cursed tongue, and damn . . . .

Well, you get the idea. This, the first of three acts, provided the opportunity to discuss issues both archaeological and historical. It raised the perennial question of what all that trash was doing in a building that supposedly was still occupied, and it needled the archaeological crew, of which I was a part, about our inability to find the road – the main road through a town we had been studying intensively for several years.

The exchange between the Rumneys, with the archaeologist as an onlooker, reminded the researchers and audience alike that not all of London's residents spoke "His Majesty's English." Elinor's comment about "the tavern down the road" where "y'll sit with the servants" grew directly out of the hypothesis that different taverns in London and nearby Annapolis catered to different clienteles, reinforcing the class structure and culture of deference that pervaded eighteenth-century Maryland and colonial society throughout North America (Thompson 1999). Those differences should be manifested in the types of vessels and food remains recovered from the tavern deposits. Elinor also clearly emerges as the principal manager of the tavern, cooperating but not wholly working with her boatwright-ferryman husband. (Regrettably, the text of the play did not make clear that Edward owned the tavern and that Elinor, under English law, could not own property: as a married woman, she was property.)

Let's now turn to method, drawing examples from my second effort.

Method

Writing a play is easier if begun with an abstract, or argument, that identifies the theme and, perhaps, a central reflector – a pivotal idea, person, object, place, or event of which all of the characters have an opinion. Here is the argument guiding the writing and production of *Revolutionary Spirits*, appearing verbatim in the playbill:

> The mood in town is tense, the residents still trying to decide where one another stand on the great issue of the day: relent and accept the will of Parliament, or hold fast to the principle of no taxation without representation. William Brown and many of his neighbors would rather boycott British imports than pay what they believe an unfair tax, but even they are hesitant to disobey their King. The mood rapidly changes, however, when news of the skirmishes at Lexington and Concord reaches town. The residents polarize, and talk turns from boycott to armed resistance. Civil war is in the offing and the characters know – although they are loath to express it – that their lives are heading for a dramatic turn; a turn forced by events seemingly beyond their control.
>
> The play begins in the main hall of the William Brown House. Anne Arundel County's Committee of Observation has just finished discussing the boycott, unaware of events that occurred in Massachusetts just days before. Join the Brown household and its neighbors as events unfold and they try to come to grips with passions that will tear apart their community.

Each act had its own abstract, although these did not appear in the playbill. They were prepared for my own benefit.

> Act I: The main room of the Browns' tavern. Susanna hurries her slave, Sall, in cleaning up after the meeting of the Committee of Observation. Some of the participants can be heard returning, having just seen off their departing colleagues. [Lacking an appropriate actor to fill Sall's role, we used the fictional indentured servant "Pamela" introduced in my first play. In either case, this character plays a more prominent role in the second act, appearing again at the end of the first to lead the audience to the kitchen, the second act.]

William Brown and Stephen West, soon accompanied by Tory Anthony Stewart, debate the issue of non-importation, discussing the loss of trade, loyalty to their king, and the new philosophy phrased in the language of ancient English rights. Stephen supports the Association, hinting at violent action, while Anthony despairs at the prospect of civil war, alluding to Proverbs 11:29 – trouble our own house, and leave nothing but waste and emptiness. William has been drawn into this whirlwind of passion, siding with the patriots, but convinced that the issue will be settled amicably, if only cool heads prevail. The act ends as William Brown, Jr., enters, a letter in hand, agitated and bold: he brings word, just received in Annapolis – British regulars and Massachusetts militiamen clashed at Lexington seven days earlier, men killed and wounded on both sides. A state of war exists, and events have overrun philosophy.

Act II: The kitchen in the basement of the Browns' tavern. Three principals – Margaret, daughter of William and Susanna Brown, Pamela, their indentured servant, and Charles Lansdale, freeman and staymaker in the employ of Elizabeth Ferguson – react to the growing schism between the King and the colonists, each against the background of their own social position tempered by their close personal relationships. Women, servants, freemen, and slaves left little record of themselves, their attitudes, or motivations. This act is less well founded on documentary records than the previous act; nonetheless, these lives must be explored.

The archival record is largely mute on how Londoners reacted to the news from Massachusetts, but enough material survives, and archaeological and architectural studies were sufficiently detailed, to mount a convincing portrayal of events, settings, and sentiments. But the piece demanded characters, both richly drawn and archetypal.

Characters and characterization

Developing characters for the play was relatively easy. The research team combed land and judgment records and compiled a list of everyone known to have been associated with the town. I selected several contemporaries about whom we had the most information and developed biographical sketches for each. The theme of London on the brink of revolution made the final choice of characters even easier, although the availability of actors necessitated some changes.

William Brown, Sr.: Born in Anne Arundel County in 1727 and descended of Scots, William Brown died in Annapolis in 1792. He is a carpenter and joiner by trade, but he runs a ferry and a tavern as well. He has taken on the construction of Dr. Upton Scott's brick mansion in Annapolis and has opted to build one for himself. He is ambitious, seeking not only material wealth but also a position of honor and prestige in the community. He may have served on the Committee of Observation in the early 1770s, possibly as recording secretary, looking carefully into the activities of his neighbors and doing his best to support the American non-importation of British goods. He lost his wealth in the economic depression after the Revolution, and his house was sold at a sheriff's sale in 1793. At the time of the play's action, William Sr. is 47.

Susanna Brown: About Susanna, or Anna, apart from her marriage to William and her children, we know virtually nothing.

Elizabeth Ferguson: Widow of the recently deceased Alexander Ferguson (died 1770), Elizabeth (age 45) had relinquished executorship over her husband's will, claiming that she was "unacquainted with Business and therefore incapable of executing the Trust." Anthony

Stewart assumed full control of Alexander's estate, with realty in both London and Annapolis, and a tailoring and staymaking shop in London. (William Brown, Sr., and Jr., witnessed his Last Will and Testament.) Nonetheless, at least from 1770 through 1773, Elizabeth ran the tavern and the tailor/staymaker shop, employing staymaker Charles Lansdale, indentured servants Joseph Gibson, John Elain, and Ruth Murphy, and Beck (a 22-year-old woman), her child Pomfrey (age 3) and a man, Abram (age 20). Alexander's probate inventory lists numerous articles of furniture indicative of an operating tavern, or ordinary. Elizabeth's household, apart from the servants and slaves, probably includes her three youngest children, Ann (16), Isabelle (14), and Elizabeth (10), and possibly her three sons, Alexander (23), David (22), and Andrew (19), all of whom would enlist in the Colonial military the following year. The Fergusons probably lived on Lot 91 since 1741, across Scott Street from the Browns and next door but one.

Anthony Stewart: Merchant and shipowner and a principal in the firm of James Dick & Stewart, Merchants, Anthony Stewart was an outspoken Tory, a supporter of King and Parliament.

Stephen West, Jr.: Although he was raised in London Town, born in 1727 the son of Stephen West (died 1752) and Martha Hall (also died 1752), Stephen Jr. moved to the Woodyard near Upper Marlboro, Prince George's County, in 1754. There he died in 1790. He was a merchant, planter, shipowner, provisioner for the Continental Army and the Maryland militia, politician, slave owner, and supporter of St. John's College in Annapolis. In 1775 and 1776 he supplied gunlocks, gunpowder, flour, blankets, and other material to the Maryland Council of Safety. Several of his letters to the council and to other prominent Marylanders survive, reporting his views on the procurement of military supplies and the prospect of manufacturing muskets in the colony.

Margaret Brown: Born in Anne Arundel County in 1759 of William and Susanna Brown, 15-year-old Margaret assists her mother in the operation of the tavern. She works alongside her friend, indentured servant Pamela – whom she affectionately calls Pammie – but their relationship is not on an equal footing.

Pamela: The fictional character Pamela was indentured to William Brown and was employed about the tavern, cleaning, serving, and generally doing the bidding of her master and mistress and of her friend, Margaret. She is slightly older than Margaret, roughly 17, and has reached a quiet, indeed unspoken, understanding with freeman Charles Lansdale.

Charles Lansdale: A freeman Elizabeth Ferguson employed as a staymaker in her late husband's tailor shop, Lansdale probably is in his twenties or thirties. We know nothing else about him; hence his character is largely fictional.

All of the characters in the second act are stereotypes, drawn largely from English-language literature of the period, in contrast to the other, more richly drawn characters for which we have some information. The actors developed each character, some in ways I had not anticipated.

Setting

Because we lacked a theater and funds for sets, venue selection became simple: we used the three-story brick mansion at the core of the historic park. The two principal areas visitors see in the house are the upstairs tavern room and the kitchen below; a pair of sets that begged a two-act play focusing on the upstairs–downstairs dichotomy and the very real social distance that existed between the characters who frequented those two places. The relatively well documented individuals played out their scene upstairs, struggling to comprehend events. The characters downstairs dealt with the very personal impact that impending civil war would have on their lives.

The tavern room was an ideal set for a very public event. It was a place in which Anthony Stewart (the preeminent Tory), Stephen West (the radical patriot), William Brown (the fence-sitter), and Susanna Brown and Elizabeth Ferguson could naturally come together and interact politically and socially. It was also the logical place to which the Brown's son brought the fateful letter from Philadelphia that reported events in Massachusetts. The audience seated around the perimeter of the room played the part of tavern guests, at times brought into the action.

The basement kitchen was darker, more private, the haunt of servants and certain members of the household. Here the Browns' daughter Margaret, freeman Charles Landsdale, and fictional indentured servant Pamela come together, exploring the meaning of freedom and confronting war's dire personal consequences. All of the characters and their relationship develop in the face of events that lie outside their direct control.

Analysis

Although the plays were not written as scientific experiments, they could be turned to that purpose. After all, as both archaeologist and playwright I was fully aware of the limitations of the available data and the kinds of questions that required answers if the London Town Foundation's staff was to fully understand and interpret London, its growth and demise. Some of these questions I addressed, if not conclusively, through dialogue; others I missed or opted not to address. Let's look at one of those questions that I only partially addressed: non-importation and the politics of things.

Revolutionary Spirits opens with Susanna Brown and a servant cleaning the main tavern room after the Committee of Observation has left, William Brown accompanying them out. Susanna, audible to the audience and half addressing them, mumbles about her husband's involvement in the committee, neglecting his family and business. She chides him when he returns with radical patriot Stephen West and argues with West over the propriety of the committee's activities: spying on neighbors, arresting those suspected of trading with the British, confiscating their goods, and denying them due process. *Things* figure more prominently in the American Revolution than perhaps in any other American conflict. The issue was representation, but embargo and home manufacturing became principal expressions of collaboration and resistance, Toryism and Republicanism, loyalty and independence (Evans 1989). Here are a few of the opening lines:

SUSANNA: Haste, wench! Clear that table and be off to the kitchen. I will see to the others myself. Mind your master's children. [Half under her breath, half to a member of the audience.] Such heated talk . . . fueled rather than cooled with drink.
[William Brown enters leading Stephen West.]
SUSANNA: Your friends are gone, then, husband?
WILLIAM: Yes, Anna. Our son accompanies them on the ferry, but not so far as Annapolis.
SUSANNA: He would do well to mind his work, sir, as would you. Don't encourage his meddling in affairs that do not concern him.
STEPHEN: Surely, Mrs. Brown, the late troubles concern your son, and all of us. A young man starting out in the world must look to his rights. He must . . .
SUSANNA: He must look to his young wife and my grandchildren. He must see his way clear of his Majesty's jail and of his Excellency the Governor's gallows! And you sir, . . .
WILLIAM: Enough, Mrs. Brown. We speak of the affairs of men. Such is not the province of women. Tend to your own affairs, and let Mr. West and I . . .

SUSANNA: [Sarcastically] and let Mr. West and I talk rubbish and neglect business.
STEPHEN: There is no business, Mrs. Brown, nor will there be until King George redresses our grievances, withdraws his troops, and repeals taxes imposed without our consultation or consent.
SUSANNA: Secret meetings and spying on neighbors will not alter the king's opinion, nor will they bring business again to our town.

Susanna and Stephen continue their argument, briefly rehearsing some of the principal issues of the boycott. William finally intercedes, cutting short their argument. He expects Elizabeth Ferguson momentarily and will try to buy her late husband's dry goods on behalf of the Committee of Safety:

WILLIAM: Peace, Mrs. Brown. Stephen, enough prattle. Mrs. Ferguson attends us soon and we've more to discuss. A militia unclothed and unarmed will little persuade the king of our convictions.
SUSANNA: If you've time later, husband, discuss the clothing and feeding of your children. [She leaves.]

While William and Stephen continue their conversation, Elizabeth arrives. Susanna offers tea to her friend and, when she sees Stephen West's shocked expression upon thinking that British tea would be served in this household, qualifies her offer: it is an ersatz tea made of herbs and grains. This scene offered an opportunity for experimentation, an opportunity I failed to recognize at the time: what did they drink tea from? Carl Steen (1990, 1999) has offered a compelling argument for the widespread use of American-made slip-decorated red earthenwares as an overt expression of American identity and, by extension, sympathies. These were vessels readily recognizable as products of American potters, particularly those of Pennsylvania. Would it have been too melodramatic if Stephen West were to snatch the Queensware cup from Elizabeth and dash it into the fireplace in the midst of an invective against English manufacturers and merchants? How might London's residents have felt about vessels of colonial manufacture? Would slip-decorated tewares have offended their sense of what was appropriate for tea, real or ersatz? Tory Anthony Stewart might have refused tea served in such a vessel: he certainly would refuse the grain beverage that passed for tea in patriot households. Patriot Stephen West might have relished ersatz tea served, for political if not necessarily gustatory reasons.

Revolutionary Spirits also touches on an important historical issue for which archaeological evidence exists and has the potential to inform upon: the political power of women in colonial society and their role in a republic. Evans (1989), for example, cites private letters and newspaper articles of the 1760s demonstrating that women increasingly spoke out on political issues and became particularly prominent in maintaining the boycotts, the latter politicizing their daily activities of shopping and home manufacturing. Groups of women pledged to abstain from tea and organized spinning bees: "Women who refused to buy British goods, who made herbal teas, spun and wove their own cloth, and insisted on 'buying American' were engaging in defiant political acts in the course of their domestic responsibilities. That some enacted their intentions in more public and formal ways through meetings and petitions demonstrates not only the reality of their political commitments but also a new level of self-perception as political actors" (Evans 1989:50). The war, explained Evans, "offered increased opportunities for women to act politically and aggressively from within their role as housewives" (1989:54). Women's consumer choices, their political choices, should be visible archaeologically, particularly in the presence or absence of British manufactured goods – ceramic dinner and tewares, for instance.

Steen has pointed out that clothing – fabrics and styles – was more important symbolically than ceramics in claiming one's allegiance in the late 1760s and 1770s: "By wearing home-spun cloth, people were effortlessly able to make a strong political statement. Ceramics, on the other hand, were relegated more to the privacy of the home and would require effort and explanation for their significance to be evident" (1999:70). For archaeologists, he continued, Philadelphia earthenwares "are a clear manifestation of a political movement that swept through the colonies" (1999:70). Steen's observations might be qualified on two points: not all ceramics were used in purely domestic settings, and all purchases during the period were public acts, regardless of how the items were actually used.

I know of no historian or archaeologist who has explored the issue of what American householders did with British ceramic tablewares in the 1770s and again after implementation of Jefferson's and Madison's embargo acts (1807–1809 and 1813–1814, respectively). Ceramics certainly were accorded political symbolism, as museum catalogs and collections demonstrate. The meaning of a chamber pot with the king's likeness on the bottom interior transcends cultural differences, and numerous examples can be cited of porcelain and faience punch bowls commemorating military victories and the new American republic (e.g. Howard 1984). Perhaps individual householders refrained from using British ceramics, but taverns and coffeehouses, hotbeds of political activity, publicly used all sorts of ceramic, glass, pewter, and treen vessels. Whether or not British wares were used in a public house, the proprietor made a statement about allegiance for all to see, as did those patrons who used or refused to use certain kinds of vessels.

On reflection, Stephen West should have grabbed Elizabeth Ferguson's teacup and saucer and hurled them into the fireplace. Recovering some vestige of gentlemanly demeanor, as defined by the day, West might have then, in gentler tones, asked Susanna Brown for another cup, but one made by American hands and more suited to a daughter of liberty. As a playwright, I can do that. I can even bring Pamela back into the scene to clear away the sherds and toss them into a slop bucket that, in the second act, might be emptied out the back door, narrowly missing the incoming lover and staymaker, Charles Lansdale. Through play writing we can identify the correlates of overt and covert use, and of public discard, and then test those correlates. But tested or not, play writing and other art forms allow us to imagine and express different attitudes and to suggest moral ambiguities and community conflicts in the past too easily dismissed in conventional archaeological analyses.

Conclusions

Play writing will never become the principal means for developing and testing hypotheses, but it can allow us to examine complex interactions where the data are too sparse or require imaginative organization. *Revolutionary Spirits* taught audiences about an important part of American history in a way that was entertaining and memorable and that suggested the emotional and social turmoil experienced by the colonists. It also allowed me to examine the relationship between people and objects in ways that cannot be duplicated through conventional analyses, and it suggested research approaches and complex relationships that I had not considered or only partially appreciated.

Play writing is not something I trained to do or that I ever had thought of doing. But archaeology has a way of introducing us to new things in unexpected ways. Completing the two plays required no Muse for inspiration: a concept, a venue, data, an understanding of historical and archaeological issues, and a deadline were all I needed. We might invoke the Muses, but it is unwise to wait for those fickle creatures: they are too easily swayed by pleasures of the moment and the demands of other gods. A workman-like hand that is turned to play writing in the same way we apply knowledge and discipline to report writing will serve well enough to help us peek over, if not scale, that wall we have inadvertently built. And, of course, one can never go amiss with a well-organized desk.

Acknowledgments

London Shades was first performed at London Town Historic Park in Edgewater, Maryland, during the last weekend in October 1998 and was reprised on Halloween weekend of the following year. *Revolutionary Spirits* was performed during the last two weekends in April 1999. I thank director Renee Tilton and producer Barbara Gimperling for their support, enthusiasm, and respect for the ideas I tried to convey through the scripts. Special thanks go to the London Town Colonial Players and technical crew: Jen Fisher, Kelly Fisher, Barbara Gimperling, Cory Gimperling, Tony Lindauer, Len Pimental, David "D.L." Smith, Greg Stiverson, Emily Strotman, Renee Tilton, Todd C. Withey, and Becki Yazel. I have benefited from subsequent discussions with independent playwright and occasional instructor Mike Field of Johns Hopkins University.

References

Davies, R. 1950. At My Heart's Core: A Play in Three Acts. Reprinted in 1991. In *Two Plays: At My Heart's Core & Overlaid*, Robertson Davies, pp. 13–92. Toronto: Simon & Pierre.

Deetz, J. 1993. *Flowerdew Hundred: The Archaeology of a Virginia Plantation, 1619–1864.* Charlottesville: University Press of Virginia.

Ehrenhard, J.E. and M. Bullard 2003. Archaeology Goes to the Opera. In *Ancient Muses: Archaeology and the Arts*, J.H. Jameson Jr, J.E. Ehrenhard, and C.A. Finn (eds). Tuscaloosa: University of Alabama Press, pp. 40–48.

Evans, S.M. 1989. *Born for Liberty: A History of Women in America.* New York: The Free Press.

Gibb, J.G. 1998. *London Shades: A Play in Three Acts.* Performed in October 1998, and October 1999, at the London Town Historic Site, Edgewater, Maryland.

Gibb, J.G. 1999. *Revolutionary Spirits: A Play in Two Acts.* Performed in April 1999, at the London Town Historic Site, Edgewater, Maryland.

Gibb, J.G. 2000a. Imaginary, But by No Means Unimaginable: Storytelling, Science, and Historical Archaeology. *Historical Archaeology* 34(2):1–6.

Gibb, J.G. 2000b. Reflection, Not Truth, the Hero of My Tale: Responding to Lewis, Little, Majewski, and McKee and Galle. *Historical Archaeology* 34(2):20–24.

Howard, D.S. 1984. *New York and the China Trade.* New York: New York Historical Society.

Steen, C. 1990. The Inter-Colonial Trade of Domestic Earthenwares and the Development of an American Social Identity. *Volumes in Historical Archaeology IX.* Columbia: The South Carolina Institute of Archaeology and Anthropology, University of South Carolina.

Steen, C. 1999. Pottery, Intercolonial Trade, and Revolution: Domestic Earthenwares and the Development of an American Social Identity. *Historical Archaeology* 33(3):62–72.

Thompson, P. 1999. Rum Punch and Revolution: Tavern-going and Public Life in Eighteenth-Century Philadelphia. Philadelphia: University of Pennsylvania Press.

Afterword

Chapter 41

Change and Creation
Historic landscape character 1950–2000

Andrea Bradley, Victor Buchli,
Graham Fairclough, Dan Hicks, Janet Miller and
John Schofield

Change and creation

In 2004 English Heritage in partnership with Atkins Heritage, University College London and the University of Bristol produced the booklet *Change and Creation: historic landscape character 1950–2000*, and launched an accompanying website (www.change-andcreation. org). The approach promulgated through Change and Creation promotes understanding of usually large scale, sometimes particular and often extraordinary cultural landscapes, for which the easiest route in is often through images, in particular photographs at the landscape scale. Alongside the following text, the reader should look out or revisit aerial photographs, long distance views or even close up images of modern cultural activities manifest in the landscape in order to engage fully the philosophy of Change and Creation.

The original booklet asked: 'What does the material legacy of the second half of the twentieth century – your century – mean to you?' This marked a new direction for English Heritage and, to a lesser extent for our partners. It still represents an innovative approach to dealing with and discussing heritage, and managing the processes of change that we (the authors) as archaeologists are most used to (see also Hayden and Wark 2004 for a comparable study in the United States). It seemed fitting to include the original text here as an afterword in the Heritage Reader. It should be noted finally that the next stage of this initiative, a book on England's post 1950 landscape, has now been produced (Penrose *et al.* 2007).

Cars and motorways, airports and tower blocks, Wimpey estates and 'prairie fields'. Nuclear weapons, power stations, windfarms and the moon landing. The Liverpool sound and Manchester, the 1966 World Cup, music festivals and the smell of fast food. TV and the web, easy travel and shrinking distance. Business parks and starter homes, the country-side as agri-business factory or city-dwellers' playground. Shopping as leisure and homo-genous high streets.

All of these defined the later twentieth-century world. Like it or not, the material remains of the last fifty years help us to recognise the major changes which we experienced in that time, brought about through innovation and rapidly developing technology. In the later twentieth century we experienced the world in new ways, which changed our perception of our surroundings, and provided the inspiration for new physical landscapes, as well as new imagined and intangible landscapes.

Understanding how the twentieth-century landscape is perceived and how it connects to the past, is an urgent task. One reason is that the structures and buildings of that fifty-year period are disappearing quickly, so that memories are already being revised and lost.

More importantly, it is difficult to understand the world we live in today, without appreciating the legacy of the recent past. This is not to say that we must protect all – or perhaps any – of the remains of the last fifty years. The study of landscape character shows the importance of change and creation to the landscape. Policies that allow the continuance of such levels of change will be more sustainable than policies that try to wipe the sheet clean every generation. Our decisions about what to lose, or what to replace it with will be better though, if they are informed by careful understanding.

In recent decades, conservation has become a driver of change in its own right, providing channels for public education, economic development and regeneration. By the end of the last century, through professional and popular interest, people had begun to engage very much more fully with the past, to care for it, and to make it part of the present. Time Team, the BBC's 'Restoration' and The Heritage Lottery Fund are evidence of this. Power of Place (Historic Environment Review, 2000) and A Force for our Future (DCMS, 2001), encapsulate this mood in public policy.

The physical structures of the later twentieth century survive in massive quantities across the contemporary English landscape, most still in their original use. Do these remains 'matter'? How are they perceived and remembered? For many people, they are unwelcome, representing the destruction of older landscapes. Yet the twentieth century has shaped who we are, and is already part of our 'heritage'. When should we start to value it? Do we leave the survival of the twentieth century to 'Nature', so that our descendants can preserve whatever rarities survive? Or do we become active agents in deciding what is passed on and why?

A database compiled for English Heritage has demonstrated the extensive scale of current historical and archaeological research on the twentieth century (Frearson, 2004). Now a new English Heritage programme – Change and Creation – aims to understand the later twentieth-century landscape: to assess the processes of change and creation in our urban and rural landscapes. It will be the first national landscape-scale appreciation of later twentieth-century heritage.

Although the programme's initial perspective is that of archaeology, the aim is to integrate a diversity of approaches. The programme will use the methods of a range of disciplines, and will engage with many perceptions of England's twentieth-century landscape, recognising the diverse, powerful and often contested nature of the very recent and contemporary past. Partnerships will be formed between professional, academic and community organisations. Various techniques for research and representation will be combined: film, photography, artistic interventions, oral histories, interviews, participant observation and public involvement, alongside archaeological fieldwork and more traditional studies of maps and aerial photographs.

The purpose of the Change and Creation document is to:

- Raise awareness and interest in the programme, by asking questions about the nature and value of the very recent heritage in the landscape.
- Provide information on the background, aims and possibilities of the programme.
- Promote the exchange of ideas and inspire the development of new projects that will contribute to the programme and drive it forward.

At the core of the Change and Creation programme lie two key principles:

- that the material remains of the twentieth century do matter; and
- that we can value, and sometimes perhaps celebrate, later twentieth-century changes to the landscape, as well as being concerned with losses.

It seems wrong to view the later twentieth century merely as a pollutant, something that has devalued or destroyed what went before. The process of landscape change – its time-depth, or 'stratigraphy' – is recognised and celebrated for earlier periods. The twentieth century should be no different.

The late twentieth-century landscape

Political, economic, social and cultural change in the second half of the twentieth century altered England's landscape in a fundamental and powerful way.

Take the expansion of the road system, and its associated infrastructure. Our car culture led to the development of the motorway network and its service areas, multi-storey car parks in all our towns, as well as controversial schemes such as the Newbury Bypass. Housing estates developed far from urban services, as did out-of-town shopping centres, and the massive sheds of regional distribution centres. A single invention – the internal combustion engine – has changed our lifestyles and our landscape.

The development of global communications also created new landscapes of television aerials, telephone masts, satellite dishes and networks of cables across cities and country-side. Perceptions of space and time changed, aided by the car and by fast travel, and an associated shrinking of distance. Airports multiplied and long-distance travel became com-monplace.

Population increase saw the infilling of space in our cities, and the development of new towns. Post-war state-led housing renewal generated new estates and high rise blocks for urban populations. The architecture was often optimistic and modernist. By the 1980s, new housing was largely provided by the private sector for the new 'middle class major-ity', for instance in cul-de-sac estates. Gated communities developed in response to the fear of crime. There was a return to historic architectural styles, perhaps reflecting disen-chantment with 'progress' and a conservatism which found 1960s architecture 'un-English'.

The city pushed into the country, with new housing, out-of-town shopping and leisure centres, university campuses, hospitals, and new schools. Urban waste became rural landfill. Town and country lifestyles were blurred, to provide for a commuting workforce, with cafes, restaurants and convenience supermarkets filling the high streets of our market towns. Country roads were modernised to take a higher volume of traffic. The countryside was suddenly urban, but we also began to reinvent 'the village' in our inner cities.

The countryside changed. It seemed that the rural and the pastoral gave way to com-modity and big business. Areas of beauty, or even any green area, became 'honey-pot' destinations, or the sites of festivals and car-boot sales. Political, technological and com-mercial change created agri-business, with consolidated farms, prairie fields and forest plantations. New settlement patterns appeared. Farm buildings and farm houses became redundant and were converted to commuter homes, with no link to their surroundings other than proximity.

Military landscapes grew, probably as never before, both in the real world and in per-ception. The strangely shaped structures and facilities associated with Britain's and the USA's Cold War nuclear capability generated social and ideological conflict in their own right (Cocroft and Thomas, 2003). Sites such as Greenham Common came and went. Our military relationship with NATO and the USA mirrored a TV-led cultural relationship. The increasing influence of American popular culture shaped our shopping malls and theme parks.

The stories in our landscape also tell of transformations in our economy. There are silent and evocative remains all around us, from which we can piece together the decline of many industries and their communities. They have been replaced by the modern service sector, housed in isolated business parks and call-centres. Collieries, steel and shipyards, textile mills, factories and nuclear power stations became obsolete, some of them now enjoying new lives as museums and visitor centres.

The social and demographic changes of the late twentieth century can be seen in the landscape. The ageing population, the changing nature of family, fragmented households, the tendency to individualism and a mobile workforce have given rise to starter homes, loft living and continuing migration from north to south.

In some places the later twentieth century saw an absence of landscape change. Sometimes economic stagnation curbed development and preserved much historic fabric, particularly in the inner cities. Elsewhere, land use policies and planning restrictions prevented change – in National Parks, for example, or Green Belt. The training and operational needs of the Ministry of Defence, meant that the half century left little new material impact in areas such as Salisbury Plain. However, just like the areas of major transformation, this absence of landscape change is also the result of human decision, and it is similarly distinct and evocative.

The later decades of the twentieth century also saw the maturing of the ideas and practice of 'conservation', and 'heritage management' and the notion of the 'historic environment' emerged. Just as nature conservation was developing an agenda for (re)creating (lost) habitats, the processes of archaeology and heritage management came increasingly to be seen as agents for change in the environment in their own right. In World Heritage Sites, Conservation Areas and Sites of Special Scientific Interest, the processes of change and creation have been given a particular direction by designation and by public policy.

Some themes and landscape types

Boundaries – Big Brother

CCTV is a feature of the later twentieth century. It highlights how boundaries have shifted and blurred. Has country become city? Green become brown? Have social as well as physical boundaries broken down and new ones arisen in their place? Has what was once public become private? Are we clear anymore about what is sacred and what is profane?

Interstitial landscapes – city waste

People have always been surrounded by their rubbish and all of our cities, towns and villages contain undeveloped wastelands, disused areas, embankments, awkward and leftover spaces. What do these landscapes on the margins tell us? Are they really empty? Should these apparently neglected areas be addressed by landscape archaeology?

Landscapes of movement – malls

These monuments to consumption also reflect our ambivalence about movement: of people, things and ideas. Do migration and asylum centres welcome new communities or do they stem influx and threat? Are motorways a scar on our landscape or a means of getting what we want, when we want it? Do we enjoy multinational brands or do we see cultural imperialism in our bill boards and shopping malls?

Transient landscapes – festival sites

Crowds, communities, even small towns, can appear and then disappear as people gather for festivals and protests. Commuters, new age travellers and the homeless are always on the move. Is it true that these transient populations leave no mark on the landscape? Should their campsites and shelters be preserved for posterity? Should their monuments now include photographs, video and satellite imagery?

Landscapes of exclusion – England's north south divide

The massive migration to southern England is twentieth-century landscape change at its broadest. It has been shaped by rivers of complex social processes: increases in both wealth and deprivation, the changing nature of the family, migration and immigration. Are we left with landscapes of exclusion? How do patterns and differences in class, ethnicity, wealth, gender, age and sexuality leave their mark on the shapes of cities and countryside?

Modern approaches to heritage

The 'heritage' of the later twentieth century, as with any other period, invites us to engage with the past. However, the abundance of material and the memories and perspectives of those who lived through the last half century mean that the recent past presents a more complex series of questions than earlier periods. What can be done with it? How can it be understood, and its resources be explored? How does it serve the needs of individuals and communities?

What new perspectives could its richness and sheer quantity provide for studies of other periods? Does it need to be managed in any way so that future generations can recognise their history in it? Or should time and nature be allowed to decide what our legacy is? Are we actors or witnesses? – a particularly acute question for archaeologists, historians and conservationists brought up in a climate of conservation and rescue.

These questions are not new. In the past decade, British archaeology, for example, has seen a new interest in the recent and contemporary past, pushing at the traditional boundaries of academic and professional archaeological interest. This has been reflected particularly in the fields of heritage management, in material culture studies and in the increasing interest in the archaeological study of historical periods. The study of the very recent past also provides the opportunity for dialogue with a particularly broad range of disciplines, such as archaeology, modern history, geography, anthropology, planning, sociology, the visual arts, design and literature. An aim of the Change and Creation programme is to enlist their perspectives and innovative techniques.

The growing appreciation of recent heritage is also reflected in public interest. Almost every day, we hear of debates over whether to keep or demolish a piece of 1960s or 70s architecture that is loved and loathed in equal measure. It is only a few decades since Victorian architecture was the subject of such conflict. Not even Victorian industrial buildings now carry the same degree of difficulty as late twentieth-century buildings. English Heritage's Post-War Listing programme was a pioneer in this field, a good example of public perceptions changing as greater knowledge and understanding was collected, leading to new ways of valuing and to an appreciation of the wider context of individual buildings.

A number of recent developments in the approach to the management of England's cultural heritage inform this programme. Reviews of the historic environment and agenda for the future – such as Power of Place (Historic Environment Review, 2000) and Force for our Future (DCMS, 2001) – reflect the increasing concern that heritage should play an active part in enriching everyone's lives and in the development of sustainable communities. Recent opinion polls have demonstrated the affection in which historic buildings and places are held. It is recognised that the past is all around us and the importance of the historic environment for economic and social regeneration, education and tourism has now been established. Thematic surveys of new monument types as diverse as Cold War airfields, shops, post-war architecture and coal mines have already been undertaken. Work can now be extended into other aspects of later twentieth-century landscapes.

A new technique, Historic Landscape Characterisation or HLC (Fairclough, this volume) was developed and promoted by English Heritage through the 1990s in order to provide high-level understanding of the time-depth of the landscape, by studying the past within the present landscape. It aims to understand the broad manifestations of human activity and history that give context to individual sites, adopting the view of landscape reflected in the European Landscape Convention (ibid.). It focuses on the semi-natural and the non-site dimensions of landscape as well as on traditional archaeological concerns, and on some of its intangible aspects as well. HLC takes present day landscape as a main object of study, documenting the historic and archaeological dimension and presenting this in GIS based plans and databases.

Most importantly, HLC draws a clear distinction between landscape and environment – between ideas and things. Landscape can be taken with you, while environment has to be left behind. Landscape is cultural in two senses: physically created by past human action and intangibly created by present human perception. Change is a critical component of both of these cultural dimensions and HLC, therefore, focuses on managing change rather than only on protection. This has particular resonance when the most recent parts of landscapes are being studied, and when there is still broad disagreement about meaning and value, such as whether new landscapes are necessarily less important than old ones. Studies of later twentieth-century landscape character can tell us about peoples' reaction to earlier layers of the landscape, and illuminate all manner of perception and myths about both the past and the present. A Force for our Future (ibid.) endorsed the characterisation approach as a leading method for managing change in the historic environment.

HLC is an enabling approach, that recognises many ways and levels of valuing, and which relies heavily on interpretation, and on human perception. It differentiates between elements of the landscape, but it does not prescribe whether something should be kept or allowed to disappear, be adapted or conserved unchanged. In this sense landscape characterisation is open ended. HLC provides information that can be used for decisions or policies to be made, but it leaves others to make choices about the future of landscape, just as they make choices about their perception of landscape.

A twenty-first-century view

Archaeologists and architectural historians working on the later twentieth century have access, in contrast to earlier periods, to an almost complete resource: one which has not been subject to the same processes of loss and change as the remains of more distant periods. Here is an opportunity to understand and record the variety of late twentieth-century monuments while they still survive in largely complete form. It is surprising how quickly things from the recent past can disappear: over 70% of the 1000 or so World War

II heavy anti-aircraft sites for instance (all substantial and extensive structures and settlement sites) have been removed since 1946, mainly as a result of post-war urban expansion.

The very proximity of the past five decades brings special problems and opportunities when considering preserving its heritage. There are issues of appreciation, detachment and clear vision. However, the study of the very recent past in the landscape offers the rewards of personal involvement with our surroundings. People live day to day in the landscape, and the legacy of the twentieth century has already been assimilated into their lives and experiences. As well as dialogue with those who currently live and work in the later twentieth-century landscape, central to the programme's methods will be engagement with those who remember this legacy when it was first created. This possibility is not open to any other period.

The programme will borrow from the ideas of 'contemporary archaeology' and it will challenge and review established conservation and cultural resource management theories and principles that are perhaps often taken too much for granted. The programme will, therefore, contribute to philosophies of heritage management, as well as to our understanding of and treatment of the landscapes of the later twentieth century. The choices we face are not whether to have a cut-off date for what should be regarded as heritage, nor how to incorporate recent change into perceptions of landscape. In England at least there is no cut-off date, and as for incorporating change, we already do this. What we need to do now is to find ways of doing so consciously and transparently, and to debate the process.

So, through a range of public engagements, Change and Creation will initially explore the diversity of popular understandings of late twentieth-century landscapes, in order to frame the questions and strategy for the programme. A principal aim of this wider consultation will be to consider matters of significance and value: which aspects of landscape from the recent past do different people value, given different ages and walks of life?

The Change and Creation programme will:

- Characterise the contribution to England's landscape made between 1950 and 2000.
- Explore this landscape layer through a series of themes, to be developed through conultation and debate with the public, academics and professionals.
- Pioneer trans-disciplinary study methods for understanding this landscape.
- Determine concepts and methods for managing the landscape as a whole and for monitoring directions of change.

The programme will provide an initial characterisation of the landscape-scale material remains from the later twentieth century across the whole of England, focussing strongly on landscape character, not the study of individual buildings or sites. The date range for the programme is broadly 1950–2000, but there will be some recognition of earlier origins of major processes and landscape creation.

The way forward

The Change and Creation programme will provide an overall structure of *dialogue*, *characterisation* and *resource management* within which individual projects will be carried out. Some projects are already underway. Others will be initiated by English Heritage or its partners. The programme will provide a forum for planning and discussion, and a means of sharing results and developing collaborations.

Dialogue

The programme will promote public and professional dialogue around the contribution of the later twentieth century to our landscape. This will be achieved through discussion, workshops, and focus groups with the public and local communities; the involvement of professional partners, such as universities, local authorities and others; and through a number of conferences.

The programme will explore peoples' own perceptions and memories, and focus discussion on issues of management and conservation at public and professional levels.

Characterisation

A nested classification system will be developed, identifying and characterising distinctive and influential late twentieth century landscape types in broad terms, and exploring major themes through which these types of landscape can be understood.

Data will be collected around these themes, and in relation to particular landscapes and landscape types. This will be largely desk-based, using historic maps, GIS, archive film, published and grey archaeological literature and aerial photographs. Data collection will aim to build upon previous English Heritage and partners' work, and upon earlier HLC projects. The programme themes will also be explored at a number of sample sites, allowing focussed area characterisation.

Resource management

The programme aims to define methods for the understanding, appreciation and management of twentieth-century landscapes.

It will produce tools to enable us to monitor the landscape based on a better understanding of recent directions of change.

It will influence other methods of landscape assessment (e.g. countryside character assessment).

References

Cocroft, W.D. and R.J.C. Thomas 2003. *Cold War: Building for Nuclear Confrontation*. London: English Heritage.

DCMS 2001. *The Historic Environment: A Force for our Future*. London: Department for Culture, Media and Sport.

Frearson, C. 2004 Twentieth Century Research Database (internal report for English Heritage) http:// // www.changeandcreation.org/ changeandcreation.html.

Hayden, D. and J. Wark 2004. *A field guide to sprawl*. London: W.W. Norton.

Historic Environment Review 2000. *The Power of Place: The Future of the Hhistoric Environment*. London: English Heritage.

Penrose, S. with contributors 2007. *Images of Change: An archaeology of the later twentieth-century landscape*. London: English Heritage.

Index